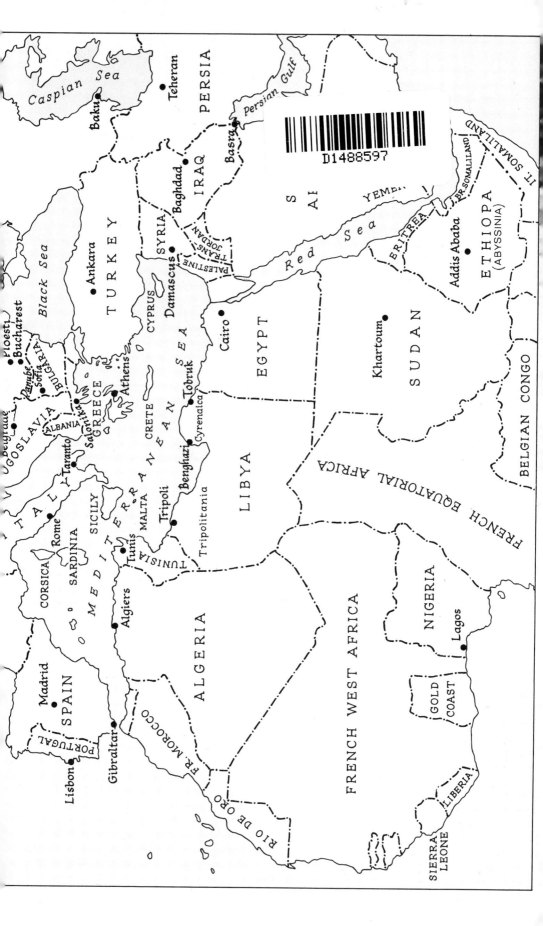

BRITISH INTELLIGENCE
IN THE SECOND
WORLD WAR

ITS INFLUENCE ON STRATEGY
AND OPERATIONS

BRITISH INTELLIGENCE IN THE SECOND WORLD WAR

Its Influence on Strategy
and Operations

VOLUME ONE

by

F.H. HINSLEY

President of St John's College and
Professor of the History of International Relations
in the University of Cambridge

with

E. E. THOMAS
C. F. G. RANSOM
R. C. KNIGHT

LONDON
HER MAJESTY'S STATIONERY OFFICE

HER MAJESTY'S STATIONERY OFFICE

Government Bookshops

49 High Holborn, London WC1V 6HB
13a Castle Street, Edinburgh EH2 3AR
41 The Hays, Cardiff CF1 1JW
Brazennose Street, Manchester M60 8AS
Southey House, Wine Street, Bristol BS1 2BQ
258 Broad Street, Birmingham B1 2HE
80 Chichester Street, Belfast BT1 4JY

*Government Publications are also available
through booksellers*

Printed in England for Her Majesty's Stationery Office
at the University Press, Cambridge
Dd 597077

ISBN 0 11 630933 4*

CONTENTS

vi

PREFACE

IN CARRYING out our brief, which was to produce an account of the influence of British intelligence on strategy and operations during the Second World War, we have encountered two problems of presentation. The first was how to furnish the strategic and operational context without retelling the history of the war in all its detail; we trust we have arrived at a satisfactory solution to it. The second arose because different meanings are given to the term intelligence. The value and the justification of intelligence depend on the use that is made of its findings; and this has been our central concern. But its findings depend on the prior acquisition, interpretation and evaluation of information; and judgment about its influence on those who used it requires an understanding of these complex activities. We have tried to provide this understanding without being too much diverted by the problems and techniques associated with the provision of intelligence. Some readers will feel that we have strayed too far down the arid paths of organisation and methods. Others, to whom such subjects are fascinating in themselves, will wish that we had said more about them.

It is from no wish to disarm such criticisms that we venture to point to the novel and exceptional character of our work. No considered account of the relationship between intelligence and strategic and operational decisions has hitherto been possible, for no such account could be drawn up except by authors having unrestricted access to intelligence records as well as to other archives. In relation to the British records for the second world war and the inter-war years, we have been granted this freedom as a special measure. No restriction has been placed on us while carrying out our research. On the contrary, in obtaining access to archives and in consulting members of the war-time intelligence community we have received full co-operation and prompt assistance from the Historical Section of the Cabinet Office and the appropriate government departments. Some members of the war-time community may feel that we might have made our consultation more extensive; we have confined it to points on which we needed to supplement or clarify the evidence of the surviving archives. As for the archives, we set out to see all; and if any have escaped our scrutiny we are satisfied that over-sight on our part is the sole explanation.

In preparing the results of our research for publication we have been governed by a ruling that calls for a brief explanation. On 12 January 1978, in a written reply to a parliamentary question, the Secretary of State for Foreign Affairs advised war-time intelligence staff on the limited extent to which they were absolved from their undertakings of reticence in the light of recent changes of policy with regard to the release of war-time records. He drew a distinction between the records of the Service intelligence directorates, which will be placed with other departmental archives in the Public Record Office, and 'other information, including details of the methods by which this material was obtained'. He explained that this other information 'remains subject to the undertakings and to the Official Secrets Acts and may not be disclosed'. And he concluded with a reference to this History: 'if it is published, the principles governing the extent of permitted disclosure embodied in the guidance above will apply in relation to the Official History'. This statement has not prevented us from incorporating in the published History the results of our work on records which are not to be opened. The records in question are the domestic records of some of the intelligence-collecting bodies. We have been required to restrict our use of them only to the extent that secrecy about intelligence techniques and with respect to individuals remains essential.

The need to apply this restriction to the published history has at no point impeded our analysis of the state of intelligence and of its impact, and it has in no way affected our conclusions. It has, however, dictated the system we have adopted when giving references to our sources. Government departments, inter-governmental bodies and operational commands – the recipients, assessors and users of intelligence – have presented no difficulty; to their intelligence files, as to their other records, we have always supplied precise references. This applies not only to documents already opened in the Public Record Office, and those to be opened after a stated period of extended closure, but also to individual files and papers which, though they may not be available for public research for a considerable time to come, nevertheless fall into categories of war-time records whose eventual opening in the Record Office may be expected. But it would have served no useful purpose to give precise references to the domestic files of the intelligence-collecting bodies, which are unlikely ever to be opened in the Public Record Office. We have been permitted – indeed encouraged – to make use of these files in our text and we have done so on a generous scale, but in their case our text must be accepted as being the only evidence of their contents that can be made public. This course may demand from our readers more trust than historians have the right to expect, but we believe they will agree that it is preferable to the alternative, which was to have incorporated no evidence for which we could not quote sources.

The above limitations have arisen from the need for security. We turn now to others which have been imposed on us by the scale on which we have worked. The first of these is that not merely when security has required it but throughout the book – in the many cases where security is no longer at stake and where readers may regret our reticence – we have cast our account in impersonal terms and refrained from naming individuals. We have done so because for our purposes it has generally sufficed to refer to the organisations to which individuals belonged; the exceptions are a few activities which were so specialised or were carried out by such small staffs, and thus became so closely associated with individuals, that it has been convenient sometimes to use names. In addition, however, we must admit to a feeling for the appropriateness of Flaubert's recipe for the perfect realistic novel: *pas de monstres, et pas de héros.* The performance of the war-time intelligence community, its shortcomings no less than its successes, rested not only on the activities of a large number of organisations but also, within each organisation, on the work of many individuals. To have identified all would have been impossible in a book of this canvas; to have given prominence to only a few would have been unjust to the many more who were equally deserving of mention.

As for the organisations, it has been impossible to deal at equal length with all. In some cases we have had to be content with a bare sketch because they kept or retained few records. With others we have dealt briefly because most of their work falls outside our subject. This applies to those responsible for counter-intelligence, security and the use of intelligence for deception purposes; like the intelligence activities of the enemy, we have investigated them in these volumes only to the extent that they contributed to what the British authorities knew about the enemy's conduct of the war. Lack of space has restricted what we have been able to say about intelligence in the field – about the work that was carried out, often in hazardous conditions, by Service intelligence officers with fighting units and by the people who were responsible in the field for signal intelligence, for reporting to the SIS and SOE, for examining enemy equipment and for undertaking photographic interpretation, POW examination and many similar tasks. As for the contribution of the many men and women who carried out essential routine work at establishments in the United Kingdom and overseas – who undertook the continuous manning of intercept stations or of cryptanalytic machinery, the maintenance of PR aircraft and their cameras, the preparation of target information for the RAF or of topographical information for all three Services, the monitoring of foreign newspapers, broadcasts and intercepted mail, and the endless indexing, typing, teleprinting, cyphering and transmitting of the intelligence output – only occasional references to it have been possible in an account which sets out to reconstruct the influence of intelligence on the major decisions, the chief operations and the general course of the war.

Even at this last level there are unavoidable omissions. The most important of these is that we have not attempted to cover the war in the Far East; when this was so much the concern of the United States, it is not possible to provide an adequate account on the basis of the British archives alone. A second derives from the fact that while the archives are generally adequate for reconstructing the influence of intelligence in Whitehall, there is practically no record of how and to what extent intelligence influenced the individual decisions of the operational commands. It has usually been possible to reconstruct what intelligence they had at their disposal at any time. What they made of it under operational conditions, and in circumstances in which it was inevitably incomplete, is on all but a few occasions a matter for surmise. And this is one matter which, after stating the facts to the best of our ability, we have left to the judgement of our readers and to the attention of those who will themselves wish to follow up our research by work in the voluminous records which are being made available to the public.

That room remains for further research is something that goes without saying. Even on issues and episodes for which we have set out to supply the fullest possible accounts, the public records will yield interpretations that differ from those we have offered. At the opposite extreme there are particular undertakings and individual operations to which we have not even referred. In our attempt to write a co-ordinated yet compact history we have necessarily proceeded not only with a broad brush but also with a selective hand, and we shall be content if we have provided an adequate framework and a reliable perspective for other historians as well as for the general reader.

□

We cannot let this volume go to press without making special reference to the contribution of Miss Eve Streatfeild. In addition to sharing in the research, she has for several years carried out with great skill and patience the bulk of the administrative work that the project has involved.

ABBREVIATIONS

ADI (Ph)   Assistant Director Intelligence (Photographic)

ADI (Sc)   Assistant Director Intelligence (Science)

ADIC   Assistant Director Operational Intelligence Centre (Admiralty)

AI   Air Intelligence

APS   Axis Planning Section

ASI   Air Scientific Intelligence

ATB   Advisory Committee on Trade Questions in Time of War

BAFF   British Air Forces in France

BEF   British Expeditionary Force

'C'   also CSS: Head of the Secret Service

CBME   Combined Bureau Middle East

CIC   Combined Intelligence Committee

CID   Committee of Imperial Defence

CIGS   Chief of the Imperial General Staff

CIU   Central Interpretation Unit

COS   Chiefs of Staff

CSDIC   Combined Services Detailed Interrogation Centre

CSS   Chief of the Secret Service, also 'C'

DCM   Ministerial Committee on Disarmament

DCNS   Deputy Chief of the Naval Staff

DD (Ph)   Deputy Director (Photography) (Air Ministry)

DDI   Deputy Director of Intelligence (Air Staff)

DDIC   Deputy Director Operational Intelligence Centre (Admiralty)

DDMI (I)   Deputy Director Military Intelligence (Intelligence)

DDMI (O)   Deputy Director Military Intelligence (Operations)

DDMO and I   Deputy Director of Military Operations and Intelligence

DDNI   Deputy Director of Naval Intelligence

DF   Direction Finding

DMI   Director of Military Intelligence

DMO and I   Director of Military Operations and Intelligence

DNI   Director of Naval Intelligence

DPR   Ministerial Committee on

DPR (*cont.*)	Defence Policy and Requirements	JIS	Joint Intelligence Staff
DRC	Defence Requirements Sub-Committee (of the CID)	JPS	Joint Planning Staff (of the COS)
		LRDG	Long Range Desert Group
DSD	Director Signals Division (Admiralty)	MEIC	Middle East Intelligence Centre
		MEW	Ministry of Economic Warfare
EP	Economic Pressure Sub-Committee (of the ATB Committee)	MI	Military Intelligence (Branch of the War Office)
EWI	Economic Warfare Intelligence	NID	Naval Intelligence Department
FCI	Industrial Intelligence in Foreign Countries Sub-Committee (of the CID)	OIC	Operational Intelligence Centre (Admiralty)
		OKH	Oberkommando des Heeres (High Command of the German Army)
FECB	Far East Combined Bureau		
FOES	Future Operations (Enemy) Section	OKL	Oberkommando der Luftwaffe (High Command of the German Air Force)
GAF	German Air Force		
GC and CS	Government Code and Cypher School	OKM	Oberkommando der Kriegsmarine (High Command of the German Navy)
GS Int	General Staff Intelligence		
HDU	Home Defence Units	OKW	Oberkommando des Wehrmacht (High Command of the German Armed Forces)
IAF	Italian Air Force		
IIC	Industrial Intelligence Centre		
ISIC	Inter-Service Intelligence Committee	PDU	Photographic Development Unit
		PIU	Photographic Interpretation Unit
ISSB	Inter-Service Security Board	PR	Photographic Reconnaissance
JIC	Joint Intelligence Sub-Committee (of the COS)	PRU	Photographic Reconnaissance Unit

PWE	Political Warfare Executive	SLU	Special Liaison Unit
PWIS (Home)	Prisoners of War Interrogation Service	SOE	Special Operations Executive
RAE	Royal Aircraft Establishment	SOI	Staff Officer (Intelligence)
RFP	Radio Finger Printing	TA	Traffic Analysis
RSS	Radio Security Service	TINA	Not an abbreviation: Study of morse characteristics of individual wireless operators
R/T	Radio Telephony		
SALU	Sub-section of Air Section GC and CS, specialising in the fusion of high and low-grade GAF Sigint. (Not strictly an abbreviation.)	TRE	Telecommunications Research Establishment
		VCIGS	Vice Chief of the Imperial General Staff
SCU	Special Communications Unit	WIDU	Wireless Intelligence and Development Unit
Sigint	Signal Intelligence	W/T	Wireless Telegraphy
SIME	Security Intelligence Middle East	Y	See definition in Chapter 1, p. 21, note *
SIS	Special or Secret Intelligence Service		

PART I
On the Eve

CHAPTER 1

The Organisation of Intelligence
at the Outbreak of War

IN THE years before the Second World War several bodies within the British structure of government shared the responsibility for intelligence. They were far from forming a single organisation. They had evolved on different lines, within different departments, and no one authority directly supervised them all. Nor could any one authority have done so, given the nature of their responsibilities and the variety of their activities. In some ways, however, they were coming to think of themselves as being parts of a single system for the first time. Perhaps the most significant development of these years is reflected in the fact that they recognised by 1939, as they had not recognised before 1918, the need to strike the right balance between the impracticability of centralisation and the dangers and drawbacks of independence and sub-division.

Steps to improve the relations between them were taken before the war began – some, as a result of experience in the First World War, as early as 1919. There is no reason to doubt that the achievements of British intelligence in the Second World War were all the greater because these measures had been adopted earlier and could then be built upon. Before the war they met with little success. Indeed, it was not until the war was more than a year advanced that co-ordination between the organisations, and even within them, developed sufficiently to produce an efficient, if still not a perfect, system. Why was this so? Why did measures which proved to have been far-sighted after the passage of time, and under the stress of war, fail to provide efficiency in peace-time, or even in time for the outbreak of hostilities? An accurate assessment of the work of war-time intelligence, of which the early short-comings were as marked as the later successes, depends upon the answer to this question.

It is only part of the answer to say that the pre-war steps were inadequate, or were implemented in too leisurely a fashion. 'If you want peace, be prepared for war.' There is no lack of evidence to the effect that Great Britain's neglect of this ancient maxim applied to her intelligence preparations no less than to her rearmament programmes. At the time, on the other hand, there was no lack of anxiety for more and better intelligence. Particularly after 1935, the anxiety was so pronounced as to suggest that the explanation must take into account the complexity of the problems as well as the fact that they were not tackled with any great urgency before that date. On closer inspection, this suggestion is confirmed: another reason why the attempts to improve matters had so little effect during the inter-war years was that they ran into difficulties which could be brought into focus, for clarification and solution, only under the stress of war-time conditions and with the help of war-time opportunities.

Some of these difficulties stemmed directly from technical obstacles which limited the amount and type of intelligence that could be obtained. We shall explain them when we discuss the sources from which information was obtained.* Those that were mainly organisational in character arose from the various pressures and resistances – administrative, psychological and political – which complicate relations whenever several bodies share responsibility in a single field. They were all the more intractable, however, because developments in the field of intelligence were setting up a conflict between the need for new organisational departures and the established, and perfectly understandable, distribution of intelligence responsibilities.

Intelligence is an activity which consists, essentially, of three functions. Information has to be acquired; it has to be analysed and interpreted; and it has to be put into the hands of those who can use it. Most of the pressures for change in the inter-war years resulted from the fact that increasing professionalisation tended to separate these functions and to call for new, specialised inter-departmental bodies to undertake them. The creation, successively, of the Special or Secret Intelligence Service (SIS) and of the Government Code and Cypher School (GC and CS) at the level of acquiring information, of the Industrial Intelligence in Foreign Countries Sub-Committee (FCI) of the Committee of Imperial Defence and its Industrial Intelligence Centre (IIC) at the level of analysing and interpreting information, and of the Joint Intelligence Sub-Committee (JIC) of the Chiefs of Staff in an effort to ensure that intelligence would be more effectively used, illustrated, as we shall see, how powerfully this tendency was at work. On the other hand, several departments of state, each having different and onerous responsibilities to the central government and to subordinate authorities at home and abroad, were naturally reluctant to exchange reliance on inter-departmental bodies for their own long-established control of the acquisition, the interpretation and the use of whatever information might bear on their work. Most of the resistance to change arose from this reluctance and – what were more commonly encountered – so did most of the uncertainty and the lethargy with which agreed changes were implemented and most of the neglect to exploit to the full the more complex structure of intelligence that was gradually emerging.

□

---

* See Chapter 2.

Of the departments most involved – the Foreign Office and the three Service ministries – the Foreign Office, the most important in peace-time, was also the one which displayed least interest in the problem we have now outlined. To the extent that it maintained close relations with the head of the SIS and an active interest in the intelligence produced by the SIS and GC and CS, it was more than nominally in charge of those organisations; but it hardly concerned itself with guiding their activities or smoothing their day-to-day difficulties. Its reluctance to participate in the JIC was not the least reason why that body was slow to develop. These are some examples, to be elaborated later on, of the ways in which the primacy of its influence gave special weight to its lack of initiative in making or accepting changes.

One reason for its attitude was its conception of intelligence as an activity. Unlike the Service departments, the Foreign Office possessed no branch or section of its own that was especially entrusted with intelligence. Attempts had been made from time to time to develop its library and its research department in this direction, but – sometimes amalgamated and at others separated – those bodies had never become more than organisations for the storage, indexing and retrieval of an increasingly voluminous archive of correspondence and memoranda because the Foreign Office's overriding interest was in the conduct of diplomacy. Although this entailed the provision of advice to the Foreign Secretary and the Cabinet on problems and choices in foreign policy as well as the execution of day-by-day detailed business, the Office made no distinction between its executive and its advisory work, but performed both by having the same geographical departments reporting upwards to the same set of higher officials. In the same way, it did not separate intelligence activities from its executive and advisory functions. The higher officials were at the same time the chief executives, the senior advisers and the ultimate assessors of the information which the department mainly derived from the daily contact with British embassies abroad and foreign embassies in London. This flow of information was not called intelligence and there were no arrangements for ensuring that it was sifted by specialist intelligence officers who, as uncommitted analysts, might have stood back from the pressures that were inseparable from the Foreign Office's work.

It was partly on this account that the Foreign Office also had no regular arrangements for comparing and collating its own conclusions with the analyses and appreciations of other ministries, particularly the Service ministries, and that it showed little interest in developing any. But its disinclination to take notice of other views was all the stronger for two other reasons. In the first place, it possessed in the shape of the reports of the diplomatic service by far the most continuous and comprehensive of all the sources of information about foreign countries, and it had the further advantage that no other department of state was in a position to develop a comparable or rival information service. Thus, it had long been laid down that the Service attachés must be attached to the embassies and that, while they could correspond informally with their departments, they must report to London officially only via the embassies and the Foreign Office. Because the attachés' reports often contained material and opinion on technical military matters, which could be competently assessed only by the Service ministries, the Foreign Office normally acted as a post-box for them, forwarding them to the Service ministries just as they were received and refraining from comment on them unless asked for its opinion. But it formed its own opinion on them and if that differed from Service opinion, and even when it concerned such essentially Service matters as the growth of the German Air Force, it by no means felt constrained from acting on its own interpretation without consultation with the Service departments. On the contrary. On the basis of a principle which finally determined its relations with other government departments in the field of intelligence – which influenced, indeed, the organisation of the British government system as a whole – it assumed the right and duty to do so.

This principle, itself the justification for the arrangements controlling the position of the attachés, had been established a long way back in British history. It was the principle that in time of peace the Service ministries should have no say, except through their representatives at the level of the Cabinet and its committees, in that field where the Foreign Office was the responsible department: the field of advising on foreign relations and on the foreign policy which would influence whether and when war would come. In modern times the principle had never been challenged by the military authorities. Even the bitter struggle which arose between the 'frocks' of the political leadership and the military 'brass-hats' about the strategic direction of the First World War had centred, rather, on the assertion by the military authorities of what seemed to them to be its corollary: the principle that in their professional conduct of the war they should be subject to no interference from civilians, not excluding even the Cabinet. It was not for that reason less carefully guarded; and it had been imposed in the field of intelligence activities, though not without friction and delay, when traditional civilian suspicions of the influence of military establishments on government were re-aroused by the modernisation of the intelligence branches of the Service departments.

This last development had begun during the last quarter of the 19th century, when the startling success of the Germans in the Franco-Prussian war was followed by the discovery that the continental states were creating large and influential intelligence organisations within their military establishments. Given this knowledge and the increase of international tension, Great Britain had to follow suit. The

Intelligence Branch of the War Office was re-organised in 1873 and empowered 'to collect and classify all possible information relating to the strength, organisation and equipment of foreign armies, to keep themselves acquainted with the progress made by foreign countries in military art and science and to preserve the information in such a form that it can be readily consulted and made available for any purpose for which it may be required'.[1] In 1887 it was further strengthened by the creation of the post of Director of Military Intelligence. The same year saw the establishment of the post of Director of Naval Intelligence at the Admiralty, which had acquired a separate intelligence branch (the Foreign Intelligence Committee) for the first time as recently as 1882, and his Naval Intelligence Department was similarly charged 'to collect, classify and record with a complete index all information which bears a naval character or which may be of value during naval matters, and to preserve the information in a form available for reference'[2]

The early DMIs and DNIs were powerful figures. Before the institution of a General Staff the DMI was responsible for mobilisation and home defence, and the DNI was similarly responsible for mobilisation and war plans, including anti-invasion plans, so long as the Admiralty resisted the establishment of a Naval War Staff. The combination of these duties with their responsibility for intelligence meant that, despite the fact that their carefully defined intelligence briefs had restricted them to collecting, preserving and analysing information, they acquired a considerable ability to influence foreign policy. Nor did their influence disappear with the decision of the government soon after 1900 to set up, with the object of ensuring that foreign policy and strategic military appreciations were more carefully integrated, the Committee of Imperial Defence (CID). If anything, indeed, the readiness with which they expressed their views on such matters as the invasion threat, the contracting and renewal of the Anglo-Japanese Alliance of 1902 and the terms of the Anglo-French Entente of 1904,[3] and the part they played in inaugurating military and naval talks with France before these were made formal at the end of 1905,[4] suggest that their influence increased at this time when Great Britain was ending her 'splendid isolation' and such departures in foreign policy as the Anglo-Japanese Alliance and the Anglo-French Entente were creating uncertainty and controversy throughout White-hall and even in the Cabinet. Even so, the CID machinery ensured

---

1. Lt Col B A H Parritt, *The Intelligencers*, p 99 (privately printed).
2. ADM 1/7166B; C Morgan, *NID History 1939–1945*, pp 3–4.
3. A R Wells, *Studies in British Naval Intelligence 1880–1945*, pp 355–361 (1972, unpublished thesis, University of London) using CAB 2/1 and FO 99/400 (1902) and FO 64/1630 (1905)).
4. C Andrew, *Théophile Delcassé and the Making of the Entente Cordiale* (1968), pp 281–285.

that the last word remained with the civilian authorities and its meetings provided the opportunity to re-assert the principle that, since the Foreign Office was primarily responsible for advising on foreign policy, it must have not only a monopoly in collecting, analysing and advising on the use of political intelligence but also, at least in peace-time, the last word in assessing the political significance of even military information.

At one level the CID proved to be a valuable, indeed an overdue, innovation. By bringing together at fairly frequent intervals members of the Cabinet and the Chiefs of Staff under the chairmanship of the Prime Minister, or a Cabinet Minister acting as his deputy, and by having a permanent secretariat to prepare for its meetings and follow up its enquiries, it did something to ensure that the different opinions of the Foreign Office and of the Service departments were reconciled, or at any rate taken into account, in policy and strategy appreciations which formed the basis of Cabinet decisions. Neither before 1914, however, nor even between the two world wars except in the limited field of appreciating industrial information on the war capacity of foreign countries, for which it established the FCI and the IIC, did its existence lead the departments themselves to collaborate in assessing and making use of intelligence. Nor was this due solely to the attitude of the Foreign Office. The Service ministries insisted *vis-à-vis* the Foreign Office that their responsibility for giving military advice meant that their say in interpreting military intelligence must be as complete as was that of the Foreign Office over political intelligence and the giving of political advice. In addition, their attitude to intelligence was such that they placed little importance, at least in peace-time, even on regular collaboration between themselves.

One reason for their attitude was diffidence lest they should cross the dividing line between military and political responsibility. Thus the Foreign Office, in its insistence on having the final say in the interpretation of political information, was inclined to rely on its own judgment of the political significance of even military information, but the Services preferred to disregard the possible military significance of political developments, and of such political information as the Foreign Office supplied to them, rather than be suspected of wishing to exert influence in the Foreign Office's field. In 1935, for example, discussing a proposed multilateral Air Bombing Pact, the First Sea Lord told the CID that the Chiefs of Staff realised that it contained 'both political and military implications...and that it was not for them to say which were the most important'. The COS had 'tried not to remark on the political considerations, but the two were so intermingled that it was difficult to keep them separate'.[5] From the

---

5. CAB 2/6, CID 268th Meeting, 25 February 1935; CAB 24/253, CP 43 (35) of 26 February.

end of 1937, when decisions on such matters as staff talks with other countries began to involve them as closely as they involved the Foreign Office, the Chiefs of Staff became less diffident on this score. But even then they continued to be inhibited in their views on the military implications of political developments, and did so for a second reason. This – which tended to limit them to the study of factual information about the military, naval or air capabilities of foreign countries – was that even in the military field they confined their interest to intelligence which immediately related to their own operational responsibilities.

In the War Office this had been a matter of principle since the formation of the General Staff in the early 1900s. Partly, perhaps, because the power of the early DMIs had aroused opposition within the Army, no less than on the part of the civilian departments, it was then laid down that intelligence should be only an advisory sub-department. From 1904 the post of DMI was abolished, intelligence was incorporated into the Intelligence and Mobilisation Department of the War Office, and that Department became part of Military Operations – the G branch of the General Staff which had executive control of troop movements and major operational decisions. During the First World War the increased importance and complexity of intelligence made it necessary to re-introduce the separate post of DMI in 1916, but the pre-war organisation was reverted to when a Combined Directorate of Operations and Intelligence was re-established in 1922. When the Air Staff was set up in 1918 the same pattern was followed: the Air Intelligence Branch was made a subordinate part of the Directorate of Operations and Intelligence.

In theory the pattern ensured that the War Office and the Air Ministry would make regular and effective use of their specialised intelligence branches. In practice, it deprived intelligence officers of the opportunity to make their views known independently, and encouraged both the tendency of operations to reach conclusions without consulting intelligence and the tendency of the intelligence branches in the different Service departments to work in isolation from each other. It must be added, however, that these tendencies were just as strong in the Admiralty as in the other two Service departments despite the fact that in the Admiralty the Intelligence branch was not formally subordinated to the Operations Division.

With the modernisation of the Admiralty from 1907, and especially after Winston Churchill's attempt to create a War Staff there in 1912 and the final establishment of the Naval Staff in 1917, the Naval Intelligence Department had been gradually restricted to intelligence responsibilities. During the First World War, however, these responsibilities had continued to give extensive influence to the DNI, not least because of his control of the Admiralty's cryptanalytical staff, and the colourful Admiral 'Blinker' Hall had wielded it so vigorously – building up his own espionage system, deciding for himself when and how to release intelligence to other departments, and acting on intelligence independently of other departments in matters of policy that lay beyond the concerns of the Admiralty – that in 1918 there was a considerable body of naval opinion, supported by the Foreign Office, in favour of abolishing the posts of DNI and DDNI.[6] Perhaps because the Admiralty exercised a more centralised control over the Navy than the War Office did over the Army, the NID survived this attack and remained a premier staff division. In the inter-war period – as throughout the war – the DNI continued to enjoy direct access to the First Sea Lord. Despite this fact, the NID's standing among the divisions of the Naval Staff was much reduced after the First World War, and its influence in the Admiralty was no greater than was that of the intelligence branches in the other Service ministries.

For what was thus a general neglect of intelligence in the Service departments, and a good deal of inertia by their intelligence branches, some weight must be allowed to the fact that, while the resources deployed on military intelligence are bound to be run down in peace-time, they were reduced after 1918 for a longer period and to a greater extent than was wise. Because this danger might otherwise have been avoided even while the over-all resources available for the armed forces were being severely restricted, perhaps even more weight should be allowed to the fact that, though men like General Wavell and Vice-Admiral Sir William James were notable exceptions, the higher ranks of the armed forces showed some antipathy to the intelligence authorities, or at least a lack of interest in their work. These sentiments have been ascribed to a variety of causes. Whatever their origin – resentment against the influence which the intelligence branches had wielded outside the strictly informational field in their early days; dislike of the officer class for the less gentlemanly aspects of intelligence work; anti-intellectualism on the part of fighting men – they certainly existed, and produced a vicious circle. On the one hand, intelligence work was thought of as a professional backwater, suitable only for officers with a knowledge of foreign languages and for those who were not wanted for command. On the other hand, the activities of the many men of average or less than average professional competence who were thus detailed for intelligence confirmed the low estimate that had already been made of the value of intelligence work.

The situation which is revealed in these various ways was not entirely surprising at a time when, with political preoccupations uppermost and military operations not imminent, static and routine information prevailed over operational intelligence in the output of the Service branches. While the Foreign Office was a department without an intelligence branch but with a tendency to regard itself as the fount

---

6. ADM 137/1630, Rear Admiral Ley's Committee on the NID, 1918; Wells, op cit, pp 42, 98–99, 100–109.

of all important information and the final arbiter in the interpretation of it, the Service departments, despite their possession of intelligence branches, had little recognition that intelligence involved more than the collection of factual information. Nor did they find it easy to change this attitude, let alone to overcome its long-term effects, when they were aroused to the need for better intelligence by the worsening of international conditions. Down to the outbreak of war, when they benefited from an intake of recruits from civilian life, their intelligence branches remained too weak in numbers and, still more important, in quality to make up for their accumulated deficiencies. Of such staff as they had, again, too many continued to be occupied on routine work of an unimaginative kind. Thus the bulk of the NID continued to be divided into geographical sections which were content to collect static or topographical information – and to be in arrears in their distribution of the information to the naval commands – while in the commands, to quote from a peace-time intelligence officer with the Mediterranean Fleet, 'the main sources were ports' consuls and ships' intelligence officers filling in NID questionnaires, usually with data quite easily available in public sources'[7] Beyond that, like its counterparts in the War Office and the Air Ministry, the NID did little more than pass on to the naval authorities, parrot fashion, the political tit-bits handed out by the Foreign Office.

At least on the organisational level, however, the Service departments made some important adjustments from 1935, and as a result of these their intelligence arrangements were reasonably ready for war by 1939.

□

These adjustments were made on two fronts. Some improved the position of the intelligence branches within their own departments. Others, equally the result of initiative on the part of the Service departments, sought to bring about co-ordination between their intelligence branches – to narrow that gap between their activities which the CID, after so many years, had failed to bridge.

Before dealing with their inter-departmental initiative it will be well to outline the changes which the Services adopted for themselves. In the War Office and the Air Ministry the first step was to grant a greater measure of independence to their intelligence branches. In the War Office this process, which was to culminate in the appointment, once again, of a separate DMI in September 1939, began in 1936: an intelligence deputy to the Director of Military Operations and Intelligence (Deputy Director of Military Intelligence: DDMI) was established after Germany's occupation of the Rhineland. In the Air Ministry this step was taken in 1935, when the resurgence of the

---

7. S King Hall, *My Naval Life 1906–1929* (1952), p 223.

German Air Force led the Air Staff to create for the head of air intelligence the post of Deputy Director of Intelligence (DDI), a promotion which placed him for the first time on a level with the Deputy Director of Operations in the combined Directorate of Operations and Intelligence and which was also followed by the creation of a full Director of Intelligence at the outbreak of war. The Admiralty moved at the same time but, because the NID was already a separate division, it did so in the opposite direction. In 1936, just when the War Office and the Air Ministry were giving their intelligence branches more independence from their operations staffs – or at least within their combined Operations and Intelligence Directorates – it began to plan the expansion of the hitherto insignificant Movements Section of the NID into the first section of what was intended to become, like its predecessor which had been brought into existence by the end of the First World War, an Operational Intelligence Centre (OIC) that would, among other things, bring its intelligence staff into closer contact with its operational staff.

The duties of the naval operational staff differed from those of its counterparts in the War Office and the Air Ministry. The Admiralty, unlike the War Office and the Air Ministry, exercised executive control over the outlying operational commands, and could at its discretion even issue orders direct to HM ships. Apart from establishing overseas Operational Intelligence Centres to serve the more distant Commanders-in-Chief, those of the Mediterranean and the China stations, the Admiralty from 1936 accordingly concentrated its efforts on ensuring that its own central OIC, with its particular responsibility for Home Waters and the Atlantic, was in a position to gather and analyse in one place the product of every source of operational information – that is, information that might have a bearing on operations or intended operations by British or Allied ships – and to transmit its findings not only to the operations staff in the Admiralty but also to the commands.

To the extent that this was a practicable objective – and we shall see later on that it had ceased to be entirely so as a result of developments since the First World War – it was being achieved from June 1937, when the OIC began to take shape. During the Munich crisis some of the civilian staff earmarked for its war-time expansion were temporarily mobilised. In February 1939 the OIC was inaugurated as such, and a Deputy Director of the Intelligence Centre (DDIC) appointed to take charge of it. When, shortly before the outbreak of war, it moved to offices alongside the Admiralty's operations staff and those responsible for convoys, it had acquired all its war-time specialised sections – dealing with surface warships and disguised raiders; U-boats; air operations concerning the Navy; merchant shipping and minefields; and wireless interception. Its communications with the operations staff, as with the other divisions of the Naval

Staff, were direct, the DNI having abandoned the requirement that his subordinates should report only through him. In the same way, it was authorised to pass immediate operational intelligence direct, without consulting the operations staff or DNI, to HQ Coastal Command and to the intelligence officers of the naval home commands, with which it was linked by telephone, and to the commands overseas by wireless.[8]

From each command, in turn, the Staff Officer (Intelligence) (SOI) was responsible for sending to the OIC whatever intelligence he could collect in his area. This service supplemented the Naval Reporting Officer network which the NID had long maintained, with the aid of businessmen and consular officials, at about 300 ports throughout the world to provide it with reports of ship movements and topographical information. In addition, the OIC was in contact by special telephone with the other intelligence organisations in the United Kingdom and with the Navy's wireless intercept and direction-finding (DF) stations there.

The War Office had no executive command function. Army intelligence doctrine laid it down that the Military Intelligence Branch of the War Office should be responsible for preparing the comprehensive, long-term intelligence required for strategic plans and appreciations as well as for organising and administering the entire Army intelligence machine, but that operational intelligence be provided to commanders by their own field intelligence staffs. These staffs were thus expected to control such sources of intelligence as they could exploit themselves. By 1939, however, it was clear that to a far greater extent than in 1914–18 they would be dependent on others for comprehensive 'background' intelligence against which to appraise that obtained locally. Thus, to oversimplify (for there was much two-way working, and short and long-term intelligence was often indistinguishable) the intelligence staff of the British Expeditionary Force was to be backed up by the War Office, while the Middle East Intelligence Centre* which was still being set up in the summer of 1939 was originally intended to back up the intelligence staff of GHQ, Middle East.

While expanding and reorganising itself to meet the growing need for long-term and background intelligence, the chief task of the MI Branch of the War Office was that of ensuring that enough trained men were available for filling field intelligence posts on mobilisation. It was a task which it was allowed to take up only belatedly and in which it only just succeeded. In peace-time intelligence officer posts existed

---

* See below, pp 40–41.

8. ADM 1/10226, NID 004/1939, 'Development of the Operational Intelligence Centre at the Admiralty'. See also D McLachlan, *Room 39* (1968), p 56 et seq; P Beesly, *Very Special Intelligence* (1977), p 9 et seq.

in the units and formations of the regular army (battalion and upwards). The extent to which they were filled, or filled effectively, depended very much on the outlook of commanders and in any case few trained officers had been available to fill them. This was in part a consequence of the abolition in 1918 of the Intelligence Corps, which had trained officers for field appointments, and in part a reflection of the low esteem into which intelligence had fallen. In the event, the Intelligence Corps was not resuscitated until 1940, and it was only as a result of desperate improvisation in the MI Branch after the Munich crisis, and with unofficial help from the Security Service (MI5), that the intelligence component of the BEF was got together in time for mobilisation.[9]

In the Air Ministry in 1935 the Air Staff, as well as creating the post of DDI, authorised a modest increase in his total staff and in the effort devoted to Germany. Until then the intelligence component of the Directorate of Operations and Intelligence, the central authority responsible on the one hand for advising the Air Staff on all information about foreign air forces and on the other hand for providing the air commands with the intelligence they needed for plans and operations, had consisted of only 10 officers ever since 1918.[10] The only area which they had studied intensively had been the Middle East, where the RAF had special defence responsibilities. Intelligence on Germany had found a place in the queue along with that on the major aeronautical powers, France, the United States, Russia and Italy. From 1935 the status and the establishment of the intelligence staff, and particularly of the German Section, were steadily improved. But since the Air Ministry, like the War Office, was not an executive command, it was still more important that steps were taken from 1936 to form intelligence staffs at HQ and lower levels in the operational commands – Fighter, Bomber and Coastal – of the Metropolitan Air Force.

Intelligence staffs at these levels, with the task of filtering intelligence prepared elsewhere down to the squadrons and of passing intelligence obtained by the squadrons upwards for analysis and interpretation, already existed in the overseas commands. In the United Kingdom they were now created for the first time. In 1938 the Air Ministry took the further step of arranging that in the event of hostilities all immediately exploitable intelligence – in practice this meant what could be readily derived from the German Air Force's tactical wireless traffic in low-grade codes, especially the prolific air-to-ground communications of its bomber and long-range reconnaissance units – would be passed directly from the main RAF interception station at Cheadle to the operational command concerned. This scheme could

---

9. Brigadier E E Mockler-Ferryman, *Military Intelligence Organisation*, pp 30–32.
10. Air Historical Branch, *Air Ministry Intelligence*, pp 6–7.

not be put into full operation immediately on the outbreak of war as it was thought necessary that the Air Intelligence Branch at the Air Ministry, which also received this wireless intelligence and mated it with information from other sources, should play a part in its interpretation. By the time intensive German air operations against this country began, however, most teething troubles had been overcome.

In the spring of 1939 the Air Ministry undertook yet another new development. On the recommendation of a committee under Sir Henry Tizard, after the committee had held discussions in February with the SIS and the DDI, the Air Ministry agreed to appoint a Scientific Officer to the staff of the Director of Scientific Research for liaison with the Air Intelligence Branch 'as a preliminary measure towards improving the co-operation between scientists and the intelligence organisation'. But although the Air Ministry approved this post in May, it was not filled until a few days after war had begun. In the Admiralty and the War Office not even this belated step was taken. Despite the fact that in February 1939 the Air Ministry reported its intention to the JIC, and expressed the hope that the other departments would join it in forming a joint scientific body, they continued to rely on their own research branches for advice on scientific intelligence.[11] Technical intelligence fared little better. In the Admiralty NID did indeed have a technical section, but it had but one officer with plans to augment it on the outbreak of war.[12] The War Office and the Air Ministry organisationally had no technical sections, although each had in their German intelligence sections an officer charged with technical matters.[13] This effort was far too small, and as the officers concerned had little authority to ask for intelligence and were able merely to collate such information as came their way, they made no extensive study of enemy weapons, and did not enquire whether advances which were already being made in the United Kingdom on such matters as radar and rockets were also taking place in Germany.

□

We must now give fuller consideration to the pressures that were bringing the Service departments to collaborate with each other and with the Foreign Office in their intelligence activities and, on the other hand, to the obstacles which impeded them.

We have already indicated in general terms the nature of these obstacles and the source of these pressures. At a time when powerful arguments continued to demand that the different functions of

---

11. AIR 20/181, CSSAD 46th Meeting, 9 February 1939; JIC 23rd Meeting, 3 February 1939; R. V. Jones, *Most Secret War* (1978), pp 52, 58.

12. Morgan, op cit, p 245.

13. Mockler-Ferryman, op cit, p 24; *Air Ministry Intelligence*, Part I, Chapter 1.

intelligence should be kept together under departmental control, within each departmental division of executive responsibility, equally powerful forces were arising in favour of separating these functions and creating specialist inter-departmental bodies to perform them. We may now add two more detailed points. These forces, which included the pressure for retrenchment and economies as well as the increasing technical complexity of the intelligence processes, came to a head at different stages according to whether the function was the acquisition, the interpretation or the use of information. And it was in connection with the acquisition of information that they first produced the acknowledgment that inter-departmental arrangements were essential. These points are illustrated by the fact that the earliest and, for several years after 1918, the only important developments were the final establishment of the Special Intelligence Service (SIS) and the formation of the Government Code and Cypher School (GC and CS).

The SIS or, as it was also called, the Secret Service was set up to be responsible for acquiring intelligence, but only for acquiring it, by means of espionage. It had in fact come into separate existence in 1909, when a Secret Service Bureau was created to serve three purposes: to be a screen between the Service departments and foreign spies; to act as the intermediary between the Service departments and British agents abroad; to take charge of counter-espionage.* The Secret Service Bureau had a Home Section (the ancestor of the Security Service or MI5) and a Foreign Section (later to become the SIS). For some time, however, its position within the structure of government had remained undecided. Though intended to be independent of any individual department, the Bureau was originally placed administratively under the War Office. In 1910 its two sections separated, the Home Section remaining under the War Office and the Foreign Section being transferred to the Admiralty, then its chief customer. In 1916, when the Home Section became part of the new Directorate of Military Intelligence as MI5, the Foreign Section was also restored to the nominal control of the War Office and named MI 1(c), but by the end of the First World War the Foreign Office had replaced the War Office as the controlling department. During the First World War, moreover, partly from dissatisfaction with the work of the Foreign Section and partly from anxiety to have control of it, the Admiralty, the War Office and even other departments had established espionage

* Hitherto, the Special Duties Division of the Military Operations Directorate had been responsible for counter-espionage. But, as the CID discovered when it examined the defects in strategic planning after 1902, intelligence in the other of these directions had been virtually non-existent. Despite the investigations of the CID, improvement did not come rapidly. In 1907 there were still no British agents in Europe, and no plans for organising an espionage system in the event of war. As the War Office commented in that year, 'the only consolation...is that every foreign government implicitly believes that we already have a thoroughly organised and efficient European Secret Service'.

systems of their own.[14] It was not until 1921, as a result of the deliberations of a Secret Service Committee first appointed by the Cabinet in 1919 to advise on post-war arrangements, that the SIS was at last made exclusively responsible for espionage on an inter-Service basis – indeed, on a national one, the Home Office, the Colonial Office, the India Office and the new Air Ministry being added to the Foreign Office, the War Office and the Admiralty as its customers – and that its relations with the departments were regularised.

By the 1921 recommendations the SIS remained under the control of the Foreign Office – and continued to be funded from the Foreign Office's secret vote – although it also retained a military intelligence title as MI6. At the same time, the intelligence branch in each of the three Services came to house one of its sections in the SIS, where it formed part of the HQ staff, and the interest of the three Services was further safeguarded by the understanding that they would take it in turns to supply its chief.* The arrangement reflected the expectation that the SIS would continue to be a supplier of military information mainly to the Service departments. It also allowed for the susceptibilities of the Foreign Office. When the SIS had first emerged as a specialised service the Foreign Office had expressly excluded the gathering of political intelligence – its own jealously-guarded field – from its activities. Now, while agreeing that the SIS might range beyond the military field, it remained anxious to safeguard two points. The first was that the espionage system should be kept operationally separate from its own political information system.† The second, secured through the Foreign Office's ultimate control of it, was that, in so far as the SIS engaged in political intelligence, it should do so as a supplier of information to the Foreign Office, under Foreign Office supervision, and not as part of a Service department which might be tempted to extend its influence beyond the field of military intelligence.

The 1921 arrangement had its strengths and its weaknesses in

---

* Known as CSS or 'C'; not, however, that 'C' was an abbreviation for chief. It derived from the surname of the first head of the Foreign Section of the Secret Service Bureau before 1914.

† Whereas previously the SIS had been at a disadvantage compared with the secret services of other countries, whose representatives had for years been posted as attachés or embassy staff, the Passport Control organisation by now provided official cover for the SIS HQ's representatives abroad. But SIS staff in the Passport Control offices, being attached to the embassies and legations, acted for the most part only as post boxes, and the secret service work itself continued to be carried out by private individuals paid out of Secret Service funds.[15]

14. Committee of Officials on Secret Service 1925 and Secret Service Committee, 1919 File, GT 6965 of February 1919, paper 5 (Retained in Private Office of Secretary of the Cabinet).

15. Hankey Report of 11 March 1940, Appendix I (Retained in Private Office of Secretary of Cabinet). See also War Office paper, 19 March 1920, in 1919 File of Secret Service Committee, copy of which in the Lloyd George Papers, House of Lords Library.

operation. Under it, the SIS received suggestions and requests for information direct from its various customers, and it reported selections from its findings direct to them without interpretation. On the debit side, with the Foreign Office exercising no day-to-day control, this meant that the SIS was not a strong enough organisation to settle priorities as between the requests that were made of it, or even to resist demands for assistance that went beyond its resources. When these demands became insistent and conflicting, as they did during the 1930s, it was over-stretched by the user departments. Nor could matters have been improved for the Service departments, which were especially critical of it for inefficiency, if they had complained to the Foreign Office, since the Foreign Office had little knowledge of the SIS's organisation and methods and refrained from taking an interest in them. But if it is beyond question that the system produced frustration in the user departments, and especially in the three Service departments, it is also true that their criticisms ignored an important point. The fundamental limitations on the efficiency of the SIS were not such as could have been overcome by administrative devices in Whitehall, as we shall see when we consider the sources of intelligence.* It is by no means impossible, moreover, that even the organisational defects of the 1921 arrangements were less serious than those that would have followed had it been feasible to adopt other solutions to the problem.

Of the obvious alternatives one was to place the SIS firmly under a single department; it was ruled out by the conflict of interests between the SIS's different users. Even more radically, the SIS could have been incorporated with other intelligence organisations in a unified intelligence centre which would have been virtually an independent body even if it had been put nominally under one of the departments. This arrangement was proposed from time to time up to 1927 but was then abandoned because it had fallen foul of the same conflict of interest and had also aroused the more fundamental, if less articulate, objection that intelligence should not be concentrated into too few hands. At the end of the First World War, when the DMI urged that MI5 and MI 1(c) should be amalgamated under the Foreign Office and provided with Service officers, CSS opposed the project and the Foreign Office supported his arguments: there was no real connection between counter-espionage and the work of the SIS; in peace-time political and economic intelligence would be more important than Service intelligence; amalgamation would increase expense and reduce secrecy. In 1920 Mr Churchill, as Secretary of State for War, suggested that economies could be effected if the SIS, MI5 and the civil Directorate of Intelligence – a security organisation that had a brief existence under the Home Office from 1919 to 1921 – were

---

* See Chapter 2, p 50 et seq.

combined. He admitted, however, that the amalgamation of 'three distinct and very secretive organisations...cannot be brought about in a hurry having regard to the peculiar nature of the matters dealt with and the importance of not disturbing the relationships which exist'; and the proposal was not considered at the Secret Service Committee meetings in 1921.[16] In 1925 and 1927, when the Secret Service Committee again reviewed intelligence arrangements, it was the turn of a new CSS to press for amalgamation under his own control. Complaining of duplication of work, inactivity and general inefficiency, he proposed that the SIS, GC and CS, MI5 and perhaps Scotland Yard's Special Branch should be combined into a single service. The Foreign Office now agreed with CSS, and some members of the Committee were mildly disposed in favour of a single organisation. But others stressed that it would be difficult to find a succession of officers who would be capable of running it, and no less difficult to settle who should exercise ministerial responsibility for it, and after taking evidence the Committee decided that as the relations between the various intelligence bodies and their customers were more important than those between the intelligence bodies themselves, it would be wise to respect 'the marked reluctance of the majority of those concerned...'[17]

The SIS thus remained under the Foreign Office and the arrangements adopted in 1921 – the arrangement by which administrative charge of it was vested in one department but by which all interested departments retained direct relations with it and some opportunity to influence its activities – at least reassured the departments that intelligence could be acquired on an inter-departmental basis without depriving them of their individual control of the interpretation of information and of the use that was made of it.

□

Where the SIS was concerned, the Service departments adjusted themselves quickly enough to this division of labour. For all their complaints about the service they received, they made no further attempts after 1921 – except for the tactical and operational purposes of their field security sections, in agreement with the SIS[18] – to organise their own espionage systems, as they had done during the First World War and as did their counterparts in Germany and other countries during the second. With the Government Code and Cypher School, the inter-departmental organisation set up to be responsible

---

16. War Office paper on Reduction of Estimates for Secret Services and covering note, 19 March 1920 (Retained in Private Office of Secretary of the Cabinet).

17. Unregistered papers in Cabinet Office Archive.

18. WO 197/97, Notes on I.b organisation in the BEF at the start of active operations in May 1940.

for acquiring intelligence from another most secret source, they found it more difficult to reconcile themselves to the same division of responsibility.

The Cabinet established GC and CS in 1919 both to study the methods of cypher communication used by foreign powers and to advise on the security of British codes and cyphers. Brought into existence as an inter-Service organisation of 25 officers recruited from remnants of the war-time Room 40 and MI 1(b), the cryptanalytical sections of the Admiralty and the War Office during the First World War,* it was initially placed under the Admiralty for administrative purposes. In 1922, on completion of the enquiries of the Cabinet's Secret Service Committee, it went with the SIS into the administrative control of the Foreign Office – and it was arranged that the cost of it, unlike that of the SIS, should be met out of the ordinary Foreign Office vote. In 1923 a further change of responsibility for it was effected. The head of the SIS was re-named 'Chief of the Secret Service and Director of GC and CS' and GC and CS, while remaining separate from SIS, came under his authority.

Perhaps because the use of wireless cypher communications by foreign armed forces was declining at that time, the three Service departments made no objection to these arrangements. But they accepted them with two important qualifications or reservations. Their reservations arose from their experiences during the First World War. As a result of the introduction of wireless since the beginning of the century, the study of the methods of cypher communication used by foreign powers had then proved to be of greater importance than ever before – and vastly superior to espionage – as a source of intelligence. What was more important, two lessons had been learned by those who had been engaged in this work. The first was that wireless had brought into existence a new field of intelligence – the comprehensive study of communications systems (later to be called Signal Intelligence or Sigint) – in which cryptanalysis, the ancient craft of reading codes and cyphers, was but one of several processes. Before wireless messages could be decyphered they had to be intercepted (the process which came to be called Y). As well as providing material for cryptanalysis, their place of origin could be discovered by means of direction-finding (DF)† and they could be studied (by the process which came to be called Traffic Analysis) as the product of communications networks whose behaviour, procedures and techniques could

---

* Room 40 (which was incorporated into the NID in 1917) and MI 1(b) had developed independently and on the basis of little, if any, pre-1914 experience, and except for general agreements like that by which Room 40 dealt with the requirements of the Royal Naval Air Service, while MI 1(b) dealt with those of the Royal Flying Corps, they had had no contact with each other during the war.

† A direction-finding station took a bearing on a transmission, and the intersection of the bearings from two or more stations – usually at least three were needed – indicated the whereabouts of the transmitter.

yield further information. In the event of their being decyphered, finally, their contents still called for interpretation by specialists if their significance was to be fully and accurately assessed; and the immediate or operational interpretation of individual messages might well depend on long-range research based on the analysis of many.

It was not until the middle of the Second World War that a standard terminology was laid down for these activities.* But already by the end of the First World War their specialised techniques had come to be well understood. So had the second lesson. If maximum use were to be made of the four main Sigint processes – interception, including DF; Traffic Analysis; cryptanalysis; interpretation – then, at least in time of war, they must be carried out in close proximity both to each other and to the operational and planning staffs who acted on the results. Only if the cryptanalysts were in close contact with those responsible for enemy wireless interception and for Traffic Analysis could the cryptanalytical obstacles be surmounted with the minimum of delay. On the other hand, only if they were aware of the needs and intentions of the operations staffs, and thus in close contact with them, could those responsible for evaluating the findings from cryptanalysis and Traffic Analysis, and marrying them with intelligence from other sources than Sigint, be fully efficient at doing their job.†

These experiences, combined with their inability to relinquish responsibility for evaluating whatever intelligence might be of use to their respective Services, explain the reservations which the Service

---

* In the foregoing paragraph we have used the terminology as it was standardised in October 1943: *Sigint* (the general term for all the processes and for any intelligence they produced), *Y Service* (the interception of signals, including the operation of DF; but this was known in the USA as the RI = Radio Intelligence Service), *TA* or *Traffic Analysis* (the study of communication networks and of procedure signals, call-signs, low-grade codes and plain language, together with DF and other technical aids). Until 1943 these terms were used in different ways and others also existed, leading to much confusion. Thus for TA itself other terms existed like W/T Intelligence, W/T Operational Intelligence, Wireless Network Research and even Operational Intelligence. Y, again, sometimes meant only interception and sometimes interception and Traffic Analysis and also came to cover the breaking and exploitation of low-grade signals in the field. It should be added that throughout this book the term 'low-grade' refers to the degree of security provided by a code or cypher and does not imply that the traffic in it was either unimportant or easy to break and interpret.

† The experience of the Admiralty illustrates the learning of this lesson. Initially Room 40 did no more than pass individual decrypts to the Operations Division. From February 1916 it began analysing the accumulation of decrypted material and issuing the Operations Division with a daily summary in addition to individual urgent messages, but this did not solve the basic problems, which were that Operations Division was swamped with material and was not sufficiently familiar with it to assess it accurately. These were the problems which hampered the efficient handling of Sigint during the battle of Jutland. Not until the summer of 1918 was a satisfactory routine established – one by which Room 40 under Captain (later Admiral) James ceased to pass individual items of intelligence to Operations Division and was made responsible both for the evaluation of operational intelligence and for long-range intelligence research.[19]

19. Beesly, op cit, p 5.

departments applied to the establishment and development of GC and CS. It was their intention from the outset that, while GC and CS might continue to be responsible for breaking new cyphers on an inter-Service basis, all readable codes and cyphers would from the outbreak of war be exploited by the intelligence branches of the departments or the HQs of the operational commands, in close proximity to the operational staffs. Thus the War Office's plan of 1926 was that:

'On the outbreak of war the War Office will be responsible for intercepting the enemy's field wireless sets and for collecting all information obtainable from this source. For this purpose it will provide, from officers on the active list and on the reserve, the necessary personnel for wireless intelligence and cryptanalysis. At this stage the help of GC and CS will only be required in the event of the enemy using a cypher which cannot be broken by the cryptanalysts in the field...when this has been done, the results will be handed over to the cryptanalysts in the field who will thenceforth decypher the messages'.

And in 1930 the War Office reserved the right 'to move the [Army] Section in whole or in part at any time if in their opinion the military situation dictates such a course'. In the same way a memorandum between CSS and the DNI of 16 November 1927 said: 'On the outbreak of war the entire naval section of the GC and CS will be transferred to the Admiralty, who may require it to go abroad...the Admiralty will always decide when transfer is necessary'. In October 1932 this agreement was modified. Thereafter it applied only in the event of war or emergency in the Far East, but in the case of war or emergency elsewhere it was agreed that the Naval Section 'will not be immediately transferred to the Admiralty and will remain at GC and CS and expand its work on its present lines...until the Board of Admiralty consider it desirable to transfer it to within the Admiralty'. On this account, the staff the Service departments contributed to the original nucleus of GC and CS, which went on to the strength of the Foreign Office in 1922, was provided on a secondment basis and such staff as they added later was organised in Service appendages – the Naval Section being added from 1924, the Army Section from 1930, and the Air Section from 1936. For the same reason this staff was cryptanalytical staff only, attached to GC and CS to work on or to be trained in working on the foreign cyphers that concerned their own Service. If the first reservation of the Services was that the crypt-analytical process should as far as possible be undertaken in their departments and commands in the event of war, the second was that even in peace-time the other Sigint processes – interception and Traffic Analysis – as well as evaluation should remain a Service responsibility.

When the Service departments undertook the improvement and

expansion of their intelligence branches, from 1935, these reservations came back into prominence. The Admiralty's plans for the development of its OIC envisaged the removal from GC and CS to the OIC of as much of the Naval Section as was feasible, and also the incorporation into the OIC of 'the enemy W/T section' (later to become DSD/NID 9) which the Admiralty had set up in 1932 to study foreign naval wireless communications and to administer the naval Y stations. In 1935 the Air Ministry added a Traffic Analysis section (AI 1(e)) to its intelligence branch, and in 1936 it began to plan for the day when, at the approach of war, it would subordinate this work and the work of GC and CS on air codes and cyphers to its Directorate of Signals and have as much of it as possible done at its main interception station. For the Army, which alone among the three Services had continued to work on low-grade codes and undertaken Traffic Analysis without a break since 1919, if only on a small scale and at its Y stations abroad, and which had invested most heavily in Sigint, the main priority was, as we have seen, the provision to Command HQs of staff skilled in the Sigint processes. By 1935, however, the earlier decision to carry out all peace-time cryptanalysis at one place, on an inter-departmental basis, had combined with the fact that Sigint was a continuum of processes, which could not easily be separated from each other, to produce a situation where powerful arguments in favour of preserving an inter-departmental basis for Sigint even in time of war cut across the plans for re-organising Service Sigint on a Service basis.

The first step towards this situation had occurred as early as 1924. 'At the request of the Fighting Services and with the consent of the Foreign Office', GC and CS had established a 'Cryptography and Interception Committee' to guide the work and settle the priorities. The Committee had met only very rarely and in 1928 had spawned a standing sub-committee to secure the better-co-ordination of wireless interception (the Y Sub-Committee). The three Service ministries were represented on these bodies alongside GC and CS,* and they retained control of the personnel and the installations of their own interception stations. But the three Services could not all have interception stations everywhere and by the 1930s a system had grown up in which the War Office undertook most of the work that

---

* The Main Committee, re-named 'The Co-ordination of W/T Interception Committee' consisted of representatives of GC and CS and the Signals branches of the Service ministries, reinforced later on by members of the Service intelligence departments. The Y Sub-Committee consisted of the Head of GC and CS and representatives from NID 9, MI 1(b) and AI 1(e), together with Scotland Yard, the GPO and the Head of the W/T Board (an inter-Service body for, among other things, technical research in the field of interception which the three Services had established in 1918). There was never any continuity in the Service membership of the Main Committee – of the 50 officers who attended during the next 14 years, only 10 attended more than one meeting. But on the Y Sub-Committee, meeting much more regularly, a greater measure of continuity was attained.

was done in the Middle East, the Navy looked after the Far East and the Air Ministry confined itself to what it could do in the United Kingdom. Even within this general sub-division of responsibility, moreover, inter-Service integration had developed. Of Middle East traffic, the Air Ministry was intercepting communications between colonial authorities in Italy and east Africa and the Navy was intercepting Italian Air Force traffic between north Africa and the Dodecanese, while the Army's interception unit at Aden was mainly engaged on intercepting Air Force material. In the United Kingdom, to take another example, the naval stations were occupied to the extent of 50 per cent on non-naval communications, while of the strategic communications of the German Air Force a large part was intercepted by the War Office on the assumption, which lasted until 1939, that it was German Army traffic.

In the same way, the influence of the Service departments on the cryptanalytical priorities adopted at GC and CS took second place to that exerted by the technical possibilities and demands of the cryptanalytical situation. Thus from 1937 the naval cryptanalysts at GC and CS worked almost entirely on non-naval Japanese cyphers, leaving the Japanese naval cyphers to be worked at Hong Kong, while in 1939 some of the Army cryptanalysts were engaged on breaking new Japanese naval cyphers. By then, moreover, although GC and CS had made scarcely any inroad into Germany's cyphers, it was clear that her Army, Navy and Air Force, not to speak of some of her other State organisations, were all using closely related cyphers based on the Enigma machine,* and that the attack on them would require a single co-ordinated effort.

In these circumstances, in the spring of 1938, the inter-departmental Y Sub-Committee decided that the next logical step was the formation of an inter-Service 'Operational Intelligence' (i.e. Traffic Analysis including DF)† section at GC and CS, and recommended the inter-connection by teleprinter and telephone of all interception and DF stations in the United Kingdom with each other and, to the extent that it did not already exist, with GC and CS. But while they did not object to the extension of the telephone and teleprinter system, which was put in hand,[20] the Service ministries resisted the centralisation of Traffic Analysis. This would have extended the work of GC and CS beyond the acquisition and provision of information and infringed their individual responsibility for appreciating and evaluating it. Instead, assisted in their arguments by the decision that it would be wise to move GC and CS from London to Bletchley on the outbreak

---

* See Appendix 1.

† See above, p 21 Fn *. The idea of such a centralised section had appeared on the agenda of the first meeting of the Main Committee in 1924.

20. See, for example, ADM 116/4080 for teleprinter links between GC and CS and the naval intercept stations.

of war, they worked out during the next 18 months separate compromise agreements in which they safeguarded this responsibility while conceding that GC and CS, by retaining Service sections, should continue to be an inter-departmental organisation in war-time to a greater extent than they had originally intended. As late as the beginning of 1939 the Admiralty, considering that the 'dress rehearsal' move of GC and CS to Bletchley during the Munich crisis had not worked well, decided that on mobilisation the whole of GC and CS's Naval Section should move to the Admiralty or go overseas. But it was finally persuaded to apply this decision in the first instance only to the German sub-section of the Naval Section, which had no cryptanalysts at the outbreak of war.

Except that they transferred more work on easily exploitable codes and cyphers to outlying Service groups on the pattern that had long operated between GC and CS and Hong Kong – some went to the main RAF intercept station at Cheadle, some to the Admiralty's Mediterranean OIC, at Malta or Alexandria – these agreements left Service cryptanalysis centralised at GC and CS. They left the control of Service interception to be exercised jointly by GC and CS and the Service departments, though the Service departments continued to staff and administer their own intercept stations. Over Traffic Analysis and the evaluation of decyphered material, on the other hand, they firmly asserted the control of the intelligence branches of the Service departments, taking away existing staff and leaving GC and CS to undertake as much duplication in these fields as it could justify for cryptanalytical purposes and taking the view that the additional staff required for such duplication should be provided by the Foreign Office.

In all these discussions the Foreign Office itself took no part. Although it paid for the civil staff of GC and CS and although this staff outnumbered that which was attached to GC and CS by the three Services put together, the Foreign Office had always been content to be represented by CSS on the Main Committee and by the civilian Head of GC and CS, a retired naval officer, on the Y Sub-Committee. According to the Head of GC and CS, this arrangement had the unfortunate result that GC and CS 'became in fact an adopted child of the Foreign Office with no family rights, and the poor relation of the SIS, whose peacetime activities left little cash to spare'. But it faithfully reflected the Foreign Office's attitude to intelligence and its lack of interest in peace-time collaboration with the Service departments in intelligence matters. Moreover, the approach of war did not necessitate new measures for that part of GC and CS's work in which the Foreign Office was directly interested. With the deterioration of the international situation the Service departments were forced to reconsider their relations with GC and CS. But until the Foreign Office began to recruit 'hostilities only' civilians, to undertake work on the diplomatic cyphers of the Axis powers as well as to increase the effort against their Service cyphers, from just before the Munich crisis, only two developments affecting the civil side of GC and CS occurred. In 1937, when the Y Sub-Committee realised that the Service interception stations would be occupied full time on military traffic in the event of war, it arranged for the GPO to erect and man the first of several stations to intercept Axis diplomatic traffic on behalf of the Foreign Office. In 1938 a specialised commercial section was added to the civil side of GC and CS to scan and select from intercepted foreign traffic, mainly in plain language or in public commercial codes, information primarily on behalf of the Industrial Intelligence Centre.

□

In the case of the specialised sources exploited by the SIS and GC and CS the Service departments had conceded that the process of acquiring information demanded the existence of inter-departmental bodies, even if they had insisted on retaining control over the evaluation of the intelligence. To aerial photographic reconnaissance, a no less specialised source, they applied the same reservation no less rigorously. In this case, however, little attention had been paid to the source until late in the inter-war period, so that in September 1939 no adequate arrangements had been made even for acquiring intelligence from it.

One reason for the delay was that, although aerial photographic reconnaissance had proved to be a valuable source of operational intelligence in the First World War, the development of it up to 1918 had taken place within technical limitations of aircraft and camera performance which had restricted operations to low heights and short photographic ranges. On this account it had come to be regarded as being essentially a source of tactical information, of real value only in association with actual or imminent military movements. It was partly for this reason that after 1918 the Air Ministry did not again resort to aerial photography for intelligence purposes until 1935, when the RAF photographed Eritrea, Abyssinia, Cyrenaica and Sicily because the possibility that the Italo-Abyssinian conflict would lead to war had aroused concern for the defence of Egypt and of communications through the Mediterranean.

Even when these flights were being made, however, other developments were suggesting that aerial photography might produce intelligence of more than tactical value. In July 1935 the DMO and I drew attention to air target intelligence as 'an outstanding example of a case in which intelligence is received from a multiplicity of sources, which necessitates careful and elaborate collation before it can be put to effective use'.[21] In January 1936 a report on the 'Central

---

21. CAB 54/3, DCOS 3 of 22 July 1935.

Machinery for the Co-ordination of Intelligence', drawn up after discussions between the Secretary of the CID and the Deputy Chiefs of Staff, recommended, among other innovations,* the establishment of an Air Targets Sub-Committee of the CID's Industrial Intelligence in Foreign Countries Sub-Committee.† As developments in aircraft were making it possible to attack industrial targets well inside Germany, and as the study of such targets was beyond the competence of the individual intelligence branches, this Sub-Committee, consisting of DDNI, DDMO and I, DDI Air Ministry and the head of the Industrial Intelligence Centre, under the chairmanship of the FCI's chairman, was made responsible for co-ordinating all target information, including aerial photography.[22] It began work in June 1936.

This step represented, as we shall see, a further stage in the development of inter-departmental collaboration in the interpretation of intelligence in the economic field. It did nothing in itself to remove the obstacles which still impeded the development of aerial photography. Not unnaturally after so long an interval, some of these arose from defects in the techniques, the training and the equipment and aircraft available, defects which were prolonged by the almost doctrinal opposition of the Air Ministry to specialisation in such matters. Others were connected, rather, with the lack of adequate preparation for the interpretation of photographs, a highly technical process which had to be undertaken before operational intelligence could be obtained or, if strategic information was to be procured, before the Air Targets Sub-Committee could do its co-ordinating work.

In the first of these directions – on equipment, research, development and training in photographic reconnaissance – the Air Ministry expended large sums from 1936. But in the time that remained before the outbreak of war, and also in comparison with the Air Ministry's expenditure, little progress was achieved with the taking of photographs. After the war the Air Ministry concluded that this was due to its continuing failure to appreciate the potential intelligence value of the source for other than tactical purposes.[23] To the extent that this judgment is valid, it was a failure which the Air Ministry shared with the other Service ministries. Thus before the winter of 1938–1939 there was little pressure from the Admiralty for more vigorous measures even though in the winter of 1936–1937 the DCNS drew attention to the importance of the 'new aeroplane reconnaissance' in memoranda in which he advocated the establishment of the OIC.[24] It may be

---

* See below, pp 34–35.
† See below, pp 30–31.

22. CAB 53/5, COS 161st Meeting, 13 January 1936; CAB 2/6, CID 273rd Meeting, 30 January 1936; CAB File 14/31/16, paper ICF/279/B of 1 June 1939.
23. AIR 41/6, *Photographic Reconnaissance*, Vol I, Part I:2.
24. See, eg, ADM 223/84, NID 0135/37 of 11 February 1937; Memorandum by Admiral Sir William James.

doubted, however, whether this was the main cause of delay after 1937, as it had undoubtedly been before 1935. On the one hand, the Air Ministry was emphasising by March 1938 that industrial as well as military installations would have to be photographed, that methods of assessing bomb damage from photographs would have to be improved and that, for the purpose of detecting changes and movements, continuous or repeated reconnaissance would have to be provided.[25] On the other hand, the other difficulties had by now come into play.

The RAF's dislike of specialisation in men or machines was a dislike bred of a long period of financial restriction. For this reason, photography continued to be regarded as one of the many functions of the all round flying man so that, although cameras were installed in aircraft and air-crews were trained to take photographs, no plans were evolved for a specially or centrally directed photographic reconnaissance programme, and little thought was given to the development of specialised reconnaissance aircraft despite the fact that from 1937 Bomber Command was insisting that these would be essential in the event of war. Equally important here, no doubt, was another consequence of earlier neglect – the fact that there were many other pressing claims for aircraft development in the last years of peace. And interlocking with these considerations, and heightening their effect, there was the fact that things had reached the point at which, if aerial photography was to meet the most pressing intelligence needs, it had to become a clandestine activity.

The reconnaissance flights of 1935–36 had used the technique of oblique photography, 'looking in from the perimeter' rather than over-flying the areas under scrutiny, and this limitation was accepted in the photographing of Pantellaria, the Red Sea, Italian North Africa and the Dodecanese that was carried out in 1937, 1938 and 1939. This technique was of no assistance against targets deep in Europe. Leaving aside the fact that vertical photographs were far more revealing, the photographing of German installations and movements necessitated the penetration of German air space, and in peace-time this was an undertaking that required secrecy. The French undertook it for the first time since 1929 in 1936, though they limited themselves to the photographing of military targets near the French frontier with Germany. Their results were made available to London through liaison between the SIS and the Deuxième Bureau de l'Armée de l'Air. One result of this liaison was that the SIS was led to take an active interest on its own account. But the Air Ministry felt unable to do so for international political reasons. Clandestine reconnaissance called for the protection of an ostensibly civilian organisation, with a cover story.

The SIS provided these by engaging an Australian, Mr F S Cotton,

---

25. AIR 41/6, Part I:5.

towards the end of 1938 to set up the Aeronautical Research and Sales Corporation, acquire a Lockheed 12A and operate as a businessman from a suitable French base on behalf of the British and French authorities.* Cotton's operational flights began in March 1939. Unlike the RAF, whose programme of research and training still took no account of the need for such specialisation, he realised that clandestine operations required high altitude, high speed, long range and a low chance of detection, as well as improved camera performance and operation. By the end of April, when his collaboration with the French came to an end and his aircraft was transferred to them, he had photographed large areas of Germany and the Mediterranean. In June, July and August, operating from England with another Lockheed, he made further sorties over Germany, where he photographed units of the Fleet for the first time, and the Italian empire, where he photographed vertically the key points from Sicily to Rhodes and Italian East Africa which had been 'previously covered obliquely by RAF machines flying discreetly beyond the six-mile limit'. His photographs surpassed all earlier ones because he had paid attention to developing the performance of his aircraft and cameras. His second Lockheed, fitted with extra tanks and painted a pale duck egg green to lessen detection, had its range increased from 700 to 1,600 miles. By using special film and arranging his RAF cameras in a frame of three, one pointing vertically down and the others set at an angle of 40°, he could photograph a strip of 11 miles at an altitude of 20,000 feet. He fitted additional concealed cameras in the wings.

At the outbreak of war Cotton and his small team – by then he had a co-pilot and a photographic specialist and had acquired a second aircraft – had just recommended to the Air Ministry that a Spitfire should be modified for reconnaissance work and added to their resources. Neither in the Air Ministry, however, which was to take over his unit, nor by way of inter-departmental arrangements, had sufficient progress been made to permit the rapid expansion of his activities.

This was especially the case with arrangements for the interpreting of photographs. After the First World War there had been a general understanding that, while the RAF should be responsible for taking all photographs, the Army was solely responsible for interpreting them. Thus, although the RAF School of Interpretation had been set up in 1922, the Army provided all its instructors and pupils until 1938. When interest in aerial reconnaissance for more than tactical or battle-field purposes began to spread, this understanding broke down and no agreement was made as to what should take its place. In March 1938 the Air Ministry announced, apparently unilaterally, that as well as being responsible for taking photographs for all three Services, it would be responsible via its intelligence branch for all photographic

---

* See Appendix 2.

interpretation.[26] In fact, however, all the Service intelligence branches maintained their attempts to interpret photographs for themselves, for their different operational purposes, when Cotton's results, which in any case infringed the RAF's monopoly in taking photographs, added to the peace-time trickle of material on which to work; and it was not until after the outbreak of war that an inter-Service unit for this specialised work, based on Cotton's pioneering activities, was organised.

□

In their arrangements for aerial photography, as in their relations with the SIS and GC and CS, the Service departments had insisted on retaining control over the evaluation of intelligence. In one specialised area of intelligence, however, that of economic intelligence about potential enemies, they came to recognise, as did the Foreign Office, that even for the task of assessing information it was necessary to develop inter-departmental bodies to complement their own activities.

The first step in this direction was taken in December 1923 when the CID set up an Advisory Committee on Trade Questions in Time of War (the ATB Committee) to ensure the readiness of administrative machinery for creating economic pressures on an enemy. From the end of 1925 this committee, under Foreign Office chairmanship, extended its activities beyond administrative matters to the assessment of economic intelligence in the field of 'economic pressure' or 'economic warfare'. From May 1933 it established an Economic Pressure (EP) Sub-Committee under the chairmanship of Mr Walter Elliott – and with a membership representing the Foreign Office, the Board of Trade and the Director of Plans at the Admiralty and including Sir Maurice Hankey, the Secretary of the CID. ATB reports thereafter represented an important part of the economic intelligence reaching the CID.

A second co-ordinating body in this field had by then been created. In 1929 the Secretaries of State for War and Air, whose departments were not represented on the ATB Committee, asked the CID to establish machinery for the study of industrial mobilisation in foreign countries, and for this purpose the CID appointed a sub-committee of itself, the Industrial Intelligence in Foreign Countries Sub-Committee (FCI), with a chairman from the Department of Overseas Trade and a membership which included the DDMO and I and the D of O and I Air Ministry.

Like the ATB Committee and its Sub-Committee, the FCI at first lacked research staff. But, in 1930, it recommended the creation of a small research centre, which came into being as the Industrial

---

26. ibid, Part I:5.

Intelligence Centre (IIC) in 1931. Until 1935, when it was 'administratively attached' to the Department of Overseas Trade, the IIC was funded from the Foreign Office's secret vote. Until 1934 it was given no formal terms of reference, but in that year the CID defined its functions as being, first, to assist in the collection, interpretation and distribution of industrial intelligence and, secondly, to co-ordinate this intelligence for the Admiralty, the War Office, the Air Ministry and the ATB Committee.[27]

By thus making the IIC the organisation which collected information and undertook research for the ATB Committee as well as for the FCI, the terms of reference avoided duplication of effort between those two inter-departmental bodies. They did not at once succeed in reconciling the individual departments to the idea that the IIC should develop into a central organisation for the assessment of economic intelligence. In order to avoid duplication between the departments and the IIC the terms of reference specified that the departments should put their requests for industrial intelligence to the IIC in the first place, and that they should communicate to the IIC any important items of industrial intelligence they received. At the same time, however, they laid it down that nothing in the new structure was to alter existing intelligence arrangements and that, in particular, memoranda produced by the IIC must be submitted to the intelligence branches of the Service departments for their approval before being distributed in Whitehall.

In November 1937, after what had clearly been a period of friction, the CID re-defined this division of function to the advantage of the IIC. From then on, while the departments remained free to collect and distribute industrial intelligence, the IIC, as the sole authority for co-ordinating this intelligence on behalf of the Service departments, the FCI Committee and the ATB Committee, was empowered to circulate or comment on any industrial intelligence it received from any quarter.[28] Nor were the Service departments any longer disposed to resist this change. In the autumn of 1935 the Deputy Chiefs of Staff had noted that 'the intelligence which it is now necessary to cover in time of peace in order to be properly prepared for the eventuality of war with any Great Power had been almost immeasurably extended and complicated by reason of:
  (1) the extent to which modern war involves the whole of the resources of the nation; and
  (2) the vast extension of the zone of operations that has been brought about by the advance of aviation'.[29]
Thereafter, the German threat having now become dominant, the

---

27. CAB 48/4, FCI 47 of 31 January 1934; CAB File 14/31/6, ICF/279/B of 1 June 1939.
28. CAB 4/22, CID 1139B of 14 May 1934.
29. CAB 54/1, DCOS 2nd and 3rd Meetings, 29 October and 29 November 1935.

ATB Committee's Sub-Committee on Economic Pressure had become the Sub-Committee on Economic Pressure on Germany from the middle of 1937, and the volume and specialisation of economic intelligence assessment had much increased. As we have already seen, it was at the request of the Service departments themselves, that the FCI Committee had established since June 1936 a further addition to the structure of inter-departmental bodies – the Air Targets Sub-Committee – 'to supervise co-ordinated interchange of information and reports between the Defence Departments and the Departments concerned in regard to air target intelligence in foreign countries'.*
The IIC was by 1937 doing most of the research work required by this Sub-Committee[30] in addition to having a special responsibility to the structure as a whole for the preparation of drafts, and a more general one for the collection at a central point of the information needed for economic intelligence research.

The IIC's responsibilities were further increased by the creation, also in 1936, of the Joint Intelligence Sub-Committee of the Chiefs of Staff.† It supplied the JIC with most of its economic information and was represented at its meetings. Lastly, by the eve of the war the IIC had added to the responsibilities with which it was formally charged by its terms of reference the preparation of material for the Joint Planning Sub-Committee of the Chiefs of Staff, whose meetings the Head of the IIC attended as required.

The extent to which these arrangements were limited to those aspects of economic intelligence that were directly relevant to the military or defence field will be obvious enough. The ATB Committee had been set up to assess the vulnerability of foreign countries to external pressure in the event of war and, particularly, in view of Great Britain's membership of the League of Nations, in the light of her obligation to apply economic sanctions against states which resorted to war in disregard of the Covenant. In the IIC's original terms of reference the province of the FCI, industrial intelligence, was defined as 'any information regarding the industrial or economic development of a designated foreign country which may throw light on the extent of its readiness for war from an industrial point of view'. The Air Targets Sub-Committee of the FCI concentrated on studying the location and structure of Germany's industrial plant. Nor was the FCI unaware that the resulting inter-departmental structure was weak on the civil side. As early as March 1934, for example, it drew attention to the fact that financial questions were beyond its competence, and proposed that it should be given a Treasury representative.[31] As

---

* See above, p 27.
† See below, p 36 et seq.

30. CAB 4/24, CID 1208B of 20 January 1936.
31. CAB File 14/31/16, ICF/279/B of 1 June 1939.

the arrangements established themselves as a part of the Whitehall machine, they built up a reasonably good working relationship between the Service departments and the specialist civil departments. Representatives from the Foreign Office and the Treasury attended the FCI from June 1935. From 1937 a representative from the Treasury joined those from the Foreign Office, the Board of Trade and the Admiralty at the meetings of the ATB's Sub-Committee on Economic Pressure on Germany. By this time the IIC had developed the practice of calling on the Treasury, the Foreign Office and the Board of Trade, as well as the Service departments, for assistance in preparing its memoranda. On the whole, however, it is perhaps true to say that the full weight of these civil departments was not brought to bear on economic intelligence assessments and that the inter-departmental system for economic intelligence which evolved under the CID remained somewhat isolated from the main stream of economic thought and discussion in Whitehall.

When we consider the state of intelligence sources in 1939, and try to assess the use that had been made of them, we shall see that in consequence of this limitation the general German economic situation escaped regular and systematic discussion by the inter-departmental system.* Thus, there is no record that the German Four Year Plan, which was directly concerned with the development of war potential, was at any time considered as a whole. It would, however, have required a very large central staff to re-examine, for their relevance to defence planning, the information and the opinions on the various aspects of foreign economies that were accumulated in the departments concerned with Great Britain's financial and commercial relations; and the result of such a re-examination might well have been too complex for defence purposes. Another of the system's short-comings was that, although it confined itself to matters most obviously relevant to defence planning, its coverage was less than complete. The IIC, with an original staff of three administrative officers and four clerical officers, which was enlarged to only eight administrative officers and a proportionate clerical establishment in 1936, was constantly in arrears with its programme of work. The size of its establishment in 1939 was fifteen, but it remained small in relation to the increase in the range of its work after 1936.

For this defect, to which the IIC did not fail to draw attention, the responsibility lay at the highest level. The assessments prepared by the IIC and the committees and sub-committees which it served were almost always approved by the CID without discussion of matters of substance. The lack of controversy, among ministers and senior officials representing departments that were entitled to make their own assessments, suggests that there was considerable confidence in the

---

* See Chapter 2, p 69 et seq.

effectiveness of the inter-departmental system at the working level,* but also that at the highest level interest in economic intelligence was at best moderate.

□

Despite the development of arrangements for the inter-departmental co-ordination of reports and appreciations in the field of economic intelligence, no steps were taken to provide machinery for the co-ordination of intelligence on a wider scale until 1935. It was not until then, at the time that they were discovering the need for the Air Targets Sub-Committee, that the Service departments began to realise that their collaboration was deficient, not to say non-existent, in two other ways, and that they began to set about repairing the deficiencies. By the outbreak of war they had devised new machinery on the one hand for co-ordinating their appreciations in every field of intelligence and, on the other, for ensuring that more efficient use was made of intelligence on inter-Service topics. At the same time, the introduction of this machinery had combined with the pressure of events to draw the Foreign Office into collaboration with the Service departments. But only a skeleton or an outline organisation existed at these levels when the war began.

The enlargement of the scope of the FCI to include air targets intelligence had itself been precipitated not only by the re-awakening of interest in aerial photography but also by a new awareness, to quote again from the DMO and I's memorandum of July 1935, 'of the increasing tendency for certain specific aspects of intelligence to develop, in which two or more separate departments are equally interested, with the result that the danger of uneconomical duplication in the collation and recording of such intelligence is tending to increase'.[33] But air targets intelligence was but one illustration of this tendency, and it was with the aim of filling a wider vacuum that in October and November 1935, in discussions chaired by Sir Maurice Hankey, Secretary of the CID, the Deputy Chiefs of Staff recommended not only the addition of air targets intelligence to the work of the FCI and the IIC, but also the establishment of an Inter-Service

---

* Some members of the CID occasionally felt that the coverage of the economic problem was not entirely adequate. On 18 November 1937 the Secretary of State for Air suggested that the CID should receive periodic reports on the economic situation in various countries.[32] He was told by Hankey that the JIC was in close touch with the IIC, which provided this information, and that the FCI Sub-Committee also made regular reports. This reply did not satisfy all members of the CID. The Home Secretary, Sir Samuel Hoare, asked the Minister for the Co-ordination of Defence, who was in the chair, to have the matter looked into. Nothing further was heard of it at subsequent meetings.

32. CAB 2/7, CID 301st Meeting, 18 November 1937.
33. CAB 54/3, DCOS 3 of 22 July 1935.

Intelligence Committee (ISIC), and that in January 1936 the Chiefs of Staff and the CID approved their recommendations.[34]

The Inter-Service Intelligence Committee, the first determined attempt* to set up an organisation in which the three Services could jointly undertake the administration and assessment of intelligence, at a level of detail which had always been impracticable at the CID, proved also to be an abortive experiment. The records of the CID, the Chiefs of Staff and the Deputy Chiefs of Staff contain no further reference to it after the agreement to set it up, and of its own meetings – if, indeed, it held any – no records have been found. This was partly due to the fact that it was premature. The CID noted when setting it up that it could not be expected to function efficiently until more money was provided for intelligence. Moreover, when it was set up, the process of improving the status of the intelligence branches within the Service departments had itself scarcely begun, and it was perhaps optimistic to expect of a committee consisting of the Deputy Director of Naval Intelligence, the DDI (Air) and the Head of MI 1 branch of the General Staff, unsupported by any staff of its own and authorised to meet merely at the request of any of its members, that it would function at all while the intelligence branches remained subordinate to the operations staffs of their own departments. But as well as being premature, the arrangements made for the committee did not go far enough.

This is clear from the list of subjects considered suitable for handling by the ISIC, whose emphasis is on factual military topics connected with operational plans.† It also emerges in a second direction. In the shape of the Joint Planning Staff (JPS), the CID and

---

* In 1934 the DNI and DMO and I had discussed the need for collaboration on intelligence appreciations between their two organisations, but the project had come to nothing.[35]

† '(a) Preparation of Intelligence Reports and provision of maps and plans for such publications.

(b) Joint appreciations on possible enemy operations from the Intelligence point of view, eg Japanese operations against Hong Kong and Singapore.

(c) Press liaison and security in combined exercises.

(d) AA defences of foreign countries.

(e) Coastal defences of foreign countries.

(f) Intelligence from Procedure Y.

(g) Signal communications and developments.

(h) Co-ordination of the work of the Intelligence Staffs of the three Services in special circumstances.

(i) Questions involving the Defence Security Service where the three Defence Departments are concerned.'[36]

34. CAB 54/1, DCOS 2nd and 3rd Meetings, 29 October and 29 November 1935; CAB 53/5, COS 161st Meeting, 13 January 1936; CAB 4/24, CID 1208B of 20 January 1936; CAB 2/6, CID 273rd Meeting, 30 January 1936.

35. Memoirs of Admiral Godfrey, Vol 5, Part I, pp 154–155 (National Maritime Museum, Greenwich).

36 CAB 54/3, DCOS 7 of 17 December 1935.

the Chiefs of Staff had possessed since the 1920s tolerably adequate machinery for co-ordinating the work of the three Services in the planning and conduct of operations. As a result of the Abyssinian crisis and a concurrent Press campaign for an improvement in defence arrangements, this machinery was strengthened from the beginning of 1936, at the time of the appointment of a Minister for the Co-ordination of Defence. Each Joint Planner was given an assistant and the scope of the JPS's work was enlarged so that it might give fuller consideration to problems before submitting them to the Chiefs of Staff. The setting up of the Inter-Service Intelligence Committee was intended to complement the strengthening of the JPS. It was not realised, however, that progress towards the co-ordination of Service intelligence depended upon establishing direct relations between the ISIC and the Joint Planners. When each intelligence branch was accustomed to serving only its own operations staff, and when the interpretation and the use of a good deal of its intelligence in fact had no bearing on the concerns of other departments, the Service departments were unlikely to consider how far they could profitably collaborate unless they were prompted to do so by having common problems submitted to them by the Joint Planners.

In June 1936 the DMO and I seized on this defect. With the help of Hankey, he succeeded in persuading the Chiefs of Staff to replace the Inter-Service Intelligence Committee with a Joint Intelligence Sub-Committee (the JIC) whose function was to assist the JPS by acting as the channel through which the Planners obtained intelligence on all subjects on which more than one Service might have something to contribute.[37] The Joint Planners were made responsible for making requests to the JIC, as necessary, and the Secretary of the JPS was made Secretary also of the JIC.* The membership of the JIC was the same as that of the abortive Inter-Service Intelligence Committee except that it was empowered to co-opt the help of the Industrial Intelligence Centre, whose head in fact attended, or was represented at, most of its meetings. From its inauguration on 7 July 1936 its meetings were held at intervals of two to four weeks except, until 1939, during the long summer break. At least to this extent, it at once established itself as a regular part of the intelligence machine, to which not only the JPS and the individual Service departments but also, if only occasionally and on military questions, MI5 and the Foreign Office turned for opinions.

---

* In the first instance the Chiefs of Staff decided that this would be too much for one man and that, lest his work for the Planners might suffer, the Secretary of the JPS should act only in a liaison capacity for the JIC. But Hankey got the original suggestion for a common Secretary restored after the JIC had pointed out that it could not otherwise perform its functions properly. The two bodies had the same Secretary until June 1939.

37. CAB 53/6, COS 178th Meeting, 16 June 1936.

Until the summer of 1939, on the other hand, it remained a peripheral body – one which had considerable difficulty in developing a function to supplement those already being performed by the intelligence branches of the Service departments, the FCI and the Joint Planners – for several reasons. The Planners did not call for its views except on topics on which intelligence was either of a routine nature or hard to come by. Nor did the JIC itself show any initiative in volunteering appreciations on more important questions like the intentions and military thinking of foreign states, partly because there was a dearth of reliable information on such questions and partly because Service opinion in Whitehall frowned on speculation. These problems are illustrated by the fact that the most extensive of the JIC's pre-war activities, and the only one of them for which it spawned sub-committees, was the attempt to discover what could be learned about air warfare by studying the available information on operations in Spain and China.* This produced some valuable conclusions – for example in showing that in both Spain and China the air fighting had been largely confined to support of land operations – but it had little impact on military thinking, perhaps because the conclusions, being unconfirmed by reliable detailed information, were also tentative. It was, however, useful both in drawing attention to the need for more intelligence and in bringing closer together individual members of the Service intelligence branches. Thus the relevant geographical section of NID was now brought into closer touch with its opposite numbers at the War Office and the Air Ministry.[40] Even so, these sub-committees aroused some hostility in the Service departments, and also from the Air Targets Sub-Committee of the FCI.† Nor was that all. The

---

* The first sub-committee, set up in May 1937 as a result of an Admiralty proposal, sat under an Air Ministry chairman and had representatives from the Admiralty, the War Office, the Foreign Office and the Air Raid Precautions Department of the Home Office. Its terms of reference were to co-ordinate the intelligence about air warfare that was coming in from Spain. It produced five reports for circulation to the Chiefs of Staff, on anti-aircraft (artillery) defence, attacks on oil fuel storage, low-flying attacks on land forces, air attacks on ships and on control of the Straits of Gibraltar.[38] The second sub-committee, set up in July 1938 as an extension of the first, attended by the same departments, except that the IIC replaced the Foreign Office, added the Far East to Spain in its field of study. It too produced five reports, on air attacks on sea communications, air co-operation with land forces, air attacks on industry, the effect of air warfare on internal communications, and on active and passive air defence.[39]

† The Air Ministry was reluctant to participate in the first sub-committee on the ground that it already had a special section at work on the subject, and the War Office joined it in resisting the setting up of the second. The War Office also objected to the first of the sub-committee reports, on anti-aircraft defence, so that the JIC had to undertake that its future reports would incorporate the views of the

38. CAB 53/33, COS 622 (JIC) of 6 October 1937, COS 623 (JIC) of 7 September 1937 and COS 624 (JIC) of 6 October 1937; CAB 53/36, COS 685 (JIC) of 17 February 1938; CAB 53/9, COS 734 (JIC) of 12 June 1938.
39. CAB 54/6, DCOS 100 (JIC) to 104 (JIC), all of 10 June 1939.
40. Morgan, op cit, p 85.

individual Service departments displayed little initiative in making use of the JIC on more urgent problems. On the subject of Germany's rearmament, for example, the subject that most pre-occupied them and the higher levels of government, they continued to make, in collaboration with the IIC, their own individual assessments for the Joint Planners and the Chiefs of Staff, as did the Foreign Office.

If the JIC played little part in co-ordinating the available intelligence and still less in analysing its implications on this and other matters of pressing importance on which the Service departments themselves were already engaged, this was no doubt because the Service departments felt that reference to the JIC would be a superfluous and time-consuming exercise. At the same time, however, they were only too ready to take this view. When asking for the establishment of the JIC they had been impressed by the importance of co-ordinating the collation of intelligence on matters of inter-Service concern to avoid duplication of effort. Having brought it into existence they effectively ensured that its work did not expand in such a way as to reduce the influence on policy and strategy which they individually derived from their responsibility for assessing intelligence for their own departments and their share in any decisions that might be based on it. In adopting this attitude, moreover, they were not discouraged by the Joint Planners. It was the Planners who, even more than the individual departments, had been expected to call on the JIC for co-ordinated studies, and it was they alone who, by engaging it in more profitable activities, could have off-set the understandable reluctance of the departments to make full use of the new organisation. With few exceptions, however, they not only confined their enquiries to the JIC to routine or unanswerable requests but also handled the replies in a manner that conveys the strong impression that on matters of first importance they regarded the co-ordination of intelligence, and of intelligence with planning, as a process which they were capable of performing for themselves.

The Planners' request were of two kinds. They were associated either with the preparation of the regular strategic appreciations and defence reviews, for the drafting of which the JPS was responsible,*

---

individual Services. A later report, on air attacks on ships, came in for fierce criticism from the Air Targets Sub-Committee which considered its practical value to be 'almost negligible' for its lack of information on essential technical details.[41]

* The first of these to involve the JIC was the Far East Appreciation of 1936–37; it supplied details on the defences of Hong Kong and Singapore, but there is neither acknowledgement of nor reaction to its contribution in the minutes of the JPS meetings at which the appreciation was drafted.[42] This pattern repeated itself during 1937 and 1938 in the drafting of the Mediterranean, Middle East and North Africa Appreciation and of an Appreciation of the Situation in the Event of War with Germany; for the revise of the latter the Planners asked the JIC for a firm estimate

41. JIC 8th Meeting, 26 April 1937; JIC 11th Meeting, 6 October 1937; JIC 15th and 16th Meetings, 25 April and 3 June 1938; JIC 18th Meeting, 8 July 1938.
42. JIC 2nd Meeting, 29 September 1936; JIC 13 of 7 October 1936; CAB 53/7, COS 207th Meeting, 18 May 1937; CAB 16/182, DP(P) 5 of 14 June 1937.

or with the provision of assessments and information to British delegations abroad and to foreign and Commonwealth governments. As the need for the latter increased the JIC did, indeed, begin to find a role and also to devote less time to the former, to which its contribution had been found to be not indispensable. During the first half of 1939 it was preparing appreciations in connection with the visit of the British delegation to Moscow and drawing up the information on the military value and possible use of Soviet and Italian forces that was used by the British delegates during the Anglo-Turkish Staff talks; in addition, although it was excluded from the preparations for the Staff talks with France and Poland, it was drawn in after those with France had begun. At an early stage in these talks a ministerial committee authorised the fullest exchange of intelligence with the French, cryptanalysis being, however, excluded, and the JIC was charged with making the necessary detailed arrangements.[46] Its last pre-war undertaking was the co-ordination down to the last detail – the wearing of uniforms, the provision of cars and drivers – of the preparations for the establishment of British Military Missions in Poland, Romania and Turkey.

Even in the development of this side of its work the JIC was not immune from the wrath of the Joint Planners, who complained that its correspondence with the French embassy was cutting across their own arrangements and who laid it down that no one committee should deal directly with the embassy on subjects in which other committees were concerned.[47] At the same time, the JIC's work had begun to impinge on that of the Foreign Office.* It was on this account that the

---

of the number of divisions Italian industry could maintain in the field, since there was a conflict between the IIC estimate of 10–15 and the War Office estimate of 36, but did not wait for its answer.[43] In fact, the JIC was unable to pronounce on this division of opinion and on later occasions, also, it was unable to supply what was wanted. Thus after the Munich crisis, when work began on revising previous appreciations on the assumption of a European war in 1939 against Germany and Italy, with possible Japanese intervention, it was asked to furnish the JPS with estimates of the strength of these powers, but there is no sign that it did so.[44] Again in June 1939 it was asked for an appreciation of the situation from the point of view of Japan, in connection with the revision of the Far East Appreciation, but had not provided one by the outbreak of war and did not subsequently do so.[45]

* Thus in December 1937 the Chiefs of Staff asked the JIC to comment on doubtful secret reports from the Foreign Office to the effect that Spain might make territorial and other concessions to Italy if Franco won the war.[48] In the summer of 1938 the Foreign Office asked for the advice of the JIC on how far Spanish fortifications in the Straits of Gibraltar constituted a menace to the fortress and to British shipping.[49]

43. CAB 53/40, COS 755 of 15 July 1938; CAB 55/13, JP 305 of 19 August 1938.
44. CAB 55/13, JP 319 of 25 October 1938; CAB 16/183A, DP(P) 44 of 20 February 1939.   45. CAB 55/3, JP 256th Meeting, 14 June 1939.
46. CAB 29/160, AFC(J) 8th Meeting, 4 April 1939, AFC(J) 35 of 21 April 1939; CAB 16/209, SAC 6th Meeting, 17 April 1939.
47. CAB 55/3, JP 267th Meeting, 11 August 1939, Item 17.
48. CAB 53/43, COS 651 (JIC) of 17 December 1937; CAB 53/8, COS 226th Meeting, 22 December 1938.
49. JIC 16th and 17th Meetings, 3 and 15 June 1938.

JIC and the Foreign Office were first brought to work together, the more so as the situation was beginning to call for co-ordination of intelligence abroad as well as in Whitehall.

As far back as the 1920s a Sigint group had been established in the Far East, on the flagship on the China Station, by collaboration between the Admiralty and GC and CS. Partly because the Navy was the only one of the three Services to have an important presence in the area, and partly because a good supply of intelligence was then being obtained from the cyphers of all three Japanese Services, this group became a factor in the development in 1935, without too much inter-Service friction, of the Far East Combined Bureau (FECB).* In the Middle East, by contrast, no progress had been made towards bringing the intelligence staffs of the three Services into closer proximity, or towards defining the division of labour that should exist between them and the Whitehall branches and GC and CS, when the Munich crisis revealed that these problems must be settled if inefficiency was to be avoided. By November 1938 the necessity for a Middle East Intelligence Centre was accepted, but agreement was still lacking as to what its scope and functions should be, and it was mainly because this question was placed on the JIC's agenda that the Foreign Office attended its meetings for the first time.

The question was one on which the Service departments still differed between themselves. The Army favoured a large degree of decentralisation of responsibility from the United Kingdom. The Air Ministry was reluctant to accept anything more than a bureau which would combine the intelligence staffs which were already at work in the area. The Admiralty's position was unsettled on this point, but it wanted to retain its own OIC, which had been at Malta or Alexandria since 1936, in addition to participating in an inter-Service centre. In the end, however, all three compromised on establishing at Cairo a Middle East Intelligence Centre to co-ordinate information and all agreed that it would be desirable if the co-ordinating centre covered political as well as military matters and thus had Foreign Office as well as Service staff attached to it. The Foreign Office objected to a political/military centre and despite signs during the spring of 1939

---

* The Bureau was formed from single-Service intelligence offices which had long existed in the Pacific area and had as its head the head of the local naval intelligence staff (COIS, China Station). It was a purely Service organisation, designed to collate and evaluate military intelligence relevant to the possibility of an attack by Japan without disturbing local single-Service intelligence arrangements. Originally housed in Hong Kong, the FECB transferred to Singapore in 1939, leaving a small support staff in Hong Kong. Though there was not much inter-Service friction there was a considerable amount between the Sigint group and the COIS on the Station, through whom, from 1937, all the group's output was handled operationally, and this friction was to continue throughout the war.[50]

50. Mockler-Ferryman, op cit, pp 198–199.

that its opinion was wavering,[51] it remained so firmly opposed that at the end of June 1939, with the Deputy Chiefs of Staff urging the need for haste, the CID approved the immediate formation of the MEIC, postponing the question of political representation on it.*[52]

By that time the need for closer collaboration between the Service departments and the Foreign Office at home had become apparent, and here, where it had long been neglected, this problem could no longer be shelved. The Chiefs of Staff had been restless for some time about the unwillingness of the Foreign Office to discuss political intelligence with their own organisation. In April 1938 they had pointed out that it would be an advantage if, before drawing up strategic appreciations, the Joint Planners could have meetings with the Foreign Office instead of merely incorporating in the appreciation a summary of the political situation provided by the Foreign Office.[53] In January 1939, by which time the Foreign Office had begun to attend some meetings of the JIC, the DDMI had opened a correspondence with the Foreign Office in which he urged that the JIC would be a more effective body if, without interfering with the liberty of action of the individual departments, its members were given a Foreign Office chairman and it was empowered to 'sift all political intelligence...and compile a reasoned analysis of international affairs'. The Foreign Office had fended off this approach.[54] But it could hold out no longer when in April 1939 the Chiefs of Staff demanded that, at the least, all intelligence, political and military, that seemed to call for quick decisions should be pooled and processed by a Situation Report Centre to which the Foreign Office should appoint a representative.

The Situation Report Centre, set up by the Minister for the Co-ordination of Defence at the instigation of the Chiefs of Staff and with the approval of the Prime Minister, consisted of representatives of the Directorates of Intelligence of the three Service departments and of the Foreign Office. It met in the offices of the CID, under the chairmanship of the Foreign Office, to issue daily reports after checking and co-ordinating all intelligence that might seem to call for emergency action. Later, for the same very limited circulation, it also produced a weekly commentary on the international situation. In these ways it was designed to fulfil in an increasingly critical situation two

---

* See Chapter 6, pp 192–193 for the further development of the MEIC.

51. JIC 77 of 20 October 1938; JIC 20th Meeting, 16 November 1938 and 21st Meeting, 11 January 1939; CAB 4/29, CID 1548B of 20 April 1939; CAB 2/8, CID 356th Meeting, 11 May 1939.

52. JIC 28th Meeting, 13 June 1939; CAB 4/30, CID 1556B of 27 June 1939; CAB 2/9, CID 363rd Meeting, 29 June 1939.

53. CAB 16/183, DP(P) 31 of 2 September 1938.

54. FO 371/23994, W 793/9 (FO to DDMI, 15 February 1939), W 5320/9 (DDMI to FO, 28 March 1939 and FO to DDMI, 21 April 1939).

requirements which the JIC, with its lack of staff, its pre-occupation with long-range issues and problems of organisation and having no regular Foreign Office member, had not been designed for. The first was the need for the departments to collaborate in ensuring that proper use was made of intelligence at the emergency or operational level, as well as at the level of planning. The second was the need to ensure, at both levels, that this co-ordination extended beyond the Service departments and at last incorporated the Foreign Office with them.

During the Munich crisis, and still more since the beginning of 1939, these needs had been becoming obvious enough. It had been becoming increasingly obvious, again, that they were closely inter-locked. On the one hand the Foreign Office, long critical of the strategic appreciations of the Chiefs of Staff and the Joint Planners, had attended a meeting of the JIC for the first time in November 1938 because the preparation of a new European strategic appreciation was on the agenda, as well as because it had serious reservations about the project for a Middle East Intelligence Centre. On the other hand, its attendance at JIC meetings had thereafter remained spasmodic and it had continued its established practice of issuing items of intelligence direct to the Service departments. At a time when these items were increasingly alarmist in tone and military in their contents, matters were made worse by the fact that they were not infrequently found to be false after they had been issued, as we shall see later on.* It was after their incautious circulation by the Foreign Office had created a series of incidents that the Situation Report Centre was set up.[55] But it was because such incidents were at last recognised for what they were – as being merely one illustration of the defects that were arising at all levels in conditions of near-war in consequence of the autonomy of the Service intelligence branches and of the peace-time separation from them of the Foreign Office – that after being in existence for two months the Centre proposed its own amalgamation with the JIC, and that in July 1939 the Foreign Office fully approved of the amalgamation.[56]

In the resulting re-organisation of June-July 1939 the JIC acquired the form which, in all essentials, it retained throughout the war. It consisted henceforth not only of the heads of Intelligence of the three Service departments, or their deputies,† but also of a Counsellor from the Foreign Office. In theory it had no chairman, the Services having

---

* See Chapter 2, p 84.
† The heads – by this time all designated Directors – did not attend regularly until 1940.

55. CAB 53/11, COS 290th Meeting, 19 April 1939; CAB 53/51, COS 935 (JIC) of 4 July 1939.
56. FO 371/23983, W 6765/108/50, W 7989/108/50; FO 371/23986, W 9715/108/50, minutes of 21 and 27 June; FO 371/23901, W 9975/9, minute of 1 August 1939.

objected to a Service committee being chaired by the Foreign Office and the Foreign Office having raised difficulties about nominating a man of suitable seniority to a subordinate position. In practice, as the members of the Situation Report Centre had initially recommended and despite the fact that it remained a sub-committee responsible to the Chiefs of Staff, its Foreign Office member chaired its meetings. It was provided with a Secretary of its own instead of continuing to share one with the Joint Planning Staff. And in its new form it was given an enhanced status as against the separate departments as well as against the Planners, as will be clear if we quote the terms of reference that were now given to it. These laid it down that the Committee 'should continue to issue the Daily Reports and Weekly Commentaries at present produced by the Situation Report Centre and should also be charged with the following duties:

(i) The assessment and co-ordination of intelligence received from abroad with the object of ensuring that any Government action which might have to be taken should be based on the most suitable and carefully co-ordinated information obtainable.

(ii) The co-ordination of any intelligence data which might be required by the Chiefs of Staff or the Joint Planning Sub-Committee for them.

(iii) The consideration of any further measures which might be thought necessary in order to improve the efficient working of the intelligence organisation of the country as a whole'.[57]

'The intelligence organisation of the country as a whole.' It was a concept that had been evolving for twenty years, but evolving slowly, haphazardly and only in response to events in the absence of a single co-ordinating authority.

---

57. CAB 53/51, COS 935 (JIC) of 4 July 1939.

CHAPTER 2

The State of Intelligence up to September 1939

F ROM WHAT we have said about the organisation of intelligence up to the outbreak of war it will be clear that not the least of the obstacles to efficiency were administrative in origin and character. As we shall see, it was in consequence of these, and particularly of the lack of co-ordination and of provision for central assessment, that information existed without being properly used. But intelligence was also impeded by difficulties arising from the nature and the state of its sources of information, and these difficulties were not only more technical than the administrative obstacles but also more intractable. At any rate theoretically, there was no restriction on the freedom to make organisational improvements; actually, if slowly, such improvements were made. Even in principle, however, by the very nature of the sources, some of the technical difficulties were insurmountable in time of peace, and this placed serious limitations on the information that intelligence could provide.

By far the most extensive system for acquiring information was the overt one by which British diplomatic missions overseas sent in a stream of despatches, telegrams and letters to the Foreign Office. It was one of the chief functions of the missions to keep London informed of political, military and economic developments in the countries to which they were accredited. Their principal sources of information were the obvious ones: the Press and other public media, of which they undertook a closer scrutiny than was attempted by the departments in London; the opportunities they had in most countries for making first-hand observations; the judgments they formed on the information they received, confidential and otherwise, in the course of their official and unofficial contacts. Their reports were not regarded as intelligence, a term restricted to information obtained from secret sources, and before September 1939, when the DNI arranged with 'C' that discreet co-operation could take place between the naval attachés and representatives of the SIS, the missions, and the Service attachés who were attached to them, were discouraged from using clandestine methods or even from having official connections with those who were using such methods – the overseas representatives of SIS.

Their opportunities for acquiring information thus varied from place to place and from time to time, according to the condition of

Great Britain's relations with the country to which they were accredited, the security measures in force there, a mission's relations with the embassies of other states and the ability of the individuals employed. From Moscow, for example, the British Ambassador often complained during 1937 that Russians never came to see him; 'as a result he gets no information and the condition of the country is a mystery to him'.[1] In October 1938 he was still reporting that 'it is impossible to obtain even an inkling of what is discussed within [the Kremlin's] walls'.[2] From early in 1939, when a change of ambassador coincided with a change in the Soviet government's outlook, the embassy was able to pass on rumours that Germany was interested in an agreement with Russia and also to report that the Soviet authorities were hinting that, although the capitulation of France and Great Britain in the Munich crisis had disturbed them, they were interested in a rapprochement with Great Britain.[3] By then, however, such hints and rumours were common currency in Europe, and neither from the embassy nor from any other source did the British government obtain reliable and timely intelligence about the Russo-German negotiations of the summer of 1939. In Berlin contacts were good up to 1937 – the embassy's opportunities being all the greater because the German government allowed British officers a wide if not an unlimited access, on a reciprocal basis, to its military establishments[4] – but thereafter they deteriorated rapidly.

The loss of official contacts in Germany was partly offset by the opening of others when the hostility of the German authorities made the task of the Berlin embassy more difficult. The British attachés themselves improved their methods of making first-hand observations of Germany's military preparations. The attachés of other states which felt threatened by Germany pooled their knowledge with their British colleagues. German citizens, and even officers of the German General Staff, fearing that Hitler's policies threatened to lead to war, passed confidential information to the embassy.[5] Increasingly, also, Germans in opposition to Hitler made visits to London to convey warnings to the British government either directly or through the agency of their private contacts with British subjects.[6]

The work of the embassies and the attachés had always been

---

1. Mr Neville Chamberlain's letters, 7 October 1937 (Neville Chamberlain Papers, Birmingham University Library). Quoted in K Middlemas, *Diplomacy of Illusion* (1972), p. 28.

2. FO 371/22289, N5764/97/38.

3. E L Woodward and R Butler (eds) *Documents on British Foreign Policy 1919–1939*, Series 3, Vol 4, pp 70–71, 123–124.

4. Major-General K Strong, *Intelligence at the Top* (1968), p 24.

5. ibid, for a good general account of the work of an attaché.

6. I Colvin, *Vansittart in Office* (1965), p 154; FO 371/21732, C8520/1941/18. See also T Prittie, *Germans against Hitler* (1964); G Ritter, *The German Resistance* (1958); P Seabury, *The Wilhelmstrasse* (Berkeley, 1964); A P Young, *The 'X' Documents* (1974).

supplemented by reports which British subjects – bankers and industrialists, merchants and merchant navy captains, politicians and journalists – passed to embassies or to their acquaintances in Whitehall. Like the approaches made by German citizens, on which they were now more frequently based, such reports also increased as the international system became more disturbed; and in 1938 and 1939, to judge by the number that remain in the files of the Foreign Office, they became a flood. Like them, moreover, they began to exert an independent influence in some official quarters, whereas they had previously been checked against information obtained from official sources and kept firmly subordinate to it.

From the end of 1932, to take one example of this development, the Foreign Office received regular assessments of the political situation in central Europe from Group Captain M G Christie, who had previously served as Air Attaché in Berlin though he was now a private citizen.* The Foreign Office occasionally asked for his advice when it was preparing memoranda, but until the end of 1935 it was comparing his assessments with the official attaché reports and sometimes commenting sceptically upon them.[7] But from the end of 1935, when they became more frequent and more detailed, Christie began to send almost all his reports direct to the Permanent Under-Secretary, Sir Robert Vansittart, and the Permanent Under-Secretary began to make use of them as part of what was virtually a private intelligence service – first by quoting telling phrases from them in his own memoranda, and attributing them to 'a very secret source', and later, especially after he was made Chief Diplomatic Adviser in January 1938, by circulating them as they stood, with only such alteration as was necessary to make it appear that they had been written by himself.[8] Nor did this collaboration stop at the official circulation of private political assessments. During 1938 and 1939 Vansittart turned several messages from Christie and other private informants[9] into insistent minutes to the Foreign Secretary in an attempt to influence the decisions of the Cabinet.[10]

The growth of these practices owed something to the uncertainty

---

* He was not, as has been claimed, employed by the SIS.

7. FO 371/15946, C8681/235/18; FO 371/17706, C2309/29/18; FO 371/17708, C4839/29/18; FO 371/18352, R3606/37/3; FO 371/18857, C891/111/18; Christie Papers, Churchill College, Cambridge, 180/1/6.
8. eg a Christie report on 12 March 1938 (Christie Papers 180/1/26A) reappears as a Vansittart memorandum. (see Vansittart Papers, Churchill College, Cambridge, 1/23).
9. See T P Conwell-Evans, *None so Blind* (1957); Young, op cit; S Aster, *1939: The Making of the Second World War* (1973), pp 57–59, 345; Middlemas, op cit, p 298.
10. FO 371/21728, C7315/1941/18 of 21 July 1938; FO 371/21729, C7648/1941/18 of 27 July 1938; FO 371/21708, C7007/1180/18 of 24 July 1938; FO 371/21708, C12655/1180/18 of 7 Dec 1938; FO 371/21729, C7560/1941/18 and C7591/1941/18 of 25 and 26 July 1938; FO 371/21664, C11164/62/18 of 29 Sept 1938.

and the disagreements about policy that accompanied the rapid deterioration of the international situation. It owed something, also, to Whitehall's lack of adequate arrangements for central and considered assessment of such intelligence as was available; and from early in 1939, by which time criticism of Vansittart's 'private detective agency' and of his impulsive response to information had become rife both in the Foreign Office and elsewhere in Whitehall,[11] it contributed to the determination to remedy that defect.* But underlying these wider explanations there were two more particular reasons for the development. The first was that when the deterioration was so closely associated with the activities of Germany, Russia, Italy and Japan, totalitarian states where intense security precautions and drastic police measures greatly exacerbated the difficulty of obtaining good intelligence, the diplomatic reporting system was unable to give advance notice of new developments with the firmness and precision that was increasingly called for. The second was that when the supply of information from the embassies was unable to meet this need, the clandestine sources were also failing to do so.

In the case of one of these sources, aerial photographic reconnaissance, we have already sufficiently explained why its clandestine use, involving the over-flying of Germany and the Mediterranean states, began only in the spring of 1939 and was not organised on a Service basis before the outbreak of war.† The others – the SIS's espionage system and Sigint – were in organised existence throughout the inter-war years and there is no simple explanation of their deficiency during the approach to war. It was due in some measure to financial stringency, in some measure to technical difficulties which could not be surmounted in peace-time, and in some measure to the fact that they could no more meet the most urgent of peace-time requirements, particularly the need for information about the intentions of foreign states, than could the diplomatic reporting system.

□

Evidence that they suffered from shortage of funds is to be found in the proceedings of Cabinet and CID committees and sub-committees. These show that from 1935, when the inability of the embassies to provide precise forward intelligence was beginning to be recognised,

---

* See Chapter 1, p 42.
† See Chapter 1, pp 28–29, and Appendix 2.

11. B Bond (ed) *Chief of Staff: The Pownall Diaries*, Vol 1 (1972), p 183 (23 January 1939, p 187 (13 February 1939); D Dilks (ed) *The Diaries of Sir Alexander Cadogan*, (1971), p 182 (18 August 1939); J Harvey (ed) *The Harvey Diaries* (1970), pp 326–327 (1 November 1939); Middlemas, op cit, pp 91, 232, 245, 320(n). We are also indebted to Mr D G Boadle who is writing a dissertation on this subject for the PhD degree in the University of Cambridge.

urgent requests were made at the highest level for a large increase of expenditure on the SIS. They also show, however, that these requests were met only in part, and with considerable delay, and this is confirmed by a series of complaints and pleas from the CSS.

In April 1935 the Cabinet set up an emergency committee to consider Hitler's claim, in his recent discussions with Sir John Simon, the Foreign Secretary, that the German Air Force had already achieved parity with the RAF. In the following month this committee, among other steps, recommended that the SIS should be given more money and that, as it was undesirable to use supplementary estimates for this purpose, the Foreign Office and the Treasury should effect an increase in some other way.[12] The Cabinet in its discussion of this report appears to have paid no attention to this recommendation.[13] Later in 1935, however, the recommendation was repeated by the Defence Requirements Sub-Committee of the CID (the DRC).

The DRC had been set up in November 1933 to report on the worst deficiencies facing the armed services. Between then and the second half of 1935 it submitted three reports to a ministerial committee.* The first DRC report concluded in March 1934 that Germany was the main potential enemy against which long-term defence must be prepared.[14] The outcome of the second DRC report was a decision by the ministerial committee in July 1935 that, as it was impossible to guarantee peace beyond January 1939, the DRC must elaborate defence programmes providing for a state of readiness by the end of the fiscal year 1938–39.[15] Intelligence from the SIS and GC and CS exercised little influence on these crucial decisions, which were mainly based on application of overt information and common sense to strategic and political assessments of the changing international situation. Essentially, the same was true of the DRC's third report. A vast series of detailed recommendations for the overhaul of British defences, this incorporated reasonably detailed information on some subjects – on foreign naval strengths and naval reconstruction and modernisation programmes, as also on the expected development of Japanese naval air power – but it stressed the meagreness of existing knowledge about Germany's offensive capacity, especially in the air, and it included in this connection a recommendation about intelligence.

---

* At first this was the Ministerial Committee on Disarmament (DCM). From mid-1935 the reports went to a Ministerial Committee on Defence Policy and Requirements (DPR).

12. CAB 21/417, FA/D/33 and CAB 21/419, FA/D/35; CAB 23/81, CAB 24 (35) of 17 April; CAB 24/255, CP 100 (35) of 13 May, CP 103 (35) of 17 May, CP 106 (35) of 20 May; CAB 24/254, Anglo-German Conservations, 25 and 26 March 1938.
13. CAB 23/81, Cab 27 (35) of 15 May, Cab 29 (35) of 21 May.
14. CAB 16/109, DRC 14 of 28 February 1934.
15. CAB 16/136, DPR 4th Meeting, 29 July 1935; CAB 4/24, CID 1215B of 2 March 1936, enclosure No 2, Vol I, Annex.

Possibly in reference to information about warship construction at
Kiel which the SIS had obtained in May 1934, and which it had
circulated as the first sign that Germany was contravening the naval
clauses of the Versailles Treaty, the report noted that 'a recent
illustration of effective concealment on Germany's part is to be found
in her naval rearmament, on which our Intelligence proved defective',
and then went on to say 'We know something of Germany's industrial
development and capacity, but it would be a dangerous illusion for
us to infer that we have a reliable measure of what she can do; still
less of what she may be able to do in the near future. The best we
can do is to strengthen our Intelligence system and our own war
potential (output capacity) so as to be able to increase our forces
correspondingly in the case of a German increase. But, although we
have included recommendations for both these purposes, we can give
no assurance, especially in regard to aircraft production, that we
may not be at a serious disadvantage compared with Germany'.[16] Its
recommendation for the strengthening of intelligence took the form
of urging more funds for the SIS. 'If [its] allowance is not augmented,
and very largely augmented, the organisation cannot be expected
to fulfil its functions, and this country will be most dangerously
handicapped. It is difficult to assign an exact figure to this service, on
which increased demands are continually being made; but nothing less
than £500,000 will be really adequate.'[17] This figure may be compared
with the one established in 1922 after economies were made following
the First World War. In 1919 the 1920 estimates for the SIS were
reduced from £240,000 to £125,000. In 1920 the Foreign Office, under
Treasury pressure, proposed to reduce this sum again, from £125,000
to £65,000. In view of objections to any further reduction from Mr
Churchill, Secretary of State for War, on behalf of the General Staff,
the Secret Service Committee, originally a ministerial committee under
the chairmanship of the Foreign Secretary, was revived as a committee
of officials under Sir Warren Fisher in 1921, when it fixed expenditure
on the SIS at £100,000. In 1922 after further discussions in which the
War Office countered a reduction to £65,000 with a demand for
£150,000, the Secret Service Committee set the figure at £90,000.[18] For
later years no figures are available; the Secret Service Committee was
reconvened in 1925 and 1931 but finance is not mentioned in the
surviving records of these later meetings.

The Defence Policy and Requirements Committee accepted the
recommendation of the DRC in principle at the end of January 1936,
thus authorising the Treasury to allow for an increase in the secret
vote in its estimates for the coming financial year. Cabinet approval

---

16. CAB 4/24, CID 1215B of 2 March 1936, enclosure No 2, Vols I and II.
17. ibid, Vol I, para 106.
18. Unregistered Papers in Cabinet Office Archive. A copy of some of these
papers is to be found in the Lloyd George Papers in the House of Lords Library.

followed at the end of February.[19] But the Committee had accepted that it would be impossible to grant so large a sum as £500,000 immediately and, apart from the fact that the Cabinet and its committees do not appear to have discussed the subject again before the outbreak of war, the complaints of the CSS make it clear that, whatever increases he did receive, he regarded them as quite inadequate.

At the height of the Abyssinian crisis in 1935 the CSS had warned that financial stringency had long ago forced the SIS to abandon its activities in several countries which would have been good bases for obtaining information about Italy; and he had complained at the same time that the SIS's total budget had been so reduced that it equalled only the normal cost of maintaining one destroyer in Home Waters. After the German occupation of the Rhineland in the spring of 1936 he attempted to get more funds than the Cabinet had approved in the previous February, or to get funds more quickly, but he met with so little success that the SIS 'had to depend more and more on French information' about Germany. During 1938, following the Anschluss of Austria, he secured some increase. But financial stringency returned after the Munich crisis in the autumn of that year.

The gravest effects of this stringency were encountered, without doubt, only when war broke out. The SIS had then to establish reporting systems and stay-behind networks in Europe in haste, and in difficult conditions, because the work had previously been impossible for lack of money.* At GC and CS, in the same way, work was impeded at the outbreak of war, and for some time afterwards, by the lack of pre-war preparations.† There was a desperate shortage of receivers for wireless interception, notwithstanding the fact that it had issued frequent warnings on this subject since 1932, while the staff was for some time less familiar than it might have been with the military communications systems of Germany and potential enemy states because by no means all the available military traffic of these states had been intercepted in recent years and even less of it had been closely studied. More immediately, for their bearing on the state of intelligence in the pre-war years, the direct consequences of the shortage of funds were less serious than the fact that the shortage accentuated the other limitations facing GC and CS and the SIS.

□

* There is no evidence that, as has sometimes been claimed,[20] a ban was placed on SIS activities in Italian territories before the war.
† GC and CS was borne on the Foreign Office Vote, and not on the Secret Service vote like the SIS, and we have traced no record of what was spent on it, or asked for on its behalf, before the war.

19. CAB 4/24, CID 1215B of 2 March 1936, covering note and enclosure No 1, para 51; CAB 16/123, DPR (DR) 9th Meeting, 31 January 1936.
20. Major General I S O Playfair, *The Mediterranean and the Middle East*, Vol 1, (1956), p. 9; CAB 79/6, COS (40) 255th Meeting, 8 August.

For some years after its establishment the staff of GC and CS and the interception resources provided for it, limited though they were, were not inadequate for the amount of work available. As a result of the phasing out of military activities and the extension of land-lines, the armed forces of foreign states made little use of wireless after the early 1920s. Until the early 1930s, moreover, most military wireless transmissions were in plain language, which in London, though not at the Sigint establishments overseas, was regarded as being of little value for intelligence purposes, and used medium frequencies which were not easily intercepted over long distances. The German armed forces were exceptional in regularly transmitting encyphered signals on stand-by wireless links for practice purposes; and it was far more difficult to intercept their signals in the United Kingdom or at British intercept stations in the Middle East than at stations in, for example, Poland and Czechoslovakia. Until 1935, for these reasons, GC and CS judged that none of the military traffic that it could decypher was worth circulating to the intelligence branches in the Service departments in Whitehall. At the same time, its research on the diplomatic cyphers of the important foreign states was yielding no results. Perhaps as a result of the notoriety gained by the decryption of the Zimmermann telegram in the First World War, those of Germany remained unreadable in the inter-war years, and those of Russia – without doubt in consequence of revelations made in the House of Commons after the Arcos raid[21] – had become unreadable after 1927.

From the mid-1930s, as a result of the introduction of high frequencies for wireless, and still more in consequence of the acceleration of military preparations and the resumption of military operations, more and more encyphered military traffic was intercepted. And GC and CS by no means neglected the increased opportunities thus offered to it. Some of its Service sections received additional staff; the Italian sub-section of the Naval Section grew from 5 in 1934 to 18 by September 1937 and the Japanese sub-section was also expanded. The ablest cryptanalysts at GC and CS applied themselves to military cyphers. They did so to some purpose despite the fact that more sophisticated cyphers were being introduced, so that the most difficult cyphers of the First World War would have barely qualified for inclusion among the medium-grade cyphers that were now being used by the important states. By 1935 GC and CS had broken the chief army and naval cyphers of Japan and some of the high-grade cyphers used by the Italian Services and colonial authorities and was beginning to make progress with Italy's diplomatic cyphers.* The resulting intelligence threw useful light on Italy's intentions before

---

* See Chapter 6, pp 199–200.

21. Hansard Parliamentary Debates Vol 206, Cols 1842–1854, 2195–2310; Cmd 2874 (1927).

and during the Abyssinian crisis and the Spanish Civil War; and in the third report of the DRC and subsequent strategic appreciations it guided the estimates made for the Chiefs of Staff of the condition and whereabouts of the Japanese and Italian forces.[22] But by 1937 the contrast between these successes and GC and CS's lack of progress against German and Russian high-grade cyphers was becoming acute. And between 1937 and the outbreak of war in Europe, while the German and Russian cyphers remained impregnable, the Japanese cyphers also became unreadable. Japan introduced a new army cypher in 1937 which was not easily mastered. During 1938 and 1939 she made greater changes, and it was not until September 1939 that, beginning with the Fleet cypher, the new cyphers began to yield to GC and CS's attack.*

There was, of course, some increase of Sigint about the Russian and German armed forces from the early 1930s. From Russia sufficient military wireless traffic was intercepted from 1932 to justify the recruitment of two cryptanalysts; they made some advance against low-grade codes. With Germany's low-grade codes progress was made from 1934, when the regular interception of German military signals was undertaken for the first time in 15 years. The German Air Force produced a large amount of tactical traffic in the course of training; some of this was readily exploitable and from 1935, in conjunction with Traffic Analysis, it greatly eased the task of estimating the current operational strength and the dispositions of Germany's bomber and reconnaissance units. It had firmly identified 60 ground stations and 578 individual aircraft by September of that year, and although this kind of information by no means removed uncertainty about the further growth of the GAF, it remained the best source on that subject when the other sources were providing conflicting and only tentative assessments. Exploitation of the German Navy's use of call-signs made it possible to establish the number and, with the assistance of DF, the movements of its U-boats and surface units. But the Germany Navy made virtually no use of medium and low-grade codes, and for lack of traffic the medium and low-grade codes of the German Army remained as unreadable as did Germany's high-grade military cyphers. About those more was known than about Russia's. By 1937 it was established that, unlike their Japanese and Italian counterparts, the German Army, the German Navy and probably the Air Force, together with other state organisations like the railways and

---

* However, some Japanese Sigint continued to be available because of the familiarity with Japan's communications systems that had been built up over the years. It remained possible, for example, to keep track of her main naval movements.

22. For various detailed papers on the Japanese Navy see FO 371/17600, A8313/1938/45; ADM 1/9587, 9589, 9649, 9713; and Wells, op cit, pp 253-254, 320-321.

the SS, used, for all except their tactical communications, different versions of the same cypher system – the Enigma machine which had been put on the market in the 1920s but which the Germans had rendered more secure by progressive modifications. In 1937 GC and CS broke into the less modified and less secure model of this machine that was being used by the Germans, the Italians and the Spanish nationalist forces. But apart from this the Enigma still resisted attack, and it seemed likely that it would continue to do so. As late as July 1939, before receiving invaluable information about it from the Poles, who had been having some success with it for several years, GC and CS could hold out little hope of mastering it even in the event of war.*

There need be no doubt that obstacles of a technical nature go far to account for the lack of progress. On the one hand, the modifications the Germans added to the Enigma machine during the 1930s were making it an instrument for cyphers far more secure than those of Italy and Japan – and so much so that by 1938 the Germans had virtually brought the success of the Polish cryptanalysts to a close and had themselves become confident that the Enigma would be impregnable even in war conditions. On the other hand, even the most sophisticated cypher is liable to become more vulnerable if heavily used on interceptable communications; and whereas Italy and Japan, with their involvement in military operations across extended lines of communication, were at last producing enough military wireless traffic to enable the cryptanalysts to make progress, the German armed forces, like the Russian, were either less active or were operating on interior lines of communication and thus resorting far less to wireless. But when this has been said it remains unfortunate that despite the growing effort applied at GC and CS to military work after 1936, so little attention was devoted to the German problem.

The volume of German wireless transmissions, in Enigma as well as in the GAF's lower-grade codes, was increasing; it was steadily becoming less difficult to intercept them at British stations; yet even in 1939, for lack of sets and operators, by no means all German Service communications were being intercepted. Nor was all intercepted traffic being studied. Until 1937–38 no addition was made to the civilian staff as opposed to the service personnel at GC and CS; and because of the continuing shortage of German intercepts, the eight graduates then recruited were largely absorbed by the same growing burden of Japanese and Italian work that had led to the expansion of the Service sections. Although plans were made to take on some 60 more cryptanalysts in the event of war, there was no further addition to staff before the summer of 1939 apart from the temporary call-up of some of the 'hostilities only' staff during the Munich crisis. Thus almost down to the outbreak of war, when GC and CS's

---

* See above, pp 47–48.

emergency in-take quadrupled the cryptanalytical staff of the Service sections and nearly doubled the total cryptanalytical staff, work on Germany's Service cyphers was all but confined to the small group which, headed by civilians and working on behalf of all three Services, struggled with the Enigma. The naval sub-section of the German Section, which was started with one officer and a clerk as late as May 1938, still had no cryptanalysts. Since virtually no military traffic was intercepted except during summer exercises, the only regular work by cryptanalysts in the army sub-section was on police traffic. In the air sub-section the communications of the GAF were being studied by only a handful of people.

□

Had more German Sigint been available, it might still have failed to illuminate the darkening scene. At least in peace-time, governments are neither inclined nor forced to refer to the highest secrets of state in their signals communications. The German authorities were taking drastic security precautions. The intelligence branches in Whitehall were as yet unpractised in the art of inferring plans and intentions from the evidence of Sigint which, if always incontestable, is also always incomplete. However that may be, the almost total lack of German military Sigint, together with GC and CS's inability to read Germany's diplomatic cyphers, added to the already considerable difficulties of the SIS. At a time when the embassies and the other overt sources were issuing conflicting warnings and rumours about Germany's intentions, when warnings and rumours that were equally conflicting and equally difficult to substantiate formed the staple content of the diplomatic cyphers that were being read, and when little or no intelligence about such things as Germany's military strength and development was coming from these sources, the fact that the Whitehall departments had no reliable intelligence on these subjects from Sigint induced them to put mounting pressure on the SIS. In the absence of the Sigint check, on the other hand, they found it no less difficult to distinguish what was reliable and what was dubious in the reports circulated by the SIS, and their mounting pressure was accompanied by mounting criticism.

By the beginning of 1938 the War Office was regularly complaining that the SIS was failing to meet its increasingly urgent need for factual information about Germany's military capacities, equipment, preparations and movements, while in that year the Air Ministry, somewhat better placed up to then as a result of the receipt of useful SIS reports and of the existence of low-grade Sigint about the GAF, dismissed SIS intelligence of this kind as being 'normally 80% inaccurate'. And both departments believed that the SIS was failing in what they judged to be its main task because its limited resources were being too much diverted to, or distracted by, the collection and distribution of political speculation about Germany's immediate intentions. By February 1939, however, the Foreign Office was also disenchanted with the SIS's performance, and so much so that Sir Alexander Cadogan, the Permanent Under-Secretary, felt it necessary to issue a minute in defence of it. 'Our agents', he wrote, 'are of course bound to report rumours or items of information which come into their possession; they exercise a certain amount of discrimination themselves, but naturally do not take the responsibility of too much selection and it is our job here to weigh up the information which we receive and try to draw more or less reasonable conclusions from it. In that we may fail and if so it is our fault, but I do not think it is fair to blame the SIS. Moreover' – and here he was referring to reports received from the embassies as well as from Vansittart's private detective agency –* 'it is true to say that the recent scares have not originated principally with the SIS agents in Germany, but have come to us from other sources'.[23]

There was some substance, naturally, in the departmental criticisms. In July 1938, defending his organisation against the Service complaints, the CSS admitted that except on naval construction, where it was excellent, the SIS's intelligence on military and industrial matters was at best fair; he also recognised that its political reports contained too much propaganda, both from Nazi sources and from the opposition groups in Germany. On this account, instead of circulating all political reports, the SIS in the immediate pre-war years was eliminating all items that were obviously of doubtful credibility. But in the attempt to use its discretion it ran the risk of introducing bias into the selection from the reports. Moreover, while the SIS received too little guidance from the Service departments in the form of requests for precise intelligence or direct questions about the SIS reports they had received on military matters, it was under increasing pressure from the Foreign Office to obtain as much political intelligence as possible, even on such matters as whether the German opposition groups could form an alternative German government.[24]† Nor, finally, did the criticisms sufficiently allow for the fact that, although in some ways the SIS found it more and more difficult to get reliable intelligence, or to get it in good time, this was because its organisation in Europe sustained a series of severe blows as the international situation became more bleak.

---

* See above, pp 47–48.

† Various references to the activities of the SIS in relation to this subject occur in documents that have been opened to the public, and they have evoked suspicions which call for a brief commentary.

The SIS's search for information as to the likelihood of a revolt in Germany widened in the spring of 1939, at his request, into preliminary discussions with a

23. Aster, op cit, pp 53–54, quoting from FO 800/270, 39/9; letter from Cadogan to Neville Henderson.
24. CAB 27/624, FP (36) 35th and 36th Meetings, 23 and 26 January 1939.

Having suffered one serious setback when the German entry into Austria in the spring of 1938 led to the arrest of the head of its Vienna station, it suffered another when the German seizure of Prague in the spring of 1939 brought about the collapse of its organisation in Czechoslovakia. Earlier still – though it remained unaware of this development until its representatives at The Hague were captured at Venlo – its organisation in Holland had been penetrated by German counter-intelligence since 1935. To make matters worse, the SIS was unable before 1939 to begin issuing W/T sets to its agents in the field even though events emphasised the need for faster communications. During the Munich crisis, for example, intelligence from some of its sources in Germany was cut off or greatly delayed by the closure of the German-Danish frontier.

Despite the difficulties, however, the SIS's performance was im-

---

German emissary about the conditions on which the British government might recognise and support the German resistance if it attempted to establish an alternative German government. These discussions became detailed only after the outbreak of war. Transferred to Holland, they culminated in the capture at Venlo, on 9 November 1939 of two of the SIS's representatives at The Hague; the German emissary was a German security official. On the basis of documents in the PRO and other open archives, it has been claimed that in these discussions the Prime Minister 'used the SIS to investigate the possibility of a compromise peace with Germany in...an operation which was concealed from the majority of his colleagues' and that 'it was only because the affair ended dramatically with the kidnapping of two British agents from Holland that this episode became known at all...'[25] Such opened documents as we have seen do not justify these claims. They show that the discussions, though carried out through the SIS, were authorised and supervised by the Foreign Office; that on 24 October 1939 the Foreign Office obtained the approval of the Prime Minister for the reply to a request for a statement of the British conditions; that when this statement prompted a further German request for elaboration the Prime Minister put the matter before the War Cabinet on 1 November; and that it was after consultation with other ministers following this meeting that the Prime Minister and the Foreign Secretary on 6 November authorised the terms of a further statement to the German emissary and that, expressing considerable doubt as to whether the German approach would lead to anything or was even genuine, the Foreign Secretary on 7 November told the French Ambassador what was taking place. Although the documents suggest that in the discussions with their colleagues from 1 November the Prime Minister and the Foreign Secretary were embarrassed by the fact that they had not reported the earlier stages of the negotiations to the Cabinet, they also suggest that the reason for this omission was not their wish to negotiate without the knowledge of the Cabinet but their scepticism as to whether anything would come out of the German request for detailed negotiations.[26]

Certain Foreign Office files referring to this episode have not been released. They are closed till the year 2015 on the grounds mentioned in our Preface: they contain references to technical matters and to individuals. We have been allowed to consult these files in accordance with the terms outlined in the Preface. In our opinion they contain nothing to modify the conclusions we have reached on the basis of the opened documents about the relationship between the SIS and the Prime Minister and between the Prime Minister and the rest of the Cabinet.

25. Letter from Dr C MacDonald, *The Times*, 1 December 1977.

26. Dilks (ed), op cit, pp 226, 228–230; CAB 65/4, WM (39) 67 CA, 1 November; Neville Chamberlain Papers (Birmingham University Library), NC 8/29/1–4 of 30 October, 7 November and 16 November 1939.

proving in some ways during the 18 months before the outbreak of war. Although Whitehall had been more than half expecting the German occupation of the Rhineland in 1936 and of Austria in the spring of 1938, the SIS, like the embassies and the other overt sources, gave no advance warning of these moves. Before and during the Munich crisis, the German entry into Prague and the attack on Poland, in contrast, it provided plentiful intelligence about Germany's plans.

The main reason why it was able to do this lay with the German moves themselves. Especially after the Anschluss with Austria in March 1938, these were creating the circumstances in which it is possible to recruit the best, and perhaps the only good, agents – those who from positions of responsibility volunteer their services from opposition to some policies or principles of government, or from devotion to others, rather than for money. One such informant, who was to continue to supply the SIS with first-class political and military intelligence during the first two years of the war, was a high-ranking officer in the Abwehr, the German military intelligence agency, who approached the Czech intelligence service in February 1936. Between then and the outbreak of war, indirectly through the Czechs at first, directly when he was exploited jointly by the SIS and the exiled Czech intelligence service in London after the German occupation of Prague in the spring of 1939, this man, Paul Thümmel, known to the Czechs as A-54, supplied not only excellent information about Germany's order of battle and mobilisation plans, and some information about the equipment of the German Army and Air Force,[27] but also advance notice of Germany's plans for intervention in the Sudetenland from the summer of 1937, for action against Czechoslovakia from the spring of 1938, for the seizure of Prague in the spring of 1939 and, from the spring of 1939, for the attack on Poland.[28]* From as early as 1936 informants of the same kind established contact with MI5. From one such source Whitehall obtained during the Munich crisis the schedules of Germany's original mobilisation plans and, as they arose, the alterations the Germans made to them. Men in similar positions offered their services to the French intelligence authorities[29] and no doubt to others also.

---

* As there will be speculation on this subject we may say that insofar as the British records are any guide A-54 was the sole Abwehr officer who collaborated directly with the Allied intelligence organisations. As will be mentioned later in the text General Oster, the second in command of the Abwehr who was also a member of the German resistance, confined himself to giving last-minute warnings to various authorities on the continent of impending German attacks, see Chapter 3, pp 113, 114, 117, Chapter 4, p 135.

27. C. Amort and I M Jedlica, *The Canaris File* (1970), pp. 11, 23; F. Moravec, *Master of Spies* (1975), pp 77–87.
28. Dilks (ed) op cit, pp 155–156, 158; Moravec, op cit, pp 123–131, 150–151, 182–183; Amort and Jedlica, op cit, pp 24, 26–41.
29. P. Paillole, *Services Spéciaux*, pp 107–108, 115, 117, 147, 152–153.

As was to be expected of informants as well placed as these, their information was as reliable as it was detailed. But it is clear from historical analyses of the pre-war crises that, as with the increasingly frequent and increasingly alarming reports coming in from the embassies, the attachés and Whitehall's various unofficial informants, so with those reaching the SIS, it was no easy task to distinguish reliable information from alarmist warnings or even from the spurious rumours that were being circulated by the German authorities.[30] More than that, it is equally clear from these analyses that, as the international scene became more critical, the over-riding problem in Whitehall was ceasing to be that of knowing what the German government intended to do next and was becoming that of deciding whether and how the British government should act, and thus of calculating how Hitler would respond to whatever the British government might do. On Hitler's intentions there was no lack of intelligence, even if it was not all reliable. As to what Hitler would do if other governments moved to check or deflect his expansionist plans, no agent, however well placed, could provide the answer, or could be believed if he professed to do so, for not even Hitler and his immediate entourage knew what the answer would be.

□

Whitehall's uncertainty as to how Hitler would react to such steps as might be initiated by other governments – an uncertainty that could not be reduced by obtaining advance information about his state of mind from political and military indications – was all the greater because Whitehall was confronted by difficult problems in assessing the state of the German economy. In a situation in which Hitler's intentions were clearly disruptive but his determination to pursue them could only be guessed at, it would at least have been helpful to know whether or not he would be restrained by economic considerations. This, too, however, was a matter on which Whitehall was in no position to make a judgement. It had established an interdepartmental body for collecting and assessing intelligence on the economies of foreign states, especially Germany. But this organisation, which in any case did not claim that political and military implications could be deduced from economic analysis, recognised that such an exercise would be especially unprofitable in relation to Germany. Even at the elementary level, despite its long experience in the routine work of collecting the facts about the economies of foreign states, the organisation found it no easy task to calculate the capacity and limitations of Germany's economy.

This task was in any case difficult because the factual evidence was

---

30. Aster, op cit; Middlemass, op cit: Dilks (ed), op cit.

incomplete. The German government, secretive about the economic information which democratic governments customarily made public, did not even publish an annual Budget after 1935, and to seek this type of information by intelligence operations was out of the question in view of the higher priority of military and political intelligence. To make matters still more difficult, by the standards of the democratic nations with market economies the German economy under the Nazi dictatorship presented unorthodox characteristics that were open to a variety of interpretation. While there could be no doubt that the economy was geared to massive rearmament and other war preparations, the degree to which resources had been mobilised for that purpose and the true costs of these preparations for the German people were very difficult to estimate. Outward signs of strain were evident in the balance of payments difficulties which marked the years immediately before 1939; full employment seemed to leave little room for further expansion of industrial output; large imports of raw materials were clearly essential if the momentum of rearmament was to be maintained. On the other hand, the civilian standard of life was reasonably well maintained and capital expenditure on civil projects continued on a very large scale. How long the economic policy of 'guns and butter' could be prolonged, especially if Hitler were to plunge the country into a major war, was a matter for debate.

In this situation intelligence faced two principal problems. One was to determine the actual level of armaments production and the scale and type of equipment being provided for the German armed forces. The second was to assess the condition of the economy as a whole, its manpower, food supplies, and raw material and fuel resources, and from readings of these basic facts to draw conclusions about Germany's capacity to sustain her military strength in war and her vulnerability to economic pressure exerted by her enemies.

None of the German armed services was of greater concern to the British government than the Air Force. The German aircraft industry was therefore the object of intense study by the Industrial Intelligence Centre (IIC) and the Air Ministry, who collaborated in producing twelve reports upon it between March 1934 and July 1939 which, after scrutiny by the Industrial Intelligence in Foreign Countries Sub-Committee (FCI), were submitted to the CID.[31] Observation of individual factories and, especially, the size and composition of their labour forces provided the basis in these reports for statistical

31. CAB 4/22, CID 1134B of 22 March 1934; CAB 4/23, CID 1151B of 5 November 1934, CID 1172B of April 1935, CID 1186B of 9 September 1935; CAB 4/24, CID 1218B of 9 March 1936, CID 1250B of 22 July 1936; CAB 4/25, CID 1284B of 30 November 1936; CAB 4/26, CID 1339B of 7 July 1937; CAB 4/27, CID 1407B of 4 March 1938; CAB 4/28, CID 1472B of 15 August 1938; CAB 4/29, CID 1541B of 20 March 1939; CAB 4/30, CID 1569B of 24 July 1939.

calculations of the current output of air frames and engines. Until 1938 access to the German aircraft industry by British aeronautical engineers was comparatively easy and they were the principal source of information; it is significant that visits by British observers to German factories, the first by an Air Ministry mission in May 1936 and the second by Mr Roy Fedden of the Bristol Aeroplane Company in the summer of 1937, are recorded as major sources of intelligence used in correcting estimates based on other material. The other sources were the SIS and the energetic Air Attaché in Berlin, who used his own plane to observe factories and GAF installations from the air.[32]

Using this type of source material the IIC and the Air Ministry drew an intelligence picture of the aircraft industry which took account of special features such as the shortage of engines which occurred before 1935, the systems used in manufacturing components and assembling planes, the number of shifts being worked, hours of work and plan reorganisation. The intelligence was sufficiently sensitive to detect periods of stagnation in the growth-rate in mid-1936 and in 1938–39 and sufficiently accurate to permit estimates of the output of complete 'military-type' aircraft (including trainers), at 550 a month in 1938 and 725–750 a month in mid-1939, which were only slightly above the figures of actual output. By the autumn of 1939 output was in fact 700 aircraft a month.[33] Reliance upon the size and utilization of the labour force as the chief factor in calculating the output of the industry was, however, to be a contributory cause of British over-estimates of the output of German aircraft in 1940 and 1941. The estimates for mid-July 1939, which were so nearly accurate, assumed that at that time the industry was working upon a one-shift system, but the IIC and the Air Ministry also calculated that, in an 'emergency', output could be increased to 1,500 planes a month if three shifts and a seven-day week were to be introduced. Without an intimate knowledge of German intentions and of the internal problems of the industry there was a natural tendency in Britain to make a 'worst case' assumption that German output would move towards its estimated full potential of 1,500 planes a month after the outbreak of war. The German authorities in fact planned to produce 2,000 planes a month at the outbreak of war, but actual output fell far short of this, partly because planning and managerial shortcomings in the industry hampered its performance. By December 1940 actual output reached only 779 planes a month.[34]

---

32. CAB 23/87, Cab 5 (37) of 3 February and Cab 9 (37) of 24 February; CAB 24/268, CP 69 (37) of 20 February (Air Vice Marshal Courtney's Mission of May 1936); CAB 16/182, DP (P) 7 of 16 July 1937 (Fedden report).

33. AIR 41/10, *The Rise and Fall of the German Air Force* (1948), p 19.

34. A S Milward, *The German Economy at War* (1965), p 137.

The difficulty of calculating the exact state of the industries producing weapons and munitions for the army was more acute, since production was dispersed over many sectors of industry and the number of factories was enormously greater. Estimates of arms production in this field, made jointly by the IIC and the War Office,[35] differed from the reports in the aircraft industry series in not setting out the basic factory information on which the global estimates were based, and they did not break down those estimates to give, for example, the number of tanks produced. The last assessment before the war, in July 1939,[36] estimated that Germany had available for immediate mobilisation a total of 120–130 divisions, of which about two-thirds would be fully armed and equipped in the most modern fashion, and that the delivery of arms and equipment was proceeding at a rate sufficient to arm 16–17 new divisions per annum.

However the calculations were made, their effect was to over-estimate the number of tanks produced for the German Army before the war. In September 1939 the War Office believed that the Germans possessed 5,000 tanks of which 1,400 were medium and 3,600 were light.[37] German Army records show that the total German stock in September 1939 was 3,000 tanks, of which 300 were medium and the remainder light (including 1,500 Pzkw I).[38]

Of the armaments industry the report of July 1939 said that 'in spite of the continued demands made upon industry by naval and air construction, the export market, the Four Year Plan...and other special activities...the average rate of output of armaments for the German Army...is slightly greater than in 1938.... At the same time the continued intensification of production, the resulting shortage of really skilled labour and the extended use of substitutes has led to a noticeable decrease in the quality of German industry which extends to the armament industry'.[39] Here, in contrast to the aircraft industry, the assessment depicted an industry already very fully extended. No attempt was made to forecast its maximum capacity, and it would almost certainly have been impossible to do so.

Pre-war estimates of U-boat production were based upon the numbers of U-boats observed to be in service with the German Navy, on SIS reports and on deductions from the German performance in building U-boats in the First World War. Under the terms of the Anglo-German Naval Treaty of 1935 Germany was allowed to build

---

35. CAB 4/23, CID 1152B of 5 November 1934; CAB 4/25, CID 1303B of 4 February 1937; CAB 4/26, CID 1345B of 26 July 1937; CAB 4/27, CID 1421B of 22 April 1938; CAB 4/28, CID 1449B of 21 July 1938; CAB 4/29, CID 1507B of 19 January 1939; CAB 4/30, CID 1571B of 24 July 1939.
36. CAB 4/30, CID 1571B of 24 July 1939.
37. WO 190/891, MI 14 Appreciation No 27 of 20 February 1940.
38. US Strategic Bombing Survey, *The Effects of Strategic Bombing on the German War Economy* (Synoptic volume 1945), pp 163–165.
39. CAB 4/30, CID 1571B of 24 July 1939.

up to 57 U-boats. The Admiralty's own 'count' of U-boats appeared to confirm that this was the number actually completed on the eve of the war, but from the autumn of 1938 onwards SIS had been reporting that Germany had built more U-boats than allowed by the Treaty and that some were already operating in the south Atlantic. Unable to prove or disprove the truth of these reports NID reluctantly accepted them and taking a worst case assumption estimated that by September 1939 the German Navy had 66 U-boats. The fact that the total was 57 at the outbreak of war was not finally established by NID until April 1940.*[40]

Using their knowledge of the number of boats on the stocks in the summer of 1939 and drawing comparisons with the first 14 months of the First World War, NID forecast in September 1939 that by March 1940 129 vessels (including the pre-war total) would have been completed. This assumed an average production rate of about 10 per month for the period and also assumed that Germany would achieve 'full mass production' by November 1939.[41] It was later to be proved that these assumptions were unduly pessimistic. In fact only 63 were completed by March 1940, though plans of course existed for an expanded output. As in the case of the forecasts of aircraft production made by the IIC and the Air Ministry, the assumption made by NID that the Germans would immediately move to the maximum production of which they were capable on the outbreak of war was mistaken. The error was due not so much to 'economic' miscalculations as to ignorance of Hitler's intentions and of his concept of the 'economics of Blitzkrieg'.†

In the attempt to assess Germany's capacity and readiness for war these specialised calculations about her armaments industries had to be supplemented by a prolonged study of her vulnerability to economic pressure. On behalf of the Sub-Committee on Economic Pressure on Germany (EPG), the IIC undertook this work in a series of memoranda, initiated in July 1937, on Germany's probable economic situation in 1939.[42] As the work proceeded the IIC brought in the intelligence branches of the Service ministries,[43] the Food (Defence Plans) Department, the Board of Trade[44] and other departments to help it with its calculations. From the outset the IIC considered that Germany's difficult external financial situation would not prevent her from waging a war of short duration,[45] and

---

* See below, Chapter 7, p 231.

† See below, p 68.

40. Memoirs of Admiral Godfrey, Vol 5, Part 2, Chapter XXXIII, 'Truth, Reality and Publicity'.

41. ADM 233/84, NID 01449/39 of 29 September 1939.

42. CAB 47/13, ATB (EPG) 2 of 5 July 1937.

43. Especially CAB 47/13, ATB (EPG) 5 of 10 October 1937.

44. eg, CAB 47/14, ATB (EPG) 34 of 16 July 1938.

45. CAB 47/13, ATB (EPG) 2 of 5 July 1937.

consideration of the financial situation played little part in later EPG appreciations. Attempts to assess the German manpower situation were soon abandoned, almost certainly because the problem was too complex and the results too speculative.* Thus the appreciations were concerned mainly with the position in food, raw materials and fuel, and were largely based on published figures inadequately supported by reliable high-grade intelligence.

The last appreciation of this type to appear before the war was prepared by the IIC for the Advisory Committee on Trade (ATB) in May 1939.[47] It concluded that although the Four Year Plan of 1936 was reducing, and might further reduce, Germany's dependence upon imports of certain commodities, she could not yet have made herself 'indefinitely self-sufficient in all raw materials and foodstuffs'. On the basis of statistics of German imports in 1936 and 1937, qualified by what was known of the stock position, the IIC identified a large number of deficiency commodities.† It noted that for the first year of a war beginning in 1939 Germany, 'failing large reserves', would have to import 9–10 million tons of iron ore from Sweden. Given suitable political arrangements manganese could be imported from the USSR. The supply of non-ferrous metals would probably suffice for six months, after which a shortage would develop, led by copper. Germany was in a strong position as regards aluminium, zinc and lead, and Yugoslavia might be a most valuable potential source of supply of several non-ferrous metals. Romania was the sole source from which the minimum import requirement of 3½–4½ million tons of petroleum and its products in the first year of war could be met. The German government claimed four-fifths self-sufficiency in foodstuffs but supplies of edible oils and fat, of which 40 per cent were imported by sea, were vulnerable.

It was clearly impossible to estimate precisely the size of the deficiencies in any one commodity in a year of war without knowing the size of existing stocks and what proportion of imports could be cut off by blockade and other measures of economic warfare. About the size of stocks there was little information, although it was known that the level had been considerably raised during 1938 and that the process was continuing. Germany's objective was believed to be to create stocks equivalent to one year's peace-time requirements.

---

* Attempts were made elsewhere, mainly in the War Office, to assess the manpower situation, but the JIC was unable to reconcile the different assessments.[46]

† Food and feeding stuffs (cereals, fruit, fish, dairy products, oils and fats, coffee and cocoa). Other vegetable produce (tobacco, timber and rubber). Textile raw materials (cotton, wool, flax, hemp, jute, manila, sisal). Miscellaneous (hides and skins, leather, tanning materials). Minerals and metals (aluminium, asbestos, chrome, copper, iron, lead, manganese, nickel, phosphates, petroleum and products, pyrites, tin, zinc and certain ferro-alloys).

46. JIC 24 of 13 January 1937.
47. CAB 47/16, ATB 181 of 22 July 1938, Appendix I (revised 24 May 1939).

Reserves of foodstuffs, aluminium, certain ferro-alloys and aviation spirit were thought to have reached that level, while those of motor spirit and oils, other non-ferrous ores and metals were not thought to exceed six months' normal supplies. Reserves of iron ore were thought to be insignificant.

This appreciation did not follow up in detail the discussion on the size of petroleum stocks which had taken place in the EPG Sub-Committee in 1937.[48] It had then been estimated that commercial storage capacity in Germany might be 2½ million tons and the state emergency reserve about another 1 million tons rising to 2 million tons in 1939. In circumstances most favourable to Germany, therefore, commercial and state reserves taken together would amount to a maximum of 4½ million tons in 1939 and Germany would require to import 2½ million tons in the first year of war. When the situation was reviewed by the IIC on 24 May 1939 the minimum import requirement was raised to 3½–4½ million tons.[49] On 1 June 1939 the IIC estimated that stocks amounted to something less than 3 million tons.*[50]

The general conclusion reached by the IIC and accepted by the ATB Committee was that, as a result of the accumulation of stocks, reserves of food and certain raw materials had probably achieved the equivalent of one year's peace-time requirement. Assuming replenishment by land routes after the outbreak of war and the continuance of iron ore supplies from Sweden, Germany might be able to maintain her industrial activity without contraction for 15–18 months of war.[51]

As well as resting on a good deal of guesswork about the size of stocks, this conclusion involved an assumption about the extent to which Allied economic warfare measures would deny to Germany her essential imports. When the ATB presented its plan for the exercise of economic pressure to the CID on 27 July 1938[52] Mr Walter Elliott, Chairman of the ATB Committee, said that the crux of the problem lay in the fact that severe economic pressure could only be exercised through a system of rationing applicable to all neutral countries exporting to Germany. Whereas in the First World War there were only five, not particularly powerful, countries of this sort there were now nineteen to be taken into account, some of which might prove very troublesome. In discussion Sir Warren Fisher of the Treasury took the view that rationing was unlikely to be effective over the whole field. Access to Germany would probably always be available from the

---

* The actual balance according to German official figures was about 2.1 million tons.

48. CAB 47/13, ATB (EPG) 5 of 10 October 1937.
49. CAB 47/16, ATB 181, Appendix I (revised).
50. CAB/HIST/G/9/1/4, ICF 284 of 1 June 1939.
51. CAB 47/6, ATB 181, Appendix I (revised).
52. CAB 2/7, CID 331st Meeting of 27 July 1938.

south-east and she would be able to bring in great quantities of supplies from that quarter, regardless of whether other neutrals were rationed. Although his criticism was directed primarily at the measures proposed by the ATB Committee it implied Treasury doubts about the economic appreciation to which the proposed measures were related. The Treasury appears to have been less optimistic about weaknesses in the German economic situation than were either the ATB Committee or the IIC.* Treasury views were taken into account during the preparation of the ATB Committee's report, but on the outbreak of war the Treasury ceased to be involved in the economic intelligence system and its opinion played little or no part in the preparation of war-time assessments.

The ATB Committee's conclusion that Germany might be able to sustain full industrial activity for 15–18 months implied that supply difficulties would begin to make themselves felt if the war was to continue for a longer period. At the outbreak of war in September 1939 the implication was that German supply difficulties should begin to be apparent in the spring of 1941 if the war lasted so long, and that they would thereafter be considerable. British assessments of the German economic situation made in the summer of 1941 were to be considerably influenced by this pre-war assumption. But in 1939 the IIC and the ATB Committee were under no illusions about the effect of the economic factor on German capabilities in a *short* war. It would hardly count at all.

Their analysis of Germany's probable war-time supply position was not, of course, a comprehensive statement about the nature of the German economy on the eve of war. On this broad and speculative issue other opinions circulated in Whitehall, and while they sometimes conflicted, their general tendency was to strengthen a belief that manpower and resources had already been so fully mobilised as to leave comparatively little room for expansion of general industrial activity under war-time conditions.

The most important defect in the evidence upon which this opinion of the German economy rested was not that factual economic information was lacking on many points, but a misunderstanding of Hitler's own conception of the nature of war and the relationship of the economy to it. Hitler was aware of the facts presented to him by his advisers about the limitations of material resources, which did not differ greatly from those appearing in British assessments, but he confidently believed that successful lightning war would provide the nation, at a minimum cost, with the material resources which it lacked. This being so, he believed that mobilisation of resources for war production need not exceed that required for short-term military operations carried out on Blitzkrieg principles, a degree of mobilisa-

---

* See further below, pp 69–70.

tion which would not involve economic hardship for the civilian population: indeed the maintenance of the best possible conditions for the nation as a whole under war-time conditions was regarded by Hitler and the Nazi Party as an important guarantee of popular support. Having ensured that by 1940 the economy would provide adequate support for the type of campaigns he envisaged, and having appointed Goering to oversee the Four Year Plan, he expected that the economy would thereafter be rapidly adjusted to his military requirements. Short periods of intense economic effort requiring rapid changes of priority within the war sector of the economy, but leaving the production of consumer goods largely unaffected, would be geared to rapid and successful military campaigns.[53]

There is no sign in the available papers that Hitler's conception of the relationship between strategy and economics was understood in London on the eve of the war, although some of its symptoms were recognized in the reporting of the British embassy in Berlin. By 1936 the embassy's coverage of the German economy had become so extensive that its annual economic review appeared as a separate print. The three large economic annual reviews for 1936–38 singled out significant and paradoxical features of the German economy, showing that, within the framework of a stringent external financial situation, the Germans were making a frantic effort to produce steel and armaments, but at the same time continuing massive civilian construction, maintaining the output of consumer goods and keeping the cost of living stable.

Even so, the tenor of the reviews was to the effect that, so structured, the economy was being subjected to increasing strain. Reporting on the situation in 1936 the embassy considered that the home market was approaching a 'war-time' condition, inflation being avoided only by governmental stabilisation of wages and prices. The iron and steel industry was working at almost full capacity, in several other industries the industrial boom was exploiting all available capacity and there was an acute shortage of skilled labour.[54] In 1937 the salient features were the subservience of all economic considerations to Wehrwirtschaft: a substantial rise in industrial output (the level of production in particular industries being determined by the rationing of raw materials) and a marked shortage of skilled labour, involving a drive for the recruitment of apprentices.[55] The last pre-war review, covering 1938 and dated 24 May 1939, used dramatic language to describe the situation as it then appeared. Germany was heading with 'demoniac persistence' towards the goal of autarky and could not turn back. She must achieve the aims of the Four Year Plan or perish.

53. See B H. Klein, *Germany's Preparations for War* (Harvard 1959); A S Milward, op cit; B A Carroll, *Design for Total War*, (Mouton 1968).
54. FO 371/20727, C3226/78/18 of 21 April 1937.
55. FO 371/21702, C3960/541/18 of 5 May 1938.

'Sooner or later further territorial expansion will be necessary'. The Chancellor was faced with a fatal dilemma: he must either accept a modification of the policy of autarky or go to war. The financial position in general had deteriorated and the government was experiencing difficulty in financing its plans. In no industry was the utilisation of labour capacity below 75 per cent and in the engineering and metals industries it was over 100 per cent (ie substantial overtime was being worked). 'The country is now practically at the limit of industrial production' and some economy measures might have to be taken.[56]

The embassy's assessments did not rely in any appreciable degree upon secret intelligence. The Press, published statistics (often defective), personal observations and off-the-record conversations seem to have been its principal sources. But the impression that Germany by early 1939 was not only suffering from serious economic difficulties, but was being driven by them towards war, was reinforced by secret reports containing substantial amounts of economic intelligence which the Foreign Secretary (Mr Eden until February 1938 and then Lord Halifax) submitted to the Foreign Policy Committee of the Cabinet (FPC) between April 1937 and January 1939. While some of these reports may have emanated from the SIS, it is clear that others, representing the views of German critics of Hitler's policies, came from the sources who were in contact with Sir Robert Vansittart and MI5.*

In April 1937 the Foreign Secretary informed the FPC that he had received a report 'from a very reliable source' concerning controversy in Germany about the pace of rearmament. Various departments of the German government had pointed to the wisdom of moderating the rate of expansion in view of the precariousness of the food and raw materials position.†[57] Extracts from reports from 'highly confidential sources' were read to the committee in November 1938. One said that the German financial position was now 'absolutely desperate' and that Dr Schacht knew that financial chaos lay immediately ahead of Germany.‡[59] A paper on 'Possible German Intentions', taken by the committee in January 1939,[61] contained a

---

* See above, p 47 and below, p 80 et seq.

† The 'very reliable source' of this report cannot be identified. The substance of the report was generally true. In April 1937 Field Marshal Keitel was telling the Committee for Reich Defence of the strain upon economic resources induced by rearmament; in the same month Dr Schacht (President of the Reichsbank) was complaining to Goering that German exports were suffering as a result of the policies being pursued.[58]

‡ The source of this report was probably Dr Carl Goerdeler.[60]

56. FO 371/23002, C8149/32/18 of 24 May 1939.
57. CAB 27/626, FP (36) 26 of 14 April 1937.
58. Carroll, op cit, p 143.
59. CAB 27/624, FP (36) 32nd Meeting, 14 November 1938.
60. Aster, op cit, p 55.
61. CAB 27/627, FP (36) 74 of 19 January 1939.

number of references to secret reports, all predicting the onset of economic catastrophe in Germany. One, from a 'high and trustworthy' source, said that economic strain was causing increased unrest among the population. 'An excellent German source' reported that the German transport system was in a very bad way and that old men and women were being used in the armaments industry. Finally there was a report of a secret speech by Dr Brinckmann, 'technical head' of the Ministry of Economics, predicting imminent economic disaster. To this Hitler had reacted by saying: 'Very well, all this means that a vital decision must come at once, and it is coming at once'.*

On 23 January 1939[63] the Foreign Secretary advised the FPC to proceed on the assumption that the information in this last paper was true. The recent dismissal of Dr Schacht supported the theory that the financial and economic condition of Germany was becoming desperate and 'compelling the mad dictator to insane adventures'. No member of the committee dissented from this opinion, which clearly influenced its judgment that Hitler might soon spring another coup.

Since these reports originated in German circles close to Dr Schacht, among others, they inevitably reflected the opinion of financial experts upon Germany's problems, more especially the external ones. These were indeed severe in the years immediately before the war. But under a dictatorship preparing for war, as the IIC and the ATB had recognised, financial issues were not of long-term significance and were secondary in importance to the state of real resources available. Even had they been wholly correct the reports would still have presented a more 'catastrophic' picture of the German situation than was, in terms of real resources, actually the case, as a comparison with the IIC and ATB findings on the supply position would have demonstrated. But the reports were circulated to the Foreign Policy Committee only and do not appear to have been collated with the views of the IIC or the ATB on the German supply position. These two bodies were inter-departmental, but they constituted an incomplete inter-departmental system, one that was not designed to examine all economic intelligence – still less to speculate on such matters as the possible effects of the German economic situation upon Hitler's political moves, which remained the province of the Foreign Office.

On 3 July 1939 the Treasury issued a paper on 'The German Financial Effort for Rearmament', above the initials of Sir John Simon, Chancellor of the Exchequer, which put the financial aspects of the German situation in perspective.[64] Drawing attention to the fact that

---

* All this information, including the report of the speech by Dr Brinckmann and Hitler's reaction to it, clearly originated with Dr Carl Goerdeler.[62]

62. Aster, op cit, pp 156–160.
63. CAB 27/624, FP (36) 35th Meeting, 23 January 1939.
64. CAB 24/287, CP 148 (39) of 3 July 1939.

no detailed statistics for state expenditure had been published for many years and that only incomplete figures for state borrowing were available, the paper concluded that Germany had an absolutely larger sum to spend on armaments than Britain mainly because far more was raised in taxation. She could probably maintain defence spending on this basis for a long period. The German government might be approaching the end of its borrowing powers, but German policy had been to acquire great stocks of imported necessities, to produce substitute materials and to establish political and economic power over adjacent territories. 'The question of the means of payment for overseas imports in war – an ever-present anxiety in our case – scarcely arises in Germany'. The paper gave no definite answer to the question: how much longer could Germany go on with her present policy. But when the Cabinet discussed the paper on 5 July the Chancellor of the Exchequer said that in the Treasury's opinion Germany was better prepared for a long war than was Great Britain, whose prospects would be 'exceedingly grim' unless she obtained US loans and gifts on a massive scale.[65]

In the absence of any central point in Whitehall at which all the threads of evidence could be drawn together in a single 'master' appreciation of the German economic situation, the IIC supplied the factual economic information for two attempts, one by the ATB Committee, the other by the Chiefs of Staff, to fill the gap. A report of the ATB Committee in July 1938[66] assumed a war beginning in April 1939 in which Britain and the Empire, France and Czechoslovakia were ranged against Germany including Austria, with Italy liable to enter the war on Germany's side at any moment. On these assumptions four economic factors would be most prominent in the probable German situation. She would be able to supply many commodities essential in war only from stocks or imports, despite efforts to attain self-sufficiency. She would have an all-round minimum of stocks equivalent to 3–4 months' peace-time supplies, although for some commodities reserves were known to be greater. She would meet increasing difficulties in paying for imports as the war proceeded. And she would be critically dependent upon the products of the Ruhr-Rhineland-Saar districts.

The second general economic appreciation was contained in the strategic assessment issued by the Chiefs of Staff in February 1939.*[67] This assumed that Germany, in alliance with Italy, would be fighting Great Britain allied to France; that the USA would be a friendly neutral; that the USSR would not intervene but that Japanese intervention on Germany's side had to be considered a possibility. On

---

* See below, p 80.

65. CAB 23/100, Cab 36 (39) of 5 July.
66. CAB 47/6, ATB 181 of 22 July 1938.
67. CAB 16/183A, DP(P) 44 of 20 February 1939.

these strategic assumptions the COS accepted that the evidence supported the following general conclusions about Germany's economic situation:

'The industrial strength of Germany may be assumed to be adequate to equip and maintain in war all the sea, land and air forces which she plans to put into the field and to maintain the essential services, provided that raw materials for these industries are available. Moreover, her mobilisation planning should enable her rapidly to expand production of war stores after the outbreak of war. . . .' 'Germany, if favoured by fortune, might maintain her industrial resistance for about a year.'* 'In April 1939 the war preparations of Germany and Italy are likely to be considerably more advanced than those of Great Britain or France. We conclude that, if war occurred, our enemies would endeavour to exploit this preparedness by a rapid victory – within a few months; and that the Allies would have no means of winning quickly.' On the other hand: 'In the past it has been after the outbreak of war that a nation's industry has been adapted and expanded and her manpower organised. In Germany and Italy these processes are now being perfected in time of peace. It seems doubtful whether these processes can be achieved without a loss of hidden reserves which normally exist in time of peace, though it is difficult to assess the extent to which this may affect the lasting power of those nations in war.'†

Thus although assessments of Germany's economic position in the summer of 1939 did not disregard the advantages Germany had secured by making early preparations, they were influenced by a general belief that Germany was about to enter a war with her economy already fully stretched. The cumulative evidence pointed to

---

* A more optimistic view than that reached by the ATB Committee which had forecast 15–18 months (see above, p 65), but bearing a resemblance to the estimates being made at that time in Germany.[68]

† Contemporary academic writing on the German economy was sparse. The most systematic analysis to appear in Britain was an article on 'The National Economy of Germany' by Dr Thomas Balogh published in the Economic Journal in September 1938. Balogh concluded that the Nazi government had evolved a system which, if the available powers of control were ruthlessly and skilfully used, maintained stable employment; that the system was based on control of costs, investment and international trade and was stable in so far as it did not involve cumulative processes undermining the standard of life. In Balogh's view the real sacrifice imposed on the German people by rearmament and self-sufficiency was very much less than commonly supposed. The penultimate paragraph of the article ran as followed: 'The German picture exhibits the signs of an economy on a war footing using fully those reserves of moral and material character which in other countries are not usually mobilised before the beginning of hostilities. The use of these reserves has hitherto yielded impressive returns. It is questionable whether a further intensification would not have different results. The intense activity, the incentive for which lies beyond the material sphere, must imply an increasing strain on the people which will inevitably have its repercussions in the longer run. And if the stability of employment is safeguarded, the flexibility of the system is being impaired'.

68. Carroll, op cit, p 177.

the conclusion that Germany was suffering serious economic stress, in itself a powerful motive for immediate aggressive action by Hitler, and that unless aggressive war were to bring substantial gains in terms of economic resources within 12–18 months Germany must run into serious supply difficulties. The extent to which on the basis of her 1939 frontiers and without an enlarged 'Lebensraum' Germany could restructure her civil economy to meet the demands of protracted war remained unclear.

On the assumptions made by the ATB Committee and the Chiefs of Staff their view of the current state of the German economy on the eve of war was not unrealistic. The principal assumptions on which their forecast rested were:

(1) that 'the war' would be between Germany and Italy on one side and France and Britain and their allies on the other;

(2) that German economic resources were equivalent to those of the Reich as it existed in the spring of 1939, after making allowance for an Anglo-French blockade and the continuance of German imports from several European countries;

(3) that the war was likely to be prolonged, since France and Britain could not win quickly;

(4) that German war mobilisation plans had depleted the 'hidden reserves' of the economy although a rapid expansion of the production of war stores after the outbreak of war must be expected;*

(5) that the supply of raw materials was the critical factor.

On these assumptions it was not unreasonable to depict the German economic situation as 'taut', a description which would have been accepted by many German economic administrators at the time. Only two of the assumptions upon which the assessment rested, however, were purely 'economic'. The first three were strategic and political and even the fourth concealed political and administrative problems in Germany which were not examined in depth by British intelligence before the war.† The fifth was narrow, reflecting the terms of reference upon which economic intelligence specialists had been working and anticipating the 'economic warfare' for which plans had been laid in London.

After one year of war the military and strategic assumptions of these assessments were to be profoundly affected by the rapid German victories on land in western Europe, and the two principal economic

---

* The implications of this assumption were not fully thought out before the war. The evident conflict between the assumption that the German economy was already fully stretched while at the same time capable of immediately expanding the supply of armaments presented the newly formed intelligence division of the Ministry of Economic Warfare on the outbreak of war with a paradox which was to remain unresolved in the first eighteen months of war.

† See Appendix 3 on German economic administration.

assumptions were themselves changed by the new strategic situation after the fall of France. None of this could have been foreseen in the spring of 1939. In the first two years of war, the economic intelligence system was to be faced with the problem of adjusting the assessments inherited from the pre-war period to situations in which the pre-war assumptions were no longer valid.

□

For economic intelligence, even so, Whitehall had at least acknowledged the need for inter-departmental assessment. In relation to intelligence which bore on the military plans and political intentions of foreign states it not only lacked machinery for central assessment but also, until the spring of 1939, the minimum amount of unity of purpose and policy that was essential before any such machinery could be set up. This was especially the case between the Service departments and the Foreign Office, but also within the Service departments, within the Foreign Office and within the Cabinet itself, the division of opinion as to what British policy should be was marked.

The need for such machinery had been partially recognised by 1936 when, however imperfectly, it was met by the creation of the ISIC (later the JIC) in an effort to improve collaboration between the Service departments and between those departments and the Chiefs of Staff.* At that time, however, the fact that it was no less essential to improve collaboration between the Service departments and the Foreign Office, and to ensure that military and political intelligence were considered together in appreciations for the Cabinet or its committees, went unrecognised, or was even resisted. To have thought on these lines would have been to affront Whitehall's deeply entrenched belief about the respective responsibilities of the Foreign Office and the Service departments for advising the government – the belief that they should tender independent advice, provided that the Service departments confined their advice to the military sphere, and have their disagreements regulated only at the Cabinet level, in Cabinet committees or at the CID.†

It was in accordance with these views that, also in 1936, in the aftermath of the Abyssinian crisis and the German occupation of the Rhineland, the Cabinet had established the Foreign Policy Committee.[69] Except when it was temporarily replaced by an even smaller inner Cabinet at critical junctures – by the Committee on the Situation in Czechoslovakia, for example, between September and November 1938 – this committee of prominent ministers, which met under the chairmanship of the Prime Minister and included the

---

* See Chapter 1, p 35.   † See Chapter 1, p 6 et seq.

69. CAB 23/84, Cab 31 (36) of 29 April; CAB 23/85, Cab 51 (36) of 9 July.

Minister for the Co-ordination of Defence, but not the Service ministers, continued to advise the Cabinet on foreign policy decisions down to the outbreak of war. The one point at which intelligence assessments were acted on, it was also the one place where military and political intelligence were brought together – for the Joint Planners continued to prepare the strategic appreciations of the Chiefs of Staff with the help only of periodic political summaries from the Foreign Office, and the Foreign Office continued to select and evaluate political intelligence, and to submit it to the committee, without consultation with the Planners or the Service departments. Yet the committee met only at irregular intervals, and had much difficulty in reaching agreement, precisely because there was so little inter-departmental co-ordination of intelligence at the lower level.

After 1936 the absence of a system whereby the Foreign Office and the Service departments co-ordinated their intelligence at the working level, and evaluated it jointly before circulating their assessments, became a greater liability with each deterioration in the international situation. But it continued to go unregarded for want of the minimum degree of unity of purpose that was essential before the departments could bring themselves to change their ways. During 1934 and 1935 the Defence Requirements Committee had at least concluded, without great acrimony, that whereas the Service departments estimated that Germany would be ready for war by 1942, it would be prudent to accept the Foreign Office's disinclination to guarantee peace beyond January 1939.* Thereafter, the division of opinion as to what British policy should be became every year more marked, and more sustained by uncertainty within the Cabinet itself, as Whitehall confronted the fact that Germany's capacity to rearm was outstripping earlier forecasts and was emphasising the threat from the existence in Italy and Japan of two other potential enemies. And although it was a division of opinion which cut across departmental lines, it also led to recrimination between the Services and the Foreign Office. The Chiefs of Staff and the Service departments, with their knowledge that British military preparations were being held back by Treasury restraint, became more and more determined to delay British involvement in military operations and more and more critical of those in the Foreign Office who seemed to be urging initiatives in foreign policy which, especially in central Europe, threatened to outrun the slow progress of British military preparations. In the Foreign Office some of the leading figures became increasingly incensed with the Chiefs of Staff for pessimism in their strategic assessments and took the view that they were exerting too much influence on the formulation of policy. In these circumstances, far from becoming reconciled to the need to pool intelligence and to reach

---

* See above, p 49.

agreed assessments, the two sides persisted in their right to render separate assessments.

It would perhaps be unjust to suggest that, in doing so, they were conscious that the institution of joint evaluation would have curbed their opportunities for emphasising or glossing over items of intelligence according to whether they chimed with or cast doubt upon their divergent views on policy. But when these views were so powerfully held there need be no doubt that they in fact influenced the selection and interpretation of the intelligence, so much of which was enigmatic and difficult to evaluate.

For the Service departments and the Chiefs of Staff an increasingly cautious assessment of the country's strategic position reinforced the traditional military understanding of the role of intelligence in peace-time – one by which it might well discover the actual and, to some extent, the future military capacity of foreign states, but could provide nothing except speculation on larger matters like the political and military intentions of foreign states that were best settled by reference to strategic and logistic considerations. In 1934 and 1935 confusion had prevailed about the current strength and probable rate of expansion of the GAF. During 1934, when the GAF already possessed 550 aircraft, the Air Ministry calculated that it had 350 and would have 480 by 1935; the Foreign Office insisted that its sources of evidence pointed to higher figures; and Foreign Office complaints of Air Ministry incompetence were answered by Air Ministry resentment at Foreign Office interference.[70] From 1936 uncertainty continued about the future size of the GAF – a matter of profound importance for the successive schemes for the expansion of the RAF – but was accepted as being to some extent unavoidable. Nevertheless the Air Ministry's estimates of the GAF's current strength improved until, as war approached, they became inflated.* In 1938, when the true figure was 3,000, the estimate was 2,640, and at the outbreak of war the estimate was 4,320 as against an actual strength of 3,647.[71] The War Office's estimates of the current strength of the German Army, and of the number of divisions it was likely to have at future dates, also improved from 1936. In February 1937 it gave the current strength as 39 divisions (plus 2 independent brigades) and the number of divisions that could be mobilised in 1938 and 1939 as 72 and 108 respectively;[72] the actual figures for 1937, 1938 and 1939 were 41, 81

---

* See Chapter 9, pp 299–300.

70. AIR 8/166 and 171; FO 371/18833, C2717/55/18, C2881/55/18; FO 371/18835, C3087/55/18; FO 371/18838, C3614/55/18; FO 371/18842, C4174/55/18; Colvin, op cit, pp 129–133.
71. CAB 4/23, CID 1151B of 5 November 1934; AI report of 31 August 1938 (retained in Air Historical Branch); D Richards, *The RAF: 1939–45*, Vol I (1953), p 7; B Collier, *The Defence of the United Kingdom*, (1957), p 66; AIR 41/10, p 21.
72. CAB 4/25, CID 1303B of 4 February 1937.

and 103.[73] In July 1939 MI was inclined to scale down the number of divisions available for immediate mobilisation from 108 to 99,[74] though out of deference to the French authorities, who had consistently over-estimated the size of the German Army,[75] the General Staff set the figure at 120–130.[76] The NID's estimates of Germany's current U-boat strength were reasonably accurate.* Like the Germans themselves, however, it had some difficulty in calculating the completion dates of the new German capital ships and it failed to discover their true displacement.† But to work out current strengths or even the rate of expansion of Germany's armed forces was a straightforward task compared with that of foreseeing how she would use them in the event of war. And yet in this direction – on important developments like Germany's preparations for the use of Blitzkrieg methods – the Service departments did not merely lack curiosity. They discouraged their intelligence branches from speculating about such intelligence as was available.

In the extant records there is no sign that the War Office circulated any study of the possibility that the German Army would use armoured Blitzkrieg methods though evidence to this effect was certainly coming in.[77] It included a report from a well-placed MI5 source giving intelligence on the constitution of a Panzer column as a self-contained unit equipped for rapid movement in battle. Furthermore, in January 1937 the Military Attaché in Berlin, in a report entitled 'German Military Equipment and the next Theatre of War', suggested that the development of the German military machine made it possible that Hitler would resort to a series of short wars with limited objectives, on the Bismarckian model, designed to frustrate the Franco–Russian pact and the operation of collective security arrangements; and though such wars were more likely in eastern Europe, they could also be directed westward. The Foreign Office was impressed by this despatch, and sought War Office agreement to its being printed and circulated in Whitehall. But the DDMI was sent over to turn down this suggestion and to explain that 'high authorities in the War Office desire to confine their activities and those of their representatives abroad to purely military matters'.[78] To the extent that, even so, this was a military matter, the War Office's response was no doubt influenced by its doctrine of deferring in questions relating to the German Army to the French, whose High Command

---

* See below, pp 62–63.   † See Appendix 4.

73. B Mueller-Hillebrand, *Das Heer*, Vol I (1954), p 68.
74. CAB 4/29, CID 1507B of 19 January 1939.
75. CAB 4/23, CID 1148B of 29 October 1934; CAB 4/29, CID 1507B of 19 January 1939.
76. CAB 4/30, CID 1571B of 24 July 1939.
77. Strong, op cit, pp 47–48.
78. FO 371/21731, MA Berlin report No 65 of 25 January 1937.

did not expect Germany to resort to Blitzkrieg. At the same time, despite the practice of deferring to the French estimates, it was sceptical of MI's lower estimates of the rate of expansion of the German Army, on the ground that the War Office could not itself have expanded the British Army at a like speed, and it may be suggested that it was influenced even more by unwillingness to heed intelligence when it pointed to possibilities which lay beyond the War Office's own experience or ideas.

This suggestion receives further support from the treatment that the Service departments gave to intelligence reports on German weapons development. After the outbreak of war the British authorities were to be surprised not only by the power and speed of German offensives, and by Germany's use of tanks or aircraft in support of what she hoped would be successful rapid campaigns, but also by encountering weapons whose existence had been reported but had been disbelieved because they were superior in performance to those which Great Britain was developing. Such intelligence as was obtained about German tanks was too incomplete, and too inaccurate, to make firm conclusions possible; even so the belief that British armour was superior was an article of faith, not a matter of evidence. As to new gun developments, an assistant military attaché reported just before the war that Germany had developed a single weapon (the MG 34) capable of serving both as a heavy and a light machine gun; but nothing could persuade the technical branches in the War Office to accept this.[79] When it was reported that the Germans appeared to be using anti-aircraft guns against tanks, they took the view that the use of weapons in this dual role was neither possible nor desirable.[80] Yet when it was encountered in the anti-tank role in 1940 the German 88 mm Flak gun was found to be superior to anything possessed by Great Britain and France. In the same way, the Admiralty refused to believe intelligence reports to the effect that Germany's *Narvik*-class destroyers mounted 15 cm (6″) guns until the base plate of a 15 cm shell was found on board a British warship after an engagement in 1943. The Air Ministry had a lively interest in discovering the characteristics of German aircraft, and it was chiefly due to the difficulty of obtaining reliable intelligence that it had failed to establish many details of known aircraft by 1939, and that in 1940 aircraft were encountered whose development had not been suspected.[81] But it still had a fair knowledge of the aircraft characteristics and the operational methods of the GAF which it failed to use when considering how Germany was likely to use her air force in the event of war.

The belief that in the event of war the main role of the German

79. Strong, op cit, p 17.
80. ibid.
81. AIR 10/1644, Handbook on the GAF July 1939, Chapter 9.

Air Force would be the independent, and perhaps the immediate, strategic bombing of Great Britain became widespread in Whitehall from the beginning of the expansion of the GAF.* 1934 and 1935 saw the establishment of two CID sub-committees on air defence – the Home Defence Committee's Sub-Committee on Air Defence Research as well as the Air Ministry's Committee for the Scientific Survey of Air Defence. At the same time, the first report of the DRC drew attention to the need to anticipate large-scale air attacks against a wide range of targets, and the danger of a German bombing offensive was the chief reason why the DRC in its third report recommended greater expenditure on intelligence.† The danger was accepted by the COS as a worst case hypothesis in October 1935.[84] These were necessary precautions – as necessary as the fear of a German 'knock-out' blow from the air was understandable. But the Air Ministry's assumptions as to how the German Air Force would be used were so much modelled on the Air Staff's own plans for the RAF that it not only neglected the available intelligence but also omitted to subject its acceptance of the prevailing opinion to technical study. Had a feasibility study been made, it might have revealed that, as Marshal of the Royal Air Force Sir Arthur Harris was to write later, the German bombers were 'not equipped for weight carrying' and were 'too small' to deliver on the United Kingdom the vast tonnages postulated.[85] From what was known of German aircraft it should have been possible to deduce that the long-range bomber force would have had to sacrifice much of its bomb load if it was to carry enough fuel for the flight from north-west Germany and back with or without over-flying the Low Countries. Again, the task of manufacturing, moving and storing the required number of bombs would have been truly vast, yet its feasibility was neither examined nor questioned. It is perhaps not surprising that these calculations were not made before 1937, for the RAF had not by then studied how its own bomber offensive was to be carried out.[86] But it is surprising that later, as the limitations on Bomber Command's own ability to attack Germany were revealed, the operational factors governing Germany's power to deliver a 'knock-out' blow were not critically examined, or the presumed scale of the attack questioned.

In the Air Intelligence branch, it appears, opinion was not unanimous in subscribing to the 'knock-out' blow thesis after 1936. The officer who was DDI3 from 1936 to 1939 has written that 'if my

---

* It was strenuously pressed by Sir Warren Fisher of the Treasury[82] and publicly endorsed by Mr Churchill.[83]   † See above, p 50.

82. CAB 16/112, DRC 22nd Meeting, 30 October 1935.
83. M Gilbert, *Winston S Churchill*, Vol V 1922–1939 (1976), passim from p 571.
84. CAB 53/25, COS 401 of 2 October 1935, para 8.
85. Marshal of the RAF Sir Arthur Harris, *Bomber Offensive* (1947), p 86.
86. Sir Charles Webster and N Frankland, *The Strategic Air Offensive*, Vol 1 (1961), p 91 et seq.

German section had been consulted about the probable employment of the GAF, they would have urged that all the indications were that the GAF was going to be used primarily for direct support of land operations, probably eastwards at first, but if the drive were to go westwards the role of the GAF would still be subsidiary to the Army role'.[87] There is some evidence in the departmental minutes that he held this view at the time,*[88] and his claim that he was discouraged from including his views in lectures may be accepted. It may be on this account that even so the AI branch did not make full use of the intelligence that might have supported his views. Aircraft of the GAF, which on training flights before the war used wireless with few inhibitions, gave no sign of being engaged in the type of exercise that would have been necessary to train a new force to undertake so difficult and unprecedented an operation as the 'knock-out' blow; and the operation would have required immense infra-structural preparations in a relatively small area of north-west Germany. Yet it does not appear that Air Intelligence emphasised the need for these developments, or initiated any search for them. Nor does it seem to have pointed out during the Munich and the Polish crises that the German bombers were deployed in eastern Germany in support of the Army, and were not available for bombing London (or Paris, as the French feared).

When positive intelligence was lacking on this and other strategic problems, and intelligence deductions, if made at all, had to be made from negative evidence, it is not altogether surprising that the Air Staff, and the Chiefs of Staff as a whole, did not press the intelligence branches for their views on this and similar subjects. That they did not do so is clear from the series of strategic appreciations which they issued between February 1937 and February 1939.[91] There was no lack

---

* It is perhaps no coincidence that he was chairman of the inter-departmental sub-committee of the JIC which made a detailed examination of the use of air power during the Spanish Civil War. It was as a result of the experience of the Condor Legion in Spain that the GAF decided to adopt support of the ground forces as its main strategic task.[89] As we have seen in Chapter 1 (p 37), one of the sub-committee's conclusions was that 'all, or nearly all, of the air effort of each combatant was primarily devoted to the direct or indirect support of the land forces', though it added the caveat that this provided no basis for judging what might happen in war between first-class powers.[90]

87. Air Vice Marshal Sir Victor Goddard, *Epic Violet* (unpublished autobiography, held in Air Historical Branch), p 33.

88. DDI3 minutes, 15 April 1937, 20 July, 9 and 21 August 1939 and, in particular, 16 May 1937, to PA/CAS (Retained in Air Historical Branch).

89. AIR 41/10, pp 13–14.

90. CAB 54/6, DCOS 101 (JIC) of 10 June 1939.

91. CAB 16/182, DP(P) 2, 'Planning for War with Germany' of February 1937, DP(P) 5, 'Far East Appreciation' of 14 June 1937, DP(P) 18, 'Mediterranean, Middle East and NE Africa Appreciation' of 21 February 1938; CAB 16/183, DP(P) 22, 'Military Implications of German Aggression against Czechoslovakia' of 25 March 1938, DP(P) 32, 'Appreciation of Situation in the event of War with Germany' of 9 October 1938, DP(P) 44, 'European Appreciation 1939–40' of 20 February 1939.

of intelligence in the paragraphs which compared the first-line military strengths of Great Britain and the other major powers, but only in the last, the European Appreciation for 1939–1940 that was drawn up in February 1939, did the Chiefs of Staff incorporate any intelligence bearing on the way in which Germany might use her armed forces; and even then it bore only on the subject of the air threat to the United Kingdom. Looking at this from Germany's point of view the Chiefs of Staff thought that the best results would be obtained by attacking the civil population, sea-borne supplies and war industries; and on balance they doubted whether Germany would initially attack the civil population as 'it is reported' that some officers in the German High Command believed that the RAF should be the first objective. But they drew attention, also, to 'recent indications' that the German Air Staff was 'tending to turn' in favour of attacking the civil population, and noted that the belief of Nazi extremists in British decadence might lead to an attempt to bring about the swift submission of the United Kingdom by demoralising the population.[92]

It is evident from this how little it was thought that intelligence on Germany's strategic planning should be allowed to modify the assumptions which the Service departments and the Chiefs of Staff based on professional calculations. And these assumptions being what they were – that, whereas Great Britain could not win a short war and had scarcely begun her preparations for a long one, Germany, being the aggressor and having, as it seemed, economic reasons for needing a short war,* would aim at a rapid defeat of Great Britain or France; that if Germany gave priority to an attack on France she would make it with reserves permitting operations on the scale of 1918, and might succeed in forcing a quick decision; that if instead she first turned on Great Britain, she would seek to reduce her by concentrated air attack[93] – it is understandable that they carried more weight with the Cabinet than did the Foreign Office's more plentiful political intelligence so long as that intelligence did not point to action by Germany in western Europe. But until the beginning of 1939 the political intelligence pointed either inconclusively (up to the Anschluss with Austria) or conclusively (in the months before the Munich crisis) to German expansion only in eastern Europe.

This is clear from the proceedings of the Foreign Policy Committee. Down to the Munich crisis only two of the papers this committee received contained intelligence material.† The first was a Foreign Office survey of July 1937 of reports, mainly diplomatic, pointing to

---

* See above, p 66 et seq.
† In addition, however, the Foreign Secretary reported verbally on intelligence about the German economy in April 1937. See above, p 68.

92. CAB 16/183, DP(P) 44 of 20 February 1939.
93. CAB 16/182, DP(P) 2 of February 1937; CAB 16/183, DP(P) 22 of 25 March 1938; DP(P) 44 of 20 February 1939.

Germany's intention to move against Austria or – though this seemed less likely – Czechoslovakia; and if the committee did not discuss it, this was because the Foreign Office had concluded that the evidence was 'not very strong', and in part contradictory, and had admitted that the British Ambassador in Berlin had poured scorn on it.[94] The second paper was submitted on 21 March 1938, in the aftermath of the German occupation of Austria. It was the strategic assessment by the Chiefs of Staff of 'The Military Implications of German Aggression against Czechoslovakia' – a paper which compiled the available intelligence about comparative military strengths; speculated as to what Germany might do if she found herself at war with Great Britain over Czechoslovakia, with emphasis on the possibility that she would attempt a 'knock-out' blow from the air; and concluded in pessimistic tones that Great Britain was unprepared for the world war that would probably develop if a crisis over Czechoslovakia was not handled with the utmost caution.[95] In the light of this appreciation, described by the Foreign Secretary as 'this extremely melancholy document', the committee recommended on 22 March, and the Cabinet accepted, that the British government should adopt the advice of those in Whitehall who had been advocating for some time that the Czech government should be pressed to come to terms with the Sudeten Germans.

For the rest of 1938, before and during the Munich crisis, the sombre conclusions of the strategic appreciation carried even more weight with the Foreign Policy Committee than did the fact that though firmly pointing to Germany's intention to move against Czechoslovakia, the political intelligence, now a flood,* could give no reassurance that she would not move against Great Britain if her intention was crossed. This did not deter the Foreign Office, where all departments were professionally inclined to be absorbed by the latest political news and some were keen advocates of British intervention, from giving prominence to such of the political intelligence reports as were insisting that Hitler would desist, or could be overthrown, if he was opposed. But these reports were by now suspect to the committee. In July 1938 the Prime Minister referred to those with this message that were coming from Sir Robert Vansittart's private contacts as being 'unchecked reports from unofficial sources'.[96] In August, when a member of the opposition groups in Germany came to London with a similar message, the Prime Minister commented that 'he reminds me of the Jacobites in King William's reign, and I think we must discount a good deal of what he says',[97] while the Foreign Secretary

---

* See above, pp 58–59.

94. CAB 27/626, FP (36) 36 of 29 July 1937.
95. CAB 16/183, DP(P) 22 of 25 March 1938. The first draft by the Joint Planners was CAB 53/57, COS 697 (JP) of 19 March 1938.
96. CAB 23/94, Cab 32 (38) of 13 July.
97. Woodward and Butler, op cit, Series 3, Vol 2, pp 686–7.

felt that all reports to the effect that the German moderates would stage an anti-Hitler coup if the British government stayed firm must be treated 'with some reserve'.[98] Occasionally, moreover, intelligence from a source of proven reliability seemed to justify this scepticism. Thus on 28 September, at the height of the crisis, a well-placed MI5 source conveyed the warning that if Great Britain declared war Germany would at once unleash an air attack on London.[99]

By November 1938 the burden of the political intelligence had begun to undergo a distinct change. On 14 November the Foreign Secretary called a special meeting of the Foreign Policy Committee to which he outlined the contents of reports received from various highly confidential informants who had proved to be reliable during the summer.[100] He mentioned that some of them were in touch with Schacht or Ribbentrop; others among them were MI5 contacts in touch with the German propaganda ministry or German offices in London. Taken together they indicated that, partly because Germany's financial situation was 'desperate'* and partly because Hitler was more than ever convinced of French and British decadence, and had received reports on the weakness of their air defences, the German authorities were preparing to take the offensive in the west as well as to extend their position in south-eastern Europe. In the Foreign Office's view the reports rang true for another reason – the gratitude of the German people to the Prime Minister for having averted war over Czechoslovakia had probably so infuriated Hitler that he now regarded Great Britain as his main opponent – and it recommended a firm attitude, which might discourage the German extremists. This meeting was followed by persistent rumours of German preparations for the bombing of London[101] and also by further reports from the same confidential sources. The Foreign Secretary presented these to the Foreign Policy Committee on 23 January 1939. Reiterating that Hitler had substituted a western for an eastern policy, they added, now, that he was contemplating another coup, the danger period being from the end of February. The meeting also considered assessments in which the Foreign Office concluded that this intelligence had to be taken seriously and suggested that, since Germany seemed to be bent on attacking Great Britain without involving France, the coup would be either an air attack on the United Kingdom or the invasion of Holland.[102]

On the strength of this assessment the Foreign Policy Committee

---

* See above, p 68.

98. CAB 23/94, Meeting of Ministers, 30 August 1938.
99. Compare Colvin, op cit, p 263 for opposite information on 27 September.
100. CAB 27/624, FP (36) 32nd Meeting, 14 November 1938.
101. Aster, op cit, p 43; I Kirkpatrick, *The Inner Circle* (1959), pp 137–139.
102. CAB 27/627, FP (36) 74 of 19 January 1939; CAB 27/624, FP (36) 35th Meeting, 23 January 1939.

asked the Chiefs of Staff to report on the implications of a German occupation of Holland. The Chiefs of Staff, though still pessimistic about Great Britain's readiness for war, replied that the move would be a direct threat to British security and had to be opposed.[103] In the light of this view, long held by the Chiefs of Staff, the committee – attended for the first time by the three Service ministers and representatives of the Chiefs of Staff – concluded on 26 January that the Cabinet could no longer defer committing itself to an Expeditionary Force and authorised the opening of staff talks with France, a step which the Cabinet had long resisted on the advice of the Chiefs of Staff.[104] On 25 January the Cabinet had given its approval in principle to these decisions, should they be recommended.[105] It reluctantly confirmed them on 22 February.[106] On 25 January the Cabinet was shown the Foreign Office assessment of the intelligence reports but not the reports themselves; the Foreign Secretary gave only a short verbal summary of them. There is no evidence that the reports were seen by the Chiefs of Staff.

In the wake of Germany's entry into Prague on 15 March reports of an even less substantial character precipitated the Cabinet's next important decision at the end of March, and did so without being considered by the Foreign Policy Committee. On 28 March the rumour reached London from the embassy in Berlin and through a British journalist who had contacts with the German General Staff that Germany would attack Poland forthwith unless France and Great Britain made it clear that they would fight. The Foreign Secretary asked for a special meeting of the Cabinet.[107] On 30 March he informed the Cabinet that there was now sufficient evidence to warrant 'a clear declaration of our intention to support Poland...' and the Cabinet agreed that the Prime Minister should make such a declaration in the Commons on 31 March.[108] So far as can be discovered, the Foreign Office had received no intelligence to support the rumour; the SIS was soon to provide a series of warnings that Germany would attack Poland some time after the middle of August, but these had not yet begun to come in.* On the other hand, the Prime Minister in his declaration of 31 March made it clear that an immediate attack on Poland was not expected. The idea that Great Britain and France

---

* See above, p 59. It may be noted that these reports were not passed on to the War Office, which received them only on 11 August after the CIGS had requested copies from CSS.

103. CAB 24/282, CP 20 (39) of 24 January 1939; CAB 27/627, FP (36) 77 of 25 January 1939.
104. CAB 27/624, FP (36) 36th Meeting, 26 January 1939.
105. CAB 24/282, CP 2 (39) of 25 January 1939.
106. CAB 23/97, Cab 8 (39) of 22 February 1939.
107. Harvey, op cit, Diary entry for 29 March 1939: Colvin, op cit, p 303 et seq. See also S Newman, *The British Guarantee to Poland* (1976).
108. CAB 23/98, Cab 16 (39) of 30 March.

should give a guarantee to Poland and Romania had been under consideration before the rumour spread, and the Cabinet had already reached its decision in principle. On 18 March, three days after the seizure of Prague, the Foreign Office having warned that Germany was now threatening Romania and the Chiefs of Staff having recommended that steps should be taken at once to co-ordinate plans with Poland and Romania, it had agreed to make approaches to those and other countries, including Russia.[109]

Unlike their earlier conclusion that an attack on Holland must be regarded as a *casus belli*, the recommendation by the Chiefs of Staff that the government should undertake commitments in eastern Europe marked the end, under the pressure of events, of an age: the views on policy of the government's strategic advisers and of the Foreign Office, or at least of some of the most prominent of the Foreign Office's staff, had ceased to diverge. Thus was removed one of the obstacles which had prevented the establishment of some machinery or procedure to ensure that military and political intelligence was brought together and jointly evaluated and assessed by the departments at the working level. But measures to fill this gap in the intelligence machine did not follow at once, as may be seen from incidents which occurred in April. One of these arose when the Foreign Office circulated warnings from the embassy in Berlin, which had felt that they could not be ignored, to the effect that GAF bombers were about to attack the Fleet; the Admiralty acted on the warnings and the Fleet's anti-aircraft guns were manned throughout the Easter week-end. At about the same time Sir Robert Vansittart informed the Cabinet that he had received a report that one or two German U-boats were on patrol off Plymouth, Portsmouth and the Thames.[110] In contrast to these alarms, which had no foundation in fact, Whitehall was taken by surprise when Italy invaded Albania on 7 April. From MI5 and other sources it had received the general warning that some such move was possible, but no precise warning of the date and form of the move was forthcoming until 7 April itself, when the NID warned the C-inC Mediterranean that on 6 April people in Durazzo had been expecting an Italian landing.[111] It was these incidents, however, and particularly the circulation by the Foreign Office, in a highly tense situation, of operational intelligence, that at last enabled the Chiefs of Staff to insist on the creation of the Situation Report Centre.*

Despite some early complaints from the Foreign Office that the Service intelligence branches were not supplying the Centre with

---

* See above, p 41.

109. CAB 53/10, COS (39) 282nd Meeting, 18 March; CAB 23/98, Cab 12 (39) of 18 March.

110. McLachlan, op cit, p 245.

111. ADM 199/392, pp 163, 166; ADM 116/3844.

enough military material the Foreign Office found its reports so useful that it welcomed its amalgamation with the JIC and assumed the chairmanship of the JIC in July 1939.* With this step the last remaining barrier to the principle that intelligence of inter-departmental importance should be assessed on an inter-departmental basis was removed, even if, as was to be amply demonstrated after the outbreak of war, Whitehall had still to learn how to translate principle into practice.

---

* See Chapter I, pp 42–43.

PART II

In the Dark

CHAPTER 3

From the Outbreak of War to the Spring of 1940

I T MIGHT be expected that after the outbreak of hostilities the
amount and variety of intelligence would have increased, and that
the evaluation of it would have begun to improve. Germany had
eliminated some of her options by embarking on operations; other
potentially enemy states had for the present reserved their positions.
In these ways the uncertainty which had hitherto dogged the work of
forecasting the strategic character and the course of a war was to some
extent reduced. The performance of Germany's military machine
could now be scrutinised, and the supply of information about it could
not but increase as a result of direct and indirect contacts. On both
levels some progress did undoubtedly take place during the first six
months of the war. But in this first phase – indeed until Germany
opened her attack on France – the improvement was more than off-set
by lack of progress, not to say by confusion, in the relations between
the many intelligence bodies, and between those bodies and the
authorities they served. In so far as a single coherent intelligence
organisation existed when war was declared, it had not been planned
and purposefully developed over many years, but had been put
together hastily and imperfectly during the short time since war with
Germany had become probable. With the outbreak of hostilities its
various sub-divisions responded haphazardly and sluggishly to the new
situation and, in the attention it paid to intelligence, the same was true
of the higher machinery of government which they served.

At first sight it may seem that the opposite was the case where this
higher machinery was concerned. By the operations divisions in the
Service ministries, by the Joint Planners, by the Chiefs of Staff, by
ministers in committees, by the War Cabinet itself, there was, as we
shall see, incessant demand for items of intelligence and incessant
discussion of them. At the same time, however, these 'user' authorities
were failing to make the best use of the intelligence bodies which were
responsible for supplying them with information, and failing to insist
on better co-ordination between them. In recent years they had
authorised the first steps to improve matters and had established, if
only in skeleton form, the appropriate machinery. With the beginning
of hostilities they kept the habit of being their own intelligence officers
or assumed it for the first time.

On the part of men who bore ultimate responsibility for the

country's political and military decisions, this attitude was to some extent understandable. In emergency conditions they felt not merely free to make their own appreciations on the basis of whatever information could be made available, but also in duty bound to do so; and even if the country's intelligence arrangements had been more advanced, they would not have found it easy to resist this temptation. But they were all the more disposed to indulge in it because the intelligence bodies had not succeeded in establishing themselves as authoritative bodies by the outbreak of war. Nor did these bodies now make very rapid strides, either separately or in concert, towards acquiring a better reputation. Although they were expanded rapidly from September 1939, they did not find it easy to make up for lost time.

Apart from the JIC the intelligence bodies were of two kinds, as we have already seen. The first comprised those charged with obtaining intelligence – the diplomatic system, including the attachés; the SIS, including the photographic reconnaissance unit that had now been taken over by the RAF; GC and CS. In this category additional bodies, inter-departmental from the outset, were established on the outbreak of war. Of these, two were formally under War Office control – the Combined Services Detailed Interrogation Centre (CSDIC), which undertook the interrogation of prisoners of war;* and an organisation which extracted intelligence for all three Services from the censorship of posts and telegraphs. A third, which eventually developed into the Political Warfare Executive (PWE), was formally under the Foreign Office but from the outbreak of war analysed enemy propaganda and compiled a digest of the foreign press and radio for circulation to all departments.[1] Except that the diplomatic system usually reported via the Foreign Office, these sent their output, as appropriate, to the Foreign Office and the Service departments. The Foreign Office and the intelligence branches in the Service departments, the second category, were responsible for interpreting what they thus received, for collating it with operational material and occasionally, as in the case of NID's naval reporting officer network, with their own sources of intelligence, and for bringing the results to the attention of the operational authorities.

After the outbreak of war, no attempt was made to disturb this division of labour. The Service ministries naturally redoubled their pre-war demands for better services from, and more expenditure on,

---

* In March 1940 CSDIC became the responsibility of MI9, the section which had by then been established to help British prisoners of war to escape and to interrogate those who succeeded. In December 1941 it was put under a new section of MI, MI19.

1. For the evolution of PWE and its intelligence-collecting activities see C Cruickshank, *The Fourth Arm: Psychological Warfare 1938–45* (1977), chapters I and IV, based on documents in the PRO and in particular on the FO 898 series.

the collectors of intelligence and, equally naturally, 'C' also demanded more money. This led the Prime Minister in December 1939 to ask Lord Hankey, now Minister without Portfolio, to investigate. Lord Hankey deferred making final recommendations until he had examined the Secret Service as a whole – MI5 as well as the SIS and GC and CS – and he had still not made a full report when he and the government of which he was a member were replaced on 10 May 1940. But on 11 March 1940 he produced an interim report on the SIS and GC and CS and on special organisations involved in sabotage and propaganda abroad. A large part of it dealt with these special organisations and had little to do with the collection of intelligence. The remainder summarised Hankey's investigation into the complaints that had been directed against 'C''s department.

It found that none of these concerned GC and CS, and it made only two recommendations relating to that body. The first was that the existing practice whereby it was never referred to in Cabinet minutes or circulated documents must be maintained. The second was that, in view of the increase in the amount and variety of wireless transmissions since the outbreak of war and the need to ensure that the Y services of the different departments co-operated efficiently in intercepting and exploiting them, the Y Sub-Committee should be strengthened. It should be given a full-time secretary and an independent, whole-time chairman, in place of the head of GC and CS, and its responsibility for co-ordinating interception should be re-defined to cover all types of wireless activity.[2]

With regard to the 'SIS proper', as Hankey called it, the report found that the dissatisfaction with its performance was all but confined to the Service departments; the Foreign Office and MEW were 'well content' except that MEW voiced a need for better trade and customs statistics from neutral countries.[3] Of the Service departments, only the Admiralty doubted whether the SIS knew enough about the requirements of its customers; it had stressed the lack of information about shipping movements in the Danish Belts and the Kiel Canal, and about the Soviet and Italian Fleets.[4] But all three departments had complained about imprecision in the SIS reports; they wanted more details about present and prospective production in Russia, Japan and Italy, as well as in Germany, about stocks and stores, about numbers and types of ships and aircraft, and they wanted to know that they were reliable, to see them backed by photostat documents or some other proof of authenticity.[5] In his summary of these points Hankey implied, between the lines, that this was easier said than done, but he also held that matters would improve if liaison

---

2. Hankey Report of 11 March 1940, paras 43–44, Appendix II.
3. ibid, paras 22, 31–32.   4. ibid, paras 24–26.
5. ibid, paras 27, 28.

between the individual Services and the SIS was strengthened and made some arrangements to this end while carrying out his enquiry. In his report he added the recommendation that liaison should be further strengthened by the institution of a regular monthly meeting between 'C', the head of intelligence at the MEW and the three Service Directors of Intelligence, under the chairmanship of the Permanent Under-Secretary at the Foreign Office, to discuss policy. At 'C''s request the recommendation allowed that these meetings should be kept separate from the JIC machinery so as to preserve the 'historic' aloofness of the SIS from the Whitehall committee system.[6] There is no evidence that, at any rate formally, such regular meetings took place.

Although relations between the suppliers and the evaluators underwent no formal change, there was some increase of expenditure on the SIS and GC and CS, in keeping with the emergency.* Nor was it long before they, together with those who were developing photographic reconnaissance, made use of the greater opportunities of war-time to lay the foundations for the immense contributions of intelligence to the course of the war. But in this first stage of the war the intelligence produced by these sources continued to be fragmentary and irregular. As was unavoidable in these circumstances, the expanding departmental intelligence branches, themselves inexperienced, often misjudged or overlooked the significance of such reliable intelligence as was available. There were exceptions to these generalisations. But they were rare.

The outcome was a vicious circle. Until the intelligence sent to them increased and their evaluation of it improved, the intelligence branches could not establish a reputation for reliability with the political and operational 'user' authorities. But until those authorities came to place greater reliance on the intelligence branches there could not be much movement towards the effective application of intelligence to the conduct of the war either within each Service or at the inter-departmental level where the JIC had been set up to serve the Chiefs of Staff and the War Cabinet.

□

On the day war was declared the Chiefs of Staff arranged for their Joint Planning Staff to be always at hand in a neighbouring room

---

* According to Hankey's report, the total Secret Vote for 1939–40 was £700,000, supplemented to bring it to £1,100,000, and the 1940–41 estimates had budgeted for £1,500,000. But the report does not show what share of these sums was intended for the SIS. Compare these figures with those in Chapter 2, pp 50–51. Hankey's report gave no details of the amount allowed for GC and CS from the Foreign Office Vote since the outbreak of war.

6. ibid, paras 19–23.

during their meetings. They made no such arrangement for the JIC. This Sub-Committee, which they had so recently established as the co-ordinating centre of the intelligence system as a whole, and as the channel through which considered intelligence assessments should reach them, was indeed made responsible for providing a summary of political and military intelligence in time for their daily morning meeting.[7] But up to the fall of France the JIC as a body only once attended a Chiefs of Staff Meeting.* Up to March 1940 it was not even shown papers prepared by the Joint Planners before they were submitted to the Chiefs of Staff.

That this situation owed something to a lack of initiative on the part of the membership of the JIC is apparent from the fact that none of the Ds of I attended regularly; not until February 1940 were all three present at a JIC meeting. Moreover, while needless delays would have resulted if the JIC had been used to prepare the intelligence the Joint Planners required for a paper or for the COS weekly summaries which they also produced, and while for this reason the JIC did not question the arrangements by which each Director of Plans obtained this information direct from his own Service's intelligence branch, the Joint Planners offered no objection when in March 1940 the JIC at last requested that each Director of Intelligence should see all their papers in draft. At this stage the Planners jibbed at making this concession to the Foreign Office[10] but a little later they agreed to extend the new arrangement to the JIC as a committee, and also to permit the chairman of the JIC to submit Foreign Office intelligence for inclusion in their papers.[11] But if the JIC was slow to assert itself, at least at the level of trying to bring intelligence directly to bear on the conduct of the war, the reasons are not far to seek.

In the first place, as before the outbreak of war, it was still heavily absorbed in supervising administrative developments within the intelligence system. The recently established Middle East Intelligence Centre gave it much trouble.† It had to oversee the conversion into a permanent body, on the initiative of DMI, of the Inter-Service Security Board, which was first set up in connection with projected

---

* This was when the COS discussed a paper from the JIC recommending the establishment of an Inter-Service Project Board to co-ordinate all sabotage and other irregular operations.[8] The only Director of Intelligence individually present at a COS meeting at this stage was DNI, who attended twice, on the first occasion to report SIS information about the whereabouts of German ships and on the second to report on the arrangements made for interrogating POWs taken from U-39.[9]

† See above, Chapter 1, pp 40–41, and Chapter 6, p 191 et seq.

7. CAB 79/1, COS (39) 2nd Meeting, 3 September.
8. CAB 79/3, COS (40) 62nd Meeting, 1 April; CAB 80/9, COS (40) 271 of 21 March.
9. CAB 79/1, COS (39) 2nd Meeting, 3 September, 17th Meeting, 15 September.
10. JIC (40) 14th Meeting, 15 March; CAB 84/2, JP (40) 17th Meeting, 16 March.
11. CAB 84/12, JP (40) 91 of 19 March; JIC (40) 18th Meeting, 1 April.

operations in Finland to look after the security and deception aspects of British war plans.*[12] When the Inter-Service Project Board was established, again on DMI's initiative, to co-ordinate all projects for irregular operations, the JIC had to consider and lay down the rules that should govern the relations of this new body with the Foreign Office and the Service intelligence branches.[13] It was also concerned, though as yet with no practical result, in a proposal to form a Scientific Intelligence Centre on an inter-Service basis, a topic which had been under consideration twelve months before.†[14]

The JIC's administrative activity was by no means unprofitable. On the other hand, it was by no means adequate for all the administrative problems that arose. In the development of some inter-departmental organisations and procedures, delays occurred at least in part because the JIC was too preoccupied to take on the work. If scientific intelligence suffered in this way, so did the problem of co-ordinating demands to the Air Ministry for photographic reconnaissance, which was not brought to the JIC until anxieties about a German invasion attempt gave special urgency to it in May 1940,‡ while the inter-departmental arrangements made for censorship and the interrogation of prisoners were evolved without JIC supervision. In yet another field, supervision of the changes that were being demanded by the increasing importance of Sigint, the JIC acquired no standing – though this was for other reasons than the fact that it was too busy, as was to be illustrated in December 1940 when conflict about the control of Sigint led to the resuscitation of the Y Board rather than to the extension of the JIC's authority to this field.§

The fact that the JIC was overburdened even with administration is one reason for believing that the war had created a crying need for two directing bodies within the intelligence system, one for guiding its organisational expansion and pronouncing on administrative policy, the other for co-ordinating from day to day, even from hour to hour, the strategic intelligence appreciations and, when this had inter-Service implications, the operational intelligence of the various intelligence bodies. For the performance of the second of these functions, moreover, the JIC, composed of representatives drawn

---

* The ISSB was finally established in March 1940. Its accommodation and secretariat were provided by the War Office, and from May 1940 its Chairman was the head of MI11, but it received policy direction from the JIC.

† See Chapter 1, p 15, and below, p 100.

‡ See below, Chapter 5, pp 169–70.

§ See below, Chapter 9, pp 271–272, and, meanwhile, p 92 above for CSS's anxiety to keep the SIS apart from the Whitehall committee system.

12. CAB 79/3, COS (40) 53rd Meeting, 14 March; JIC (40) 13 (S) of 12 March.

13. CAB 82/2, DCOS (40) 19th Meeting, 29 April: CAB 80/10, COS (40) 305 (JIC) of 26 April.

14. JIC 23rd Meeting, 3 February 1939; JIC (40) 2nd Meeting, 31 January; JIC (40) 5 of 24 January.

from the individual departments, depending on intelligence selected and passed to it by those departments, and having no staff of its own for the evaluation of intelligence, was even less adequate than it was in its administrative role.

This, the second reason why the JIC was slow to develop, was made plain enough whenever – and this was only occasionally – it issued appreciations. As often as not, these dealt with matters on which intelligence about the enemy had little bearing, and they might as well have been compiled by the Foreign Office or by operational or planning sections in the Service departments as by an intelligence staff. They included an enquiry into how far German actions in Poland constituted violations of international law, requested by the War Cabinet in September 1939 and important to the Ministry of Economic Warfare (MEW) in connection with its decision as to the extent to which economic sanctions were to be applied to Germany;[15] and a joint study with MEW, also requested by the Cabinet, of what resources in the Low Countries it was desirable to deny to Germany in the event of invasion.[16] When JIC appreciations did call for knowledge of the enemy's operations or strategic intentions, on the other hand, they contained little or nothing that the political authorities and the operational staffs could not provide for themselves.

In November 1939, for example, asked to report on German concentrations of shipping and on German reconnaissance and mine-laying activity over the British and French coasts, the JIC agreed with the Joint Planners that it was impossible to do more than guess at their significance.[17] Its first assessment of the action that Germany might take in the spring of 1940 was scarcely more informative. Undertaken from December 1939 for the Allied Military Committee, which met in London and consisted of the French and British Permanent Military Representatives of the Supreme War Council, this considered various alternatives before concluding that 'which of these courses Germany will select will depend less upon logical deduction than upon the personal and unpredictable decision of the Führer'.[18] Not unnaturally, perhaps, the Joint Planners were not impressed. As well as disputing this conclusion and insisting that Germany would be guided by strategic considerations, they noted that 'this exhaustive examination reveals no new and unexpected feature in possible

---

15. CAB 65/1, WM (39) 10 of 10 September; CAB 79/1, COS (39) 13th Meeting, 12 September; CAB 65/1, WM (39) 14 of 13 September; CAB 66/1, WP (39) 23 of 12 September; JIC (39) 8th Meeting, 20 October; JIC (40) 13th Meeting, 12 March.

16. CAB 65/3, WM (39) 40 CA, 7 October; CAB 66/2, WP (39) 72 of 30 November.

17. CAB 84/9, JP (39) 94 and 95 of 30 November and 5 December.

18. JIC (39) of 18 December; CAB 80/7, COS (40) 217 of 24 January. See also, for the Allied discussion of an agreed draft, CAB 85/1, MR (39) 97th Meeting, 20 December; 105th Meeting, 30 December 1939; CAB 85/3, MR (40) 4th, 7th, 8th and 9th Meetings, 4, 8, 9 and 10 January.

German intentions', and commented unfavourably on the report's lack of precise intelligence on German industries, particularly the aircraft industry.*[19] On two further appreciations from the JIC, in February 1940, the Planners' comments are not available. As the reports canvassed in a purely tentative fashion the possibility of German action against Sweden in the coming spring, perhaps no comments were made.[20]

When towards the end of February 1940 the Joint Planners criticised the paper prepared for the Allied Military Committee, they coupled with their criticism some suggestions as to how the evaluation of intelligence might be improved, and the Chiefs of Staff drew the JIC's attention to these.[21] MEW should concentrate on studying whether Germany's industry was capable of producing weapons for the large forces she was supposed to have or to be preparing; the JIC should test the machinery for 'concerting' industrial intelligence; German propaganda might throw some light on German intentions if its trends were carefully watched. These ideas were somewhat gratuitous, as the JIC pointed out when it reviewed the arrangements which already existed for studying German propaganda.[22] But the fact that they were offered marked the beginning of a change in the outlook of the Planners and the Chiefs of Staff – a change that was to be continued when, on the one hand these authorities agreed in March that the JIC might see all planning papers in draft, before these were submitted to the Chiefs of Staff,† and when on the other, again in March, the Joint Planners urged the JIC to expedite the report on German industry's armaments potential which it was undertaking jointly with MEW at their prompting, and which they needed for their own appreciation of the strategic outlook.[23] Until then, they had received the JIC's daily situation report but had asked the JIC for little in the way of additional intelligence, factual or appreciated. Partly because the JIC had little competence in making appreciations, and partly because the Service intelligence branches were already passing factual information to the Joint Planners via their own plans or operations divisions, the Joint Planners had assumed that they could undertake the appreciation of strategic and operational intelligence for themselves.

This attitude was the third reason for delay in developing the JIC machinery. And all the more so because, characteristic of the Chiefs of Staff and the Joint Planners until the catastrophes of the spring of

---

* For this aspect of the report and for later assessments on this subject, see below, p 101 et seq.   † See above, p 93.

19. CAB 80/8, COS (40) 241 (JP) of 14 February.
20. CAB 80/104, COS (40) 247 (S) of 19 February (JIC (40) 10 (S)).
21. CAB 79/3, COS (40) 41st Meeting, 27 February.
22. JIC (40) 11th Meeting, 5 March.
23. CAB 84/2, JP (40) 17th Meeting, 16 March.

1940 were almost upon them, it was almost equally characteristic of the War Cabinet itself, and for quite as long. From the first days of the war the Cabinet's first care was to have itself continuously supplied with innumerable summaries, including intelligence summaries, in order both to keep itself informed and to enable it to reach its own conclusions. In addition to a weekly résumé of Allied and enemy military developments from the Chiefs of Staff, these included separate weekly reports by each Service ministry,* monthly intelligence reports from the MEW, political intelligence reports as and when the Foreign Office chose to distribute them, two reports a day by the Cabinet War Room, and the daily and weekly situation reports incorporating secret material which the JIC had taken over from the Situation Report Centre before the war and for which it continued to be responsible.†[25] Not content with this, the War Cabinet insisted on receiving a daily weather forecast for some time from October 1939, when it was alarmed by reports that the Germans were considering an invasion. In addition to the flow of paper, the War Cabinet heard at each of its meetings – and it met at least daily – verbal statements from the Service Ministers or the Chiefs of Staff and, often, also from the Foreign Secretary. Even so – and perhaps because of the flow – it found it necessary to establish the Military Co-ordination Committee at the end of October 1939. Chaired by the Minister for the Co-ordination of Defence, and consisting normally of the three Service Ministers with the Chiefs of Staff as advisers, this was charged with keeping under review the strategic situation and the progress of operations, and with reporting back from time to time its recommendations on the conduct of the war.[27]

Apart from the weekly Chiefs of Staff résumé and the daily situation reports, the War Cabinet dispensed with all reports in February 1940; by this time, as well as being swamped with paper, it had perhaps become sceptical of their value.[28] Those from the Foreign Office distinguished between information received from the diplomatic system and information received from secret sources, but often included from both sources mere rumours of German intentions

---

* The Admiralty issued only one weekly report[24] before withdrawing from the system.

† But the weekly situation reports were abandoned at the end of 1939 as containing nothing that could not be included either in the daily situation reports or in the Foreign Office summaries.[26]

24. CAB 66/5, WP (40) 36 of 28 January.
25. CAB 65/1, WM (39) 7 of 7 September. The weekly reports from the departments other than the War Office and the Air Ministry were issued in the WP (R) series (CAB 68). The War Office and Air Ministry reports and the COS résumés were in the main WP series of Cabinet papers (CAB 66).
26. JIC (30) 18th Meeting, 29 December.
27. CAB 65/11, WM (39) 66 of 31 October.
28. CAB 65/5, WM (40) 46 of 19 February.

or of domestic trouble for the Nazi government without assessing their worth or collating them with the information available in other departments.* The weekly reports from the Service ministries mixed up information about British forces and operations with information about the enemy, and included in the latter such details as the location of U-boats and minefields and the movements of troops. Like the daily situation reports, even the Chiefs of Staff résumés, the most serviceable of the regular statements, made no attempt to integrate the statements of the Service departments; each Director of Intelligence approved his own department's intelligence contribution and the Joint Planners did little but add them to paragraphs dealing with allied operations. And as the résumés expanded in scope – they began by covering only France, Great Britain and Germany, but were gradually extended to Italy, Japan, the Soviet Union and the Baltic, the Balkans, the Mediterranean and the Middle East – their intelligence content became more miscellaneous and their function became more uncertain.

To the factual reporting of enemy operations, they began to add interpretations which reflected all the difficulties and all the dangers arising from that unfortunate combination – the combination of shortage of reliable information with lack of an adequate mechanism for relating scarce information to current developments – which marked this stage of the war. They had started as a retrospective weekly summary of Allied and enemy operations. But they were now increasingly used by the Service intelligence branches as a vehicle for peering into the future, in comments on strategic trends, small essays on enemy operational practice, and pronouncements on such matters as the stability of the Soviet regime or the relations between the Party and the Army in Germany, with results that were at best superficial.† Their political judgments were reached without consultation with the Foreign Office. Their military assessments were made without close consultation between the Service branches. To make matters worse, they interrupted the discussion of the German war with items about the Sino-Japanese war or the situation in Persia, and their presentation as three separate Service reports not only permitted the adoption of single-Service interpretations of German naval, military and air activities, but also obscured the significance of such little relatedness between these activities as was observed.

□

---

* This was also true of the non-routine items which the Foreign Office continued to send in. Thus in June 1940 the Foreign Secretary reported an anonymous letter to the Consul General, Barcelona, which claimed that Hitler's 'secret weapon' was the painting of German aircraft in Allied colours.[29] For the secret weapon scare see below, p 99.   † Cf footnote * on pp 111–112.

29. CAB 65/7, WM (40) 157 of 7 June.

Despite the fact that it was ultimately concentrated in the War Cabinet, and co-ordinated for the Cabinet by the machinery of the Chiefs of Staff, operational responsibility was necessarily delegated to several government departments and, in the case of the Services, even beyond the departments to commands. It followed that the situation we have just described was not confined to relations between intelligence and the central or inter-departmental executive authorities. In microcosm, as it were, it existed within each department and between each department and its commands.

Each separate intelligence branch had two responsibilities within its own department. It had to supply the information which the operations, plans and policy staff would require when taking strategic decisions. At the same time, it had to build up that intimate knowledge of the enemy which was indispensable if his activities were to be effectively monitored and if – what was of crucial importance – reliable inferences about his intentions were to be drawn from his departures from his normal behaviour. Until it was efficient at these tasks its relations with the operational and planning staff were beset with problems. So long, moreover, as the separate intelligence branches were preoccupied with these problems within the sphere of their own immediate concerns, they had little time to exchange their findings and co-ordinate their opinions – to bring about that closer collaboration which war-time conditions made more than ever essential not only for the inter-departmental authorities but also in the interests of each individual Service.

In one limited but important field, that of scientific intelligence, closer co-operation was rejected by some of the Service departments as being undesirable or inopportune. Because they had never pressed for it, and because the SIS had lacked staff with the scientific knowledge that would have enabled it to meet departmental enquiries, intelligence about new weapons and scientific developments was a scarce commodity in Whitehall.[30] This was made plain enough by the scare created by Hitler's 'Secret Weapon' speech of 19 September 1939. After much investigation the JIC suggested that Hitler had been referring only to the German Air Force, as would have been clearer from the outset but for faulty translation of Hitler's remarks and as later proved to be the case, but because little was known of what had been happening in Germany it could not exclude the possibility that some unknown kind of weapon was involved.[31] The same deficiency was to be underlined again in November 1939, when the so-called Oslo report first lifted the veil of ignorance which surrounded Germany's most important scientific and technological advances.

---

30. *Air Ministry Intelligence*, p 289.
31. JIC (39) 7th Meeting, 6 October; JIC (39) 18 of October. See also R V Jones, op cit, Chapter 7.

The Oslo report,* one of the most remarkable intelligence reports of the war, was sent anonymously to the British Naval Attaché in Oslo by a source who had previously taken the precaution of asking the Attaché to indicate that it would be welcomed.[32] The very fact that the report dealt with many topics on which no information had been collected led many to disbelieve it – that and the conviction that one man could not possibly know so much and must therefore have passed on planted information. But its truth was to be proved in nearly every detail and it served to alert scientific intelligence to several developments of which no previous knowledge existed.[33]

An attempt to improve matters in this field came to nothing in January 1940. The Air Ministry then proposed to the JIC the formation of an Inter-Service Scientific Intelligence Centre.[34] The JIC invited the Service Directors of Scientific Research to consider the suggestion. But, chiefly as a result of Admiralty opposition, nothing was done; apart from the Air Ministry, where a scientific intelligence officer had been appointed at the beginning of the war, the departments did not even establish their own scientific intelligence sections during the first four years of hostilities.[35]

In the field of economic intelligence inter-departmental co-operation declined, rather than improved, on the outbreak of war. Here the ATB and FCI Committees and the IIC, the inter-departmental bodies which had kept the German economy under review in the inter-war years, were abolished and their functions passed to a single department, the Ministry of Economic Warfare (MEW), which had its own Intelligence Branch. Many months were to pass before methods of collaboration between the new intelligence organisation and the existing ones could be hammered out.

The organisation of the Intelligence Branch of MEW was planned by Major Morton, then head of the IIC, between February and July 1939.[36] When the Ministry opened in September 1939 this branch, with Morton as its head, comprised six sections which were re-grouped in November into two departments. One of these, Blockade Intelligence, was designed to serve the day-to-day activities of the rest of the Ministry and in particular to provide information needed by the contraband control system. The other, Economic Warfare Intelligence (EWI), was intended to inherit the inter-departmental role of the pre-war FCI Committee and the IIC and to provide intelligence for the Services and other agencies of government.

The relationship between the work of the EWI department of

---

* It is reproduced as Appendix 5.

32. Collier, op cit, p 331.
33. AIR 20/1716; Jones, op cit, Chapter 8.
34. JIC (40) 2nd Meeting, 31 January; JIC (40) 5 of 24 January.
35. *Air Ministry Intelligence*, p 287.
36. CAB/HIST/E/1/6/2 (memo by N Hall).

MEW's Intelligence Branch and the Service ministries was not formally defined when the new Ministry came into existence and it was left to the department to establish the central position in its own field within the Whitehall intelligence system to which it aspired. Its purpose was 'to keep under constant observation the enemy's economic potential for war with the object of assisting other branches of intelligence in detecting in advance his possible intentions, in estimating his strength and his weaknesses and in selecting points vulnerable to attack by any weapon that we could command – blockade, pre-emption, submarine warfare, air attack, political and psychological propaganda...'.[37] The pre-war inter-departmental system, incomplete though it was, had demonstrated the value of focussing the assessment of intelligence bearing upon this group of economic problems at a central point but in the first months of war other departments of government were reluctant to relinquish to a new ministry the work they were themselves doing in this field.*

Under the pre-war system the Service ministries had retained the right to receive and process economic intelligence for themselves.† These departments were less disposed than ever to abandon this right when the importance of intelligence and its relevance to operations were heightened by the outbreak of war. In consequence, competing papers on general economic questions concerning Germany were written for the JIC by MEW, the War Office and the Air Ministry during the autumn of 1939 and the spring of 1940 and it was beyond the powers of the JIC to adjudicate between them. The first steps towards centralisation were taken at a higher level. At the end of February 1940 the Minister for the Co-ordination of Defence, prompted by the discontent of the Joint Planners with the weakness of industrial intelligence exposed during the Allied Military Committee's discussions of Germany's intentions for the spring of 1940, ordered a joint JIC-MEW analysis of German industrial capacity,[39] which was put in hand but had not been completed when Norway was invaded. In April the War Cabinet Secretariat called a meeting of Directors of Intelligence to discuss the work of the various intelligence branches with special reference to German manpower which, although it did not result in an agreed appreciation on manpower, brought about a greater awareness of the need for collaboration.[40] But it was

---

* EWI also found difficulty in recruiting staff, especially as Blockade Intelligence naturally received priority. By June 1940 Blockade Intelligence had a staff of 152 administrative and 357 clerical officers whereas Economic Warfare Intelligence had 61 and 22 respectively.[38]

† See above, Chapter 1, p 31.

37. Ibid.
38. CAB/HIST/E/2/6/3/6.
39. CAB 79/3, COS (40) 41st Meeting, 27 February; JIC (40) 9th Meeting, 28 February and 11th Meeting, 5 March.
40. Hall, loc cit.

not until May 1940, in the shadow of impending military disasters in western Europe which were to elevate economic warfare to the front rank in British strategic planning,* that MEW was given a seat on the JIC.

It was not only in the field of general economic assessments that the division of responsibilities remained unclear. In the more specialised work of estimating the output of German armaments the relationship between the EWI department of MEW and the Service ministries differed as between the Services. Before the war the War Office had left the estimation of tank production very largely to the IIC and this arrangement continued when EWI was established, although intelligence on the subject was so poor that no firm estimates could be made. For U-boat production EWI was responsible for the study of productive capacity while NID estimated the output of vessels. With the Air Ministry, however, no satisfactory division of labour was arrived at in relation to German aircraft production.

After the outbreak of war the pre-war practice of producing joint IIC-Air Ministry surveys of the industry gradually fell into disuse. Although MEW continued to study the subject, the Air Ministry claimed final authority, partly on the ground that the low-grade Sigint which it received, and which MEW did not, threw a light on the delivery of aircraft from the factories to the German Air Force. Prepared in isolation from each other, MEW and Air Ministry estimates began to diverge, ultimately leading Mr Churchill as Prime Minister, when he became aware of the divergence, to call for an enquiry by Mr Justice Singleton in the winter of 1940–41.†

Collaboration between MEW and the Air Ministry on target intelligence fared no better, and it again required the intervention of the Secretariat of the War Cabinet to bring the two departments into a reasonable working relationship on this subject.[41] Both MEW and the Air Ministry issued bomb damage reports from the early months of 1940 which, until photographic reconnaissance flights were able to supply reliable intelligence, were based on unreliable sources and differed considerably in their conclusions.[42]

In contrast to the hesitancy with which inter-departmental working arrangements were arrived at in other fields of economic intelligence, swift and effective action was taken to establish an inter-departmental body to study the German oil situation. At the request of the Chiefs of Staff, a special committee was established in October 1939, under the chairmanship of Mr Geoffrey Lloyd, Secretary for Mines, to keep the situation under continuous review. The members of the committee

---

* See below, Chapter 7, p 234 et seq.
† See Chapter 9, p 299 et seq.

41. Webster and Frankland, op cit, Vol I, p 262.
42. Ibid, p 267.

were drawn from the Foreign Office, Admiralty, War Office, Air Ministry, Mines Department, Petroleum Department and MEW. It issued its first report on 13 October. The Lloyd Committee reported to the Hankey Committee, established by the War Cabinet on 17 October 1939 to review the organisation and action required to prevent oil supplies from reaching Germany. The Lloyd Committee and its successor, the Hartley Committee,* proved to be a very effective means of preparing 'master' assessments for Whitehall, based upon all available information.

The appreciations of the German economic situation in the first year of war, as prepared by the organisation just described, are the subject of a later chapter.†

□

If the intelligence branches in the Service departments had little interest in inter-departmental co-operation, this was because they were absorbed by problems within their own Service. Of all of them, this was most true of the NID. On the one hand, it was more fully occupied by operations than Air or Military Intelligence. The Admiralty, alone among the Service departments, exercised direct operational control; for some months, apart from limited operations by the RAF, it was only the war at sea that brought German and British forces directly into conflict. On the other hand, the NID was least well supplied with information.

Its naval reporting system worked well, ensuring from the outset that information about a high proportion of the sailings of merchant ships for German ports reached the Admiralty in time to be useful in enforcing the blockade against Germany. By contrast, its information on German naval movements came mainly from contacts by British forces, whose reports were incomplete and often inaccurate. Items from the SIS and from diplomatic posts about naval movements were rarely confirmed and often contradictory. Except for highly localised and routine purposes, within ports and in in-shore waters, the German Navy used only a high-grade cypher, and this was not broken by GC and CS until the spring of 1941.‡ To make matters worse it went over to war-time wireless procedure shortly before the attack on Poland, putting an end to the possibility of following its movements by correlating call-signs with the results of direction-finding, and it was to be months before work on the German naval signals system at GC and CS and in the Operational Intelligence Centre (OIC) at the Admiralty made it possible to produce even tentative deductions on the basis of Traffic Analysis. The first step was to distinguish U-boat

* See Volume Two.
† Chapter 7.
§ Apart from a short period in the spring of 1940, see below, p 163.

from other German naval communications, and it is some indication of the extent of the black-out that this elementary advance was not made until the end of 1939. The first Sigint of any importance to the Admiralty was to be obtained from GC and CS's success against the GAF Enigma, and special arrangements were made as early as January 1940 for relaying the results of this to the Home Fleet. But little intelligence bearing on naval operations was obtained from this source before the opening of the Norwegian campaign in April.

In the absence of Sigint or of reliable reports from the SIS, aerial photography would have been invaluable if it had been possible to survey the enemy's main bases and harbours at frequent intervals. Unfortunately, although the first RAF sortie of the war was a photographic reconnaissance of Wilhelmshaven by a Blenheim of Bomber Command, the high rate of casualties, a consequence of using operational aircraft for PR purposes, made regular cover by Blenheims impossible,[43] and in addition, because of bad weather or heavy defences, their sorties often produced no photographs. From the beginning of 1940 the special flight taken over by the RAF, now known as the Photographic Development Unit (PDU), undertook reconnaissance of the German bases as a high priority as soon as it had acquired and modified its Spitfires. But it was not until February that the unit photographed Emden and Wilhelmshaven using a modified Spitfire (Type B). Kiel could not be reconnoitred until a longer-range Spitfire (Type C) became available in April; and bases east of Kiel remained beyond range at that date.[44] Meanwhile the PDU in co-operation with a private company, the Aircraft Operating Company, was improving the standards of photographic interpretation by using the 'Wild' machine, a Swiss device which made it possible to calculate the dimensions of even small vessels from vertical air photographs. In the absence of frequent sorties, however, progress remained slow on this front also. It was following disagreement with the Admiralty about the identification of barges and submarines that the Air Ministry took over the company, after the Admiralty had offered to do so, in July 1940, turning it into a branch of the PDU that subsequently developed into the Photographic Interpretation Unit (PIU).[45]

The Navy was not the most formidable part of Germany's military machine. As against that, her surface ships were new, fast and powerfully armed, her U-boat crews were well trained, and Great Britain's shipping, like the Navy which had to protect it, was so dispersed that the opportunities open to a power which possessed the initiative were very wide. This was all the more the case because, while the NID's sources were poor, the German Navy at this time was

43. AIR 41/6, p 83.   44. Ibid, p 78.
45. Ibid, pp 125, 202–203. See also Barker, op cit, pp 171–173.

supplied with Sigint about British merchant ship and naval movements.* But when there was thus a heavy premium on obtaining early warning of sorties by warships and surface raiders, and of the departure and patrol areas of U-boats, no such indications were forthcoming from those in the OIC who maintained plots of enemy surface ships and U-boats, as also of German mine-laying operations. No sign whatever betrayed Captain Prien's penetration of Scapa Flow in U-47 in October 1939, when he sank the *Royal Oak* there;† or the return of the *Deutschland* to Germany in November from the first raid by heavy units into the Atlantic; or the sortie of the *Gneisenau* and the *Scharnhorst* in which, in the same month, they sank the *Rawalpindi;* or the next sortie of these battle-cruisers with the cruiser *Hipper,* in February 1940, which was, however, cut short by a chance sighting by an aircraft of Bomber Command. The engagement which led to the destruction of the *Graf Spee* in December 1939 was brought about without any assistance from the NID; she eventually steamed into the area where Commodore Harwood had concentrated his ships on the basis of his own appreciation after considering where she had made her attacks, what she might expect in the way of counter-measures, and the relative attractiveness for her of the various shipping lanes in the South Atlantic.[47] It was not until she entered Montevideo that the OIC first identified her as the *Graf Spee.* Before then she was thought to be the *Scheer,* and the Admiralty had announced early in November that the *Scheer* had returned home. A week later it had reversed this view. The Admiralty received from United States broadcasts the first news that the *Graf Spee* had entered Montevideo, and also the first news of her final sailing from there.[48]

In February 1940 intelligence contributed somewhat more to the interception of the *Altmark,* the *Graf Spee's* supply ship, and the rescuing of her prisoners of war, as she was about to leave Norwegian waters on her return to base. On 15 February, when she was nearing the end of her long journey from the South Atlantic, the Naval Control Service Officer at Bergen, part of the organisation which the Admiralty kept in foreign ports to furnish friendly ships with convoy instructions and other information, reported that she had passed there at noon. That evening the British embassy in Oslo forwarded confirmation of the news, which it had received from the French Naval

---

* See Chapter 4, p 141.

† Indeed, the OIC was not sure that the *Royal Oak* had been sunk by a U-boat until the announcement was made by the German radio; and after the event an Admiralty Board of Enquiry concluded that Prien could not have entered the Flow by the channel he in fact used.[46]

46. ADM 186/799, BR 1736 (48) (1), *Home Waters and the Atlantic,* p 27.
47. These operations are surveyed in ADM 186/799; ADM 186/794, BR 1736 (19), Battle Summary No 26; AIR 41/45, *The RAF in Maritime War,* Vol 1; Captain S K Roskill RN, *The War at Sea,* Vol 1 (1954).
48. For the *Graf Spee* see also ADM 1/9759, NID 02356/39.

Attaché's network of agents on the Norwegian coast. These reports were followed up by Coastal Command aircraft, and their sighting led to her interception.[49] By then, however, there had been frequent occasions on which the OIC, acting as best it could on the kind of information that was available, had sent the ships of the Home Fleet to sea, or off their course, on fruitless errands. The OIC's first war-time report to the Home Fleet, to the effect that the German Fleet might have moved to Icelandic waters just before the declaration of war, had turned out to be wrong, as had a sighting by a Coastal Command aircraft on 3 September 1939 which reported that German major units were apparently leaving harbour. In October such units, which by selecting darkness and the right weather conditions could in fact pass north with little fear of detection, had been sighted off southern Norway on an occasion when they wanted to be sighted, in order to tie down forces from the Home Fleet which might otherwise have joined in the hunt for the *Graf Spee*. In December the Admiralty's suggestion that the Germans might attack one of the Norway convoys in an attempt to off-set the loss of prestige caused by the sinking of the *Graf Spee* had been assumed by the Home Fleet to be more than a suggestion, and had led to yet another false chase.[50]

The inability of the intelligence division to assist in current operations was also illustrated by the way in which it was discovered that Germany was using a magnetic mine. Early in September 1939 ship damage caused by an underwater explosion strongly indicated that Germany might be laying mines of a kind for which the Admiralty was unprepared. Thereafter, increasing sinkings of, and damage to, coastal shipping caused grave concern, as did the lack of success in devising a method of sweeping.[51] But it was not possible to acquire a mine for examination until towards the end of November when, as well as being laid by submarine, the mines began to be dropped by the German Air Force, and a mine which had been seen to fall close inshore by coast watchers was recovered from land accessible at low tide. This was inspected by a team from HMS *Vernon* and its method of operation determined.[52] Partly because counter-measures were then possible and partly because Germany was running short of mines, the campaign was brought under control. But the required technical intelligence had been obtained without help from the NID, which had not known that the British Admiralty had used a magnetic mine in 1918 and was by 1939 ready to put one of a new design into production.

---

49. Roskill, op cit, Vol 1, pp 151–152.

50. ADM 186/799, pp 20, 49–50, 56.

51. CAB 65/1, WM (39) 18 of 17 September; CAB 65/2, WM (39) 88 of 19 November.

52. Roskill, op cit, Vol I, pp 55, 100–102. See also W S Churchill, *The Second World War*, Vol I, (1949), p 397.

In contrast to these indications, positive and negative, of the frailty of naval intelligence, one minor advance was achieved. From the slow accumulation of sighting reports by Coastal Command aircraft and British submarines the OIC was able to piece together by December 1939 the routes then being followed by the U-boats on passage from Germany to the Atlantic, and to use the information to guide mine-laying operations against them. The 'continuous chain' patrols flown by Coastal Command between Scotland and Norway, supplemented by submarine patrols, could not be relied on to sight fast-moving surface sorties in the frequent thick weather or to help in narrowing down the search for U-boats, but their sightings of U-boats, though not always reliable, were the sole supply of regular information about the German Navy at this stage.

□

Against the maritime operations of the German Air Force against east coast shipping the OIC received assistance from AI and from the operational intelligence units at Cheadle, the Air Ministry's intercept station, and in the RAF Commands. Part of the price paid by the German Air Force for its rapid expansion was a considerable dependence on the use of radio aids for navigation and low-grade tactical transmissions for such things as weather and reconnaissance reports. Despite improved German radio security these transmissions could be exploited and interpreted, as before the war, without great difficulty.* From the same sources AI, as early as the end of October 1939, was able to trace the return of some of the long-range bomber units from Poland to their normal German bases. Thereafter, it was often possible to detect the take-off of German aircraft from their bases in advance of their detection by the British radar chain, which

---

* The main systems in use were –

i.   The Air Safety Service which controlled aircraft on medium frequencies in certain phases of their flights and which had enabled Air Intelligence to build up before the war a fairly complete tally of GAF aircraft numbers and transfers between bases. Shortly before war began the GAF changed the aircraft markings and the call-signs. But fairly rapid progress was made in identifying the new call-signs, and those of most operational units had been established by the end of 1939.

ii.   Air-to-ground coded traffic used on HF during operations. Six codes were in use when this was first intercepted in December 1938 and all were soon partly solved at GC and CS. This traffic used coded call-signs the first of which were solved only in September 1940. The solution was helped by the process of correlating this traffic with that on the Air Safety Service.

iii.   The GAF navigational beacons on medium frequencies, not to be confused with the VHF navigational beams which are discussed below (see Chapter 10). These started up shortly before the war and numbered 50 by March 1940. From January 1940 their call-signs and frequencies could generally be predicted in advance, and they were used by Bomber Command aircraft for navigational purposes until 1943. They were sometimes useful in forecasting GAF operations.

was as yet incomplete, to identify the bases and to spot transfers between them. By the end of 1939 it had, further, become possible to identify, once again, many GAF units and to indicate in advance the type of some of the operations they intended.[53]

After the defeat of Poland most of the GAF's operations during the winter months consisted of bombing and mine-laying directed against the Fleet and, more particularly, the east coast shipping. In the absence of adequate defence preparations against these activities, of which the GAF itself had foreseen the importance only in the few months before the outbreak of war,[54] the operational intelligence from low-grade Sigint sources – virtually the only operational intelligence available – was increasingly valuable from the end of 1939. Until then some of the Fighter and Coastal Command stations had too little knowledge of the good use that others were making of it to give attention to it. For example, on 14 October 1939 RAF low-grade Sigint warned Fighter Command that a raid on the Firth of Forth was imminent. (It was, in fact, the first sizeable raid on this country.) Since Fighter Command was unwilling to accept deductions made from intercepted messages without confirmation, of which there was none, the raiders succeeded in surprising the defences.[55] Thereafter, however, Fighter Command regularly husbanded its scarce resources by using low-grade Sigint to enable it to despatch fighters to the most favourable interception positions and to warn the convoys. By the time of the Battle of Britain, these sources were to be still more valuable, indeed invaluable. On the GAF's preparations for the invasions of Norway and France, however, which the German authorities took special care to conceal, they threw no light, and, for reasons which we shall discuss, they were to be of little or no use to British forces during those campaigns. Nor as yet were their limitations overcome by the fact that as early as January 1940 GC and CS made the first great cryptanalytic advance of the war by breaking into the GAF's Enigma keys.

Between the middle of January and late March 1940 GC and CS solved by hand about 50 Enigma settings.* They belonged to three different series – that used by the Army in Germany's 20 military districts (named the Green by GC and CS); that used by the GAF for practice purposes (the Blue); and that used by the GAF for the operational and administrative communications of all its Commands (the Red). By the end of May it had greatly enlarged these first successes. On 10 April traffic was first intercepted in a new key (the

---

* See Appendix 1.

53. *Air Ministry Intelligence*, pp 67, 80; AIR 41/14, *Air Defence of Great Britain*, Vol 1, pp 56, 68.
54. Collier, op cit, p 80; AIR 41/10, pp 96, 97, 109.
55. *Air Ministry Intelligence*, p 80; Collier, op cit, p 82.

Yellow). This was a relatively simple key introduced for the Norwegian campaign. Its traffic was mainly concerned with GAF operations and it was broken continuously – the first to be so – from 15 April until it lapsed in the middle of May. By then it had become clear that the Green key would seldom be breakable and that highest priority should be given to the Red; and GC and CS was taking delivery of the first British-built Bombe.* On 22 May, despite the fact that on 1 May, in preparation for the French campaign, the German authorities introduced new indicators for all Enigma keys except the Yellow, the Red key for 20 May was broken. From 22 May 1940 until the end of the war GC and CS was to read its settings daily, with few interruptions, and to do so with little delay. Nor was that all. Based on a machine and broken on a machine, the Enigma's cyphered messages were mechanically converted direct into plain language; so that it yielded up its end-product in cornucopian abundance once the daily setting had been solved. But until the final conquest of the Red key the Enigma was broken by hand with a delay of several days, sometimes even weeks. To make matters more difficult, its plain language end-product, while it opened up to British eyes for the first time an intimate view of a vast German organisation, presented British intelligence with immense problems in evaluation on account of the intricate procedures, the code-names, the pro-formas and the other conventions which it employed for the sake of brevity or in the interests of internal security – not to speak of the difficulties sometimes created by poor interception and other sources of textual corruption. In addition, the process of handling and disseminating the results of so sensitive a source raised complicated difficulties for British internal security. For all these reasons high-grade Sigint was not flowing regularly from GC and CS to Whitehall until after the outbreak of the Norwegian campaign, and GC and CS had hardly put its Enigma sections onto watches throughout the 24 hours when the campaign began. Until then, again, the Enigma remained of long-term rather than of operational interest. For all the light the cypher threw at once on the organisation and the procedure of the German Air Force and sometimes, as a by-product, on German Army affairs, the communications of the GAF were not yet so stretched that it had to use wireless for other than administrative purposes. In advance of such a move as the invasion of Norway, moreover, or the attack on France, the GAF authorities naturally kept all references to their preparations even from their own cypher communications for security reasons.

In these circumstances Air Ministry intelligence and GC and CS were no more able than the OIC in the Admiralty to provide warning of the move against Norway, and their contributions to strategic intelligence were limited in value. Although Air Ministry intelligence,

---

* See Appendix 1.

unlike that of the Admiralty, was not seriously criticised until the summer of 1940, when the GAF's operations against the United Kingdom began in earnest, its assessment of the size of the GAF continued to be seriously exaggerated in two directions. First – although it did become increasingly mystified by its inability to locate where the huge reserves were stored and on more than one occasion requested photographic reconnaissance of German factory airfields in an attempt to find them[56] – it estimated the reserve strength, during the first winter fewer than 1,000 machines, at five times the true figure. In the second place, it also over-estimated, though less seriously, effective GAF front-line strength, particularly in long-range bombers. In December 1939 these were estimated at 1,750 when in fact there were just over 1,000 at this time.[57] It was because the Air Ministry calculated that the Home Fleet at Scapa was threatened by 800 bombers, when the GAF had less than 300 within range, that the Fleet was based on the west coast of Scotland, with all the grave limitations which that imposed, at the end of 1939.[58] For similar reasons, instead of reflecting on why the GAF had not launched the expected knock-out blow on London (or Paris if you were French), AI offered no resistance to the view that, in the modified form of raids aimed at the destruction or neutralisation of the RAF and the aircraft industry, and at ports and shipping, the main purpose for which the GAF was preparing remained the bombing of the United Kingdom.

To the extent that it held that the GAF would have to establish air superiority as a prelude to a German invasion of Great Britain, this view was sound enough. But it obscured the improvised character of Germany's plans when she did eventually turn an Air Force trained to support the Army to the bombing of London and the night bombing of British cities. More important, in the period before that point was reached it obscured the Air Ministry's appreciation of the use to which Germany's air power might be put by closing its mind to other and more likely alternatives – and even to such evidence as was accumulating in support of alternatives. As late as March 1940 the Air Intelligence branch was still assuming that only a small proportion of the GAF was trained and intended for support of the Army, and was still concluding that, since Hitler's main aim was to subdue Great Britain, the objective of his spring land offensive would be limited to the intermediate stage of seizing Holland as a base for an all-out air attack on Britain.[59]

□

---

56. For example AIR 40/2321, A13 Minutes of 30 December 1939.

57. Collier, op cit, p 78; AIR 19/543, Report from Mr Justice Singleton to the Prime Minister, 3 January 1941, (Appendix A). AIR 40/2321, A13 Minute of 4 October 1940.

58. ADM 186/799, p 23.

59. AIR 40/2321, A13 Minute, 21 March 1940.

In watching for the enemy's next strategic moves the War Office was more active than the other two Services. AI 3(b), the Order of Battle Section of the Air Intelligence Directorate, regarded the assessment of enemy intentions and strategy as one of its main tasks, but it was as yet too preoccupied with building up from Sigint its knowledge of the strength and order of battle of the GAF, and with developing more efficient ways of evaluating Sigint for operational use, to give much thought to the matter. For undertaking strategic assessments the NID was poorly organised. Because of the Admiralty's executive responsibility the OIC's main interest was in applying intelligence to the day-to-day conduct of the naval war, and this became even more the case when the supply of intelligence from Sigint became excellent. On the other hand, in the geographical sections of NID, unlike the country sections in MI and AI, desk officers did not have access to Sigint and were thus severely handicapped in the task of assessing strategic developments. The section responsible for co-ordinating these two sides of NID, and for drawing strategic conclusions, was NID 17, DNI's executive office;* although this was to make a valuable contribution to strategic evaluations when the JIC eventually developed an effective system of bringing intelligence to bear on them in the spring of 1941, it was until then without much influence on the Admiralty's plans and policy divisions. But the War Office's Intelligence Directorate was not only not involved in operations, at any rate before the Norwegian campaign; because the Army was the principal strategic instrument in the continental states, the MI country sections tended to regard strategic appraisal as their chief task. Indeed, at this time when the JIC was failing to perform it, the work of seeking out information from the other Services, of making rounded appraisals and of circulating them to the Foreign Office and the other intelligence branches appears to have been attempted only in the War Office.

Its appreciations on subjects other than Germany's military intentions need not delay us. They dealt with Italian reinforcements to Libya in the early months of the war and to Albania in March 1940; with Russian concentrations on the Polish frontier before the Russian move into Poland in September 1939; and with the Russian build-up on the Finnish frontier during October 1939. During the Russo-Finnish war, which was watched as closely as the western front, there were numerous accounts of poor morale and military inefficiency among the Russian forces, which were judged to be incapable of a serious offensive war. But the sudden end of the Russo-Finnish war was not foreseen.[60] The Head of the MI Directorate's German section neglected no opportunity of warning his superiors in late 1939 that

---

* For the further development of NID 17 see below, Chapter 9, pp 286–287.

60. CAB 80/2, COS (39) 32; CAB 80/4, COS (40) 77 and 112; CAB 80/8, COS (40) 228 and 262 (COS Résumés, Nos 2, 6, 9, 22, 25, 27).

Russo-German amity was superficial only, and that friction between them was inevitable.[61] This section (MI 3(b)) also dismissed Foreign Office ideas of a split between the Nazi Party and German Army in March 1940: there would be no split as long as there were victories, and after defeat the German Army would retain enough cohesion to deal with neo-Spartacist uprisings.[62] The section was not at this stage free of a general intelligence infection which a later C-in-C Home Fleet was to call 'a propensity for digging holes and then filling them in again'. Thus the German railway system was severely over-strained – but would nevertheless be able to cope:[63] the Russian people were hungry and disaffected – but the Communist Party would not be overthrown:[64] the Finnish situation was dangerous – but not critical;[65] the Germans were constructing gigantic fortress works in the east – which a fortnight later were found (and reported to be) insignificant.[66]

When reporting on Germany's intentions MI's chief sources were the Deuxième Bureau, French and British missions in Poland, the SIS, neutral attachés in Germany, and the German Press and radio.*[67] These made it possible to draw up full reports on the fighting in Poland and, by correlating these with pre-war intelligence, to highlight the main lessons of the campaign, namely the German use of armour and air support.[68] The same sources enabled MI to trace the return of German divisions from Poland to the western front between the end of September and the end of October 1939. By 21 September, the date on which General Gamelin gave up thoughts of launching an offensive, it calculated that Germany had 42 divisions in the west, and the actual figure was 46 or 47.[69] By the end of October MI put this strength at 77 divisions, the French estimate being 85–90 and the true figure being 'over 80'.[70] By the spring of 1940 it had also produced

---

* At a time when the German authorities were overjoyed by success in Poland, and unable to suppress the belief that it would be followed by the end of hostilities, the Press and radio were more revealing about the composition and the movements of German units than they were to be later on, when stricter censorship was imposed.

61. WO 190/874 and 883.
62. WO 190/891, MI3(b) Minute of 23 March 1940.
63. WO 208/2256, MI Weekly Commentary of 1 February 1940.
64. CAB 80/7, COS (40) 219; CAB 80/8, COS (40) 233 (COS Résumés, Nos 21 and 23).   65. CAB 80/8, COS (40) 262 (COS Résumé, No 25).
66. CAB 80/7 COS (40) 187 and 206 (COS Résumés, Nos 18 and 20).
67. WO 190/891, MI14 Minute, 14 August 1940; Général Gauché, *Le Deuxième Bureau au Travail* (1953), p. 162.
68. WO 191/861, DDMI's press conference 21 September 1939; WO 190/865, MI3 Appreciation, 29 September 1939; WO 190/871, MI3 Notes of the War in the West, undated but evidently October 1939; WO 190/874, MI3 Minute to MO4, 18 October 1939.
69. CAB 80/3, COS (39) 44 (COS Résumé, No 3); J R M Butler, *Grand Strategy*, Vol II (1957), p 60.
70. CAB 80/4, COS (39) 103 (COS Résumé, No 8); Gauché, op cit, p 178; Butler, op cit, Vol II, p 61.

accounts, detailed if not wholly accurate, of the characteristics and the performance of German tanks, artillery and armoured cars.[71] But even if MI itself was becoming alert to the implications of the fighting in Poland, its reports made little impact on thinking in the Army, where deficiencies in equipment and in tactical doctrine could in any case not be rectified in a short time. A good indication of the mind of the War Office is to be found on the cover of its booklet entitled 'Order of Battle of the German Army' and dated April 1940: it is marked 'Not to be taken into front line trenches'. From the COS papers it appears that no systematic study was made before May 1940 of the relevance of MI reports on the Polish campaign to earlier reports of Germany's interest in Blitzkrieg methods,* or of the possibility that she would use them in western Europe. According to General Gauché, who rendered similar reports from the Deuxième Bureau stressing the autonomous role played by Panzer divisions and the priority given by the German forces to the destruction of enemy forces, rather than to the capture of political objectives, the French High Command also paid little attention.[72] But General Gauché, like MI in Whitehall, could not be sure that methods used in Poland, which had had no frontier fortifications and had been attacked by a greatly superior force advancing on broad fronts, would be applicable against the British and French armies.

In the same way, MI could only guess at what the next German move would be. At the outbreak of war MI3's conjecture was that Germany would over-run Poland in three weeks, would then make overtures to the western powers and, when these were rejected, would launch an offensive in the west between the end of October and the beginning of December.[73] At the time of the Polish surrender the Czech intelligence services's contact in the Abwehr, A-54,† warned that this offensive was planned for 12 November.[74] The same warning was given via the Vatican and to the Dutch Military Attaché in Berlin by General Oster in October and again early in November[75] and the German concentration on the western front had reached such proportions that MI's initial appreciation seemed to be confirmed. British and French intelligence thus concluded that the offensive was imminent, with the main weight of the German armour centred on the German frontier with Belgium and Holland, and Allied forces were brought to battle stations.[76] This conclusion was correct: on 5 November Hitler did order a state of readiness for the offensive. On

---

* See Chapter 2, pp 76–77.   † See Chapter 2, p 58.

71. WO 190/891, Nos 20, 21, 22.   72. Gauché, op cit, p 177 et seq.
73. WO 190/844 of 4 September 1939.   74. Moravec, op cit, pp 185–186.
75. H Deutsch, *The Conspiracy against Hitler in the Twilight War* (1968), pp 94–97, 144, 244; R Manvell and H Fraenkel, *The Canaris Conspiracy* (1969), pp 82–83.
76. Gauché, op cit, p 183; CAB 80/4, COS (39) 77 and 103 (COS Résumés, Nos 6 and 8; L F Ellis, *The War in France and Flanders 1939–40* (1954), p 32.

the one hand, however, Hitler, who cancelled these orders two days later, at this time frequently brought his forces to a state of readiness without giving any evidence to Allied intelligence. And on the other hand intelligence lacked any firm indication of what kind of offensive was being planned. Apart from the possibility that the activity might have been bluff or cover for some other operation,[77] it could have been in preparation for an attack on both France and the Low Countries, or for one on the Low Countries only, or even for one limited to Holland.

Speculation about these alternatives continued throughout the winter. Nor was it confined to them. As we shall see, MI3 first mooted the possibility of a German invasion of Norway and Sweden in December 1939.[78] But attention swung back to the Dutch and Belgian frontiers in the same month, and the renewed expectation of activity there seemed to be borne out when a German aircraft force-landed in Belgium on 10 January 1940. The Allies retrieved from this a copy of GAF instructions relating to an offensive by the German western armies across the central Belgian plain to the North Sea. This incident had been preceded by another report by the Czechs' Abwehr source (A-54); he stated at the end of November 1939 that the offensive was now set for mid-December, though he doubted whether it would take place before the end of the year.[79] At about the time of the incident a member of the US embassy in Moscow heard in Berlin that the offensive was timed for 13 January, and passed the news to Brussels and Paris,[80] and General Oster again used his links with the Dutch and the Vatican to send a similar warning.[81] These other clues led intelligence, again correctly, to infer that a German invasion had been ordered, and a second major alert was called. But again Hitler postponed, after three days, the fresh orders for the offensive to open on 17 January which he had issued on 10 January.[82] It should be added that even on this occasion MI could not be certain that the captured document had not been planted. The PR Flight had begun to make operational sorties with one of its two Spitfires over the Siegfried line and Belgium on 18 November. Between then and 10 January it flew 15 sorties. But as the aircraft was impeded by bad weather and navigational difficulties, not all of these succeeded in obtaining photographs. Apart from the fact that the photographs were small-scale and difficult to interpret, the results were thus too discontinuous to be useful in reducing the operational uncertainty.[83] Nor was Sigint contributing any operational intelligence at this stage.

---

77. CAB 80/5, COS (39) 124 (COS Résumé, No 11).
78. WO 190/885.
79. Moravec, op cit, p 189; Amort and Jedlica, op cit, p 53 et seq.
80. C Bohlen, *Witness to History 1929–1969* (1973), pp 97–98.
81. Deutsch, op cit, pp 98, 139–146.
82. WO 190/886; Ellis, op cit, p 32.
83. AIR 41/6, pp 88–89; Barker, op cit, p 163 et seq.

As we shall see, the capture of the GAF instructions was to have important repercussions on the German planning of the western offensive, but this was now deferred for three months. During that time Sigint and air photography still produced little intelligence, and British troops had direct contact with the enemy only on a limited part of the French front. Nevertheless, thanks largely to the SIS and, from January 1940, to valuable if random items from the Enigma, British knowledge of German order of battle – that is, of identifications and locations of formations, of their composition and status (active, reserve, special category), of their movements, and of the Army's manpower resources and call-up policies, all of which was the essential foundation for accurate strategic appreciation – remained good enough for assessing the general strength and area' of the German offensive of May 1940, though not for predicting its precise time and place (something that probably no intelligence organisation could have done in the circumstances of the time).* During this time the British Army had the further advantage of exchanging intelligence with the French. This brought many benefits, but also led Whitehall into over-estimating the total number of German divisions. The error was soon corrected and had no unfortunate strategic consequences; nor was it until late in 1940 that MI's calculation of the divisional strength of the German Army began to go astray.†

□

In all the circumstances, given the organisation of intelligence and the state of its sources as we have described them, we can scarcely be surprised that the significance of the many indications that Germany was preparing the invasion of Norway and Denmark eluded the individual intelligence bodies and the inter-departmental authorities, at the intelligence, planning and political levels, to whom they reported. What clues were available then? And how was it that they came to be misinterpreted or overlooked? The answer to these questions will complete what there is to say about intelligence up to the point at which it began to be improved, and will bring into focus what we have said already.

Admiral Raeder first urged the seizure of Norway in October 1939. But it was not until 14 December that Hitler authorised a plan – primarily on defensive grounds and because Quisling was warning that a British occupation was imminent – and not until 17 January 1940 was the preparation of a detailed plan put in hand. Hitler's decision to implement the plan was sealed, effectively, by the *Altmark* incident of 16 February, and his order to complete arrangements for executing it on 20 March was signed on 1 March.[84] On 3 March he finally

---

* See below, Chapter 4, p 128 et seq.   † See below, Chapter 9, pp 303–304.

84. T K Derry, *The Campaign in Norway* (1952), pp 16–18.

decided that the operation should precede the attack on France, to
protect the northern flank of the German western offensive, and
approved a speeding-up of preparations so that by 10 March the
operation could be launched at four days' notice.

In the light of this timetable, it cannot be said that warning was slow
to reach Whitehall. By the end of December 1939 a number of SIS
reports asserted that a German expeditionary force was assembling
and carrying out combined operations exercises in Baltic ports, and
that merchant vessels there had been fitted out for the transport of
troops and vehicles.[85] During January similar reports continued to
come in.[86] Early in February the Military Attaché in Stockholm
forwarded the view of his Romanian colleague that Germany was
preparing to occupy the Swedish ore-producing areas and naval and
air bases in south Norway as part of a strategy of encircling Great
Britain.[87] By 11 March the Foreign Office had received from a German
source a warning that action was being planned against Denmark and
Norway.*[88] But no reference to this appeared in the intelligence
documents and it seems that it was disregarded in the Foreign Office.
On 26 March – by which time the German move had been deferred
to April because of the persistence of ice in the Baltic – three telegrams
were received from the Stockholm embassy. According to the Air
Attaché, the Swedish Naval Staff believed Germany to be ready to seize
Norwegian ports and airfields under the pretext of responding to
Allied intervention. The Assistant Naval Attaché reported that a
concentration of ships in Kiel included fast merchant vessels with AA
armament and with flying personnel on board, and that 50 merchant
vessels had that day passed the Kiel Canal into the Baltic. The
Ambassador commented that 'these preparations may have been
merely intended for a counter-stroke to our Finnish expedition or they
may foreshadow a fresh German initiative'.[90] The circulation of these
reports by the Foreign Office to the Service intelligence branches
prompted the MI section dealing with Scandinavia to inform the
Foreign Office that DMI had recently received a further item from
the Military Attaché in Stockholm: German officers there had hinted
that the Swedish government was free to negotiate alliance arrangements with Finland, but must omit Norway as Germany intended 'to

---

* The source is named as Foerster, presumably the Gauleiter of Danzig who in the
summer of 1938 had been in touch with the PUS at the Foreign Office.[89]

85. CAB 80/7, COS (40) 187 and 206; CAB 80/8, COS (40) 228 (COS Résumés, Nos
18, 20 and 22).
86. FO 371/24381, C 5835/5/18 (Foreign Office digest of JIC Daily Summaries
prepared for the Prime Minister).
87. CAB 65/11, WM (40) 32 CA, 3 February.
88. Woodward and Butler (eds), op cit, Series 3, Vol I, pp 653–655.
89. D Dilks (ed), op cit, p 86.
90. FO 371/24815, N 3602/2/63; N 3603/2/63.

take care of Norway in a very short time'.[91] Oster once again warned the Dutch and the Vatican at the last minute that Germany would attack on 9 April[92] and similar warnings were reaching the Foreign Office from the Danish and Norwegian authorities and were no doubt also influencing the reports of the British attachés. On 2 April the Naval Attaché in Oslo sent in a report, graded AI, to the effect that large numbers of troops were being concentrated at Rostock.[93] By 3 April Whitehall had received information from the Swedish government that German shipping and troops were concentrating at Stettin and Swinemünde and unconfirmed reports that ships were loading war material, including tanks, in Hamburg. And by 4 April it had received the report that 117 German aircraft were in north-west Germany after night flying and navigational training in the Baltic area.[94]

On the part of the intelligence branches, again, there was no undue or, operationally speaking, fatal delay in bringing these reports to the notice of the Chiefs of Staff. It was at this stage, however, that complications arose. On three occasions up to 3 February 1940 the COS résumés included items drafted by MI3 which summarised the SIS reports but hedged them about with qualifications. The latest of these dismissed the idea that the reports justified the view that an expeditionary force was being prepared.[95] MI3 had already concluded in December that Germany would need 25 to 30 divisions for an invasion of Norway and Sweden.[96] It could now trace only 6 divisions in the area to which the reports had drawn attention.* In an appreciation of 21 January, after noting that the many reports it was receiving about Scandinavia varied from suggesting that Germany intended no move, through suggesting that she was preparing against an Allied threat to suggesting that she was planning an invasion, it was inclined to discount the positive ones. It recognised the strategic importance of Norway to Germany; indeed, the appreciation quoted Admiral Wegener's *Die Seestrategie des Weltkrieges*, a book published in 1929 which Sir Robert Vansittart had brought to the notice of the Admiralty in April 1939, and which criticised German strategy in the First World War for its failure to see the importance of seizing Norwegian and French Atlantic bases.[97] But it thought the build-up

---

* In fact for Norway Germany made do with six.

91. FO 371/24815, N 3602/2/63.
92. Deutsch, op cit, pp 318, 323, 334–335; Manvell and Fraenkel, op cit, p 85.
93. FO 371/24815, N 3776/2/63.
94. FO 371/24381, C 5835/5/18.
95. CAB 80/7. COS (40) 187 and 206; CAB 80/8, COS (40) 228 (COS Résumés, Nos 18, 20 and 22).
96. WO 190/885, MI3 Minute, 11 December 1939.
97. Derry, op cit, pp 16–17. ADM 100/39; ADM 1/9956, for Vansittart to CNS 14 April 1939 and Admiralty Summary of Wegener 15 May 1939.

could have other implications. On the one hand, 6 divisions was the normal peace-time strength of the area. On the other, while 6 divisions was a sufficient force for 'immediate action', the assembly might have other objectives than Norway even if an operation was being planned.[98] In February MI was no less sceptical about the Romanian Attaché. His report was the subject of much minuting in the intelligence branches and was brought to the attention of the War Cabinet, where the Prime Minister found it of 'particular interest'. But MI warned that in a previous post the Attaché had often supplied inaccurate information.[99] After January it made no further reference to Wegener or to Norway's possible strategic importance to Germany.

By 3 April MI was beginning to hesitate, and it advised the Chiefs of Staff and the War Cabinet that the latest reports 'might portend an invasion of Scandinavia'.[100] The next day, however, it concluded in another appreciation that, while the picture could change rapidly, the evidence did not at the moment support the probability of a German invasion.[101] Nor did the other departments disagree with this conclusion. Air Intelligence had earlier been more inclined to heed the intelligence reports. In January, when SIS reports were warning, also, of the presence of paratroop brigades and transport aircraft in the amphibious training area, AI had thought it possible that an invasion of Norway was being prepared as a response to intervention by Great Britain.[102] On 13 March an Air Intelligence minute had quoted a neutral visitor to Germany, who had recently found there a widespread expectation of military action, and AI had suggested that his report was borne out by an SIS report that the German government had called for the completion of contracts by 15 March.[103] But MI's 4 April appreciation put together the information supplied by all three Services. Its conclusion was also in line with opinion in the Foreign Office. On 26 March the Head of the Northern Department minuted on the telegram from the Air Attaché in Stockholm: 'I wish I could believe this story. German intervention in Scandinavia is just what we want.' On 28 March, on the copy of the Military Attaché Stockholm's report received from the War Office, he commented that 'there may be, after all, something in this story'. On 31 March, however, he was dismissing rumours of German action as 'the usual threats....'.[104]

If the SIS and the diplomatic warnings were thus largely discounted,

98. WO 190/891, No 10 of 21 January 1940.
99. CAB 65/11, WM (40) 32 CA, 3 February.
100. CAB 65/12, WM (40) 80 CA, 3 April; CAB 79/85, COS (40) 63rd Meeting SSF, 3 April.
101. WO 190/891, No 49 of 4 April 1940.
102. AIR 40/2321, AI3 Minutes, 27 December 1939, 5 and 6 January, 2 February 1940.   103. ibid, 13 March 1940.
104. FO 371/24815, N 3602/2/63; N 3741/2/63.

it was partly because of the failure to find confirmation for them. After the event we can see that while there was no confirmation of an unambiguous kind – from Sigint sources, for example – and no photographic reconnaissance to help in interpreting the other evidence, the intelligence branches might have found considerable indirect support if they had collated all the evidence that was available to them and if they had jointly, or even individually, considered it carefully. In its contribution to the résumé for 29 February to 7 March the MI branch had informed the Chiefs of Staff that Germany was paying attention to her defences on the Danish frontier.[105] On 27 March it had noted that she had called up six different classes of Danish-speaking Germans.[106] Its Military Commentary of 28 March had recorded a stoppage of German Army leave similar to that which had preceded the alerts of the previous November and January on the western front.[107] By 24 March, again, the OIC in the Admiralty had noticed – though without commenting on so unusual a development – that U-boat activities against the trade routes, and also U-boat and destroyer mine-laying, had ceased after the second week of the month.[108] GAF attacks on the Fleet Air Arm base at Hatston in the Orkneys, on 16 March, and on the convoys to Norway, of which Cheadle had given advance notice, had correctly been seen by AI as a change in German policy, and reported as such to the Chiefs of Staff.[109] But the connection between these clues was overlooked. The different intelligence branches, and even the individual sections within each branch, were as yet unaccustomed to collating information received from different sources. In the Admiralty NID 1, the geographical section dealing with Germany, was responsible for interpreting the SIS and diplomatic reports bearing on German intentions in Scandinavia, but the OIC, which was responsible for operational intelligence, including that derived from studying the movements of German ships and aircraft, received by no means all of the SIS and diplomatic information. To make matters worse, relations between NID 1 and the OIC were not good, and NID 17 was not properly co-ordinating their output. In MI a similar situation prevailed. MI 2, responsible for interpreting reports received from Scandinavia about German intentions there, did not receive reports of preparations in Germany. The latter were studied by MI 3, which did not see the evidence from Scandinavia. Relations between the two sections were poor. More serious still, although MI 2 was privy to plans for British intervention in Norway, MI 3 was not.

In addition, being by no means immune from the strategic and

---

105. CAB 80/8, COS (40) 262 (COS Résumé, No 27).
106. WO 190/49, MI3(b) Minute, 27 March 1940.
107. WO 208/2257, MI Weekly Commentary, 28 March 1940.
108. ADM 186/798, BR 1736 (46), *Naval Operations of the Campaign in Norway*, p 10.   109. CAB 80/9, COS (40) 273 (COS Résumé, No 29).

operational assumptions of the operational divisions which they served, the intelligence branches tended to fit their information together within a framework dictated by their expectations. Air Intelligence, for example, thought that the Hatston raid might indicate a German decision to work up gradually to an all-out GAF attack on the United Kingdom, 'thus softening the effect on neutral opinion', and missed the fact that Hatston was the British air base nearest to Bergen and Trondheim. In the Admiralty, in the same way, no intelligence section, until it was too late, dissented from the belief of Mr Churchill, the First Lord, that a landing in Scandinavia was beyond Germany's powers[110] or from the conclusion reached by the First Sea Lord and the Naval Staff when it at last became obvious that some move was afoot – the conclusion that what Germany intended was another break-out by heavy ships into the Atlantic or against British convoys to Norway.[111] Up to 7 April the daily summaries of the OIC leave no doubt that it was on the alert only for these possibilities. As it happened, moreover, the planning and operational divisions in the Service departments were absorbed, as were the Chiefs of Staff, in preparing for British intervention in Norway, and both they and the intelligence branches looked at the reports of German preparations, which were so far silent about their timing and conflicting as to their objective, in that context. For example, on 30 March the DNI informed the Naval Staff about the activities of a German spy ship which during the past few weeks had been carrying out observations in Norwegian territorial waters; he recommended that she be left unmolested because of the cryptanalytical value of her transmissions.* DNI did not link her activities with other evidence of German preparations for the invasion of Norway and their significance was not grasped until after the event. At the time the Naval Staff connected them only with the British plans to lay mines.[112]

Intelligence had little influence on the origin and the evolution of the plans for British intervention.[113] While pre-war intelligence appreciations had of course drawn attention to the importance of Swedish iron ore for Germany's industries,[114] the project for cutting

---

* These messages, intercepted by MI5's Radio Security Service (RSS) after a tip-off by a double agent and decrypted by GC and CS, were the first examples of intelligence from the cyphers of the Abwehr. In December 1940 GC and CS broke the hand cypher of the main Abwehr group and continued to read the Abwehr traffic, which later adopted a machine cypher and increased enormously in amount, until the end of the war (see, for examples, Chapter 4, p 131, Chapter 11, p 358 and Chapter 14, p 447). It was on the basis of these decrypts that the double agent system was built up – see J C Masterman, *The Double Cross System* (1968).

110. CAB 65/12, WM (40) 80 CA, 3 April.
111. Roskill, op cit, p 158; ADM 186/798, pp 12, 147.
112. ADM 223/24, NID 01259/40, DNI minute 30 March 1939; E Montagu, *Beyond Top Secret U* (1977), p 34.   113. Butler, op cit, Chapter V.
114. eg CAB 47/13, ATB (EPG) 6 of 11 October 1937; CAB 47/14, ATB (EPG) 35 of 18 July 1938; CAB 47/6, ATB 181 of 22 July 1938.

off Germany's supplies originated in ministerial pressure, mainly from Mr Churchill. Thereafter, the MEW took the view that the stoppage of only the Narvik route would produce only limited embarrassment for Germany, the implication being that, to be effective, action would have to extend to the seizure of the Swedish orefields. Before mounting so drastic a measure the Chiefs of Staff wanted to be assured that its effects on Germany would be decisive. The MEW could not guarantee this. Under ministerial pressure, which increased with the outbreak of the Russo-Finnish war, planning continued despite this impasse.[115] The initial intention had been to carry out a purely naval operation to stop the passage of Swedish ore to Germany via Narvik by mining Norwegian waters. This was expanded to embrace land operations in Norway and Sweden, partly from the wish to help Finland in her struggle with Russia and partly from the need to secure the Swedish orefields and to counter probable retaliation from Germany. But the plan was reduced to something nearer its original scope from the middle of March, when the collapse of Finnish resistance had created the latest in a long series of hesitations and delays. On 1 April the Cabinet decided that the naval action should at last proceed but that there should be no landings in Norway unless 'the Germans set foot on Norwegian soil, or there is clear evidence that they intend to do so'. It further decided that, in case Germany moved, Allied forces should be ready to secure Narvik, in order to pave the way for the seizure of the Swedish orefields, and to occupy Stavanger, Bergen and Trondheim in order to deny them to Germany. On 3 April, the day on which they were advised that intelligence pointed to the possibility of German action somewhere in Scandinavia, the Chiefs of Staff were making preparations in accordance with these instructions. They were also operating on the assumption that, provided they avoided delay in despatching an invasion force on the first news of a German move, Germany, though she might forestall this force at Stavanger, would be unable to forestall it at points further north. Moreover, they entertained the hope, a product of this assumption and of much earlier frustration, that Germany would retaliate when the mining took place.

Carried out so late in the winter, when the Baltic supply routes from Sweden to Germany were about to unfreeze, this mining would not

---

115. CAB 65/1, WM (39) 20 of 19 September; CAB 65/2, WM (39) 99 of 30 November, WM (39) 122 of 22 December; CAB 66/4, WP (39) 162 of 16 December, 164 of 15 December, 168 of 20 December, 169 of 20 December, 170 of 21 December; CAB 67/4, WP (G) (39) 153 of 18 December; CAB 80/6, COS (39) 168 of 20 December, 181 of 31 December; CAB 65/5, WM (40) 1 of 2 January, 2 of 3 January, 8 of 10 January, 10 of 12 January, 11 of 13 January, 21 of 23 January, 55 of 29 February; CAB 65/6, WM (40) 64 of 9 March, 65 of 11 March, 73 of 20 March; CAB 66/4, WP (40) 11 of 9 January; CAB 66/5, WP (40) 35 of 28 January; CAB 68/4, WP (R) (40) 22, undated but covering 7–14 January; CAB 80/7, COS (40) 218 of 28 January; CAB 80/104. COS (40) 268 (S) of 29 March.

seriously damage the German economy. It was by no means certain, then, that Germany would 'take dangerous retaliatory action'. But the purpose of the Chiefs of Staff meeting on 3 April, when the mining was due to be carried out on the morning of 7 April, was to complete the arrangements by which the Admiralty would give the order for the despatch of the British land forces if it became evident that Germany was attempting landings in Norway.[116] On 5 April, again, they secured Cabinet approval for proposals intended to start the expeditions at once if news was received of a German move, and on 6 April they informed the Cabinet that, except that the Narvik force was not now to cross into Sweden without further orders, the instructions for the expeditions were substantially the same as those drafted before the Finnish collapse.

It was in these circumstances, the authorities in Whitehall half doubting and half hoping that German action would still justify the expansion of their own mining project into a larger undertaking, that the next developments took place. At 0025 on 6 April the Minister in Copenhagen sent a further diplomatic warning. His American colleague had been told by a well-placed source that Hitler had given 'definite orders to send one division in ten ships moving unostentatiously at night to land at Narvik on 8 April occupying Jutland on the same day, but leaving Sweden [alone]', and that German moderates were said to be opposing the plan.[117] Despite the fact that throughout the departments people were watching for a German move, they did not expect one until the British minelaying had begun and they did not expect it to be so daring. Incredulity was thus the first response in Whitehall to the Copenhagen message. The desk officer in the Foreign Office minuted: 'A German descent on Narvik is surely out of the question' and the head of the Northern Department minuted for the second time 'I wish I could believe this'. In NID it was first believed that Narvik must be a mistake for Larvik, a port in southern Norway.[118] At 1417 on 6 April the Minister in Copenhagen sent a second telegram: 'US Minister [considers] the report in principle fantastic, but he felt it could not be ignored. Troops actually embarked 4 April, but military authorities hoped to have the order rescinded'.[119] Nor was incredulity dispelled when, more than 24 hours after the first Copenhagen message was received, aircraft of Coastal Command made the first sighting of German ships: in the forenoon of 7 April what was at first thought to be a cruiser force was reported to be moving towards Norway. The sighting prompted the Admiralty to pass the substance of the first Copenhagen message to C-in-C Home

---

116. CAB 65/12, WM (40) 80 CA, 3 April; CAB 79/85, COS (40) 63rd Meeting SSF, 3 April.
117. FO 371/24815, N 3990/2/63.
118. Derry, op cit, p 66.
119. FO 371/24815, N 4002/2/63.

Fleet, who received it at 1420 on 7 April, but DNI added – or allowed to be added – the comment that 'all these reports are of doubtful value and may well be only a further move in the war of nerves'.[120]

In doing so he was unaware not only of some of the evidence that had accumulated before the early days of April, but also of more recent indications. Some of these were scattered about in other departments. Aircraft of Bomber Command had observed intense activity during the night of 6/7 April in the wharves at Kiel, Eckernförde, Hamburg and Lübeck and on the roads leading to them.[121] The first photographic reconnaissance of Kiel made on 7 April had reported a heavy concentration of shipping there.[122] The Military Attaché in Copenhagen now estimated the German strength on the Baltic coast as 12 divisions: and during 4 and 5 April he had reported that military traffic, including sealed trains, was being given precedence between Hamburg and Bremen, and that a large number of transports were collecting at Kiel, Stettin and Swinemünde.[123] Items available in the Admiralty itself included reports, noted in the OIC Daily Report of 6 April and probably derived from the Norwegian Foreign Office, that a German flight, believed to be photographic reconnaissance, over the west coast of Norway – a unique event – had been made on 4 April; a report that the *Scharnhorst* and the *Gneisenau* had been seen in Wilhelmshaven, also on 4 April; and the fact, noted in the OIC Daily Report of 7 April, that exceptional German naval wireless activity in the Bight and Jutland areas and the Baltic entrances had begun during the night of 6/7 April.* But these items, taken by themselves, were consistent with a German plan to do no more than pass the battle cruisers into the Atlantic and it is clear that, although a few officers in the Admiralty were coming to believe by 7 April that the Copenhagen message was reliable,[124] they had not marshalled the wider evidence in such a way as to enable them to feel sure, or to present a convincing case to those who took the decisions.

When the Admiralty's signal of 7 April was received at Scapa, with DNI's comment on it, the Home Fleet was brought to one hour's notice for steam. It sailed at 2015, and might have done so earlier but for

---

* This information went by telephone to the OIC, from the Naval Section at GC and CS. It was GC and CS's first contribution to naval operational intelligence and inaugurated its close collaboration with the OIC, but the Naval Section could do no more than state that the activity was without precedent in the history of the German naval wireless system since the outbreak of the war, the study of which it had just completed. As yet, moreover, the OIC and the Naval Section were unknown to each other except as voices on the telephone, and GC and CS did not receive copies of the information received by the OIC from other sources or copies of Admiralty telegrams to the Commands, and therefore worked in a void.

120. ADM 186/798, p 10.
121. WO 190/891, No 51 of 8 April 1940.
122. CAB 80/9, COS (40) 292 (COS Résumé, No 32).
123. WO 190/891, No 51 of 8 April 1940.
124. ADM 186/798, p 12.

the DNI's comment and a failure in air to ground communication which delayed the receipt of a second and fuller sighting report which indicated that the German force included a ship of the *Scharnhorst* class and 10 destroyers. Early in the afternoon of 7 April a Bomber Command aircraft reported the German ships to be two cruisers, one battle cruiser and 10 destroyers. The report did not reach the Home Fleet until 1727.[125] What was still more unfortunate, the Fleet sailed on the north-easterly course which would enable it to intercept ships attempting to break out into the Atlantic, but which left the central North Sea uncovered.[126] Nor was this decision questioned by the Admiralty during 8 April, when a redisposition might still have frustrated the German plans. Although it informed the C-in-C at 1115 that the Copenhagen report might be true, it did not firmly conclude that an invasion of Norway was in progress until, early on 9 April, reports came in of the German landings – and this despite the fact that the northward passage of German warships from the Kattegat was reported during the afternoon of 8 April by HM submarines, as well as by the Naval Attaché at Copenhagen and by the SIS, and despite the receipt in the Admiralty, also in the early afternoon of 8 April, of information from survivors of a German transport, sunk by the submarine *Orzel*, to the effect that they had been on their way to Bergen 'to protect it from the British'.[127]

During 8 April, indeed, the Naval Staff, which had earlier been charged with ordering the despatch of British troops to Norway if it received any information indicating that Germany was moving troops in response to the British minelaying, took two operational decisions in the conviction that its information still pointed to a German attempt to break out into the Atlantic. The first withdrew from Vestfjord the destroyers which had laid mines there the previous day, with the unhappy consequence that the approaches to Narvik were open when the German ships arrived. The second abandoned that part of the plan for moving British troops – and it was the larger part of it – which had involved the use of cruisers of the Home Fleet. This had a further unfortunate outcome. The forces which might otherwise have been in position to counter German landings at crucial places like Bergen and Stavanger remained on the wrong side of the North Sea.[128] But the preconceptions underlying these decisions – that against Norway Germany would act only in response to the British mining and that, since she could not hope to scize and retain Norway in the face of British supremacy at sea, the action she took would be something less ambitious – were not confined to the Admiralty, with its concern for the trade routes, or even to operational staffs with their reluctance

---

125. ibid, p 10, footnote 4.
126. Roskill, op cit, pp 159–160.
127. Derry, op cit, p 30; ADM 186/798, p 13.
128. Roskill, op cit, pp 160–162; ADM 186/798, pp 13–15.

to be converted by intelligence reports which were unconfirmed and, individually, inconclusive. Also on 8 April, MI issued another appreciation entitled 'The Possibilities of German Action against Scandinavia'. Except that it had none of OIC's naval operational intelligence, this surveyed the information that had recently accumulated in the Service departments and the Foreign Office. It claimed that the dispositions of German forces did not then 'support any probability of a Scandinavian invasion'. But it based its conclusion – that Germany was ready to carry out 'limited operations' on the Norwegian coast, but that it was 'by no means certain' that she would undertake such action 'except to counter a similar expedition by the Allies' – not so much on the information as on general assumptions. One of these was that little advantage was to be gained by Germany from occupying Denmark. As for the advantages she would derive from forestalling the British by occupying Norwegian ports, these were grudgingly admitted and considerably qualified.[129]

It was a conclusion which reflected the outlook of the whole of Whitehall at this time when, in the absence of incontestable intelligence, from Sigint and from regular photographic reconnaissance, there was also no adequate machinery, within the departments or between them, for confronting prevailing opinions and lazy assumptions with rigorous and authoritative assessments of the massive but miscellaneous information about the enemy that was nevertheless available.

---

129. WO 190/891, No 51 of 8 April 1940.

CHAPTER 4

From the Invasion of Norway to the Fall of France

T HE GERMANS achieved total surprise by their invasion of Norway. In concealing their intention to take the offensive in western Europe they could scarcely be so successful. After the alerts of November 1939 and January 1940* the intelligence branches in London and in Paris remained convinced that Germany was poised to launch an offensive between the Moselle and Holland. After the beginning of operations in Norway they warned that this further assault was imminent and that it could be made with little warning at short notice.[1] A minute written by DMI in January 1941 records that the French did not wholly agree at first, but also that they came into line by the end of April 1940: 'On 15 April...the British Liaison Officer with the French reported that they did not consider an invasion imminent: and only after a meeting with the French Deuxième Bureau (29 April) did the latter agree to subscribe to our view of the imminence of invasion by possibly the whole of their [the German] armoured divisions....'[2] These strategic warnings were not ignored by the operational authorities. It is true that on 13 April the Prime Minister wrote: 'The accumulation of evidence that an attack [in the west] is imminent is formidable...and yet I cannot convince myself that it is coming'.[3] But it was generally held that the main indications – the deployment of the bulk of the German Army and Air Force in the west, the logistic preparations visible on the German western frontiers, and the fact that only a small proportion of the German forces had been diverted to Norway – supported them. During the April full moon period a third alert was called for the Allied troops. But intelligence was unable to say where and when the blow would fall, and thus to save the Allied commanders from being tactically surprised.

As to where the attack would come, four main possibilities were kept under review – an attack limited to the seizure of the Low Countries,

---

* See Chapter 3, pp 113–114.

1. JIC (40) 18 (S), 11 April; WO 190/891, MI3 (b) Appreciation No 53B, 12 April 1940.
2. WO 190/893, MI14 Appreciations File, DMI minute to VCIGS of January 1941 (exact date not preserved).
3. Chamberlain Papers, University of Birmingham Library; Chamberlain to sister Ida, 13 April 1940.

and perhaps of Holland alone; an attack through the Low Countries aimed at turning the Maginot Line in the north; an attack on the Maginot Line; an additional thrust through Switzerland. Neither alone nor in their various possible combinations did these alternatives include the option which Germany finally selected. Initially, in October 1939, she had intended to thrust across the central Belgian plain to break the Allied armies, to seize as much as possible of the Low Countries and northern France as a base for warfare against England, and to provide a protective *glacis* for the Ruhr. But then in January the knowledge that the Allies had captured documents* led the Germans to conclude that, as the Allies would have been strengthened in their opinion that 'our only concern is to occupy the Channel coastline of Holland and Belgium',†[4] they should modify their plans. Issued on 24 February, the new plans specified that the main thrust would be through the Ardennes with the aim of cutting off the Allied armies north of the Somme. They involved the transfer of 20 divisions (including 7 armoured and 3 motorised) from Army Group B, which was to have been responsible for the original thrust in the north, to Army Group A which, further south, faced the weak French forces defending the Meuse crossings.

The fact that the Allied authorities did not allow for the possibility of a break-through in the Ardennes determined the course and the outcome of the subsequent campaign. When it began the Allied armies moved eastward into Belgium and so played into the hands of the German main forces, which pierced the frontier further south and advanced westward into France. The chief reasons for the oversight were two-fold. Certain preconceptions, based on other considerations than intelligence, kept attention elsewhere. Intelligence was unable to unearth sufficient information to undermine these preconceptions.

At an early stage General Gamelin appears to have allowed that an attack through the Ardennes was one of several options available to Germany.[6] Later the belief that the Ardennes were impassable, an assumption dating from the First World War and invested with all the prestige of Foch and Pétain, prevailed. In London, where it was in any case shared by the Chiefs of Staff,[7] there was no inclination to challenge this assumption. On the contrary, over and above the doctrine of deferring to French views in army matters, British preconceptions reinforced it. After the event there were those who

---

* See Chapter 3, p 114.

† In fact MI's first instinct was to think that the January captured material, with its full information on the German plan for a thrust in the north, was a German plant.[5] But this suspicion did not persist.

4. Ellis, op cit, p 340.
5. CAB 44/66; BEF Narrative, Part I, Section III, p 5.
6. Ellis, op cit, p 318.
7. CAB 16/183, DP (P) 44 of 20 February 1939, paragraph 421.

recalled that there had been some disquiet in London that the Ardennes option was not being studied.[8] There is no evidence that at the time there was any sustained questioning of two widespread beliefs. Needing a quick end to the war on account of the state of her economy, Germany would try to secure this by means of intense air and naval attacks on Great Britain and her supply lines – and especially by the strategic bombing of the United Kingdom, the GAF's primary mission. On this account, and also because her army was inadequate for an all-out attack on France, she would direct her land assault against Belgium and Holland, and would probably limit herself to seizing them.

A paper embodying these beliefs, coupled with the warning that the Germans remained ready to undertake operations at short notice, was circulated by MI on 6 March to the CIGS, to GHQ BEF, and to all departments represented on the JIC: the most probable area for the offensive was the Low Countries.[9] On 11 April this view was endorsed at an urgently summoned meeting of the JIC, the first such meeting to consider the subject. The JIC recorded that 'there are such strong reasons for assuming that a German invasion of Belgium and Holland is likely that arrangements must be made to implement, at shortest possible notice, the Allied precautionary measures already agreed upon'.[10] On 12 April MI insisted that, 'as we have repeatedly said, Germany is in a position to invade Holland and Belgium at the shortest possible notice'.[11] On 19 April the JIC again concluded that the most likely objective of the next German move was the invasion of Holland.[12] Early in May the Chiefs of Staff endorsed this view, though also allowing that it was possible that a major German attack would be made against France.[13] The JIC issued no further appreciation. Nor is this surprising. No subsequent information received, or at any rate noticed, in London suggested that as a result of their knowledge of the capture of their documents the Germans had changed their original plan.

From this statement the evidence supplied by French intelligence cannot be excluded. Ever since the beginning of 1940 the Deuxième Bureau had been reporting that a German offensive could be launched at short notice and that warning as to its time and place would only be possible if reliable information could be obtained during the very limited period of the first move forward. By the end of April, as well as concluding that the offensive was imminent, it had

---

8. W S Churchill, op cit, Vol II (1949), p 33.
9. WO 190/891, No 31 of 6 March 1940.
10. JIC (40) 18 (S) of 11 April.
11. WO 190/891, No 53B, 12 April 1940.
12. JIC (40) 23 (S) of 19 April.
13. CAB 66/7, WP (40) 145 of 4 May; CAB 65/7, WM (40) 109 of 1 May, WM (40) 114 of 7 May.

established that by the end of March the great bulk of the German divisions in the Saar sector, including all the best ones and most of the armour, had been re-deployed north of the Moselle, between Luxembourg and Wesel, and that the German sector against Switzerland continued to be weakly held. On this basis it confidently predicted that no attacks could take place against the Maginot Line or through Switzerland without lengthy preparations of a kind which could not go undetected. But it had not detected the scale on which Germany was transferring divisions from the Dutch frontier* to the Eifel-Moselle area† and, beyond saying that it would be north of the Moselle, it still could not tell where the offensive would come. Nor was it able to judge this from its incomplete knowledge of the deployment of the German armour. The German main thrust against France was in the event mounted along the axis Euskirchen-Bastogne-Bouillon-Sedan. But Euskirchen was equally accessible to the part of the Belgian frontier where the original German thrust was to have been made and where, to the end, it was expected to come.[14] The post-war account by General Gauché, Chief of the Bureau, gives the following as the Deuxième Bureau's estimate of the German order of battle, and we give the actual figures in brackets:

Opposite the Dutch frontier (Army Gp B), 37 (29)
Eifel-Moselle (Army Gp A), 26 (45)
South of Koblenz, 41 (20)
In German rear areas 27–32 (45)

The Bureau estimated German armoured divisions correctly enough at 10–12, but these were thought to be equally available for Group A or Group B.

Allied knowledge of the German order of battle was based on air reconnaissance and reports from agents and diplomats. Among the reports were some which might have challenged the deep-rooted belief in the impassability of the Ardennes. On 7 April the French learned from a German who had defected to Luxembourg that an attack on Luxembourg was planned for 14 and 15 April and that maps of the Grand Duchy had been distributed to German formations.[15] On 4 May the British Military Attaché in Berne sent in a report from a Polish intelligence officer to the effect that an offensive between Basle and Holland was imminent and that circles close to Goering were confident of over-running France in 4 weeks.[16] But these warnings can hardly be called precise, and they were but a few among a large number of reports of which most pointed in other directions. At the time, moreover, it was impossible to distinguish which reports

---

* Later discovered to be Army Group B area.
† Later discovered to be Army Group A area.

14. Gauché, op cit, pp 188, 222–223.
15. ibid, p 211.
16. AIR 40/2321, p 88.

were genuine, which were guesswork and which were inspired by the Germans, for none of them came from sources that were known to be completely reliable.

It has been claimed that A-54, the Czech Intelligence Service's source in the Abwehr, whose reliability had been established before the war,* warned Paris and London as early as 25 March that the main German attack would be launched through the Ardennes, the Panzer units crossing the Meuse north of Sedan and driving towards the Channel, and that while the French were sceptical of the report, the SIS was impressed by it. But it has also been claimed that earlier in March the same source had reported that an attack on Holland was still included in the German plans.[17] It is perhaps for this reason that in the British records there is no evidence that any precise warning was received about the Ardennes. These records do establish that during the spring of 1940 MI5's Radio Security Service (RSS) intercepted the traffic on a German Secret Service wireless link connecting Wiesbaden with France, Belgium and Luxembourg; when decrypted the traffic, which was originally restricted to Gestapo affairs, began to carry enquiries about defences, road blocks, troop dispositions and other military topics in the area where the Germans later made their attack. There is no reference to this evidence in any contemporary MI document. Nor do clues of this nature appear in the uninhibited summary of evidence of German interest in the Ardennes supplied to the Deuxième Bureau during April and May 1940 by the French Service de Renseignements (SR), responsible for agent information and cryptanalysis, which is included in General Gauché's post-war account.[18] This tends to confirm the conclusion to which RSS came in November 1940 that the strategic significance of its information had not been grasped at the time. It is now no longer possible to be certain that the information reached the German section of MI. Had it reached the Deuxième Bureau it is possible that it might have prompted Gauché to give more weight to the possibility of a major German thrust through the Ardennes. As it is, his post-war account makes no reference to any discussion of this possibility.† As far as can

---

* See Chapter 2, p 58.

† Nor does it refer to a similar and also apparently reliable report of German interest in this sector which reached the SR on 12 April. A double-agent then disclosed that he had been ordered to provide, as a matter of urgency, a report on French troops, obstructions, bridges and depots on the axis Sedan–Charleville–St Quentin–Amiens. On 13 April the head of SR, Colonel Rivet, disclosed this information personally to General Georges, C-in-C of the North-East Front, and his chief of operations who observed that it ran counter to other reports which led them to believe that the main German thrust would be made against northern Belgium and Holland. The officer who accompanied Rivet states in his post-war account, which makes no mention of Gauché or any disclosure of this report to him, that it produced no change of attitude at the French HQ.[19]

17. Moravec, op cit, pp 189–190.
18. Gauché, op cit, pp 211–212.
19. Paillole, op cit, pp 186–187.

be traced, this was the only Sigint evidence of German interest in the Ardennes to be received before 10 May 1940. As such, it would have helped provide a corrective to the general run of espionage and diplomatic reports about German intentions coming in at the time. That it did not do so is evident from the assessments made by the intelligence authorities towards the end of April. By 20 April, according to the head of the French counter-espionage, all the signs pointed to an attack on the Low Countries.[20] An MI appreciation of 1 May indicated a greater state of uncertainty but reached the same conclusion. It noted that of eight recent reports on German plans, five spoke of an offensive between 1 and 15 May, and that three gave Holland as the main objective, two England, one Belgium and Luxembourg, while two merely referred to the western front in general. MI preferred the reports which pointed to Holland and England but conceded that all might be true – or all false, designed to deter the Allies from reinforcing Norway.[21]

That intelligence thus obtained no information about German planning from some of the other possible sources – field Sigint, prisoners of war, captured documents, even the GAF Enigma that was being broken from time to time from January 1940 to 1 May* – is in no way surprising. The Germans were taking the strictest precautions and there was next to no contact between the German and Allied forces.[22] Nor need we be surprised that air reconnaissance – in the circumstances potentially the most useful source[23] – failed to detect the final moves of the German formations which would have disclosed their battle plan. The main responsibility for air reconnaissance lay with the French. But for various reasons – among them bad weather, the superiority of the GAF, the need to preserve good pilots, and the political undesirability of overflying Belgium – the effort of the French Air Force in this direction remained restricted.[24] Nevertheless, such reconnaissance as was carried out, taken together with the Deuxième Bureau's other sources of information, succeeded in establishing the disposition of the majority of the German formations between the Moselle and the lower Rhine which were to carry out the attack.[25] The chief failure of air reconnaissance was that it did not detect the southward transfer of the divisions from Army Group B to A. We may assume that the main reason for this was the bad weather during early 1940 which prevented the regular reconnaissance necessary to detect such moves. It cannot be accounted a failure that the last-minute moves

---

* See Chapter 3, pp 108–109, and below, p 43 et seq.

20. ibid, pp 186–187.
21. WO 190–891, No 73 of 1 May 1940.
22. Major General K Strong, *Men of Intelligence* (1970), p 60.
23. ibid, p 58.   24. ibid, pp 58, 60.
25. ibid, p 58.

of the German armoured divisions to their take-off points remained undetected in view of the precautions taken by the Germans.* That British air reconnaissance, which by now was more experienced than the French, did not succeed in filling the gaps left by its ally, sprang from a variety of circumstances. Part of the explanation is to be found in the fact that although a unit of the PDU (212 Squadron) was detached to France, and placed under the operational control of the AOC-in-C British Air Forces in France (BAFF), with the PDU remaining responsible for technical development, it was largely employed on tasks that were not directly related to the German Army's dispositions. Because the BEF had no recent maps of Belgium – and because the Belgians, hoping to preserve their neutrality, were not disposed to help[26] – 212 Squadron obtained the necessary information by using the methods developed by the SIS Flight before the war. By the end of March 1940, in spite of bad weather, it provided sufficient photographs to bring up to date the old maps; and at the same time its clandestine programme produced airfield intelligence of some 30 Belgian airfields for the RAF.†[27] The unit also over-flew Germany, partly to get new intelligence, partly to develop new techniques, but the main purpose of this activity was the production of the first war-time mosaic of the Ruhr in preparation for Bomber Command's strategic bombing offensive, which began in the middle of May.

The main photographic reconnaissance effort in France before the German attack was carried out by operational squadrons of the Air Component of the BEF, which were equipped with Blenheims. One of its main objects was to discover signs of bridging across the Rhine and of German movement westwards. The results were disappointing. Up to May 1940, 82 sorties had been flown of which 44 were for various reasons unsuccessful. The remainder produced little intelligence of operational interest. And losses – 18 aircraft – were high. The Spitfires of 212 Squadron were available to BAFF HQ for special tasks in support of the Blenheims' programme, and their sorties were much more successful. Though their frequency was severely limited

---

* See below, p 135.
† The reluctance of the Belgians to co-operate in advance of the German offensive also made it necessary for the intelligence organisation at GHQ BEF to set up, with the agreement of SIS, a small espionage organisation in Belgium for sending topographical information direct to GHQ.[28] In addition GHQ formed combined Army–RAF reconnaissance missions which were to enter Belgium when the fighting began. These missions – No 3 Air Mission and the Hopkinson Mission for ground reconnaissance – were to establish themselves at the Belgian Army HQ and collaborate with Belgian formations as soon as this became possible.[29]

26. AIR 41/6, p 132.
27. ibid, pp 131–135.
28. WO 197/97, Notes on I.b organisation in the BEF at the start of active operations in May 1940.
29. Ellis, op cit, p 28.

by poor weather, they contributed to knowledge of the location of the German formations west of the Rhine. The AOC-in-C later reported that 'an immense number of extremely valuable photographs were taken prior to and during the battle, 10 May–17 June, both for the French GHQ, GHQ BEF, and my own use'.[30] For all that, PR had clearly not been sufficiently regular to help to establish where the German advance might come.

It was partly, perhaps, on account of the lack of decisive intelligence as to where the German attack would fall that the Deuxième Bureau failed to convince General Gamelin that there could be no surprise assault against the Maginot Line or through Switzerland. Up to the beginning of the offensive General Gamelin retained strong forces south of the Moselle and distributed his reserves evenly behind the entire front. It is impossible to establish with certainty whether this was because the Deuxième Bureau's conclusion (that German dispositions ruled out an attack against the Maginot Line or through Switzerland, at any rate without good warning) was not clearly presented to him, or whether he had reasons for overruling it. But one element in the situation was the receipt of German-inspired reports to the effect that their offensive would come against those parts of his front. At the same time, the Deuxième Bureau weakened its own argument by its tendency to over-estimate the German Army's total strength in armour. In January 1940 Gamelin expected Germany to be able to put 160 out of a total of 200 divisions into her western offensive.[31] By the beginning of May, after frequent exchanges of views between French and British intelligence, the French estimates had been brought nearer to the lower ones of the War Office; they now put the total at 190–200, with 120–125 available in the west, when the British figures, which had themselves moved upwards in deference to French opinion, were 189 and 124.[32] The actual figures were 157 and 134.[33] By assuming that in addition to 40 Panzer battalions in 10–12 armoured divisions, as was roughly correct, the Germans had 25–30 further such battalions in army troops, when no such further battalions existed, the Deuxième Bureau reached the figure of 7,000–7,500 as against an actual figure of 2,445 tanks,[34] and this gigantic estimate cannot but have had an inhibiting effect on French dispositions. In March the British estimate had been that Germany's seven armoured divisions and eight light and motorised divisions would be equipped with 5,800 tanks.[35]

---

30. AIR 41/21, *The Campaign in France and the Low Countries*, p 147.
31. CAB 80/104, COS (40) 228 (S) of 11 February.
32. Gauché, op cit, pp 188, 213; CAB 80/10, COS (40) 339, paragraph 34.
33. Butler, op cit, p 177.
34. Gauché, op cit, p 189; General Ulrich Liss, *Westfront 1939–40* (1959), p 133.
35. WO 208/2914, *Periodical Notes on the German Army*, No 12 of 12 February 1940, Appendix B; No 14 of 18 March 1940, Appendices A and B.

As well as concealing the direction of their offensive, the German authorities took Allied intelligence by surprise with the arrangements they made for the final timing of the attack. In November 1939 and January 1940 German orders for the offensive had allowed six days for the approach march and the final concentration of troops, but the Germans had noticed that these preliminary moves had given the Allies good notice that the offensive was due. After February 1940 they took the precaution of effecting the preliminary closing up by gradual stages. When the offensive was finally ordered on 9 May their troops were already near the frontier, in a position to move off on 10 May without affording the Allies an opportunity to observe or learn about their last-minute preparations.* Allied intelligence gave notice from the end of April that the offensive was imminent and that, delivered anywhere except against the Maginot Line or in Switzerland, it could be launched with little or no notice.† So general a warning was of no assistance against tactical surprise: the Allied High Command could not keep its forces on permanent alert; the subordinate commands could only await another order to bring their forces to immediate readiness. In the event, the High Command issued no such order after the April alert and, as their war diaries record, the formations of the BEF were surprised by the German attack. I Corps's war diary states that 'so well had the date of the blow been concealed that a number of key personnel were on leave'.[37]

It is impossible to decide whether this outcome resulted from a continuing lack of firm intelligence or from disregard by either the intelligence or the operational authorities of last-minute evidence of a sort that merited their attention. That such evidence was available has been claimed in several accounts. It is said that A-54 gave notice via The Hague on 1 May that the German offensive would begin on 10 May;[38] that Oster, in the last of his series of warnings, notified the Dutch Military Attaché on 3 May and the Vatican at about the same time that an invasion of the Low Countries was due in the following week, and that Oster confirmed the warning to the Attaché on the eve of the attack.[39] On the first of these occasions the Attaché did not pass the message to The Hague because in the preceding months the many similar warnings from him had been received with disbelief. Even his last-minute warning was treated with some scepticism. According to

---

* Major Kielmansegg's account records that the commander of his armoured division received notice that the offensive would start at dawn on the following day only at 1315 on 9 May. The division remained dispersed until 1800; it moved to the frontier during the hours of darkness.[36]

† See above, p 127.

36. Kielmannsegg, *Die Wehrmacht, 1941*, quoted in Gauché, op cit, p 216.
37. CAB 44/66, p 7.
38. Moravec, op cit, p 190; Amort and Jedlica, op cit, pp 77–78.
39. Deutsch, op cit, pp 327–330, 335–342; Manvell and Fraenkel, op cit, p 85; K H Abshagen, *Canaris* (1956), pp 178–179.

Cotton's account, a Spitfire of 212 Squadron photographed German armour along the Luxembourg border with Germany, in the wooded country that forms an extension of the Ardennes, on 6 May. It adds that 400 tanks were seen there on 7 May when the AOC-in-C BAFF ordered a low-level sortie; that a report from the AOC-in-C failed to convince the Air Ministry; that Cotton himself, returning to the United Kingdom, failed to convince the C-in-C of Bomber Command.[40] The war-time head of French counter-intelligence has claimed that intercepts provided his organisation with intelligence on the GAF's preparations and, on 7 and 8 May, showed that the German Army was ready and waiting for its final orders.[41] But to the obvious truth that no action was taken on these particular warnings we can only add the suggestion that they were perhaps less precise or outstanding at the time than they have been made to seem after the event – if, indeed, they were given. In Whitehall – whatever the French authorities may have thought of them – none of them was singled out for special comment by the intelligence authorities, who were at least expecting the Germans to move at any time. The War Office's daily intelligence summary for the twenty-four hours to 1100 on 8 May stated that there was still no sign that an invasion of France or Belgium was imminent; but it went on to say that various reports indicated that some action was to be expected in the immediate future and to warn that Germany's dispositions would enable her to move against Holland at any moment with a minimum of notice.[42]

□

When Germany's armed forces moved against France their invasion of Norway had already made possible a great improvement – for the first time – in British intelligence about them. The improvement came too late to counter or, even, to reduce the advantages which Germany derived from possessing the strategic initiative and safeguarding the element of surprise. In the best of circumstances it may be doubted whether intelligence, however plentiful, could have altered the outcome of the campaign. Once Germany had secured footholds in the main ports, the outcome was decided by operational and logistic considerations – above all by Germany's superiority in the availability and use of air power. But there was a further problem. Of the flow of intelligence that became available after the first week, the amount put to operational use remained strictly limited.

The Chiefs of Staff, who retained direct control of the British forces until 22 April, when General Massy assumed what was little more than

---

40. Barker, op cit, p 187. See also Winterbotham, *Secret and Personal* (1969), p 138.
41. Paillole, op cit, p 188.
42. WO 106/1644, WO Daily Intelligence Summary No 248 of 8 May 1940.

titular command of Allied operations in central Norway, took their earliest and most crucial decisions on information that was 'little better than that of the newspaper reader'.[43] It is true that reports about German intentions and movements now began to flood into Whitehall from diplomatic and SIS sources; but the reports were too vague and too conflicting to provide a clear picture of the unfolding of the German moves. From 15 April, however, the day after Allied forces began to go ashore, GC and CS produced a dramatic addition to Whitehall's sources.

On 10 April the Germans introduced a new Enigma key (the Yellow) for use by the GAF and the Army during the Norwegian operations. GC and CS broke this as early as 15 April and continued to read it daily by hand methods until the traffic ceased on 14 May. The traffic was voluminous and highly operational and, as well as carrying GAF and Army communications, it contained information about such naval movements as concerned the other two German Services. It was normally decrypted within a few hours – and sometimes within an hour of its transmission by the German stations – so that it not only reported the operational situation of the German forces, and the state of their organisation and supplies, but also gave notice of their intentions. For two reasons, however, little or no immediate use could be made of it.

It had not been foreseen that the Germans would make use of wireless at high-echelon levels for operational purposes. There had been no high-echelon operational Sigint in the First World War, when operational traffic had been confined to field units and operational intelligence had been derived from field cyphers and other local sources of information. As late as 1939 GC and CS had feared that the outbreak of war might be followed, not by an increase in the use of wireless by enemy states but by the imposition of wireless silence on their armed forces for all except tactical signalling. Since January 1940 GC and CS had broken the GAF general Enigma key with some regularity, though also with some delay; but as was only to be expected in the absence of operations the decrypts had dealt only with administrative and organisational questions. For the enormous volume of the operational decrypts it yielded, no less than for the speed at which it was possible to find the daily settings, the breaking of the Norwegian Enigma thus came as a complete surprise. And the first consequence was that neither GC and CS nor the Whitehall departments were equipped to handle the decrypts efficiently.

At GC and CS, quite apart from the fact that it had as yet little experience with the many textual difficulties that impeded the elucidation of the decrypts,* the staff was quite inadequate either in

---

* For these problems see Chapter 3, p 109, and below, p 144 et seq.

43. Derry, op cit, p 66.

numbers or in its understanding of military matters; and the same was true of the communications between Bletchley and Whitehall. Emergency arrangements were made to recruit military advisers and other additional staff and to install additional teleprinters; nor was it long before the most urgent decrypts were being teleprinted to Whitehall without great delay. But these were not problems that could be completely solved before the end of the short-lived Norwegian campaign. In Whitehall the intelligence branches were similarly overwhelmed by the volume of intelligence, and handicapped by their unfamiliarity with it. Moreover, delay and confusion were imposed by the internal security arrangements which were in force for safe-guarding the confidentiality of the Enigma material.

These arrangements had been introduced in January 1940, when translations of GAF Enigma decrypts were first circulated in Whitehall. The Admiralty then insisted that such translations as were sent to it should be sent to the OIC direct from GC and CS and in undisguised form; but MI and AI received the decrypts via the SIS disguised as SIS reports – initially from agent 'Boniface', later prefixed 'CX' – and this system was retained in those branches when they began to receive the decrypts direct from GC and CS. This had the effect that the un-indoctrinated intelligence staffs tended to give them the sceptical reception which they habitually applied to espionage reports, rather than the absolute trust they might have accorded to Sigint. It seems probable that the breaking of the Norwegian Enigma key necessitated some relaxation in the procedure. In the War Office, for example, the head of the section (MI8) responsible for distributing the material to the country sections of MI, who had hitherto been kept in ignorance of the true source, was apparently admitted to the ranks of the indoctrinated, which apart from the OIC included the three Directors of Intelligence and, we must assume, the Chiefs of Staff and the War Cabinet. But the relaxation did not extend to the sections which drew up the briefings for the indoctrinated authorities, and it does not appear that these authorities had any way of distin-guishing the Enigma from the other ingredients that went into the briefings.

The Admiralty's different procedure did not obviate the difficulties that followed from the need for security precautions in Whitehall. Because the OIC received the decrypts in their undisguised form the desk officers of the country sections of the NID did not receive them in any form. The Admiralty did, however, avoid a second consequence of the unexpectedness of the Enigma windfall. In January 1940 it had alerted the C-in-C Home Fleet and other selected senior naval officers to the possibility that they might receive intelligence derived from high-grade Sigint; and it had made arrangements by which this material would be sent to them in the Flag Officer's cypher in messages prefixed 'Hydro'.* But the other two Services had not taken the precaution of briefing their commanders and introducing such arrangements. When GC and CS broke the Norwegian key the War Office and Air Ministry no doubt made the full facts available to the appropriate commanders in the United Kingdom – General Massy and the Cs-in-C of Bomber and Coastal Commands, who were responsible for most of the air operations over the North Sea and in Norway – but the short-lived Norwegian campaign afforded them no opportunity for indoctrinating the commanders in the field. In signals sent to them, intelligence derived from the Enigma could be taken into account in Whitehall's instructions, but otherwise it could be quoted only as intelligence received from less sensitive sources, and was most commonly described as 'information from own forces'.

How much Enigma was passed to Norway in this way cannot, for this reason, be established without immense difficulty. Nor would it serve any purpose, except an academic one, to attempt to disentangle the Enigma from other intelligence items that featured in Whitehall's signals. It is clear that the field commanders were in no position to profit from it – clear, indeed, that, given their circumstances, it could have made little difference to the outcome of the campaign even if efficient arrangements had been made in advance to get it into their hands. In the same way it was a lamentable fact, but one that had negligible effect on the outcome, that the Army units in Norway and the short-lived RAF effort in support of them were poorly equipped for deriving operational intelligence from local sources. Either because the requirements of the Army and RAF field Sigint units in France had made it impossible to spare operators and equipment, or because field units had been prepared for the Norwegian expedition but were left behind when emergency re-arrangements were made at the last minute, the British forces sent to Norway were not equipped to intercept the enemy's field wireless transmissions. If they had been so equipped, they would still have been unfamiliar with the field codes and cyphers used by the German Army; GC and CS had broken two of these by the end of 1939, but given the virtually total lack of intercepts it remained uncertain whether these systems were still being used. Some GAF tactical traffic from Norway was intercepted in the United Kingdom, both in readable low-grade codes and in plain language, and the resulting intelligence was of some use to the operational authorities in London. But no arrangements had been made for passing it to Norway as it was received. With other local sources, the Norwegian forces and population, contacts had to be

---

* In June 1941, when the German naval Enigma was first read currently, 'Hydro' was replaced by 'Ultra' and the traffic was transmitted in total security in one-time cypher (see Chapter 10, p 346).

improvised during the fighting. The SIS had no organisation ready when the campaign began, though it now began to develop a stay-behind network in the main Norwegian towns.

The British forces were hampered even by a shortage of topographical intelligence. MI and NID had assembled information on such matters as terrain, roads and railways, harbour works, airfields, fixed defences and weather conditions since the end of 1939, when British intervention in Norway was first considered. But the work had been done hastily, and the results had been so poor that the DNI had advised against a campaign in Norway in the belief that the topographical intelligence was inadequate.[44] In any case, the work had concentrated on areas selected for British intervention, whereas the German initiative forced the fighting elsewhere. We can see why Whitehall was at last shocked into improving the topographical intelligence service* when we learn that the topographical summaries prepared by MI did not reach the commands owing to mistakes in loading, or that Baedeker's *Scandinavia* (revised 1912) was all that was available to pilots of Bomber Command for their raids on airfields in southern Norway,[45] or that the naval pilots from HMS *Furious* who attacked Narvik had to rely on Admiralty charts which showed no contours.[46]

At sea the Navy was in one respect fortunate. At an early stage of the operations, on 14 April, U-49 was sunk near Narvik. As well as providing details of the total number of U-boats in commission, she yielded up a chart marking the dispositions of the U-boats which had been concentrated in the North Sea for the protection of the German expedition, and this was of some assistance in enabling the Home Fleet to avoid them[47] Otherwise, however, the Home Fleet was no better served than the Army and the RAF. For information about the whereabouts of the German surface forces it was dependent on sighting reports and, as a result of the weather, the distances involved and the lack of suitable aircraft, air sighting reports were unreliable. Nor was the Admiralty able to do much to supplement this inadequate source. At the outset of the campaign the Admiralty's own ignorance was complete. When it intervened to give the orders which resulted in the first battle of Narvik on 9 April, it did so in the belief, based on Press reports, that one German ship had arrived there, whereas the German expedition to Narvik had reached the port in ten destroyers.† On the other hand, the Admiralty orders incorporated

---

* See below, p 161.

† However, before launching his attack Captain Warburton-Lee learned from the pilot station in the Narvik approaches that six ships larger than his own had passed in.

44. WO 106/1840; Mockler-Ferryman, op cit, pp 2–3; Morgan, op cit, p 24; Godfrey Memoirs, Vol 7, Part 2, pp 228–229; Wells, op cit, pp 405–406.
   45. Derry, op cit, p 54.   46. ADM 186/798, p 36.
   47. ibid, pp 99–100; Roskill, op cit, Vol I, pp 164, 190.

information on coastal defences which, as it transpired, did not exist.[48] From 15 April the Norwegian Enigma traffic produced some intelligence about German naval movements. Although none of the messages has survived, the OIC sent this intelligence to the C-in-C Home Fleet in 'Hydro' signals. But it was of no operational value, as may be judged from the fact that at the end of the campaign the C-in-C Home Fleet complained that 'it is most galling that the enemy should know just where our ships. . .always are, whereas we generally learn where his major forces are when they sink one or more of our ships'.[49] Whether or not he suspected it – and it seems unlikely, for exceptional British security measures were not to be adopted till much later – the German Navy had indeed read the main British naval cypher to a limited extent from the end of 1938 and, by the beginning of the Norwegian campaign, following a temporary black-out after the outbreak of war, it was reading over 30 per cent of the traffic it intercepted in the North Sea and the Norwegian area.*

Towards the end of the campaign, when the British evacuation was in full swing and operations in Norway were drawing to a close, matters had in no way improved. This was demonstrated by the circumstances in which the *Gneisenau* and the *Scharnhorst*, leaving Kiel on 4 June, sank the aircraft carrier HMS *Glorious*, homeward bound as part of the evacuation of Narvik, on 8 June. By that time the OIC had lost the assistance, such as it was, of the Norwegian Enigma, which had faded out in the middle of May, but the Naval Section at GC and CS, assisted by the geographical extension of the German naval signals system to Norway, had devised techniques for making inferences about German naval movements from the external behaviour of the wireless traffic. A fortnight before the German battle cruisers made their sortie it began to report to the OIC that this behaviour indicated that German main units were preparing to move from the Baltic northwards up the Norwegian coast. In time GC and CS's persistent warnings found their way into the OIC Daily Reports. On 29 May these recorded that 'from a study of German naval W/T traffic. . .there would appear to be a movement of certain enemy ships, class and type unknown, from the Baltic to the Skagerrak'. On 7 June they went so far as to say that 'WTI indicates that German naval forces in Norwegian waters may in future be associated in any offensive action taken by German units in the North Sea'. But the OIC was far from being convinced by such evidence, and not even a qualified warning was issued by the Admiralty to the Home Fleet. The *Glorious*, which carried aircraft capable of flying defensive patrols and launching a

---

* Enemy cryptanalysis continued to enjoy this degree of success against the naval cypher until the end of August 1940; from that date until September 1941 it read a much smaller proportion of the traffic. See Volume Two for further details.

48. Derry, op cit, p 43; ADM 186/798, pp 21–22, 26.
49. Quoted in Roskill, op cit, Vol I, p 198.

limited torpedo strike and which might have had these in the air if she had been alerted to the possibility of encountering enemy heavy ships, was caught unprepared.[50]

It is not difficult to understand the OIC's scepticism. Traffic Analysis (WTI) was an untested technique, and one that yielded only broad hints and inferential clues. The Admiralty, like the other Service departments, firmly insisted that its own intelligence branch must be solely responsible for the interpretation that was put on any intelligence material within its sphere – still retained in the OIC, indeed, for the purpose of watching the German naval signals system, the staff which it had taken back from GC and CS at the outbreak of the war.* But although this staff itself was sceptical about GC and CS's claims for Traffic Analysis, and although the evidence of Traffic Analysis was unsupported by other indications, the OIC had no good reason for resisting GC and CS's suggestion that it should issue at least a qualified warning to the Fleet. To make matters more difficult, the fact that the evacuation of Narvik was in progress was being kept extremely secret. Not only was GC and CS, then as for a long time later, uninformed of British movements. Coastal Command had not been alerted, and did not in consequence carry out reconnaissance of the area through which the evacuation convoys, and the *Glorious*, were to pass.[51] Though barely conceivable, it also appears to have been the case that even in the OIC only the senior staff was aware that important British movements from Norway were taking place. Shortly after the *Glorious* was sunk, with no chance to make a signal herself, a German ship transmitted four signals, one of them marked 'Immediate', from a position which poor DF fixes placed off the Norwegian coast. The Duty Officer in the OIC saw no significance in them and took no action. A day or two later, when it became clear that these signals had been reporting the sinking, an enquiry revealed that the Duty Officer had not known of the British naval movements from Norway, and that contacts between the operational and the intelligence staffs in the Admiralty were far from perfect.[52]

As a result of this disaster, steps were taken not only to improve the working relations between the operational and the intelligence staffs in the Admiralty, but also to bring the OIC and the Naval Section at GC and CS closer together. It was as a direct result of the loss of the *Glorious* that regular visits between the two groups were instituted and that the OIC, returning its WTI staff to GC and CS, recognised that it had to rely on the Naval Section's greater familiarity with the German naval wireless system and to co-operate with the Naval Section in

---

* See Chapter 1, p 25.

50. Roskill, op cit, Vol I, p 195.
51. Roskill, op cit, Vol I, p 197; ADM 186/798, pp 63, 129.
52. ADM 233/84, NID 02297/40, DNI Minute of 11 June.

relating this knowledge to other operational information. It did so with a will – even to the extent of sending a representative of the Naval Section to Scapa to explain the Section's work to the Home Fleet. In the meantime, the Admiralty and the C-in-C Home Fleet received the first news of the loss of the *Glorious* and of the identity of her attackers from a German broadcast. To the poverty of naval intelligence during the Norwegian campaign – to the failure indeed of the entire intelligence system up to this point – perhaps no testimony could be more eloquent.

□

From the intelligence point of view the experiences of the Norwegian campaign were repeated during the campaign in France. The German success in obtaining complete tactical surprise was again followed, from 10 May, by a first phase in which Whitehall was in the dark. For a fortnight ignorance of what the enemy was up to was so great that, in the records of the Cabinet and the Chiefs of Staff, discussions of the fighting continued to be headed 'The Netherlands and Belgium'. Thereafter, again, there was a dramatic improvement in the supply of intelligence; but because events had by then gone so far, and were still moving so fast, it was an improvement from which neither Whitehall nor the commands could derive any immediate advantage.

Virtually all the records of the BEF and of Air HQ in France were destroyed during the British retreat. Of the day to day records of the intelligence branches in Whitehall few survive for this period. But the historical accounts later drawn up by the departments and the commands make it clear that there was no intelligence to speak of until 25 May, when two highly secret documents were captured from the staff car of the liaison officer of the C-in-C of the German Army with Army Group B. These accounts indicate that this piece of good fortune influenced, perhaps decisively, what has been called C-in-C BEF's 'most fateful action during the whole campaign'. The retirement of the Belgian Army had left a gap between Menin and Ypres which Lieutenant General Brooke, commanding the British II Corps, was anxious to fill. One of the captured documents revealed that the Germans planned to attack in this gap with two corps. On this evidence Lord Gort poured into the gap two divisions which were preparing to attack elsewhere. 'By doing so', writes the official historian of the campaign, 'he saved the British Expeditionary Force'.[53]

The most important reason for the lack of intelligence during the first fortnight lay in the fact that on 1 May, in preparation for the attack on France, the Germans had made changes to the Enigma machine. Except in Norway, where they did not apply, these changes affected

53. Ellis, op cit, pp 148–149.

all the Enigma keys and made it impossible for GC and CS to read the traffic in the GAF general key (the Red) which it had broken on and off since January. Correspondingly, what chiefly transformed the situation from the last week of May was the fact that GC and CS, assisted by German mistakes in the few days after the change of 1 May and by a huge increase in the daily traffic from the beginning of the German offensive on 10 May, succeeded in breaking the new Red key for 20 May on 22 May, from which date it broke it virtually every day until the end of the war.

During the remainder of the campaign in France this cypher, which before the German offensive had been used lightly, and mainly for administrative purposes, produced a flood of operational intelligence. GC and CS decrypted, translated, amended and interpreted the messages at the rate of 1,000 a day. With unimportant exceptions it despatched all of them by teleprinter or courier to Whitehall and, as a result of its experience in handling similar material during the Norwegian fighting, did so more promptly than had then been possible. In Whitehall, moreover, arrangements were made to forward the intelligence to commanders in the field. Except for those made by the Admiralty for the C-in-C Home Fleet, no such arrangements had been made in time for the Norwegian campaign. But between 24 May and 16 June the most important Enigma items were passed direct from GC and CS to GHQ BEF and Air HQ in special cypher on a special signals link via an SIS mobile unit which assisted in the interpretation of the material and advised as to the handling of it.

Despite these measures, and despite the operational character of the Enigma signals, it still proved impossible to make much use of the intelligence for immediate – as opposed to longer-term strategic* – purposes. Delays inevitably attended the process by which the intercepts had to be got to GC and CS, to be decyphered, translated and sorted there, and then passed to Whitehall and the HQs in France. Despite GC and CS's growing experience, these delays were added to by the difficulties it still encountered in elucidating the decrypts. Apart from their sheer bulk, the texts teemed with obscurities – abbreviations for units and equipment, map and grid references, geographical and personal code names, pro-formas, Service jargon and other arcane references. One example is furnished by the fact that the Germans made frequent use of map references based on the CSGS 1:50,000 series of France. This series had been withdrawn from use in the British Army. Unable to obtain a copy of it, GC and CS was obliged to reconstruct it from the German references to it. Transmitted in the heat of battle, and having to be re-transmitted after interception to GC and CS, the texts were also frequently imperfect or corrupt. Nor were these the only difficulties. The operational situation in France was constantly changing; the arrangements made

---

* See Chapter 5, p 161 et seq.

to keep the staff at GC and CS in touch with the operational situation, and to reinforce it with advisers who had experience of military matters, were necessarily rudimentary. It is small wonder that in these circumstances much of the most urgent intelligence reached Whitehall and the commands too late to assist the forces in the field.

Over and above the unavoidable delay, some loss of operational efficiency continued to be accepted in the interest of security. As in Whitehall itself (except at the Admiralty), the main security precaution adopted when Enigma was sent to the field HQs was the procedure whereby the intelligence was disguised as SIS reports. In Whitehall the disguise was beginning to break down, many beyond the 30 or so individuals there who were in the secret now suspecting the true source of such abundant material. This was not the case with the intelligence officers in the field, who received only selections from it. For them the effect of the device was that the intelligence 'attracted . . . the scepticism with which agents' reports were normally viewed'. Despite the SIS disguise, security considerations also dictated that the material should have only a limited circulation at the HQs. As a result the intelligence staffs at GHQ BEF and at AHQ were unable to co-ordinate the product of the Enigma with the low-grade Sigint and the other field intelligence for which they were responsible.

These severe restrictions were to be subsequently, though also cautiously, relaxed. The decision to abide by them during the German offensive against France was, it can scarcely be doubted, doubly justified. On the one hand, the German authorities did not discover, as they might otherwise have done after their great successes, any evidence that the Enigma had been compromised.* On the other hand, the fact that the Enigma was rarely of operational value to the British forces during the campaign was due far less to the security precautions, or to the other problems connected with the production of its intelligence, than to two other considerations. Of these the first was the fact that when the Enigma became available the BEF's intelligence organisation was already so seriously disrupted that it was in no position to ensure that intelligence would be acted on. The second was still more serious. The BEF itself was already in full retreat in circumstances in which no intelligence service, however good, could have done much to help it.

---

* The material sent to the British GHQ and AHQ was repeated to the Howard-Vyse Mission to the French GQG. Despite this fact, and despite the fact that they captured the archives of the French High Command, the Germans uncovered no evidence that the Enigma had been compromised. Nor did they derive any grounds for suspicion from the French authorities. Some of these authorities had co-operated closely with GC and CS in the work on the Enigma up to the middle of June (see Appendix 1) and in October 1940 they resumed work on it in unoccupied France.[54] Like the Polish authorities who were in the secret, they never divulged information to the Germans.

54. Bertrand, *Enigma ou la plus grande Énigme de la Guerre* (1973), pp 115–138.

The BEF's intelligence organisation had been mobilised at very short notice.* During the winter of 1939–40 it had been built up – no mean feat – to comprise 1 major general, 80 officers and 120 other ranks, and it had prepared itself for busier times by conducting intelligence exercises, organising security, censorship and the regular briefing of the operational staffs, and developing liaison arrangements with the RAF and the French. But within days of the beginning of the German offensive this large organisation was overwhelmed. It could make little of the German field army's complex signalling network and could not exploit its low and medium-grade codes. Neither the network nor the codes had been much used before the campaign, and the difficult task of building up familiarity with them was not one that could be undertaken while the fighting lasted. On the one hand, it called for close collaboration between GC and CS and MI8 in research on intercepts and captured documents. On the other hand, while traffic below corps level could not be intercepted in the United Kingdom, partly because it used low transmission power and partly because of shortage of intercept receivers, the British intercept units in France could not find time to send their intercepts back to the United Kingdom because they were swamped by the volume of the traffic and busy with more urgent work. In the event, indeed, the research did not begin until the fall of France. If the field intercept stations logged the traffic which they intercepted during the campaign they destroyed their records before being evacuated to the United Kingdom, so that analysis had to be based on intercepts made in the second half of 1940. Even then, while progress was made in understanding the procedures of the German Army's fixed W/T stations, the unravelling of the complex operations of its field networks had to await Germany's penetration of the Balkans and the arrival of her forces in north Africa.

The urgent tasks which preoccupied the intercept units in France arose from the fact that a good deal of the German tactical traffic – that which passed in plain language, or in plain language thinly disguised, and that which used the GAF codes, which had either been captured or sent out to them from GC and CS – could be exploited locally. The intelligence obtained from these messages was, indeed, 'ample and easily deduced', and it gave a clear idea of the course of the battle on the entire front. It came primarily from GAF intercepted traffic in low-grade codes and plain language. Arrangements had been made for the GAF codes to be worked at GHQ and although the call-signs and frequency systems of the GAF had not been fully established at this stage, the messages were initially of considerable operational value. Thus the GAF broadcasts of bombing safety lines enabled GHQ to determine the rate and extent of the German

* See above, Chapter 1, p 17.

advance, while signals from aircraft enabled some of the advancing divisions to be followed and identified, and indicated some of the areas in which French resistance was crumbling. But little of the material dealt with the comparatively small sector of the front covered by the BEF, and before long even that lost its operational value as communications between the intercept stations and the intelligence staffs at GHQ, at AHQ and at the Army's two corps HQ, and, also, communications between the HQs and the inteligence staffs and the forward operational formations, proved to be quite inadequate for the war of movement which had been unleashed.

The breakdown was all the more complete because the GHQ intelligence staff was itself broken up at the beginning of the campaign. On 10 May, judging that GHQ had become too large and elaborate for battle conditions, the C-in-C took a small staff, comprising his DMI and two senior intelligence officers, with him to a command post 50 miles away, leaving the bulk of his intelligence staff at Arras. When the Germans broke through he sent the DMI, accompanied by one of these officers, to command an *ad hoc* force, leaving only one intelligence officer at the command post. As a result of these unrehearsed measures, and of poor communications between GHQ and the command post, information collated at GHQ often failed to pass from the command post to the lower formations in time to be of use to them, while much of the information which divisions at the front sent into the command post was never passed back to the GHQ.[55] The only part of GHQ intelligence that was able to function as planned was the sub-section which had been set up to collect and assess all types of intelligence bearing on possible bombing targets before passing it by direct line to the Allied Central Air Bureau; even so the Bureau itself was unable to make much operational use of the information that was sent in to it about the movements of the German columns. Furthermore, of the Sigint obtained locally, much of which was at least valuable in revealing the extent and seriousness of the German threat on the whole front, by no means all got through from GHQ to the command post. At the command post it was thought at the beginning of the offensive that an alarmist GHQ was greatly exaggerating the scale of the German attack[56] and the C-in-C's knowledge of what was happening outside his own sector remained 'scanty, vague and often inaccurate'.[57]

As early as 18 May, on account of the advance of the German forces south of the BEF, GHQ's intelligence organisation was ordered back to Hazebrouck, and 'all effective work' on its own account came to an end.[58] With the BEF in full retreat, the intelligence staffs attached to

55. Ellis, op cit, pp 64–65; Mockler-Ferryman, op cit, p 118.
56. Ellis, op cit, p 63.   57. Mockler-Ferryman, op cit, p 119.
58. ibid, p 118.

the British formations were also unable to function. Thus the task of providing even tactical intelligence to the BEF was, like the control of operations, already moving from France to London by the time the Enigma began to reach GHQ from 24 May. It was the Y organisation in the United Kingdom which, during the withdrawal of the British forces and their evacuation from Dunkirk, jammed the communications of the German dive-bombers with decisive effect and supplied from GAF intercepts the intelligence which helped the naval authorities at Dover to control the shipping off the beaches.

Y also provided a solitary reference to Hitler's decision to halt Kleist's Panzer forces on the canal line outside Dunkirk on 24 May – the decision which gave respite to the British forces and made the evacuation possible. At 1142 on that day a plain language message announced that the attack on the line Dunkirk–Hazebrouck–Merville was to be 'discontinued for the present'.[59] From the surviving records it is impossible to say whether this message was intercepted in the United Kingdom, or only in France, or even whether its operational significance was recognised at the time. But the records contain no evidence that other intelligence was received about the German decision, and they establish that the Enigma made no reference to it. The first Enigma decrypts containing intelligence of operational value were obtained on 26 May when they gave eight hours' notice of the time and place of a meeting between the Chiefs of Staff of four GAF Fliegerkorps – and there was much disappointment at GC and CS that the meeting was not attacked.

Photographic reconnaissance, the only important source of intelligence for the BEF apart from field Sigint and the Enigma, continued to function from French bases after the BEF's field Sigint had closed down. During the BEF's withdrawal it had, like the other sources, produced little intelligence that could be put to operational use. An Anglo-French plan for reconnaissance, drawn up prior to the battle, proved to be inadequate when the Germans attacked. Much of the reconnaissance was visual, although photographic sorties were flown to obtain strategic intelligence. Severe losses were incurred from the outset, and by 19 May 'the difficulties of organised reconnaissance were now very great, as many units were on the move and communications were failing'.[60] By 20 May the Air Component's Blenheims had left for England, and reconnaissance was attempted by a new organisation, 'the Back Component', in England. The Lysanders remained in France for visual reconnaissance, but by 22 May it was virtually impossible for them to continue tactical and artillery reconnaissance. Thereafter, with the exception of 212 Squadron, the detachment of the PDU equipped with Spitfires, reconnaissance was carried out only

59. Churchill, op cit, Vol II, p 68.
60. AIR 41/21, p 273.

by the Back Component, and only up to 4 June. But 212 Squadron now concerned itself more than ever before with tactical reconnaissance.

The squadron carried out close support sorties entirely with its own resources until 18 May. Thereafter it was reinforced by the rest of the PDU. Although the PDU as a whole had only 8 Spitfires at this stage, it not only assisted the AOC-in-C in obtaining information of tactical value, but also undertook tasks for Bomber Command* and made a preliminary reconnaissance of north Italy before being withdrawn to the United Kingdom in the middle of June. In the 36 days from the invasion of the Low Countries to the end, sorties were flown on all but seven days by 212 Squadron. Forty-two were more or less successful out of a total of 52. The squadron lost no aircraft on these operations.

□

Two British operations against French forces followed the campaign in France† and completed the tragedy of France's collapse – the bombardment of the French Fleet in the harbour of Mers-el-Kebir near Oran on 3 July, and the ill-fated attempt to make an opposed landing at Dakar in the last week of September.

To the decisions which led to the first of these operations, decisions which were prompted by the government's anxiety lest the enemy would otherwise get his hands on the French Fleet, the intelligence organisations made no contribution. Indeed, as was perhaps fitting when the objective could be secured only with co-operation from the forces of a recent ally or, failing that, only by subjecting them to duress, intelligence in the strict sense of the word did not exist when the decisions were reached. The British authorities depended for information on their contacts with the French naval authorities and, in particular, on reports sent in by British liaison officers with the French Fleet at various Mediterranean bases who were being shown French naval orders, or were otherwise getting access to them.

The information so received was all to the effect that the Cabinet's anxiety was misplaced. On 22 June the British Naval Liaison Officer at Toulon sent the Admiralty the gist of a signal in which Admiral Darlan had instructed the fleet to fight to the last, surrendering no ship and obeying no order other than from himself, and had nominated certain admirals to succeed him in the event of his

---

* As a result of offensive operations by Bomber Command, demands arose for damage assessments. Firstly to check the effect of buoyancy mines dropped in the Rhine, and secondly to assess the results of bombing of communication centres and industrial objectives in the Ruhr.[61] The first Bomber Command attack on an industrial target took place on the night of 15/16 May.

† See below, p 161 et seq for intelligence during the final stage of the campaign in France.

61. AIR 41/6, p 158.

'becoming unable to function satisfactorily'.[62] On 23 June No 8 Military Mission (the Army liaison body in Syria) reported that some ships in the area had been ordered to French ports, but that the local admiral had no intention of carrying out the order.[63] On the same day C-in-C Mediterranean reported that Darlan had urged the commander of the French Alexandria squadron to fight on.[64] On 26 June Vice-Admiral Malta reported that he had seen an order from Darlan dated 20 June; it had ended by saying: 'Whatever orders be received, never abandon to the enemy a ship of war intact'.[65] In the papers of the CNS there is a report from the Naval Liaison Officer at Mers-el-Kebir to the effect that Darlan had ordered the fleet to destroy any instruction to surrender ships intact that it might receive from the French government.[66] On 28 June all British Naval Liaison Officers in the Mediterranean, meeting at Casablanca, informed the Admiralty of their joint opinion: the officers of the French Fleet were unanimous in wishing to continue the war; the ships' companies would follow them if given an immediate lead; this lead would best take the form of the appearance of a British squadron outside territorial waters off Oran; its arrival would probably induce the French battleships to put to sea and all other forces would probably follow them.[67]

By that date none of the liaison officers had learned – or none, at least, had reported – that on 24 June Admiral Darlan had sent a signal ordering that all French ships were to be sailed to the United States or to be scuttled if there was any danger of their falling into enemy hands. The Admiralty had received the gist of this signal from the head of the French Naval Mission in London – its only direct link with the French authorities since the departure of the British Ambassador with the Naval Mission to the French government from Bordeaux on 22 June – but had not been reassured by it.[68] In the same way, it was not disposed to put its trust in the reports it was receiving from the Mediterranean.[69] It gave its assessment of the situation to the commands in two signals on 26 June. The first accepted that Darlan was genuinely determined to let no ship fall into enemy hands, but doubted whether he would be able to prevent this. In the second it reported that it had received 'evidence to show that the Germans have obtained French naval codes and are issuing instructions to the French Navy purporting to come from Admiral Darlan. It can be assumed that this procedure has been used since 20 June'.[70]

---

62. ADM 186/800, BR 1736 (49) (1), *Operations against the French Fleet at Mers-el-Kebir*, Appendix E 21.

63. ibid, Appendix 33 (c).   64. ibid, Appendices 33 and 39.

65. ibid, Appendix 39. See also A J Marder, *From the Dardanelles to Oran* (1974), p 199 note 35, quoting the text of Darlan's message.

66. ADM 205/4.   67. ADM 186/800, Appendix 41 (b).

68. Butler, op cit, Vol II, p 220. See also Marder, op cit, p 211, note 48.

69. Marder, op cit, p 205 et seq.

70. ADM 186/800, Appendix 40 (b).

The second signal was based on Vice-Admiral Malta's report of 26 June; this had said that Darlan's message of 20 June was his 'last genuine order' because 'Germany has got French codes and is passing out messages purporting to come from Admiral Darlan'. Except that No 8 Military Mission had in its signal of 23 June voiced the suspicion that Germany was issuing orders in the French cyphers, there was no other evidence. Vice-Admiral Malta had reported the development as being a matter of fact; the source of his information was presumably the French submarine *Narval*, which arrived at Malta on 26 June and put herself at the disposal of de Gaulle. It seems reasonable to suppose that she based what can have been no more than a suspicion on the text of Darlan's message of 24 June, which stated that he was using the cypher for the last time, and on the fact that, as well as nominating successors in case he ceased to be able to act, he had issued a code-word to enable the fleet to distinguish genuine signals from false ones.[71] Against this suspicion, justifiable as it may have been, the Admiralty might have set the fact that, unless the British liaison officers were being deceived, the contents of the signals reaching the French Fleet after 20 June were clearly not German-inspired. If it stopped to have this thought, however, it remained unimpressed. In a report drawn up for the CNS towards the end of June Captain C S Holland, an officer renowned for his knowledge of and admiration for the French who had till recently been Naval Attaché in Paris, argued that if Admiral Darlan had designated successors and issued a code-word, it was because he had expected his hands to be tied; and it concluded that it would be unsafe to rely on assurances from the French admirals that they would scuttle their ships if need be.[72]

The Admiralty had not seen the text of Darlan's signal of 24 June.[73] It did obtain, however, the text of a further signal from him on 26 June which among other things enjoined the fleet not to listen to the British.[74] Nor was its anxiety allayed when it learned on 1 July, after a period of uncertainty, the final terms of the French armistice. By 27 June the British government had heard that one of the stipulations of the armistice was that, with certain exceptions, the ships of the French Fleet were to be recalled to their home ports, there to be demobilised and disarmed under German or Italian supervision. The home ports of many of the ships were in occupied France; the Admiralty feared that they, at least, would be virtually handed over to the enemy intact if the French government accepted the stipulation.[75] On 30 June Admiral Darlan, who had been pressing for

---

71. Playfair, op cit, Vol 1, p 462; W Tute, *The Deadly Stroke* (1973), p 97.
72. ADM 205/4.   73. Marder, op cit, p 211, note 48.
74. ibid, pp 215, note 57 and 241, note 155.
75. Playfair, op cit, Vol 1, p 125; ADM 205/4, CNS interview with Admiral Oden'hal on 27 June 1940, CNS meeting of 29 June.

modification of the terms, reported the results of his efforts to the head of the French Naval Mission in London. As received by the French Naval Mission, the message was imperfect; on 1 July the head of the Mission could assure the Admiralty only that his government had 'firm hopes of obtaining permission to station the Fleet at Toulon or in north Africa'.[76] But an uncorrupt version of the signal was intercepted by the British authorities and decrypted at GC and CS. Its text, sent from GC and CS to the DNI on 1 July, made it clear that the Italian government had authorised the stationing of the fleet 'à demi effectif' at Toulon and in north Africa, and stated that the French Admiralty firmly expected the agreement of the German government to this arrangement.

It is not known whether the Cabinet was aware of this text when, on the evening of 1 July, it decided to despatch Force H from Gibraltar to Mers-el-Kebir and drew up the options it would offer to the French naval commander there. Nor is the point of any importance. As the offical history has said, 'in the view of the Cabinet not even North African ports, and still less Toulon, could be regarded as outside the German reach'.[77] It is clear, indeed, that at a time when the Italian Fleet had just entered the war, when the *Bismarck* was expected to commission in August and when it was widely feared that all the resources of the Royal Navy might soon be needed to repel an invasion of England, the Cabinet's decision to attack the French ships if they rejected the British conditions was taken in the conviction that the acquisition of them by Germany or Italy would determine the whole course of the war. Nor was it disposed to accept that this outcome would be avoided if it put its trust in orders from, or reassurances by, French admirals. On the contrary, it was convulsed by the shock of the French defeat, embittered because the French government had broken faith by concluding a separate armistice, and driven on by the wish to prove to the neutral world, and especially to the United States, that 'Britain at bay...could be tough to the point of ruthlessness'.[78]

Darlan's message of 30 June was the first Vichy signal to be decrypted at GC and CS. There is no truth in the suggestion that the British authorities had been obtaining from Sigint a considerable amount of advance information about the armistice terms and the contents of Admiral Darlan's signals to his fleet, and that this information had confirmed them in the view that, contrary to the advice of the liaison officers with the French Navy, ruthless action was inescapable.[79] Copies of the French cyphers had been provided

---

76. Playfair, op cit, Vol 1, p 137; Butler, op cit, Vol II, p 220.
77. Butler, op cit, Vol II, p 220.
78. ibid, p 227. See also Playfair, op cit, Vol I; Sir Llewellyn Woodward, *British Foreign Policy in the Second World War*, Vol I (1970); Churchill, op cit, Vol II.
79. Tute, op cit, p 105.

voluntarily by the commander of the submarine *Narval* after her arrival at Malta and flown to the United Kingdom. But it was not until 1 July that GC and CS, having arranged the necessary interception, completed the complicated task of sorting out the intercepts and began decrypting them. No Sigint about the French Fleet was obtained from other cyphers; neither the German Enigma nor the Italian Service cyphers mentioned the subject, and the traffic of the Italo-French Armistice Commission was as yet unreadable.*

GC and CS decrypted the next French signal of any importance on 3 July. The signal, timed 1250 and sent out from the French Admiralty, recapitulated the British conditions, as these had been reported to Paris by Admiral Gensoul from Mers-el-Kebir after his negotiations with Force H earlier in the day, announced their rejection and ordered all French naval forces in the Mediterranean to proceed to Oran and place themselves at Gensoul's disposal. The decrypt showed that Gensoul had represented the conditions as an ultimatum to join the British Fleet or scuttle by omitting the other alternatives offered to him – notably the option of sailing to the United States. GC and CS teleprinted it to the Admiralty at 1809, 15 minutes after Force H had begun its bombardment of the French ships.

Had this decrypt reached the Admiralty sooner or had Gensoul's earlier signals to Paris been intercepted in the United Kingdom – they were not – it is remotely possible that the London authorities would have delayed the bombardment while Force H tried to clarify the British terms. But it is most unlikely. For one thing, the French Admiralty had told Gensoul in a plain-language signal at 1300 to inform the British force that French naval forces had been ordered to Oran; and, in the hope that the French would make last-minute concessions, Force H had already delayed opening fire until the Admiralty had repeated this intelligence to it at 1613.[80] Furthermore, the parleying on board the *Dunkerque* at Mers-el-Kebir can have left the British negotiators in little doubt about the French attitude to their conditions. In the course of the discussions the British had been shown the full text of Darlan's message instructing the fleet to sail to the United States or to scuttle if it were in danger of falling into enemy hands; and on account of the rumours about the German use of the French cyphers they had questioned its authenticity.[81] And they can scarcely have remained unaware that the French negotiators drew a sharp distinction between sailing to the United States to avoid falling into enemy hands and sailing to the United States under duress applied by the British government.

After Force H's bombardment GC and CS's French decrypts were briefly of some importance. They included on 3 July the text of the

---

* See Volume Two.

80. ADM 186/800, p 144.   81. ibid, p 43.

order – already received in plain language – that the French naval forces were to make for Oran; of the order, made at 1953, that all submarines and aircraft in the vicinity were to attack Force H; and of the order to all French naval forces, made at 2045, to attack all British warships they encountered and to seize merchant ships. By 5 July, however, further decrypts showed that the danger had passed: the orders of 3 July had been replaced by instructions that French ships were to adopt a defensive attitude. Another decrypt of 3 July ordered ships in British ports to sail at once for France, using force if necessary; but during 4 and 5 July the decrypts included signals from the Alexandria squadron announcing that it was unable to comply, but would scuttle if need be, and on 6 July the squadron reported that it had reached an understanding with the C-in-C Mediterranean which avoided the use of force. But no messages from the ships at Mers-el-Kebir were decrypted, presumably because they were not intercepted in the United Kingdom. Sigint thus played no part in the decision of Force H's commander to carry out on 6 July a second and more successful attack on the *Dunkerque*, which had received only slight damage on 3 July, and gave no warning of the departure of the *Strasbourg*, the one ship that escaped.

Although GC and CS continued to decypher French naval signals down to the Allied landings in north-west Africa in November 1942, its files show that the decrypts threw no light on the purpose of the French naval authorities in sending cruisers from Toulon through the Straits of Gibraltar on 11 September 1940, a movement which gravely complicated the attempt to land a Free French expedition at Dakar, and they contributed nothing of value to the planning and execution of that ill-fated undertaking.

The suggestion that the vacillating French forces in Africa could be rallied to de Gaulle by an occupation of Dakar, or at least a show of force, was first mooted by British governors and consular officials. The idea was initially resisted by the Chiefs of Staff. After the bombardment at Mers-el-Kebir and attacks on the battleships *Richelieu* at Dakar and *Jean Bart* at Casablanca, which also took place early in July, the Chiefs of Staff wished to take no further action against the French unless hostilities broke out with France.[82] But de Gaulle won over the Prime Minister and he, with greater difficulty, won over the Cabinet to the idea that an unopposed landing would be feasible at Dakar;[83] and this modest project then evolved into operation *Menace*, the plan for an opposed landing to which the Cabinet gave its final approval on 27 August.[84]

---

82. CAB 80/13, COS (40) 459 of 13 June, 465 of 15 June: CAB 80/14, 536 of 7 July, 543 of 16 July; CAB 79/5, COS (40) 212th Meeting, 8 July, 233rd Meeting, 25 July, 237th Meeting, 29 July; CAB 80/15, COS (40) 577 (JP) of 27 July. See also Marder, *Operation Menace* (1976), p 10 et seq.

83. CAB 65/14, WM (40) 219 CA of 5 August; Marder, op cit, p 24, note 36.

84. CAB 44/150, Hist (A) 2, May 1942; Marder, op cit, passim.

That the project did so evolve is in itself evidence that uncertainty prevailed about the probable reactions by the garrison, the naval force and the local population to an attempt to land at Dakar. From first to last, moreover, the authorities in Whitehall recognised that this was a matter on which they did not have reliable information. Nor is this surprising: the results of what the army commander of the operation subsequently called attempts to assess the inassessable[85] varied from the highly optimistic view of de Gaulle's emissaries[86] to the conviction that a landing would be resolutely resisted, a conviction which was expressed by two British Service liaison officers* who were brought back to London from west Africa to make a special report.[87] But despite the contradictions between the political reports, the more optimistic ones were given the greater weight as the planning proceeded; and this was particularly the case when, even after the expedition had sailed, it had still to be decided whether it should continue or be called off as a result of unforeseen complications.[88]

More serious, perhaps, and certainly less excusable, was the fact that as the success of the undertaking, whatever the truth about the political situation in Dakar, would very largely depend on effectiveness and surprise in carrying it out, the plans were based on inaccurate operational and topographical intelligence. Not until the expedition was at sea did the commanders discover that the army liaison officer who had been brought back to London had sent a copy of the complete French West Africa Defence Scheme to the War Office in June, and that they had neither seen it nor heard the gist of it in their discussions with him.[89] Having done their planning on out-of-date information – some of it dating back to the First World War – they had gravely under-estimated the defences: the troops available in the area were about three times what they had assumed, the coast defence artillery twice as strong. Intelligence about the state of the *Richelieu* was no less defective. As was only to be expected, it proved impossible to find out what damage she had sustained during the attack that was made on her on 7 July; but this mattered little compared with the fact that on 23 June SNO Dakar had reported that her main armament

---

* The naval liaison officer was to become the second war-time DNI.

85. CAB 106/771, covering note to General Irwin's report, 7 October 1940, paragraph 3 (c).
86. CAB 85/23, CFR (40) 16 of 22 August, summarised in CAB 44/150, Hist (A) 2, p 6; Marder, op cit, pp 39–40; P M H Bell, *A Certain Eventuality* (1974), p 107, quoting FO 371/24329, C8342/7372/17.
87. CAB 44/150, Hist (A) 2, pp 9–10 and fn; CAB 106/772, Folder 2 of historian's meeting 13 November 1940 with Major Poulter and Poulter letter 30 January 1941, Folder 5, commanders' comments on draft history and historian's note on Irwin's comment, 26 November 1940, Folder 4, 'Devant Dakar' (the account of the GSOI), p 5.
88. CAB 106/771, Irwin report, pp 15 para 7, and 25 paras 5 and 6; CAB 44/150, Hist (A) 2, p 14 and Annexes 12 and 13; Marder, op cit, pp 64, 88–89, 91–92.
89. CAB 44/150, Hist (A) 2, pp 5, 11 fn; CAB 21/1465, historian's note 3 February 1941; CAB 106/772, Irwin lecture, p 8.

was incomplete.[90] In the event the effectiveness of her main armament contributed decisively to the failure of the operation. On other difficulties to be overcome – searchlights, booms, the state of the beaches – the commanders knew that they were working with obsolete and woefully inadequate information.[91] For this reason, on the other hand, the departure of the expedition had to be postponed, and the operation recast, as new evidence about topography and installations reached Whitehall. Thus on 19 August a postponement was necessitated by additional information about surf conditions which ruled out four of the six beaches hitherto chosen for landings, and in the light of a report that hydrophones were installed to the seaward of the net defences it was decided that the landing craft carrying the landing parties would have to journey eleven instead of eight miles to the beaches if they were to escape detection and achieve surprise.[92] This report proved to be wrong during the fighting.[93]

All hope of achieving surprise was destroyed during the second week of the expedition's voyage to west Africa. As a result, it appears, of leakages by the Free French and the Poles in London during the planning stage, Vichy had learned by 8 September that a Free French force was at sea en route for Africa.[94] It remained uncertain of the expedition's dates and destination, however, when on 9 September it despatched a squadron of 3 cruisers and 3 destroyers from Toulon to west Africa. The squadron was in fact under orders to make for Libreville in Gabon, from which base it might help to deter other French territories from following the lead of Chad and transferring their allegiance to the Free French.[95] Nor did Vichy make any secret of the squadron's departure; it officially informed the British embassy in Madrid on 10 September that the ships had left Toulon and would be passing through the Straits of Gibraltar. But from no source, including the French naval cyphers that were being read at GC and CS, was any intelligence received about their destination or the purpose of their move. In these circumstances the authorities in Whitehall jumped to the conclusion that they were making for Dakar and decided that they must be intercepted. But they reached the decision tardily. For one thing, a movement by French ships had not been foreseen and this led to delay in passing the information within Whitehall. For another, the COS hesitated at the thought that war with Vichy might result if force was used to deflect the squadron. Partly

90. ADM 186/800, p 140.
91. CAB 44/150, Hist (A) 2, Annex 3; ADM 186/800, p 62 n; ADM 186/799, p 169 n; Marder, op cit, pp 42–44.
92. CAB 80/16, COS (40) 643 of 19 August; Marder, op cit, p 34.
93. Marder, op cit, p 146, note 4.
94. Butler, op cit, Vol II, p 318; CAB 44/150, Hist (A) 2, p 8 and Annex 4 (ISSB report); PREM 3/276, FRACO telegram No 177, 14 September 1940; Marder, op cit, p 49, note 18.
95. Roskill, op cit, Vol I, pp 311, 315.

on this account they had made no prior arrangements for the eventuality with the authorities at Gibraltar – where confusion was confounded by an ill-defined chain of command, by an incomplete knowledge of the plans for operation *Menace* and by the feeling that the French purpose in moving the ships was to get them away from the reach of the enemy, not to speak of the fact that the senior naval officers were among those who thought that the attack at Mers-el-Kebir had been 'a deplorable blunder' – and attempts at interception came to nought before the three cruisers reached Dakar. Together with a fourth cruiser, which was already at Dakar, they tried to leave on 19 September – no doubt because the chase for them had alerted the French authorities to the probability that Dakar was the objective of the expedition[96] – and the Cabinet decided that they must be prevented from returning there at all costs. After a further chase two of the four were intercepted and escorted to Casablanca; the other two got back to Dakar.[97]

Notwithstanding Whitehall's assumption that the cruisers had taken Vichy reinforcements to Dakar, operation *Menace* went into effect on 23 September. And notwithstanding that the assumption was unfounded,[98] the operation was called off, a total failure, on 25 September. Intelligence obtained during the fighting made no difference to the outcome. Locally, the intelligence arrangements were inadequate: the Free French delegation to the garrison had no means of reporting back the vital news that the garrison was determined to resist, and intelligence from the Free French ships to the command ships was so delayed in transmission as to be useless.[99] From Whitehall the commanders received no intelligence of any value during the operation. On the afternoon of 23 September they were informed that naval forces in Dakar had been ordered to resist;*[100] and on 24 September they learned from the Admiralty that the *Strasbourg* had sailed from Toulon.[102] The second report was inaccurate; on 23 September the German authorities had refused a French request for permission to send the *Strasbourg* to west Africa.[103]

Much later, in December 1941, Whitehall was told by a member of the US mission in north Africa that when operation *Menace* was called

---

* It has also been claimed by French sources that the British intercepted an encouraging message from Pétain to the Governor in Dakar.[101] It has not been possible to confirm this from GC and CS records.

96. Marder, op cit, pp 96–97.
97. ibid, pp 68–76, 198–201; Roskill, op cit, Vol I, pp 309–315.
98. ADM 186/800, p 79; Marder, op cit, pp 85, 160.
99. Marder, op cit, pp 109, 165.
100. CAB 21/1463; summary of events.
101. Marder, op cit, p 135, note 4.
102. Marder, op cit, p 138.
103. CAB 65/9, WM (40) 260 of 27 September; Marder, op cit, p 96, note 17, pp 172–173.

off on 25 September 1940 the French garrison and ships were down to their last few rounds of ammunition and the Governor of Dakar was writing out his surrender. If this claim were correct it would be difficult to know whether it would complete a tale of avoidable errors or close a list of unavoidable misfortunes. But the JIC was not inclined to accept the story[104] and the best comment on it is probably that given by Professor Marder:

'I find the story highly improbable. French writers do not even mention it, and there is no reference to it anywhere in the British records'.[105]

---

104. JIC (41) 456 of 2 December; JIC (41) 458 of 6 December; ADM 186/799, pp 179, 182.
105. Marder, op cit, p 149, note 9.

CHAPTER 5

The Threat of Invasion and the Battle of Britain

FOR THE operational and the intelligence authorities in Whitehall the Dakar débâcle completed a succession of failures which had begun in the spring. From the invasion of Norway to the following autumn there had, indeed, been little outward sign that the intelligence system was becoming more efficient or that the operational authorities were ready to place greater confidence in its findings or its judgments. Over this same period of time, however, the intelligence bodies had been taking decisive steps along the path that would one day bring them to mastery in the work of acquiring and assessing intelligence and the operational authorities, renewing their efforts to improve the arrangements for making use of intelligence, had made some progress in creating what would subsequently become a correspondingly effective structure.

In the second of these directions the Military Co-ordination Committee of the Cabinet (MCC)* on 12 April, among the first responses to the invasion of Norway, hastily took what would have been a retrograde decision if it had been allowed to stand. It made the War Office's intelligence branch, not the JIC, responsible not only for meeting the urgent need for co-ordinated intelligence about the German forces in Norway by issuing a daily Scandinavian intelligence summary, but also for reviewing and revising the whole system by which intelligence would be brought to the attention of the government during the campaign.[1] In fact the JIC at once took over this responsibility from the War Office, and for the preparation of these intelligence summaries arranged special meetings of the Service intelligence departments, the SIS and, when appropriate, the Foreign Office.[2] On 11 April, moreover, the Joint Planners, themselves galvanised into action, had already asked the JIC to hold an emergency meeting to consider the possibility that a German attack on the Low Countries would follow that on Norway;†[3] and a week later, again at the suggestion of the Joint Planners, the Chiefs of Staff

---

* See above, Chapter 3, p 97.
† See Chapter 4, p 129.

1. CAB 63/3, MC (40) 20th Meeting, 12 April.
2. JIC (40) 21st Meeting, 13 April.
3. CAB 84/12, JP (40) 100 (S) of 11 April; JIC (40) 18 (S) of 11 April.

authorised the JIC to include in its daily intelligence summaries brief regular appreciations of Germany's probable intentions.[4]

These provisional changes were reconsidered when Mr Churchill, the new Prime Minister, ordered the Chiefs of Staff to review the system by which intelligence was related to the government's procedure for taking operational decisions. The outcome of this enquiry was to confirm the JIC as the central body responsible for producing operational intelligence appreciations and for bringing them to the attention of the operational authorities. The Chiefs of Staff strengthened the JIC's secretariat. They directed the JIC to take the initiative in issuing, at any time of day or night, and only to the Prime Minister, the War Cabinet and the Chiefs of Staff, urgent papers on any strategic development on which any of its members wanted to report in the light of any information received from the Foreign Office or the Service departments. The Chiefs of Staff emphasised the need to prepare the papers rapidly, so as to prevent action from being taken on information not properly assessed by the intelligence authorities, and wished them to contain assessments by those authorities of the value of the information they contained.

These arrangements were adopted in response to GC and CS's success in breaking the Enigma used in Norway no less than to failures of the operational authorities in Norway. They were not implemented, however, until after the invasion of France. The Chiefs of Staff directive was dated 17 May.* Even then, they could not be effective without further delay. In the first place their proper functioning entailed a fundamental revision of the relations between the JIC and the other intelligence bodies. The insistence that the JIC should make urgent strategic reports only to the Prime Minister, the War Cabinet and the Chiefs of Staff carried with it the implication that the other intelligence bodies, including the Foreign Office, should no longer report separately to those authorities on these matters. For this reason the JIC arranged on 24 May that the MEW, the SIS and MI5 should have full membership.†[5] But, as we shall see, some time was to pass before the other bodies became fully reconciled to the strengthening of the JIC and to the principle of the single central assessment of strategic intelligence. In the second place, even a strengthened JIC still depended for its supply of intelligence upon the

---

* See Appendix 6.

† Continuing the pre-war practice by which the IIC had attended JIC meetings, the MEW had hitherto normally been represented at the meetings on an informal basis. Since 8 December 1939 the SIS had received JIC papers dealing with current and future developments overseas but had succeeded in keeping aloof from JIC meetings (see Chapter 3, p 92).[6]

4. CAB 79/3, COS (40) 86th Meeting, 19 April.
5. JIC (40) 34th Meeting, 24 May.
6. JIC (39) 15th Meeting, 8 December.

separate government departments, as these in their turn still depended on what they received from the inter-departmental bodies responsible for procuring intelligence. It was one thing to strengthen the JIC machinery, but quite another to secure a substantial improvement in the procurement of intelligence, in the standards which the departments brought to its evaluation and in the promptness with which they brought their evaluations together for central assessment at the JIC.

The difficulties which existed in these other directions may be illustrated by the attempt to improve the supply of topographical intelligence. In the second half of May, appalled by the paucity of topographical information which had been brought to light in Norway, the Chiefs of Staff instructed the JIC to consider what measures could be taken to improve it in relation to possible future theatres of war. The outcome of the JIC's enquiry was not the establishment of a new body but the introduction of better arrangements for the inter-departmental collection, analysis and distribution of topographical intelligence. The NID's topographical section was enlarged and began to supply information to the other Services. Increased staff was also sanctioned for the other Service departments, the attachés, and, if necessary, the Foreign Office. The JIC assumed responsibility for indicating the areas where British operations were being planned and for eliminating duplication between the different departments.[7] Under these arrangements the NID section, which moved to Oxford in October 1940, gradually developed into the Inter-Service Topographical Department (ISTD).*[8] But there was no guarantee against further unpreparedness so long as Germany retained the strategic initiative. It was not until 1942 that the ISTD came into its own in circumstances in which the initiative had passed to Great Britain and her allies and it was Germany's turn to be unable to be ready for every contingency.

Thanks largely to GC and CS's success in breaking the Enigma regularly and currently, first in the key used in the Norwegian campaign and then in the general GAF key during the operations in France, substantial improvement in the supply of operational intelligence was less slow in coming. For reasons which we have already discussed, it did not begin in time to assist British forces in the field during the Norwegian and French campaigns. By the time the French campaign was drawing to a close, however, Whitehall's strategic decisions were at last profiting from the accurate assessment of general developments which the Enigma material made possible.

Helped by the second of the two documents captured on 25 May

---

* See Chapter 9, p 292.

7. CAB 79/4, COS (40) 131st Meeting, 14 May, 161st Meeting, 1 June; CAB 80/10, COS (40) 347 of 12 May; CAB 80/12, COS (40) 412 (JIC) of 30 May.
8. ADM 223/90. Bassett and Wells, *History of ISTD*, paras 1, 17–19, 22, 29, 40.

– a document which gave the War Office 'an authoritative picture of the German Army'*[9] – it ousted rumour and guesswork from Whitehall's strategic appreciations of the development of the campaign and put in their place hard factual knowledge and confident assessments. By 30 May MI† had formed tolerably accurate estimates of the strengths of the German Army Groups A and B, of the transfers which had taken place between them and of the reserve divisions immediately available for further operations, and it recognised that these so outnumbered the remaining French formations that Germany would probably continue the offensive against France, using the threat of an attack through Switzerland to force her to retain large forces on the Upper Rhine while seeking her destruction further west.[10] During the second German offensive, which started on 5 June, the British had no intelligence from field Sigint, the BEF's resources having been evacuated at Dunkirk, there was even less photographic reconnaissance than had been available in the earlier phase, and regular contact with the French intelligence bodies was maintained by a single SIS representative, who even so was able to report on the German advance and on the French plans only up to 10 June.‡ But Whitehall was able to follow the progress of the battle currently and in detail with the aid of the Enigma traffic. Nor need we doubt that the evidence of an irresistible German advance which this provided was one of the factors which determined the British government's refusal of French requests during these last days for the despatch of further RAF contingents.

What was even more important, it was the Enigma decrypts, flowing in in such enormous amounts first from Norway and then from France, that enabled GC and CS and the Service intelligence branches to start accumulating the expertise that would ensure the accurate interpretation and efficient use of the material in the future, and that prompted the operational authorities to prepare more efficient procedures for the future distribution of the results.

The decrypts threw most light on the organisation and the methods

---

* See Chapter 4, p 143. The official historian adds that the document was the basis of the War Office's grasp of the composition of the German Army, a grasp 'which it never subsequently lost'. Much indeed was owed to the document but this comment exaggerates the War Office's later ability to keep its knowledge of the German order of battle up to date and does not allow for the fact that, to the extent it succeeded, it was mainly indebted to the Enigma.
† This paper was prepared by MI 14. On 15 May 1940 MI 3(b), the German sub-section of the European country section, became a separate section as MI 14.
‡ Since the outbreak of war SIS in Paris had had no sources of its own and had been entirely dependent on its excellent liaison with the French Ve Bureau – the new organisation for intelligence-gathering which had been split from IIe Bureau at the beginning of the war.

9. Ellis, op cit, p 148.
10. MI14 Appreciation, 30 May, incorporated in CAB 80/12, COS (40) 417 (JIC) of 1 June.

of the GAF. During the operations in France they also revealed for the first time the scope and importance of the German Flak (anti-aircraft) organisation which, under the GAF's control, furnished anti-aircraft protection for GAF and German Army units and installations. On the German Army's methods and order of battle the Enigma was nevertheless almost as revealing, since the GAF was necessarily kept informed of the Army's operational requirements and movements. It was of far less value to the Admiralty. Against the naval Enigma, moreover, GC and CS remained unable to make progress despite the fact that the first capture of material relating to it had occurred during the Norwegian campaign.

On 26 April the Navy captured the German patrol boat VP2623, while she was on passage from Germany to Narvik, and took from her a few papers which enabled GC and CS, building on its earlier work, to read the naval Enigma retrospectively for six April days during May. More might have been achieved if VP2623 had not been looted by her captors before she could be carefully searched; and the Admiralty at once issued instructions designed to prevent such disastrous carelessness in the future. As it was, except that they provided some information on the extent of the damage sustained by the German main units during the Norwegian campaign, the decrypts were of no operational use. And though they increased GC and CS's knowledge of the naval W/T and cypher organisation, months were still to elapse before the naval Enigma, like the Army Enigma, could be read currently or in large amounts.*

It later became clear that, until the fall of France, Germany enjoyed not only the strategic initiative but also the advantage of good operational intelligence. During the Norwegian campaign the German Navy's Sigint service supplied valuable information about the movements of the Home Fleet and, as was revealed by the Enigma decrypts, advance knowledge of the British landings at Aandalsnes, Namsos and Narvik.† During the planning and the carrying out of the attack on France the work of the enemy intelligence department of the General Staff of the German Army was of crucial importance and its value fully justified the prestige which the department had always enjoyed. The work has been described by General Ulrich Liss, head of the department from 1937 to 1943. He emphasises that partly on the basis of British army documents captured in Norway, which provided all it needed to know about the British order of battle, and partly from the cypher traffic between the French War Ministry and the army groups, armies and home authorities, most of which it read from soon after the outbeak of war until 10 May, the department had a very comprehensive and accurate knowledge of the dispositions and

---

* See Chapter 10, p 336 et seq.
† See Volume Two for further details.

qualities of the Allied forces. This influenced the selection of the precise point of the German break-through on 9 May; established that on the eve of the campaign German forces exceeded the French by two to one; helped the Germans to appreciate that the Allied armies would advance to the Dyle when the attack began; and reduced German anxiety by strengthening the assessment that the French would be unable to launch an effective counter-attack on the flank of the main German thrust. In addition to the successful exploitation of captured documents and Sigint, the department made good use of photographic reconnaissance in determining in advance of the offensive such things as road capacities, defences, physical obstacles and floodable areas. During the campaign its intelligence continued to be good, and Sigint continued to be the best source.[11]

At the time, while the results of British unpreparedness were only too apparent, the authorities in London could only guess at the extent of these German intelligence achievements, and there is no sign that they even did this. Nor could they foresee that, from now on, while the British intelligence system, after its poor start, would slowly succeed in bringing its many parts into closer unity and in obtaining for itself from government and planners an undisputed authority, the much fragmented German intelligence machine would become more divided and less influential as the war expanded. But although the future remained impenetrable, the hope was beginning to form by June 1940 that, before too long, the gap between German success and British failure, in intelligence as in the field of strategy, would be reduced.

□

Little occurred to substantiate this hope between June and the autumn of 1940. The interval, which was brought to a close by the failure at Dakar, was dominated by the threat of invasion and the Battle of Britain. That Germany lost the battle and was forced to abandon the attempt to land in England – this outcome, contrasting with her successes so far, owed much to the difficulty of the German under-taking and perhaps still more to the tenacity of the British resistance. It owed less to the fact that British intelligence was at last beginning to improve.

When the French collapsed, and Germany had seized the French coasts, Hitler was unprepared for the next move. On two occasions, in quick succession, Germany had now struck against the West with ambitious and well-prepared plans, but the extent and the rapidity of her successes had surprised even the High Command. On the other hand, her successes had been so dramatic that the German authorities hoped that Great Britain would decide not to fight on alone. It was

---

11. Liss, op cit, Section B.

not until 2 July that Hitler ordered his three Services to prepare plans for an invasion. Even then he remained unconvinced that the plans would have to be implemented. He also remained uncertain whether an invasion attempt could succeed: in the middle of July further directives from him gave the German Air Force the task of preventing all air attacks on the invading forces, but set early September as the earliest date for the attempt and laid it down that no crossing would be made until the RAF had been robbed of the power to intervene. But the authorities in Great Britain not only had no doubt that Germany's next move would be to invade. Perhaps inevitably, but also ironically at this time when Germany was forced to delay and was reduced to improvising, they also assumed that she was poised to strike again at once.

The War Cabinet had considered the possibility of an invasion of the United Kingdom, for the first time since the outbreak of war, on 30 October 1939, after a spate of diplomatic and SIS reports that Germany intended this.[12] In November 1939, at the request of the Cabinet, the Chiefs of Staff had reconsidered the danger. On both occasions it had been dismissed as unlikely to materialise so long as British naval and air forces remained in being.[13] During April 1940 the old view that the objective of Germany's western offensive would be the occupation of Holland in preparation for an all-out air assault on the United Kingdom, rather than an invasion of France, was reinforced by Germany's successes in Norway.[14] More important, however, these successes shattered previous – and reasonable – assumptions as to what was operationally practicable for her in relation to the United Kingdom. On 10 May, the day on which Germany had moved against France and the Low Countries, the chiefs of Staff had introduced measures against an invasion attempt, rumours of which were again appearing in SIS reports,[15] by setting up the Home Defence Executive to co-ordinate the anti-invasion preparations of all the Service and civilian departments.[16] They were already looking beyond the long-expected bombing offensive against the United Kingdom and fearing something still more drastic. And by the end of May, confronted by the proved strength of the GAF, by the rapid advance of the Germans to the Channel ports and by the depletion of the RAF and the absence in France of the Army's main fighting strength, they had come to the conclusion that, as was being suggested by a flood of diplomatic and SIS reports, an invasion might

---

12. For these see WO 190/879 Appendix A, MI3 Minute, 1 November 1939.
13. CAB 65/1, WM (39) 65 of 30 October; CAB 80/5, COS (39) 125 of 18 November.
14. JIC (40) 18 (S) of 11 April; JIC (40) 23 (S) of 19 April; CAB 66/7, WP (40) 145 of 4 May.
15. WO 190/891, No 74 of 3 May 1940.
16. CAB 80/10, COS (40) 332 of 10 May; CAB 65/7, WM (40) 132 of 21 May.

be attempted at any moment. The diplomatic reports included one containing Prince Bernhard's belief that the Germans could launch an airborne invasion of the United Kingdom even while the land campaign was still in progress, and even though air support for it was limited, and among the reports from the SIS were warnings that barges were being prepared in German ports.[17] For what it was worth, there was also a single diplomatic decrypt on the subject – a message from the Japanese Minister in Budapest to the effect that the Hungarian Prime Minister believed Germany had a plan for invading Britain.

On 10 May the Chiefs of Staff had still assumed that Germany would attempt invasion only after she had succeeded with a major air offensive. Increased GAF activity over the United Kingdom would thus give general warning that an expedition might be expected. But they had already stressed that the Germans had revealed an 'unexpected ability to carry out large-scale overseas operations' and had shown themselves to be 'past masters in the secret preparation and rapid execution of a plan'. In the worsened circumstances at the end of the month they felt that they had to allow for the possibility of a large-scale raid with the object of establishing a foothold, to be followed by full-scale invasion if a foothold was established. By using 'a fleet of 200 fast motor boats, each carrying 100 men', the Germans might even make such a raid without warning, and it could not be excluded that they had developed 'specially buoyant landing craft' for putting AFVs ashore on open beaches. With these arguments, 'as a matter of urgency and as military advisers to the Government', they warned the War Cabinet on 29 May that it was highly probable that a full-scale attack on the United Kingdom was imminent. 'The late C-in-C Home Forces asked us to inform him when the Chiefs of Staff considered an attack imminent. We think that General Ironside should be so informed now'.[18]

Within a few days of giving this advice the Chiefs of Staff were able to countermand it with the assistance of intelligence. By providing evidence that was incontrovertible so far as it went – if also, as was to be the case on many later occasions, fragmentary – Sigint gave notice of a major enemy move for the first time in the war when on 1 June, much influenced by the GAF Enigma material which had been coming in since 22 May, MI concluded that the Germans were likely to complete the overrunning of France before turning against the United Kingdom.[19] On 3 June, the JIC having endorsed this appreciation,[20] the Chiefs of Staff accepted it to the extent of recommending that reinforcements should be sent to France despite the fact that the

17. WO 190/891, No 100 of 25 May; CAB 65/7, WM (40) 133 of 22 May.
18. CAB 80/12, COS (40) 406 of 29 May.
19. WO 190/891, No 98 of 1 June.
20. CAB 80/12, COS (40) 417 (JIC) of 1 June.

United Kingdom was 'dangerously exposed to the risk of decisive air attack and/or invasion'.[21] Their worst fears returned, however, when the French collapse was complete.

Against these fears the intelligence authorities were in no position to provide reassurance. For one thing, they had come to share them. As late as 23 April the JIC had reconsidered the Chiefs of Staff report of November 1939 and agreed with its conclusion: 'An invasion of this country by sea and air will be a most hazardous undertaking so long as our air forces remain comparatively intact and the control of the North Sea, even by light forces, is maintained'.[22] By the beginning of May, however, it was submitting evidence in support of the Chiefs of Staff calculation of 10 May that the provision of adequate shipping and troops for an invasion would present Germany with no problem.[23] At the same time it was assembling evidence on German subversive activities in foreign countries. This supported the stress which, by the time of their meeting on 10 May, the Chiefs of Staff were beginning to lay on the need to take measures against the Fifth Column danger.*[24] On 24 May, asked for its views on the implications of an Allied withdrawal from Norway, which the Chiefs of Staff were now considering, the JIC was inclined to suggest that the move would encourage Germany to think that the conditions were favourable for a descent on Great Britain. It listed, it is true, some of the difficulties which Germany would be faced with. The only small craft at her disposal were tugs, barges, ferries and other slow-moving craft. Possible assembly ports in France and the Low Countries were either destroyed or not yet captured, and it would take a fortnight to prepare airfields for the necessary air support. No more than the Chiefs of Staff, however, did it question that Germany was fully prepared with plans for an invasion: she could invade at any time she considered the conditions to be suitable.[26]

Once they had made this assumption the intelligence authorities had no choice but to take a further step. On 26 May they warned the Chiefs of Staff that it was unlikely that intelligence would provide advance notice of a landing, and did so without distinguishing between strategic warning of the fact that invasion was intended and tactical warning of the extent to which an expedition was prepared, or of the

---

* At this point the JIC was doubtful of the propriety of making recommendations for action against aliens and sabotage. After the invasion of the Low Countries, however, it threw its scruples aside and made detailed recommendations against the Fifth Column menace.[25]

21. CAB 79/4, COS (40) 166th Meeting, 3 June; CAB 80/12, COS (40) 421 of 23 June.
22. JIC (40) 24th Meeting, 23 April; CAB 80/10, COS (40) 314 (JIC) of 3 May.
23. CAB 80/10, COS (40) 332 of 10 May.
24. ibid, Appendix to Annex II.
25. JIC (40) 26th Meeting, 1 May; CAB 80/11, COS (40) 359 (JIC) of 16 May.
26. CAB 80/11, COS (40) 384 (JIC) Revise of 24 May.

fact that it was on its way.[27] Before the attack on France intelligence had provided strategic warning that an offensive was intended, but tactical notice of the date and point of the attack had not been possible, and these things had remained in doubt until the end. It had at least to be assumed that this would be the case again. But in advance of the invasion of Norway intelligence had not even provided strategic warning; and if the operational authorities had under-estimated Germany's capacities, intelligence had failed to correct their misconceptions. Now, the operational authorities might be exaggerating the enemy's capacities, but the mistake of under-estimating them was one that the intelligence authorities dared not risk making again. Until they had firm evidence to the contrary, they would not depart from the assumption that invasion might come at any time and from any direction.

On the other hand, no such evidence was forthcoming until Germany embarked on her preparations, and this she did not do until she launched the preliminary phase of the Battle of Britain in the second week of July. Until then – until somewhat later, indeed – the intelligence authorities remained in a quandary. Working on the assumption that an invasion might be launched at any time, without any general warning from the stepping-up of air attacks on the United Kingdom, they could nevertheless unearth no evidence as to the form it would take or the areas where it might be assembling. And unearthing no evidence – failing to discover the undiscoverable – they suspected their sources rather than questioning their assumption.

□

If, given their previous experience, this unwillingness to trust negative intelligence was only to be expected, so was their other response to the new emergency. Recalling that experience, they now made further organisational improvements.

In advance of the invasion of Norway intelligence had failed because, under-estimating Germany's capacities, it had been too much disposed to discount evidence. It had also failed because it had been too loosely organised to ensure that all the available evidence was properly weighed on an inter-departmental basis. Having guarded against the first of these mistakes on 26 May by confessing that intelligence could not be counted upon, the JIC guarded against the second, after a series of discussions between 26 and 30 May, by setting up in the Admiralty's OIC an inter-Service sub-committee of five (later six) officers to be responsible for co-ordinating all intelligence, including information gained at first hand by British forces, that might

---

27. JIC (40) 35th Meeting, 25 May; JIC (40) 84 of 25 May; CAB 80/12, COS (40) 410 (JIC) of 30 May.

have a bearing on the threat of invasion.[28] This, the Combined Intelligence Committee (CIC), was not a permanent inter-Service intelligence staff of the kind that came into being later in the war. Until the beginning of July its members spent most of their day in their own intelligence departments and only one of them – the War Office member – gave his full time to collecting the information that might possibly bear on the danger of invasion. But from 31 May, until the danger had passed, it met daily as a committee to scrutinise the information and to issue an appreciation. It continued to meet, though less and less frequently, until 1943.

A further organisational improvement followed soon after the establishment of the CIC, and was closely associated with it. On 26 May the JIC had recommended that systematic and continuous air reconnaissance, including photographic reconnaissance, should be organised over all coasts and seas from which an invasion might be launched. When the JIC itself was seriously suggesting that even Vigo was a possible point of departure for an expedition, and when the Chiefs of Staff were agitated by the danger that a raid might be launched from Norway,[29] this was an obvious recommendation; already on 10 May, when setting up the Home Defence Executive, the Chiefs of Staff had particularly charged it with providing special naval and air reconnaissance to ensure the earliest possible warning of the assembly and passage of an expedition. But after the establishment of the CIC important new departures did take place. Hitherto, the Service departments and the home operational commands had failed to lay down any procedure either for notifying and deciding the priorities between their competing demands for air reconnaissance or for co-ordinating the interpretation and use of the information obtained. On 10 June a meeting of Air Ministry and Admiralty representatives agreed that the CIC should be the sole authority for making requests for reconnaissance and for setting the priorities. A little later the Air Staff upheld this decision, and also stipulated that the CIC should alone be responsible for collating invasion intelligence from air reconnaissance with information from other sources. At the same time the Air Staff made Coastal Command, hitherto responsible for reconnaissance flights over the open sea, responsible also for carrying out all reconnaissance over enemy ports and coasts.[30] A further change affected the organisation for photographic reconnaissance. On 18 June the PDU,* hitherto under the control of the Director of Air Intelligence at the Air Ministry, was transferred as an

---

* For the creation of the PDU out of the pre-war SIS Flight see Chapter 3, p 104.

28. JIC (40) 35th Meeting, 25 May; CAB 80/12, COS (40) 410 (JIC) of 30 May.
29. CAB 65/7, WM (40) 144 of 28 May, WM (40) 146 of 29 May, WM (40) 148 of 30 May.
30. AIR 41/6, Part III: 2.

operational unit to C-in-C Coastal Command and re-named the Photographic Reconnaissance Unit (PRU).

Thereafter it was a notable feature of the CIC's activities that, after reviewing the evidence from the latest flights and mating it with other information, it indicated directly to Coastal Command the areas to be reconnoitred in the next flights and the type of cover required. This task it performed well enough. Nor is there any doubt that in the work of collating and appreciating information it became a useful body, whose regular short-term assessments left the JIC free, as it had never previously been free, to concentrate on more considered apprecia-tions – on any significant developments that the CIC might bring to light or on such broader questions as the probable scale of the German attack and the place of the invasion project in Germany's general strategy. But, as we shall see, it cannot be said that the JIC greatly distinguished itself or that intelligence emerged from the crisis with its reputation much improved.

□

If one reason for this was that the intelligence authorities brought to the crisis misleading assumptions about Germany's capacities and state of readiness, another was that beyond establishing the CIC, which was set up to serve limited, tactical purposes, they achieved little or nothing by way of the better co-ordination of the various intelligence bodies. Even when they were faced by the supreme threat of invasion, which threw up many problems obviously calling for inter-departmental treatment, they continued to rely largely on separate departmental contributions to JIC papers, and the JIC still acquired no drafting staff of its own. In the middle of July the machinery for co-ordinating the action to be taken by the individual Services was improved; the Vice Chiefs of Staff were made responsible for agreeing what action was needed and the Directors of Intelligence for bringing to the attention of the Vice Chiefs of Staff any item of intelligence that called for action[31] But it was judged that no change was needed in the system by which the CIC and the JIC pooled, assessed and issued intelligence. Nor is it difficult to see why. The flow of reliable intelligence was painfully slow to improve; and reliable intelligence, the sovereign remedy for false assumption, is also a pre-condition of profitable collaboration.

On 26 May, in the paper in which it announced that intelligence could not be relied on to give advance notice of an invasion, the JIC had pointed to air reconnaissance, especially photographic reconnais-sance, as offering the only immediate hope of guarding against

31. CAB 79/5, COS (40) 232nd Meeting, 24 July; CAB 80/15, COS (40) 564 of 22 July.

surprise and had singled out Sigint as the only other source that might prove valuable. Diplomatic reports from the neutral countries were, as always, conflicting; as well as suffering from the same defect, SIS's operational information had been gravely reduced since Germany had overrun so much of Europe, and its receipt much delayed. From the middle of June aerial reconnaissance was steadily improved and expanded. By the end of June, although its volume had tailed off since the end of the fighting in France, high-grade Sigint began to give some colour to the hope which had earlier been based on it. Until the middle of July, however, these two sources did little to remove the uncertainties which plagued the intelligence authorities, and in some ways they added to their confusion.

Cotton's services were dispensed with when the PDU was reorganised as the PRU. But his departure coincided with the final victory of his methods of photographic reconnaissance. Even before the campaign in France the inexpensive success of a handful of Spitfires, contrasting sharply with the costly failure of the Blenheims, had undermined the pre-war Air Ministry doctrine that air reconnaissance must be undertaken by operational aircraft which were capable of fighting for air-space. During that campaign the superiority of the doctrine of relying on speed and altitude to evade conflict was once more demonstrated. As early as 13 May C-in-C Home Forces had advised the Chiefs of Staff that 'the most effective method of keeping a watch by air on German movements will be a high altitude reconnaissance as often as practicable'.[32] On 10 June the Air Ministry–Admiralty conference which granted control over the direction of reconnaissance to the CIC also decided that high altitude flights by the PDU would be the best means of obtaining results. When the Air Staff transferred the PDU to Coastal Command this view had everywhere won acceptance.

Despite this advance the work of the PRU was still limited, not so much by the number of its Spitfires – though they were few – as by their range. Of the 11 aircraft available up to the end of July, only 3 were long-range Spitfires (type C). From the end of July the introduction of type F increased the range only by 100 miles to 650 miles. During July priority was restored to work on 2 Spitfires of type D, designed for a range of 1,700–1,800 miles, but the first of these did not become available until the worst of the emergency was over, and it was not until 29 October that it secured photographs of the more distant Baltic ports – Stettin, Warnemünde, Swinemünde and a part of Rostock. Before the end of July, by basing one of its flights at Wick and another at St Eval, the PRU could just reach south-west Norway and Kiel (from Wick) and the Gironde estuary (from St Eval). Not until 18 July, however, was its coverage sufficiently regular to enable the

---

32. CAB 80/10, COS (40) 349 of 13 May.

CIC to conclude that there was probably no foundation for the many rumours that Germany was preparing a major expedition from Norwegian ports, and not until 24 July did it succeed in photographing the Bordeaux area for the first time and thus discount the anxiety that shipping might be assembling there for a descent on south-west England or Ireland.

It might be expected that the fear of a surprise attack from these more distant areas would have been scotched at an earlier date by the absence of any sign of abnormal preparations at the ports which lay between. On 26 May the JIC noted that reconnaissance even of the Belgian, Dutch and German North Sea ports was only occasional. From the middle of June the PRU was covering them and the French channel ports sufficiently regularly to establish the absence of any unmistakably warlike concentrations of shipping there. But the CIC and the JIC did not suggest that this negative evidence made it unnecessary to expect what was *prima facie* unlikely: a large-scale invasion carried out by a single fast expedition from the Baltic, Norway or the Gironde. On the contrary, they insisted that negative evidence could not be accepted as proof that invasion was not imminent, and they applied this warning to a descent from the nearest ports no less than to one from those which remained beyond the range of reconnaissance.

The CIC gave the warning in its first assessment on 31 May.[33] Until the middle of July it repeated it without qualification whenever it announced that there were no signs of impending invasion. From the middle of July it began to hazard some slight qualification. On 14 July and again on 19 July it reported that in view of the increased regularity of photographic reconnaissance it should now be able to detect a mass departure of barges from the coasts opposite England; but it continued to emphasise that an expedition might be lying ready and undetected in the Baltic. On 23 July the JIC pronounced in much the same terms. It should now be possible to give some warning of expeditions starting from the Dutch, Belgian or French coasts, since the collection of the necessary shipping could probably not be concealed from air reconnaissance, but 'under modern conditions an expedition could, if the shipping were available, be collected and despatched at very short notice, and we cannot count on being able to give any substantial amount of prior warning'. Nor was that its only hesitation. 'In the case of an expedition from the Baltic it is quite possible that, given thick weather, the first intimation we should receive would be the interception of the enemy ships by our own coastal patrols only a few miles off-shore. It is even possible that under certain weather conditions landings might be effected without previous warning'[34]

---

33. AIR 40/1637; CIC Report No 1 of 31 May. All subsequent references to CIC records in this chapter are similarly filed.   34. JIC (40) 174 of 23 July.

In these circumstances the JIC did not feel able to guarantee the operational authorities the respite they would have liked to have; thus at the end of June the JIC would not guarantee the three days' notice of invasion which the Home Defence Executive wanted while it put its coastal evacuation plans into effect.[35] On the other hand these authorities were kept in suspense by several warnings from the CIC that invasion might be imminent. Reports of shipping concentrations from Norway, where the SIS organisation had now begun to operate, were on several occasions up to the middle of July taken to indicate that a raid or an invasion from there or from the Baltic must be expected. In the middle of July the fact that all U-boats appeared to have been withdrawn from patrol, as they had been in advance of the invasion of Norway, was singled out as a pointer to the imminence of invasion.

These false alarms were contained by the JIC; they reached the Chiefs of Staff and the Cabinet but were withdrawn or watered down before they had caused much disturbance. The JIC realised, as the DMI told the Chiefs of Staff on 3 July, that the CIC, an intelligence watch set up to look for signs of invasion at a time when invasion was expected, would be too prone to find them,[36] and that, as the DNI noted on 23 July, the need to report quickly meant that its reports were 'inevitably sometimes rather undigested and thus occasionally tend to over-stress scare reports'.[37] But the JIC itself was not always able to avoid these dangers. Indeed, the DMI's recognition on 3 July that they existed prefaced his announcement to the Chiefs of Staff that the evidence was nevertheless beginning to suggest that invasion might come at an early date, and on 5 July his verbal report was followed by a JIC appreciation to the effect that, while 'full-scale invasion' was not to be expected before mid-July, large-scale raids must be expected at once.[38]

This alarm, the first to be issued by the JIC, was precipitated – a particularly ironical twist of circumstances – by the fact that indications from low-grade Sigint of the redeployment of GAF bomber units and PR evidence of extensions to airfield runways were at last supplemented by indirect references to the beginnings of German preparations in the GAF Enigma. As German operational activity subsided and as the higher-echelon communications of the GAF went over to land-lines, the volume of Enigma signals intercepted in the United Kingdom had slumped sharply after the fall of France, and though GC and CS had continued to read them, they had in any case been silent on the subject of invasion until German preparations were put in train. From the last week of June, however, items from this source

---

35. CAB 80/13, COS (40) 487 (JIC) of 24 June.
36. CAB 79/5, COS (40) 205th Meeting, 3 July.
37. ADM 233/84, NID 002729/40, DNI Minute of 23 July 1940.
38. CAB 80/14, COS (40) 529 (JIC) of 4 July.

attracted the notice of the CIC. On 23 June the Enigma established that some GAF units were resting and refitting in preparation for operations against the United Kingdom from airfields in the Low Countries and north-west France, where aerial reconnaissance had already revealed runway extensions and other preparations. On 25 June it reported the concentration of dive-bombers in the same area. At the end of June it provided evidence that the Germans were postponing a ceremonial parade in Paris. At the same time, and for the first time, high-grade Sigint information was used to guide the photographic reconnaissance programme, for the Enigma now reported that long-range guns were being set up opposite Dover and thereafter the PRU provided detailed information of progress at the sites. On the basis of further Enigma information the CIC reported on 4 July that the majority of GAF units would have completed refitting by mid-July, the date from which the JIC on 5 July warned that 'full-scale invasion' might be expected.*

Even if the guns were intended to provide covering fire for a Channel crossing, this evidence by no means necessarily pointed to an early invasion attempt, particularly as the PRU had still found no sign that invasion shipping was being assembled in the Channel ports. The JIC allowed that the evidence of GAF preparations was equally consistent, if not more so, with the preparation of a major air attack. This is what materialised, in the shape of the opening of the Battle of Britain, in the second week of July. But the JIC judged it better to assume the worst. It had little doubt, as it had reported on 2 July, that invasion would be Germany's next move.[39] It had received no evidence, from any source, that Germany had on 2 July made air supremacy a precondition of invasion and that she was working to early September as the earliest possible date. Nor was it allowed to forget that Germany had resorted to unorthodox methods in earlier campaigns. On 5 June MI had warned the CIC to avoid thinking of the invasion threat in such conventional terms as 'bases, covering forces, sea power etc' and to allow for an attack on a wide front by tanks carried in motor boats. On 25 June the DMI was still pressing the DNI to consider whether the JIC was giving enough attention to this danger.[40] By then, it is true, the NID was distinctly sceptical: its reply to the DMI emphasised that motor boats, of which none had yet been sighted or reported by a reliable source, were in any case so operationally limited that they would at most be used as a diversion.[41]

---

* It should be noted that while the SIS disguise for the Enigma material was now wearing thin in Whitehall, the security precautions later adopted for protecting the source – special code-words and restricted circulations – were not yet enforced. In the CIC reports it is referred to as information from an 'A1' source. War Office papers containing it were marked 'by hand of officer' at this stage.

39. CAB 80/14, COS (40) 518 (JIC) of 2 July.
40. ADM 233/84, DMI letter to DNI, 25 June 1940.
41. ibid, DNI to DMI, 30 June 1940.

But MI remained unconvinced by these arguments, and for some time after the DMI had led the way in issuing the warning of 5 July it continued to believe that the Germans had intended to invade early in July but had postponed the attempt.

We might wish to attribute MI's views to the fact that, its staff being soldiers, they were ignorant of the difficulties involved in organising a seaborne expedition against powerful naval and air defences. Unfortunately for this argument, MI's views were shared by the Naval Staff.

It had first adopted them on 29 May, in the alarmist atmosphere which had then prevailed.[42] Since then it had used them to justify the retention of large numbers of destroyers and smaller ships, most of which were suitable for escorting convoys, as inshore patrols and striking forces on the south and east coasts. Early in July the Chief of the Naval Staff re-affirmed his acceptance of them in a memorandum to the Prime Minister. This began by saying that 'we cannot therefore assume either that special craft will not have been provided, or that past military rules as to what is practicable and what is impracticable will be allowed to govern the action undertaken'. It went on to allow that the enemy might get as many as 100,000 men ashore with little or no warning by making a number of separate attacks and feints, at widely dispersed points in a carefully chosen combination of calm weather and low visibility, from ports as far apart as Biscay and Norway, hundreds of fast motor boats having assembled undetected by reconnaissance in French and Dutch ports and expeditions using larger vessels and tank-landing craft having assembled beyond the range of reconnaissance in Biscay and the Baltic.

Despite their serious effect in depriving the Atlantic convoys of anti-submarine escorts, the views of the Admiralty did not change before the end of 1940, although it was prevailed upon to change its dispositions from the end of October* in view of the extent to which the U-boats were profiting from the reduction in convoy escorts. Despite the Admiralty's views, on the other hand, the Chiefs of Staff did not order an invasion alert on the strength of the warnings from the DMI and the JIC, one reason being that as a whole, as was clear during their discussion with the DMI on 3 July, they attached great weight to the probability that an invasion attempt would be preceded by a major air battle. On 10 July, moreover, the Prime Minister paid no attention to these warnings when commenting on the CNS's memorandum.[43] He found it 'very difficult to visualise the kind of invasion all along the coast by troops carried in small craft, and even in boats', which the CNS, like MI, was still allowing for, and he seriously doubted whether the enemy could assemble an effective

---

* See Chapter 10, p 335.

42. ibid, M 010329/40 (Appreciation of Invasion) of 29 May 1940.
43. CAB 80/14, COS (40) 550 of 15 July.

invading force without it being detected by photographic reconnaissance. The Prime Minister had already expressed this opinion in the House of Commons on 18 June.[44] On the other hand, he supported the Admiralty in its refusal to change its emergency dispositions, on the ground that one had to allow for the worst. Beyond Whitehall the C-in-C Home Fleet opposed the Admiralty's policy of immobilising so many destroyers and escorts on the ground that warning of invasion would be given by a preliminary battle for air supremacy as well as with the argument that the Germans would be unable to assemble an expedition without detection.* The operational authorities were thus throwing off the worst fears that had assailed them at the end of May, and were doing so with less hesitation than the intelligence authorities.

□

They cannot but have been strengthened in their earlier views – those they had held before the French collapse – by the onset and the outcome of the air battle. By British reckoning, the preliminary phase of the Battle of Britain began on 10 July. It became obvious by that day, after a month of scattered night raids, that the GAF had embarked on a programme of concentrated daylight attacks on ports, coastal convoys and aircraft factories with the object of wearing down the RAF's fighter defences in the south-east. By mid-August it had failed in this object but could no longer defer the decision to increase the scale of its attack and seek the direct destruction of the RAF on and over its airfields. Unless this was achieved without delay, the landings in England could not take place, as planned, early in September. Within a fortnight this larger effort – operation *Adler* – was beginning to fail. On the night of 24–25 August the GAF went over to widespread night bombing; its last big daylight effort for several weeks came between 26 and 31 August. On 1 September the diversion of part of its remaining daylight raids from airfields to the docks at Tilbury heralded the opening of a further phase in which from 7 September, in a final attempt to break British morale, it switched its main attack to London and made it mainly at night.

The Enigma material gave general warning, as we have seen, of the approach of the Battle of Britain. In the Air Ministry, which even in the alarmist atmosphere at the end of May had continued to believe

---

* And in September he was quicker than the intelligence authorities to see that the German failure to win air supremacy meant that Germany must abandon the attempt to invade during 1940. Admiral Cunningham in Alexandria also concluded at an early stage that the practical difficulties of invasion would be too much for Germany.[45]

44. Churchill, op cit, Vol II, p 250.
45. Roskill, op cit, Vol I, pp 258–259; Admiral of the Fleet Viscount Cunningham, *A Sailor's Odyssey*, (1951), p 276.

that Germany would have to establish air superiority before attempting a landing,[46] the warning did not go unheeded. AI summed up in a minute of 28 June the evidence that was coming in: 'Reports indicate that the majority of the long-range bombers will have completed refitting at home bases by 8 July...In view of one report that a Fliegerkorps has been ordered to bring into force new W/T instructions from 2200 on 30 June, the opening of the offensive on this country must be anticipated from 1 July onwards'.[47] From the outset of the battle the fact that the Enigma had now been producing intelligence for some months on the GAF's organisation,* order of battle and equipment was also of great strategic value.

The intelligence consisted of fragmentary and often disconnected items in the signals of the main users of W/T, the lower-level operational units of the GAF. For AI and for GC and CS – which initially undertook the analysis for the help it gave to cryptanalysis and the interception programme, but which soon found that the results were of immense assistance to AI – it was no easy task to piece these clues together, and to collate them with intelligence from other sources that were of varying and often unknown reliability. It was not until 5 August that GC and CS completed its first attempt to compile from the Enigma a detailed GAF order of battle. But by the beginning of July the work of identifying and locating the GAF's operational units, and of understanding the GAF's organisation, methods and equipment, was sufficiently advanced to enable AI to accept a major revision of its estimate of the GAF's first-line bomber strength. In June it had estimated the first-line strength at more than 5,000 (including 2,500 bombers) and the reserves at 7,000, when actual figures were about 2,000 (including 1,500–1,700 bombers) and 1,000.†[48] At the beginning of July, prodded by Professor Lindemann's‡ reluctance to believe that the GAF, as suggested by the JIC, would be able to deliver 4,800 tons of bombs per day,[49] AI scaled down the first-line figures drastically, reducing its estimate of bombers likely to be available in the first week of full-scale operations from 2,500 to 1,250 and its estimate of the possible daily bomb load from 4,800 to 1,800 tons.§ Not least because they were based on the Enigma information, which was

---

* For the operational chain of command of the GAF see Appendix 10.

† See Chapter 3, p 110 for earlier estimates.

‡ Professor Lindemann had in June 1940 been charged by the Prime Minister to look into technical matters, both British and German.

§ These figures were still too high in Professor Lindemann's view. After considering the sortie rate achieved by the GAF in August and September, he returned to the attack on Air Intelligence. The outcome was the Singleton enquiry, see Chapter 9, p 200 et seq.

46. AIR 40/2321, Minutes of 11, 14, 15, 30 May.
47. ibid, 28 June.
48. Collier, op cit, p 112.
49. CAB 80/12, COS (40) 432 (JIC) of 6 June.

described as 'heaven-sent' and 'apparently sure', the new figures enabled the Air Staff to 'view the situation much more confidently than was possible a month ago'.[50]

Valuable as it was, the Enigma's order of battle intelligence was of no assistance to AI in its attempts to answer the supreme question – could the RAF outlast the GAF? – because it threw no light on the losses and effective strengths of the GAF's units or on the size of their reserves. At the beginning of September, asked to predict how long the GAF could keep up its effort, Air Intelligence calculated that if German fighter losses continue at the August rate, 'the German fighter strength will be ineffective in 6 weeks',[51] and that the escorted daylight raids would have to be abandoned by then. In fact the GAF was forced to go over to night bombing within a week of this reply, and to do so because the serviceability of its aircraft had fallen so low.[52] The main reason for AI3's caution lay in its continuing over-estimation of GAF total strength in operational and reserve aircraft. This was too great to be offset by the over-estimation by Fighter and AA Commands of the losses they had inflicted on the GAF. AI was suspicious of these claims, but they were even more exaggerated than AI suspected. The Commands claimed 1,112 GAF aircraft destroyed and 400 probably destroyed between 9 August and 2 October, but the actual losses totalled 635.[53]

For similar reasons the Enigma was of no help in forecasting the shifts that occurred during the battle in the GAF's methods and objectives. Communications between Berlin and the GAF formations in France went by land-lines, so that strategic decisions were rarely spelled out in W/T signals. From time to time it could be deduced from the decrypts that a change in the GAF's intentions was to be expected, but the deductions were of no operational value to the C-in-C Fighter Command. For one thing, there was no knowing how widely they applied – for not all the forward GAF formations used W/T. For another, they were too vague. Thus the decrypts made several references to 'Adlertag' between 9 and 13 August, and it was obvious that some new development must be expected, but neither GC and CS nor AI could unravel what the code word 'Adlertag' stood for. For all his major decisions C-in-C Fighter Command accordingly depended on his own strategic judgment, with no direct assistance from the Enigma. This may be further illustrated by the events of 15 August, the day on which the GAF sustained the defeat which is sometimes taken as marking the turning point in the Battle of Britain. The GAF attempted on that day to throw Fighter Command off balance by

---

50. AIR 40/2321, Minute of 6 July 1940.
51. ibid, 2 September 1940.
52. AIR 41/10, p 91.
53. Collier, op cit, Appendices X, XII, XIV; AIR 41/15, *The Air Defence of Great Britain*, Vol II, pp 225–6; AIR 40/2321, p 60.

combining diversionary attacks north of the Humber with the main attack against southern England. But there is no evidence in the surviving records that Fighter Command got advance warning of the GAF's intention either from Enigma or from the GAF's low-grade transmissions; brief forewarning of the two attacks was received, it seems, only from radar.

In the day-to-day fighting, by giving notice of the time, the targets and the forces committed to individual raids, the Enigma provided an increasing amount of intelligence as the GAF moved into its all-out effort. But this intelligence was sometimes obtained too late to be of operational value. Moreover, the GAF made last-minute alterations of plan which were not disclosed in the decrypts, or were not disclosed in good time. As an example of this difficulty, which sometimes undermined confidence in the source, the Enigma decrypts revealed on 14 September that a big raid on London was to take place that day, and gave an indication of the forces that would take part in it; but they had previously announced that the raid was scheduled for 1800 on 13 September, and in the event the raid was made on the morning of 15 September without any further Enigma warning.[54] Nor were these the only limitations.

For all that it was incomplete, and often gave scant warning, if any at all, the Enigma's tactical intelligence could still have been put to better use if the organisation for handling operational intelligence had not been defective in one important direction. Before the war, the Air Ministry, like the War Office, had built this organisation around the exploitation in the field of low-grade tactical codes. It had thus centred it at Cheadle, where most of the traffic in such codes was intercepted.* But because it had not expected the GAF to use high-grade cyphers, or at least to use them for operational traffic, it had made no arrangements either for AI to participate in operational intelligence, beyond supplying Cheadle with details about the GAF's order of battle, or for GC and CS to pass high-grade intelligence to Cheadle or the operational commands. When the Enigma began to produce tactical intelligence, that intelligence was distributed only to that section of AI which dealt with the long-term problem of the GAF order of battle, but that section, unlike Cheadle, was not organised or staffed for the exploitation of operational intelligence. The result was a separation of the tactical information obtained from the high-grade and the low-grade sources, the former occasionally revealing the GAF's orders and intentions, the latter reporting them as they were carried out, which prevented both sources from being used to the full during 1940, when the GAF effort against the United Kingdom was at its height. Not until considerably later, indeed, and

---

* See Chapter 1, p 14.

54. CX/JQ 214/T1, 220/T1, 8, 306/T4, 5.

then largely by GC and CS and on its initiative, was an adequate system developed for integrating the two.*

Notwithstanding this defect, AI's rapidly growing understanding of the GAF's organisation and order of battle – which it owed largely to Enigma – was of increasing help to Fighter Command as background for its conduct of operations. It also broadened the background against which Cheadle interpreted the low-grade traffic which it intercepted. This was of considerable operational importance during the Battle of Britain. We have already outlined the methods by which Cheadle exploited the GAF's heavy reliance on tactical signalling in low-grade codes during operations.† By the beginning of the Battle of Britain the interception of this traffic on medium and high frequencies was being supplemented by the interception of plain language radio telephony (R/T) on high frequencies at a chain of stations on the east and south-east coasts, known as Home Defence Units (HDUs).‡ Manned by German-speaking WAAF and WRNS staff, their activity managed by the RAF centre at Kingsdown, these stations telephoned their intercepts direct to the local RAF command, as well as to HQ Fighter Command at Stanmore, where they were co-ordinated with incoming intelligence from Cheadle, the radar chain and the Observer Corps and with the work of the Operations Room.§

By and large German fighters used R/T, and were covered by the Kingsdown system, while the bombers and reconnaissance aircraft used the MF and HF systems. The MF Safety Service controlled, amongst other things, the take-off, approach and landing of German aircraft. Interception of its transmissions thus gave early notification of the departure of aircraft for operations or other movements, and DF gave the bases involved. But the transmissions did not identify the unit or its mission. Information about the units or their missions came from other types of low-grade Sigint. Before the start of the operation the aircrafts' W/T control would frequently make dummy messages, for calibration purposes, on the high frequency which would be used by the aircraft for operational purposes while airborne. Interception

---

* Certain members of the Air Section of GC and CS, which as well as breaking low-grade GAF codes studied the daily traffic returns of Cheadle and the Kingsdown organisation, had access to the Enigma. In late 1940 they realised the potential value of fusing the two for illuminating the pattern of GAF operational activity against Britain. This work was not attempted by AI because of its preoccupation with correlating Enigma information with that from other sources, and with the management of the RAF Y service. AI at first opposed these attempts but later acknowledged their value.

† See Chapter 3, pp 107–108.

‡ Search for this kind of traffic had begun in January 1940 but it was first intercepted in the United Kingdom during the evacuation from Dunkirk in May. Thereafter the HDUs were rapidly set up in the belief that the Germans would use R/T heavily, eg for their tanks, in the event of invasion.

§ The HDUs were also in telephonic touch with the naval commands in their areas, which received the R/T traffic of German E-boats as well as air intelligence.

of this was a further indication that operations were afoot. The code used for this HF traffic had been broken by GC and CS and was read by Cheadle: but, unlike the MF traffic, it used daily-changing secret call-signs which during the first weeks of the Battle of Britain still could not be identified and this – for all that the transmissions could be DFd – made it impossible to be sure which unit was using them. Cheadle's experience since the beginning of the war had by now, however, taught it much about the habits and external characteristics of the W/T traffic of most GAF units and formations. During these first weeks, therefore, it was able to make early and, for the most part, correct guesses as to the identity of the units about to operate. Moreover, using its knowledge of the unit's previous habits and its observation of the navigational beacons switched on for the operation, Cheadle could sometimes foretell the intended target area. And since it was known that a unit would normally return to the same base, it was possible, once the target had been confirmed or identified by the actual attack, to establish the probable line of the enemy's return flight.

Had Cheadle been able to solve the secret HF call-signs at this stage it would have been able to learn more about the operations in progress. For, while GAF aircraft were instructed to keep W/T silence during operations, this rule was frequently disregarded – most often on completion of their mission, but sometimes before. Thus Cheadle would report their position, course and height and give information about their attack and about the target. But, except in the case of convoy sightings by aircraft, no operationally useful information could yet be obtained. By September 1940, however, Cheadle had made such progress in correlating the indications on MF with those on HF that it could identify the majority of bomber units 'very soon after the start of each operation'. From then on the operational reports from aircraft could be interpreted with increasing confidence and much useful information about the nature of the operation was forthcoming.* During the summer low-grade Sigint units were set up in Fighter and Coastal Commands; and the former was increasingly able, as the Battle of Britain progressed, to match the low-grade Sigint indications with those from radar.

During the later stages of the Battle of Britain – those marked by heavy attacks on RAF bases and on London – the GAF aircraft paid little heed to radio security. R/T intercepts in particular now increasingly supplemented the information from radar and Cheadle. Thus the HDUs could, on occasion, determine where enemy aircraft were forming up for a raid outside radar's detection range, give the altitude of the aircraft as they approached, and indicate which incoming groups on the radar screen were fighters and which bombers. All this was urgently needed information. And by their

---

* See Chapter 10 below, p 319 et seq.

frequent ability to intercept and pass on the orders given to the enemy fighter escort – orders which sometimes specified the areas for main and diversionary attack, gave information about the enemy's appreciation of RAF activity and furnished details of where the bombers would rendezvous for the return flight and the routes to be taken – they were able to be useful in directions where radar could not help. In such ways, and with growing regularity and accuracy as the battle proceeded, the organisations exploiting the GAF's low-grade signals traffic were able to give advance information about the purpose, type and scale of the enemy's attacks.

Without making a detailed comparison between the operational records of the units of Fighter Command and the war diaries of Cheadle, Kingsdown and their satellite interception sections – a complex piece of research which has not been undertaken and for which the surviving records are probably inadequate – it is not possible to gauge the precise impact of this intelligence on the day-to-day operations or to compare its value with the value of the intelligence derived from radar. There can be little doubt, however, that it made an important contribution to the effectiveness of Fighter Command during the crucial weeks of August and the first half of September, when the fighter strength of the RAF was limited and greatly outnumbered.

After the middle of September, when the GAF had abandoned the battle for air supremacy, the low-grade Sigint continued to be valuable. But by then other methods that were of equal importance in countering the efforts of the GAF were being developed, notably the system of countering the GAF's navigational beams.* By then, again, the chief preoccupation of operational intelligence was switching from the Battle of Britain back to the German preparations for invasion.

□

We have seen already how the intelligence authorities had responded to this danger up to July, on the one hand warning that negative evidence could not be relied on as proof that invasion was not imminent, and on the other hand finding it difficult to resist suggesting that invasion might be imminent when they were alarmed by any indications of unusual activity. We have noticed, too, that they clung to the first of these positions until well into July. We may now add that they retreated from the second after raising between 3 and 5 July their first serious alarm. Between early July and early September they issued no further alert.

One reason for the change was the onset of the Battle of Britain. This put their fears of invasion into better perspective. It is noticeable,

---

* See Chapter 10, p 322 et seq.

for example, that from the middle of July the assessments of the CIC began to pay more attention to the information that was coming in about the state of readiness of the GAF. On 14 July it noted that the GAF had still not completed its redeployment after the Battle of France; on 27 July it stressed that the GAF was not yet at full serviceability. On 14 August it went further, pronouncing for the first time the view that no final decision had been or would be taken by the German authorities 'pending the result of the present struggle for air superiority'. On 16 August it repeated this judgment and on 27 August it was still more positive. 'On the success of this operation will depend the decision as to the invasion'.

These conclusions were supported by the Czechs' source, A-54. He reported on 12 August that there would be no invasion for at least 14 days, and that it might even be three weeks before expeditionary forces assembled in Paris, Brussels and The Hague could be dispersed to their ports and airfields.[55] The CIC gave prominence to this information and used it as the basis for its pronouncement of 14 August. At the same time the CIC was far more sceptical than before of reports from diplomatic and SIS sources to the effect that invasion was imminent, several of which it now dismissed out of hand, and it was acquiring growing confidence in the information provided by aerial reconnaissance. The service performed by the PRU was subject to the weather. As the CIC stressed on 9 August, it could not yet with absolute reliability distinguish movements that might be invasion preparations from the enemy's everyday activities. But on the coasts opposite England it had revealed no unmistakable invasion preparations and its coverage, reaching out to the Gironde, the Baltic approaches and Norway from the third week in July, was at last expanding. Again as late as 9 August, the CIC was still voicing the suspicion that unseen invasion preparations might be in train in the Baltic itself, which the PRU could not bring into its range until October, but even that suspicion was somewhat allayed early in August when the Naval Attaché in Stockholm, who had been able to organise a source of information in Stettin, reported that ' all was quiet' there.[56] From the middle of August, however, the two most trusted sources, Sigint and photographic reconnaissance, revealed a marked change in the situation.

Since the end of July the GAF Enigma had yielded occasional but strong indications that German preparations for a landing were in progress. In an Enigma decrypt of 29 July GAF bombers were forbidden to bomb harbour facilities in British Channel ports, and the CIC drew attention to the fact that the GAF had imposed a similar restriction in relation to the French ports in advance of the attack on

55. Moravec, op cit, p 196.
56. AIR 40/1637, No 71 of 9 August 1940.

France. A further Enigma clue followed on 11 August – and the use that was made of it showed that the intelligence branches which stood behind the CIC were beginning to use their growing store of information and experience to improve the interpretation of the latest intelligence. On that day the CIC noted that GAF units earmarked for a special undertaking had been transferred to a Fliegerkorps commander who had been associated with close support during the French campaign. On 12 August the same commander was told that 30 men with a perfect knowledge of English were also being transferred to him.* Thereafter the Enigma indications continued to mount up; and in the first days of September they revealed that dive-bombers were about to assemble at airfields near the Straits and that long-range bombers had instructions to transfer from Norway to France.[57]

In themselves these indications, which GC and CS was producing with less delay after taking delivery in August of the first of the machines developed for finding the Enigma settings, did nothing to indicate that invasion might at last be imminent. But they coincided with another development. The PRU had hitherto failed to find unmistakable evidence of unusual assemblies of shipping in or near the Channel ports. From the first day of September it detected a striking increase of barges in the Ostend area, and their gradual movement westward. At Ostend the number increased from 18 on 31 August to 270 on 7 September. In the course of that week barges, motor-boats and larger vessels were seen or photographed on passage from the North Sea to the Channel ports. Between 1 and 4 September about 100 arrived at Flushing; at Dunkirk and Calais substantial numbers arrived in the next two days. At the same time, as the CIC noted on 2 September, photographic reconnaissance revealed that work on the long-range batteries at Gris Nez was proceeding at a great pace.

The JIC was not convinced that these shipping movements were in preparation for an invasion.[58] Even so, as the CIC was suggesting on 7 September, the purpose of the activity in the Channel might be to supply or in other ways support a main assault delivered from north-west Germany, where presumed invasion preparations were now noted, or from the Baltic. With this possibility in mind, the JIC warned the Chiefs of Staff on 5 September that seaborne raids must be expected at any moment, though it added that the Germans would probably renew their attempt to win air superiority before risking a

---

* Perhaps from the wish to restrict the circulation of at least the most tell-tale Enigma items, the CIC did not reproduce this information in the daily report, but it was certainly aware of it. The item was given due emphasis in an MI14 appreciation of 20 August.

57. 9 CX/JQ 218, 221, 238, 244, 249, 261, 262, 264, 266, 268.
58. JIC (40) 57th Meeting, 5 September.

major seaborne invasion.[59] And on 7 September, asked to be more precise,[60] it abandoned its hesitations in the light of further evidence.

On 5 September the PRU had recorded another increase of barges in Ostend, and a report had been received that German army leave had been stopped from 8 September. On 6 September Sigint had revealed that the transfers recently ordered by the GAF had taken place. On 7 September itself the PRU warned that a large-scale and disciplined movement of barges was taking place to forward bases in the Channel. Judging that the enemy would not bring the barges within range of RAF attack unless invasion was imminent, observing that conditions of moon and tide on the south-east coast would be particularly favourable for landings between 8 and 10 September, and bearing in mind also that these dates were being mentioned in the increasing number of invasion warnings that were being received from diplomatic and SIS sources, the JIC decided to advise the Chiefs of Staff that a full-scale invasion might be attempted at any moment. And 'as if to clinch the matter', as it added in its report, four Germans caught landing from rowing boats on the south-east coast had confessed that they were spies whose task had been to be ready at any time in the next fortnight to report the movement of British reserve formations in the quadrilateral Oxford-Ipswich-London-Reading.[61]

The Chiefs of Staff and GHQ Home Forces accepted this assessment. At seven minutes past eight in the evening of 7 September the GHQ issued codeword *Cromwell*, bringing all home defence forces to 'immediate action'.

□

At that point the Germans remained uncertain when, indeed whether, to attempt a landing. As long ago as the end of July Hitler had set the middle of September as the date for the completion of all preparations, but had not decided when he would order the preparatory 10-day count-down. On 11 September he abandoned any intention of giving this order before the 14th. On 13 September he informed the commands that, in view of the fact that the state of the air battle, though hopeful, was still uncertain, the moment for the order had not yet arrived. On 14 September he postponed the warning date for three more days, thereby renouncing the prospect of invasion before 27 September, the last day until 8 October when moon and tide would favour a landing. On 17 September he postponed it again, and also ordered a partial dispersal of the invasion shipping, which had been battered by the RAF since 5 September. But he maintained other preparations against a possible

59. CAB 80/18, COS (40) 713 (JIC) of 5 September.
60. CAB 79/6, COS (40) 296th Meeting, 6 September.
61. CAB 80/18, COS (40) 721 (JIC) of 7 September; CAB 79/6, COS (40) 300th Meeting, 7 September.

decision to invade in October. On 12 October he put off the operation until the following spring but instructed that the threat of invasion should be kept in being as a means of exerting military and political pressure on Great Britain.

Of these delays and deliberations some hints began to reach Whitehall from as early as 15 September, as we shall see. Until well into October, however, these hints were less powerful than were the indications that preparations for invasion were at an advanced stage, if not actually complete. The liners *Bremen* and *Europa* were sighted, camouflaged, in Bremen on 10 September. The PRU detected the extension of assemblies of shipping to Le Havre and Cherbourg, and its evidence at last contained numerous reports of specially converted invasion craft. The Enigma supplied plentiful details of the enemy's administrative preparations. On 13 September the Naval Section at GC and CS judged by Traffic Analysis, from its study of the behaviour of the new naval wireless network set up by Germany for the Channel area during the summer, that 'everything was ready'. But during the whole of the period in which invasion remained a serious possibility neither the Enigma nor any other source gave any precise indication as to when an assault would be made.

As to where and in what strength the assault would come, intelligence was equally unable to help. The size of the German transport aircraft fleet was known from call-sign evidence. This enabled the JIC to put a ceiling on the scale of airborne attack. But although the whereabouts of some of this fleet was identified from PR and Sigint, it was not possible to say how much of the force would be committed. In the same way, although the maximum size of at least the first wave of the seaborne assault across the Channel could be judged once the shipping had begun to assemble and to be photo-graphed, such calculations were of little value in the light of the assumption that a large part of the expedition would come from the Baltic. In its turn, this assumption arose from pre-suppositions as to where the expedition would be delivered. In its final form the German plan was in fact to put the whole force ashore within a fairly restricted area in Kent and Sussex. But the British planners assumed from the first that the main assault would be made on East Anglia, the best direction from which to envelop London, with only diversionary raids and landings farther north, on the south coast and against Eire. Even after the invasion shipping had moved to its forward embarkation ports in France, they continued to allow for a main landing on the east coast and a secondary assault in the south. As late as 28 October, the day before the PRU reached the Baltic ports, GHQ Home Forces was still working on this assumption and disposing its formations accordingly,[62] and apart from MI's early emphasis on the probability

---

62. WO 199/911A.

that the enemy would use unorthodox methods, and that these might include surprise landings at widely dispersed points, intelligence had still produced no evidence which cast doubt on it.* On this problem, as on the subject of the probable scale of the attack, the papers produced or approved by the JIC were as strong in speculation at the end of September, and as weak in their information, as they had been in May.[64]

In their effort to discover the date of the invasion the intelligence authorities resorted after 7 September to every conceivable source, and to some devices that are barely conceivable. As well as arranging to have cages of carrier-pigeons (with instructions for use) dropped on the other side of the Channel,[65] they consulted Channel tunnel experts,[66] listened to a water diviner who claimed to be able to forecast the enemy's movements[67] and, aware of Hitler's interest in astrology, paid some attention to his horoscope. Though the views of an astrologer on Hitler's horoscope were quoted to the Chiefs of Staff,[68] the Vice Chief of the Naval Staff was surely being sarcastic when he suggested on 1 October that the NID should set up an astrological section,[69] and it may be allowed that the more recondite of these enquiries were not seriously pursued. But the fact that they were considered at all reveals the absence of reliable information. Of the many diplomatic and SIS reports a few came close to the mark. As was usual, however, they were few among many that were widely contradictory, and they encountered the problem that, the more accurate they were, the less could they be precise. On 22 September, to illustrate their mixture of inaccuracy and precision, the CIC announced that, according to a report from the British embassy in Washington, invasion had been ordered for 1500 on that day. On 27 September, to illustrate the imprecision of the more accurate few, the CIC reproduced an SIS report to the effect that preparations for the invasion had been completed on 10 September, but that no date had been fixed as the decision was to be reached in the light of

---

* A-54 had given two warnings that the landings would be in the south. In August he had reported that they would be around Brighton and Ramsgate and on 21 September had given Dover as the main point of the attack.[63] By that time, however, Sigint had begun to reveal the existence of a large-scale German administrative organisation for invasion in the Scheldt which countered this and similar reports by tending to confirm British operational assumptions.

63. Moravec, op cit, p 196.
64. CAB 80/10, COS (40) 326 (JIC) of 6 May; CAB 80/11, COS (40) 371 (JIC) of 21 May; CAB 80/12, COS (40) 432 (JIC) of 6 June; CAB 80/13, COS (40) 473 (JIC) of 18 June; CAB 80/14, COS (40) 533 (JIC) of 5 July and 550 (JIC) of 15 July; CAB 80/15, COS (40) 551 (JIC) of 16 July, 566 (JIC) of 22 July and 567 (JIC) of 25 July; CAB 80/16, COS (40) 611 (JIC) of 7 August; CAB 80/18, COS (40) 740 (JIC) of 13 September.   65. Strong, *Intelligence at the Top*, p 68.
66. ibid, p 69.   67. ibid, p 69.
68. CAB 79/15, COS (40) 353rd Meeting, 18 October.
69. ADM 233/84, NID 003462/40.

circumstances. And further to complicate matters, it was just between the middle of September and the middle of October, when Hitler was gradually abandoning the attempt to invade, that evidence from the most trusted sources emerged to sustain the belief that invasion might be attempted at any moment.

The PRU's photographs of the Channel area were at last revealing the existence of invasion devices that had so far gone undetected – embarkation and disembarkation ramps; twin-barges of novel design. The Enigma decrypts, consisting as they did of the signals of subordinate formations, were silent about the enemy's strategic thinking but were providing more details than before of the complex invasion organisation, involving all three Services, which the Germans had brought into existence, and there was no lack of evidence that the organisation remained at a high state of readiness. On 21 September the Enigma vouchsafed the code word *Sealion* for the first time; and other Enigma decrypts of 24, 25 and 27 September referred to first, second and third crossings.[70] As late as the middle of October, indeed, information from this source about the invasion preparations of Luftflotte 2 convinced MI and AI that the enemy remained fully ready and determined to attempt a large-scale invasion if conditions turned favourable.* And on 18 October, on the basis of these appreciations, the Chiefs of Staff, who had previously permitted some slight relaxation,[71] ordered a return to the highest state of readiness.[72]

In the light of this evidence indications that Hitler had decided against invasion, at least in the immediate future, were treated with caution. The first such indication was provided by Traffic Analysis. On the morning of 15 September an identical signal was transmitted on every German naval frequency, an unprecedented occurrence.† This signal was followed, not by an increase of wireless traffic on the Channel area frequency, but by a marked decline in it. Later on 15 September, somewhat prematurely as it turned out, the Naval Section at GC and CS reported to the OIC in the Admiralty that this unusual German naval wireless behaviour was probably in some way associated

---

* These appreciations are reproduced in Appendix 7. They are noteworthy (a) as being the earliest in which the intelligence branches brought together a large number of indications from a wide range of sources, though notably from Sigint, in a sustained attempt to reconstruct the state of enemy planning, but also (b) as revealing the extent to which the branches were still applying a single-Service approach and reaching their conclusions independently. In addition, though they were given a very limited circulation, they played a part in alerting the authorities to the need for new security procedures to deal with the growing profusion of Enigma intelligence. It was for reasons of security that the cover-name *Smith* was used in Whitehall in place of *Sealion*, as can be seen in the AI appreciation.

† This signal presumably conveyed the decision reached by Hitler on 14 September, see above, p 185.

70. CX/JQ 324, 326, 333 and 343.
71. CAB 79/7, COS (40) 338th Meeting, 7 October, 346th Meeting, 11 October.
72. CAB 79/7, COS (40) 353rd Meeting, 18 October.

with the postponement of the German initiative. By 20 September this inference, which the Admiralty did not forward to the CIC, was being supported by photographic reconnaissance. The PRU noticed on that day that 5 destroyers and a torpedo-boat had withdrawn from Cherbourg and that the assemblies of barges had begun to disperse. By the end of the month the total of barges photographed in the five main ports between Flushing and Boulogne had declined from 1,004 on 18 September to 691. But even this evidence was judged to be inconclusive: the withdrawal might be only a tactical move to avoid losses from RAF bombing, which was clearly taking its toll.* Not until 28 October did the CIC, reporting that photographic reconnaissance had detected the first considerable movement of shipping eastward out of the Channel, risk the comment that this movement 'if maintained, could reduce the risk of invasion'. By then, on 25 October, it had received the first firm indication from the Enigma – the disclosure that the GAF had disbanded one of the special administrative units attached to the invasion forces.

During October the CIC was equally reserved towards the increasingly frequent diplomatic and SIS reports that invasion had been postponed. A report from A-54 on 30 September, to the effect that invasion had been deferred until early October, was not mentioned by the CIC. On 13 October, the day after Hitler had so decided, SIS circulated another report from the same source, dated 9 October, which said that the invasion had been put off until 1941. But it graded the information as being of only B3 quality – possibly correct from a usually reliable source – and this was noted when the report was reproduced by the CIC on 17 October. By that time the Foreign Office had learned that Hitler had told Mussolini at their Brenner meeting on 4 October that *Sealion* was postponed until the spring;[74] and as early as 9 October, on the strength of a report from the Madrid embassy, the Cabinet had called for a study of the possibility that Germany would advance through the Balkans into the Middle East.[75] But the CIC did not comment on these diplomatic reports.

Despite the conflict of evidence and the absence of what alone could have resolved it – an unambiguous indication from a Sigint source that the invasion had been abandoned – a sense of relaxation gained ground slowly in Whitehall from the beginning of October. It was then that the CIC changed the formula used in its reports from 'invasion could come at any time' to 'situation unchanged: no indication that a decision to invade has been taken'. On 10 October the CIC's

---

* It later transpired that more than one-tenth of the transports and barges had been sunk or damaged in or en route to their assembly points by 21 September.[73]

73. Collier, op cit, pp 227–228.
74. Woodward, op cit, Vol I, p 488.
75. CAB 65/15, WM (40) 268 CA of 9 October.

assessment came close to depicting the actual situation: as well as keeping everything ready in case conditions favoured a landing, the enemy was probably continuing his administrative preparations in order to contain British forces and to avoid the fall in German morale that would follow if the operation were abandoned. On the same day the JIC concluded that, while the danger of invasion would remain so long as Germany had numerical superiority in the air, the enemy's failure to win the air battle, the shortening days, the worsening weather and the growing strength of the British defences were now combining to make invasion a 'hazardous' undertaking.[76] These assessments were based on operational considerations, rather than on intelligence indications, and the operational authorities were not so confident. On 21 October, three days after the last of the intelligence alarms, the Chiefs of Staff, and especially the CIGS, were perturbed about the widespread feeling that the danger had passed.[77] But on the last day of October the Defence Committee* agreed with the Prime Minister that the danger was now 'relatively remote' and adjusted the dispositions and state of readiness of British forces to what it judged would remain a diminished threat throughout the winter.[78]

---

* The Defence Committee, set up in May 1940, carried out the same functions of keeping under review the strategic situation and the progress of operations as its predecessor, the Military Co-ordination Committee: it was normally chaired by the Prime Minister as Minister of Defence. It remained in being for the rest of the war.

76. CAB 80/20, COS (40) 819 (JIC) of 10 October.
77. CAB 79/7, COS (40) 354th Meeting, 21 October.
78. CAB 69/1, DO (40) 39th Meeting, 31 October.

CHAPTER 6

The Mediterranean and The Middle East to November 1940

TO IMPROVE the contacts between the many bodies engaged in procuring and evaluating intelligence; to see that their contributions were brought together for the benefit of the operational authorities; to ensure that those authorities made the best use of whatever was being provided – these tasks were difficult enough within the United Kingdom. Extended to the Mediterranean and the Middle East they were still more daunting. Apart from the fact that intelligence was procured in the Middle East as well as in the United Kingdom, and that it was by no means easy either to achieve a logical division of labour between the two theatres or to arrange for their output to be exchanged, there were two main problems. The Service intelligence staffs in the Middle East, which were immediately responsible for assessing intelligence for the three commands there, were at the outbreak of war far more widely separated from each other, physically and institutionally, than were the intelligence directorates of the Service departments in Whitehall. And the preparation of intelligence for the operational authorities was further complicated by the fact that strategic decisions had to be the outcome of a dialogue between Whitehall and the Commanders-in-Chief in the Middle East. Each party to this dialogue needed to receive all available intelligence that was not strictly tactical.

The CID went some way towards meeting these problems by setting up the Middle East Intelligence Centre (MEIC) in Cairo in June 1939 and authorising it:

'(a) to furnish the Commanders-in-Chief and representatives of the Civil Departments in the Middle East with co-ordinated intelligence and to provide the Joint Planning Staff in the Middle East with the intelligence necessary for the preparation of combined plans;
(b) to provide the Joint Intelligence Sub-Committee in London for the information of HMG with co-ordinated intelligence in respect of the area allotted to it.'[1]

The emphasis in the terms of reference on 'co-ordinated intelligence' reflected the anxiety of the three Services to keep the responsibility for exploiting and assessing operational intelligence in the hands of their separate intelligence hierarchies in the Middle East. Limits were

---

1. CAB 2/9, CID 363rd Meeting, 29 June 1939; CAB 4/30, CID 1556B of 27 June 1939.

set, moreover, to what the MEIC should co-ordinate. The Foreign Office declined to participate in the Centre, and trusted that it would not be responsible for assessing political intelligence.* Security intelligence in the Middle East was already co-ordinated for the three Services by the Defence Security Officer, Egypt. In the autumn of 1939 the C-in-C ME proposed that MEIC should take over this responsibility.[2] The Foreign Office and the SIS disliked this proposal, and in December 1939 a new inter-Service body, Security Intelligence Middle East (SIME), was established as part of GHQ, ME. The JIC excluded the Balkans from the purview of MEIC; until May 1940, on instructions from the Cabinet, it was itself at work on plans for a separate intelligence organisation for that area in collaboration with Turkey.[3] But the MEIC was not greatly inhibited by these restrictions, and between the summer of 1939 and Italy's entry into the war in the summer of 1940 it developed more rapidly in some directions than Whitehall had expected – and than its nearest equivalent in Whitehall, the JIC, was able to do.

Denied a diplomatic component and excluded from political intelligence on the insistence of the Foreign Office, and therefore set up as a 'combined' staff of army, navy and air force officers, it nevertheless established a foreign affairs section. And despite frequent complaints from the Foreign Office and the heads of missions in the area, particularly the Cairo embassy,[4] it co-ordinated diplomatic with military intelligence in its appreciations. By the end of 1939, again, it had established a Balkan section, although it was not until May 1940, in response to its agitation, that the JIC authorised it to include the Balkans in the area for which it was responsible.[5] By the spring of 1940 it was issuing not only strategic appreciations but also background reports on a great variety of subjects – frontiers, climate, resources, communications, hygiene – for more than twenty countries, and it was indexing and collating information from more sources than any British intelligence body had previously tried to do. It is clear, indeed, that it regarded information from any source as grist to its mill – and that it established the right to receive everything – high-grade Sigint, field Sigint, PR and other reconnaissance, SIS reports, POW intelligence, as well as appreciations sent out from Whitehall and by the many intelligence organisations in the Middle

---

* Chapter 1, pp 40–41.

2. Mockler-Ferryman, op cit, pp 155–159.
3. JIC (39) 4th Meeting, 22 September, 13th Meeting, 1 December; CAB 65/2, WM (39) 108 of 8 December; CAB 66/3, WP (39) 150 of 8 December; CAB 65/5, WM (40) 41 of 14 February; CAB 66/3, WP (40) 47 of 14 February; JIC (40) 5th Meeting, 16 February; JIC (40) 53 of 5 May and 69 of 16 May.
4. Mockler-Ferryman, op cit, pp 155–157.
5. JIC (40) 28th Meeting, 7 May.

East, and reports from British diplomatic, consular and colonial authorities.[6]

In Whitehall it was not only the Foreign Office that disliked the way in which the MEIC was developing. The JIC was sometimes exasperated by complaints from the MEIC about Whitehall's failure to send it information and to exchange strategic appreciations with it.[7] The JIC and the Services in London were also incensed by some of the MEIC's initiatives – its demand, for example, that it should be responsible for the Balkans, and its attempt to monopolise the exchange of Mediterranean and Middle East intelligence with the French. For information and opinion about Italy Whitehall was far more dependent on overseas organisations than it was where Germany was concerned. But it was by no means wholly so; and the London authorities were anxious that the MEIC should not become so comprehensive and so powerful that it excluded them from the field of strategic intelligence for the theatre.

This anxiety was a large factor in delaying consideration until 1943 of the need for a full-scale JIC in the Middle East. In May 1940 the War Office did, indeed, move to abolish the MEIC and have it replaced by a small committee consisting of a single representative of each of the three Services that, with a secretary, would function as a miniature JIC. But the C-in-C Middle East vetoed this proposal. Such a committee, he insisted, would be incapable of digesting the seventy-odd separate and often conflicting intelligence summaries that were regularly circulated in the theatre. These summaries provided much of the raw material for the MEIC's broad appreciations, and those appreciations, which were themselves circulated to some sixty addressees, had become indispensable to the theatre's operational and planning authorities,[8] who had previously had to digest many of the often conflicting summaries and make their own appreciations.[9] But if, in the absence of anything approaching a regular series of Middle East appreciations from London, this argument saved the MEIC, it was still the case that the MEIC could not meet all the needs and the interests of the operational authorities in the theatre.

From May 1940, when the naval OIC finally moved to Alexandria and the three Service intelligence HQs came to be situated closer to each other, there was a good deal of informal consultation between them. It is clear, indeed, that by the autumn consultation had produced an inter-Service body for the exchange and discussion of intelligence appreciations consisting of representatives of the three

---

6. WO 106/5074, 13 July 1941; Playfair, op cit, Vol 1, p 34.
7. eg, JIC (40) 226 and 227, both of 6 August; JIC (40) 277 of 17 September.
8. Playfair, op cit, Vol 1, p 34; Field Marshal Lord Wilson, *Eight Years Overseas* (1948), p 22.
9. Mockler-Ferryman, op cit, p 155.

Service HQs, with DDMI of GS Int GHQ, MEF as secretary,* which lasted until a JIC (Middle East) was formally set up in 1944.[10] But this body was no more than an unofficial forum. In October 1940, after the war had extended to the Middle East, the Cs-in-C in the theatre recognised that informal co-operation was inadequate by recommending to the Chiefs of Staff that a Joint Planning Intelligence Committee should be established to serve the Joint Planners there: the separate Service HQs were too busy with day-to-day operations to fulfil this role, and the MEIC, though it was represented at meetings of the Middle East Joint Planners,[11] was too removed from operational intelligence to be able to perform it.[12] Early in 1941, again, the new DMI in Whitehall suggested that the JIC should make MEIC its counterpart in the Middle East.[13] Perhaps because the London authorities felt that they should themselves provide such co-ordination of intelligence for planning purposes as was beyond the scope of the MEIC, these proposals were not taken up in Whitehall.

The proposal of the Cs-in-C envisaged the need for something like a Middle East JIC in addition to the MEIC, but it stopped far short of advocating a merger of their intelligence staffs. Nor is this surprising. In Whitehall itself the sections of the three Service intelligence directorates which were responsible for the Mediterranean or Middle East were numerically small compared with the intelligence staffs at the Service HQs in the theatre, but the chief functions of each of them were to keep its own department abreast of the information that was coming in from those HQs and to ensure that such intelligence as was produced in the United Kingdom reached the theatre HQ of its own Service with the least possible delay. Applied to the Middle East, the insistence that the three Services should retain separate and self-sufficing intelligence HQs was strongly reinforced by two other considerations. Unlike the Whitehall intelligence directorates, they were part of operational commands – even the C-in-C Mediterranean was in practice free from Admiralty intervention in operations of the kind that could take place in Home Waters and the Atlantic – and they naturally regarded it as their first responsibility to provide intelligence to their own C-in-C. Then there were the huge distances and the poor communications of the theatre, and the extraordinarily diverse nature of its problems. Any attempt to centralise in one place, for three dissimilar and powerful commands, the work of such various bodies as GS Int, which was responsible for an area stretching from Libya to India, the naval OIC

---

* For the formation of GS Int GHQ, ME see below, p 195.

10. ibid, p 157.
11. WO 169/3, War Diary of G Branch, GHQ ME, 23 September 1940.
12. ibid, 10 October 1940.
13. JIC (41) 1st Meeting, 2 January; JIC (41) 13 of 7 January.

attached to C-in-C Mediterranean, whose area extended westwards to Gibraltar, and the intelligence staff of HQ RAF, ME, whose centre of gravity had until recently been in Iraq, must have involved grave difficulties.

In the course of the discussions which led to the establishment of the MEIC the idea had been mooted that there should be a single centre responsible for co-ordinating operational intelligence for the three Services in the Middle East, on the lines of the Far East Combined Bureau (FECB). This suggestion had come to nothing on account of the insistence of the fighting Services that the Middle East commands must have separate intelligence staffs at their HQs doing operational intelligence independently of each other.[14] Instead, an intelligence staff responsible for co-ordinating operational intelligence for all the air forces in the theatre had been attached to AOC-in-C Middle East when his command was set up in Cairo in March 1939;[15] a naval OIC had been set up, in the first instance at Malta, in April 1939; and in April 1940 the C-in-C Middle East was provided with an intelligence staff of his own (GS Int GHQ, ME) headed by a DDMI.* As GOC-in-C from June 1939 until his post was up-graded to C-in-C ME, in February 1940, the Army Commander had relied for operational intelligence on HQ British Troops, Egypt, and on the MEIC, but it had never been intended that that arrangement should be more than temporary. On the contrary, with the approach of war in the Middle East the Army was brought into line with the practice of the other two Services, and with Service principles. Nor did practice and principles change when the war extended to the Middle East. For if it increased the need for collaboration between the Service intelligence staffs, it also emphasised their separate needs by bringing operational intelligence into greater prominence.

A further complication existed. Partly as a result of the special features of the theatre that we have already mentioned, and partly because Sigint had been plentiful in the Middle East for several years, the Services had organised the control of Sigint in the theatre through all its stages – procurement (including interception and

---

* By October 1940 the expansion of Gs Int was such that some decentralisation was found necessary. The DDMI retained responsibility for operational, signals, topographical and POW intelligence, while another Brigadier was appointed to take charge of personnel security, censorship, publicity and certain offshoots of the newly formed Special Operations Executive (SOE). (The latter were handed over as soon as a representative of SOE arrived in Cairo.) The two parts of the organisation remained, 'for some unexplained reason', entirely separate, though maintaining close touch, and dealt direct with the Chief of Staff or the C-in-C. There was no co-ordination until, in June 1941, a Brigadier was appointed as DMI. The two parts of GS Int each then came under its own Colonel (DDMI(I) and DDMI(O)). The total strength was then about 140 officers.[16]

14. Mockler-Ferryman, op cit, p 156.
15. AIR 41/44, *The Middle East Campaigns*, Vol I, p 3.
16. Mockler-Ferryman, op cit, pp 159–160.

cryptanalysis), interpretation and use – on single-Service lines. From 1924 the Army had centred its Sigint organisation on No 2 W/T Company at Sarafand; from 1937 the RAF, which had previously concentrated its intelligence at Baghdad, had built up Heliopolis (Cairo) into the Cheadle of the Middle East; by the spring of 1939 the Navy was preparing to do Italian Traffic Analysis and to exploit Italian low-grade codes and cyphers at its OIC in Malta. When the Italians were making liberal use of plain language, when Italian low-grade codes were easy to read and when even Italian high-grade codes could be exploited locally after the initial work on them had been done at GC and CS, it seemed obvious to the Services that the whole Sigint process should as far as possible take place in close proximity to their operational HQs. On the other hand, when those HQs and their intelligence staffs were widely dispersed, and physically remote from their subordinate operational authorities and their intercept and Y stations, they naturally gave priority to improving their own Sigint networks – a programme made all the more urgent by the need to develop their field Sigint organisations. Thus in August 1939 that part of the Sarafand unit which dealt with Italian Army Sigint was moved to Mersa Matruh to begin work on material intercepted in the field, and in the first half of 1940 the RAF was undertaking similar work at Cairo as well as setting up additional intercept stations in Aden, Khartoum, Malta and the south of France. In these circumstances they resisted suggestions that in the Middle East, as in the United Kingdom, the exploitation of Sigint should be centralised as far as possible at a single inter-Service centre.

In the United Kingdom the conflict between GC and CS, with its view that all high-grade cryptanalysis and at least the direction of all interception programmes should be concentrated at one inter-Service centre, and the Service intelligence directorates in Whitehall, with their insistence on their own responsibility for evaluating intelligence and their fear that this responsibility would be eroded if they did not resume control of their own cryptanalysis on the outbreak of war, was by 1939 coming to be settled by a compromise which largely, though by no means entirely, favoured the GC and CS thesis.* In 1938, and again at the end of 1939 and the beginning of 1940, GC and CS advocated the creation of a Combined Sigint Bureau in the Middle East in the hope that its thesis would be extended to that theatre – that whatever arrangements the three Services might make to preserve their right to assess for themselves all intelligence affecting them, at least they would consent to pool their cryptanalytical resources in one place, modelled on GC and CS, able to help GC and CS with the growing problem of getting locally intercepted traffic back to London without delay, and empowered to negotiate with GC and CS a satisfactory division of labour between the United Kingdom and the

---

* See Chapter 1, p 21 et seq.

theatre. But the intelligence staffs in the Middle East rejected this proposal, and even persuaded GC and CS that there were grave obstacles to a centralised Sigint centre. Nor did these obstacles disappear when Italy entered the war. After debating since 1940 the need for a theatre Y Committee to advise them on Sigint policy and co-ordinate their separate Sigint activities – and to deal with problems like those that arose from the fact that they could not avoid doing some wireless interception for each other – the three Service HQ intelligence staffs in the Middle East did, indeed, form a Sigint policy committee (the W Committee) in August 1940. Beyond that their old views still prevailed. The W Committee recognised the need for better liaison between the three Services but decided in favour of continuing on single-Service lines and against an inter-Service Combined Sigint Bureau.

The attitude of the Middle East intelligence staffs rested not only on their concern for the interests of their own Service, but also on their jealousy of each other – thus RAF intelligence feared that in a combined bureau it would be dominated by the larger and longer-established Army intelligence organisation. But their mutual jealousies gave way to a common front when it came to arguing with GC and CS about how the work on the Italian cyphers, and the limited stock of cryptanalysts trained in Italian work, should be divided between the United Kingdom and the Middle East. Until the war extended to the Middle East the division of labour – one by which, while immediately exploitable intercepts were decrypted at the intelligence HQs in the theatre, intercepts in cyphers which GC and CS had not fully solved were sent back to GC and CS, and by which GC and CS's decrypts of this material and of material intercepted in the United Kingdom were sent to the intelligence branches in Whitehall for selection and forwarding to the intelligence HQs in the Middle East – worked well enough. With the outbreak of war with Italy in June 1940, however, the communications links between the United Kingdom and the Middle East proved quite inadequate to meet the need to exchange a growing body of intercepts and decrypts without delay by W/T and, not unnaturally, the complaints of the Middle East authorities that the product of GC and CS was reaching them too slowly were accompanied by calls for the transfer of cryptanalytical staff from GC and CS to the Middle East.

In July, in response to a special request from C-in-C Middle East and in the hope that the step would further the development of a combined bureau there, GC and CS sent out to Cairo a small party containing cryptanalysts from all three Services as well as civilians. In August the party was joined by another group of cryptanalysts under the head of GC and CS's Italian military section who became Director of the Combined Bureau Middle East (CBME) in November.* At that

---

* See below, p 219 et seq.

point, while GC and CS became reluctant to release more of its staff and resources to the Middle East, the Middle East authorities became still more critical of the division of labour, their criticism taking the form of increasingly bitter complaints about the delay with which they received the results of GC and CS's cryptanalysis and increasingly vigorous suggestions that GC and CS was giving too little priority to work on Italian cyphers.

As we shall see, a new problem, coming on top of existing organisational difficulties and long-standing differences of opinion, went far to explain this atmosphere of mounting recrimination. From the intelligence point of view the most serious consequence of the outbreak of war with Italy was the fact that it was followed by a wholesale change in Italy's codes and cyphers. But before considering this development, which was to have important repercussions on the organisation of intelligence, we must outline the state of intelligence about the Middle East up to Italy's entry into the war and during the first few months of hostilities.

□

For most of the period between September 1939 and Italy's entry into the war on 11 June 1940 the British authorities were less preoccupied with the danger from Italy than with two other possible threats to the Middle East – a German move through the Balkans and a Russian advance against the Anglo-Iranian oilfields. It was these threats which induced the Cabinet to authorise the JIC in the autumn of 1939 to try to make arrangements for an exchange of intelligence with the Turks,* and which led to the establishment at Istanbul, under the wing of the Military Attaché at Ankara, of a small inter-Service Balkan Intelligence Centre in December 1939. In setting up this Centre the greatest secrecy was observed, but the Germans knew of its formation and they broadcast the fact within a week.[17]

The Istanbul Centre acted as the collecting agency for information from the British attachés at Belgrade, Bucharest, Budapest, Sofia and Athens. It probably supplied most of the many reports about German troop movements towards south-eastern Europe and Russian troop movements in the southern USSR which found their way into the intelligence summaries produced in London, by the MEIC and at GHQ, Middle East at this time. These reports, derived from the observations of the attachés, from the SIS and from the Press, were not yet being supplemented by information from better sources. In the spring of 1940 PR of the Caucasian oilfields was carried out covertly after the Supreme War Council had discussed their possible

---

* See above, p 192.

17. ibid, p 156.

destruction. The PDU, using the techniques and an aircraft of the SIS flight, photographed Baku without opposition on 30 March. On 3 April an attempt to photograph Batum encountered AA fire but sufficient material was obtained from these two sorties to provide target maps.*[18] Apart from this brief activity there was no photographic reconnaissance of the area. During most of 1940 the GAF Enigma, as yet the only important Sigint source about Germany's activities, was uncommunicative about eastern Europe and the Middle East. As for Russia, the available military Sigint threw no light on her intentions. In the pre-war years work on her Service codes and cyphers had been confined to a small unit in India and to No 2 W/T Company, the Army's Sigint unit at Sarafand, until GC and CS took it up after the conclusion of the Nazi-Soviet Pact in August 1939. Since then GC and CS had broken the Russian meteorological cypher, read a considerable number of naval signals and decoded about a quarter of some 4,000 army and police messages; but like that which had long been exploited in India and at Sarafand, this was local traffic and, though useful for tactical information, it yielded nothing of strategic importance.[†]

If British intelligence could thus do little more than speculate about Germany's and Russia's intentions, it was better placed in relation to Italy's. In the period before she entered the war the RAF authorities in the Middle East complained of the shortage of intelligence about Italy.[19] Admiral Cunningham, the C-in-C Mediterranean, was later to assert that 'intelligence about Italy was sparse', and that 'we had no subterranean access to Italian secret documents or decisions'.[20] These claims have to be set against the fact that in the years immediately before Italy entered the war GC and CS had all but completely mastered her cyphers. The diplomatic and colonial cyphers had been read for several years. Both the most secret and the general book cyphers of the Italian Navy were largely readable from 1937, as was one of Italy's two naval attaché codes. The high-grade book cypher used by the Italian Air Force in east Africa was solved in 1938; a second, in use in the Mediterranean, became readable in the summer of 1939. Of the six Army book cyphers used in Libya, three were easily readable and the others largely so, and the same applied to a military attaché cypher and to the cyphers used by the Italian mission and the

---

* Papers about the project to destroy these oilfields were captured by the Germans in France in June 1940 and referred to publicly by Hitler on 10 July and by Molotov in August 1940.

† All work on Russian codes and cyphers was stopped from 22 June 1941, the day on which Germany attacked Russia, except that, to meet the need for daily appreciations of the weather on the eastern front, the Russian meteorological cypher was read again for a period beginning in October 1942.

18. AIR 41/6, pp 136–8.   19. AIR 41/44, p 2.
20. Cunningham, op cit, p 203.

Italian intelligence services in Spain. As we have already noticed, Sigint, even when in plentiful supply, is less revealing about a government's intentions than is sometimes supposed. But Sigint in fact gave good notice of Italy's entry, if only for a month before the event,* as well as providing over a much longer period detailed information about the organisation, the strengths and the order of battle of Italy's armed forces.

The detailed information was of immense value in helping to check and interpret reports about her state of readiness that were coming in from the diplomatic service, the attachés, the SIS and overt sources. From Sigint the British authorities possessed up to June 1940 a close knowledge of the Italian Navy[21] and they estimated with a fair degree of accuracy the resources and dispositions of the IAF and the Army. Their assessment of the strength of the IAF in metropolitan Italy was 1,393 aircraft in April 1939, when the true figure was 1,200.[22] They estimated the IAF strength in Libya at the end of May 1940 as 140 bombers (plus 36 in the Dodecanese) and 144 fighters (plus 12 in the Dodecanese) – a total of 284 operational aircraft at a time when the true figures for these two areas were 140 bombers and 101 fighters, a total of 241.[23] Of the IAF strength in east Africa their information was somewhat more accurate. In relation to the Army, as well as having a very full order of battle for east Africa,[24] they knew that there were 15 divisions in Libya at the end of April 1940 and that 60,000 more troops had arrived there between 1 May and 10 June, though they did not know where and in what units these reinforcements were deployed.[25] As for the state of readiness in all three Services, they knew that it was poor – in particular, that the IAF's maintenance organisation was defective, that only about one-third of its pilots were up to RAF standard and that, on account of deficiencies in tanks, artillery, motor transport and training, the Army in Libya was in no condition to go over to the offensive at an early date.

In February 1939, when the Chiefs of Staff concluded that Italy remained anxious to preserve her neutrality, they could thus base their assessment on considerable knowledge of her military unpreparedness for a long war.[26] But British planning down to September 1939 still had to proceed on the assumption that on the outbreak of war with Germany Italy would come in on Germany's side. Sigint was no more

---

* See below, pp 202–203.

21. ADM 186/800, pp 18, 22, 161; ADM 223/83, OIC Daily Report, 1 July 1940.
22. AIR 41/44, Appendix XII; Richards, op cit, Vol I, p 243.
23. AIR 23/6756, HQ RAF, ME Weekly Intsum, 5 July 1940; Playfair, op cit, Vol I, p 95.
24. WO 169/18, GS Int GHQ ME, Weekly Review of Military Situation (WRMS) 15 July 1940.
25. ibid, 1 July 1940; Churchill, op cit, Vol II, p 370.
26. CAB 16/183, DP (P) 44 of 20 February 1939, Appendix I, paragraph 315.

revealing than the other sources about what she would do in that eventuality. We have already seen that in April 1939, when she invaded Albania, there was, if not a complete lack of notice, at least no sign of her intentions in any of the cyphers the British were reading.* It had to be assumed that there would again be no warning if and when she made another move.

In the event, Italy's stance during the crisis of September 1939 was reassuring, and an agreement between Great Britain and Italy to exchange information about their major military movements[27] ushered in something of a détente between the two countries. But uncertainty as to whether and when Italy would enter the war revived in the spring of 1940. This was not because British intelligence got wind of the fact that Mussolini was then moving towards a decision. At the Brenner meeting on 18 March he told Hitler that he would be ready in three or four months,[28] and on 31 March he outlined his strategic plans to the Italian Chiefs of Staff,[29] but no reports of his statements on these occasions found their way into the intelligence summaries circulating in Whitehall. What first caused anxiety was evidence of unusual Italian movements. By the end of February it was known that the Italian Army in Libya had been brought close to full war establishment.[30] A further large contingent arrived there on 19 March.[31] By the end of March information about Italian naval dispositions had led the C-in-C Mediterranean to begin negotiations with the Admiralty for the reinforcement of the Mediterranean Fleet.[32] All this evidence was being obtained from Sigint. The intelligence résumés reaching the Chiefs of Staff at this time show that it was plentiful and detailed; it permitted a close watch to be kept, for example, on the movements of individual squadrons of the Italian Fleet. It was by no means conclusive, however, and it was not detailed intelligence so much as the shock of the German attack on Norway that made the anxiety about Italy acute.

Reports from other sources than Sigint – from agents and visitors to Italy – had carried rumours since the end of March that Italian moves were imminent.[33] After the invasion of Norway, with its revelation of German efficiency and Allied unpreparedness, such rumours multiplied. They also began to find their way into the diplomatic reports. These had previously contained repeated assertions from a variety of missions that Italy would in no circumstances

---

* See Chapter 2, p 84.

27. Playfair, op cit, Vol I, p 47.
28. Butler, op cit, Vol II, p 296.
29. Playfair, op cit, Vol I, p 89.
30. CAB 80/8, COS (40) 262 (COS Résumé, No 27), paragraph 26.
31. ADM 186/800, p 13.
32. ibid, p 14.
33. Loc cit.

go to war. Now they conveyed warnings that Italy would enter the war shortly. In such a context the rumours could not be ignored: as was revealed by the decrypt of his message of 30 April, the Italian Ambassador was advising Rome that 'responsible British circles thought that the outcome in Norway would influence the Italian decision to enter the war'.[34] On 18 April the Admiralty's OIC started a daily Italian situation report. On 27 April the Admiralty decided that the situation was serious enough to justify precautionary measures, including partial closing of the Mediterranean. On 4 May the C-in-C Mediterranean, accompanied by the Mediterranean OIC, left Malta for Alexandria. At this juncture, also, steps were taken to repeat the special operations for photographic reconnaissance of the Mediterranean which had been adopted during June 1939.* After discussions between the PDU and the Deuxième Bureau at the beginning of May, a single Spitfire was transferred from No 212 Squadron to Le Luc near Toulon and between 12 and 14 May it photographed all but one of the main ports in the Gulf of Genoa, the port of Bari, the Milan area and the approaches to the Franco-Italian border.[35]

By the time these flights began the alarm had temporarily subsided. On 22 April an earlier warning to the effect that the Italian Air Force had been set to war readiness was cancelled.[36] On 5 May the OIC's situation report announced that Italian warship movements remained normal, and there had been no important developments in Italy's overseas territories. On 6 May the Foreign Secretary informed the War Cabinet that Mussolini's military advisers had dissuaded him on 17 April from entering the war on account of the state of the Army and the lack of armaments.[37] On 8 May the Cabinet rescinded the partial closure of the Mediterranean. But the Mediterranean was again closed on 16 May. Although it remained impossible to be sure that Italy would enter the war, the presumption that she would do so was now strong; and although the three Service intelligence departments informed the Chiefs of Staff on that day that her intervention 'might take place without warning',[38] in fact there was an accumulation of reliable Sigint indications that it was imminent.

On 19 May RAF HQ, Middle East, notified C-in-C Mediterranean and C-in-C East Indies that Italy had ordered the immediate mobilisation of her Army and Air Force in east Africa; and on 23 May the Chiefs of Staff received confirmation that this was a secret mobilisation and that it also applied to the Air Force in Libya.[39] On

---

* See Chapter 1, p 29.

34. ADM 223/82, OIC Daily Italian Sitrep, 30 April 1940.
35. AIR 41/6, pp 168–9.
36. CAB 80/10, COS (40) 314 (COS Résumé, No 35).
37. CAB 65/7, WM (40) 113 of 6 May.
38. CAB 80/11, COS (40) 362 of 16 May.
39. CAB 80/12, COS (40) 412 (COS Résumé, No 39), paragraphs 30, 55.

21 May an unusual cypher message, judged to be a warning, was sent from Rome to 15 Italian tankers in the Mediterranean.[40] On 5 June the Italian Navy formed a new cruiser squadron. On 7 June it was known that 17,000 army reinforcements had reached Libya since the end of May[41] and that 122 modern bombers had arrived in Sicily.[42] On 7 June, again, the Italian Fleet ceased to use plain language in its W/T traffic. These warnings were received from Italian Service decrypts. Others came from decrypts of Italian diplomatic and attaché traffic. On 22 May one of these disclosed that the Italian Foreign Ministry was instructing the London embassy to get young scholars in the United Kingdom to return to Italy by any means available. Beginning on 22 May several messages from Italian Service authorities in the Italian attaché cyphers announced that the call-up of personnel was necessary to ensure the functioning of units in the first month of war activity. By 3 June it had been learned that Italian consular officials in British colonies had been ordered to destroy their cyphers.[43] By then the indications were no longer confined to Sigint. There were diplomatic reports of Italian troop concentrations on the French and Yugoslav borders, of the evacuation of Rome, of defence preparations in the Dodecanese. Some of these were confirmed by photographic reconnaissance; after the first aircraft had been called away by more urgent work elsewhere, two Spitfires returned to Le Luc and between 28 May and 15 June completed the coverage of north-west Italy and photographed several areas further south.[44]

By the end of May, well before all these signs had built up, all three British Services in the Middle East were ready for war to break out at any moment, and in Whitehall, despite some uncertainty as to whether Italy's activities were being undertaken in order to put her in a position to attack or merely to threaten war, the JIC had decided that she intended war. On 24 May, in its first comprehensive attempt to assess Italy's intentions, the JIC reviewed the considerations that might keep Italy out of the war, and thought they provided a good argument for believing that Mussolini would be content with extreme pressure short of war or might at least temporarily postpone his entry. But it concluded that, on balance, war was at last likely.[45] On 29 May in a further paper it was again tempted by the thesis that Italy might be hoping to secure her aims without having to go to war, but it decided in the end that war was definitely intended.[46]

---

40. ADM 186/800, p 16.
41. ADM 223/89, Titterton, Report of Med Intelligence Centre, Appendix XI, Diary of Events, 7 June 1940.
42. ibid, 7 June.
43. ADM 223/82, OIC Daily Italian Sitrep, 3 June 1940.
44. AIR 41/6, p 170.
45. CAB 80/11, COS (40) 387 (JIC) of 24 May.
46. CAB 80/12, COS (40) 407 (JIC) of 29 May.

It was less easy to answer other questions. Would Italy remain on the defensive on the outbreak of war or adopt an offensive strategy? If she took the offensive where would she strike? Since Italy in fact planned no immediate offensive apart from IAF bombardment of Malta, the evidence, or at any rate the reliable Sigint evidence, contained no information on these points. But early Italian offensives could not be ruled out on the basis of negative evidence. In July 1939 the Sigint organisation had followed in detail an exercise off Derna in which the Italian Fleet had rehearsed with submarines and the IAF a plan designed to intercept the British Fleet in the eastern Mediterranean.[47] In August 1939 the NID had obtained from the French government a most secret document, purporting to be an Italian Admiralty directive, which listed various offensive operations – the systematic harassing of the enemy in every section of the Mediterranean; the severance of the eastern from the western Mediterranean; the isolation of Malta; attacks on the Suez Canal from Libya – as the principal objectives of the Italian Navy.[48] This document, together with its knowledge of Italy's numerical superiority at sea, undoubtedly influenced the JIC's first attempts to assess Italy's probable strategy. In a paper dated 19 April 1940 it concluded that Italy's most likely course would be an early offensive against the Allied fleets.[49] It still took this view on 29 May, though also admitting that a naval offensive might be combined with any one of a wide variety of other assaults – against Malta, Egypt, Crete, Corfu, Salonika, Yugoslavia, the Balearics, Corsica, Jibuti, or France.[50] At that point the C-in-C Mediterranean held the different view that Italy would in the first instance take no risks with her fleet,[51] and military intelligence at GHQ, ME did not believe that the Italian Army in Libya was ready to take the offensive.[52] But the Chiefs of Staff would not exclude the possibility of land offensives against Somaliland, southern France and Yugoslavia,[53] while RAF circles preferred the view that Italy's first move would be to reinforce the IAF in Libya and deliver a knock-out blow against the Delta and Malta.[54]

Uncertainty similarly prevailed until the end about the date on which Italy would declare war. On 24 May, when the JIC concluded that war must be expected, it was unable to say when it would come.[55] On 6 June, summarising the latest intelligence for the Chiefs of Staff, the three Service departments in Whitehall could still hazard no guess as

---

47. ADM 186/800, p 18; ADM 223/89, Appendix XI, 26–28 July 1939.
48. ADM 233/84.   49. JIC (40) 23 (S) of 19 April, Section 7.
50. CAB 80/12, COS (40) 407 (JIC) of 29 May.   51. ADM 186/800, p 20.
52. WO 169/18, GS Int GHQ ME, WRMS, 1 July 1940.
53. CAB 80/12, COS (40) 412 (COS Résumé, No 39), paragraph 35.
54. AIR 41/44, pp 3, 18–19, 21.
55. CAB 80/11, COS (40) 387 (JIC) of 24 May.

to the date.[56] It has been claimed that on 7 June the Czech Intelligence Service's reliable A-54 gave the night of 10–11 June as the date of Italy's entry but it is impossible to say whether, if Whitehall received this report, it attached any significance to it. On 4 June, however, the Admiralty had selected the days from 10 June to 20 June as the danger period. Later, on learning that Mussolini was to make a speech on 12 June, the Admiralty believed that war would follow on 13 June. But the C-in-C Mediterranean adhered to the Admiralty's earlier and broader estimate. At 0400 on 10 June, twelve-and-a-half hours before Ciano informed the British and French ambassadors that Italy would be at war from 11 June, the C-in-C Mediterranean ordered an anti-submarine sweep to leave Alexandria and attack submarines which attempted to leave their declared areas without escort.[57] As a result HMS *Decoy* attacked a submarine two hours before Ciano's declaration of war took effect.

□

In some ways – those in which it benefited from contact with an enemy – intelligence about Italy improved with her entry. The intelligence HQs in the Middle East made reasonably rapid progress in the exploitation of captured documents; their summaries show that much intelligence was obtained from these from an early date about enemy order of battle, tactical dispositions, airfields, equipment and defences. The same was true of the arrangements made for the interrogation of POWs. These had their teething troubles, but in August it was decided to set up a CSDIC(ME) on the model of CSDIC in the United Kingdom, and by December 1940 an interrogation centre capable of handling 60 POWs at a time had opened on an inter-Service basis near GHQ, ME for the collection of longer term information from selected POWs. Information of more immediate importance was obtained by posting officers from the centre to the forward divisions. As this could not be done in time for the British offensive of December 1940 officers from the United Kingdom were sent out at that time to do this work at advanced HQ.[58] The censorship organisation was even quicker off the mark.* This organisation, already in existence before the war, was expanded at the end of 1939 and placed under GHQ, ME. It at once extended its activities from

---

* Apart from the 'invaluable' MEIC, this was the only component of Middle East intelligence which Field Marshal Lord Wilson singled out for praise in his memoirs.[59]

56. CAB 80/12, COS (40) 435 (COS Résumé, No 40) paragraph 29.
57. ADM 186/800, p 21.
58. Mockler-Ferryman, op cit, pp 102, 106–108, 184–185.
59. Wilson, op cit, pp 22, 29.

the scanning of civilian and British Services' mail to the interception of mail from Italian territories and Italian POWs. Before long – so poor was the Italian sense of security – this type of interception was a principal source of information on Italy's order of battle. As early as the end of July 1940 captured private letters revealed much of the army order of battle in Cyrenaica.[60] Thereafter it was mainly with assistance from this source that those working on Italy's high-grade cyphers were able to keep in touch with the order of battle of the Italian Air Force and thus recover the ground they lost when, with the outbreak of hostilities, Italy changed her most important cyphers.

GC and CS went on reading the cyphers used by the Italian diplomatic service, and in some ways the value of this traffic increased. Soon after Italy's entry, for example, the Royal Navy cut the cable from Malaga to Genoa, forcing the Italian embassy in Madrid to put its communications on the air. At the same time, other Italian diplomatic posts greatly increased their use of wireless, especially the legations in the Balkans. But the information obtained was chiefly useful for the light it threw on Italy's economic transactions and espionage activities, and the trickle of intelligence it provided about her operational plans and strategic intentions was poor consolation for the fact that all her Service cyphers were now changed. A new Italian general Army cypher was introduced on 10 June, and somewhat later the Army cyphers in use in east Africa were also changed. Of the two Air Force high-grade systems, that used in the Mediterranean area was changed on 10 June, while the one in use in east Africa was changed in November. The Italian Navy was slower to act; on 29 June, moreover, the new general code book which it planned to introduce in July was captured, complete with recyphering tables, from the submarine *Uebi Scebeli*. By then, however, no less than ten Italian submarines had been sunk or captured since the beginning of war – and one of those captured had been pictured in tow in the British Press – and on 5 July the Italians introduced a separate cypher system for submarines, which had previously used the largely readable general code book. On 17 July they brought in new cypher tables for their surface fleet. On 1 October their most secret naval cypher was equipped with new tables. To make matters worse, all three Italian Services changed their lower grade codes and cyphers and, though these continued to be read, they became more difficult to break – not least because the Italians drastically reduced the use of plain language in their wireless communications.

At a time when Italy was expected to take the offensive with greatly superior forces, and when the operational value of Sigint would have been greater than ever before, these reverses came as a great shock to intelligence authorities long accustomed to receiving a steady supply

60. WO 169/18, GS Int GHQ ME, Intsum No 71, 30 July 1940.

of Italian Sigint. Less serious, but still disturbing, was the fact that the tightening of security in Italy on the outbreak of war had dealt a blow to the collection of overt intelligence there. Just as the Italian Services had been lax in their W/T and cypher discipline in peace-time, so Italian security in general had not been very effective, and a good deal of information had found its way out through the diplomatic corps and the attachés of France and the neutral states as well as of Great Britain herself. Furthermore, the other sources that might have provided some information about Italy's intentions, the SIS and air reconnaissance, were in no position to do so. We have seen already that SIS activities in Italian territories had been limited before the war, and that last-minute attempts to infiltrate agents and arrange stay-behind networks had been unsuccessful.* We may now add that although the SIS attached senior men to the Army staff at GHQ, ME in the early months of 1940, little had been achieved by the end of 1940 either by way of putting the SIS in the area on a war footing or in improving liaison with the Service intelligence authorities in the theatre. As for air reconnaissance, the theatre commanders were highly critical of the resources available to them, particularly for long-range work, during the first months.

A number of aircraft in the theatre could be equipped with cameras and were able to do some aerial photography while on normal reconnaissance duties. These included flying boats based on Alexandria and Gibraltar, and from the end of September – the first aircraft in the theatre that were suitable for PR – a few Glenn Martins (Marylands) in Malta. They were useful in several ways. Thus the unit at Gibraltar made its first photographic sortie over parts of Spain and the Spanish coast on 25 June and was thereafter able occasionally to reconnoitre the French Fleet. But there were not enough of them to meet the most pressing strategic needs – those for early knowledge of Italian Fleet movements, for close watch on the routes and the frequency of convoys sailing between Italy and Libya, and for coverage of preparations in Italian ports and at the Italian bases in Libya.[61] On account of the threat of invasion, on the other hand, few aircraft, and certainly no special PR unit, could be spared from the United Kingdom for the Mediterranean theatre, or for any overseas command, before the Air Ministry undertook the reorganisation of photographic reconnaissance in the RAF in the autumn of 1940.[†]

At that point, in September and October 1940, it was decided that No 2 PRU (PRU, ME), initially using Marylands, should be formed at HQ RAF, ME and that, in addition, the Marylands already at Malta

---

* See Chapter 2, p 51.
† See below, Chapter 9, p 278 et seq.

61. AIR 41/44, p 73; AIR 41/19, *The RAF in Maritime War*, Vol VI, pp 12, 48, 57, 63–9.

should be reinforced. But these decisions were not implemented by the end of the year. The aircraft allotted to No 2 PRU were not despatched from the United Kingdom until January 1941; even then they were lost at sea, and a second instalment was found to be unsatisfactory when it arrived in April.[62] At the end of 1940 and early in 1941, in view of these delays, stop-gap measures were adopted. As a result of Admiralty pressure for regular reconnaissance of north African ports, No 1 PRU in the United Kingdom took over two Marylands and operated them from Gibraltar as a detachment from the PRU.[63] In an attempt to supplement the Blenheims and Lysanders of RAF, ME, which were providing photographic reconnaissance for Wavell's desert offensive, three Hurricanes were converted for PR (for which they were not really suited) and sent out by the Takoradi route. On arrival in Egypt, however, these were converted back to fighters, the need for which was even greater.[64]

If the provision of PR aircraft proved to be difficult during 1940, the supply of skilled PR interpreters was even less satisfactory. Until No 1 PRU sent a detachment from the United Kingdom to Gibraltar at the beginning of 1941 the RAF had no trained interpreters overseas. And until GHQ, ME set up a small Army Air Photographic Interpretation Unit,* also early in 1941, the Army and the RAF in the Middle East had only one trained interpretation officer between them.[65]

□

Of the three Services the Navy, perhaps, most needed intelligence in the first phase of the war. Its main bases at Alexandria and Gibraltar were distant from the Italian Fleet. The Italian Fleet in fact abstained from offensive operations, but this was against the expectations of most people. When the Italian Fleet did move, moreover, a good intelligence service helped it at this stage to avoid encounters with the British forces; air reconnaissance and Sigint both provided it with information about British naval movements.[66] On the British side, on the other hand, the decline of intelligence was most complete in relation to the Italian Navy. Like the sources which had benefited from the outbreak of war – captured documents, POW, censorship – the diplomatic reporting system and Sigint, the sources which had suffered the most serious setbacks, told more about the Italian Army and Air Force than about the Fleet.

It is true that the level of naval intelligence remained good during the first few weeks after Italy's entry. Until 5 July – so long as Italian

---

* See Volume Two.

62. AIR 41/7, *Photographic Reconnaissance*, Vol II, p 59.
63. ibid, p 47.   64. AIR 41/44, p 73.
65. AIR 41/7, p 59; AIR 41/44, p 73.
66. Playfair, op cit, Vol I, pp 302–303.

submarines continued to use the general fleet code book – the Mediterranean OIC was able to identify Italian submarines and provide advance information about their patrol areas, as well as about their numbers and order of battle, and these facts played a large part in bringing about the destruction or capture of ten submarines by that date.[67] This blow to their morale does much to explain why so large a force – 100 submarines – achieved so little. The seizure of documents from the first of these captures, that of *Galileo Galilei* which was hunted, attacked and surrendered in the Red Sea on 19 June, produced further intelligence. It is not known whether she was located with the aid of decyphered messages; but her documents gave the sailing orders of four more of the eight submarines in that area, of which three others were sunk. They also contained cypher material on which a special section at the Mediterranean OIC, staffed from GC and CS, was able to work for three weeks.[68]

Intelligence about the Italian surface fleet was similarly not lacking to begin with. Within a few hours of Italy entering the war Admiral Cunningham left Alexandria for a sweep of the central Mediterranean with the object of attacking any enemy forces found and countering any Italian action against Malta. No enemy was encountered; but during the Fleet's return voyage the OIC at Alexandria received DF bearings revealing the presence of Italian units north of Derna, one of them the cruiser *Garibaldi*. A signal to the C-in-C was at once drafted. Unfortunately, owing to congestion in the W/T office the signal was sent off too late to precipitate what might well have been a successful interception. The incident was 'most regrettable', signalled the C-in-C, for the bearing showed *Garibaldi* to have been very close to his ships. Bad visibility prevented any aircraft sighting. In consequence of this episode arrangements were made for signals conveying DF bearings to have priority in the Fleet,[69] and these arrangements worked well during the first encounter between the Mediterranean Fleet and the Italian Navy, which took place off the Calabrian coast in the second week of July. In this engagement the C-in-C Mediterranean derived intelligence from signals in the Italian Fleet code and in plain language. Together with the fact that low-grade Sigint – the identification of call-signs and direction-finding – was also useful, this enabled him to establish the intention of the Italian C-in-C, which was to lure his opponent into a submarine and aircraft trap by waiting back off the Italian coast.*[70]

---

* It was during this engagement that C-in-C Mediterranean, on being shown the request of the Italian cruiser admiral to his C-in-C for permission to return to harbour, remarked: 'Reply: "approved" '.[71]

67. ADM 223/89. Section II.   68. ibid, Section III.
69. ADM 186/800, BR 1736 (49) (1), pp 23, 136.
70. ADM 186/796, BR 1736 (36) (6), p 22; ADM 223/89, Section III and Appendix IIIa; Playfair, op cit, Vol I, p 153.
71. ADM 223/89, Section III.

A very different situation prevailed, however, during the next fleet engagement, that between the Italian Fleet and the Gibraltar-based Force H off Cape Spartivento on 29 November. On that occasion Admiral Somerville's first evidence that the enemy was at sea came from aircraft sighting reports, and they were the first intelligence he had received about the whereabouts of the Italian Fleet for fifteen days.[72] And in the same month the slump in naval intelligence was revealed in another incident. The 7th Cruiser Squadron of the Mediterranean Fleet entered the Adriatic to attack the regular convoy from Italy to Albania. It had made contact and sunk four ships when it received a report from the Naval Attaché, Ankara that the Italian Fleet was about to sail to bombard Corfu. It broke off the action on the basis of this report, which was wholly without foundation.[73]

The main reason for the decline in naval intelligence was the change on the cryptanalytical front. The new Italian Army and Air Force book cyphers were recovered fairly quickly and, although they underwent further changes and were eventually to become unreadable, they were still read for long periods for some time.* But Italy's main naval book cyphers, which were the cyphers used by her fleet for most of its important communications, were never read again after July 1940 except for a few brief intervals as a result of captures after the middle of 1941. Whether or not an earlier and bigger effort at GC and CS would have been possible, or successful, is debatable. The fact is that after the end of July the black-out of Sigint from Italian naval communications was 'broken only by fitful gleams from the systems of the lower grades' and by GC and CS's first success against an Italian naval machine cypher. The Italians had used a version of the Enigma machine carelessly during the Spanish Civil War.† In 1940 they brought an improved version of it into use for the Navy, and it was this which was broken in September 1940. Unfortunately, it carried only one or two messages a day up to the summer of 1941, when it was withdrawn from naval use and confined to the traffic of the Italian SIS. During the early months of 1941 its few naval messages were to be invaluable: they contained especially good information about Italian submarines and it was they which provided the vital clue to Italian movements before the battle of Matapan.‡ But between September 1940 and the end of the year they vouchsafed little of interest, and operational intelligence about the Italian Navy was restricted to what little could be obtained either from low-grade Sigint or from air reconnaissance and the traditional look-out.

Low-grade Sigint made it possible to identify submarine call-signs

---

* See below, p 212 et seq.   † See Appendix 1.
‡ See below, Chapter 13, p 403 et seq.

72. ADM 199/392, Force H War Diary, pp 170–171, 205, 221; ADM 186/796, p 55n.
73. ADM 186/796.

and to establish the number of submarines on patrol, but rarely revealed submarine positions.[74] About submarine intentions it gave no information at all. Thus no warning was obtained either of the attack on Gibraltar by two midget submarines on 30 October 1940 – which, though unsuccessful, was the first use made of this weapon – or of the fact that the Italians had developed such craft. Against the Italian surface fleet low-grade Sigint was still less useful than against the more exposed submarines. Traffic analysis, virtually the only source of advance information about the Fleet's movements, 'was at best inadequate and on occasions led to quite false conclusions'. The Italians were also often successful at concealment. 'At most...W/T inference showed main units about to put to sea. This in itself was valuable when greatly outnumbered British forces were maintaining control of the Mediterranean...[but] there was little indication of the direction or location of a naval movement'. In general it was of little operational value unless backed by decrypts. In these circumstances the Mediterranean Fleet and Force H were reduced to relying on air and other sightings in their main tasks – protecting British convoys and seeking out the Italian Fleet – and of the extent to which the reconnaissance aircraft at their disposal were inadequate there had been many indications before the November episodes to which we have already referred. Between June and October the Mediterranean Fleet had made 16 sweeps in search of the enemy, but had sighted his ships only three times.

But if both admirals justifiably complained on this score, they found that in some of their operations photographic reconnaissance, though limited, could be turned to good use. Photographic reconnaissance provided the up-to-date information that was required before the numerous naval bombardments of the north African coast,[75] while the aircraft-carrier attacks made on naval targets in Italian harbours – as at Tobruk on 6 July 1940, Bomba on 22 August[76] and, still more important, Taranto on 11 November – depended entirely on this source for their success. The carrier attack on Taranto, though contemplated for a long time, was postponed from October to November and this delay allowed Malta's newly arrived Glenn Martin reconnaissance aircraft to take photographs of the harbour and the ships with which the attack was planned in detail. Last-minute photographs taken by these aircraft, and flown from Malta to HMS *Illustrious* while she was making for the flying-off position, materially altered the plan of the attack by revealing that the anchorage was now protected by a balloon barrage and the battleships by nets – and it was these photographs which ensured the success of the operation by

74. ADM 223/89, Section II.
75. AIR 41/44, p 113; ADM 186/800, pp 44, 70.
76. ADM 186/797, BR 1736 (38), pp iv, vi.

enabling most of the British aircraft to avoid the air defences.[77] Hardly less important, photographic reconnaissance alone made it possible after the attack for the Admiralty to reap the full strategic benefit by re-deploying some of the Mediterranean Fleet. The Italians sent to their Naval Attaché in Peking in one of the diplomatic cyphers a muted account of the damage done, and this was read by GC and CS. But the chief check on the many contradictory and inaccurate reports received from British diplomatic sources and the SIS was provided by the photographs of the damage taken by the Glenn Martins after the raid.

In one direction, however, air reconnaissance and naval sweeps proved to be just as inadequate as they were in the search for the Italian Fleet. Between June and December 1940 the Italian Fleet failed to gain any notable victory, and it sustained at Taranto one serious set-back, but it succeeded in its main strategic aim by passing 690,000 tons of shipping in fast convoy to Libya with less than 2 per cent losses.[78] Several factors contributed to this outcome. The Italian Navy's intelligence service enabled it to move the convoys when British forces were out of range.[79] This was all the easier because of the weakness of the Malta-based British striking forces. But this weakness, itself a consequence of pre-war British over-estimates of the Italian air threat to the island, was compounded by two other considerations: the lack of intelligence other than what could be obtained from reconnaissance, and the fact that reconnaissance, hampered by the existence of too many demands on too few aircraft and submarines, was unable to make up for other deficiencies. By the first week in October, when the Italian Army's advance to Sidi Barrani had made it a matter of great urgency that the convoys should be intercepted, only one had been sighted, and it was still not known whether they were using the inshore route via Tripoli or the direct route to Cyrenaica.[80] Had British operational intelligence been better, the few striking forces kept at Malta would have been more effective.

□

Against Italian air reconnaissance and the constant danger of Italian air attacks, British naval forces benefited from the fact that air intelligence suffered a less serious decline. The codes used by Italian aircraft for their sighting reports continued to be readable for much of the time. Signals transmitted by shadowing aircraft to indicate the position of British forces could be used to intercept the shadowing

---

77. Cunningham, op cit, pp 283–284; Playfair, op cit, Vol I, p 222; Roskill, op cit, Vol I, p 301; ADM 186/801, BR 1736 (49) (2), p 10.

78. Roskill, op cit, Vol I, p 307.

79. ADM 186/800, p 61.

80. ibid. p 115.

aircraft, or jammed to prevent the arrival of enemy bombers, or simulated in order to mislead the bombers.[81] More generally, regular enemy air activity charts compiled by the Mediterranean OIC from a variety of sources – Sigint, POW, sightings – showed the principal areas covered regularly by Italian reconnaissance and were used to guide the routeing of British convoy and naval movements.[82] But what chiefly distinguished the state of air intelligence from that of naval intelligence was the fact that within a month GC and CS broke into the new high-grade cypher introduced by the Italian Air Force for the Mediterranean area at the outbreak of war, and the RAF and Army authorities in the Middle East profited more than the Navy from this achievement.

Because of the inadequacy and insecurity of communications, GC and CS found it difficult to keep Cairo abreast of its progress against the Italian cyphers until special arrangements were made in September, and because the communications problem was compounded by the fact that a good deal of the Italian traffic was intercepted only in the Middle East, Cairo derived little benefit from GC and CS's decrypts until the same date. But GC and CS sent the new IAF keys out to the Middle East in August, and by the last week of that month, after some weeks of ignorance about what changes were taking place in the IAF order of battle in Libya and what reinforcements were arriving from Italy, HQ RAF, ME had accumulated enough material to enable it to identify all IAF units there. At the beginning of October the new order of battle worked out in August was confirmed in almost all details by a captured document.[83] On the eve of Italy's September offensive, however, HQ RAF, ME greatly exaggerated the IAF's strength in Libya. It estimated this to be 600 aircraft, an increase of 175 over the June figure, and it calculated from the numbers and types of reinforcements received since June that the IAF had particularly increased its superiority in fighters. In fact the number of serviceable bombers, fighters and ground attack aircraft was about 300.[84] This over-estimate was due partly to the inclusion of reconnaissance and transport aircraft but mainly, as in Whitehall's calculations of GAF strength, to exaggeration of the level of serviceability which the enemy could maintain. Even so, the new assessment was an improvement on the guesswork of June and July when, in the absence of any reliable evidence, RAF intelligence in the Middle East had accepted a report to the effect that the entire IAF had been transferred to Libya after the fall of France.[85]

---

81. ibid, pp 58, 62; ADM 223/89. Section I.
82. ADM 186/800, pp 58, 62; ADM 223/89, Section II and Appendix IX.
83. AIR 23/6767, HQ RAF, ME, Weekly Intsums, 26 August and 7 October 1940.
84. ibid, 17 October 1940; AIR 41/44, p 56; Playfair, op cit, Vol I, p 208.
85. WO 169/18, GS Int GHQ ME, WRMS, 15 July 1940; AIR 23/6767, HQ RAF, ME, Weekly Intsum No 1 of 21 June, and No 4 of 15 July.

On 20 September, a week after the beginning of Italy's advance in north Africa, the IAF cypher was changed again. But again it was quickly recovered, and by the time the British counter-offensive (*Compass*) was launched in December 1940 the British estimate of IAF strength was far more accurate. When the actual strength stood at 140 bombers and 191 fighters, the estimate was 300 combat aircraft, and it was based on a highly detailed reconstruction of the IAF order of battle.[86] The improvement was partly the result of the accumulation of Sigint information. But it was brought about chiefly by the better co-ordination of that information with battlefield photographic reconnaissance. The procedure by which the high-grade Sigint gave the identification of units and photographic reconnaissance then confirmed their locations and made it possible to count their aircraft – a procedure that was used to great advantage in all theatres later in the war – was developed in north Africa during these weeks between the Italian and the British offensives.

□

As well as profiting from air intelligence, at any rate at the strategic level, the Army authorities in the Middle East were better served than the other two Services by their field Sigint organisation. The Army's No 2 W/T Company at Sarafand had long experience with the Italian Army's medium and low-grade codes and cyphers. By September 1940, when No 2 Company moved its Italian section to Egypt, it had organised four sections for work in forward areas.

One of these went to Mersa Matruh in August and was able during Graziani's brief advance in the following month to obtain a fairly comprehensive picture of the Italian forces from its work on their cyphers. Helped by this experience, the forward section attached to Western Desert HQ during the British counter-offensive in December was even more useful. Nevertheless, despite the windfalls brought by field Sigint during the advance against the Italians, its recondite character and liability to interruption prevented it from being treated by operational commands on a par with regular, orthodox, non-Sigint sources. Rather, its products were treated as a bonus. This reacted on the non-Sigint sources in that their results could not yield their full value unless integrated with the depth of reliable information which it was Sigint's characteristic property to provide. At this stage of the war it had not yet become the practice of forward HQs systematically to record and collate Sigint evidence in order that at least some depth of information was immediately available to them. Thus intelligence, despite its occasional big bonuses, remained for the first years of the desert war 'the Cinderella of the Staff and information about the

---

86. AIR 41/44, Appendix XIV.

enemy was frequently treated as interesting rather than valuable'.[87] Despite the advent of better field Sigint and a better supply of high-grade German Sigint to the Middle East on a direct service from GC and CS* from March 1941, this attitude was to change only slowly. Partly because stricter security precautions were applied to German than to Italian Sigint, and partly because of the blunted impact of its fragmentary and often less than self-evident character, the commanders and the regular officers who held the senior intelligence posts at forward HQs could not quickly grasp the relevance and value of Sigint information. But if it was not until the summer of 1942 that intelligence came to be regarded as an integral part of the conduct of war, and that field Sigint came to be fully integrated with other intelligence sources at Army level and to be a major source of tactical information, the foundation for this belated development was laid by the pioneering work of the forward sections which worked in the desert from the autumn of 1940.

In their cryptanalytical work the forward units were backed up by No 2 W/T Company and, from November 1940, by the Army section of CBME,† which among other things did the same work as the forward units for the benefit of GS Int GHQ, ME in Cairo. But GS Int was chiefly concerned with operational intelligence at the strategic level. At this level, despite an initial period of 'increasing difficulties owing to changes of cyphers',[88] it was able to give good general warning of Italy's first land offensive, but was less successful, as was Whitehall, in foretelling the day of the attack.

British intelligence had an accurate knowledge of the strength of the Italian Army in north Africa, though not of its detailed dispositions, when Italy entered the war.[89] During June and July, when the change in the Italian Army cypher reduced it to reliance on air reconnaissance and on observation and the capture of documents by British troops, its knowledge of what was going on in Libya became very uncertain.[90] But during August GC and CS was making progress in breaking the new Italian Army cypher, and it became clear that Italy was preparing an advance from Libya. By the end of the first week of August the War Office informed the Chiefs of Staff that Italy's strength on the Egyptian border was sufficient to permit her to invade at any time.[91] On 23 August a directive from the Prime Minister to the C-in-C, ME insisted that 'a major invasion of Egypt must be expected at any time now'.[92] At that stage Cairo took a different view.

---

* See Appendix 13.   † See below, pp 219–220.

87. WO 208/3575, Williams *The Use of Ultra by the Army*, p 3.
88. WO 169/18, GSInt GHQ ME, War Diary, 27 June 1940.
89. Playfair, op cit, Vol I, pp 117–118.
90. WO 169/18, GS Int GHQ ME, Intsums Nos 38, 82; WRMS, 1 July and 12 August.
91. CAB 80/16, COS (40) 616 (COS Résumé, No 49), paragraph 19.
92. CAB 80/17, COS (40) 653 of 23 August.

The intelligence staff there believed that the Italian advance would be a limited one, to Sidi Barrani at the most, on account of supply difficulties.[93] On 25 August the three Cs-in-C reported to London on the basis of the latest reconnaissance: unless the enemy had concealed his preparations with remarkable skill, he could not be ready for several weeks.[94] This judgment settled the routeing of the armoured and other reinforcements which, earlier in August, the War Cabinet had agreed to send to the Middle East from the United Kingdom. It had been agreed that some of the reinforcements would be sent through the Mediterranean if, by 26 August, the Italian advance seemed imminent. They were now sent round the Cape.

Thereafter neither London nor Cairo gave warning of the beginning of the Italian advance on 13 September. In London the intelligence summaries for the Chiefs of Staff noted the despatch of IAF reinforcements to Libya and the eastward movement of one Italian division, but continued to refer to the 'delayed offensive'.[95] From Cairo as late as 12 September Wavell reported to the War Cabinet that he was not expecting a big offensive for a few more days, perhaps not till 20 September,[96] though both GS Int (since 9 September)[97] and the Desert Force HQ (since 10 September)[98] had been noticing evidence of much increased Italian Army activity.

The failure of Cairo and London to give last-minute notice must be put down to several factors. Hesitation on the part of the Italians was one source of confusion: throughout August Graziani had dragged out his preparations and he remained reluctant to move even when Mussolini ordered him to do so on 9 September. At the same time the Italians were naturally taking pains to conceal their intentions. On this occasion, to illustrate how this made it difficult to give precise tactical notice even of an expected enemy initiative, there was no increase in Italian Army W/T traffic and, as this was contrary to precedent in the experience of the British intelligence staffs, they may have been misled by their conviction that such an increase would take place. Even so, it is clear after the event that the available evidence about the Italian Army would have assumed greater significance if it had been more carefully co-ordinated with other signs, particularly of increasing preparations by the IAF. In London, however, the need for an inter-Service body to review evidence from all sources as a matter of routine had as yet been recognised only to the extent of establishing the Combined Intelligence Committee (CIC) in connec-

93. WO 169/18, GS Int GHQ ME, WRMS, 22 July, 19 August, 26 August, 28 August, 16 September 1940.

94. Churchill, op cit, Vol II, pp 396, 417.

95. CAB 80/18, COS (40) 716 (COS Résumé, No 53), paragraph 56, COS (40) 740 (COS Résumé, No 54) paragraph 23.

96. CAB 65/9, WM (40) 249 of 13 September.

97. WO 169/18, GS Int GHQ ME, WRMS, 9 September; Intsum, 11 September 1940.

98. WO 169/53, HQ Western Desert Force, Intsums 70–73, 11–14 September 1940.

tion with the invasion danger.* In the Middle East, similarly, all intelligence appreciation was still done on a single-Service basis except at the MEIC which was increasingly confined to the collection and co-ordination of non-operational political and economic information. In the absence of a body responsible for strategic appreciation on an inter-Service basis GS Int GHQ, ME regarded itself as being responsible for appraising not only the intentions of the armies that opposed it but also the strategic situation in the theatre in all its aspects, as did the Intelligence Branch in the War Office in relation to all theatres, and its daily and weekly summaries were less single-Service minded than those of the other intelligence HQs. But its co-ordination of army intelligence with intelligence received from the other Service HQs remained spasmodic, and it was most likely to break down when it was most urgently called for.

As had been expected by GS Int the Italian advance stopped when it reached Sidi Barrani on 16 September. Chronic uncertainty as to whether and when it would be resumed – an uncertainty that was not reduced by the fact that air reconnaissance and Sigint were throwing more and more light on Italy's strength and order of battle in Libya[99] – was now compounded by mounting evidence of Italy's preparation for an attack on Greece. The possibility of an Italian campaign against Greece or Yugoslavia, or against both, a possibility that had been canvassed in London and Cairo since Italy's entry into the war,[100] had been much discussed since the middle of August, when a submarine, presumed to be Italian, sank a Greek cruiser off Tinos and fired torpedoes into the harbour. The incident precipitated Greek enquiries as to what assistance Great Britain would provide if Greece were attacked and, in London, stimulated the first paper on the subject from the JIC. This concluded that an Italian invasion was likely if Greece resisted Italian pressure for permission to make use of Crete and other islands; it also forecast that the invasion would come before the expected Italian thrust from Libya.[101] In fact Mussolini was being advised at that time that the five Italian divisions in Albania were insufficient, and he did not decide on the move until October, by which time he was pressing Graziani to push on to Mersa Matruh to divert British attention from the invasion of Greece.

Perhaps because it contained no positive evidence in support of its

---

* See Chapter 5, p 169.

99. WO 169/53, HQ Western Desert Force, Intsums 83, 86, 88 of 24, 28 and 30 September 1940; WO 169/19, GS Int GHQ ME, Intsum of 8 October 1940, DDMI, GS Int GHQ ME, 31 October, GS Int GHQ ME to War Office, 5 November and GS Int GHQ ME, WRMS, 25 November 1940; CAB 80/21, COS (40) 890 (COS Résumé, No 61) paragraph 30; CAB 80/22, COS (40) 915 (COS Résumé, No 62) paragraph 62; Playfair, op cit, Vol I, pp 258–259.

100. CAB 80/12, COS (40) 412 (COS Résumé, No 39) paragraph 35; WO 169/18, GS Int GHQ ME, Instums 28 May and 17 June 1940 and GS Int GHQ ME, WRMS, 24 June.

101. CAB 80/17, COS (40) 656 (JIC), 23 August 1940.

conclusion, the JIC report was ignored by the Chiefs of Staff. Fortified by the fact that the Foreign Office did not yet expect Italy to move against Greece,[102] they preferred the view that Italian pressure on Greece was bluff, aimed perhaps at diverting attention from Graziani's preparations in north Africa.[103] But from early in September the intelligence authorities in London and Cairo made it abundantly clear that Italy was preparing a Greek campaign. On 2 September GS Int GHQ, ME correctly reported the despatch of troop reinforcements to Albania,[104] and by the end of September, when it was known that these reinforcements amounted to three divisions and that the Greeks expected the attack at any time,[105] GS Int was confident that it was imminent, though unable to suggest a date.[106] On 14 October RAF Intelligence HQ, ME first noted the despatch of air reinforcements to Albania.[107] Some of this information was coming from the SIS and various IAF codes and cyphers provided details about the units and the personnel that were being transferred. In Whitehall the intelligence branches kept the Chiefs of Staff informed of these developments.[108] On 22 October the Chiefs of Staff instructed C-in-C ME to hold forces in readiness to occupy Crete.

The timing of this decision was good. Mussolini finally decided on the Greek move on 13 October; on 15 October he selected 26 October as the date for the attack; and the attack began in the early hours of 28 October. It is true that intelligence authorities had not yet hazarded any forecast of the date. Nor did they do so when last-minute information was received. This came from a variety of sources. On 23 October the British embassy in Washington reported that, according to information from Rome, the attack was due on 25 October.[109] On 27 October the Malta intercept station reported greatly increased Italian W/T traffic with Albania.[110] On 28 October at 0558, at about the time the Italians moved, the Chief of Intelligence Staff (COIS) Mediterranean announced by telegram that the attack was about to start.[111] In this last case the source of the information cannot now be traced. It is impossible, also, to say whether there were other clues that went unnoticed. But the fact that such as were noticed were quickly reported suggests that, while it is strictly true that the date of the attack was not foreseen, neither the intelligence nor the operational

---

102. Woodward, op cit, Vol I, p 509.
103. CAB 79/6, COS (40) 278th Meeting, 23 August.
104. WO 169/18, GS Int GHQ, ME, WRMS, 2 September 1940.
105. Playfair, op cit, Vol I, p 224.
106. WO 169/18, GS Int GHQ, Intsum, 23 September 1940.
107. AIR 23/6767, HQ RAF, ME, Weekly Intsums, 14 and 28 October 1940.
108. eg CAB 80/19. COS (40) 783 (COS Résumé, No 56) paragraph 29; CAB 80/10, COS (40) 820 (COS Résumé, No 58) paragraph 31 and COS (40) 840 (COS Résumé, No 59) paragraph 25.
109. CAB 79/7, COS (40) 357th Meeting, 23 October; ADM 186/800, p 92.
110. Wm 169/19, GS Int GHQ ME, Intsum, 27 October.
111. ADM 223/89, Appendix XI, 28 October 1940.

authorities were taken by surprise, as they had been by the first Italian advance in September.

□

If the intelligence bodies were thus becoming more efficient in assessing the available evidence, and in bringing it to the notice of the operational authorities, this was not because they had been persuaded of the need, either in Whitehall or in the Middle East, for a single committee that would undertake regular appreciations on the basis of all sources, and for all the Services, on the lines adopted for the CIC. That this was not the case – that, on the contrary, the improvement that had taken place by October resulted only from the better supply of evidence and particularly, despite changes in the Italian cyphers, of Italian Army and Air Force Sigint – was shown when the conflict between GC and CS and the Middle East intelligence staffs came to a head in November.

As we have seen,* this was a conflict about the arrangements that should be made for producing or procuring Sigint, rather than for interpreting and using the product. Though there were other issues, like complaints from the Middle East at the delays involved in the system by which GC and CS's decrypts were despatched to the Whitehall intelligence departments for onward transmission to the theatre, these were subsidiary to the main bones of contention, which were, first, how much cryptanalysis should be done at GC and CS and how much in Cairo and, secondly, whether GC and CS was devoting to the Italian cyphers as much effort as it should. GC and CS emphasised that the cypher changes that had taken place since the entry of Italy into the war necessitated the concentration of high-grade cryptanalysis in the United Kingdom, and used its considerable success against the new cyphers to justify its position. The Middle East intelligence authorities, on the other hand, stressing the losses that had been inflicted on them by the cypher changes, became more and more convinced that the new cyphers would be broken with less delay and their product used with more effect if the main cryptanalytical effort was moved to the Middle East and undertaken within their separate Service intelligence organisations. And during October they prevailed on the Cs-in-C in the Middle East to demand London's agreement to this solution: the transfer of the work from GC and CS to Cairo.

On 31 October the Chiefs of Staff rejected this request. More than that, they at last insisted on the establishment at the RAF station in Helipolis of a Combined Bureau Middle East (CBME) and defined the functions of the Bureau and GC and CS in such a way as to preserve GC and CS's control of cryptanalysis. The Bureau, administered by the Army, was to be composed of the cryptanalytical sections of the

---

* See above, p 195 et seq.

separate Service intelligence staffs in Egypt, together with the cryptanalysts who had been sent out from GC and CS in July and August. GC and CS was to remain responsible for the basic research and the initial attack on the high-grade Italian cyphers, while the Bureau was to work on lesser cyphers and, with the aid of GC and CS's results, to be responsible for exploiting readable high-grade cyphers for the benefit of the Service intelligence staffs in the theatre. There was to be a direct communications link between GC and CS and the Bureau on which the Head of the Bureau could raise technical problems with GC and CS but was not to challenge its policy decisions.

The Chiefs of Staff took these decisions on the advice of the Directors of Intelligence in the Whitehall Service departments. Those departments had hitherto supported the resistance of the Middle East commands to a Combined Bureau. But they now had powerful reasons for supporting GC and CS against the wish of the commands to control the work on Italian cyphers – and thus for accepting GC and CS's claim that in the Middle East, as in the United Kingdom, cryptanalysis should be concentrated in a single bureau. For one thing, they themselves needed Italian Sigint for the Middle East as much as did the Middle East commands, if not quite so urgently. For another, as GC and CS pointed out, the Middle East was not the only area in which the Italian forces might operate. Not less important, the time was fast approaching when German forces might be operating in the Mediterranean and north Africa, and while it was arguable that the Italian high-grade book cyphers could be handled in the Middle East as efficiently as at GC and CS, there was no question that work on the machine cyphers of the German forces was beyond the resources and the experience of the cryptanalysts in the Middle East. It demanded the concentration of effort at one place, and that place must be in the United Kingdom. This point was reinforced in September 1940 when GC and CS first broke an Italian machine cypher,* and this success in its turn lent added weight to the argument that the basic work on different cyphers should not be dispersed – that it was impossible to say when progress with one cypher might not be the key to success with another.

For all these reasons a recurring struggle – the struggle between the principle of concentrating as far as possible in one place the production of Sigint, and especially the processes connected with high-grade cryptanalysis, and the policy of dispersing those processes in order that they might be carried out in close proximity to the intelligence staffs who were responsible for judging the significance of the product and to the operational authorities who depended on the judgment of those staffs – was again settled in favour of the principle of concentration. As the Service departments in the United

* See above, p 210.

Kingdom had yielded their claims to those of GC and CS, however reluctantly, with the approach of war with Germany, so now they conceded that the Service intelligence staffs in the Middle East must accept in the shape of CBME a miniature version of GC and CS which would also be an out-post of GC and CS under GC and CS's policy control; and the W Committee in Cairo reluctantly accepted their decision on 13 November. But just as the Whitehall intelligence directorates, when yielding the control of cryptanalysis and the management of interception to GC and CS, had insisted all the more vigorously on their right and their need to remain responsible for interpreting and appreciating the products of Sigint for their own Services, so the intelligence staffs at the Middle East commands, after bowing with great reluctance to the decision to set it up, remained determined to limit CBME strictly to cryptanalytical work.

In terms of the relations between GC and CS and CBME the arrangements made in November 1940 worked out somewhat less tidily than had been expected. In practice CBME comprised only an Army and an RAF section, as a result of the failure of GC and CS to break into the new Italian naval book cyphers and the continued concentration in Alexandria of such other naval Sigint as was done in the Mediterranean. In practice, again, these sections did not leave all basic research to GC and CS: as we shall see, it was they who were mainly responsible for recovering the IAF high-grade cypher in east Africa when this was changed in November 1940.* On the whole, however, except that GC and CS and the CBME were often to criticise each other for failing to interchange captured code and cypher documents, recrimination between the Middle East and GC and CS about the problems connected with the procurement of Sigint now came to an end. But it was otherwise in terms of relations between CBME and the Army and RAF intelligence staffs in Cairo. These were long to be bedevilled by the determination of the two Services to resist encroachment by CBME upon their individual control of their own intelligence components – a determination which gave rise to pro-longed demarcation disputes concerning security, the exploitation of low-grade Sigint and the allocation of interception priorities. Nor was this issue the only factor which prevented CBME from developing, as some hoped that it might do, into a full-blown inter-Service Sigint centre which both produced and appreciated Sigint for all the Middle East commands. If the Service intelligence HQs were anxious to restrict the CBME to cryptanalysis, they were also insistent that the other Sigint processes – interception, the exploitation of low-grade Sigint and the interpretation of its product – should continue to be carried out on a single-Service basis under their own control in close proximity to their own operational commands. This was soon to lead to further strife.

---

* See below, Chapter 12, p 380.

CHAPTER 7

Intelligence on the German Economy, September 1939 to the Autumn of 1940

UNDER WAR conditions economic intelligence served two main purposes. One was to provide support for British economic warfare operations – the blockade of Germany's external trade and the negotiation of agreements designed to limit her economic relations with neutral states – by activities which extended from the compilation of information on the origins and destinations of goods down to detailed case work on individuals and firms involved in trade with Germany and in conflict with the British economic warfare system. The other purpose was to study the economic condition of Germany in order to assess not only the impact on her of Allied economic measures but also the significance of the economic factor in her military capabilities and intentions. It called for the compilation of factual information about current performance in particular sectors of the German economy – the manufacture of war equipment; the supplies of food, fuel, materials and manpower; German economic policy; the operation of the economic system; trends in the size and distribution of the gross national product. It also involved attempts to forecast the enemy's future economic performance, a task of great complexity and one in which there was much scope for uncertainty and error given the absence of proven methods in economic analysis and forecasting.

The Ministry of Economic Warfare accordingly divided its Intelligence Department into the Blockade Branch and, to use its ultimate title, the Enemy Branch. And in the war conditions of late 1939 and early 1940 it gave priority in staff and resources to the establishment of the Blockade Branch, to enable it to handle the flow of statistics, statutory listing and information on commodities that supported the day-to-day actions of MEW departments on prize, foreign relations and other current issues of the blockade system. The Enemy Branch of the MEW Intelligence Department, which had absorbed the pre-war Industrial Intelligence Centre (IIC), grew much more slowly. Demands for intelligence on the German economy were less insistent than demands for blockade intelligence until Germany's victories in western Europe in May–June 1940 elevated hopes and beliefs about her future economic performance to front rank in British strategic thinking.

□

The Blockade Branch, fully developed by the summer of 1940, was in general effective throughout the rest of the war. Its objectives were reasonably limited and its work more manageable than that of the Enemy Branch. The problems involved and the effort deployed were nevertheless considerable.

The task of watching the conduct of consignors and consignees in neutral states was a delicate one, having something of the character of police or security work, and information from many different sources had to be collated and interpreted. Official trade and other statistics published by the neutral states (which, in the circumstances, could not be uncritically accepted); censored mail, cable traffic and telephone conversations; intercepted neutral mail, reports from British diplomatic missions and consulates, from the French Ministère du Blocus, from private firms and from the examination of ships detained at Kirkwall and other control ports – these sources provided a very large flow of raw intelligence material. SIS posts in neutral states were briefed to assist in the collection of information; they reported on suspect ships and firms, oil cargoes passing the Dardanelles, barge and rail traffic between Belgium, Holland and Germany. With the coming into force of the cable censorship organisation in September 1939, the small unit set up by GC and CS in 1938 to supply the IIC with foreign commercial intercepts began to provide MEW with a large new input of material. Shortly after the outbreak of war the intake of this section, mainly in plain language or in public commercial codes, rose to between 6,000 and 8,000 telegrams a day, of which about 10 per cent was found to be worth circulating to MEW. MEW was also served by a network of War Trade Reporting Officers – consular officers or specially appointed agents in neutral countries. They sometimes acted as Naval Reporting Officers* but also had the responsibility for collecting statistics of exports to Germany and information on the movement of suspect contraband. This operation, conducted very often in the face of the hostility of neutral states in which they worked, contributed a substantial flow of intelligence.

The deployment of this extensive intelligence-collecting capacity produced so large a volume of blockade intelligence that the Blockade Intelligence Branch was not in a position until June 1940 to digest it all.[1] Much of the product, of course, contributed to the casework character of this type of intelligence and was, in detail, unremarkable, but part of it also contributed to the study of the German economy.

Italy was treated by the British government as a genuine neutral until the eve of Mussolini's declaration of war in June 1940. As early as December 1939, however, MEW knew that Germany hoped to use Italy as a base for transit trade and that some influential Italians were

---

* See Chapter 1, p 13.

1. W N Medlicott, *The Economic Blockade*, Vol I (1952) p 124.

prepared to acquiesce in the plan.[2] Italian arrangements for large-scale evasion of British contraband controls were discovered; the extent of Italian collusion with Germany could be judged from the volume of commercial wireless communications between the two countries.[3]

Economic relations between Germany and the USSR were obviously an important subject for MEW to study both for possible economic warfare operations and for their contribution to German economic capacity. Though they were a difficult target, MEW knew in the spring of 1940 that Germany was supplying the USSR with heavy machinery, machine tools and semi-manufactured goods.[4] In investigating the leak in the blockade through Vladivostock and Dairen (the Siberian Leak) MEW had access to good information on the capacity of the South Manchurian Railway for traffic to Germany.[5] It was known that by the time of the Russo-German trade agreement of February 1940 the Germans had formed an extensive organisation in the Far East, involving Japanese firms, to further trans-Siberian trade.[6] The supply to Germany of oil from the USSR and Romania and of chrome from Turkey was well covered by Sigint and SIS sources. The existence of a German blockade-breaking organisation in the Iberian peninsula (the Sofindus-Hisrowak organisation) was revealed by the decrypts of telegrams using a relatively simple commercial cypher machine. The foregoing examples will suffice to illustrate the work of the intelligence-collecting system which directly supported British blockade operations.

□

The Enemy Intelligence Branch was at first called Economic Warfare Intelligence (EWI), then, after re-organisation and expansion in June 1940, Enemy and Occupied Territories (EOT) and finally Enemy Branch in 1941. Its functions were described as follows:*[7]

'To collect, collate, appreciate and present to the Service and other departments concerned...all information about the enemy's economic strength, dispositions and intentions, which may be of use in attacking him; in particular –

(a) to estimate the enemy's capacity to keep his forces armed, equipped, provisioned and mobile;

(b) to collect economic information which throws light on his military intentions;

---

* For simplification the title 'Enemy Branch' is used throughout this chapter.

2. ibid, p 295.
3. ibid. p 289.
4. ibid, p 326.
5. ibid, p 404.
6. ibid, pp 404–405.
7. CAB/HIST/E/1/6/2; Paper on Enemy Branch in Economic Warfare Intelligence Policy and Planning.

(c) to identify the points at which the enemy's supplies, industry, transport and administration are most sensitive to attack, and to estimate the relative importance to him of these economic objectives;

(d) to estimate the limits which economic factors such as industrial capacity, manpower, transport, shipping, may impose on the enemy's ability to attack or to resist attack in different theatres of war;

(e) to estimate the value to the enemy of the resources of territories which he might occupy and to supply information for our own forces regarding the resources of territories which we might occupy;

(f) to appreciate the enemy's economic situation and plans and its influence on his strategy.'

The complexity of these tasks was such that, to carry them out effectively, MEW would have needed both reliable methods of economic forecasting and a great store of accurate information. As it was, the methods did not exist and the information was not forthcoming. About the flow of goods into Germany and about firms and individuals involved in efforts to break the blockade, the Blockade Branch could obtain intelligence outside Germany. But accurate information about the behaviour of the German economy could come only from inside the Reich, from sources reporting at first hand on the system as a whole or on its principal economic sectors; and it was even more difficult to acquire this type of intelligence under war conditions than it had been before the war and no prior arrangements had been made to do so.

As in pre-war days, expert advice and specialised knowledge were used for constructing estimates in the absence of good information. In the first year of the war, indeed, mainly because it was in a better position to call on industrial experts as consultants, MEW's Enemy Branch handled much more information than the IIC had obtained in the last years of peace. But by November 1940 it had to acknowledge that this source was out-dated.[8] Until the fall of France dependable neutral commentators provided an important source of basic material;[9] but official and secret contacts with this source were lost as a result of Germany's victories in the west. Nor did agents or Sigint make up for the deterioration in the service provided by these overt sources.

The outbreak of war severely curtailed the flow of economic intelligence supplied by SIS. SIS information on German tank production and other armaments manufacture had been voluminous before September 1939; by January 1940 (owing to the loss of sources in German undertakings) it had dried up.[10] By the spring of 1940 there

---

8. JIC (40) 371 of 9 November.
9. ibid.
10. WO 190/891, MI3(b) note of 8 January 1940.

was a serious lack of intelligence on the output and types of German land armaments and reserves of war material. In the same way, whereas SIS had made a significant contribution to British knowledge of the German aircraft industry before the war,* its reporting on German aircraft production after the outbreak of war was of little value.[11] As for Sigint, Germany's conquests in Europe caused a steep decline even in commercial telegraph and cable traffic, leading to a reduction in the staff of GC and CS Commercial Section from 100 to 25 in the summer of 1940 (later expanded to 50 for the rest of the war). Thereafter, the traffic on the German police radio networks threw some light on economic conditions of the German people, and indirect evidence was obtained from what the commercial traffic said about various aspects of the blockade, but otherwise Sigint supplied very little intelligence about the German economy at this stage.

Given the shortage of first-hand intelligence, there was naturally a tendency to carry over into war-time conditions assessments based on pre-war statistical data and to rely on 'common sense' conclusions. In particular it was assumed that Germany would now devote her economic strength to the largest output of war material of which she was capable. On this assumption early British intelligence estimates of German output of aircraft, tanks and U-boats were too high. In the case of U-boats the acquisition of reliable information during 1940 led to substantial corrections and brought the estimates of output close to reality. But no reliable evidence was obtained on the output of aircraft and tanks, and intelligence estimates here remained too high throughout the year.

British estimates of German military aircraft production, which had been approximately correct in July 1939, began to exceed actual output soon after the war began and the discrepancy increased during 1940. Despite the unsatisfactory state of collaboration between MEW and the Air Ministry,† a number of estimates of German aircraft output were agreed between them in the first months of war. Intelligence officers working on this problem had inherited a joint estimate of July 1939 by the IIC and the Air Ministry of an output of 725–750 military aircraft per month.[12] In September 1939 the figure agreed between MEW and the Air Ministry stood at 800 per month.[13] In December 1939 it was 975 per month.[14] By April 1940 it had risen to 1,000,[15] in June to 1,250.[16] In August it had settled at 1,200.[17] Based upon these

---

* See Chapter 2, p 55.   † See Chapter 3, p 101.

11. *Air Ministry Intelligence*, p 228.
12. CAB 4/30, CID 1569B of 24 July 1939.
13. AIR 8/463, Paper by Professor Lindemann comparing the RAF and the GAF, Feb 1941.
14. FO 837/437, MEW Intelligence Branch paper I 51/1 of 6 May 1940.
15. ibid.   16. JIC (40) 130 of 20 June.
17. AIR 8/470, MEW-Air Ministry paper L/50/Z of 26 August 1940.

estimates of monthly averages, total output for 1940 amounted approximately to 13,300 military aircraft, as against the output of 10,826 aircraft of all types given in official German statistics published after the war.*

In 1940 the Air Ministry, making independent calculations of German production based upon basic material different from that used by MEW, reached much higher figures of output than those formally agreed with MEW. A paper prepared for the Prime Minister on 'Present and Future Strength of the GAF', dated about 7 December 1940,[19] estimated that monthly output had been 1,100 military aircraft between 3 September 1939 and 1 April 1940, and 1,550 between 1 April and 1 December 1940. The paper went on to forecast 1,435 for the period 1 December 1940 to 1 April 1941, and 1,825 for 1 April to 1 July 1941. Upon these estimates of monthly averages it can be roughly calculated that the Air Ministry estimate for total output of military aircraft in 1940 amounted to 19,000, a total much higher than that based upon the average agreed between MEW and the Air Ministry in August 1940 and much above actual output given in the German official statistics.

A number of factors contributed to British over-estimates of German production of war planes in 1940. In the first place the supply of first-class intelligence material was sparse, especially after April 1940. It is significant that the agreed MEW-Air Ministry estimates after April used no detailed information on German factories. Although very little had been forthcoming since the beginning of the year, in April it was at least possible to obtain some information from neutral journalists who had visited German factories. From May onwards no material based upon even this kind of direct observation appears to have been available. Secondly, the calculations, based on Y material, that AI was making of the numbers of new aircraft delivered to the GAF proved to be misleading largely because AI was exaggerating the front-line strength of the GAF.† It is significant that the Air Ministry paper on 'Present and Future Strength of the GAF' contained the following: 'We estimate that to maintain the front establishment from 3 September 1939 to 1 April 1940 monthly rate of production *should have*‡ reached 1,600 aircraft of all types of which 1,100 *would be*‡

---

* The official German statistics of output for 1939 and 1940, reclassified by the United States Strategic Bombing Survey,[18] and published after the war were as follows –

	Fighters	Bombers	Transport	Trainers	Others	Total
1939	1,856	2,877	1,037	1,112	1,413	8,295
1940	3,106	3,997	763	1,328	1,632	10,826
1941	3,732	4,350	969	889	1,836	11,776

† See Chapter 9, pp 299–300.   ‡ Our italics.

18. US Strategic Bombing Survey, (Synoptic Volume), Appendix Table 102, p 277.
19. AIR 8/463; AIR 19/543.

operational types'.[20] Thirdly, an important pre-war assumption about German aircraft output now began to affect British estimates.

In 1938 and 1939 it was assumed that the number of working shifts in the German factories would be substantially increased in war-time.* The agreed MEW-Air Ministry estimate dated April 1940, though relying only upon an 'impression', nevertheless assumed that German aircraft factories were working two shifts in each 24 hours.[21] The French disagreed with the British on this point. In a note submitted to the Allied Military Committee on 25 May 1940[22] the French Air Staff believed, on the basis of information obtained in March and April from a very good source, that the large German aircraft factories (except those producing prototypes) were working only one 8-hour shift per 24 hours and that the rate of production, limited by a shortage of certain rare metals and insufficient finance, did not exceed 850–900 a month. In the French view maximum German output on the basis of two 10-hour shifts could not be reached during the summer of 1940. There is no sign that this French report affected British intelligence estimates of German aircraft production.

In justice to both MEW and Air Intelligence it must be recorded that the actual output of German aircraft in 1940 was less than that expected and called for by Hitler. Even within the framework of his own economic strategy Hitler was dissatisfied with the performance of the aircraft industry. On 13 July 1940, as part of the preparations for the invasion of Britain, he gave priority in war production to aircraft, mines, torpedoes, tanks and troop carriers. At that time the total monthly output of fighters and dive-bombers, which made up the bulk of the total monthly production of aircraft, was 642. The July directive demanded that it should be raised to 1,080. The directive was not fulfilled. Nor did the industry respond adequately to Hitler's demand on 28 September 1940 for additional aircraft for the campaign against Russia in 1941.[23] If Hitler's requirements had been met MEW-Air Ministry estimates of the total output of the aircraft industry would have been much nearer to reality. Discrepancy between British estimates and reality is partly to be explained by failures in the German aircraft industry itself.

Germany's output of tanks was even more difficult to assess than her aircraft production. The industry was widely dispersed over metal and engineering firms, details of which could not be collected. Intelligence material was very poor. No figures for output or stocks of tanks were inherited from reports prepared before the war for the CID by the

---

* See Chapter 2, p 61.

20. AIR 8/470, paper L/50/Z of 26 August 1940.
21. FO 837/437, paper I 51/1 of 6 May 1940.
22. WO 193/852, Allied Military Committee, DF No 174.
23. Milward, op cit, pp 38, 42.

War Office and the IIC.[24] The Enemy Branch of MEW Intelligence Department continued the study of tank production during 1940 but, lacking adequate factual knowledge about German output, was driven to guesswork based on information about British factories, floor space, the amount of steel available and manpower requirements.[25] The assumption that the production of war material would be sharply increased after the outbreak of war, combined with errors about the tank establishment of the armoured formations in the German Army, led the War Office to believe that the stock of tanks was rising sharply in the first six months of war. In March 1940 it was believed to be 5,800 (1,800 medium and 4,000 light).*[26] A total of 7–8,000 AFVs of all types was estimated for June 1940.[27] Even the lower figure of 7,000 implied a rate of output from German factories considerably in excess of 2,000 for the 10-months period September 1939–June 1940. The true figure was in fact 755.† Total production was 247 in 1939 and 1,458 (an average monthly output of 121) in 1940.

British estimates of U-boat production in the early stages of the war were too high, but in the course of the year 1940 were brought close to reality. NID estimates in September 1939[29] of the numbers of boats expected to be completed in 1940 were distorted by the same mistaken assumption that the Germans would make maximum use of their capacity that had led MEW and the Air Ministry astray in their estimates of aircraft production. NID estimated that by November 1939 87 boats would be completed, by January 1940 109, and by March 1940 129. The actual number of boats completed by the end of March 1940 was 67. In reaching its estimate the NID had assumed a monthly production of 10 boats, a figure which in the absence of reliable intelligence, including photographic reconnaissance, could not be checked. Analogy with the performance of the German yards in the First World War also helped to inflate the estimate.[30]

Before the estimates were reviewed in July 1940 documents

---

* Compare the estimates and actual figures for September 1939 in Chapter 2, p 62.

† Since the performance of German industry in responding to Hitler's requirements for tank production is of interest in relation to his abortive plans for the invasion of Britain and his instructions in September 1940 to prepare for the attack on Russia the actual monthly output figures as set out by the United States Strategic Bombing Survey are given below[28] –

	1939				1940											
	Sept	Oct	Nov	Dec	Jan	Feb	Mar	April	May	June	July	Aug	Sept	Oct	Nov	Dec
Output of tanks	51	77	57	62	66	70	78	68	116	109	140	153	145	170	138	205

24. CAB 4/29, CID 1507B of 18 Jan 1939; CAB 4/30, CID 1571B of 24 July 1939.
25. CAB/HIST/E/1/6/2; Memo by W A Burton, August 1945.
26. WO 190/891, No 44 of 23 March 1940.
27. ibid, No 113 of 17 June 1940.
28. US Strategic Bombing Survey, Synoptic Volume, Appendix 104.
29. ADM 233/84, NID 01449/39 of 29 September 1939.
30. Godfrey Memoirs Vol V, Chapter XXXIII, 'Truth, Reality and Publicity'

revealing the actual numbers of boats at sea and losses sustained by the U-boat fleet since September 1939 were recovered from U-49, sunk in Vaagsfjord on 15 April 1940. These documents proved that Germany had entered the war with 57 U-boats completed. Taking these documents into account NID sharply reduced its estimate of German output. With 57 as the starting figure and with the addition of an estimated 38 boats completed between 3 September 1939 and July 1940,[31] NID now reached a total of 95 boats completed. The actual number was 79.

On 25 November 1940 the figures were again revised.[32] It is clear that information obtained from prisoners captured from U-32 in October 1940 played a crucial part in this re-assessment. Their information, believed by NID to be 'reasonably correct' and 'roughly in accordance' with the number of U-boats then thought to be operating, indicated that 30 U-boats had been lost since the beginning of the war and that some 60–70 boats were now available. According to the prisoners there had been considerable delays in the construction programme. This information, in combination with an estimate of the capacity of the yards agreed with MEW, led NID to believe that 90 boats had been completed by 3 November 1940, only 33 having been added since the beginning of the war. It was, however, noted that the output of 22 in the second seven months (3 April to 3 November 1940) was double that produced in the first seven months (3 September 1939 to 3 April 1940) and, moreover, it was certain that an initial war programme of up to 215 boats had been envisaged.[33] The estimate in November of 90 boats completed was in fact slightly too low. The best available information on actual production indicates that by the beginning of November 1940 98 boats had been completed. The POW evidence of delays in construction may have exerted too much influence upon the estimate and have obscured the fact that by August 1940 U-boat construction was beginning to take a firm upward turn. NID had deduced that an expansion was taking place but POW intelligence from U-32 and also from the commander of U-31 appears to have caused an under-estimate of the rate of expansion.*

---

* Actual monthly figures, compiled from official statistics, published in the German Naval Handbook on U-boats[34] and used in the text above, are as follows –

	Pre-war Total	1939 Sept	Oct	Nov	Dec	1940 Jan	Feb	Mar	Apr	May	June	July	Aug	Sept	Oct	Nov	Dec
No of U-boats commissioned	57	1	–	2	3	1	1	2	3	3	3	3	5	7	7	6	9

31. ADM 233/84, NID 002673/40 of 18 July 1940.
32. ibid, NID 0449 of 25 November 1940.
33. loc cit
34. ADM 186/802, BR 305 (1).

In a paper written in 1947 the former DNI wrote 'We never guessed that so little effort was being put into naval construction during the first year'.[35] This self-criticism is justifiable for the period September 1939 to July 1940 but thereafter progressive scaling-down had brought the estimates very close to reality by November 1940.

□

As in establishing the level of German production of war equipment, intelligence was faced with difficulties in discerning trends in other sectors of the enemy economy, particularly in the supply of materials. The Enemy Branch of MEW Intelligence Department inherited in September 1939 the pre-war estimates that the supplies of basic materials to the German economy would be threatened after some 12–18 months.* These estimates were not challenged by developments in the military situation between September 1939 and May 1940, while the Enemy Branch was being slowly established and enlarged, but they were brought under scrutiny when Germany's victories in western Europe introduced a new economic situation. By April 1940, on the other hand, on the eve of the military campaigns in the west, although general estimates credited Germany with more war production than she was in fact achieving and with excessive consumption of scarce resources, MEW intelligence appreciations of the German supply situation under blockade were already cautious, sometimes even pessimistic.

A MEW situation report submitted to the War Cabinet[36] (covering the period November 1939 to January 1940) insisted that because of its dependence on foreign supplies the German economy was 'brittle' and lacked 'the hidden reserves of the 1914–1918 war'. It nevertheless concluded that 'no sign of serious change in the German supply position' was observable; in a number of directions Germany's economy was demonstrating great strength and her war potential was still increasing. In a report of April 1940[37] MEW noted the 'directional flexibility' of German foreign trade: 'as a weapon of war it can be moved almost as quickly to exploit the opportunities of time and place as any military force'. The same caution was voiced in an evidently authoritative internal MEW memorandum[38] entitled 'The Progress of the Economic Campaign: the Condition of the German Economy at the end of April 1940'.† Reflecting a point of view widely held in the

---

* See Chapter 2, p 65.
† The author of the memo has not been identified.

35. Godfrey Memoirs, loc cit.   36. CAB 68/4, WP (R) (40) 43 undated.
37. Quoted in Medlicott op cit, Vol I, p 48.
38. CAB/HIST/E/2/6/3/4.

Enemy Branch, the paper contains the following passage: 'Germany is not comfortable today, but the question for the Allies is, how comfortable is she likely to be in a year's time? The present outlook on the economic warfare front gives little reason to suppose that her discomfort will have greatly increased'. It went on to emphasise the effectiveness of counter-blockade measures prepared by the Germans before the war, and assessed the position in regard to German 'deficiencies' as discouraging. Mastery of the Scandinavian peninsula had given Germany an assured supply of high-grade iron ore and, supplemented by supplies coming via Siberia and Italy, adequate sources of non-ferrous metals; petroleum stocks were at a level which could be maintained by imports from the USSR and Romania; the supply of textiles was adequate; economic dominance of the Balkans and the help given by Japan had overcome at least part of the deficiency in animal fats. Synthetic production was beginning to relieve an acute shortage of rubber.

If none of the MEW assessments of the raw material position at this time could be described as excessively optimistic, the same was true of reports on the oil situation, which the pre-war assessments had correctly identified as a crucial sector of the German economy. The Lloyd Committee, in its reports to the Committee that was responsible under Lord Hankey for proposing measures to deprive the enemy of supplies,* treated the oil situation with caution after an initial burst of optimism. It based its early estimates upon material prepared before the war by the IIC which, largely on the basis of SIS reporting, had listed and described Germany's secret storage capacity[39] and accurately estimated stocks.[40] The Lloyd Committee was comparatively well supplied with current intelligence from the consular service, contraband control, SIS reports on oil freight crossing the German frontier, and material from GC and CS Commercial Section.[41] Its first report, issued in October 1939,[42] concluded that 'it would appear that in the spring of 1940 Germany's oil position will be critical, as she will by then have expended an amount equivalent to all her incoming supplies and two-thirds of her war reserves'. The second report, issued in March 1940, was much more restrained. It concluded that if German forces were to remain inactive for the next six months, and if Russian and Romanian imports were maintained, Germany should be able to maintain stocks above the critical level until the winter.[43] As the Hankey

---

* For the establishment of the Hankey and Lloyd Committees see Chapter 3, pp 102–103.

39. CAB 77/29, AO (46) 1 of 9 March 1946, quoting ICF/950 of 3 January 1938.
40. ibid, quoting ICF/284 of 1 June 1938 and ICF/294 of 1 June 1939.
41. CAB 66/3, WP (39) 134 of 20 November 1939.
42. CAB 66/2, WP (39) 90 of 16 October.
43. CAB 66/6, WP (40) 108 of 28 March.

Committee commented in its own third report: 'The German position is serious, but not so critical as we had hoped at the time of the Sub-Committee's first report...'[44]

□

Up to May 1940, for all that the intelligence bodies suffered from a lack of current information and still depended on many pre-war assumptions, they could study the German economy in a period of comparative calm. From May 1940, with the onset of the military crisis on the western front, they were forced to operate in a quite different atmosphere.

On 19 May the Defence Committee ordered an immediate examination of the means by which Great Britain would continue to prosecute the war if by 1 June France had collapsed and the French Fleet had passed into enemy hands. This called for a reappraisal of the German economic situation in conditions to which pre-war assumptions no longer applied. The Chiefs of Staff paper which fulfilled the Defence Committee's instruction was, however, to be drafted in the utmost secrecy and with great haste. A senior official of MEW was instructed to join in a personal capacity with the Directors of Plans in preparing the draft, and was specifically forbidden to consult anyone including his Minister.* The main object of the paper was to discern the broad lines of strategy by which Britain might survive the impending military disaster in western Europe and ultimately win the war. The resulting draft, 'British Strategy in a Certain Eventuality',[45] took the view that 'upon the economic factor depends our only hope of bringing about the downfall of Germany' and that 'Germany might still be defeated by economic pressure, by a combination of air attack on economic objectives in Germany and on German morale and the creation of widespread revolt in her conquered territories'. If the economic factor was to play this role two crucial assumptions had to be made. The first was that Britain could count on the full economic and financial support of the USA 'without which we do not consider we could continue the war with any chance of success'. The second was that with full Pan-American co-operation Britain should be able to control German deficiency commodities at source. It was assumed also that the Dutch, Belgian and French Empires would be at British disposal.

Upon these assumptions the economic annex to the paper concluded

---

* The official, at that time responsible for Enemy Branch in MEW, is of the opinion that an intelligence assessment of the effects of German occupation of new territory could not have been completed by MEW in less than three months.

44. ibid.
45. CAB 80/11, COS (40) 390 of 25 May.

that all overseas supplies could be denied to the enemy. There would be a shortage of food in German-occupied Europe if, as was expected, the 1940 harvest were proved to be poor. Germany's war potential must be expected to decline through a deficiency in oil; if synthetic plants could be destroyed German garrisons in Europe would be largely immobilised and German striking power cumulatively decreased. Finally, deprived of seaborne imports of certain essential non-ferrous metals, alloys, rubber and fibres, Germany would not be able to maintain a high rate of replacement of war equipment, the quality of the equipment must be expected to decline and a large part of the industrial plant of Europe would stand still.

The economic paragraphs of the 'Certain Eventuality' paper, originating from a senior official of MEW, had set out to provide not an objective economic analysis so much as some indication of the hopeful possibilities for British strategy. In the critical situation of the war with Germany the paper was not primarily an intelligence assessment but a search for means of winning the war. Even so, at the time the paper was drafted British economic intelligence assessments exaggerated the results that might be expected from economic warfare. According to MEW's information the food situation in Germany was deteriorating; the Lloyd Committee regarded the German oil position as being at least serious; Germany's territorial conquests were expected to increase pressures upon her resources of scarce materials. At the same time the paper had put economic warfare in the forefront of British strategy and it had done so in the belief, largely inherited from pre-war intelligence assessments, that the German economy was vulnerable. But with Poland subjugated, Czechoslovakia a German Protectorate, Norway and the principal industrial states of western Europe occupied, the USSR in trading relations with Germany and south-eastern Europe in fear of German might, the economic situation in Germany and German-occupied Europe had to be reappraised. By the summer of 1940 the assumptions upon which pre-war assessments had been based had been undermined.

The first attempt to re-assess the situation by the JIC, on which MEW was now represented, was undertaken in June. Its paper, 'The Present Situation in Germany',[46] although bearing some resemblance to the economic section of the paper on 'A Certain Eventuality', forecast economic developments in Germany with greater caution. It assumed that the German economy was fully mobilised for war. 'Germany has, for long, been throwing all her available resources of manpower, equipment and supplies into her supreme effort to defeat the Allies outright'. On the other hand: 'The losses incurred by all three branches of the German Fighting Services have not interfered

---

46. JIC (40) 130 of 20 June.

with her ability to carry on the war against any foreseeable combination of enemies, on any scale likely to be required, until the early autumn and probably until the end of the year'.

Assuming that Germany pursued her military, naval and air operations at their present intensity, and that with the wholehearted co-operation of the American continent it would be possible to maintain an effective British blockade of Germany's overseas trade, the JIC concluded that by the end of 1940 '*there may be** a progressive deterioration in the quality of German war equipment' and that the German war effort could be expected to be '*seriously affected*'* by the combined effects of a shortage of oil, a shortage of ferro-alloys and certain non-ferrous metals and textiles, and a further deterioration in the food situation. The JIC did not, however, think that any of these factors, 'except shortage of food, and possibly oil', were likely to bring about the military collapse of Germany in the spring of 1941. Moreover, if Germany were for any reason able to lessen her present military effort, 'her powers of resistance will, as far as we can see, be limited only by the food situation reacting on the civilian morale'. In more detail its report allowed that as the result of transferring labour from civil employment to the armament industries, a shortage of skilled labour 'necessitated very severe conditions of work', but did not forecast critical effects of labour shortage upon industrial production in the near future. 'The exhaustion of labour thus resulting is reducing the output per head and in some cases the total output. It is doubtful whether food supplies have, as yet, seriously affected output, at least in the heavy industries, nor does mobilisation seem to have been allowed to affect the production capacity of, at any rate, the key factories. While there is little evidence of any serious labour troubles, some significant concessions have had to be made in regard to working conditions'. 'If the total number of men in the armed forces is to be maintained at 7.6 million, the manpower available to maintain this force, to provide for essential civil needs and for minimum exports, should be forthcoming'. Communications in Germany had stood up well to the demands made upon them.

A survey by MEW of the German supply position was included in the JIC report. It identified serious shortages of industrial raw materials only in rubber, petroleum (where 'the position is serious') and textile fibres. 'There is no likelihood of any quantitative shortage of war stores as a whole. The most that can be hoped for is some falling off in quality if the war continues on the present scale'. As for food: 'The German people are at present fairly adequately, if monotonously, fed' but as from the beginning of the winter of 1940–41 the prospects indicated a marked change for the worse since the harvest would not be a good one, the supply of feeding stuffs had

---

* Our italics.

dwindled and skilled agricultural labour was scarce. All the occupied territories, a food liability for Germany, were facing the prospect of 'something approaching famine' and could make no contribution to Germany's food supplies.

In July the JIC issued a note by MEW on the 'Probable Supply Position of German Europe'[47] which compared the supplies of the principal commodities likely to be available up to June 1941 with consumption in the same area in the year 1938.* The note concluded that only in coal, iron and steel would supplies suffice to meet 1938 rates of consumption. It did not speculate on the methods by which Germany would deal with the impending shortages but it served to reinforce the impression that, in the short term at least, the newly acquired Lebensraum was a liability rather than an asset. By August, however, evidence was strong enough to modify the earlier forecast of food shortages. A MEW memorandum to the War Cabinet, dated 7 August 1940,[48] concluded: 'If the Germans distribute reserve, plus this year's harvest, equitably among the populations under their control, there will be, even if the harvests are very light, enough grain and potatoes to sustain life, with a margin of calories in hand, until the harvest of 1941 is gathered'. By mid-1940 specialised study of the German oil position by the Lloyd Committee similarly tended to show that shortages due to purely economic factors would arise less rapidly than formerly expected.†

Despite the modifications that were introduced in June and July into the intelligence assessments of the German economy, the Joint Planners in August extracted more optimistic conclusions from a survey presented to them by MEW.[49] After June 1941 they felt, when present stocks would have been exhausted, Germany's oil position would have become so serious that she must before then have attempted to end the war or make some move, such as driving the British Fleet from the eastern Mediterranean, to ensure seaborne supplies from Russia and Romania; and difficulties would increase in respect of food, transport and industrial employment. Germany would

---

*	Maximum Supplies plus net stocks (tons)	1938 Consumption (tons)
Petroleum	13.2 m	23.5 m
Rubber	140,000	300,000
Copper	580,000	850,000
Nickel	23,000	32,000
Chrome	170,000	380,000
Cotton	280,000	1,200,000
Wool	203,000	425,000

† See p 240 et seq.

47. JIC (40) 197 of 25 July.
48. CAB 67/8, WP (G) (40) 208 of 7 August.
49. CAB 80/16, COS (40) 647 (JP) of 21 August.

have to act quickly to achieve victory before shortages immobilised her armed forces. Her economy would be at a low ebb by the spring of 1941 and by the end of 1941 her oil position might well be disastrous.

The principal themes in the economic assessments undertaken in the summer of 1940 were re-examined in the Chiefs of Staff report on 'Future Strategy' issued on 4 September,[50] of which the Planners' August paper was the forerunner. This report, the most important general review of the German economic situation to appear in the later part of the year, pointed out that the security of the United Kingdom remained primary but recommended that: 'The wearing down of Germany by ever-increasing force of economic pressure should be the foundation of our strategy'.[51] 'It is not our policy to attempt to raise and land on the Continent an army comparable in size with that of Germany. We should aim, nevertheless, as soon as the action of the blockade and air offensive have secured conditions when numerically inferior forces can be employed with good chance of success, to re-establish a striking force on the Continent with which we can enter Germany and impose our terms'.[52] 'The general conclusion, therefore, is that our strategy during 1941 must be one of attrition... *But the general aim which should govern our strategy and determine the scope and rate of development of our expansion programmes should be to pass to the general offensive in all spheres and in all theatres with the utmost possible strength in the spring of 1942*'* [53]

While not giving a precise forecast of the date by which weakening economic conditions in Germany would permit the employment of numerically inferior British forces against the German Army, taken together these recommendations implied that an economic/military balance might be achieved as early as 1942. The paper recognised that several of the assumptions in the 'Certain Eventuality' paper had not yet been realised. It now seemed likely that earlier hopes of inducing the French colonies to continue to fight at Britain's side would be disappointed, the extent to which Britain could count upon American economic and financial support was still uncertain, and control of the supply of deficiency commodities at source had not yet been achieved. Nevertheless, the economic argument of the paper forecast that the deterioration of economic conditions in Germany and German-occupied Europe after June 1941 would be serious enough to affect the mobility of the German armed forces and to restrict German strategic flexibility.

Neither the JIC review of June 1940 nor the COS strategic paper of September foresaw any future *increase* in German economic

---

* Original italics.

50. CAB 80/17, COS (40) 683 of 4 September.
51. ibid, para 211.   52. ibid, para 214.
53. ibid, para 218.

strength. While the JIC review was cautious about the rate of inevitable economic *decline* in Germany, it held to an assumption that Germany's total war economic mobilisation would be in excess of available resources. The COS paper stated even more forcefully the underlying assumption of full mobilisation of the German economy; indeed, this argument was central to its economic forecast. 'The prediction of Germany's intentions regarding armaments is extremely difficult, but it is possible that she may now be content with a comparatively modest programme, except in aircraft and submarines. For this her present supplies of ferro-alloys, copper etc and even tin may prove sufficient, though a more ambitious armament programme will become increasingly difficult without loss of quality and dislocation of other European industries'.[54] 'The economic system of Greater Germany has produced spectacular results because it was based on an imposed discipline covering all activities down to individual trans-actions. This engendered a degree of compliance without which distribution would have proved impossible and the Nazi economy would have spontaneously collapsed.* Germany is now faced with the difficult problem of imposing her administrative system and economic discipline upon hostile populations, and particularly upon under-organised peasant communities'.[55] 'The time factor is most complex. Germany had a long start over the British Empire in war production and, consequently, she started the war vastly better prepared. Apart altogether from whether certain vital deficiencies may make it imperative for Germany to endeavour to finish the war quickly, it must be to her advantage to exploit her existing lead, which, when our war production gets into full swing in 1941, will be rapidly caught up. Her deficiencies in food, textiles and oil, which may prove disastrous to her in 1941, point to the conclusion that her courses of action may well be restricted either to an early attempt to secure victory before supplies run out, and while she has the military lead, or else to turn to the East to obtain additional supplies of oil and natural fibres, without which she can neither hope to establish self-sufficiency in Europe nor undertake major operations after the summer of 1941'.[56] 'Unless Germany can materially improve her position, particularly with regard to oil supplies, we believe that her economic condition will be at a low ebb by the spring of 1941'.[57]

□

---

* These two sentences strongly suggest that one of the main reasons for reference to the 'tautness' of the German economy so frequently described in MEW intelligence documents at this time was the belief that the economy was totally subjected to authoritarian planning. This belief was at variance with the facts, see Appendix 3.

54. ibid, para 41.   55. ibid, para 44.
56. ibid, para 47.   57. ibid, para 50, sub-para V.

The September paper on 'Future Strategy' registered the high-water mark of British expectations about the effects of economic restraints on the enemy's strategic position. By the end of 1940 its conclusions had been considerably modified. As a result of the calculations carried out by MEW in August* it was no longer expected that extreme shortages of food would develop in Germany and the occupied territories during 1940–1941. Further examination by the Lloyd Committee undermined belief in the probability of an early oil crisis. As for German stocks of other basic raw materials, MEW's revised estimates showed that the rate of decline was not so rapid as to bring about a major setback during 1941, least of all in the early part of the year.

The 'Future Strategy' paper considered Germany's oil stocks might be exhausted, and Germany's situation disastrous, by June 1941.† 'After this date...', it said, 'when present disposable stocks should be exhausted, her shortage of oil will become so serious that it seems inevitable that she must before then have attempted to end the war or at least make some move to improve her oil position. Apart from ending the war by the defeat of Great Britain, Germany can only improve her oil position to any material extent by driving our fleet from the Eastern Mediterranean, thus ensuring seaborne supplies from Romania and Russia'. From this the Chiefs of Staff concluded –

(a) that a combined German and Italian attack on Egypt during the next six months was likely;

(b) that in the spring of 1941 Germany would still be able to meet her estimated minimum requirements, though the situation would rapidly be approaching a danger point;

(c) that after midsummer the position would become precarious even if Germany had succeeded in obtaining all possible seaborne supplies from Romania and Russia;

(d) that by the end of 1941 Germany's oil position might well become disastrous and, therefore,

(e) that any steps that could be taken to deprive Germany of oil would be of the utmost importance in hastening her defeat.[58]

It is clear that, except as a means of hastening an economic process that was in any case leading to a danger point in the spring of 1941 and possibly German disaster by the end of the year, these conclusions did not rely on any effects that might be obtained by British bombing.

In June 1940, however, the Lloyd Committee had already taken a more sober view.[59] It had believed, it is true, that the balance of supply and consumption in Germany, dependent as it was upon imports from Russia and Romania, was precarious; that, while in the short term Italy

---

* See above, p 237.   † See above, p 239.

58. ibid, para 50 (i).   59. CAB 66/8, WP (40) 191 of 4 June.

could provide some assistance from her own stocks, she too was likely to run into deficit; and that the acquisition of conquered territories would greatly add to the long-term difficulties of maintaining the balance for enemy and enemy-occupied Europe as a whole.[60] On the other hand, it had refrained from giving a probable date for a breakdown in German oil supplies because the time during which shortages would develop seemed to have lengthened. In the first place the German stock position had been reinforced by a net addition of 600,000 tons of loot taken from Norway, Denmark, Holland, Belgium and northern France. Secondly, Germany's military successes in the west had so greatly enhanced her political power in eastern Europe that even the theoretical possibility of diverting Romanian supplies from Germany by British negotiation had ceased to exist.[61] Instead, the committee had stressed the vulnerability of Germany's oil installations to air attack. And the Hankey Committee, also in June, had followed suit, refraining from forecasting when the balance between supply and consumption might become critical for economic reasons alone, but advocating bombing attack on the installations. 'If sufficient damage can be done to German oil the war is won. No refinement of statistical estimates can dispose of this simple proposition'.[62]

In December 1940, after intensified study of the intelligence over the past three months, the Lloyd Committee, in the fifth and most influential of its reports, attempted to forecast the oil situation in German-occupied Europe for the period from October 1940 to September 1941.[63] It estimated consumption between October 1940 and September 1941 at 12,400,000 tons and, after deducting production by synthetic oil plants, output from crude oil and imports from Romania and Russia, calculated total stocks under German control as being 5,800,000 tons at 1 October 1940, 3,775,000 tons at 1 April 1941 and 3,400,000 tons at 1 October 1941. Assuming that a minimum of 2,500,000 tons would be locked up in the distribution system, it concluded that the tonnage available for immediate use would be 1,275,000 tons at 1 April 1941 and 900,000 tons at 1 October 1941.[64]

The Lloyd Committee's estimates for consumption* and stocks†

---

* The forecast consumption of 12,400,000 tons compares with the official German figure of 12,598,000 tons actual consumption for 1941, including consumption during fighting in Russia from June to December.[65]

† The Lloyd calculations of the total stocks in October 1940, April and October 1941 cannot be put against comparable German official figures which, however, indicate a decline in the stocks of aviation spirit, motor gasoline and diesel oil from 1,535,000 tons at the end of 1940 to 797,000 tons at the end of 1941. The Lloyd forecasts of the margin stocks of all types of oil at 1,275,000 tons on 1 April 1941 and

60. CAB 66/9, WP (40) 267 of 14 July.
61. CAB 66/8, WP (40) 191 of 4 June.   62. ibid.
63. CAB 66/14, WP (41) 2 of 2 January.   64. ibid.
65. CAB/HIST G/9/1/4; Paper on Economic Warfare, p 45.

were reasonably accurate. In both cases, however, the accuracy was fortuitous; Germany's invasion of Russia was not foreseen. The committee was also close to reality in its estimate of the German production of synthetic oil in 1940 and was right in foreseeing the increase in it in 1941.* But its estimates of total 'new supplies' (ie total addition to existing stocks) were only approximately correct,† and they incorporated errors in forecasting the level of imports from Romania and Russia.‡ Even so, it seemed clear that new supplies, from synthetic production and from imports, would be higher in the period April–September 1941 than in the period October 1940–March 1941 and that, as consumption would remain unchanged, consumption would exceed supply by less in the second period than in the first. Although total stocks would continue to decline, they would do so less rapidly in 1941 than they had done in 1940. The committee accordingly concluded that purely economic limitations would not reduce the Axis oil position to 'a breaking point' by October 1941, and it did not expect that oil shortage would restrict the military effort of Germany and Italy before that date unless special action was taken by the British government.

900,000 tons on 1 October 1941 were not greatly at variance with the official statistics, although in two respects the British estimate had gained advantages from errors. In the first place the estimate of the margin stock resulted by deducting 2,500,000 tons distribution minimum from gross stocks: German official figures, however, regarded the distribution at 800,000 tons in the first half of 1941 and 1,300,000 after the invasion of Russia.[66] In the second place German stocks were drawn upon by warfare in Russia at a rate not foreseen by the Lloyd Committee.

* The committee estimated that output per month of synthetic oil was 300,000 tons in the period July to September 1940, equivalent to an annual rate of 3,600,000 tons. The official German statistics show that the output in 1940 was 3,348,000 tons.[67] For the year October 1940 to October 1941 the committee forecast a total production of 6,050,000 tons, of which 4,550,000 tons would be synthetic oil and 1,500,000 tons refined from imported and domestic crude. Actual synthetic production for 1941 was 4,116,000 tons according to official German statistics[68] or 3,930,000 tons according to figures compiled by the British from German official sources.[69]

† Its estimated total of new supplies for October 1940–September 1941, at 10,000,000 tons, compares with German official estimates of 7,600,000 tons for 1940 and 10,000,000 tons for 1941.[70]

‡ The Lloyd Committee estimates of imports in the period October 1940–September 1941 somewhat exceeded the actual increase in supply from Romania. Total imports by Germany were 2,050,000 and 2,756,000 tons in 1940 and 1941.[71] The fifth Lloyd Report estimated 3,950,000 tons for October 1940–September 1941 from Romania and Russia. In 1940 Romania exported 1,930,000 tons to Germany, and 2,067,000 tons in 1941 to the Reich and the Wehrmacht in Russia,[72] a rate of flow below that forecast by the Lloyd Committee.

66. ibid.
67. US Strategic Bombing Survey, Synoptic Volume, Table 37.
68. ibid, Table 37.
69. Webster and Frankland, op cit, Vol IV (1961), Appendix 49, quoting CAB 77/29, AO (46) 1 of 9 March.
70. US Strategic Bombing Survey, Synoptic Volume, Table 37.
71. ibid, Table 37.
72. ibid, p 74.

Even more emphatically than in its report of June 1940, the Lloyd Committee in its fifth report thus stressed the vulnerability of Germany's oil installations to air attacks and other operations. 'The present statistical position within the Axis is not by any means satisfactory enough to relieve them from serious concern for the future. Particularly, there must be an ever-present fear that, even on the existing relatively inactive scale of land operations, a more concentrated air attack on their synthetic plants and a failure for any reason of their channels of supply from Romania and Russia, might cause a critical deterioration in their position'. It again received strong support from the Hankey Committee. Both the fifth report of the Lloyd Committee and the accompanying sixth report of the Hankey Committee argued forcefully that an air attack on German oil supplies, especially synthetic production, would be more decisive earlier than later. If not attacked from the air the German supply position would recover in certain respects. The Hankey Committee drew from the Lloyd Committee the conclusion that '...the time factor is of the greatest importance. The Germans are now engaged in completing new synthetic plants and in reorganising transport of oil from Romania with a view to greatly increasing their supplies. It is only by early action that we can obtain full value for our effort'.[73] The Chairman of the Lloyd Committee added a personal note to his committee's fifth Report: 'I know the difficulties, but it is worth repeating that the only way to get a quick death clinch on the whole enemy oil position is both to destroy the synthetic plants and to interrupt Romanian supplies'.

The force of the two committees' reports was that oil, as the single immediate weakness of the entire economy of the German military and civil system, justified exceptional and concentrated assault. Their argument, supported by belief in German dependence for high octane aviation fuel upon synthetic oil plants, the details of which were known and logged,[74] was to play an important part in giving oil targets primary place in the British bombing directive of January 1941.*[75]

While the investigations of the Lloyd Committee were discounting earlier expectations of a sharp deterioration in the German oil position, reconsideration by MEW of German stocks of other basic raw materials was showing by the end of 1940 that their rate of decline was not so rapid as previous forecasts had suggested. During the summer MEW had argued that the stock position was already limiting the expansion of German war production.† By the end of the year there

---

* For the place of oil targets in the RAF's strategic bombing offensive against Germany see Volume Two. † See above, p 236 et seq.

73. CAB 66/14, WP (41) 2 of 2 January.
74. CAB 66/8, WP (40) 191 of 4 June.
75. Webster and Frankland, op cit, Vol I, pp 158–162.

had been little improvement in its ability to make reliable stock calculations. As well as requiring information on supplies, it had to make estimates of the consumption of materials by industry in Germany and German-occupied Europe, and intelligence on industrial production was so defective that Enemy Branch could not establish statistical indices. In these circumstances, MEW calculations about the German stock situation in December 1940 were approximate only as to quantities and rates of change,* but the trends they pointed to were not in doubt, and they in effect excluded the possibility that shortages of materials would in themselves precipitate an economic crisis in Germany by early 1941.

□

MEW's revised view of the stock position reflected the fact that, with respect to raw materials, the German situation had changed

<hr>

*

MEW Estimates of materials in German Europe[76]
(000 metric tons)

	Stocks at 1.1.40	Current Supplies	Consumption in 1940	Stocks at 1.1.41
Chrome ore (all grades)	215	86	178	123
Molybdenum (metal)	5.1	1.3	2.5	3.9
Wolfram	12.7	4.2	8.5	8.4
Manganese (50% Mn ore)	1,110	140	630	620
Copper	200	350	325	225
Nickel (metal)	9.1	14.1	11.0	12.1
Tin (metal)	17.9	12.8	10.5	20.2
Asbestos –				
Textile	5.0	2.7	4.0	3.7
Other	2.5	17.5	10.0	10.0
Bauxite	1,500	1,150	1,300	1,350
Alumina	very small	–	–	very small
Aluminium	mainly scrap	–	–	mainly scrap

Official German Statistics showing stocks 1939–40[77]

	Stocks at 1.1.40	Current Supplies 1940	Consumption in 1940	Stocks at 1.1.41
Chrome ore	56.3	13.8	35.3	36.8
Molybdenum	3.2	0.3	2.2	1.9
Wolfram	5.0	0.9	3.7	3.1
Manganese ore	–	50.7	130.2	164.8
Copper	183.0	318.0	292.0	209.0
Nickel	9.2	13.7	11.6	11.3
Tin	7.0	11.5	8.5	10.0
Bauxite	–	–	–	–
Aluminium	–	–	–	–

Large divergencies between tonnages of chrome and manganese ores in the MEW and official German statistics reflect the use of different percentages of the metal contents of the ores.

76. FO 837/15, MEW Intelligence Summary No 45 of 24 December 1942.
77. US Strategic Bombing Survey, Synoptic Volume, Table 83.

considerably during 1940. At the outbreak of war, despite efforts during the 1930s to increase imports and accumulate stocks, available raw materials were inadequate for a long war. By 1939 many critical materials apart from coal were not sufficient to meet current consumption levels for longer than one year. While stocks of manganese were large enough for 18 months, other materials such as rubber and magnesium could only meet current consumption for a few months more.[78] Pre-war British intelligence assessments of the situation had corresponded closely with assessments of the German government. The conclusion reached by the IIC, and accepted by the ATB, to the effect that Germany could not sustain full industrial activity in war-time for more than 15–18 months before supply difficulties would make themselves felt, was close to reality.* Hitler was receiving similar assessments of the raw material situation, but he rejected the advice of the head of the Wehrwirtschafts-und-Rüstungsamt, General Thomas,† whose views were shared by Dr Schacht and many others, that Germany was not prepared for a long war of attrition;[79] a long war and attrition were excluded by his concept of Blitzkrieg. Already by the autumn of 1939, however, the German authorities had reviewed the raw material situation; as a result of the maintenance of trade with Sweden, Romania, the USSR and Yugoslavia, of the looting of Poland and of unexpectedly slight strains upon economic resources they had concluded that the available supplies of raw materials would meet current consumption for two years rather than the one year estimated in the summer of 1939.[80] The success of Blitzkrieg strategy in western Europe in the summer of 1940 further reinforced their confidence in the supply situation; the acquisition of France and the Low Countries augmented steel capacity by 50 per cent, French iron ores were under German control, Polish coal was added to German production and stocks of non-ferrous metals were seized from occupied territories.

MEW had no access to German estimates of the situation, and on the evidence at its disposal it could not itself reach firm conclusions about the effect on Germany's economy of her seizure of the occupied territories. Thus the JIC, in October 1940, after examining the munitions industries of the territories newly occupied by Germany concluded that they could not significantly add to the production of armaments for the German forces.[81] It estimated that if the industries of all the occupied territories could be supplied with raw materials the

---

* See Chapter 2, p 65.
† See Appendix 3.

78. ibid, pp 68–69.
79. Carroll, op cit, p 191.
80. ibid, p 199.
81. JIC (40) 319 of 14 October; JIC (40) 328 of 20 October.

production of aircraft could, theoretically, be increased by 400 (rising later to 800) a month, shipping construction by about 1 million tons a year and land armaments in quantities sufficient to equip 40–50 divisions, but that these goals could not be achieved because supplies of raw materials were inadequate. But it is scarcely surprising that, after Germany's military victories, MEW's estimate of Germany's position in raw materials, as in oil and food, became markedly less optimistic. Even at the end of 1940, on the other hand, its forecasts failed to move close to reality because they continued to suffer from a more serious limitation. Before its forecasts could be accurate MEW had to understand the nature and the peculiarities of the German economy as a system. As yet, however – indeed until the beginning of 1942 – its Enemy Branch did not merely lack reliable intelligence about economic policy and economic administration in Germany; it did not recognise that the study of those subjects was central to intelligence work on economic problems. Still in the process of establishment when thrown into crisis by the events of the summer, and provided with little or no assistance either from published research or from current intelligence, it was less equipped to analyse the behaviour of the German economy than to collect information on such matters as armaments, oil, raw materials and food, and was content to regard the system through a veil of inherited or common-sense assumptions.

In particular, it still assumed, as the 'Future Strategy' paper had assumed, that the German economy was inflexibly disciplined and fully mobilised for war, and that its resources, especially oil and raw materials, were under stress from the total use of its industrial capacity. In fact, the German economy was not yet centrally planned by a single agency; the General Bevollmächtigter für die Wirtschaft was abolished on 7 December 1939.* Pre-war investment in industrial expansion had largely been directed towards the production of armaments to suit Hitler's belief in Blitzkreig to be waged against single and isolated enemies, rather than in preparation for prolonged war and attrition. When war began in September 1939 Hitler had insisted on exploiting the existing industrial basis; rather than approve major investments in the industrial basis itself, he was determined that military potential should be built up as required in the shortest possible time – the policy described by General Thomas as 'armament in width'.[82] Despite the inefficiency of the methods used by the German administration in allocating resources and requirements as between industries, the available capacity of factory plants and machine tools had been ample to meet the military demands of the German campaigns in Poland, Norway and western Europe during 1939 and 1940, and the German economy had proved flexible enough to respond to changes in priorities laid down in directives from Hitler.

---

* See Appendix 3.

82. US Strategic Bombing Survey, Synoptic Volume, p 20.

Hitler had frequently issued such directives demanding rapid economic adjustment to his military priorities,* but MEW's weekly intelligence reports and the appreciations of the JIC made no reference to them. In October 1940 one of MEW's reports expressed interest in an American suggestion that German production programmes had been adapted to a new stage of the war,[90] but there is no evidence that this clue was followed up. In the same way, the process by which Hitler reluctantly agreed to accept changes in methods of economic management, a process which began early in 1940, eluded the attention of MEW until 1942.

The first stage of this process occurred before the military successes in Norway and western Europe had strengthened the confidence of the German government in its ability to obtain adequate supplies of raw materials. Concern with the wastage of resources led, on 17 March 1940, to the appointment of Dr Fritz Todt as Reich Minister for Weapons and Munitions, primarily responsible for economising the consumption by the arms industries of scarce metals, especially copper.[91] His creation of a new system of committees to supervise the allocation of materials and introduce improvements in factory management paved the way for an expansion of the production of armaments under Albert Speer, who succeeded Todt in February 1942. 'Todt's reforms of the administration had shown the way, even during the Blitzkrieg, to a better system should the German economy have to be changed to a policy of full-scale war production'.[92] London knew of Todt's appointment but received no reliable intelligence about his objectives in the administrative reforms which he initiated. As late as February 1942 MEW believed that Todt was no more than a 'professional remover of bottlenecks'.†[93]

While Hitler's adjustments to Germany's economic priorities could not be detected in London, the British belief that the German

---

* Upon the attack on Poland in September 1939 Hitler dropped naval construction from its position as first priority.[83] In October he gave the motorisation of troops priority over all other programmes.[84] Munitions having become short after the campaign in Poland Hitler ordered that they should be produced in greater quantities, and by the third quarter of 1940 the output was increased by 90% above the level of 1939.[85] In mid-1940 their production had already been increased to meet requirements for *Sealion*.[86] Following military success in France Hitler ordered withdrawal of production from requirements of the Army[87] and, in June, the transference of effort to other sectors. Having decided in July 1940 to invade Russia in May 1941 Hitler demanded on 28 September 1940 that preparations be begun for the invasion[88] but, expecting quick success from the Blitzkrieg, he called for no major economic planning.[89]   † See Volume Two.

83. Carroll, op cit, p 194.   84. ibid, p 106.
85. ibid, p 220.   86. ibid, p 226.
87. Milward, op cit, p 37.
88. ibid, p 41.   89. ibid, p 32.
90. FO 837/439, MEW Survey No 58 of 28 October 1940.
91. Milward, op cit, p 57.   92. ibid, p 63.
93. FO 837/15, MEW Intelligence Weekly No 1 of 19 February 1942.

economy had been stretched from the outset and was 'lacking the hidden reserves of the 1914–18 war'[94] remained unaffected by the passage of time and the course of events in 1940. It was one of the reasons why MEW, in its attempt to use intelligence about the German economy to throw light on Germany's strategic intentions, concentrated on calculating and – as we have seen – re-calculating when and to what extent economic factors would set limits to her military capability and mobility. In comparison with its many meticulous appreciations on this question, its use of economic intelligence to indicate Germany's forthcoming military moves was infrequent and highly tentative. In January it produced for the Allied Military Committee a memorandum suggesting that, as her industrial capacity and stocks might be expected to reach a peak in the spring, Germany might invade Holland, Belgium and Denmark to obtain stocks, or Sweden to obtain iron ore, or Romania to secure oil, or the Balkans for food and raw materials.[95] Not unnaturally, the Joint Planning Staff was unimpressed; it complained of the lack of intelligence on German industrial production.[96] By the end of the year economic intelligence had only once made a positive contribution to a strategic appreciation – in September, when the evidence about oil supplies had led the COS to conclude that a combined German-Italian attack on Egypt was likely during the next six months.* But if the contribution of MEW to political and strategic assessments was so slight, it has to be remembered that not only was intelligence about the German economy in short supply but also that political and strategic intelligence was failing to diagnose the two special characteristics of the total German situation which above all provided the framework within which the German economy was managed.

Throughout 1940, as in the years before the outbreak of the war, the British military and political authorities did not appreciate the extent to which Hitler's strategy rested on the concept of Blitzkrieg. If Hitler's purpose and methods had been better understood in London and if, above all, it had been known in July 1940 that Hitler had decided to attack Russia in the following spring, the Enemy Branch of MEW's Intelligence Department might well have put aside, for the time being, attempts to forecast the performance of the German economy. As it was, until towards the middle of 1941, when military intelligence at last established that Germany intended to turn on Russia,† intelligence about the German economy was carried out in ignorance not only of the essential character of Hitler's strategy, but also of the approach of another great turning point in the development of the war.

---

* See above, p 240.   † See below, Chapter 14.

94. CAB 68/4, WP (R) (40) 43, undated.
95. CAB 85/7, MR (J) (40) 10 of 22 January.
96. CAB 80/8, COS (40) 241 (JP) of 14 February.

CHAPTER 8

Strategic Intelligence during the Winter of 1940–1941

I F LONDON was unable to make accurate estimates of what would be the state of Germany's economic war potential during the winter of 1940–1941, reliable intelligence about her military planning was equally difficult to come by. This was all the more the case because, between the postponement of *Sealion* and the spring of 1941, the German authorities themselves remained undecided about all but the most important of their strategic options in Europe and the Mediterranean – the attack on Russia.*

In June 1940, long before *Sealion* was postponed – before, indeed, the decision to attempt invasion was finally reached – the German naval authorities, with their preference for a less direct assault, were already advocating the occupation of the Atlantic islands and an advance into the Middle East with Italian and Russian help. During July Hitler, preoccupied by then with the invasion project, allowed no diversions other than the offer to Italy of support for bomber raids on Suez. But by the end of that month, by already speaking of his interest in an attack on Russia in the following spring, he had stimulated in the naval and the army commands a livelier concern to promote alternatives both to this attack and to the invasion of England. From the end of July the Army was examining the possibility of sending a Panzer force to strengthen Italy in north Africa, of launching an attack on Gibraltar and of mounting a northabout thrust through Turkey and Syria to seize Suez. On 6 September the Navy was stressing the vital importance of taking Suez as well as Gibraltar in any plan to eliminate Great Britain from the Mediterranean, and was urging that such a plan was preferable to *Sealion*.

Thus far, *Sealion* remained the main objective, and the planning of *Fritz* (then the code name for the attack on Russia in 1941) was the next most active project: an OKH plan for the latter had been ready since 5 August. However, Hitler's determination to launch *Sealion* was already wilting when on 11 September he decided to send Army and Air Force missions into Romania. This step was taken after he had received from the new Romanian government requests for help against other Balkan countries and Russia, who had occupied Bessarabia, north Bukhovina and the Baltic states in June. The missions entered Romania openly on 7 October, their ostensible

---

* See below, p 258 and Chapter 14.

purpose being to train the Romanian forces but their real task being to protect the Romanian oil and to prepare Romania's facilities for use in future operations. By 7 October *Sealion* had further receded and other diversions had claimed Hitler's attention. On 14 September, the day after the Italians began their offensive in north Africa, he had ordered preparations for the despatch of a Panzer force to Libya – though he had rejected on 26 September Admiral Raeder's plan for an advance through Egypt to Syria. On 16 and 17 September, during a visit to Berlin by Suner, who was soon to become the Spanish Foreign Minister, he requested Spanish assistance or connivance in an attack on Gibraltar. On 19 September Ribbentrop, on a visit to Rome, was confronted with Mussolini's interest in making an attack on Greece.

On 12 October Hitler put off *Sealion* for the first time, except as a deception operation to divert attention from the preparations for the attack on Russia, and made those preparations the Army's first priority. Germany's other projects were by then running into difficulties. The move into Romania was increasing Hitler's anxiety that the Balkans, an important source of raw materials, should remain quiet until the spring, and made it necessary to try to prevent further Russian moves while his preparations against her continued. The British failure at Dakar and the course of Germany's negotiations with Spain were suggesting to him that Vichy France might be a more promising partner than Franco's Spain. For this reason at the Brenner meeting on 4 October he persuaded Mussolini to abandon territorial claims against France. At that meeting, on the other hand, Mussolini, as well as declining the offer of German help in Libya, was strengthened in his determination to occupy Greece. On 15 October, furious on account of Hitler's unilateral move into Romania, he fixed a date for the invasion without informing Germany.

On 4 and 12 November the Germans reviewed and attempted to fix their immediate plans following Hitler's round of talks between 22 and 28 October with Laval, Pétain, Franco and Mussolini and in the light of the Italian attack on Greece on 28 October. They decided that, although GAF units would go to the Mediterranean, no Panzers would now be sent to Libya, at least before Italy had taken Mersa Matruh, and no collaboration would be sought from Vichy France beyond her consent to the discussion of measures for the protection of her African territories. With Spain, on the other hand, at a time when Italian reverses in Greece increased the importance of a drive on Gibraltar as a means of safeguarding the position in Libya, Hitler persuaded himself that prospects of partnership were brighter. Preparation for this advance (*Felix*) was thus given high priority, though its extension to the Canaries and the Cape Verde islands was reserved for further consideration. In the Balkan direction there was to be no action against Turkey and beyond as this would be incompatible with the preparations for attacking Russia. But British air forces had moved into Greece immediately after the Italian attack, and since it was feared that they might attack the Romanian oilfields, the missions in Romania were to be reinforced and preparations begun for the occupation of continental Greece with 19 divisions via Bulgaria with the object, at this stage, of securing bases for attacks on such British forces as might threaten the Romanian oil.

□

In London while these developments and alterations of plan were taking place the intelligence authorities continued to be preoccupied with the invasion threat. As compared with the flurry of interest they had shown in the Balkans before the German offensive in the west* and in the Mediterranean before Italy's entry into the war,† they paid little attention to these areas between June and September 1940. At the same time, such was their conviction of Germany's ability to conduct more than one offensive concurrently, and so obvious did it seem that she would try by every means to defeat Great Britain with the least possible delay, that they allowed that *Sealion* might be accompanied by enemy action in these other directions.

On 2 July the JIC expected that while Germany would make peace overtures to the United Kingdom, she might be planning one or more of the following projects: invasion of the United Kingdom; operations against Russia; an advance into south-eastern Europe, perhaps as far as Syria and Palestine; and an attack in the Mediterranean to Egypt or Gibraltar. It calculated that except that she could not invade the United Kingdom and attack Russia simultaneously, she could carry out more than one of these moves at the same time. As to which of the moves were the most likely, the JIC acknowledged that there was 'at present little direct intelligence', but its general conclusion was that Germany would do her best to avoid intervention in south-eastern Europe before eliminating Great Britain.[1] In briefs for the JIC, MI and the Foreign Office had supported this conclusion with slightly different arguments. In MI's view Germany could deal with the Balkans at leisure if she succeeded against Great Britain by the winter; if not, she would still have time enough to decide whether to occupy the area as it would offer little resistance. From concern to avoid another winter of war, she would give priority to invading the United Kingdom. Russia was 'hardly a possibility', therefore, though Germany might also turn her attentions against the Ukraine if by the autumn she realised that a quick defeat of the United Kingdom was out of the question. The Foreign Office agreed that Germany was

---

* See Chapter 6, pp 198–199.   † See Chapter 6, p 201 et seq.

1. CAB 80/14, COS (40) 518 (JIC), of 2 July 1940.

unlikely to move against the Balkans – she could get what she wanted by political and economic means, and more direct action would embroil her with Russia. It also agreed that 'on the face of it it seems improbable that she would wish to take on the Soviet Union before she had finished with us'. But it felt it probable that sooner or later Germany intended to dominate the Ukraine, and its feeling that she would eventually strike in eastern Europe was strengthened by its suspicion that she would not attempt *Sealion*. There were weighty arguments against the attempt being made, not least the German preference for striking at 'the soft spot' – a preference that MI itself had often stressed.[2] It was very much the opinion of the Foreign Office at this time that Hitler would not 'be fool enough to attempt invasion'.[3]

In its general conclusions of 2 July the JIC leaned more towards the opinion of MI than to that of the Foreign Office. It accordingly devoted such attention as it spared from Germany's invasion preparations to the danger of developments in the Mediterranean rather than in south-eastern Europe. Nor did it change its assessments when the attachés and the SIS in the Balkans began to send in evidence of increasing German infiltration there. In June these sources had persuaded MI, correctly, that Germany had set up 'Gestapo cells' at the Ploesti oil wells and other strategic points in Romania.[4] During July they left little doubt that, following Russia's occupation of Bessarabia, the Romanian government was becoming pro-Axis.[5] They were warning that enemy action could be expected by the end of September, despite a report at the beginning of July, from a contact 'considered completely reliable', to the effect that Germany was not for the present considering armed intervention 'in the SE region'.[6] On 26 September Whitehall had received 'specific reports of the imminent arrival of German motorised AA units at Ploesti' and 'more general reports of German personnel and material' at other places in Romania.[7] On 29 September Czech intelligence's A-54 predicted a German march into Romania at the beginning of October, in preparation for an attack on Turkey that would be accompanied by an Italian attack from Libya and a German attack through Spain.[8] And early in October, three days before the German missions entered Romania, the SIS added that Germany had begun to redeploy her divisions in south-eastern Europe and had offered Romania fighter-squadrons.[9] Throughout these months, however, opinion in Whitehall

---

2. JIC (40) 143 of 27 June, appendices.
3. Dilks (ed), op cit, p 318, entry for 31 July 1940.
4. WO 208/2257, MI Weekly Commentary of 6 June 1940.
5. ibid, Nos 48 and 49 of 11 and 18 July.
6. AIR 40/2321, Minute of 1 September 1940.
7. CAB 80/19, COS (40) 783, (COS Résumé, No 56).
8. AIR 40/2321, Minute of 29 September 1940; Moravec, op cit, p 202.
9. CAB 80/20, COS 801 (40) (COS Résumé, No 57).

remained unchanged. A German advance in the Balkan direction was much less likely than a German attack on Egypt from north Africa in conjunction with Italy or a German advance to Gibraltar through Spain. It would lead to complications with Russia and Italy, would overstrain the German economy and would in any case be unprofitable unless the Royal Navy had previously been driven from the eastern Mediterranean. This assessment of the Chiefs of Staff of 4 September[10] reflected the views expressed by MI during July and August.[11] It was repeated at the end of September by AI, which doubted whether a German move even into Romania was to be expected.[12] On 3 October, moreover, the Cabinet had 'certain indications' – the source of which cannot now be traced – that the next German move would be an attack from Libya, rather than into the Balkans or through Spain,[13] and on 9 October its initial reaction to the German entry into Romania was to regard it as an isolated step and to feel that German support for the Italians in Libya was more likely than a German advance through the Balkans.[14]

Further reflection on the German entry into Romania produced a change of mind about German intentions in the Balkans, the more so as it was followed by reports which seemed to confirm the accuracy of the warning received from A-54 at the end of September. On 9 October London was advised by the Madrid embassy that, according to the Spanish Foreign Minister, Hitler and Mussolini had at their Brenner meeting agreed on an advance through the Balkans and Syria to Egypt.[15] On 9 October GC and CS decrypted a report from the Vichy French Naval Attaché in Athens to the effect that the Yugoslav General Staff feared that German action against Yugoslavia and Greece was imminent. On 10 October the Foreign Secretary told the Cabinet on the basis of this and other reports that the Germans were studying the possibility of action against Greece and Yugoslavia and thinking of postponing the invasion of the United Kingdom until the spring.[16] These rumours had an immediate effect on Whitehall's appreciations. On 10 October the JIC, in its first assessment since July of German intentions, allowed that the move into Romania would be followed by expansion into Bulgaria – though it did not expect any advance to the Middle East by this route before the late spring of 1941 and still thought that the immediate dangers were German assistance to an intensified Italian attack on Egypt, an Italian invasion of Greece and German political pressure on Spain.[17] On 11 October the COS

10. CAB 80/17, COS (40) 683 of 4 September 1940.
11. WO 190/891, MI Minute to MOI, 10 July 1940, Appreciations Nos 126 and 129 of 16 and 30 July, Nos 134 of 5 August, 131 of 8 August.
12. AIR 40/2321, Minute of 29 September 1940.
13. CAB 65/9, WM (40) 265 of 3 October 1940.
14. CAB 65/15, WM (40) 268 CA, 9 October 1940.   15. loc cit.
16. CAB 65/9, WM (40) 269 of 10 October 1940.
17. CAB 80/20, COS (40) 819, 10 October 1940.

résumé suggested that the move into Romania might point to a larger scheme in which an Italian attack on Greece was combined with a German thrust through Bulgaria against Turkey.[18]

Before these appreciations were received the Cabinet had on 9 October, as a result of the Madrid report and in spite of its first reaction to the news from Romania, asked the Chief of Staff for a comprehensive study of the implications of a German advance through the Balkans to the Middle East.[19] This study was completed by the Joint Planners, with assistance from the JIC, on 1 November, four days after the Italian invasion of Greece. It envisaged that Italy's attack would be accompanied by a peaceful German occupation of Bulgaria by mid-November and be followed by a German advance to the Turkish straits by the end of the year and a thrust into Syria and possibly Iraq in the middle of 1941. It reckoned that Germany had ample land and air forces to enable her to undertake these operations without reducing the threat of the invasion of the United Kingdom.[20]

At the departmental level AI raised no objections to this last conclusion: Air Ministry estimates of the strength of the GAF had not yet been deflated by the Singleton and the Lindemann enquiries.* However, it was just at this time that the GAF Enigma began to reveal the move to the Balkans of GAF units which had been engaged against the United Kingdom, and to mention their interest in Bulgaria.† Moreover, MI, which had in any case been sceptical since July about the ability of the GAF to undertake operations elsewhere without reducing its capability against Great Britain,[21] had begun to accumulate evidence both of an increase in the size of the German Army, and especially in the number of its motorised and airborne divisions, and of its concentration in eastern and south-eastern Europe. On 31 October it reported that a vast programme of motorisation was being undertaken and that there had been a steady movement of divisions from western Europe to Poland, so that there were now 70 divisions in eastern and south-eastern Europe. The new and numerically increasing mechanised divisions, which would be fully trained by the spring, were probably intended for Blitzkrieg operations in Russia or the Middle East.[22] By 13 November it had learned from 'a good source' that Germany planned to motorise a third of all her divisions, making a possible total of 70 armoured and motorised divisions, and that she was also increasing her paratroop

---

* See Chapter 9, p 299 et seq.
† See below, p 259 et seq.

18. CAB 80/20, COS (40) 820 (COS Résumé, No 58).
19. CAB 65/15, WM (40) 268 CA, 9 October 1940.
20. CAB 80/21, COS (40) 871 of 1 November 1940.
21. JIC (40) 143 of 27 June, Appendix A.
22. WO 208/2258, No 63 of 31 October 1940.

and airborne divisions.[23] Between these two dates, moreover, on the basis of SIS and attaché reports from the Balkans, it had calculated that 2 German divisions had already completed the occupation of Romania and that they would eventually be increased to 18 divisions, a figure that exceeded that which was needed to train the Romanian forces and provide ground and air defence for the Romanian oil.[24] There was no evidence as to what Germany's wider purpose might be, but on 6 November MI reinforced the recent conclusions of the Joint Planners and the JIC by opting firmly for the view that she intended a drive on the Middle East to deprive Great Britain of Iraq's oil. The Axis subjugation of Greece, in which Italy would receive assistance from Germany in Albania, would be followed by a German move into Bulgaria, Thrace and beyond; and Germany's purpose in transferring divisions to Poland, as also to north Norway and Finland, was to deter Russia from interfering.[25] Once the German entry into Romania had been followed by the Italian attack on Greece there was a strong temptation in the Middle East, also, to assume that these were the opening moves in a concerted Axis plan to overthrow the British position in the Middle East by pincer thrusts aimed at Suez through the Levant and from north Africa. The DDMI at GHQ ME made this assumption on the day of the Italian invasion.[26] On 5 November the Chiefs of Staff in Whitehall agreed.[27] It is true that the Chiefs of Staff allowed for the possibility that Mussolini had acted without Germany's knowledge, or at least without her approval. But MI discounted this possibility and on 4 November the Joint Planners, accepting that Germany was planning an advance into Turkey through Bulgaria in 1941, suggested that the Italian attack on Greece might be intended to divert British forces from the defence of Alexandria.[28] And on 5 November the Chiefs of Staff entertained the same suspicion: Italy might be luring British forces into Greece to be destroyed by a German offensive through Bulgaria.[29]

□

The conclusion that Germany was preparing for a thrust to the Middle East through the Balkans was reached a few days before Hitler's rejection of the project on 4 November.* But it did not rule out the

---

* See above, pp 250–251.

23. ibid, No 65 of 13 November 1940.
24. CAB 80/21, COS (40) 890 (COS Résumé, No 61): WO 190/892, MI14 Appreciations of 6 and 12 November 1940.
25. WO 190/892, Minute of 6 November 1940.
26. WO 169/19, 28 October 1940.
27. CAB 79/7, COS (40) 374th Meeting, 5 November 1940.
28. CAB 80/22, COS (40) 901 (JP) of 4 November 1940.
29. CAB 79/7, COS (40) 374th Meeting, 5 November 1940.

danger that she would also strike elsewhere. On the contrary, A-54 had warned that Germany was planning to attack Turkey concurrently with an Italian advance from Libya and a German drive through Spain;* and within days of concluding that Germany was preparing to strike against Turkey the intelligence authorities were warning the Cabinet of the danger of an imminent German advance into Spain and against the Canaries.

Troops and transports had been kept in readiness since the summer of 1940 for a preventive occupation of the Atlantic islands should Spain join the Axis or Germany move into Spain, but until October there had been no firm evidence that either of these dangers was imminent. In that month, however, there had been a number of diplomatic reports of increasing pressure from Berlin on the Spanish government and of increased readiness on the part of German units near the Spanish frontier, and Whitehall had also been made uneasy by information from Spanish authorities.[30] Beigbeder, the man who had been replaced as Foreign Minister in Madrid by the pro-Axis Suner on 17 October, maintained clandestine relations with the British Ambassador.[31] From him Whitehall learned that Franco had evaded a definite commitment to Germany when he met Hitler at Hendaye on 24 October – that Franco had, indeed, been alienated by Hitler's insistence that something had to be done to conciliate the Vichy authorities.[32] But the Ambassador also reported that Beigbeder himself now expected Germany to demand at least the right of passage through Spain,[33] and the danger that Spain would at last consent to this despite the dependence of her economy on supplies allowed in by Great Britain, and despite the possibility that her army would resist a German move, seemed all the more real when, on 3 November, the Spanish government abolished the international administration at Tangier, formally announcing a Spanish protectorate, and when, on 19 November, Suner returned to Berlin for further negotiations. On 25 November the Defence Committee considered the occupation of Ceuta as a contingency measure.[34]

At that point the Chiefs of Staff were opposed to taking any action. But the danger was kept alive – was indeed replaced by the threat that Germany would make a descent on Spain without Spanish connivance – when Italy's set-backs in Greece were followed by the opening of

---

* See above, p 252.

30. CAB 65/10, WM (40) 281 of 1 November 1940; CAB 80/23, COS (40) 966 (COS Résumé, No 64) and COS (40) 968 of 23 November; CAB 80/24, COS (40) 1040 (JIC) of 13 December 1940.
31. FO 800/323, Hoare to Halifax, 30 October 1940.
32. FO 371/24517, C 11790/113/41.
33. FO 371/24508, C 11460/40/11.
34. CAB 69/1, DO (40) 40th Meeting, 25 November; CAB 80/23, COS (40) 987 (JP) of 27 November.

Wavell's offensive in north Africa. By the end of the first week of December the Prime Minister felt sure that Hitler would retaliate, and that he would probably do so in Spain. The JIC was inclined to agree, though it ruled out the danger of a German attempt to take the Atlantic islands as photographic reconnaissance had revealed no naval forces in the Biscay ports,[35] and the CSS thought that Germany would 'do a Norway' on the west coast of the Iberian peninsula.[36] On 14 December, however, the Chiefs of Staff and the Foreign Office opposed the Prime Minister's wish to occupy the Cape Verdes and the Azores as a precaution; the Chiefs of Staff stressed that the available resources were insufficient for the operation, and the Foreign Office held that Spain's actions in Tangier had not been undertaken in collusion with the Axis powers.[37] The decision was deferred; but the possibility of taking action was kept under review. On 16 December the Prime Minister still believed that a German descent on Spain was more likely than an attack in the Balkans.[38] On 20 December AI believed that the GAF was still being reserved for another attempt at invasion of the United Kingdom, but that if aircraft were diverted it would be for an attack in the Iberian peninsula.[39]

On 8 January 1941 the Naval Attaché, Madrid, attended a meeting of the Defence Committee. He reported that it was now becoming increasingly unlikely that the Spanish authorities would assent to the entry of German forces. But he still recommended that preparations should be made for opening contact with Spanish resistance forces and sending a support group to them in the event of a German invasion.[40] The proposal was adopted.[41] Thereafter the Madrid embassy provided increasingly reassuring evidence: the Spanish government was resisting German and Italian pressure on it to enter the war, and the Spanish Army was preparing to resist if Germany moved into Spain.[42] And on 22 January the Future Operations (Enemy) Section (FOES)* reached the conclusion that a German move into Spain was no longer imminent.[43]

This appreciation was close to the mark. On 5 December 1940 Hitler

---

* For the establishment of FOES in December 1940 see below, Chapter 9, p 297.

35. CAB 80/24, COS (40) 1035 (JIC) of 11 December 1940 and COS (40) 1040 (JIC) of 13 December; JIC (40) 417 of 13 December.
36. Dilks (ed), op cit, p 340, entry for 14 December 1940.
37. CAB 79/55, COS (40) 32nd and 33rd Meetings (o), 14 December 1940; Dalton's Diary, 17 December 1940 (held in Library of London School of Economics).
38. CAB 65/16, WM (40) 306 CA, 16 December 1940.
39. AIR 40/2321, p 94.
40. FO 371/26904, C 460/46/41; CAB 80/56, COS (41) 2 (o) of 8 January 1941; Churchill, op cit, Vol III, (1950), p 7.
41. CAB 69/2, DO (41) 1st Meeting, 8 January 1941; CAB 84/26, JP (41) 29 (S) and (o) of 12 January.
42. FO 371/26904, C 896/46/41; FO 371/26945, C 2065/306/41, C 2420/306/41.
43. CAB 79/8, COS (41) 28th Meeting, 22 January.

had insisted that operation *Felix* and the German attack on Greece (*Marita*), if begun, must be completed within weeks so that his forces could be deployed for the attack on Russia (now to be known as *Barbarossa*) by mid-May 1941. On 11 December he had postponed *Felix* because he did not think that the political conditions were yet favourable. It was with some reluctance, however, that he abandoned the operation. On 20 January 1941 he and Mussolini agreed to renew the pressure on Franco. They met with another rebuff but until March, when the operation was finally deferred until after the first phase of the attack on Russia, the German authorities continued to make staff studies for it. This situation, too, was accurately reflected in the British appreciations. Until 25 March, when it finally conceded that an advance through Spain had become unlikely, MI stressed from time to time that the Germans were continuing their preparations.[44] But at the inter-departmental level this fact was offset by the knowledge that the Spanish government continued to be unco-operative and by the evidence of increasing German involvement in the Balkans. And on 5 and 19 March the JIC and FOES again dismissed the danger.[45]

The JIC and FOES were also correct in discounting the likelihood of a German occupation of Vichy France and Tunisia. On 10 and 11 December 1940 Hitler, as well as postponing *Felix*, had ordered contingency planning for the occupation of Vichy France and the seizure of the French Fleet (operation *Attila*) in case the French colonies should secede. On 17 January 1941 London received via Washington a report from the United States Naval Attaché in Rome to the effect that the Axis powers intended to attack Vichy France and invade Tunisia from Sicily, the object being to bolster the crumbling Italian position in north Africa. On 19 January the JIC was sceptical of this report but, aware by then that the GAF had arrived in Sicily* and that there was evidence that German divisions were in southern Italy, it conceded that a German move into Tunisia was not impossible.[46] In the next two weeks, moreover, the report did something to deflect the attention of Whitehall from the fact that German troops were crossing to Libya.† But by the beginning of March a steady trickle of reports from British and United States diplomatic sources, revealing the arrival of Germans in French north Africa disguised as tourists or as Armistice Commission staff,[47] persuaded the JIC and FOES that infiltration was all that the Germans intended and

---

* See Chapter 12, p 384.
† See Chapter 12, p 387.

44. WO 190/893, Nos 24D, 29A and 33A of 6, 18 and 25 March 1941.
45. JIC (41) 90 of 5 March 1941; CAB 81/64, FOES (41) 5 of 19 March 1941.
46. JIC (41) 32 of 19 January 1941.
47. JIC (41) 69 of 8 February 1941; JIC (41) 84 of 2 March 1941; CAB 65/17, WM (41) 19 of 20 February 1941; CAB 65/18, WM (41) 22 of 3 March 1941; CAB 80/26, COS (41) 145 (COS Résumé, No 79).

that, at least in advance of an occupation of Spain, a military operation against Tunisia or French Morocco was improbable.[48]

□

From the last days of October 1940 the intelligence authorities began to receive incontrovertible evidence that Germany was actively preparing a large-scale Balkan campaign. Until then British intelligence about German intentions in south-eastern Europe, as in other theatres, had been almost entirely confined to what could be derived from the reports received from the British diplomatic posts and Service attachés, the SIS and decrypts of Axis diplomatic cyphers.* In western Europe it had become increasingly possible to check these sources against the evidence, largely negative, of photographic reconnaissance, which was occasionally able to cover the Franco-Spanish border and was soon to be helpful in dismissing the threat to the Atlantic islands,† and of the GAF Enigma. In the south-east photographic reconnaisssance was not available, no indications of enemy preparations had appeared in the GAF Enigma and the only evidence of Germany's intentions had been a spate of rumours from the British diplomatic posts, from the SIS and from GC and CS's decrypts of the Axis diplomatic and attaché traffic. But the intelligence picture was transformed from the end of October. In consequence of the GAF's preparations for operations there, the Balkans began from that date to figure for the first time in the GAF Enigma traffic. And in February 1941 the situation was further improved when GC and CS, using hand methods, broke another variant of the Enigma – that used by the German railway administration – and from the Czechs the SIS began to receive warnings from A-54.‡

As a result, the British intelligence authorities were to provide, in the words of the official historian, 'timely and accurate'[49] warning in advance of the attacks on Greece and Crete; and these were to be the first German campaigns of the war for which such warning was possible. But while it was an immense advance to be able to chart in detail Germany's preparations for the attacks on Greece and Crete, Whitehall still failed to discern that the strategic purpose underlying these attacks was to safeguard the southern flank of Germany's invasion of Russia. Throughout the spring the impending Balkan campaign remained for the British authorities what it had been when they had first concluded early in November 1940 that it must be

---

* See Chapter 11, pp 348–349.
† See above, p 257.
‡ See Chapter 11, p 357.

48. JIC (41) 90 of 5 March 1941; CAB 81/64, FOES (41) 5 of 19 March 1941.
49. Playfair, op cit, Vol I, p 348.

expected – part of a strategy which sought, with the help of Italy and, if possible, Spain and Vichy France, to overthrow British positions in the Middle East and the Mediterranean and to divert British resources from the defence of the United Kingdom.

For this misconception – the major failure of intelligence at the strategic level at this time – one explanation is to be found in the fact that even the Enigma traffic was, as usual, silent about the nature of OKH and OKW planning and the purpose of Hitler's decisions. It yielded voluminous information about the movements and order of battle of the German forces in the Balkan area from the beginning of November 1940, and left no doubt that they were massing for an attack on Greece. But it did not reveal that the attack was fundamentally a defensive operation – one which Hitler had ordered initially to safeguard the Romanian oil* – which on 5 December he made dependent on the failure of Italy to reach a negotiated peace with Greece and which, in a new directive of 13 December, when he feared that Italy's setbacks had laid the way into Greece wide open to British forces, he finally ordered to go forward as a means of securing the flank of the projected assault on Russia. Some indication of the German frame of mind was, indeed, obtained from Italian diplomatic Sigint. In a despatch decrypted on 9 November the Italian Minister at Sofia reported that Germany was considering an advance through Bulgaria to Greece 'to guard against possible British attacks from Greek bases against Romanian oil'. It was not on the basis of any intelligence, however, but as a result of their own speculations on the effects of the Italian setbacks, that the British authorities came close to recognising the defensive purpose of the impending attack on Greece in the early days of 1941. On 9 January, in the first attempt by the intelligence bodies since October to provide an independent assessment of German intentions, FOES cast doubt on the existence of a plan to drive to the Middle East, regarded the plan to invade Greece through Bulgaria as a precautionary step made necessary by Italian defeats and judged that for a similar reason, in order to prevent collapse there, Germany might even be preparing to occupy part of Italy.[50]

Like the earlier *tours d'horizon*, this FOES report considered the possibility of a German attack on Russia. Like them, it dismissed it. Indications from the GAF Enigma of German operational preparations for an attack on Greece, hitherto sparse, were by now accumulating rapidly. In contrast the Enigma traffic not only remained silent about the purpose of the Greek campaign but was also devoid as yet of any indications from which preparations for an attack on Russia could have been inferred. But this contrast was not the only further

---

* See above, p 251.

50. CAB 80/25, COS (41) 23 of 9 January 1941.

consideration that continued to avert Whitehall's eyes from the true situation for, even when good indications of the intention to attack Russia began to come in, the Whitehall authorities greeted them, as we shall see, with pronounced scepticism.* Nor is it difficult to diagnose the other, more general, factors that helped to mislead them during the early months of 1941.

The first of these factors, and the most general, was a reluctance to believe that Hitler would go so far to reduce British difficulties as to attack Russia before he had defeated Great Britain – a reluctance amounting almost to incredulity. The least general was the operation of Germany's own deception measures. There is no doubt that these were effective in presenting the earliest preparations for *Barbarossa* as preparations for the assault in south-eastern Europe, and no less so in simulating the retention of *Sealion*.†[51] A third lay in between. As winter gave way to spring the threat of invasion returned and, at a time when the Whitehall authorities still calculated that Germany had the capacity to carry out concurrently with *Sealion* any of several other moves excepting only a campaign against Russia, they had insufficient knowledge not only of the planning for *Barbarossa*, but also of Germany's parallel abandonment of *Sealion*.

□

On 12 November 1940, having put off *Sealion* for the first time a month before, Hitler ordered improvements to be made to the plans for the invasion of the United Kingdom: changes in the general situation might still make invasion possible in the spring of 1941. On 10 January 1941, except as a means of providing deception cover for the *Barbarossa* preparations, he again, and for the last time, put *Sealion* off. But in the minds of the British intelligence authorities the invasion, which was also the great preoccupation of the political and operatiolial authorities, continued to be Germany's main objective. At the end of December MI forecast that invasion preparations would continue on 'a massive scale', concentrating on the construction of special landing-craft and troop-carrying aircraft and 'certainly' including the use of gas.‡[52] On 10 January the Combined Intelligence Committee (CIC)§ still believed that invasion would come as soon as the Germans had achieved air superiority, and on 24 January it stressed that, while the German Army was large enough to threaten all fronts, there was no certainty of receiving advance information

---

* See Chapter 14, pp 438–439.
† See Chapter 14, p 440.
‡ For intelligence on chemical warfare see Volume Two.
§ See Chapter 5, pp 168–169.

51. Enemy Documents Section Appreciation/5, pp 105–106.
52. JIC (41) 10 of 5 January, Annex A (Report of MI14).

about its movements. Outside a limited area, SIS reports about German dispositions and movements continued to be slow and inaccurate; only the invasion front was being regularly covered by photographic reconnaissance.[53] Since photographic reconnaissance and Sigint showed the Germans to be still engaged on invasion exercises, these were understandable conclusions, and this was all the more the case because there were occasional reports of Germany's intentions from other sources that could not easily be ignored. Thus A-54 had recently reported that he had attended a meeting at the end of December at which Keitel had announced Hitler's decision to remount the invasion in the spring.[54] Certainly, they were conclusions that were not challenged by the senior inter-departmental intelligence bodies. In its report of 9 January 1941 FOES maintained that Germany would permit no diversions from the invasion preparations beyond the measures she was planning in support of Italy, though there might possibly be a descent on the Straits of Gibraltar via Spain;[55] and on 22 January and 18 February it thought that she would not permit her Balkan operations to do more than delay her invasion attempt.[56] On 31 January the JIC concluded that only the renewal of the invasion attempt could provide Germany with the chance of victory in 1941 which she badly needed. This was the outcome of a massive review of the probable scale and objective of an invasion attempt, and of its likelihood, to which all the intelligence directorates contributed.[57]

The JIC report of 31 January nevertheless contained some indication that scepticism was setting in. It was confident – as confident as it was of the fact that a successful invasion was the only means by which Germany could be sure of obtaining victory in 1941 – that the danger of invasion would not return before 1 April. It suggested that by then the improvement in British defences and the relative decline in the strength which the GAF could deploy against them would have made an invasion attempt too risky for Germany unless she had developed some secret weapon or was bent on using gas. It did not speculate on the nature of the secret weapon, but was not inclined to believe that any secret weapon existed or that gas would be used. Further signs of a change of attitude in the intelligence bodies soon followed. On 3 February, commenting on an increase since the beginning of the year in SIS and diplomatic reports to the effect that invasion would come in the spring, and perhaps as early as February, the CIC allowed for the possibility that the reports were based on rumours planted by the Germans.[58] From 15 February its summaries began to stress on the one

53. AIR 40/1638, No 225 of 10 January 1941, No 239 of 24 January 1941.
54. Amort and Jedlica, op cit, p 100.
55. CAB 80/25, COS (41) 23 of 9 January 1941.
56. CAB 79/8, COS (41) 28th Meeting, 22 January 1941; CAB 81/64, FOES (41) 2 of 18 February 1941.   57. JIC (41) 35 of 31 January 1941.
58. AIR 40/1638 No 249 of 3 February 1941.

hand that Germany would continue the invasion preparations in order to keep up the threat, but, on the other, that she was increasingly directing her energies into the Battle of the Atlantic.[59] By then, however, the Chiefs of Staff had embarked on a rigorous examination of the JIC assessment of 31 January.[60]

Recognising the assessment for what it was, a strategic appreciation rather than an intelligence offering, the Chiefs of Staff in their examination of it were critical of the state of intelligence. They noted that the JIC, lacking reliable information on such matters as the embarkation of troops and the sailing of ships, had admitted that it was still unable to guarantee to give advance notice of the date of an invasion, and they recommended that 'the SIS should take every possible step to remedy this extremely unsatisfactory state of affairs'. At the same time, they accepted a similar intepretation to that which the JIC had placed on the economic evidence, such as it was. The fact that Germany would reach maximum production by the summer of 1941, and seemed to be making no reasonable provision for 1942, suggested that she would attempt invasion during 1941.* The Chiefs of Staff also agreed with the JIC that, with the passage of time and the build-up of British forces, invasion would from now on be a great gamble for Germany. For this reason she would probably delay the attempt, possibly till the autumn, while she sought to deplete British resources by direct attacks on shipping and industry and by operations through Spain, from Italy and in the Balkans. By the same token, however, they expected her to put her every resource behind the attempt should she decide to renew it. The JIC had advised that the GAF would commit about 4,620 aircraft. In their report the Chiefs of Staff allowed that Germany might throw in her entire Air Force and, approving the final draft on 3 March before AI had absorbed the findings of the Singleton enquiry, they calculated that with reserves this would amount to as many as 14,000 aircraft. They thought it 'reasonable to assume that we would be certain to get indications' if an invasion attempt on this scale was remounted; they expected three weeks' strategic notice. They therefore decided against any diversion of naval forces from trade-protection until the alarm was sounded. But, because they judged that the country must remain ready to resist invasion, they opposed the despatch overseas of any armoured formations, or of any divisions at all beyond those already earmarked for the Middle East and Northern Ireland, for the time being.[61]

On 24 March, at a meeting with the Prime Minister, they found him

---

* See Chapter 9, p 310.

59. ibid, No 261 of 15 February 1941. See also No 276, 2 March, No 284, 10 March, No 293, 19 March, No 299, 25 March, No 302, 28 March.
60. CAB 79/9, COS (41) 41st and 46th Meetings, 4 and 8 February 1941.
61. CAB 80/27, COS (41) 109 of 26 February, approved at CAB 79/9, COS (41) 79th Meeting, 3 March 1941.

determined to send reinforcements abroad, and this led them to soften their findings.[62] On 27 March they issued the final version of their assessment with a covering note to the effect that the danger of invasion had become less likely during the two months since they had begun their investigation.[63] But it was now the turn of the JIC to drag its feet. By 25 March, after giving several reminders during February that invasion must still be expected, MI had decided that there would be no invasion attempt unless and until Germany failed in her intensified attack on ports and shipping; by 7 April the CIC was concluding that evidence 'from all sources' showed that Germany was concentrating on operations in other theatres and against shipping, rather than on preparations for a full-scale attack on England.[64] On 10 April, however, in a commentary on German strategy during the remainder of 1941, the JIC considered that Germany was still giving priority to an invasion of the United Kingdom. Its conclusion was that, so long as this continued to be the case, an advance through the Balkans and Syria to the Middle East and an attack on Egypt from Cyrenaica were unlikely, as was an attack on Russia in spite of recent reports to the contrary.[65] Not until April, after much disagreement between the War Office and the Foreign Office,* did the JIC modify these opinions. On 27 April, reconsidering the invasion threat on the instructions of the Chiefs of Staff, it conceded that the danger had declined: Germany was continuing to despatch troops to the Balkans and the Middle East, and was increasingly devoting her efforts against the United Kingdom to the Battle of the Atlantic rather than to preparations for a direct attack.[66]

---

* See Chapter 14, p 456.

62. CAB 79/55, COS (41) 8th (o) Meeting, 24 March 1941.
63. CAB 80/26, COS (41) 162, covering note of 27 March 1941.
64. WO 190/893, Nos 22C and 33A of 26 February, 25 March 1941; AIR 40/1638, No 312 of 7 April 1941.
65. JIC (41) 144 of 10 April 1941.
66. JIC (41) 180 of 27 April 1941.

PART III

Daylight Comes

CHAPTER 9

Reorganisation and Reassessment during Winter of 1940–1941

BY SEPTEMBER 1939 the Whitehall directorates had conceded that cryptanalysis in the United Kingdom must continue to be undertaken on an inter-Service basis at GC and CS. But they had done this reluctantly and with reservations. At the same time, they had insisted, as powerfully as ever, that they must retain total and individual responsibility for assessing the product of cryptanalysis, as also for undertaking Traffic Analysis, and for passing the resulting intelligence to the operational authorities.* After the outbreak of war they had made no attempt formally to disturb this division of labour, and up to the spring of 1940 their discontent with it had had but one result – Hankey's recommendation for strengthening the Y Committee at which the Service departments and GC and CS jointly discussed the needs of the interception stations and supervised GC and CS's direction of interception programmes.† As a result of this recommendation the Y Committee was given an independent chairman and two joint secretaries (one Army and one Air Force) and empowered to report on how best to combine and develop the country's Sigint resources.

By the end of the year the Y Committee, though now meeting more frequently, had produced no recommendations of its own. One reason for its silence lay in the fact that its independent chairmanship was only a part-time appointment. Another was more fundamental. In practice, on the day-to-day level, relations between GC and CS and the Service intelligence directorates were changing continually. Moreover, while some changes were common to all these relations, others affected the three Service directorates to different extents and induced each of them to look on GC and CS in a different way.

GC and CS had produced no significant success with Germany's naval cyphers by December 1940, and what it produced from those of the Italian Navy had been reduced to a trickle after July 1940. For such decrypts as it did make, however – as for example those belatedly obtained from the German naval Enigma for occasional days in May 1940‡ – its Naval Section had adopted the practice of

---

* See Chapter 1, p 21 et seq.　　† See Chapter 3, p 91.
‡ See Chapter 10, p 336.

despatching to the Admiralty's OIC a translation of every text. This procedure had reassured the OIC that its responsibility for interpreting intelligence was not being undermined. But the civilians of GC and CS's Naval Section had studied the same intelligence; and, being free from the operational responsibilities of the OIC's naval officers, they had studied it not only for a different purpose – to assist the work on the cyphers – but also in a different fashion. By the autumn of 1940 it was they, not the OIC, who had become the experts in interpreting the linguistic nuances and the specialised terminology of the decyphered texts and who were best placed to analyse such information as the texts provided about the enemy's organisations and habits, including his wireless habits. By the same date, on the other hand, the OIC was recognising that its own greater operational experience and GC and CS's expertise were complementary – that, given that the OIC retained the last word, there was much to be gained from debating with GC and CS even about the evaluation of Sigint and from encouraging GC and CS to make suggestions. In a process that may be dated from the sinking of the *Glorious* in June 1940,* relations between the two bodies became steadily closer and more harmonious. This fact was marked in December 1940 by the return to GC and CS of responsibility for Traffic Analysis. Staff for this work, taken from GC and CS into a section of OIC (NID 8G) at the beginning of the war, now returned to GC and CS. Responsibility for instructing and administering the naval interception stations remained with another section of the OIC (NID/DSD9), but from this date until the end of the war the naval interception programme was settled by close consultation with the Naval Section of GC and CS, whose relations with DSD9 were particularly amicable.

Like the Admiralty, though for different reasons, the Air Ministry was reasonably content with the way in which its relations with GC and CS were developing. Of the three Service intelligence directorates, AI had benefited most from GC and CS's cryptanalytical successes since the beginning of the war and especially since the first breaks into the GAF Enigma in January 1940. In addition, it had secured and maintained what proved to be the most productive exception to the general arrangement that cryptanalysis should be concentrated at GC and CS – the provision by which low-grade Air Force Sigint, including the exploitation of tactical codes and cyphers broken at GC and CS, should be undertaken at the main RAF interception station at Cheadle. It was the problem of how best to use the sheer bulk of the Air Force Sigint produced by Cheadle and by GC and CS which led to such limited friction between AI and GC and CS as did occur.

AI, with its responsibility for co-ordinating air intelligence from all sources, and from concern to safeguard its control of interpretation

---

* See Chapter 4, p 141 et seq.

and assessment, frowned on the efforts of GC and CS's Air Section to mate the low-grade Sigint from Cheadle and R/T intercept stations with the Enigma decrypts. Other difficulties were to come from the attachment of RAF officers to GC and CS to advise it in the work of interpreting the Enigma decrypts and selecting them for transmission to Whitehall: apart from the fact that these officers and the GC and CS civilians did not always see eye to eye, both groups occasionally upset some sections of AI by having dealings with other sections which did not know the true source of the Enigma intelligence. But these problems were unimportant compared with AI's recognition that the Enigma was the most valuable of its sources. And far from leading the Air Ministry at this stage to think that relations between AI and GC and CS were in need of fundamental revision, they were more than off-set by steadily increasing collaboration in which AI benefited from the research which GC and CS undertook on the GAF's communications and the more specialised features of its organisation and order of battle.

It was otherwise with the War Office. MI had received a good deal of military intelligence from the GAF Enigma during the German offensives in western Europe, but since June 1940 this traffic had contained little of value to it. Still more disappointing, GC and CS had had no more success with the German Army Enigma than with that of the German Navy. Like the Admiralty, again, and unlike the Air Ministry, the War Office lacked the consolation of a supply of lower-grade Sigint. For lack of time during the fighting in Norway and France, and for lack of traffic since, none of the German Army's low and medium-grade codes had been broken. And yet in return for what was undoubtedly a poor yield from cryptanalysis, the War Office was saddled with the work of intercepting the Enigma transmissions of the GAF. It had initially undertaken this work on the mistaken assumption that the transmissions were those of the German Army, and until towards the end of 1940 the Air Ministry was unable to take much of the load off the Army's interception stations.

Responsibility for the work of these stations lay with MI8. As the branch of MI set up at the beginning of the war to supervise the Army's Y activities and to be the channel through which Sigint would pass to the branches doing substantive intelligence, MI8 had also become the centre for all Army Traffic Analysis and since the summer of 1940 this work had become increasingly important. During the operations in France the work of the Army's field Sigint units on the enemy's low-grade W/T communications had been handicapped by MI's ignorance of the German Army's complex W/T system; after Dunkirk, and the return of officers with first-hand experience and a wealth of captured documents, it became possible to study the system. Given the dearth of good military intelligence it also became essential to do so, and before very long MI8's progress was contributing significantly not only to the understanding of the German Army's W/T networks, and thus to the more efficient interception of them, but also to MI's knowledge of the German Army's order of battle. Nor was the work confined to the German Army. Although AI had a small party at GC and CS which passed to a few people at Cheadle the call-sign identifications and other Traffic Analysis items that it derived from studying the Enigma, it did no sustained Traffic Analysis on the high-echelon W/T networks of the GAF. Partly for this reason, and partly because the traffic on these networks was still being intercepted at Army stations, MI8 undertook Traffic Analysis on GAF as well as on German Army high-echelon communications. In addition – and this consideration helps to explain why MI8 became an important centre for Traffic Analysis – GC and CS's Army Section, unlike its Naval and Air Sections, displayed little interest in the work, its cryptanalysts being inclined to regard it as 'a fad'.

If these developments were understandable enough, so were their consequences. From the middle of 1940 MI, like AI, attached a small Traffic Analysis team to GC and CS, to work at the point where the GAF Enigma was being decyphered and processed. MI8's work benefited so much from this step that in December 1940 it demanded that its entire Traffic Analysis staff, by then a force of 70 officers, should be accommodated at GC and CS. Recognising that the day was long past when it was possible to decentralise high-grade cryptanalysis and transfer it to the Whitehall departments, it justified the demand with the argument that Traffic Analysis and cryptanalysis must be done in the same place. But the Director of GC and CS opposed the demand on the ground that his establishment should continue to be a cryptanalytical centre. Considering that GC and CS had long advocated a combined centre in the Middle East, which would analyse all types of Sigint in one place and communicate the results to all three Services,* this was an odd response, the more so as it came at just the time that GC and CS's Naval Section was taking over responsibility for Traffic Analysis from the Admiralty. It can be presumed that the Director was swayed by the differences between his staff, sceptical of the value of TA, and MI8's officers, and even by fears for his own control of GC and CS, as well as by such practical matters as the grave shortage of accommodation at Bletchley. For MI, on the other hand, where the MI8 Colonel in any case fervently believed that the Services should control Sigint in time of war, GC and CS's attitude provoked the DMI into writing to the other Directors of Intelligence about 'the vexed question of the balance of interception between cryptographic needs on the one hand and operational needs on the other'. Behind this question, however, lay a wider issue, the control of Sigint policy and production. The DMI's letter went on to complain that 'with

---

* See Chapter 6, p 196.

distribution [of Sigint] governed by "C" and [with] direct control from GC and CS to the [interception] stations, the Services have little or no responsibility except to administer their stations'. Its purpose was to acquire for the Service intelligence directorates a greater say in the management of GC and CS, and it formally demanded an investigation by the Y Committee and suggested that the Y Committee should report back to the JIC.

This, the first attempt during the war to involve the JIC in the discussion of Sigint policy and organisation, foundered on the opposition of 'C'. Instead, the Main Committee* (of which the Y Committee was a sub-committee) was called together for the first time since the outbreak of war. During February and March 1941 this committee, composed of 'C' and the three Service Directors of Intelligence and now rechristened the Y Board, reached agreement on broad principles. It decided that Y – this vague term being now defined as the exploitation and development of all means of interception that might produce intelligence, and thus as including such things as non-communications radio,† navigation aids, R/T, RFP‡ and TINA§ – must remain under the control of the Services, but that cryptanalysis must continue on an inter-Service basis under separate management by 'C' and GC and CS. The work of GC and CS involved so many technicalities, and so much of its output interested more than one of the Services, that direct intervention by the individual Service departments in the running of the organisation was seen to be impracticable. But if the Services accepted this, they were successful in providing for the better co-ordination of cryptanalysis and interception and for the more effective presentation to GC and CS of their requirements.

The revised terms of reference for the Y Board established that the Chiefs of Staff were ultimately responsible for the co-ordination of Y and cryptanalysis. Acting on their behalf, the Y Board was in future to meet every six or eight weeks. To help relate everyday decisions to operational requirements an intelligence officer from each of the Service directorates joined the signals officers who had hitherto formed the Y Committee; the Y Board set up a parallel Sub-Committee for cryptanalysis on which the Services were similarly represented; and the Chairmen of the Y Committee and of the cryptanalysis committee were both made members of the Y Board. For his part, the Director

---

* See Chapter 1, p 23.

† By this time other organisations than the Y service were intercepting enemy signals. No 80 Wing RAF was undertaking the airborne interception of navigational beacons and beams (see below, Chapter 10) and the Telecommunications Research Establishment (TRE) and the Royal Aircraft Establishment (RAE) were examining these intercepts as they were later to examine enemy radar and infra-red.

‡ A process which filmed the type and peculiarities of a transmitter.

§ The study of the morse characteristics of individual wireless operators.

of GC and CS made amends by setting up there an 'Inter-Service Distribution and Reference Section', at which the Service intelligence directorates were to be fully represented, as a means of assuring the Directors of Intelligence that their interests in the circulation of the results of cryptanalysis were met.

These decisions of the spring of 1941 brought to an end the period in which misunderstandings and emergencies resulted from inadequate high-level direction of Sigint policy. One example of these had arisen when Hankey was called in to investigate the difficulties which came to a head at the end of 1939. Another had occurred in September 1940. At the peak of the invasion danger, and at a time when GC and CS was beginning to provide vital information about German penetration into the Balkans, the capacity of the Services to intercept the GAF Enigma traffic had begun to lag behind GC and CS's decrypting capacity from shortage of wireless operators. The facts had reached the Prime Minister through personal channels; on his instructions Hankey had met the emergency by ordering the transfer of operators from the Radio Security Service, MI5's intercept service, overruling RSS's protests. After the activation of the Y Board and the strengthening of its structure of committees, problems of this scale and character were kept under review and dealt with more effectively. The structure underwent minor changes. The cryptanalysis committee died out in August 1941, largely because it was replaced by a special Enigma sub-committee of the Y Committee, set up at AI's suggestion in March 1941. During 1941 further sub-committees were formed for such matters as the development of technical equipment. But at the higher levels, although disagreements were inevitably to arise from time to time, this system proved to be adequate for the efficient development, co-ordination and control of Y and cryptanalysis, and for maintaining good relations between GC and CS and the Service directorates, after the volume and importance of Sigint increased from the spring of 1941.

The more detailed controversies which had precipitated the enquiry were less easily solved. Thus, the Y Board made a special investigation into the relationship of Traffic Analysis to cryptanalysis and concluded that the two activities were inextricably bound up with each other, but the Services still treated Traffic Analysis differently, MI8 continuing to do it for MI while the Admiralty and the Air Ministry left it to staffs at GC and CS. Through difficulties at the working level the Inter-Service Distribution Section at GC and CS failed to achieve its purpose – that of stilling the resentment felt by the Service departments, and especially by the War Office, at the fact that 'C' and GC and CS remained in charge of the distribution of the results of cryptanalysis. It turned out to be impossible for a single section to extract for each of the three Services what was significant in a daily flow of thousands of signals of very many different kinds. This was all the more the case because several groups of experts had grown up in different parts of GC and CS, each interpreting and combining different types of Sigint in a great variety of appropriate ways and each developing direct links with the different branches of the Service directorates in Whitehall. This last development was one which should have comforted the Whitehall directorates, and which in fact did so. But it was a development which also gave them further cause for disquiet. Within the Whitehall directorates it led to rivalry between the different branches as to which of them should provide the liaison officers at GC and CS. At the same time, it was providing the serving officers of the directorates with their first close acquaintance with a body of men and women that must to them have seemed extraordinary for its lack of uniformity in outlook, organisation and procedure.

GC and CS had increased in size four-fold in the first sixteen months of the war. At the beginning of 1941 it was by Whitehall standards poorly organised. This was partly because the growth in its size and in the complexity of its activities had outstripped the experience of those who administered it. Reflecting the pre-war constitution and priorities of GC and CS, these were Foreign Office civilians and Service officers who had been trained for cryptanalysis and who still doubled their administrative responsibility, as the Head of GC and CS or as the heads of its sections, with the role of cryptanalyst. But there were other reasons why GC and CS remained a loose collection of groups, rather than forming a single, tidy organisation. New sections had had to be improvised into existence in response to the needs and opportunities thrown up since the outbreak of war. Some of them were subordinate to outside activities, including the Services themselves, and were cut off from the others by security barriers as well as by chains of command. Not less important, many of the new recruits had been drawn from the universities and similar backgrounds. Professors, lecturers and undergraduates, chess-masters and experts from the principal museums, barristers and antiquarian booksellers, some of them in uniform and others civilians on the books of the Foreign Office or the Service ministries – such for the most part were the individuals who inaugurated and manned the various cells which had sprung up within or alongside the original sections. They contributed by their variety and individuality to the lack of uniformity. There is also no doubt that they thrived on it, as they did on the absence at GC and CS of any emphasis on rank or insistence on hierarchy.

It was difficult for the Service directorates to distinguish between the real and growing need for a stronger higher administration at GC and CS, one that would be more effective in negotiating with them about the unavoidable clashes of priority and personality that accompanied GC and CS's increasing importance to the intelligence effort, and, on the other hand, the value of accepting and preserving the condition of creative anarchy, within and between the sections, that distinguished GC and CS's day-to-day work and brought to the front the best among its unorthodox and 'undisciplined' war-time staff. The difficulty was all the greater because the monopoly of the directorates in the interpretation of Sigint was being threatened. The staff at GC and CS, recognising no frontiers in research, no division of labour in intelligence work, invaded the field of appreciation. The Whitehall directorates, regarding this as their province, were nevertheless ill-equipped and untrained for some at least of the research on the Sigint data that the work demanded. Between GC and CS and the Admiralty, as we have seen, this problem produced less friction than was the case with the other two Services. But until February 1941 even the Admiralty hankered after the idea of appointing a senior naval officer to take charge of GC and CS's Naval Section.

In March, after the investigation by the Y Board, the Admiralty adopted a different solution. It appointed an assistant director of the OIC (ADIC) 'to be responsible to DNI for the co-ordination of the results of the work of the Naval Section at [Bletchley Park] and for the action taken by NID on the material provided by BP'. This appointment, held by an RN Captain who was based in OIC but made regular visits to GC and CS, supplemented on the one hand the day-to-day telephonic contacts that had already grown up between the OIC and the Naval Section and, on the other, the network of the Y Board and its committees that now began to function in Whitehall. It did so to such good effect that discord never again flared up between the OIC and GC and CS's Naval Section. They shared the work of handling Sigint, GC and CS in some matters duplicating or double-banking the OIC and in others dividing the responsibility with it, in close agreement till the end of the war and with no further regard for the demarcations between cryptanalysis and Y and between the procurement and the evaluation processes. With AI and MI, GC and CS's relations remained less smooth. Neither of these directorates made an appointment similar to ADIC. Both continued to chafe against the large measure of control which GC and CS had established over the Sigint effort and to complain through their advisers at GC and CS about the supply and selection of decrypts which they still received via the SIS. Even by these directorates, however, the arrangements made by the Y Board in February and March 1941 were accepted as constituting the proper channel for ventilating complaints and removing friction.

□

In contrast to their increasing interest in the work of GC and CS, the Service departments displayed no concern to interfere in the other part of 'C''s empire – the SIS.

That this was so was partly, but only partly, because they respected 'C''s claim that the SIS must be allowed autonomy and secrecy of operation for security reasons. It was on this account that during the second half of 1940 the SIS was excluded from the enquiries of a committee set up to try to reduce the demand for W/T transmitters, then in short supply, by investigating the work done and the equipment needed by the various departments. For the same reason the working of SIS as an organisation was rarely considered by the normal inter-departmental intelligence machinery. Up to the spring of 1941 this took place on only one occasion – in February 1941, when the JIC and the Chiefs of Staff considered the shortage of transport aircraft that was gravely hampering the SIS's operations.[1] As we have seen, however, the management of Sigint and of the affairs of GC and CS enjoyed a similar immunity without escaping criticism from and intervention by the Service departments. If there was no such criticism of the SIS, and no investigation of its affairs comparable to that which led to the activation of the Y Board, this was because another factor was at work.

This other consideration, reinforcing the continuing remoteness of the SIS, was a growing indifference on the part of the SIS's chief customers, the Service departments, to the greater part of its product. In August 1940 the SIS was complaining that the departments were not incorporating in their intelligence summaries and appreciations all the information that it was supplying to them. As we shall see, the complaint prompted the Prime Minister to instruct the departments to pass all items of intelligence about occupied Europe to his personal staff.* The Service ministries were less easily moved by the complaint. In February 1941, again, when they considered the SIS need for aircraft, the Chiefs of Staff recognised the problem but were not disposed to alleviate it by giving the SIS any special priority. The fact was that since the previous summer, while the supply of Sigint, POW reports and PR had steadily increased in amount and significance, the ability of the SIS to acquire reliable information had not improved, and had in some areas markedly declined.

By the spring of 1941 the SIS had made but little progress in overcoming the difficulties that sprang from pre-war inactivity in the eastern Mediterranean and the Middle East, as also in north Africa. In Spain and Portugal at that time these same difficulties were still being exacerbated by other considerations; in Portugal by acrimonious SIS disputes both local and with London; in Spain by the British Ambassador's conviction that the stability of the Franco regime was the best guarantee of Spanish neutrality and by his insistence that British intelligence organisations should therefore be kept on a tight

---

* See below, p 295.

1. JIC (41) 57 of 6 February: CAB 79/9, COS (41) 55th Meeting, 14 February, COS (41), 95th Meeting, 12 March.

rein lest they get involved with anti-Franco forces.[2] In most of the rest of Europe the SIS's recovery from the set-backs that had followed upon German occupation was necessarily slow. It was not until the spring of 1941 that, beginning with the formation of coast-watching cells in Norway, of a reporting organisation in the French Atlantic ports and of new links with Berlin via Switzerland, it began to get results from the recent re-establishment of its networks there. Even then there were many technical difficulties associated with getting agents into the occupied areas. It was not always easy to find the right type of agent, there was a lack of trained W/T operators, and the extremely severe German control of invasion areas and security measures against easy identification of troops had also to be contended with.

In these circumstances, its wish to remain autonomous reinforced by the decline in the value of its service both absolutely and relative to the supply of information from other sources, the SIS was left alone to solve its problems. Of these the shortage of the transport – ships as well as aircraft – now needed for its missions into occupied Europe was not the least serious. A new section of SIS responsible for acquiring transport succeeded in forming in the summer of 1940 a flotilla of Norwegian fishing boats, which later developed into the famous 'Shetland Bus' shuttle service, but it was unable to provide a regular service to France until the spring of 1942. Until then except that an irregular fishing boat service to Brittany produced sporadic intelligence from as early as July 1940, infiltration into France was possible only by submarines, which were rarely made available, or by special craft, which the SIS requested without success until, again only in 1942, the Admiralty provided an MTB flotilla, or by aircraft. From the summer of 1940 the SIS had a Special Flight – No 419 (SD) – at its disposal. But missions were few and far between until the spring of 1941, when the Flight was replaced by Squadron No 138 (SD), and even then the situation only slowly improved. There were only 18 successful missions using aircraft in the first seven months of 1941, as compared with 38 in the following six months.

Transport difficulties loomed large because the SIS had been driven back upon the United Kingdom as the base for its operations. This was also true of the various governments-in-exile that had now arrived in London, and their arrival presented the SIS with another set of problems – those arising from the fact that it was made responsible for liaison with their agent-running organisations. With that of the Poles, who were already operating an extensive network of agents in Europe, with efficient W/T channels, liaison presented few difficulties. The Polish government agreed to hand over to the SIS all

2. FO 800/323, Halifax Papers; Hoare to Halifax 15 August 1940; Templewood Papers (Cambridge University Library), 13, 20; PREM 4/21/2A, Dalton to Churchill 17 January 1941.

the intelligence it gathered, except that dealing with Poland's internal affairs, and in January 1941 the Polish IIe Bureau became the sole link for passing this material and for receiving British requests for information. A similar arrangement was possible with the Czechs until 1943. The other European secret services were less well-founded, and less secure, and the SIS sought to control the situation by denying them their own communications and codes and by assuming responsibility for their funds and logistics. The arrangements worked reasonably well with some of them – with the Norwegians, for example, who easily agreed to a division of labour by which they collected military intelligence while the SIS confined itself initially to ship-watching for the Admiralty. With others it produced strained relations and involved the SIS in tortuous and unproductive complications. The Dutch, with Venlo still fresh in their minds,* were highly critical of the SIS (unjustly, as it later transpired) when an operation to send additional agents to Holland, which they carried out jointly with the SIS from August 1940, ended in failure in the following October. With the Belgians relations were made difficult by the existence of a second Belgian organisation which was at loggerheads with the Belgian Sureté-in-exile. A similar problem bedevilled relations with the French, and it was made all the more intractable by the failure or the inability of the SIS to make a clear division of responsibility between two of its own sections – that which dealt with de Gaulle's Free French SIS, and that which was trying to revive contacts in Vichy France and establish a British network there. It is claimed, however, that in some ways the rivalry between these sections had a beneficial effect on the intelligence produced.

Unlike the other problems besetting the SIS's relations with these European intelligence bodies in London, this last, which was to exist till the end of the war, had its origin in British organisational rivalry and confusion. It was matched in this respect – though in scale and as a source of irritation to the SIS it was far outweighed – by another development. At the hands of the British government departments the SIS suffered no more than indifference to its results and a resulting lack of priority for its requests. With its old counterpart, MI5, it had to forge closer links when it was carrying out most of its activities from the United Kingdom and when MI5 was tapping new sources of intelligence by establishing interrogation centres for spies, from July 1940, and, from January 1941, for alien refugees. Even so, friction between the two bodies was not avoided, particularly about the RSS, control of which passed from MI5 to the SIS in May 1941. On the whole, however, an arrangement whereby SIS established a new section within MI5 worked amicably enough. This was not the case with the adjustments that were forced upon the SIS by the creation of a new

---

* See Chapter 2, pp 56–57.

body, not unlike itself in mode and sphere of activity, in the summer of 1940. Its relations with this body got off to a poor start in August 1940 when what was to become the Special Operations Executive (SOE), on being made responsible for sabotage activities overseas, took over the SIS's sabotage section without consulting 'C'. Thereafter the SIS found itself having to share with the SOE such limited transport facilities as were available to it in the United Kingdom – though in the Mediterranean the two groups relied mainly on developing their own private navies and operated independently. On the other hand, the SIS feared that sporadic sabotage would endanger long-term intelligence plans, and also felt, often with justification in the early days, that SOE's methods were insecure. It thus insisted on conducting the SOE's communications, and in April 1941 it defeated a demand by the SOE to be allowed its own codes and signals network.

By the spring of 1941 these early grounds for mutual recrimination were being joined by another. Inevitably the SOE was beginning to gather items of intelligence as a by-product of its sabotage activities. In Denmark, for example, it had established by then a link, via Sweden, with the MI authorities, whose pre-war liaison with the SIS had been interrupted by the German occupation, despite the efforts to continue it made by the Danes and the SIS in the autumn of 1940. From the middle of 1941, when the Danish network was producing excellent intelligence, the SIS agreed that the SOE should act for it in Denmark. Until 1942, when the two organisations finally agreed that SOE's intelligence should be passed to the user departments only via the SIS, this further overlap of their activities was to be the cause of especially bitter rivalry between them; and even then, as we shall see, the SIS remained in the somewhat humiliating position of having to pass on intelligence obtained by its younger competitor from areas which it had failed to penetrate with its own agents.

□

As a source of intelligence the value of photographic reconnaissance, particularly high altitude, high speed reconnaissance with Spitfires, was fully recognised by the autumn of 1940, but its development was still held back by inadequate resources and difficulties of organisation. For the Admiralty, especially, less favoured than the Air Ministry by the supply of Sigint and more desperate than the War Office, whose needs for operational intelligence declined as the threat of invasion receded, the expansion of these resources had become a matter of first priority, and the Air Ministry's apparent inactivity – at least its inability to meet the Admiralty's requests – was becoming the subject of intense criticism. Aware of this, and anxious in any case to delegate its own operational control of PR to the RAF Commands, the Air Ministry began in October to investigate two proposals: the creation of a single Photographic Reconnaissance Group which would direct all operations by Coastal and Bomber Commands and be of sufficient size to meet the needs of all three Services; and the formation of a single Photographic Interpretation Unit with which all three Service intelligence directorates should have direct and close contact.

Of these projects the second was implemented without great difficulty, if not without some delay. On 7 January 1941 the PIU* was re-christened the Central Interpretation Unit (CIU) and, subject only to administration by Coastal Command and technical supervision from the Air Ministry, set up as an independent organisation responsible for interpreting all air photographs from all sources and for issuing all reports on interpretation to the Service ministries and the commands. In the following April it was moved from Wembley to Medmenham, where it remained for the rest of the war. At this point, although the Air Ministry insisted that the unit be made entirely RAF, its civilians being replaced or given appropriate Service rank, it became the centre for all training in interpretation, the headquarters of a central photographic library, and the supplier to all three Services of charts, plans and models as well as of the operational intelligence derived from PR.[3] By that date friction between the three Services about interpretation had come to an end and the only remaining disputes were between the Air Staff, the CIU and Bomber Command as to which would be responsible for interpreting and reporting on bomb damage.

The plan to establish a single Photographic Reconnaissance Group for all PR operations and development met with opposition from Coastal and Bomber Commands. Accordingly it was in the first instance rejected 'in favour of [separate] operational control by Coastal and Bomber Commands tempered by Air Ministry co-ordination on a technical level'. In order to carry out this co-ordination the Air Ministry created a Deputy Director (Photography) and an advisory committee. With this qualification, three separate PR units emerged. No 1 PRU, the original unit, remaining substantially unaltered except for some aircraft changes, continued to be responsible under Coastal Command for the intelligence requirements of the CIC and for meeting the Admiralty's needs. No 2 PRU was the Middle East unit, based in Egypt, the establishment of which had been decided in September 1940.† No 3 PRU, a reorganised unit under Bomber Command, retained primary responsibility for taking the photographs required for targetting and for assessing bomb damage.[4] Bomber Command also retained responsibility for night photography, an activity which, partly for policy reasons, partly on account of

---

* See Chapter 3, p 104.   † See Chapter 6, p 207.

3. AIR 41/6, p 252.   4. ibid, pp 244–252.

shortage of equipment and partly because its Spitfires were unsuitable, the PRU had not undertaken. The need for night photography arose chiefly from the fact that, as was revealed by reconnaissance, Bomber Command's raids were achieving poor results and from the wish to photograph the bomb-bursts in relation to the targets during an attack.

These steps proved satisfactory as far as technical matters and aircraft modification were concerned. The improvement of night photography proved to be difficult, and its development was transferred to the Aircraft and Armament Experimental Establishment at Boscombe Down when No 1 and No 3 PRUs were amalgamated in the summer of 1941. But in other directions – particularly in meeting earlier criticism of the small scale of the photographs taken by the high-level Spitfires – good progress was now made.[5] The standard F.8 cameras with 20″ focal length lenses were replaced by Fairchild cameras with 24″ lenses, which produced the scale of 1/15,000, and even better results were obtained with two German telephoto 30″ lenses which were put into use in November 1940. At the operational level, on the other hand, matters remained unsatisfactory. Neither DD(Ph) nor any other authority in the Air Ministry had any responsibility for ordering reconnaissance or for co-ordinating and settling the priorities between the requests for it that came with increasing frequency from the Service ministries, and particularly from the Admiralty. At the end of 1940 and in the early months of 1941 the Admiralty complained repeatedly that its needs for coverage of the U-boat yards and the main units of the German Fleet were not receiving sufficient attention under the existing system by which it put its requests for PR direct to Coastal Command. Coastal Command, it argued, was being neglected at the expense of Bomber Command's needs, and the expansion of photographic reconnaissance was being held up by the reluctance of the Air Ministry and the Ministry of Aircraft Production to divert any resources from the aircraft programme.[6]

The Air Ministry took the view that the intelligence authorities should decide these matters on an inter-departmental basis, and in February 1941, D of I Air Ministry having appointed an adviser on photographic reconnaissance to attend its deliberations, the JIC gave substantial backing to the Admiralty's complaints in a memorandum for the Chiefs of Staff.[7] On 14 February the Vice-Chiefs of Staff considered this paper and invited the Air Ministry to consider whether the solution might lie after all in amalgamating the photographic units under a single centralised operational control.[8] The outcome of these discussions was that on 1 March the Air Ministry

5. ibid, p 194; AIR 41/7, p 25.
6. ADM 233/84, Monograph on Photographic Reconnaissance.
7. JIC (41) 63 of 10 February.
8. CAB 79/9, COS (41) 55th Meeting, 14 February.

decided to assume operational control of the PR units in the United Kingdom, as well as of CIU. The intention was that the control should be exercised by the D of I, who was strengthened by the appointment of an ADI (Photographic), and the opportunity was taken to insist that the CIU should be responsible for all interpretation, including bomb damage assessment. DD (Ph) was to remain in existence as technical adviser to the new ADI (Ph)[9] and was to be responsible with RAE Farnborough for the development of cameras and associated equipment.

This plan, in its turn, was implemented only in part and with some delay. The amalgamation of No 1 and No 3 PRU was announced in April but did not take place until 16 June; not until September 1941 was responsibility for bomb damage assessment finally transferred from Bomber Command to the CIU. In the end, moreover, it proved impracticable to vest control of operations in ACAS (I), as the D of I became in April 1941.* The amalgamated unit was placed under Coastal Command, though ADI (Ph) remained responsible on behalf of ACAS (I) for overall co-ordination and the sole channel for the supply of reconnaissance photographs. More important, the new arrangement did little to solve the problem of competing demands for reconnaissance between the Admiralty, Bomber Command and Fighter Command, which now stemmed less from organisational problems than from the continuing shortage of PR aircraft and the delay in introducing PR aircraft with a longer range.†

On this issue the Admiralty's dissatisfaction reached new heights during March. On 22 March it noted that 'for ten months strong pressure has been brought on the Air Ministry to enlarge the scope of PR' and that 'every effort direct or through the JIC and COS has failed'. About the same time – at a time when it was being baffled in all its attempts to locate the *Scharnhorst* and the *Gneisenau* – it began to talk about taking independent action, either the rebuilding of a photographic unit under the SIS of the kind it had supported before the war‡ or a plan by which the Navy would 'built up an organisation itself to supplement the PRU, adapting American types of aircraft...and enlisting personnel at once to operate them'.[10] The Air Ministry rejected these suggestions, and objected to DNI's further proposal in April 1941 that Cotton, who had resigned his RAF commission in March, should be re-employed in the Fleet Air Arm.

Despite these rebuffs, the NID continued to pursue such ideas into the summer, and by September 1941 the Admiralty had decided to

---

* See below, p 284.
† See Chapter 5, p 169, and Chapter 10, p 332.
‡ See Chapter 1, pp 28–29.

9. AIR 41/6, p 257 et seq.
10. ADM 233/84.

develop a long-range system and had employed Cotton. He was provided with an American bomber of a new type (DB7), but because the Admiralty had no authority to operate and control shore-based aircraft he was restricted in what he could do. Moreover, others besides Cotton flew the aircraft, causing accidents and damage which further hampered him. But by the time the aircraft was written off at the end of the year the slow expansion of PR resources during 1941 was yielding a great improvement in photographic intelligence for all three Services.[11]

□

During the first year of the war the interrogation of prisoners of war and the scrutiny of captured documents and crashed aircraft had contributed to the solution of some important problems – the clarification of the U-boat order of battle, the identification of GAF units and, in ways that we still have to describe,* the understanding of the GAF's systems of navigational beams – and sometimes they had even yielded the first clue or the essential detail. From the autumn of 1940 these sources were providing so much valuable and up-to-date intelligence that they could be used as 'cover' for the dissemination of intelligence from Sigint, which might otherwise have had to be withheld for security reasons. Reciprocally, the provision under strict control to interrogation officers of facts known from Sigint was making for the more effective interrogation of prisoners.

Direct interrogation – one of three techniques adopted for getting intelligence from POW – was most effective when the prisoner was at all co-operative, either initially or after persuasion by offers of better treatment or other inducements. (It was found that most prisoners who did co-operate did so after a period of two to nine days). The success of interrogation depended heavily on the brief of the interrogator, as well as on his experience, skill and understanding of the prisoner. The brief contained all information about the prisoner's units, Service personalities and technical matters that could be gathered from other prisoners and from different secret sources. To this end a substantial library was rapidly created. A second technique was eavesdropping with the aid of concealed microphones. This enabled interrogators to overhear conversations between prisoners of the same unit or crew, who were kept apart immediately after capture and until they had been first questioned. It proved to be of considerable value, not only for the new intelligence it produced but also in suggesting new lines for further interrogations, but it allowed of no stage management. Hence the development of a third method, the introduction of stool-pigeons. These had to be briefed in detail about the character they adopted,

---

* See Chapter 10, p 332 et seq.

11. Morgan, op cit, p 283.

as well as about the prisoner and his likely areas of knowledge. Their use was to some extent limited; they were under considerable strain and could not be used in all cases. They were originally recruited from refugees, four of whom had been trained and used by the end of 1940. It was also found possible to use some prisoners, when from ideological reasons or otherwise they were prepared to co-operate. In all, 49 were selected for this duty during the war.

At the outbreak of war these activities had been concentrated in the Tower of London and they had later been moved to Cockfosters Camp in Barnet. By the autumn of 1940 it became obvious that, with the growth in POW numbers, the fullest use of these techniques would necessitate a move to new quarters. It was now arranged that they should be transferred to Latimer and Beaconsfield, though the move did not take place until the second half of 1942, when these centres had been properly equipped. At the same time steps were taken to put the handling of POWs in the Middle East on a better footing.*

At the beginning of the war the work in the United Kingdom had been organised on an inter-Service basis, under the administration of the War Office, through the Combined Services Detailed Interrogation Centre (CSDIC).† In July 1940 the CSDIC had been supplemented by another system when the War Office set up the Prisoners of War Interrogation Service, the PWIS (Home). This consisted of a body of officers posted to commands throughout the United Kingdom to undertake the preliminary interrogation of prisoners arriving in their areas. It formed an important link between the CSDIC and field units, and it also provided the interrogators who were attached to the raids made on occupied territories. By then, however, the CSDIC itself had evolved as three Service sections, all working closely together in the exchange of information and the development of the techniques for getting it, but each responsible to its own Service intelligence directorate for seeing that the department received whatever intelligence might concern it and receiving from it briefs and priority instructions. As the numbers of POW increased, it had become clear that separation on Service lines was to this extent unavoidable.[12]

□

The Service intelligence directorates continued to be organised, as before the war,‡ largely on geographical lines. The geographical division had perhaps been the appropriate one in peace-time, when the Services had been required to bring together the various types of

---

* See Chapter 6, p 205.   † See Chapter 3, p 90.
‡ See Chapter 1, p 11 et seq.

12. Mockler-Ferryman, op cit, Section II, Chapter 6; *Air Ministry Intelligence*, Part II, Chapter 7; Naval History of POW Intelligence 1939–1945 (draft).

intelligence that could throw light on the military capacities and plans of individual foreign countries. But under war conditions it had been subjected to increasing strain.

During the first year of the war all three directorates had responded to the new conditions by setting up specialised or functional sections alongside the main country sections. In the autumn of 1940 the Air Intelligence directorate – expanded by then to 240 officers as compared with 40 at the oubreak of war – embarked on a series of reorganisations which by the summer of 1941 were to replace its geographical sub-divisions by functional sections.[13] Hitherto, apart from introducing a watch-keeping section to handle urgent intelligence throughout the 24 hours, it had set up new sections only for specialised purposes. One collated the intelligence required for AI's contribution to JIC papers; another procured intelligence from the censorship organisation; a third maintained contact with the bodies which conducted clandestine operations. In November 1940 the entire directorate was reorganised into four new deputy-directorates. Three of these, those dealing with substantive intelligence, were still organised on geographical lines – one for the neutral unthreatened countries; one for Germany and the countries occupied or threatened by her; one for Italy, the Balkans and other areas likely to be involved in the Italian war – but the second of them was further sub-divided into specialised sub-sections to deal with such subjects as the GAF's order of battle, organisation, aircraft production, airfields, communications and technical intelligence. A still greater departure from the geographical principle followed in April 1941, when the German and the neutral sections took over the countries of the Italian area and were subordinated to a single Director of Intelligence (Operations). At the same time the post of Director of Intelligence was up-graded to that of Assistant-Chief of Air Staff – ACAS(I) – and the functional sections of AI were directly subordinated to him as directorates or deputy-directorates. A directorate was created to take over the work of the Deputy-Director of Signals (Y) and to supervise all aspects of air Sigint other than the handling of the end product. An assistant-directorate was set up for PR. And AI's scientific intelligence officer became an independent Assistant-Director as ADI (Science) and was given a small group of scientists to assist him. In August 1941, in a further reorganisation, the whole of the substantive work of AI was put on a functional basis, the Director of Intelligence (Operations) becoming responsible for strategic and operational intelligence in respect of all foreign air forces.

Neither the reorganisation of AI, nor the improvement in its status which followed when its head was promoted to be ACAS(I), was paralleled at the Admiralty or the War Office. In the case of the

---

13. *Air Ministry Intelligence*, Part I, Chapter 1.

Admiralty the main reason is to be found in the existence of the OIC, and in the arrangements that had governed its relations with the remainder of the NID, since the beginning of the war. What chiefly brought about the reconstruction of AI was the immense importance and mobility of the GAF – the fact that its every move might be significant operationally and for the light it threw on Germany's strategic intentions. When these considerations made it imperative to centralise all available intelligence about the GAF, and when much of the increasing wealth of information was of a kind which, like the results of the detailed research being done at GC and CS, could not be transmitted to the commands, AI was becoming the unique authority and the commands were depending on its collation and assessment of intelligence about enemy air forces to a far greater extent than had been expected. It was from the beginning of 1941 that it began to issue to the commands the series of bulletins that, with their ever-increasing frequency and accuracy, were to be of crucial importance to the conduct of air operations in all theatres. But it was precisely in order to provide such a service to the naval commands that an OIC had been set up in the Admiralty, as also with the Mediterranean Fleet, at the outbreak of war. Nor was that all. In AI the product of Sigint, the most important source of intelligence, had been handled from the outset only by the main, and initially geographical sections, and the source was disguised in the interests of security. In the NID, in contrast, this type of intelligence was undisguised, but for reasons of security was restricted to the OIC and, except to selected individuals, was not made available to the country sections. The head of NID 3 (the Mediterranean section) was not included among these individuals until February 1941.[14] And it was only in January 1941 that the officer responsible for studying U-boat construction in NID 1, the section responsible for Germany and northern Europe, was given access to it.[15]

These arrangements did not necessitate the preservation in the NID of the geographical system of division. There were other grounds for keeping it, arising out of the nature of the naval war. In the second half of 1940, for example, a new geographical section was carved out of the existing country sections to deal with Scandinavia, where the need to watch German activity, the planning of possible British raids and the importance as a source of information of the Naval Attaché in Stockholm were all considerations calling for separate study of the area. Beyond doubt, however, the relationship already established between the OIC and the rest of NID acted as a barrier against larger-scale reorganisation. In addition, it did much to shape such alterations as were made. Its general consequence was that the

---

14. Morgan, op cit, p 97.
15. ibid, pp 28, 30.

country sections, staffed and equipped to do research but virtually cut off from Sigint, were restricted largely to the collation and assessment of political and strategic information from other sources, whereas the OIC was poorly equipped to do long-term research on the Sigint which contained so much of the essential information about the enemy navies. In organisational terms this had two particular results.

The first, which we have already noticed, goes far to explain why the NID staff did not increase as much as AI's or MI's: GC and CS's Naval Section developed into the body on which the OIC relied for a good deal of the long-term research on naval Sigint.* The second was that only a few functional sections were added during the war to those set up in the NID long before the autumn of 1939 – the technical section; a signals section; and the OIC itself. One of these, a *de facto* section for the study of coastal and other fixed defences in European countries, was formed in 1943 when it was decided that the NID section studying Scandinavian defences should work alongside those studying this subject in the War Office.[16] Another was a section attached to the DNI–NID 17.

NID 17 was set up early in 1940 as a small section of two or three officers 'to co-ordinate intelligence' within the NID and to liaise between NID and other intelligence bodies. One of its officers concentrated on scrutinising the SIS reports, the Axis diplomatic decrypts and Sigint from high-grade Service cyphers for intelligence that was of strategic importance to the Admiralty but that was not being handled by the OIC or GC and CS, because it was not relevant to naval operations, or by NID's geographical sections because they were cut off from Sigint.[17] In mid-1940 this officer formed a sub-section – NID 17M – which exploited GC and CS's reading of the Abwehr cypher† and, by acting as the link between MI5 and the Naval Staff, helped to break up at the end of that year a German attempt to set up a weather-reporting system in Greenland and Jan Mayen. Thereafter, NID 17 (later NID 12) not only continued to act for the Admiralty in the work of countering German secret service initiatives and conducting deception operations – for example, it helped to check the sabotage of British ships in Spain – but also became responsible for issuing to the Naval Staff, the C-in-C Home Fleet and a few other authorities regular summaries of strategic intelligence, based on the decrypts which it handled, of the kind that had a bearing on the deliberations of the War Cabinet and the Chiefs of Staff. As the flow of intelligence from these and other sources increased, and the machinery for inter-departmental assessment of it became more

---

* See above, pp 267–268, 274.
† See also Chapter 3, p 120 and Chapter 11, p 358.

16. ADM 233/84, *Development and Organisation of the NID.*
17. Morgan, op cit, p 145 et seq.

developed, NID 17's numbers greatly expanded as did its work of representing the Admiralty at the JIC, the Joint Intelligence Staff (JIS)* and other inter-Service bodies.[18]

In the War Office the organisation of the MI directorate continued to conform more closely to the Admiralty pattern than to that adopted in AI.[19] On the one hand, war-time conditions made it necessary to form some functional sections. The creation of MI8 at the outbreak of war was soon followed by that of special sections for technical intelligence, for propaganda and for prisoners of war.† During 1940 the sub-section studying German rail movements acquired a *de facto* responsibility for studying the railways of the whole of Europe. In December 1940 another sub-section took over from AI the responsibility for collating all intelligence about enemy AA defences and for disseminating it not only in MI, but also to the RAF commands and, later on, to the United States Army Air Force as well. On the other hand, the most important change during 1940 was the establishment of a new country section, MI14.‡ This was made responsible only for Germany and German-occupied Europe, areas which had hitherto been covered by a geographical section responsible for most of the European continent. But if for its main sections MI, like the NID, retained the principle of geographical division, it did so for different reasons.

Chief among them was a consideration reflected in the fact that it acquired no section equivalent to the OIC and that, as in AI as long as that directorate remained on a geographical basis, its country sections were the sole recipients of Sigint. The War Office, always as we have already noted the least operational of the Service departments, continued to be so. During 1940, in order to free itself for the task of concentrating on enemy intelligence, its intelligence directorate shed some of the administrative responsibilities with which it had been saddled before or on the outbreak of war. It transferred its press censorship section to the War Office's Directorate of Public Relations, its postal and telegraph censorship section to the Ministry of Information, its production of ordnance survey maps to DMO, and its responsibility for staffing and equipping intercept stations to the Signals Directorate. But except for the period up to the evacuation from Dunkirk, when it supplied intelligence to C-in-C Home Forces, it did not acquire the responsibility for supplying operational intelligence to the commands. On the contrary, the commands in all the active theatres acquired during 1940 their own virtually self-contained

---

* See below, p 298.
† See above, p 283 and Chapter 3, p 90.
‡ See Chapter 5, p 162, fn †.

18. ibid, pp 145–147.
19. Mockler-Ferryman, op cit, Chapter 3.

intelligence staffs, with their own PR and POW arrangements, and from March 1941 they received Sigint direct from GC and CS.* Moreover, in the light of the long-established relationship between the War Office and the Army commands, it is unlikely that this system would have been altered even if the German Army Enigma traffic had been broken earlier in the war instead of only in 1942.

In these circumstances the improvement of arrangements for selecting, training and administering field intelligence officers for the expanding field army became a major task for the MI directorate, and in this direction important developments took place at the end of 1940. The Intelligence Corps, formed in July of that year, became operational in December, when a Commandant and an Assistant Commandant were appointed to supervise the I Corps Depot. MI selected the officers for the Corps. The Corps Depot acted as a central holding unit for all field intelligence units and personnel, and it provided the initial training of the members of I Corps before they went on to the Intelligence Training Centre at Matlock for more specialised training in such matters as field intelligence, field security, photographic interpretation and POW interrogation.[20]

It was from this time, too, that the Intelligence Training Centre, developed out of the Intelligence School which had been established in September 1939, began its great expansion.[21] In January 1941 its interrogation wing was moved to Cambridge. The I Corps then comprised 390 officers and 2,257 other ranks, most of them untrained. By the end of the war it totalled 11,000 – not including the ATS who, like the WRNS and the WAAF, now began to perform a variety of important intelligence roles – and during 1941 its expansion and the excellence of its training were already bringing about at the Army commands a livelier recognition of the value and potentialities of intelligence.

MI's involvement in the expansion of field intelligence did not alter the fact that its main task lay elsewhere. In so far as it promulgated information about foreign armies to the Army commands, its role was secondary or supplementary; but it was directly responsible for providing intelligence to the Operations Directorate of the War Office and to the General Staff. Before the war the operations and the intelligence divisions had been fused in a single directorate. In November 1940 a committee report on the organisation of the War Office recommended that they should once again be amalgamated in the interests of greater efficiency and as a means of saving staff.[22] By that time the number of officers in MI had increased from 49 at the outbreak of war to 219. The expansion had required the same intake

---

* See Appendix 13.

20. ibid, Chapter 4.   21. ibid, Chapter 5.
22. ibid, Chapter 3, p 15.

of civilians, from similar walks of life, as had taken place at GC and CS, but the demand that the Whitehall departments should be combed for officers needed by the commands was nonetheless acute. The recommendation was not proceeded with, the ostensible reason being that the geographical divisions in the two directorates were not compatible. More important were two other considerations. One was the security of Sigint – the wish to restrict the knowledge of its existence and the handling of its product to the intelligence directorate. The other was the existence of intelligence directorates in the other Service departments. The value of intelligence, the importance of inter-departmental collaboration in that field – these things were receiving increasing, if still imperfect, recognition, and it was feared that the first would be reduced and the second impeded if MI were to lose its separate identity.

In the Ministry of Economic Warfare a not dissimilar problem was under discussion during the winter of 1940–41. MEW's Economic Warfare Intelligence Department had become the Enemy and Occupied Territories Department after the fall of France. By April 1941, when it became known as Enemy Branch, a title it retained for the rest of the war, it was divided into four sections: financial transactions; commodities; shipping; enemy and occupied territories. Blockade intelligence had meanwhile remained with the General Branch, the operational side of the Ministry, where a records and statistics department was responsible for providing the information required for the interruption of traffic between enemy and neutral countries.[23] The General Branch was otherwise divided into geographical, not functional, sections. In these circumstances Enemy Branch and the General Branch were gradually drifting apart.

By the spring of 1941 the Director of Enemy Branch was considering two solutions to this problem. The first was to reorganise the branch into sections which would be complementary to the territorial sections of the operational side of the Ministry, and thus more closely integrated with its activities. For a variety of reasons, which no doubt again included concern for the security of the most important sources of intelligence, this plan proved to be impracticable. The operational and the intelligence sides of MEW continued to become increasingly self-contained 'so that in April 1944, when Enemy Branch was administratively transferred to the Foreign Office, nobody noticed the difference'.[24]

The alternative course of action was to recognise that the General Branch required only general assistance from Enemy Branch and to develop the latter mainly as an organisation that was designed to work

---

23. CAB/HIST/E/1/6/2; Memo by N F Hall, November 1942.
24. C G Vickers, 'MEW: The Study of Enemy Intelligence', November 1943, reproduced in Medlicott, op cit, Vol II, Appendix IV, p 677.

with the intelligence directorates of the three Service ministries for the better co-ordination of enemy intelligence. But in this direction, too, there were serious obstacles to overcome. By the end of February 1941 the NID had agreed to base its estimates of enemy naval construction on MEW figures of the capacity of the yards.[25] But MI continued to make such estimates of German production of land armaments as were possible, and relations with AI were scarcely more satisfactory. Although the MEW was officially the authority on the capacity of enemy industries, AI made its own estimates of German aircraft production. Nor was the MEW content with its share in the preparation of inter-departmental assessments. In November 1940 its Director of Intelligence was complaining that being represented at JIC meetings did not prevent his branch from being presented with more or less completed papers at too late a stage to do more than make hurried comments on them. By that date he already felt that there could be no improvement unless the Service directorates could be persuaded to appoint members of their staff to work in Enemy Branch.[26]

By the spring of 1941 the Service departments had made it clear that they would not consent to this proposal. Enemy Branch regretted this decision. 'If we had been able', wrote its Director later on, 'to arrange an adequate degree of Service penetration into Enemy Branch, so that at least a fair proportion of those who most often met the Services were themselves Service personnel, who had worked in Service Intelligence Departments, we should have been immensely helped in knowing what was wanted, in knowing how to present it, in persuading the Services of its importance and in inducing them to rely upon it.'[27] But the decision meant that the only way by which the Branch could make a more effective contribution lay in obtaining better co-operation with the Service directorates at the inter-departmental level of the JIC.

On this level, progress was still being delayed by two further difficulties. One of these was related to the state of MEW's information about the enemy's economy. Inter-departmental assessments, drawn up to be read by the central authorities, needed to make their point briefly and decisively. But by the spring of 1941, as we shall see later on,* Enemy Branch's picture of the German economy was so changing and unsettled that it had become reluctant to generalize and predict in the manner of 1940, and thus to provide broad statements of the kind that could make their mark in JIC, Joint Planning and COS papers. In the economic sections of these inter-departmental papers, even so, if only because it was the only department which attempted to assess the state of the German economy over the whole range of

---

* See below, p 305 et seq.

25. ADM 233/84, NID 0714 of 27 February 1941.
26. CAB/HIST/E/1/6/2; Hall, op cit.
27. Vickers, op cit, in Medlicott, op cit, Vol II, Appendix IV, p 676.

its resources (other than oil), MEW's views invariably predominated, and the second difficulty lay in the manner in which these papers were prepared and circulated. The functions of the machinery that produced them were to ensure proper co-ordination between all the intelligence directorates and branches and to meet the even more complex problem of channelling co-ordinated intelligence to the central authorities responsible for political and strategic decisions, but it was not yet performing them efficiently.

□

On 5 November 1940 the Prime Minister had asked – whether from ignorance or in provocation – how *the* Intelligence Service (Naval, Military and Air) was organised and who was the man responsible for it.[28] In their reply the Chiefs of Staff conceded that the idea of a single intelligence department had its attractions, but they emphasised its 'many grave disadvantages'. That it would divorce the intelligence branches from the operational authorities in the individual Service departments was only one of these. 'Even if this difficulty could be surmounted – and it is only one of many – it seems to us very undesirable that a drastic reorganisation of this magnitude should be attempted at the moment when we are fighting for our lives'.[29] The fact that the Chiefs of Staff took the implications of the Prime Minister's question seriously and the tone in which they laid aside the idea of a single service are equally indicative of their dissatisfaction with the working of the machinery which they had set up to ensure inter-Service co-ordination in the evaluation of intelligence and in the provision of intelligence to themselves and the other central authorities, the Cabinet, the Defence Committee and the Joint Planners. But neither they nor anybody else had yet given prolonged thought to why that machinery was defective.

The main difficulty was that the machinery hinged on a single body – the JIC – which was burdened with too many different responsibilities. In particular, it remained responsible for a wide range of activities and arrangements which, whatever their importance, were purely administrative. It was still deeply engaged in the organisation of such matters as internal and operational security, deception, propaganda, the dissemination of information about air raid damage in the United Kingdom, the treatment and exchange of POWs. In relation to topographical intelligence, to take a further problem, it retained the supervisory role laid down for it in the spring of 1940* and thus accumulated a good deal of work both in handling the

---

* See Chapter 5, p 161.

28. CAB 80/22, COS (40) 932 of 14 November, para 2.
29. ibid, paragraph 15.

Planners' requests for this kind of information and in watching over the continuing attempt to develop an inter-departmental topographical intelligence service. Even after September 1940, when it set up in the Admiralty an *ad hoc* sub-committee to act as a clearing house for all requests for topographical information, [30] complaints about the quality of the service continued to come in, [31] and in February 1941, when the Chiefs of Staff established a permanent co-ordinating committee under the DNI, they reaffirmed the JIC's responsibility for supervising the work. [32]

From time to time miscellaneous additional duties of an administrative kind added to the JIC's burden. In the summer of 1940 it was helping the Foreign Office to examine what could be done to organise British communities overseas to collect intelligence and at the beginning of 1941 it was advising the Chiefs of Staff to establish a centre in the United Kingdom at which people could be trained in the methods of stimulating the work of the overseas communities. [33] From September 1940, after some dispute as to how much intelligence should be circulated to the Dominions and British diplomatic missions, the old system whereby they were kept informed by separate telegrams from the Foreign Office and the Service ministries was replaced by a single daily telegram, and the compiling of this became another charge on the JIC. [34] During the autumn of 1940, to take another example, its work in making arrangements for the United States delegation to the 'Standardisation of Arms' talks* to tour the home front was virtually that of a travel agency, [35] and it performed the same function when these tours were later extended to the attachés of neutral countries. [36] In December 1940, however, the JIC firmly rejected a proposal from MI5 that it should take charge of the system that was being developed for passing information to the enemy through double agents.

These activities reduced the attention the JIC could give to its other work. In this other work moreover – the co-ordination of the intelligence available in the separate government departments, and the

---

* See below, p 312.

30. JIC (40) 58th Meeting, 6 September; 59th Meeting, 25 September.
31. CAB 69/1, DO (40), 40th Meeting, 5 November; CAB 80/22, COS (40) 932 of 14 November; CAB 84/2, JP (40) 148th Meeting, 1 December.
32. JIC (41) 5th Meeting, 7 February; JIC (41) 56 of 8 February. See also Godfrey Memoirs, Vol 5, Appendix E.
33. JIC (41) 1st Meeting, 2 January; JIC (40) 432 of 27 December; CAB 79/8, COS (41) 17th Meeting, 14 June.
34. JIC (40) 55th, 56th, 59th Meetings, 15, 17 August and 25 September; JIC (40) 240, 253, 284 of 13 and 25 August, 13 September.
35. CAB 79/6, COS (40) 256th Meeting, 9 August; CAB 80/16, COS (40) 621 (JIC) of 10 August.
36. CAB 79/6, COS (40) 296th Meeting, 6 September; 315th Meeting, 18 September 1940; CAB 80/19, COS (40) 754 (JIC) of 17 September.

presentation of it to the central authorities – the JIC was encountering another difficulty. This arose from the fact that the demand from the planning bodies for what was often called static intelligence – for information on the organisation and infrastructure of foreign armed forces, coast and other fixed defences in enemy and other overseas territories – was growing as the war expanded and as new authorities were created which needed this kind of intelligence. As far as possible the JIC insisted that 'static' intelligence should be supplied by the individual Service intelligence directorates. Thus, when the Director-ate of Combined Operations was set up in June 1940 the Chiefs of Staff instructed the JIC to help it in the choice of suitable objectives, but the JIC left this assignment and the provision of intelligence about ojectives to the separate Service departments.[37] Again, the JIC undertook no responsibility for supplying information to SOE, though it did agree from November that SOE might receive some of its summaries and appreciations.[38] When the Joint Planning organisation was remodelled in August, and a Future Operational Planning Section (FOPS) was established alongside the sections responsible for strategic and executive planning, the JIC took the same attitude.[39] FOPS was told that, like the rest of the planning staff, it should make its requests for intelligence direct to the Service departments except when it wanted topographical intelligence or a co-ordinated report;[40] and when FOPS nevertheless incorporated such requests in its demands to the JIC for topographical intelligence the JIC simply farmed them out to the Service directorates.[41] But these commendable attempts to ensure that such time and manpower as it could devote to intelligence were spent on bringing co-ordinated intelligence to bear on important operational and strategic questions did not entirely succeed in saving the JIC from routine intelligence activity.

More important, they were not accompanied by a determined effort to give priority to what had already been singled out in May 1940 as the weakest link in the intelligence machine. The JIC's secretariat had then been strengthened in order to make it capable of taking the initiative in alerting the central authorities to significant new devel-opments, and the JIC had been instructed to issue special bulletins whenever it seemed desirable.* From then on, and noticeably from the early autumn, the number and frequency of its inter-Service intelligence appreciations had increased. It had not been involved in

---

* See Chapter 5, p 160 and Appendix 6.

37. CAB 79/4, COS (40) 172nd Meeting, 7 June, 173rd Meeting, 8 June; CAB 80/12, COS (40) 468 of 17 June; JIC (40) 257, 29 August, JIC (40) 295, 24 September.
38. CAB 66/10, WP (40) 271 of 19 July; CAB 79/6, COS (40) 276th Meeting, 21 August, Annex (Paper by Dalton); JIC (40) 631 (S) of 26 October.
39. CAB 80/18, COS (40) 727 of 8 September.
40. JIC (40) 279 of 12 September, Annex A.
41. JIC (40) 59th Meeting, 25 September.

the preparation of the first strategic appreciation made on the assumption that France would collapse, which was issued in May,[42] or in the Far East appreciation written in August, when circumstances had made the despatch of a fleet to Singapore – hitherto the basis of Far Eastern strategy – temporarily impossible.[43] But it made a considerable contribution to the enormous survey of the future course of the war which the Chiefs of Staff completed on 4 September, supplying for it the calculations of the military strengths of Germany and Italy up to 1942 and the assessments of the readiness and ability of the occupied territories to arise against the Nazi regime.[44] It then went on to issue special papers with greater regularity on such subjects as the state of Italo-Greek relations,[45] the implications of a German advance through the Balkans and Syria,[46] the military value of the Vichy forces,[47] the consequences in north Africa should Weygand join the Allies,[48] the possibility of enemy operations against the Atlantic islands,[49] future Axis intentions in the light of the German move into Romania.[50] But these appreciations were of a routine character and made no unique contribution. They were either merely speculations of the kind which the Planners and the central bodies could make for themselves, or the intelligence they contained added nothing to that which had already appeared in the many daily and periodical summaries issued by the JIC itself and other bodies. At the same time the JIC was not fulfilling its instructions to draw attention to new developments.

Discontent with both aspects of this situation mounted during the autumn. In August a series of JIC reports on the situation in the French colonies had been instituted. As JIC reports these were stopped at the beginning of November after complaints from the Prime Minister about their length and frequency.[51] Apart from the JIC's occasional appreciations, there still remained the JIC's daily summary, the twice-daily Cabinet War Room record, the Chiefs of Staff résumés, an inter-Service operational intelligence summary on the Greek situation, prepared in the War Office, and innumerable summaries and telegrams from the Foreign Office and the individual

---

42. CAB 80/11, COS (40) 390 of 25 May.
43. CAB 80/15, COS (40) 592 of 31 July.
44. CAB 80/17, COS (40) 683 of 4 September, Annex, paragraphs 26–50, 51–57; Appendix I, paragraphs 58–81, 90–92; Appendices II, III and IV.
45. JIC (40) 249 of 23 August.
46. JIC (40) 318 of 17 October.
47. JIC (40) 256 of 31 August; JIC (40) 375 of 18 November.
48. JIC (40) 382 of 23 November.
49. JIC (40) 358 of 10 November; JIC (40) 372 of 13 November.
50. CAB 80/20, COS (40) 819 of 10 October.
51. JIC (40) 260 of 29 August; PREM 3 254/1; CAB 79/7, COS 79/7, COS (40) 341st Meeting, 9 October, 367th Meeting, 31 October, 378th Meeting, 7 November, 387th Meeting, 13 November.

Service directorates. On 12 November the Prime Minister complained again in more general and more explosive terms in a minute to the Secretariat of the War Cabinet –

'Please look at this mass of stuff which reaches me in a single morning, most of it having already appeared in the Service and FO telegrams. More and more people must be banking up behind these different papers, the bulk of which defeats their purpose...'[52]

And during November 1940, in an attempt to meet this complaint, the afternoon Cabinet War Room record and the JIC daily summary were suspended – though the JIC continued to provide items of inter-Service intelligence for the remaining CWR daily record.[53] The Prime Minister's dissatisfaction was not confined to protests at the number of summaries in circulation. In August 1940, prompted by the SIS complaint that some of its information on occupied Europe was not getting into the summaries,* he had revealed his discontent with appreciations and summaries as a 'form of collective wisdom' in the following minute to General Ismay –

'I do not wish such reports as are received to be sifted and digested by the various Intelligence authorities. For the present Major Morton will inspect them for me and submit what he considers of major importance. He is to be shown everything, and submit authentic documents to me in their original form.'[54]

In October 1940 he asked to see lists of those in Whitehall who had access to the 'special material' and expressed indignation at 'this vast congregation who are invited to study these matters', and he was not easily persuaded that the circulation was the minimum required if the material was to be properly used. At the end of September 1940 the Prime Minister had instructed 'C' to send him 'daily all Enigma messages'. It is not known how far this request was complied with, but it is clear that the Prime Minister came to accept that it was impracticable. The surviving archive shows that by the summer of 1941 he was receiving from 'C' at least daily a special box containing only a selection of up to 20 GAF Enigma decrypts, a summary prepared in GC and CS of the principal revelations from naval high-grade Sigint, and occasional decrypts of Abwehr, Axis diplomatic and German police signals, together with memoranda on the progress, procedure and security of the cryptanalytic programme, and that it was on this selection that he based calls for action or comment from the Chiefs

---

* See above, p 275.

52. JIC (40) 376 of 12 November, Appendix A.
53. JIC (40) 378 of 16 November; JIC (40) 391 of 30 November; CAB 79/8, COS (40) 407th Meeting, 27 November.
54. CAB 120/746, PM Registered File 413/2, Minutes of 3 and 5 August 1940; Churchill, op cit Vol III, pp 319–320.

of Staff or the Foreign Office and sent signals direct to the operational theatres and individual commanders.

In its modified form the arrangement with 'C' was to remain in force for the rest of the war, and it was to have one beneficial result. It produced a close relationship between 'C' and the Prime Minister, whose knowledge of the products of 'C''s organisation, particularly of GC and CS, proved valuable when strategic decisions and intelligence priorities were being debated. But it was also to have its drawbacks – not least for the Chiefs of Staff, the Directors of Intelligence and the Permanent Under-Secretary at the Foreign Office, who found that the Prime Minister was liable to spring on them undigested snippets of information of which they had not heard. Above all, it was no substitute for an efficient and regular procedure for co-ordinating intelligence and channelling it to the central authorities in such a way that what was truly important caught their attention, and as the JIC was still failing to establish such a procedure in the last months of 1940, other steps had to be taken. In October, disturbed by the German move into Romania, the Chiefs of Staff were again urging the JIC to 'make a practice of initiating reports when a fresh situation developed' or when there was new intelligence on questions under discussion at the Chiefs of Staff Committee.[55] And at the beginning of November the feeling that the JIC, as it was constituted, was unable to meet all the requirements placed on it played its part in the decision to establish a new inter-departmental intelligence organisation.

As first outlined by the Joint Planners, on the initiative of the Director of Plans at the War Office, the new organisation was to be an 'Enemy Syndicate' which would try to anticipate the enemy's intentions by studying the situation from the enemy's point of view, and it would be independent of the JIC.[56] At the discussion of this proposal between the Joint Planners and the JIC the DNI preferred a new or a strengthened body that would still be responsible both for the adminstration and the appreciation of intelligence, but the other Service Directors of Intelligence, recognising that the JIC's intelligence work had suffered from this combination, welcomed the plan. They fought hard, however, to have the new organisation set up as a section of the JIC, under the JIC's control, and succeeded in reaching a compromise. As put to the Chiefs of Staff, the plan was that the Future Operations (Enemy) Section (FOES) would owe allegiance both to the Planners and to the JIC but would be administered by the JIC, which would comment on its reports before they were passed to the Planners. It would have access to all relevant digested intelligence, but not to Allied plans, and would consist of a senior officer from each

---

55. CAB 80/18, COS (40) 727 of 8 September.
56. CAB 84/2, JP (40) 122nd Meeting, 3 November; 125th Meeting, 5 November. See also McLachlan, op cit, pp 251–4 for the early history of the project.

Service and representatives from the Foreign Office and from MEW. On 28 November the Chiefs of Staff decided to add three junior Service officers to the FOES staff. They also introduced a further modification: they themselves would receive FOES reports in the first instance and would remit them to the JIC or the Planners if they saw fit.[57]

FOES started work on 9 December 1940 with the following terms of reference –

'To watch continually, on behalf of the Chiefs of Staff, the course of the war from the enemy point of view, and in particular to prepare enemy appreciations and work out possible enemy plans under the general direction of the Chiefs of Staff.'[58]

At his first meeting with the Chiefs of Staff on 10 December its spokesman explained that in order to get into the 'skin of the Germans' the Section would require a few weeks before completing its first appreciation.[59] Despite the early optimism the experiment was not destined for a long life. Within a month a new DMI was protesting that its existence involved a ridiculous duplication of the work of the JIC.[60] By February he was pointing out that some body like FOES was needed within the JIC, and the JIC had agreed that the creation of FOES did not relieve the Directors of Intelligence of the duty to provide appreciations of enemy intentions for the Chiefs of Staff.[61] And in March 1941, after discussions with the JIC and representatives from the Joint Planners, the Chiefs of Staff finally recognised that to have set up a body reporting to themselves and separate from the JIC, and even more removed than the JIC from the raw material of intelligence, was not the way to go about correcting the deficiency of the JIC as the organisation responsible for co-ordinating the intelligence done in the individual departments and preparing it for the attention of the authorities responsible for political and strategic decisions. FOES was disbanded and replaced by the Axis Planning Section (APS).[62]*

APS had much the same composition as FOES, and it was charged with much the same function, but it was set up as an integral part of

---

* See Appendix 8 for the new section's terms of reference.

57. CAB 84/2, JP (40) 128th Meeting/JIC (40) 68th Meeting, 6 November, JP (40) 127th Meeting, 6 November, 128th Meeting, 8 November, 134th Meeting, 19 November; JIC (40) 69th Meeting, 18 November; CAB 84/2, JP (40) 639 of 8 November; JIC (40) 70th Meeting, 21 November; JIC (40) 381 of 18 November; CAB 79/8, COS (40) 401st Meeting, 25 November; CAB 80/23, COS (40) 982 (JIC) of 26 November.
58. CAB 79/8, COS (40) 407th Meeting, 28 November.
59. CAB 79/8, COS (40) 422nd Meeting, 10 December.
60. Davidson Papers (King's College, London, Archive), Section G, Part I.
61. JIC (41) 5th Meeting, 5 February; JIC (41) 58 of 6 February.
62. CAB 79/9, COS (41) 93rd Meeting, 11 March.

the JIC. Its papers were to be seen by the Service intelligence directorates or considered by the JIC before being circulated, and they were to be circulated as JIC papers. On the other hand, it could study a subject or write a paper on its own initiative, without waiting for instructions from the JIC, and in this way its establishment was to lead to a reform of procedure within the JIC. Since June 1940 the JIC had agreed that its papers would be drafted by its junior secretariat, briefed by the Directors of Intelligence, or by an *ad hoc* drafting sub-committee, and would be discussed by the main committee only if wide divergences came to light.[63] Since then, while the main committee had rarely met for the joint consideration of operational developments and important trends, no drafting sub-committee had developed that was strong enough to appraise and reconcile the amendments to papers, as made by the individual Service directorates through their Directors of Intelligence, and thus to avoid delay in completing the final drafts of JIC papers. In these circumstances APS soon became the inner committee of the JIC that was responsible for digesting everything that had a bearing on enemy intentions and for drafting all JIC papers in that field. By 29 March the Secretary of the JIC was referring to APS as the JIC's drafting committee; on 8 May the JIC decided that APS should be its drafting sub-committee. And from 15 May, in recognition of this change, the name APS fell into disuse and the JIC's inner committee began to be known as the Joint Intelligence Staff.[64]

By that time the Chiefs of Staff had enhanced the status of the JIC by introducing a further organisational change. Until the spring of 1941, though the Directors of Intelligence had individually or collectively been called in somewhat more frequently, the JIC as a body had still attended Chiefs of Staff meetings only on rare occasions. In the second half of 1940 it had been present only on two occasions, and on one of those the problem under discussion had been the establishment of FOES, a step which increased the distance between the Chiefs of Staff and the JIC during the early months of 1941 instead of improving the contact between them.[65] On 22 April 1941, however, the better to ensure that they were informed of 'any dangerous development that had been observed', the Chiefs of Staff decided that the JIC should in future have a regular (normally weekly) meeting with them.[66]

□

---

63. JIC (40) 47th Meeting, 28 June.
64. APS (41) 9 of 28 April; JIC (41) 12th Meeting, 8 May, 13th Meeting, 15 May.
65. CAB 79/7, COS (40) 341st Meeting, 9 October; CAB 79/8, 401st Meeting, 25 November.
66. CAB 79/11, COS (41) 143rd Meeting, 22 April.

We shall see later on* that as a result of these developments, and particularly after the emergence of the Joint Intelligence Staff (JIS) with its freedom from the JIC's heavy involvement in administration and the daily circulation of intelligence bulletins, the effectiveness of the JIC as the machinery for co-ordinating, assessing and disseminating strategic intelligence steadily increased. Up to May 1941 its work in this field had been hampered not only by the paucity of information about enemy capacities and intentions but also by the failure of the JIC, as also of the bodies that were represented on it, to bring to bear on the available intelligence that came to it a proper sense of priorities and a sufficiently rigorous scrutiny.

How much this was so is brought out by the investigation that was made after the Battle of Britain into the strength of the GAF. The investigation originated in some instinct or sixth sense which assured Professor Lindemann† that the scale of the German bombing attack upon the United Kingdom expected after the fall of France by the JIC 'was all wrong'.[67] It brought to bear upon a single intelligence problem the personal attention of a most formidable group of persons, few of whom were members of the 'intelligence community'. Apart from Professor Lindemann and his Statistical Office, the Prime Minister himself, a Judge and the Chief of the Air Staff were all involved at one time or another between December 1940 and March 1941 in technical arguments with the specialist intelligence staffs of MEW and the Air Ministry. Neither the JIC nor the COS Committee played any part in the proceedings.

As we have seen, the Air Ministry, which in 1938 had under-estimated the total strength of the GAF, issued in September 1939 an estimate of 4,320.‡ This, at a time when the true figure was 3,647, represented an over-estimate of about one-sixth and showed a sudden change of approach on the part of the Air Ministry's intelligence branch which in January 1939 had forecast that the total would be 3,700 by October 1939.[68] The September 1939 estimate also put the total number of German long-range bombers at 1,650 – an over-estimate of one-third.[69] Thus the Air Ministry abandoned the view underlying its earlier under-estimations of GAF strength, which was that the best criteria for judging Germany's rate of expansion were those which governed the rate at which the RAF could itself form efficient units. This view also prompted the Air Ministry's tendency to exaggerate the size of the GAF's reserves – a tendency which was not to be modified. Its

---

* In Volume Two.   † See Chapter 5, p 177.
‡ See Chapter 2, p 75.

67. The Earl of Birkenhead, *The Prof in Two Worlds* (1961), p 220.
68. CAB 53/44, COS 831 (JP) of 26 January 1939.
69. AIR 40/2321, Minute of 20 September 1939.

estimate of September 1939 put the current size of the GAF's reserve at 4,900, when the true figure was between 400 and 900 aircraft.[70] These errors continued to accumulate, gave the Air Ministry anxious moments during the Battle of Britain, and, in the end, precipitated the crisis with the Prime Minister.

In May 1940 Air Intelligence estimated that the first line establishment of the GAF was 5,350 planes with 7,000 in reserve[71] and the JIC took the view in June that this force was capable of dropping 4,800 tons of bombs a day upon the United Kingdom.[72] On 5 July Lindemann made known his disbelief to Air Intelligence[73] but before he could launch a major assault AI lowered its estimate on the grounds that the force operationally available would be only 50 per cent of establishment and not 80 per cent as assumed in the JIC paper.* This revision reduced the expected scale of the attack without altering the estimates of the first line establishment of the GAF, and, since it was the establishment estimate which was Lindemann's real target, he remained dissatisfied. On 1 December 1940 he succeeded in arranging a conference on German air strength and production with the DCAS. On the following day the Prime Minister asked the Secretary of State for Air and the CAS for a paper on the potential increase of the GAF in the next six months.[74]

The Prime Minister, Professor Lindemann and representatives of AI and MEW discussed the paper produced by AI[75] at a meeting on 7 December which lasted for four and a half hours but failed to reconcile differences between estimates presented by the two ministries. Subsequently, in a memorandum upon which he had spent many hours, the Prime Minister concluded that MEW estimates of aircraft production were compatible with a GAF front line strength of no more than 3,000 machines whereas the AI estimates were nearly twice as high. He circulated his memorandum to all the parties concerned, with the instruction that they were to treat it as a questionnaire and reply to it separately. At the same time he proposed that an impartial inquiry should be conducted by Mr Justice Singleton.[76]

The enquiry was put in hand at once and after sitting through the remainder of December the Judge issued an interim report on 3 January and a final one on 21 January 1941. The Singleton report set

---

* See Chapter 5, p 177.

70. ibid; Collier, op cit, p 78; AIR 41/10, p 21.
71. CAB 80/11, COS (40) 390 of 25 May.
72. JIC (40) 101 of 6 June.
73. AIR 40/2321, Minute of 6 July 1940.
74. AIR 19/543, letter from the Prime Minister to S of S for Air and CAS, 2 December 1940; Churchill, op cit, Vol III, pp 34–35.
75. ibid, Present and Future Strength of the German Air Force (undated).
76. ibid, letter from the Prime Minister to S of S for Air and CAS, 9 December 1940.

out to establish a rather general comparison between the strengths of the GAF and the RAF. Although it considered several aspects of the evidence available, its positive conclusions owed most to an examination of the 'strength' of the GAF at the beginning of the war (without attempting to disentangle 'establishment', 'identified first line strength' and 'serviceability'), of the output of aircraft and of its allocation to first line units, training and reserves. By assuming allocation ratios similar to British practice it reduced from 4,900 to 2,000 aircraft the size of the 'reserve' which AI believed the GAF to have possessed at the outbreak of war. Adding a net increase of 2,281 aircraft between 3 September 1939 and 30 November 1940 to an original front line strength of 3,741, and employing the new reserves figure of 2,000, the report concluded that the GAF at 30 November had a total of 8,022 operational aircraft as against 6,216 in the RAF. The strength of the GAF in relation to the RAF was therefore roughly 4 to 3.[77]

Without attempting to draw firm conclusions from the facts, the report noted that British 'Wireless Telegraphic interception' (a reference to the low-grade Sigint acquired by Cheadle) covered 80–90 per cent of call-signs emitted by German long-range bombers when on sortie, from which information AI was able to identify the Geschwader, Gruppen and Staffeln* to which the aircraft belonged, and that the numbers so identified in September–November 1940 fell short of the first line bomber strength of the GAF as estimated by AI, a discrepancy which indicated that that estimate was also too high. Shortly after the enquiry British estimates of German air strength were presented to the Americans at staff conversations[78] in a document which, after referring to a recent special enquiry in London, gave GAF strength as 5,710 first line establishment, 4,900 estimated actual strength and 3,230 estimated serviceable. Reserves were now estimated at about 50 per cent of establishment. While it had influenced the estimate of 'total' strength by reducing the scale of reserves, the Singleton enquiry had thus had little impact upon AI's estimate of the first line establishment. It was the further investigations of Professor Lindemann which were to reduce it.

In the period following the Singleton report, Lindemann paid special attention to the significance of the call-sign evidence referred to by Singleton. Early in February 1941 he sent to the CAS a paper entitled 'Comparative Strength of the British and German Air Forces'[79] which began by showing that if AI's estimates of GAF

---

* For the operational chain of command of the GAF, see Appendix 10.

77. ibid, report to the Prime Minister by John E Singleton, 21 January 1941.
78. CAB 99/5, BUS (J) (41) 11 of 4 February.
79. AIR 8/463, undated letter from Lindemann to CAS and comment by AI, 18 February 1941.

strength were correct the actual number of sorties flown by any one German bomber at the height of the raids in August–September 1940 must have been only one every six days and in October–November one every ten days – figures incompatible either with POW reports or with common sense. The estimates of the size of the enemy force must therefore be re-examined. Lindemann then made possibly the most important of all the points in his paper. AI believed that the fighting establishment of the Staffel was 12 aircraft. Linemann's reading of the call-sign evidence was that the establishment was in fact 9. On this basis, and accepting that 134 Staffeln had been identified, he concluded that the establishment of the German long-range bomber force was 1,200–1,300, the difference between this and the AI estimate of 2,000 being due to the inclusion of three non-operational machines per Staffel. If one-third of the GAF consisted of long-range bombers, as was generally accepted, its total establishment was not 5,710 but 3,900, a figure which made sense of AI's estimate of 3,230 as its serviceable strength (ie 83 per cent of an establishment of 3,900). A second major point made by Lindemann was that a sound comparison between two air forces could be made only by relating the number of active machines in operational squadrons; it was misleading to include immediate reserves.

Clearly impressed by Lindemann's arguments the CAS remained unmoved by his Director of Intelligence's rearguard action in defence of the original AI estimates of GAF first line establishment when Lindemann's paper was examined in the Air Ministry.[80] He called a meeting on 20 February 1941 attended by the Director of Plans, the D of I, other AI officers and Professor Lindemann; this agreed that, subject to further calculations by the Directorate of Intelligence, the basic unit of the GAF should in future be regarded as the Staffel of 9 aircraft.[81] On 24 March 1941 (the D of I's further calculations having failed to alter this conclusion) the CAS wrote to the Prime Minister asking for approval to adopt the new establishment of the Staffel and proposing a front line GAF establishment of 4,284. It was in fact 4,508 at the time.[82] Reserves (no longer included in the tables but dealt with in a secondary manner in the text) were put at about 4,000 aircraft. The total, close to Singleton's, amounted to 8,300 aircraft as on 1 January 1941.[83] The Prime Minister signified his approval on 25 March.[84]

□

80. ibid, D of I Minute of 18 February 1941.
81. ibid, draft Minutes of meeting.
82. *Air Ministry Intelligence*, Appendix Chapter 11 (1) C.
83. AIR 8/463, CAS letter to Prime Minister, 25 March 1941.
84. ibid, PS to Prime Minister letter to R S Crawford, Air Ministry, 23 March 1941.

Estimates of the size and order of battle of the German Army did not, like those of the GAF, arouse the suspicions of the political and operational authorities: as yet, British strategic calculations were less dependent on great accuracy in this field. Here too, however, British intelligence in the months after the fall of France began with an over-estimate and carried on into the spring of 1941 with calculations that were too high.

On 9 June the total number of German divisions was 156, of which 6 were motorised (including SS formations) and 10 armoured.[85] In broad outline, this establishment underwent the following changes during the next 12 months. On 15 June Hitler ordered a reduction of 35 divisions, but these did not include the 'schnell Verbände' (ie the motorised and armoured divisions), which were to be doubled. During July and August 17 divisions were disbanded; but the remaining 18 earmarked for disbandment were kept in being at the request of OKH, and during September, following Hitler's decision of 31 July to begin to prepare for an invasion of Russia, reduction was replaced by a programme to build up to 180 divisions by the spring of 1941.[86] By October and December 1940 the divisional totals were 155 and 184 respectively. By June 1941 the total was 208 divisions, including 10 motorised, 20 armoured (including one cavalry) and 4 SS (motorised).[87]

MI's estimates over these months began by putting the total at 200 divisions at the end of May 1940 – an exaggeration of 25 per cent.[88] In July and again in November it continued to believe that the number would be maintained at 200–215 until the spring of 1942.[89] Thereafter its estimates of divisions-in-being rose steadily from 217 on 12 December to 225 on 6 February 1941 and, on 3 April and 21 May 1941, to 250, 'the maximum number she [Germany] can maintain without serious risks to war production and supply'.[90] Within these totals, however, it correctly assessed the number of motorised and armoured divisions. These were assumed to be 5 and 10 respectively at the end of May 1940, 6 and 10 at the end of August, 8 and 11 by the end of October.[91] By the last of these dates, though it had little information about the number of tanks in service or of their rate of production,*

---

* See below, pp 309–310.

85. Mueller-Hillebrand, op cit, Vol II, (1954), pp 48–49.
86. ibid, pp 62–64, 76; Butler, op cit, (1957), Vol II, p 537.
87. Mueller-Hillebrand, op cit, Vol II, pp 188–191.
88. WO 190/891, No 95 of 29 May 1940.
89. ibid, MI14 Note to MO 1, 10 July, and No 131 of 8 August; WO 190/892, No 24A of 11 November.
90. CAB 80/22, COS (40) (Résumé, No 63); CAB 80/24, COS (40) 1038 (Résumé, No 67); WO 190/893, No 13B of 6 February 1941; CAB 80/27, COS (41) 221 (Résumé, No 83); JIC (41) 212 of 21 May.
91. WO 190/891, notes for a lecture, 27 August 1940, by VCIGS; WO 190/892, No 18 of 31 October 1940.

it had reason to believe that a big increase in mechanisation was afoot, and that there might be 14–15 armoured divisions by June 1941 and 10 motorised and 19–20 armoured divisions by the spring of 1942.[92]

We do not know where MI obtained its early information about the motorised and armoured divisions. Perhaps A-54 provided it; the MI records refer to the existence of one good SIS source on German Army plans.[93] For its estimates of total divisions, however, it is clear that it was dependent on fragmentary and unreliable evidence. The valuable document captured shortly before Dunkirk* was rendered out of date by the demobilisation and expansion that followed each other in the second half of 1940. There was no repetition of such windfalls and no taking of Army POW until the start of Rommel's offensive in Libya in February 1941; and the information obtained from the early contacts with his forces made little impact on the broad picture. Information from the German Press and from PR rarely indicated the nature or location of an Army formation. The German Army's Enigma and its lower-grade cyphers were still unbroken, and in the inactive period between the fall of France and the build-up in the Balkans the GAF Enigma material contained little intelligence about the Army. As for SIS reports, for reasons we have already discussed† these were for most areas either lacking or unreliable. In December 1940 MI was receiving good reports from Denmark, Norway, Poland and the Czech Protectorate and some useful information from Romania, but very few identifications from Germany and Austria, none from Slovakia and, from France, the Low Countries and Italy, only highly dubious statements.[94] At the end of February 1941 SIS reporting from France and Belgium began to increase but MI recognised that 'the great majority of reports are from a single unproved source in each country' and that it had 'no confirmed evidence of the number of divisions located at any time in these countries, still less of their exact location or divisional numbers'.[95]

Given the state of evidence, it was perhaps natural that MI's estimates should err on the generous side despite its attempt to apply rigorous tests before accepting that a unit or a formation had been identified. Certainly the figure of 250 divisions, which it adopted after getting wind of the call-ups of October and December 1940, was little more than its estimate of the maximum Germany could sustain after meeting the manpower needs of the GAF and the Navy and of war production.[96]

□

---

* See Chapter 4, p 143, Chapter 5, p 162.   † See above, pp 275–276.

92. WO 190/891, MI14 note to MO 1 of July 1940; WO 190/892, No 13 of 31 October 1940.
93. WO 190/892, No 42B of 19 December 1940.
94. ibid; WO 190/893, No 1A of 3 January 1941.
95. WO 190/893, No 24C of 28 February 1941.
96. ibid, No 13A of 30 January 1941.

The state of intelligence about Germany's capacity at sea had less bearing on the problem of deciding which of her various strategic options she would choose next. In this direction, moreover, some reliable evidence was forthcoming and there was less margin for error.* In both of these respects the opposite was true of the state of intelligence about Germany's economy.

By the early months of 1941 there was a growing recognition in Whitehall that the German economic situation was not as critical as it had seemed up to the summer of 1940: for a number of reasons Germany's collapse was further off than had previously been hoped. The blockade was leaking badly, through Russia and Vichy France. Secondly, by March 1941 the major air offensive against synthetic oil plants in Germany, so strongly advocated by the Hankey Committee, had been abandoned and the German oil situation appeared to be comparatively strong. Thirdly, study of the situation in German-occupied Europe was beginning to show that the economic assets obtained by the Germans from their conquests were more substantial and the liabilities smaller than had been estimated. The deflation for these reasons of the hopes of 1940 was in itself an advance, but it gave rise to a host of uncertainties.

Shipping from French north Africa to Marseilles was supplying the Axis powers with larger quantities of valuable commodities. For example, MEW estimated that between 1 October 1940 and 1 March 1941 enough groundnuts had been shipped by this route to supply the Germans and Austrians with their margarine ration for six months.[97] The magnitude of this leak was to lead the Joint Planners to conclude in June that it threatened to postpone the breakdown of the German economy.[98] At the same time goods of Russian origin, or in transit from the Far East and south eastern Asia, were moving to Germany at a rate of 1,700 tons a day[99] via the Trans-Siberian Railway and meeting several of her most urgent needs, especially of copper, rubber, tin, tropical produce and fibres. It was judged politically unwise to try to stop the first leak and it was physically impossible to stop the second.

The Hankey and Lloyd Committees had hoped to bring Germany to her knees by destroying her synthetic oil plants,† and their destruction was made the sole primary aim of Bomber Command for six months on 15 January 1941.[100] But the plan was frustrated by bad weather. It required 3,400 sorties to be flown but since operations could only be carried out at night, and there was little chance that targets would be hit except in moonlight, the actual number of sorties

---

* See below, p 309 and Chapter 10.
† See Chapter 7, p 241.

97. Medlicott, op cit, Vol I, p 579.
98. CAB 84/31, JP (41) 444 of 14 June.
99. Medlicott, op cit, Vol I, p 650.
100. Webster and Frankland, op cit, Vol I, p 162.

flown was only 221, less than in the period July–September 1940. Moreover, photographic and other evidence about the Gelsenkirchen, Scholven, Leuna and Politz plants, which had been attacked before the oil offensive began, showed when examined by the Lloyd Committee in May 1941 how greatly earlier forecasts had exaggerated the extent of bomb damage.*[101] Despite continuous pressure by the Hankey Committee the offensive, halted in March, was not to be resumed in 1941.

By the beginning of 1941 MEW's study of the consequences of the German occupation of Europe was beginning to show that, whatever hardship the occupied territories were suffering, the economic position of Germany herself had been strengthened by the assets syphoned off from those territories. It was now appreciated that the whole area was being administered on a Reichsmark basis and that the banking system was completely under German control. While there was no sign as yet of a comprehensive German plan for the utilisation of the manufacturing industries of the occupied territories in support of German war production, trade agreements had been signed between Germany and each of the territories, and these ensured a flow of commodities into Germany greatly in excess of the outflow.[102] The 1940 harvest in Europe was good and by supplementing their own production with supplies from the occupied territories the Germans were maintaining a strong food position. By the late spring important new sources of raw materials had become available – nickel from Greece and Finland, chrome from Greece, Yugoslavia, Bulgaria and Romania, refined cobalt from Belgium and France. There was no shortage of coal or of iron and steel. On paper at least, there was a large surplus of aluminium and even for copper no critical situation was foreseen before the end of 1942.

MEW considered that after the call-up for the armed forces, which had been observed from the autumn of 1940 onwards and was assumed to be bringing the strength of the Army up to 'at least 250 divisions',[103] the manpower situation was 'exceedingly strained'.[104] The 1,411,000 civilian foreign workers believed to be employed in Germany by the end of 1940 were no real substitute for the irreplaceable specialists from the armaments industries who had been called up for the armed forces.

In fact the manpower situation in Germany, although difficult, was less black than MEW painted it. Despite the call-up there had been no significant increase in hours worked in industry, a fact which MEW

---

* For further details of the offensive see Volume Two.

101. CAB 66/16, WP (41) 85 of 23 May.
102. FO 837/441, Summary of Enemy Economic Developments No 95 of 14 July 1941.
103. ibid.
104. ibid.

acknowledged. Moreover MEW noted that although armaments production had been 'geared up to an unprecedented level', leaving no margin for expansion by converting non-essential civil industry,[105] Germany was still exporting machine tools, which were 'the key to all engineering production'.[106] These apparent paradoxes were an indication that in a truly critical situation a good deal of 'slack' could still be taken up without an increase in the labour force. British information on the number of machine tools used in the German metal-working industries and on the numbers of employees using them was inaccurate. While the number of machine tools in Germany in 1941 was 1,840,000 the MEW estimate put the total at 760,000. On an average, in Britain each of the 740,000 machine tools employed over 5 men whereas in Germany each of the 1,840,000 machine tools employed less than half that number of men.[107] Man for man, therefore, the productivity of the German industrial worker for industry as a whole tended to be much higher than the productivity of the British industrial workers and much higher than that allowed for by MEW. Ignorance of the extent of this difference would obviously lead to an exaggeration of the effect on output of the withdrawal of men from industry. Lastly, the incorrect assumption that Germany was building up an army of 250 divisions exaggerated the numbers of men which it was thought were being withdrawn from industry and so made the difficulties of the labour situation appear worse than they were.

Of the performance of German industry, MEW confessed, 'only the sketchiest outline' could be discerned.[108] Source material in relation to stocks, expenditure and the use of substitute materials was incomplete:[109] the basic raw material for economic intelligence in general was 'a variety of conflicting reports and statistical analyses', published documents, reports from SIS, low-grade Sigint and escapers. For economic intelligence no new single source of illumination comparable with Enigma had been, or ever would be, discovered.

The available information was interpreted to mean that although there was some 'slack' left in parts of the German economic system, the management of controls had been efficient enough to prevent any important wastages[110] or misdirection of resources in war production. One industry in which it was considered that a good deal of 'slack' still existed was the aircraft industry. It was known that it was encountering difficulties in introducing new types of aircraft and

---

105. ibid.
106. JIC (41) 212 (Final) of 21 May.
107. US Strategic Bombing Survey, Synoptic Volume, p 44.
108. FO 837/441, No 95 of 14 July 1941.
109. ibid, No 119 of 29 December 1941.
110. ibid, Summary No 95 of 14 July 1941.

meeting increasing demands for replacement of wastage and re-equipment, and that maximum capacity had not been reached. No expansion in front line strength was expected in 1941.[111] Nevertheless the true state of affairs was unknown in London, and would have been hard to credit if it had been known. The industry was in fact failing to meet the requirements placed upon it, not so much because manufacturers were incapable of producing planes as because the direction of the aircraft programme was in a state bordering on chaos. In the early months of 1941 Göring and Field Marshal Milch (the Inspector General of the GAF) awoke to the fact that the Directorate of Air Armament under Ernst Udet, a 'rabbit-warren of colonels, bureaucrats and engineers responsible for everything but responsible to nobody',[112] was so mismanaging the production programme that the new aircraft upon which the Air Staff had been relying for 1941 were not yet operational. Göring was later to say of the Directorate 'Never have I been so deceived, so bamboozled and so cheated as by that office. It has no equal in history'.[113]

Relying upon information about manpower employed and factory capacity (quantities quite insensitive to variations in the level of productive efficiency), and unaware of the crisis of management, MEW and the Air Ministry continued greatly to over-estimate German aircraft output. The available British estimates put German monthly output of fighters at 550 for January 1941[114] and 545 for April.[115] The output of bombers in the same two months was estimated to be 705[116] and 785.[117]

A simple comparison of these estimates with actual output for the two months in question would be misleading since actual output spurted from a low level in January to a peak for fighters in April and for bombers in August, from both of which months the level of production subsequently fell away.*

By comparison with an average monthly output for the whole year of 311 for fighters and 363 for bombers the British estimates are manifestly much too high. If, however, it is assumed that the two peak

* Actual Output[118]	Jan	Feb	March	April	May	June
Fighters	136	255	424	476	446	376
Bombers	255	326	392	355	269	325
Actual Output	July	Aug	Sept	Oct	Nov	Dec
Fighters	320	285	258	261	232	263
Bombers	446	454	416	382	331	379

111. JIC (41) 212 (Final) of 21 May.
112. D Irving, *The Rise and Fall of the Luftwaffe* (1974), p 120.
113. ibid, p 122.
114. AIR 19/543, D of I Notes on Fighting Value of the GAF, 10 February 1941.
115. AIR 8/463, CAS to Prime Minister, 1 April 1941.
116. AIR 19/543, D of I Notes on Fighting Value of the GAF, 10 February 1941.
117. AIR 8/463, CAS to Prime Minister, 1 April 1941.
118. US Strategic Bombing Survey, Synoptic Volume, p 277 and Appendix, Table 102.

figures represent approximately the maximum German capacity for producing existing types of aircraft the British estimate of 545 fighters in April as against a peak actual production of 476 appears less exaggerated. For bombers, however, even a comparison on these lines (ie a British estimate of 785 for April as against an actual peak of 454 in August) still leaves a wide discrepancy. It was not until the GAF was shown to be unexpectedly depleted and weak after the first six months of the Russian campaign that serious doubts were cast upon the estimated reserves of front line aircraft available to the GAF, and hence upon the accepted production estimates.[119]

Photographic reconnaissance, of little value as a source on the aircraft industry, was by the spring of 1941 providing the principal evidence on U-boat building, although even with so good a visual source there was room for differences of interpretation, particularly of the length of time required to build and commission the boats and of the maximum potential capacity of the yards. In March 1941 the construction-time was believed by NID to be about 12 months,[120] and the maximum capacity of the yards was put at 12 per month by MEW. The estimate of construction-time was too short, and was later to be adjusted by NID.[121] MEW's estimate of capacity coincided almost exactly with actual output for March 1941 but was soon to be overtaken by an expansion of output to 19 per month in May and 24 in October – showing that there was more 'slack' to be taken up within the whole complex of yards now available to the Germans than seemed possible in the early months of 1941. A contemporary American estimate, based on information from the United States Naval Attaché in Berlin,[122] put the rate of production at 25 per month in January 1941, which was twice as high as the actual output or the MEW estimate but was in fact the output planned by the Germans in August 1940. Irregularity in PR coverage, periods of dearth in SIS reporting and difficulties of interpretation conspired to keep the NID estimates of boats completed somewhat below the real figure. The estimate was that at the end of February 1941 63 new boats had been added to the 57 with which Germany started the war, giving a total of 120.[123] The actual number was 132.[124] By the beginning of April another 11 boats had been added to this total.*

For land armaments production, including tanks, in the spring of 1941 no statistical intelligence estimates can be traced. MEW had noted the possibility of some slowing down in the production of land

---

* See Chapter 10, p 333.

119. *Air Ministry Intelligence*, p 169.
120. ADM 233/84, NID 001089/47 of 27 March 1941.
121. ibid, NID 002322/41 of 16 June 1941.
122. Morgan, op cit, p 28.
123. ADM 233/84, NID 0714, 27 February 1941.
124. ADM 186/802, BR 305 (1).

armaments after the campaigns of the summer of 1940[125] and was aware of the drive to increase the degree of mechanisation in the German Army which began in the autumn of 1940, but the rate of increase in tank production, from 200 per month at the end of 1940 to 300 per month in May 1941,[126] was unknown. One thing seemed to be certain: that the output of essential armaments was not being restricted by lack of raw materials.[127]

By the late spring of 1941, therefore, the prospects for a serious German economic crisis seemed much less promising than they had appeared to be in the summer of 1940. It is true that in January and February 1941, before the German conquest of Yugoslavia and Greece, MEW had correctly detected a deficiency in non-ferrous metals (especially chrome) in Germany and it may well have been with the non-ferrous metal situation in mind that the JIC emphasised in January, in its review of the state of the German invasion threat,* 'the lack of essential commodities' as an economic reason why Germany must seek victory in 1941.[128] Having lived under war-time conditions for five years Germany would reach the peak of war productive effort in March 1941. The JIC's view was therefore that the current German drive in war production would decline after March 1941 because basic deficiencies in material resources would at last begin to tell. When, however, the Chiefs of Staff reviewed the JIC paper,[129] the Director of Enemy Branch, MEW, who took part in the meeting, added another interpretation of the current economic performance of Germany. He expressed the view (subsequently proved to be correct) that Germany was building up for the use of maximum striking power in the summer of 1941, without regard to 1942, although he did not of course suggest in which direction it would be used. He forecast that under these circumstances, unless Germany had access to world trade within the next four to five months, the quality of production would fall. This did not, however, amount to a prediction of crisis in the near future.

By May 1941 it no longer appeared probable that even if the peak of German war production were to be passed in 1941 a serious crisis would occur in that year. The crucial question which had to be answered was not merely when a crisis might be expected to occur but above all whether it would be serious enough to affect German military capabilities. The JIC, when it reviewed the situation in May,

---

* See Chapter 8, p 262 et seq.

125. FO 837–439, Summary of Enemy Economic Developments No 55 of 7 October 1940.
126. US Strategic Bombing Survey, Synoptic Volume, pp 162–3.
127. FO 837/440, Summary of Enemy Economic Developments No 70 of 20 January 1941.
128. JIC (41) 35 of 31 January.
129. CAB 79/9, COS (41) 51st Meeting, 12 February.

concluded that: 'Lack of raw material and supplies, with the possible exception of oil and rubber, is unlikely to limit the enemy's flexibility during 1941. But the conflict that already exists between military and civilian demands for manpower may become acute in the autumn, and it is questionable whether Germany can maintain as many as 250 divisions permanently under arms'.[130]

This pronouncement left the crucial question unanswered and it was not until June that the Joint Planners made a forecast based upon a consensus of views, including that of MEW.[131] This forecast was that, if pressure on Germany could be maintained, 'a marked deterioration' of the German economic situation would occur in the winter of 1941–42 and continue throughout 1942, leading in 1943 to strains so great that they could not be supported without 'a drastic reduction in the power of the armed forces'. This seems to mean that the economic factor could not be expected to have a noticeable military effect for at least another two years.

□

During the winter of 1940–41 items of intelligence provided by the United States began to make a contribution, if as yet an insignificant one, to Whitehall's appreciations. More important, though the full benefits would not be reaped till much later, the basis for Anglo-American co-operation in the intelligence field had been laid down by the spring of 1941.

Discussions between the two countries about defence programmes, equipment and staff plans went back at least to the early months of 1937.[132] Before the summer of 1940 these discussions had rarely extended to intelligence matters. Such exchange of Service intelligence as took place was confined to the two navies. Beginning with the visit to London of the director of the War Plans Division of the United States Navy in January 1938, this had been conducted on an informal and a one-sided basis, the DNI supplying the American Naval Attaché with regular information about the Japanese Navy in return for material on such matters as boom defences.[133] At the diplomatic level there had been only occasional exchanges of confidences. Early in 1939 the Foreign Office had informed Washington in considerable detail of the intelligence which was leading the Foreign Policy Committee to fear a German attack on Holland.*[134] Later that year the United States government had passed to London information about the

---

* See Chapter 2, pp 82–83.

130. JIC (41) 212 (Final) of 21 May.
131. CAB 84/31, JP (41) 444 of 14 June.
132. Matloff and Snell, *Strategic Planning for Coalition Warfare 1941–1942* (Washington 1953). See also Dilks (ed), op cit, pp 33–34; Aster, op cit, p 82.
133. ADM 233/85, File 002711/40, DNI minute 19 July 1940; Dilks, op cit, pp 33–34.
134. Dilks, op cit, pp 141–144.

Russo–German negotiations that led to the Russo–German pact.*[135] In the early months of the war these pre-war contacts were supplemented in only one direction. Early in 1940, in the interests of SIS's counter-espionage work in the United States, 'C' had made contact informally, though with the President's approval, with the FBI, and in May 1940 the SIS had appointed Colonel Stephenson to be its liaison officer with the American intelligence services.

In July and August 1940 matters were taken further mainly on American initiative. In July, prompted by the new SIS representative in the United States, a special envoy of the President, Colonel Donovan, made an informal visit to London. One of his objects was to assess the determination and the ability of the British to continue the war, both of which were being doubted by the American Chiefs of Staff. Another, on behalf of the United States Navy Department, was to see whether closer collaboration could be arranged with the Admiralty on intelligence. At the end of August, the British government having invited a United States delegation to come to London for the 'Standardisation of Arms' talks about supply and defence programmes and staff plans with the Chiefs of Staff and the Service departments, and the Prime Minister and the President having agreed in principle to the pooling of all information on these subjects, however secret, an Army representative on the United States delegation outlined the progress his Service was making against Japanese and Italian cyphers and formally proposed to the Chiefs of Staff that the time had also arrived for the free exchange of intelligence.[136]

The President's special envoy returned to Washington to recommend a full exchange of intelligence by direct liaison between the two naval intelligence departments and to urge that United States consular reports, particularly from French ports, should meanwhile be made available to the NID.[137] His recommendations were favourably received. From the middle of August the relations of USN representatives in London with various sections of the NID became very close.[138] Nor was it long before these first steps were extended and put on a more formal footing. At the end of August – by which time President Roosevelt was already seeing the British Ambassador's copy – the JIC reluctantly agreed that the United States Ambassador should receive a copy of the Dominions Wire, the regular bulletin of which the intelligence content was based on the JIC's daily intelligence summary.[139] On 7 September 1940 the President agreed that the American intelligence services might make available to the British

---

* See Chapter 14, p 430.

135. Aster, op cit, pp 314–317.
136. CAB 79/6, COS (40) 289th Meeting, 31 August.
137. ADM 233/85, File 002376/40, DNI note of 2 August 1940 on Donovan's visit.
138. McLachlan, op cit, pp 216, 218–219.
139. JIC (40) 56th Meeting, 27 August.

attachés in Washington any relevant information from United States diplomatic and consular sources. At the same time he assured 'C''s representative in the United States that he would be given every assistance in obtaining information on any topics he might raise. By then, on the other hand, the British intelligence bodies had become disappointed in the quality of the information that came to them. Especially from the Axis and Axis-occupied countries, it was only too clear that the Americans were themselves finding it difficult to collect reliable intelligence.[140]

In February 1941 two FBI officers were received as pupils at SIS's London office and the opportunity was taken to advise the United States that GC and CS's work on Axis cyphers was leading to an increased output of intelligence. In the exchange of the results of intelligence between Washington and Whitehall the arrangements made in September 1940 were also extended in the spring of 1941. The outcome of further staff talks held in Washington between the end of January and the end of March was that the British and American governments established in each other's capital a military mission whose members jointly represented their Chiefs of Staff and individually represented their Service departments. It was agreed that the intelligence organisations of each power would continue to operate independently but that, in order to maintain close links between them and to ensure the 'full and prompt exchange of pertinent information concerning war operations', the staff of each mission should include intelligence officers from all the Services. In London the Defence Committee gave this agreement its formal approval on 31 May. The British mission, initially called 'Advisers to the British Supply Council' but subsequently named the British Joint Staff Mission in Washington, was directed 'to maintain constant touch with the plans, operations, intelligence and communications branches of the United States Service Departments'.[141]

The scope of this directive enabled the Service intelligence directorates in Whitehall to appoint staff to Washington and to strengthen their links with the United States mission in London, originally known as the United States Special Observers Group. Officers from MI arrived in Washington to form the intelligence component of the British Army Delegation to the Joint Staff Mission in April 1941.[142] The naval intelligence staff of the mission was set up as an integral part of the NID (NID 18) at the same time.[143] The Air Ministry moved more slowly, no doubt because the USA had no separate air force. It was

* See Volume Two.

140. ADM 233/84, NA Washington to DNI, 14 January 1941.
141. CAB 80/27, COS (41) 255 of 22 April, paragraphs 15–19, Annex I; CAB 80/28, COS (41) 312 of 17 May; CAB 69/2, DO (41) 30th Meeting, 31 May.
142. Mockler-Ferryman, op cit, p 95; Davidson Papers Series H, Part 1.
143. Morgan, op cit, p 115.

not until after the American entry into the war that AI set up a special section – AI3 (USA) – to act as a clearing house for the exchange of intelligence with Washington.[144] Until the American entry into the war, on the other hand, not to speak of that phase of the war which ended with the German attack on Russia, these activities added nothing of value to the stock of British intelligence except for the information derived from the exchange of Japanese Sigint between Washington and Whitehall. Apart from this and some dubious diplomatic and consular intelligence about enemy and enemy-occupied Europe, Washington still had little to offer, and their closer contacts with the United States intelligence organisations left the British authorities in no doubt that it would have little to offer for many months.[145]

In June 1941, for these reasons, the JIC was still adopting a cautious attitude. The JIC had played no part in making the intelligence arrangements that resulted from the staff talks. Until June it was involved in these arrangements only in an administrative capacity.[146] In May it had agreed to use an impending visit to Washington by the DNI as an opportunity to investigate whether the exchange of intelligence with the United States might be extended to its own activities and cover the exchange of inter-Service appreciations.[147] When it approved in principle the proposals brought back by the DNI in June – proposals which envisaged the creation of a JIC within the British Joint Staff Mission in Washington in the hope that this would induce the United States authorities to set up a JIC of their own* – it was less impressed with what might be gained from them than with what might be lost. It instructed the British Mission's JIC to be critical of what it received from the United States departments and to take care lest its daily report to London was merely a summary of what London had already received from Washington and of what London would already know for itself. Out of concern for the security of its own papers, on the other hand, it placed restrictions on which of them could go to the JIC (Washington) and on what use the JIC (Washington) could make of them.[148] But by the end of September it would be relaxing these restrictions and allowing its papers to be seen by the United States defence departments, as well as by their attachés in London.†[149] At this level, as at every other, the further development of Anglo-American co-operation in the intelligence field was the outcome of arrangements that had been all but completed by the summer of 1941.

---

* See Volume Two.   † See Volume Two.

144. *Air Ministry Intelligence*, Part 1, Chapter 1, p 12; Chapter 3, p 21 et seq.
145. FO 371/26518; C 3670/19/18 of 17 May 1941.
146. JIC (41) 12th Meeting, 8 May.
147. ibid.
148. JIC (41) 253 of 14 June; JIC (41) 17th Meeting, 17 June.
149. JIC (41) 27th Meeting, 23 September.

CHAPTER 10

The Blitz and the Beginning of the Battle of the Atlantic

THE BLITZ involved both the gradual transfer of the bulk of the GAF's effort from day-time to night bombing and a change in its targets, from the RAF's installations and aircraft factories to the big cities. It underwent two phases. From 7 September to the middle of November 1940 night bombing supplemented the continuing daylight battle and London bore the brunt of both. By the middle of November the attempt to bring about the collapse of the British will to fight on by dislocating the capital had failed, and from then to the middle of May 1941 the attack was extended to the chief industrial and communications centres, ports in particular, with the double aim of preventing Great Britain from repairing her losses and of checking the expansion of her war production.

For the GAF the undertaking was a huge improvisation, embarked on at short notice. It was preceded not only by public declarations from Göring, who warned in August that 'air warfare against Britain would soon start to play its primary role', and from the commander of the GAF's anti-shipping forces, to the effect that Germany intended to combine aerial Blitzkrieg and economic warfare,[1] but also by indications which left no doubt that these threats had to be taken seriously. By the beginning of September the intelligence authorities, notably the section which AI had set up to study the characteristics and use of enemy airfields, were reporting to the Chiefs of Staff that Sigint evidence pointed unmistakably to logistic preparations for a long and heavy bombing campaign against the United Kingdom. Communications of all kinds were being developed with the main airfields in northern France, where runways were being lengthened to take heavy bombers; stocks of bombs and fuel were being accumulated and new bomber units were moving in.[2] Since June, moreover, Cheadle had observed a rapid extension of the GAF's network of navigational beacons to new sites in the occupied territories, and in that month, as we shall see, AI had detected the introduction of a new beam system of navigation known as *Knickebein* which offered much greater accuracy in the location of targets, and which could be used at night as well as by day. Nor was this the only pointer to the likelihood of

---

1. AIR 41/17, *Air Defence of Great Britain*, Vol III, pp 40–41.
2. AIR 40/2321, Minutes of 28 August and 2 September 1940; *Air Ministry Intelligence*, pp 213, 220 et seq; CAB 80/17, COS (40) 684 (COS Résumé, No 52), para 31.

increased night attack. Again in June 1940, Sigint had revealed that
in 'no less than 6 Kampfgruppen' the GAF was building up a nucleus
of crews with experience of night flying over the United Kingdom.[3]
Throughout the summer, as well as providing vital information about
Knickebein and the two improved aids to navigation that were to follow
it (*X-Gerät* and *Y-Gerät*), evidence from low-grade Sigint, POW and
documents from wrecked aircraft showed that the GAF was extending
this experience to all its units – bombers and fighters alike.[4]

On 18 October, noticing that the scale of night flying was increasing,
AI predicted that the GAF would soon concentrate on night operations
and use as many as 600 long-range bombers in its raids.[5] And just over
three weeks later it received from the GAF Enigma and from a POW
the warning that the GAF was about to embark on the new strategy
of making large-scale attacks at night, preceded by pathfinder
fire-raising units, over industrial centres. The fact that this warning
was received three days before the first of the new-type raids, that on
Coventry on 14 November, has been made the basis of much
speculation about the extent and the nature of the intelligence that
was available before Coventry was attacked. The truth, by no means
uncomplicated, is as follows in its essential features.*

On 11 November an Enigma decrypt disclosed that the GAF was
preparing an unusually important operation. It was to be led by KG
100† using the *X-Gerät* beams, and from its code-name ('Moonlight
Sonata') it appeared that it was in some fashion to be carried out in
three stages and to be a night attack at or near full moon. The decrypt
gave no date for the operation and it contained no evidence about the
target or targets beyond a list of four target numbers and, among the
meanings of a number of radio code groups, one which was not
self-evident – the single word 'Korn'. On 12 November AI learned
from a POW that the GAF planned to make a very heavy night raid
with every available long-range bomber between 15 and 20 November,
and that the targets were to be Coventry and Birmingham. In
assessing this intelligence for the Directorate of Home Operations AI
took it that the POW's dates, which coincided with a full moon, fitted
in with the information from the decrypt; but for two reasons it set
aside his reference to Coventry and Birmingham. In the first place,
it believed from the evidence of a captured map that the four targets
listed in the decrypt were located in London and the Home Counties.
In the second place, it concluded that these were the targets for the
impending raid because it did not realise – and had no grounds for
suspecting – that 'Korn' was also the code-name for a target.

---

* See Appendix 9 for details.
† See Appendix 10 for the operational chain of command of the GAF.

3. AIR 41/14, p 24.   4. ibid, p 59.
5. AIR 40/2321, p 50.

Between 12 and 14 November, while the Directorate of Home Operations was drawing up counter-measures in the belief that the raid was to take place against London and the south-east, AI was twice given an opportunity to revise its conclusion about the targets. It overlooked the first clue. This was contained in a second Enigma signal, from KG 100, decrypted on 12 November. The decrypt gave beam bearings from *X-Gerät* transmitters for three targets; and as the transmitters had already been located, it showed – or could have shown – that the bearings intersected at Wolverhampton, Birmingham and Coventry. But signals similar to this had been not uncommon since September in connection with the GAF's experiments with *X-Gerät*, and of the targets they had referred to many had been located in the industrial Midlands. There is thus no difficulty in understanding why no one in AI or at GC and CS associated the second decrypt with the unusual decrypt which had announced the 'Moonlight Sonata' operation. Although it was suspected that the introduction of the *X-Gerät* system and of the pathfinder technique for GAF raids was imminent, it was not obvious in advance that operation 'Moonlight Sonata' would be the first such raid. The second clue came from the POW. By 13 November, under interrogation, he had stated that the operation was to consist of three separate attacks on consecutive nights, and had repeated that the targets were to be in 'the industrial district of England'. AI brought both of these items of intelligence to the attention of the operational authorities. The first modified the initial judgment of those authorities, to the effect that 'Moonlight Sonata' was to be a single operation, to the extent that the operational instructions issued by the Air Ministry in the early hours of 14 November stated that 'the operation will be carried out in 3 phases in a single night or on 3 consecutive nights. It is, however, considered that the former is more likely, and that the attack will be concentrated in a single night'. The POW's evidence about the targets did not find its way into the operational instructions. There was, however, some debate as to whether or not the instructions should mention Coventry and Birmingham, and later on the morning of 14 November the Air Staff alerted the Prime Minister to the coming raid in a memorandum which concluded by saying: 'We believe that the target areas will be...probably in the vicinity of London, but if further information indicates Coventry, Birmingham or elsewhere, we hope to get instructions out in time'.

The Air Staff had good reason to expect further information. The 'Moonlight Sonata' decrypt had made it clear that the night of the attack would be indicated by GAF beam tunings between 1300 and 1500 of the day finally chosen, and from study of GAF procedure it was known that intelligence on beam paths and beam intersection points, obtained from intercepting the beam transmissions, would establish the GAF's approach routes and targets. Notice to this effect was incorporated in the Air Ministry's operational instructions, which ordered that a specially close watch should be kept on the GAF's W/T and beam transmissions. And so it turned out. As the Directorate of Home Operations minuted in a summary of the operation on 17 November, at about 1300 on 14 November GAF W/T and beam transmissions indicated that the operation was to begin that night, and by 1500 No 80 Wing RAF had found that the beam transmissions were intersecting over Coventry.

Although this information was at once relayed to the RAF commands and to other authorities involved, the British counter-measures proved ineffective: of the 509 bombers the GAF despatched to Coventry, 449 reached the target and only one was certainly destroyed.[6] It has been suggested that the defences would have been more successful if there had been less delay in accepting the POW's evidence that the target was to be in the Midlands, or if AI had not accepted the POW's date, 15 November, for the operation when the full moon period in fact began on 14 November. However, from the fact that preparations for the counter-measures had been completed well before the operation took place, and from the fact that it was learned during the afternoon that Coventry was to be the target, it is equally possible that the failure of the defences was due to operational deficiencies which intelligence, even if it had been better than it was, could have done little to off-set. It has further been pointed out that, while the beam frequencies used by the GAF pathfinder force were detected before the raid began, and jammers switched on, the jammers were ineffective because the audible signal frequency had been wrongly reported and they were incorrectly set.[7] But again it is impossible to say whether this mistake made any difference to the outcome.

Whatever may be the truth on these questions, it is certainly the case that there was a steady improvement in intelligence, as in operational counter-measures, equipment and methods, from the time of the Coventry raid. The effort which the GAF put into the Blitz, in terms of aircraft, numbers of sorties flown and casualties incurred, was measured with an increasing degree of confidence and accuracy. Of the extent of this improvement one example must suffice. AI's estimate of the number of bombers engaged in the raid on Coventry was 340[8] whereas, as we have seen, 509 were despatched and 449 reached the target. On the night of 13 December, in contrast, it estimated that 95 aircraft of Fliegerkorps II were active over the United Kingdom and a document captured shortly afterwards established that the actual number had been 97.[9]

---

6. Collier, op cit, p 264.
7. AIR 20/1627, Air Scientific Intelligence Report No 10 of 12 January 1941; Jones, op cit, p 151.   8. AIR 40/2321, p 50.
9. *Air Ministry Intelligence*, p 70.

The reason for the improvement was growing British knowledge about the GAF's order of battle – and not only about the number and whereabouts of its operational units but also, and even more important, about which of the units were over or under strength and how many bombers they had available for immediate operations. For this improvement AI was increasingly indebted to the Enigma decrypts, but advances in the techniques by which the intelligence bodies exploited the low-grade Sigint, already described,* also made an important contribution. There had never been much difficulty in decoding the GAF's low-grade codes and cyphers, and by the end of 1940 GC and CS had broken some 75 air to ground codes, 18 airfield serviceability codes, cyphers used by the German Sigint service and two systems used for encyphering map references. Hitherto, however, there had been some difficulty in intercepting all the traffic, for which there was a change of frequency every 24 hours, and the value of the messages on HF had been reduced by the impossibility of identifying the unit of the transmitting aircraft. Their operational HF call-signs were secret and were also changed daily, and intelligence had not succeeded in correlating them with the open call-signs that were used on the MF Safety Service. But in September 1940 Cheadle had made a start on this task of correlation, and in the next few months, with some assistance from captured documents, the solution of the secret call-signs was completed by a combination of Cheadle's empirical methods and analysis at GC and CS.

From the beginning of the GAF's night raids, as the solution proceeded, Cheadle could trace with ever-growing accuracy the whereabouts, movements and operational strengths of GAF units, thus supplementing – and providing a convenient cover for – the valuable strategic intelligence that was coming in an increasing amount from the Enigma. More immediately important, it was increasingly able to identify the GAF bomber units soon after the start of an operation. It thus provided indications of the imminence of raids in advance of radar notification from the early-warning radar, and also supplied information about them of the kind which radar could not obtain – on the sorties of the attacking aircraft, their numbers, their alternative targets, the results of their fire-raising attacks and the outcome of attacks by RAF fighters. The Kingsdown chain also contributed, for the German bombers sometimes used R/T for formation-keeping.

As low-grade Sigint supplemented the background intelligence derived from the Enigma, so the Enigma made a highly important contribution to tactical intelligence from November 1940. By that time most of the GAF's HQs and bases in north-west Europe had long ago ·reverted to land-lines, but KG 100, the pathfinder unit which led the big industrial raids and was associated with the operation of one of

---

* See above, Chapter 5, p 179 et seq.

the new GAF navigational aids (*X-Gerät*), continued to transmit and receive W/T signals. In September 1940 GC and CS broke the Enigma key used for these signals.* And from the middle of November, after previously divulging technical information about the navigational beams,† the decrypts of this key, to which GC and CS gave the highest priority, frequently divulged during the afternoon the beam settings to be used by KG 100 during the coming evening. In addition, in the course of developing counter-measures against the beams, it was found that the beam transmissions themselves could be intercepted on the ground by the VHF stations of the Kingsdown network. In these ways it proved possible to predict with growing accuracy, though not always with sufficient notice for operational purposes, where the next GAF attack would fall.[10]

So long as the Blitz lasted the availability of this method of predicting the GAF's 'target for tonight' went far to off-set the fact that the high-grade and the low-grade Sigint were still not being fully co-ordinated. Even so, this fact continued to limit the use that was made of the available tactical intelligence. No machinery had yet been devised by which GC and CS, Cheadle and Kingsdown could exchange immediate tactical Sigint before and during operations, though these organisations did exchange intelligence after the event on a limited scale, and no one body was set up to be responsible for integrating all Sigint of operational value with information derived from radar and other operational sources. At the end of 1940 the Air Section at GC and CS set up two parties – one for research on the pattern of GAF fighter activity and the other for research on the behaviour of the other units of the GAF – which mated high-grade with low-grade Sigint and which later integrated Sigint with intelligence from other sources like photographic reconnaissance. Their reports were valued by AI. But partly because its prime concern was to assemble long-term intelligence as background for strategic decisions, and partly because it was reluctant to let GC and CS share the work of interpreting intelligence, AI would not agree till a much later date that the reports should be circulated to the command intelligence staffs which were studying the GAF's tactical activities on the basis of low-grade Sigint, combat reports and other non-Sigint information, and which would have greatly benefited from GC and CS's research.

KG 100 itself provides a good illustration of the handicaps which resulted. Like many other GAF units it normally gave warning of forthcoming operations by opening up its low-grade W/T transmissions half an hour before its aircraft left the ground, and its aircraft

---

* See below, p 326.   † See below, p 322.

10. CX/JQ 215, 225, 249, 306, 320, 322, 379, 381, 384, 387, 389, 391, 392, 399, 401, 408, 409, 412.

made free use of W/T while in flight. With Cheadle's assistance Fighter Command was thus able to identify its pathfinder sorties on the radar screen. But Cheadle worked in ignorance of KG 100's targets obtained at GC and CS, as GC and CS's Enigma watches worked without the benefit of Cheadle's information, which went only to the Air Section for use in its long-term research, and Fighter Command received the Cheadle and the Enigma information through separate channels. Moreover, only one or two individuals at Fighter Command received the advance Enigma intelligence about the GAF's targets.

If delay in solving this organisational problem was mainly due to organisational resistances, we need not doubt that they were strengthened by security considerations. Nor could these be lightly set aside. In the series of raids which, beginning with Coventry, marked the intensification of the Blitz, Wolverhampton escaped despite the fact that it had been scheduled among the targets in the Enigma decrypts. POW revealed why this was so: the Germans had learned from deciphering British W/T traffic that the AA defences there had been strengthened in anticipation of an attack, and, after confirming their Sigint by reconnaissance, had called off the raid. It must be added, moreover, that operational limitations were no less important than organisational defects and the security problem in preventing the maximum operational use of the available intelligence. In the autumn of 1940 the shortage of night-fighter squadrons was acute and AA Command was not fully equipped. And between then and the late spring of 1941, when the GAF's offensive was faltering and it was transferring the bulk of its bombers to the east, these limitations were only gradually overcome.

In proportion as they were reduced, however, intelligence played an increasingly valuable role in limiting the effects of the Blitz and in raising its costliness for Germany, and did so in spite of continuing problems of organisation and communication. Nor were Fighter Command and AA Command the only beneficiaries. In the many ways in which its sources, Sigint especially, supplemented the early-warning radar, it was useful to the fire-fighting and other Civil Defence services, which were sometimes able to send reinforcements to threatened areas before the German bombers struck. By the ability to identify the bases used by the GAF units that were most active, and particularly the bases to which bombers were returning after their raids, intelligence contributed to Bomber Command's many successful attacks on the bases. And by foretelling the time at which the German bombers were likely to return, it assisted the intruder operations against the returning raiders which Fighter Command undertook from the end of 1940. There was some delay before arrangements were made for this intelligence to go direct from Cheadle to those who could make use of it, but Fighter Command later estimated that the forecasts from low-grade Sigint used in these operations 'maintained an accuracy of about 90 per cent'.[11] Low-grade Sigint also helped to frustrate GAF intruder attacks on returning Bomber Command aircraft. From October 1940 German night fighters scored many successes with this form of attack, which was a German innovation; but they abandoned it at the end of 1940 when, after a study of their radio traffic, the RAF introduced a method of confusing them by transmitting deceptive signals.[12] By the spring of 1941 low-grade Sigint, particularly that from the Kingsdown chain, was contributing to the operations by Bomber and Fighter Commands in yet another way. As a result of GC and CS's growing understanding of it, Kingsdown became able to interpret the traffic of the German ground-controlled night-fighter units which had first been intercepted accidentally by the BBC in September 1940. But the full value of this traffic was only to be realised later on, in connection with the RAF's large-scale bombing of Germany. During the winter of 1940–41, when the most important problem was the defence of the United Kingdom against German bombing, the most important contributions made by intelligence came from its ability to give notice of the GAF's 'target for tonight', which we have already discussed, and from the part it played in frustrating the GAF's navigational systems, to which we now turn.

□

Before the war the British authorities knew nothing about the GAF's experiments with more advanced radio aids to air navigation, but they were aware that it had created a network of Medium Frequency (176–580 kc/s) beacons for this purpose. From 1940 until as late as 1943 observation of this network – a network which by 1 September already stretched from Norway to France, included 38 beacons and 11 broadcasting stations, as well as the network within Germany, and was being improved by the introduction of a fan system of beams known as *Elektra* – was of great assistance to the RAF, whose aircraft could use it for locating their own targets in the absence of any comparable British radio aids. From an early date the switching on of the German beacons had been one of the indications which had enabled low-grade Sigint to give notice that German raids were imminent.[13] But what was more important – for, as we shall see, this use of the beacons, as of other forms of low-grade Sigint, was not fully exploited till later* – Cheadle's knowledge of the location of the beacons and of the operating procedure and the frequency changes of the network was already making it possible to develop effective radio counter-measures during the Battle of Britain.[14]

---

* See Volume Two.

11. *Air Ministry Intelligence*, p 84.
12. ibid, p 72.   13. ibid, pp 84–85.
14. AIR 41/46, No 80 Wing RAF, Historical Report 1940–45, Appendix C.

The counter-measures rested on the deployment of 'meacons' – masking beacons which had been developed by the Post Office as a precaution against any attempt by the GAF to use illicit beacons in the United Kingdom. They could change frequency rapidly and, by re-radiating the enemy's beacon signals, could render them useless, even misleading, to his aircraft.* The first 'meacons' were installed at three sites in August 1940. Their effectiveness was thereafter demonstrated in two ways. POWs admitted that the beacons were often useless,[15] and enemy aircraft from time to time landed or crashed in the United Kingdom when their crews thought they were near their own bases.[16] Secondly, the GAF was forced to introduce more elaborate systems for its MF call-sign and frequency changes in an effort to make it more difficult for the British authorities to intercept and exploit the signals. It adopted this evasive measure for the first time at the beginning of December 1940. During 1941 four further changes of system followed, each more complex than the previous one.

After each of these changes, while Cheadle was working out the new call-signs and frequencies, there was some interruption in the supply of the rapid intelligence which played the crucial part in the operational control of the counter-measures. On the whole, however, the interruptions were short-lived, at any rate before April 1941.[17] They were less significant, moreover, than they might have been. The MF network designed for general navigation on the way to the target and on the return flight was not a sufficiently accurate system to provide a bombing aid. But since 1937, with the double aim of speeding up the training of pilots and of improving their day-time bombing in poor weather, the GAF had been developing more sophisticated navigational aids.[18] By the middle of 1940 it had gone a long way with its experiments and was introducing the systems for use in its night-bombing offensive.†

By the same date British intelligence had gone a long way towards understanding how the new systems operated, and was providing the research establishments and the operational authorities with the information they needed for the design and deployment of counter-measures. Dr R V Jones, the scientist attached to the Air Ministry for intelligence purposes, was responsible for this advance. In the course of making it, he demonstrated what could be done if the entire range

---

* Those German beacons likely to be required by RAF Commands were not 'meaconed' when the others were being interfered with.
    † The above summary of the work on the MF beacons and the following paragraphs on the work against the other navigational systems are supplemented in Appendix 11, where fuller technical details will be found.

15. AIR 41/17, p 28.
16. Churchill, op cit, Vol II, p 339.
17. AIR 41/46, Appendix C.
18. AIR 41/10, pp 92–96.

of intelligence sources was carefully co-ordinated. That the Germans already had some form of radar and a knowledge of radio direction finding techniques was first suggested to him in 1939 by, among other slight indications, a reference to the existence of a German coastal air raid warning system in the Oslo report* which, as it happened, had contained no direct reference to the beam devices which were to be the essential features of the GAF's three navigational and bomb-dropping devices. In March 1940 the interrogation of prisoners of war yielded references to equipment known as *Knickebein* and *X-Gerät*, which appeared to be navigational aids to blind bombing, and documents referring to *Knickebein* were recovered from two crashed Heinkel 111 aircraft. These names having been brought to the attention of the intelligence collectors, the next clue was provided by GC and CS. On 5 June a GAF Enigma message of Fliegerkorps IV reported that a *Knickebein* transmitter at Kleve was being directed at a position in the United Kingdom over which it was learned that KG 27 had operated that night. An earlier examination of the He 111, the only type of aircraft used by that KG, had revealed that, while the aircraft carried no specialist equipment, they were fitted with a blind-landing radio receiver in the 30 Mc/s band that was unduly sensitive for its purpose.

On all the evidence Jones advanced the theory that beam transmissions from the *Knickebein* station in Germany, aimed at given co-ordinates, were intercepted by the He 111 on their blind-landing receivers, and that a second transverse beam would indicate the target position.[19] The theory was supported by further POW information in the middle of June, particularly by a POW who described a two-beam system and hinted that the bombs were dropped automatically, and on 16 June the Night Interception Committee decided that the evidence was sufficient to justify a search for the beams and the initiation of a counter-measure programme. On 18 June the Wireless Intelligence and Development Unit (WIDU) was formed from a disbanded Blind Approach Training and Development Unit to search for the beams. On the same day documents from a crashed aircraft established the location of the transmitters at Bredstedt and Kleve. On 21 June another captured document gave the location and frequencies of the transmitters at Kleve and Stollberg. On that day the Prime Minister was informed of the conjecture and of the evidence for it, and he ordered that absolute priority should be given to counter-measures. There were still some objections to the conjecture, based on known properties of HF transmissions, but the beam transmissions were found that evening by an aircraft from WIDU. They were in a

---

* See Appendix 5.

19. AIR 40/1532, *History of Air Scientific Intelligence*, (1946), p 4; AIR 20/1623, ASI Report No 6 of 28 June 1940; Jones, op cit, Chapter 11.

narrow beam, 400 to 500 yards wide, and were intersected by a secondary beam. So far as is known, this was the first occasion on which enemy signals were intercepted in a British aircraft. With assistance from a wide variety of intelligence sources, the understanding of *Knickebein* was thus advanced from conjecture to certainty with so little delay that its transmissions had been discovered within days of its first known introduction.

Photographic reconnaissance played a part in completing the investigation in September by locating a transmitter and showing that it was suitable for the frequencies used by the beams.[20] By that time five transmitters had been identified and it had been found possible to intercept them on the ground, using the VHF stations of the Kingsdown network. This greatly assisted the operation of counter-measures; by the end of August the jamming of transmitters had been tested but the further development of these counter-measures necessarily took some time, requiring as it did the provision of high-power jamming transmitters in numbers sufficient to cover the whole country and the establishment of a special organisation – No 80 Wing RAF which incorporated the Wireless Intelligence and Development Unit and, after an experimental period, opened at Radlett on 14 October.[21] Even before the end of September, however, the preliminary efforts to interfere with *Knickebein* were having some effect, as was shown when two of the stations exchanged frequencies during an attack on London on the night of 24–25 September.[22]

The *Knickebein* was not the only blind-bombing aid under development in Germany. But whereas it did not require the bombers to be equipped with specialist equipment, the next device to be encountered – the *X-Gerät* – did. *Knickebein* was designed to locate the point of bomb release with good accuracy, which was initially assessed to be within 400 yards, and it could be used by large forces of bombers. But it remained subject to errors on account of uncertainty about the aircraft's velocity at the release point. To overcome this limitation the *X-Gerät* directed a main beam to the target and intersected it with transverse beams. By recording the transit time between the cross beams, equipment in the bomber could determine the true ground speed and bomb automatically. On the other hand, its use required more complex training and equipment and was thus restricted to a specialist unit. The GAF first used it in attacks on coastal targets, from mid-August, It was first used by pathfinder aircraft in a major raid during the attack on Coventry on 14 November, the tactic being that the aircraft using the system made an incendiary attack and the following bombers bombed on the fires.

---

20. AIR 20/1626, ASI Report No 9 of 18 September 1940.
21. AIR 41/46, pp 6, 9–10.
22. ibid, p 11; Jones, op cit, Chapter 16.

During September 1940 progress in acquiring intelligence about the *X–Gerät* became very rapid. As a result of the fortunate circumstance that KG 100 operated from Brittany, where GAF units continued to use W/T for some time after the rest of the GAF had returned to land-lines for its communications, GC and CS was able to break in mid-September a new Enigma key (the Brown) introduced for communication between KG 100 and the Sixth Company of the GAF Signals Experimental Regiment, responsible for the development of *X-Gerät*. Until May 1941 when it died out, this was read almost every day and, as well as giving advance warning of KG 100's targets on many occasions by disclosing the beam settings to be used in the next night's operations,* it provided a considerable body of information about *X-Gerät* in the form of equipment returns. It was this information which gave the exact location of some of the transmitters and played the major part in solving the *X-Gerät* system. Its references to the supply of quartz crystals enabled the frequency range to be established as 65–75 Mc/s. Its references to an *Anna* equipment with 'grad' settings or scale marks led to the discovery that the number of *Anna* grads announced in Enigma messages was related to the particular frequency within that range that was to be used. By giving the works numbers or factory markings of the *Anna* apparatus it guided the examination of the equipment in a crashed Heinkel to the discovery that *Anna* was a complete VHF receiver.[23]†

The counter-measures based on these discoveries were not at first effective. Apart from the fact that there was some delay while jamming transmitters in the 65–75 Mc/s band were obtained, an error was made when their necessary modification was undertaken. As it happened, information was still lacking about another component of the system – a device called APV – to which the GAF Enigma was referring. It was not until the middle of November that, as well as yielding a document giving a comprehensive description of the *X-Gerät*, the crash of another Heinkel (brought about by 'meaconing') disclosed that this device was an audio filter and established the correct modulation frequency used by the system. From December 1940 counter-measures rapidly improved. Studies by the Air Ministry of the accuracy of bombing by aircraft using the *X-Gerät* showed a serious deterioration in February 1941 as compared with November 1940. On one calculation the total effect of the counter-measures, despite the delay in bringing them into force, was that not more than

---

* But the beam-setting signal was not decrypted on 14 November 1940, the day of the Coventry raid.

† This was the first time that the analysis of factory markings, a method extensively used later in the war, was employed in the solution of an intelligence problem: see Appendix 11 (v).

23. AIR 20/1627; Jones, op cit, Chapter 17.

one-fifth of German bombs fell within the target area.[24] In March 1941 the crew of a crashed aircraft of KG 100 revealed that interference with the *X-Gerät* had been noticeable since the previous November and that since February, when the British authorities had at last acquired sufficient transmitters to enable them to jam the cross beams, it had been very serious. By the end of March, when KG 100 had gone back to independent bombing and the GAF was making its raids by moonlight only, the GAF's lack of confidence in the system was confirmed.

There was even less delay in countering the next navigational aid which the Germans introduced. In this system, the *Y-Gerät* or *Wotan*, a single beam* was used to give the aircraft its direction and the order to bomb was given from a ground station, where the exact range of the bomber on its bearing was determined by the time taken for the station's signals to be re-radiated from the bomber. The system first came to the knowledge of the intelligence authorities when the Enigma reported on 27 June 1940 that the GAF was setting up *Wotan* and *Knickebein* stations near Cherbourg and Brest.[25] This evidence led Dr Jones to associate it with an item in the Oslo report which had referred to a method by which the distance of an aircraft from its base could be determined by radar and the pilot informed of his position. A message of 6 October in the GAF Enigma[26] to a new station *Wotan II*, giving co-ordinates for 'Target No 1 for Y', supported the theory that the *Y-Gerät* was a single beam system. Similar messages were decrypted on 13 October and 2 November, and later in November signals were intercepted on about 42.2 Mc/s and it was noted that base and aircraft transmitters had simultaneously transmitted a modulated signal. Subsequently a POW divulged that *Wotan* indeed consisted of only one beam. The GAF unit involved was III KG 26. The first photographs of a *Wotan II* site were taken by PRU on 22 November in the Hague peninsula.[27] By that time counter-measures were in preparation. They included the centralised co-ordination of the work of Kingsdown's HDUs. Originally the HDUs had reported only to the RAF and naval commands;† by the end of 1940 Kingsdown had become the R/T collecting centre, with direct lines to the principal HDUs. By January 1941, when only a few German aircraft had made use of it, the general principles of the *Y-Gerät* system were fully understood.

By February counter-measures had been instituted. By March these

---

* Wotan was the one-eyed god.
† See Chapter 5, p 180.

24. Churchill, op cit, Vol II, p 343.
25. CX/JQ 92.
26. CX/JQ 248.
27. AIR 20/1624, ASI Report No 7 of 17 July 1940; AIR 20/1627; Jones, op cit, pp 120–121, Chapter 21.

were adding to the teething troubles which the GAF was still experiencing with the system. During April and May the GAF used it in raids over a wide area, and this made counter-measures difficult, but it was noted that on only two occasions did more than 25 per cent of the bombers receive the dropping signal. At the beginning of May the crews of three crashed aircraft admitted that III KG 26 was losing confidence in the system on account of British jamming. At that point, the recovery from one of these aircraft of a damaged *Y-Gerät* apparatus having completed the British knowledge of the system's operating details, further refinements in the British jamming measures made them still more effective.[28]

□

By the late spring of 1941, largely in consequence of a rapid improvement in British scientific intelligence, Germany had lost the first battles in the radio war. *Knickebein* was discredited, though it was later to be modified. The *X-Gerät* was about to be withdrawn from service, to undergo modification before being used again in the west during the Baedeker raids on the United Kingdom in 1942. The *Y-Gerät* was still being developed but was subjected to regular interference. In Great Britain, at the same time, an intimate co-operation had been established between the intelligence authorities and No 80 Wing RAF which was to prove invaluable for the rest of the war. By the same date the GAF's bomber offensive against the United Kingdom was being greatly reduced. From the middle of April it became clear that, in order to maintain even its declining level of activity, the GAF was finding it necessary to send aircraft on second sorties during the same night. On 16–17 April Cheadle established that about 60 aircraft made double sorties; on the night of 10–11 May, during the last big raid on London, a considerable number again made two sorties and some made three.[29]

The GAF's offensive against British shipping had begun to decline much earlier. Indeed, its mass attacks on east coast shipping, suspended since July 1940 for the duration of the Battle of Britain but resumed in October, had been abandoned altogether in the middle of November, when the GAF withdrew from the daylight battle in order to concentrate on the night-bombing offensive. They were replaced by small isolated raids and mine-laying sorties. These, which continued after the bulk of the GAF had been transferred to other theatres, produced less GAF W/T traffic than the mass attacks had done. On the other hand, the technique of matching the GAF's low-grade signals with radar steadily improved. By February 1941

---

28. AIR 41/46, pp 20–22; AIR 20/1627.
29. *Air Ministry Intelligence*, p 70.

Sigint was being used to alert the radar stations and the Observer Corps; and by April it was possible on the basis of the low-grade Sigint to give advance warning of mine-laying operations.[30] The intelligence provided by the RAF and naval R/T intercept stations was similarly valuable against the fighter and fighter-bomber attacks on coastal shipping and coast towns and against the E-boat attacks which also went on after the departure of the main GAF bomber force for the east.

Against another of the threats to shipping which continued after the GAF had withdrawn from the Blitz, intelligence was less effective. As early as February 1940 POW had mentioned that a new unit (KG 40) was being equipped with Focke Wulf 200 aircraft and trained for long-distance anti-shipping operations. From August 1940 these aircraft made weather flights between Bordeaux and Stavanger, to the westward of the British Isles, and attacked independently routed ships during their flights. With the coming of winter they worked from Bordeaux only, supplementing their attacks on shipping by reconnaissance work for U-boats and experiments in homing U-boats on to targets.

Cheadle detected KG 40's move to Bordeaux and from the beginning was able to keep a close watch on its activities. With this information and with the assistance of intelligence from prisoners and other non-Y sources the Air Ministry built up an accurate picture of the unit, establishing the areas in which the reconnaissance was carried out, calculating the unit's losses and its average monthly intake of new aircraft, and tracing its gradual expansion from 8 to 29 aircraft (including a known number of transport aircraft). Some use was made of this intelligence when Bomber Command raided the Bordeaux base on 22 November and brought about a reduction in KG 40's activities for three weeks. But intruder operations against the unit, though recommended by Air Intelligence, proved impracticable, and full knowledge of the unit's habits, while illustrating the growing ability of the intelligence service to keep GAF units under observation, was of little avail when it came to intercepting the aircraft or reducing their depredations.[31] By the end of 1940, when KG 40 was making three or four sorties daily, it had sunk over 108,000 tons of shipping and damaged over 168,000 tons for the loss of one aircraft. In January and February 1941 it achieved still greater success. With only 15 operational aircraft, it sank in those two months 47 ships, totalling 168,000 tons, and damaged a further 19.[32]

In Whitehall the seriousness of these losses, and indications that collaboration between KG 40 and the U-boats was increasing, now

---

30. ibid, p 68.
31. ibid, p 71; AIR 40/2321, pp 8, 100; AIR 40/2322, AI 3 Summary of Minutes, Vol II, p 44.
32. Roskill, op cit, Vol I, pp 362–363.

produced special measures. By the end of January the problem of how best to protect shipping against KG 40 was being discussed at meetings of the heads of the German sections in the different intelligence departments. Early in March, shortly after Air Intelligence had reported that KG 40 had resumed its routine of shuttling between Bordeaux and Stavanger, and had emphasised the implications of this change for convoy routeing, the Prime Minister decreed that the defeat of KG 40 and the U-boats must take priority over all other tasks.[33] The problem seemed all the more urgent in that Air Intelligence was still ascribing the GAF's failure to reinforce KG 40's activities to the fact that 'the German High Command has never been really enthusiastic over this type of offensive' rather than to the real cause – the fact that the GAF's resources were severely strained – and was thus urging that the GAF would have no difficulty in finding the necessary aircraft and crews should it change its mind.[34]

For a time from the end of February these fears appeared to be confirmed by new intelligence. At this juncture, when the Blitz was becoming increasingly costly to the GAF and increasingly unpopular with its crews, the German authorities converted a night-bombing unit to the anti-shipping role. From 24 February low-grade Sigint revealed that III KG 27 had moved to Brest. During March this unit extended the daylight raids on shipping into the southern Irish Sea and the Bristol Channel. By the end of that month it was known that it was being reinforced by the transfer to Brest of I and II KG 27 and the GAF Enigma had disclosed that the GAF was creating a special authority to co-ordinate its Atlantic anti-shipping activities from France and Norway, and that it was about to allocate further units exclusively to this work.[35] Before long, however, these plans were abandoned in favour of the transfer of units to the east, and in the meantime, while attempts to intercept KG 40's FW 200s west of Ireland remained consistently unsuccessful, KG 27's He 111s suffered heavy losses and achieved poor returns. As a result in part of their inexperience and in part of the fact that, since they operated closer to the British coasts than the FW 200s it proved possible for the British defences to make use of the advance intelligence of their raids, their activity was greatly reduced from the end of March.[36]

□

By the end of March 1941 the GAF's attacks on British high-seas shipping had reached, and passed, their peak. As yet, on the other hand, the successes against the British trade routes of the German

---

33. AIR 40/2322, p 44; Churchill, op cit, Vol III, p 107.
34. AIR 40/2322, p 6.
35. Roskill, op cit, Vol I, p 362; AIR 41/10, pp 105–109.
36. AIR 41/10, p 106.

surface fleet and the U-boats continued to mount, and there seemed to be little prospect of bringing them down.

At the outbreak of the war the German authorities had decided to complete those surface ships which had already been laid down, but to undertake no new construction. Although this meant that their major units, if lost, would be irreplaceable, they also decided to make a bold use of such as they had, both to supplement the U-boat assault on British shipping and achieve that dislocation of British naval dispositions which the presence at sea of even one or two warships would bring about. Undeterred by the loss of the *Graf Spee* in December 1939, they were able to extend operations after the seizure of Norwegian and French bases and the development of a supply-ship organisation in Biscay during the autumn of 1940. During the winter of 1940–41 the pocket-battleship *Scheer*, the battle cruisers *Scharnhorst* and *Gneisenau* and the cruiser *Hipper* all left home ports for raids in the north Atlantic. In addition, the first six German auxiliary cruisers – converted merchant ships – had sailed by July 1940 for the south Atlantic, the Indian Ocean and Australasia where, disguised as Allied or neutral ships, and aided by the knowledge of British shipping codes, they carried out attacks on independently routed ships.*

During the first three months of 1941 these activities produced a marked increase in the sinkings of British ships by the German surface fleet. Indeed, such sinkings now ran at a higher rate than at any other period of the war, and the main reason was that the increase in German operations was not yet matched by any significant improvement in British naval intelligence. Occasionally, as when it revealed in September 1940 that the *Hipper* was making a reconnaissance cruise in the Barents Sea,[37] the GAF Enigma yielded a clue to German naval movements; but the naval Enigma remained unbroken. Somewhat more frequently the behaviour of the German naval W/T network indicated that unusual preparations were afoot. It was on the strength of signs from Traffic Analysis that main units were about to leave the Baltic that the Home Fleet put to sea on 20 January 1941, and thus came close to making contact with the *Scharnhorst* and the *Gneisenau* after the Traffic Analysis indications had been confirmed on 23 January by an attaché report to the effect that battle cruisers had been sighted in the Great Belt.[38] But the results of Traffic Analysis were rarely judged to be positive or accurate enough in themselves to justify sending the Home Fleet to sea. As for the remaining sources of intelligence – photographic reconnaissance and agents' reports – they were even less able to give reliable advance warning of naval movements.

---

* See Volume Two.

37. ADM 223/78, Admiralty signal of 27 September 1940.
38. Roskill, op cit, Vol I, p 373.

In the number and range of its aircraft the PRU was still expanding far too slowly for the Admiralty, as we have already seen.* From November 1940 the prototype of a new Spitfire (type D) brought more distant bases – Toulon, Oslo, Trondheim – within range, but it was not until April 1941 that this and other types were available in sufficient quantity to provide frequent, if not continuous, cover of a few priority targets. In March the photographs of German shipbuilding yards became sufficient in number and quality for work to begin on what was later to become 'one of the most outstanding services rendered to naval intelligence by photographic reconnaissance'[39] – that of estimating the rate and understanding the methods of U-boat construction. Beginning on 28 March, again, when the *Scharnhorst* and the *Gneisenau* were first photographed in Brest, 87 sorties were flown over them there by the end of April, though many were unproductive on account of bad weather. But until the spring, in still poorer weather and with the other Services competing with the Admiralty for the use of the few available aircraft, anything approaching a regular watch on Germany's naval bases was impossible. This reduced the value of such information as PR managed to obtain. On 29 November 1940, for example, just before she made her first sortie into the Atlantic, the *Hipper* was photographed in Brunsbüttel, but the OIC did not appreciate the significance of her presence there.[40] The fundamental problem, however, was that for operational purposes the coverage was too infrequent to be valuable. Thus the *Scharnhorst* and the *Gneisenau*, first photographed at Kiel on 15 and 21 October and seen there again in 21 December, were missing when Kiel was next completely photographed on 9 January. Except by the ships they attacked, they were not seen again until the end of March. Aircraft from HMS *Ark Royal* then sighted them on their approach to Brest, but in part owing to delays and accidents in the transmission of the sighting report the *Ark Royal* was unable to make an attack.[41]

From Brest between the end of March and June 1941 SIS agents were able to send daily reports about the positions and the sea-worthiness of the *Scharnhorst* and the *Gneisenau*. These reports were especially useful because it was difficult to judge from photographic reconnaissance the effect of bombing raids on the ships. On 20 June 1941 'C' was to send a collated report on both ships to the Chiefs of Staff with a warning that, although the *Gneisenau* was out of action, the *Scharnhorst* could get home at any moment, probably through the Channel.[42] As events were to prove, however, they could

---

* Chapter 9, p 281 et seq.

39. AIR 41/6, p 262; ADM 233/84, NID 001089, 27 March 1941.
40. Roskill, op cit, Vol I, p 291.
41. ibid, p 377.
42. AIR 22/74, Air Ministry Weekly Intelligence Summaries, Nos 85, 90 and 91 of 16 April, 14 and 25 May 1941.

not be relied on for advance information should the ships move from Brest. Unless supported by other indications, reports on intentions and movements from this source, like those that came from agents in the Baltic entrances via the Naval Attaché in Stockholm, were generally too vague and too conflicting, or else were received too late, to be useful for operational purposes.

If the German surface ships were thus able to carry out their cruises with little or no danger of interception, so were the U-boats. Even before the spring of 1941, when photographic reconnaissance of the yards first provided intelligence about the rate of construction, the NID's estimates of the number of operational U-boats had not been far from the truth, particularly after the recovery of documents from U-49 had enabled it to correct its evaluation of the number available at the outbreak of war and its guesses about U-boat losses up to April 1940.* At 1 March 1941 it calculated that 63 had been added to the 57 available in September 1939 and that at least 30 had been lost, giving a force of 90.[43] The actual figures at 1 April, when 143 boats had been commissioned, were 32 operational boats and 81 in training, 30 having been lost.[44] By the same date it had accumulated a considerable amount of accurate information about the tonnage, propulsion and general performance of the different types of U-boat – though less about their armament and listening equipment – and the U-49 documents had established the correct type classification of all boats commissioned up to the spring of 1940. POW from U-32 (sunk in October 1940) had provided it with further information of this kind, especially about torpedoes.[45] But NID continued to lack operational intelligence about the U-boats, as opposed to background information about them. Thus it remained unaware of the considerable trouble with torpedo failures which the U-boats experienced up to the middle of 1940 – as it did of Germany's plans to introduce the acoustic mine before that was encountered in August 1940 – and it had no reliable information about U-boat operations. From early in 1941 the Polish intelligence network in France, co-operating with the SIS, was able to report to London the departure of U-boats from Bordeaux, and by June this service had been extended to Brest and Le Havre. But it could say nothing about U-boat destinations and patrol areas. Like the rest of the German Fleet, the U-boat arm used only the Enigma for encyphering its communications. Like the rest of the Fleet, the U-boats kept wireless silence at sea except on sighting a convoy, when they reported for the benefit of others on patrol, or if reporting a success, when their attacks had already betrayed their positions. Apart from DF fixes on their

---

* See Chapter 7, p 231.

43. ADM 233/84, NID 0714 of 27 February 1941, NID 00687/41 of 1 March.
44. ADM 186/802.
45. ADM 233/85, NID 00379/40 of 9 November.

sighting reports, the U-boat plotting room in the OIC had no information as to their whereabouts and movements other than the attacks they made and the occasional sighting of them by British ships and aircraft. On this evidence the plot could keep a fairly accurate tally of the number on patrol but it could do little more than guess where to route the convoys in its attempt to steer them clear of the U-boats.

Against the U-boat danger, even more than against the raids by surface ships, the lack of operational intelligence constituted a grave and a mounting handicap. In the first nine months of the war, despite the bold use that was made of it in minelaying and other operations close to the United Kingdom, the U-boat arm had presented only a limited threat to the British trade routes. The number of boats on patrol at any one time, never more than 10, had often been as low as 2; at some periods – in the second half of December 1939; from the end of February to the end of May 1940, when they had been withdrawn for the Norwegian campaign – their attacks on shipping had been entirely suspended. Losses of boats, at the high figure of 14, had barely been made up by additions to the operational fleet. Moreover, even if in proportion to their numbers their results had been good, they had been meagre in relation to the total available shipping. To the end of February 1940 they had sunk 664,931 tons of shipping since the outbreak of war, an average monthly rate of 133,000 tons. Defects in their construction and equipment were not easily overcome. Their commanders and crews were still short of experience and they were hampered by legal and political restrictions on submarine warfare which, notwithstanding the sinking of the *Athenia* and other incidents that led the British authorities to fear the early introduction of unrestricted warfare, the German government only gradually abandoned. Above all, the early introduction of the convoy system for the bulk of British trade proved to be an effective counter-measure. Of the 169 ships sunk by U-boats up to the end of February 1940, only 7 were in convoys escorted by anti-submarine vessels. But between June 1940 and March 1941, in the second phase of the U-boat war, the threat from the U-boats increased alarmingly. Between June and October 1940 their monthly sinkings increased steadily from 268,000 tons to 350,000 tons. By the U-boat commanders, among whom several 'aces' began to distinguish themselves, this period became known as the first of their 'happy times'. After October they were somewhat less successful for some months. Except in December, their sinkings did not reach 200,000 tons in any month from November to February. But over the whole period from June 1940 to February 1941, inclusive, they still sank an average of 260,000 tons of shipping a month, at double the rate they had previously achieved. During the same period, compared with the figure of over 2 million tons sunk by U-boat, German surface ships sank a total of 609,000 tons and the GAF somewhat less than 500,000.

The better performance of the U-boats was not due to any marked increase in their operational numbers. Practically without replacement, the pre-war fleet still bore the burden. After the fall of France, however, they were able to work from bases in Brittany instead of from Baltic and North Sea ports. This transfer, bringing them several hundred miles nearer to the Atlantic, enabled them to stay longer on patrol, so that the number at sea at any one time now averaged 15, or to patrol wider areas. From August 1940 they were making the first experimental cruises to the distant area off west Africa. By that time they had acquired another advantage: in the middle of August Germany finally declared unrestricted submarine warfare and a total blockade of the United Kingdom. In conjunction with the growing experience of their commanders and crews, the removal of restrictions facilitated their adoption of new tactics. From the end of August, instead of attacking at periscope depth and mainly by day, they adopted night attack on the surface, and did so to such advantage that it was not until three years later, and then reluctantly, as a result of being forced to submerge by Allied superiority in radar and intelligence, that they abandoned the new method. By attacking on the surface they could make use of their greater surface speed and mobility and could conserve their batteries. They could also elude the British Asdic, which was devised to detect U-boats when they were submerged. Finally, and not least as a result of the fact that so many of the available British escort vessels were retained in the Channel as part of the anti-invasion measures, the U-boats became bolder in attacking convoys. It was in September 1940 that the proportion of attacks on convoys began to rise. Already in that month 40 of the total of 59 U-boat attacks on merchant shipping were attacks on convoys.

For the relative decline in U-boat successes from November 1940 British counter-measures were mainly responsible. At the end of October, in view of the mounting frequency of attacks on convoys and the decline of the danger of immediate invasion, the Defence Committee ordered the recall to convoy escort duties of more than half of the naval forces that had been retained in Home Waters to deal with the approach of a seaborne expedition.[46] At the same time, more of Coastal Command's aircraft were transferred to anti-submarine work. Until March 1941, in spite of the continuing lack of operational naval intelligence, these measures sufficed to contain the threat to the flow of British supplies. But at that juncture the U-boat Command, its operational fleet about to enter at last upon a fairly rapid growth and its commanders prepared for the introduction of the new tactics of hunting and attacking the convoys in 'wolf-packs', was embarking on the next stage of the Battle of the Atlantic with every expectation of achieving a decisive victory.

□

---

46. CAB 69/1, DO (40) 39th Meeting, 31 October.

That it was denied this success was largely, if not wholly, due to an advance on the part of British intelligence. In fits and starts during March and April 1941, just when the first great battle of the convoy routes was beginning, the German naval Enigma at last yielded to the efforts of GC and CS.

Since the outbreak of war GC and CS had continued to give work on the GAF variant of the Enigma priority over its attack on the naval traffic. It had done so for two good reasons. The GAF traffic was more voluminous. Over and above that, those who worked on the naval Enigma had been held up first by the fact that the German Navy used the machine more carefully than the GAF, so that by the beginning of 1940 GC and CS had been able to break the settings for only 5 days of 1938, and then by the discovery that, sometime about the outbreak of war, the naval machine had undergone more radical modification than had the GAF's. During 1940 small amounts of captured naval cypher material had confirmed that, while both still used only three wheels at a time, the naval Enigma's wheels were now selected from a larger number than were the GAF's: it used from 8 instead of from 5.[47] It thus seemed probable that not even an increase in GC and CS's cryptanalytical machinery, which was soon to make possible the regular reading of the GAF's traffic, would bring success against the less vulnerable naval cypher, and that further advance would depend on capturing more naval material – or at least on obtaining detailed information from knowledgeable prisoners of war.

From December 1939 GC and CS had left the Admiralty in no doubt about the urgency of this last requirement, but the Admiralty had had little opportunity to meet it. Three Enigma wheels had been recovered from the crew of U-33 in February 1940, but these had not provided a sufficient basis for a further advance. Nor had the chance capture of cypher settings from VP2623 in April 1940* been much more useful to the cryptanalysts. It had enabled GC and CS to read during May 1940 the naval Enigma traffic for six days of the previous month, and thus to add considerably to its knowledge of the German Navy's W/T and cypher organisation. GC and CS was able to confirm that, though the Germans resorted to fairly simple hand codes and cyphers for such things as light-ships, dockyards and merchant shipping, their naval units, down to the smallest, relied entirely on the Enigma machine.† More important still, it established that they used only two Enigma keys – the Home and the Foreign – and that U-boats and surface units shared the same keys, transferring to the Foreign key only for

---

* See Chapter 5, p 163.

† All carried a hand cypher for use in case the machine broke down but except in the Mediterranean this was rarely used.

47. Jürgen Rohwer, *The Critical Convoy Battles of March 1943* (1977) Appendix 10 ('Notes on the security of the German cipher systems'), p 233.

operations in distant waters. The Foreign key was used only by the pocket-battleships and armed merchant cruisers, and was never broken. As against this, however, the advance in knowledge had also confirmed GC and CS's worst fears about the difficulty of breaking even the Home key, in which over 95 per cent of German naval traffic was encyphered, and only five further days' traffic, for dates in April and May 1940, had been broken by February 1941. But in March 1941 the need for more captures was at last fulfilled, and fulfilled on a sufficient scale.

In advance of the Lofoten raid of 4 March a special effort to seize the Enigma machine and its settings was concerted between the NID and GC and CS. It was rewarded by the capture in the course of the operation, from the armed trawler *Krebs*, of material which enabled GC and CS to read the whole of the traffic for February 1941 at various dates from 10 March. Thus fortified, GC and CS broke the whole of the traffic of April 1941 by cryptanalytical methods between 22 April and 10 May and was able to read much of the May traffic with a delay of between three and seven days. Nor was that all. The capture made in March and the cryptanalytical progress made during April provided the basis for a series of further advances.

These further advances were brought about in three ways. The first was opened up when the intelligence staff at GC and CS's Naval Section discovered an unexpected opportunity to capture more Enigma material. After studying the decyphered traffic of February and April, GC and CS was able to show conclusively that the Germans were keeping weather-ships on station in two areas, one north of Iceland and the other in mid-Atlantic, and that, though their routine reports were transmitted in weather cypher and were different in outward appearance from Enigma signals, the ships carried the naval Enigma.* The upshot was that the Admiralty organised not one, but two, special cutting-out operations. On 7 May 1941 the weather-ship *München* was captured; and it was with her settings that GC and CS read the June traffic practically currently. On 28 June the weather-reporting trawler *Lauenburg* suffered the same fate. She did so at a carefully chosen time, near the beginning of another month and the entry into force of the next monthly sheet of Enigma settings. With her settings GC and CS read the traffic currently throughout July. In between these two operations U-110, captured by chance on 9 May, had yielded a haul which included the special settings used in the Navy for 'officer-only' signals and the code book used by the U-boats when making short-signal sighting reports (Kurzsignale). This made it possible for the first time for GC and CS to read these two important types of traffic and to reconstruct later editions of them, but the Home

---

* See Appendix 12 for the GC and CS reports which provided the evidence for these operations.

Waters settings taken from her were those for April, of which most of the traffic had already been decyphered, and those for June, which duplicated the *München* material. She had destroyed the settings for May.

For the rest of the war captured documents continued to be of great assistance from time to time to the work on the naval Enigma, as they were to that on other cyphers, and procedures were laid down to ensure that no opportunity of taking them was missed when Allied forces were in contact with the enemy. Beginning with the landings in north-west Africa in November 1942, moreover, the Allied offensives were accompanied by teams formed and trained for this work. After June 1941, however, no further operations were undertaken for the special purpose of capturing naval Enigma material. The wish to capture it gave place to apprehension lest even fortuitous capture, by alarming the enemy, should compromise the fact that GC and CS had now mastered the cypher. For in the breathing space provided by the captured material for June and July 1941 GC and CS had recruited more cryptanalytical staff and obtained more machinery. By the end of June it had increased the number of its anti-Enigma Bombes to six, of which at least one was always available for naval work. The cryptanalysts had also used the mounting experience that came from their daily reading of the Enigma to perfect their methods. It was as a result of this progress on the cryptanalytical front that, without the assistance of further captures, they were able after the first week of August to decypher all but two days of the Home Waters traffic down to the end of the war. Except during December 1941, moreover, when the delay temporarily increased to about 80 hours, most of this traffic was read within 36 hours.

In making this break-through GC and CS was assisted not only by the hauls from the weather-ships and the improvement in GC and CS's supply of machinery. In the spring of 1941 it made an advance in a third direction. It had broken several hand codes and cyphers of the German Navy since November 1939 – a cypher that was briefly used between Berlin and the naval attachés at Madrid, Tokyo and Buenos Aires for signals about supply ships; a new merchant navy code; some light-ship codes; a naval-air code, after its capture during the Norwegian campaign; an air-sea rescue code. From the spring of 1941, assisted first by a captured document and then by the discovery that some of the signals were repetitions of decrypted Enigma messages, it broke a dockyards and fairways hand cypher ('Werft'). From August 1941, as a result of the fact that some of its signals were re-encyphered in the Enigma and re-transmitted, and of GC and CS's ability to isolate these signals, the 'Werft' decrypts made, in return, an invaluable contribution to the daily cryptanalytical assault on the naval Enigma settings. At the same time it was as a result of breaking into the Enigma that GC and CS was able to complete its mastery of the dockyard cypher and to read it, too, for the rest of the war. Of many that were encountered during the war, in connection with the GAF and Army Enigma as well as with the naval, this was perhaps the outstanding illustration of the importance of concentrating all cryptanalytical effort in one place. It emphasised, too, the wisdom of attacking all codes and cyphers, even the ostensibly insignificant. The cryptanalytical value of the dockyard cypher was enormous. But it could not have been foreseen; and the cypher might have been neglected if its operational value had been the only consideration. Like the other minor systems of the German Navy, it yielded no important operational information.

From the same date, the spring of 1941, a similar bonus was derived from GC and CS's work on the systems which most countries had introduced at the outbreak of war for encoding the reports transmitted by their meteorological stations. As the reading of these cyphers was in any case of operational importance, and indispensable for the weather forecasting of the Meteorological Office, it required careful organisation and absorbed an increasing amount of labour; although the cyphers were relatively simple, large numbers of them existed and they had to be read with next to no delay. But one of them, the German naval meteorological cypher, turned out to be of especial importance. It was first broken in February 1941 and in May of that year the Meteorological Section at GC and CS discovered that it carried weather reports from U-boats in the Atlantic which had originally been transmitted in the naval Enigma. Thereafter its decrypts were no less useful than those of the dockyard cypher in helping to break the Enigma keys. As we shall see, they were also to be valuable by providing direct statements of the positions of U-boats when the U-boat Command decided that the U-boats must disguise the positions they announced in their Enigma signals.*

□

Of the advantages that followed from breaking the Naval Enigma the most fundamental were reaped in the struggle against the U-boats during that phase of the Battle of the Atlantic which began when Germany launched the first concentrated attacks on the convoy routes in April 1941 and closed in December 1941 with the temporary collapse of her anti-commerce operations.† The earliest, and the most dramatic, took another form. To the sinking of the *Bismarck*, which brought to an end commerce raiding by the main units of the German Navy, the naval Enigma traffic made only an isolated contribution, but it was a contribution of some importance. It was entirely due to this traffic, moreover, that the Admiralty was able to destroy the tankers and supply ships that Germany had sent out in advance of *Bismarck's* cruise.

---

* See Volume Two.   † See Volume Two.

The *Bismarck* sailed from Kiel on 19 May 1941 with the *Prinz Eugen*, a new 8″ cruiser, to continue the surface-ship offensive in the Atlantic. Up to that time, as well as experiencing great difficulty in tracing the whereabouts of Germany's operational surface fleet, the Admiralty had obtained no reliable evidence about the state of readiness of the ships that were under construction. At the outbreak of war it had estimated that the two battleships, the *Bismarck* and the *Tirpitz*, would complete by the end of 1940, that the aircraft carrier *Graf Zeppelin* could commission by the middle of that year, that two 8″ cruisers, the *Blücher* and the *Eugen*, were virtually ready and that of two further 8″ cruisers, the *Seydlitz* and the *Lützow*, one would complete in the autumn of 1940 and the other at the end of 1941. During the next 12 months it was able to keep some PR check on the progress of the *Tirpitz*, which lay at Wilhelmshaven till March 1941; it learned that the *Blücher* had been lost during the Norwegian campaign; and it received some rumours that the *Lützow* had been sold to Russia, a transaction which happened in February 1940 after the pocket-battleship *Deutschland* had been renamed *Lützow*. But about the other ships it received no firm information and, while their construction was if anything falling behind schedule, the Admiralty was inclined to bring forward the dates of the commissioning. Of the *Bismarck* this was especially true after she left her dock in Hamburg, first for Kiel in the middle of September 1940 and then further eastward, beyond reconnaissance range, from the end of that month. Earlier in the summer the Admiralty had allowed that she might take part in the attempt at invasion. From September it paid full attention to any indication that she might be leaving the Baltic.[48]

One such indication had been received in April 1941, and the Home Fleet had put to sea, but the rumours had proved to be false.[49] On the night of 20 May another report came in. The Naval Attaché Stockholm signalled the Admiralty that he had obtained 'possibly true' information 'from a usually reliable source' – it was in fact the Norwegian Military Attaché in Stockholm, who had heard from his Swedish connections that the ships had been sighted by an aircraft of the Swedish cruiser *Gotland* – to the effect that two large German warships had passed through the Kattegat that afternoon on a north-westerly course.[50] On this occasion, moreover, the OIC had additional grounds for being on the alert.

During the previous week German reconnaissance aircraft had paid more than usual attention to Scapa Flow.[51] Still more important, the GAF Enigma had revealed that FW 200 aircraft of the GAF had been

---

48. Roskill, op cit, Vol I, pp 37, 57, 257, 260–261, 368, 483; AIR 41/39, *The Bombing Offensive*, Vol I, pp 172–173.
49. Roskill, op cit, Vol I, p 393.
50. Morgan, op cit, p 74; Beesly, op cit, pp 75–76.
51. Roskill, op cit, Vol I, p 395.

carrying out unusual reconnaissance of the ice conditions between Jan Mayen and Greenland. On the morning of 18 May the OIC had informed the C-in-C Home Fleet that they had done so again, north-west of Iceland, during the night of 17–18 May.[52] Later the same day, a report from Flag Officer Commanding Iceland of 14 May on the ice conditions there having ruled out the conjecture that the Germans were preparing to attack Jan Mayen island, the C-in-C had taken his first steps to counter the other possibility – that German ships were planning to break through to the Atlantic – by ordering special preparations and heightened vigilance on the part of the Denmark Strait patrol. His preparations included instructions to HMS *Suffolk* to pay particular attention to the ice-edge. It was in these circumstances that, on receipt of NA Stockholm's report, the Admiralty asked for air reconnaissance of the Norwegian coast. Two Spitfires of No 1 PRU, stationed at Wick, were sent to reconnoitre. One of them found and photographed a battleship and an 8″ cruiser at 1300 on 21 May. Interpretation of the photographs showed the ships to be the *Bismarck* and the *Prinz Eugen*, who were then off Bergen.[53] They had arrived there less than two hours earlier at 1115.

Thus far the naval Enigma had played no part in raising the alarm. The traffic for April and May was being read, but none of it was being read without a delay of several days and it had as yet contained no information about current or future operations. But during the morning of 21 May, just before the German ships were sighted at Bergen, messages for some April days came to hand which put it beyond doubt that the *Bismarck* intended to raid the trade routes. They showed that she was carrying out exercises with the *Prinz Eugen* and had embarked prize crews and appropriate charts. At 1828 on 21 May the OIC issued this information to all the naval commands, adding this comment: 'One *Bismarck* and one *Prinz Eugen* class reported by reconnaissance at Bergen on 21 May. It is evident that these ships intend to carry out a raid on trade routes'.[54] The C-in-C Home Fleet made further dispositions on the strength of this signal and on the assumption that the *Bismarck* might proceed from Bergen immediately after fuelling. He was also influenced by an unreliable report that a U-boat was north of Iceland and by a GAF attack on the Fleet W/T station in the Faroes.[55]

During the next twenty-four hours no intelligence source threw any light on the remaining uncertainties: when would the enemy ships leave the Norwegian coast; what route would they take? Now, as throughout the *Bismarck's* cruise, the naval Enigma was of no

---

52. ADM 223/78, Admty signal 0955/18 May 1941.
53. AIR 41/7, p 93.
54. ADM 223/78, Admty signal 1828/21 May 1941.
55. C-in-C Home Feet's Despatch, Supplement of 17 October 1947 to London Gazette of 14 October 1947.

assistance, the delay in reading it being still between three and seven days. Air reconnaissance, the source which in the end made the next contribution, was for some time unable to do so. From first light on 22 May aircraft of Coastal Command tried to establish whether the ships had left the Bergen area. They failed on account of fog and low cloud. It was not until 2200 on 22 May that a torpedo-trainer aircraft of RN Air Station, Hatston, despatched on the initiative of the Commanding Officer and flown by the station's executive officer, penetrated the fog belt by flying almost at surface level and established that Bergen and its approaches were clear of warships. The *Bismarck* and the *Prinz Eugen* had in fact left at 1945 on 21 May, six hours after the PRU had sighted them there and about an hour after the Home Fleet had received the naval Enigma evidence about their intentions.

The next development was a further sighting. On the evening of 23 May the C-in-C's dispositions bore fruit when HMS *Suffolk* made contact with the *Bismarck* in the Denmark Strait. Together with HMS *Norfolk* she kept contact throughout the following night. At that time there was no intelligence to add to the vital evidence provided by visual contact and radar observations. This remained the case during the engagements which followed on 24 May, when the *Bismarck* sank the *Hood* and damaged the *Prince of Wales* and was herself damaged by the *Prince of Wales* and hit by torpedo by an aircraft from the *Victorious*, and for so long as she was then shadowed by HMS *Suffolk*. In the early hours of 25 May, moreover, the *Suffolk* lost touch and there followed a crucial period during which, uncertain whether and how far the *Bismarck* had been damaged and what her movements and intentions might be, the British authorities depended entirely on such information as they could derive from studying her unreadable signals.

She had made 22 signals to Germany while British ships had been in contact with her, some announcing her change of plans. These signals were not readable at GC and CS until 28 May, after she had been sunk. But the positions indicated by DF bearings on them had been compared in the OIC with her positions as reported by the British ships, and the errors of the DF readings had been tabulated and analysed. In addition, the British intercept stations had submitted the signals to analysis by RFP, which filmed the type and the peculiarities of a transmitter, and by TINA, the process which studied the morse characteristics of individual wireless operators. These precautions proved valuable when the *Bismarck*, slow to grasp that she had shaken off her shadowers and possibly misled by false intelligence, which included a reconnaissance report to the effect that part of the Home Fleet was still in Scapa Flow,[56] transmitted three further signals during the forenoon of 25 May. It was the DF bearings and the RFP

---

56. For the intelligence sent to the *Bismarck*, see McLachlan, op cit, pp 143–162.

and TINA characteristics of these signals that in the end enabled the British authorities to decide correctly which option of the three available to her the *Bismarck* had adopted.* But it was only after considerable delay that this decision was reached.

When she threw off HMS *Suffolk* it was obvious to the British authorities what the *Bismarck's* choices were. She might go on with her operation, or double back to Norway north or south of Iceland, or make for Brest. For several hours during 25 May the C-in-C Home Fleet remained uncertain which course she had taken. Indeed, while the Admiralty at 1023 ordered Force H to move up from Gibraltar on the assumption that the *Bismarck* was making for Brest, and instructed other ships to act on that assumption, he himself adopted a course that took him towards the Iceland-Faroes gap. One reason for this was that the DF bearings of the first signal made by the *Bismarck* after she had shaken off the *Suffolk* – she made it at 0854 – were wrongly plotted in the flagship when they were received from the OIC: at this time – apparently because the C-in-C Home Fleet had requested this[58] – the Admiralty supplied the Fleet with the bearings of enemy transmissions, not with the positions worked out from the bearings by the OIC, and while the OIC placed the signal at 55° 30' N and 30° to 32° W, the flagship placed it at 57° N and 30° W. Another reason was that the Admiralty, though noting the discrepancy between its own fix and the more northerly and westerly position broadcast to the Fleet by the C-in-C at 1047, did not draw his attention to it. It was deterred from doing so by uncertainty about the accuracy of its own fix and by the possibility that one of the flagship's destroyers had been able to take a closer and hence more accurate bearing. Nor did the confusion end there. It was prolonged not only by the C-in-C's extreme reluctance to break wireless silence – and help the *Bismarck* – by asking questions of the Admiralty, but also by further hesitation on the part of the Admiralty.

The Admiralty learned of the discrepancy at 1116, when it received the C-in-C's signal of 1047. By then it had obtained on a second and third transmission, made at 0948 and 1054 on the frequency being used by the *Bismarck*, fixes indicating positions (55° 15' N 30° to 31° W and 55° N 31°W) slightly south and east of that of 0854. On the strength of these it repeated at 1100 its earlier instructions to Force H. At 1158 it also ordered HMS *Rodney* to act on the assumption that the enemy was proceeding to a Bay of Biscay port. At 1244 Flag Officer Submarines disposed his force on the same assumption. But at 1428

---

* It is recorded that before the *Bismarck* sailed the OIC had received an SIS report to the effect that arrangements were being made at Brest for the reception of a battleship.[57] This item of intelligence could hardly have influenced the Admiralty's assessment of what the *Bismarck* might do after she had shaken off the Home Fleet, and the remainder of this account makes it clear that it did not do so.

57. Beesly, op cit, pp 74–75, 93.
58. L Kennedy, *Pursuit*, (1974), p 130.

the Admiralty ordered the *Rodney* to act on the assumption that the enemy was proceeding to Norway via the passage between Iceland and Scotland. It is no longer possible to reconstruct the reason for this change of mind, or to say whether it was related to the fact that at 1419 the Admiralty had signalled to the C-in-C that it had intercepted at 1320 a signal, from a position estimated on good DF bearings to be within 50 miles of 55° 15′ N 32° W, from an enemy vessel using a submarine frequency but with a strength of signal indicating that the transmission was from a surface ship. But it is clear that this conjecture originated from the Admiralty and it may be said that GC and CS's Naval Section would have been sceptical of it had it been consulted, even though it would have been unable to rule out the possibility that the *Bismarck* was resorting in an emergency to a highly unusual device. As it happened, the Naval Section's close watch on the German naval W/T system yielded only one piece of evidence in the course of 24 May, and this was discovered at a time which cannot now be precisely established. It informed the OIC by telephone that, whereas the normal W/T control station for the *Bismarck's* frequency was Wilhelmshaven, the control had been transferred to Paris, a good sign that the *Bismarck* was moving south.[59] German naval records establish that the *Bismarck* was ordered to shift to the Paris control at mid-day on 24 May.[60]

It was not until 1507 that the Admiralty followed up its signal of 1419 with a report to the C-in-C to the effect that RFP indicated that the 1320 transmission was not from the vessel which had transmitted at 0948 and 1054, and was probably a U-boat, and not until 1805 did it cancel its latest instructions to the *Rodney* and order her again to assume that the *Bismarck* was making for a French port. In the flagship, meanwhile, the C-in-C appears to have decided by 1548, after previously steering a middle course which would enable him to turn either north to the Faroes or south to Biscay, that Biscay was the most probable destination – he had, of course, received the bearings on the 0948 and 1054 signals, and the instructions to Force H and the *Rodney* had been repeated to him – but to have wavered again on receipt of the Admiralty's signal of 1428 to HMS *Rodney*. At 1621 he asked the Admiralty, with reference to this signal, whether it considered that the enemy was making for the Faroes. At 1810, before receiving a reply and before getting the Admiralty's 1805 instructions to the *Rodney*, he decided independently that the *Bismarck* was making for Brest and at last made the change of direction that put him on the right course.[61]

---

59. Morgan, op cit, p 139 contains the evidence passed to OIC but no record remains of the time at which it was passed.

60. Naval Historical Branch letter to Cabinet Office Historical Section, NHBL 2473A of 28 January 1977.

61. For a full analysis of the signals exchanged between the Admiralty and the Fleet during 25 May, see ADM 233/88, Colpoys, *Admiralty Use of Special Intelligence in Naval Operations*, pp 53–73.

Within minutes the correctness of the 1805 and 1810 decisions was confirmed for the OIC. In answer to an enquiry from the Chief of Staff of the GAF who was in Athens in connection with the invasion of Crete, the GAF authorities had used the GAF Enigma to inform him that the *Bismarck* was making for the west coast of France.[62] At 1812 the Admiralty advised the Home Fleet accordingly, in a signal which the Fleet received within an hour. But even without this confirmation the air searches for the ship would probably have located her. During daylight on 25 May they had been hampered by uncertainty as to her intentions. On 26 May, when they would in any case have been flown on the assumption that she was making for Brest, she was sighted (at 1030) by a Catalina which had been briefed in the light of the GAF Enigma signal and by aircraft from Force H at 1115 about 130 miles south of the Home Fleet. Nor was intelligence of any further assistance in the operations which ended with her destruction at 1027 on 27 May. Her fate depended on whether her speed could be so reduced as to enable British battleships to catch up with her, and it was sealed when aircraft from the *Ark Royal* secured two hits and jammed her rudder on the evening of 26 May. Of the *Prinz Eugen's* movements no information was obtained, and she evaded detection until she was located at Brest by a PR aircraft on 4 June.[63]

Against the network of tankers and supply ships which the German Navy had prepared for the cruise of the *Bismarck* and *Prinz Eugen*, and also for the growing number of U-boats in the north Atlantic, intelligence was, in contrast, plentiful. The naval Enigma for May was not being read soon enough to assist during the chase for the *Bismarck* and the *Prinz Eugen*, but it was building up a comprehensive picture of the movements of these support ships, and from the first day of June it was available currently. By 25 May the OIC knew that 8 ships were in the Atlantic and of 4 of these it knew the precise patrol areas. By 21 June all but one of the 8 were disposed of – 6 of them as a direct result of using the Enigma information.[64]

Between 21 June and 11 July a further 7 supply or weather ships were sunk or captured, including the *Lauenburg*. Except in the case of the *Lauenburg*,* however, their interception owed nothing to the Enigma. Even when this divulged their whereabouts, which was not always so, the Admiralty decided not to make use of it. If the interception of these ships was thus fortuitous, it was also embarrassing. The Admiralty's decision had resulted from growing concern lest the sinking of so many ships in so short a time, on top of the loss of the *Bismarck*, might alert the Germans, not to speak of British forces, to the fact that the naval Enigma had been compromised. So far as

---

* See above, p 337.

62. CX/JQ 993 of 26 May; ADM 223/78, Ultra signal 1812/25 May 1941.
63. AIR 41/7, p 93.
64. ADM 223/88, pp 74–83.

British personnel were concerned – and also to guard against the possibility that the Germans might be reading British naval communications – great care had been taken from an early date to specify that Admiralty orders were based on DF fixes and to word Admiralty appreciations in guarded language except when they were issued to ships that were carrying the Flag Officers' Cypher. In January 1940 selected Flag Officers had been advised that they might receive in that cypher, in messages prefixed 'Hydro', intelligence from a particularly sensitive and absolutely reliable source, and this system for distributing to them the results of high-grade cryptanalysis, inaugurated in January 1940, was still in force during the chase of the *Bismarck.** But even this system had to be used with circumspection and it was not until the middle of June 1941, the first month in which the naval Enigma was read currently, that the Admiralty was able to replace it with one using the prefix 'Ultra' and messages based on a special one-time pad cypher, which gave total protection, and to introduce stringent new security regulations governing the handling of 'Ultra' material. Against German suspicions, moreover, even these measures might be of no avail if British successes continued at their recent rate.

In the event, as we shall see, Germany's suspicions were, for a variety of reasons,† deflected away from concern for the naval Enigma. Ironically, the reasons included the conviction that the Enigma was impregnable. No less ironically, this conviction was sustained by Germany's own intelligence sources. On 21 May, for example, the day after the British Naval Attaché in Stockholm had reported the *Bismarck's* movement out of the Baltic, the head of the German Abwehr had informed the Naval High Command (OKM) that he had positive proof that the Admiralty had received such a report.[65] Had OKM been more attentive, the opportunity to sink the *Bismarck* would not have arisen but, the more so since it knew that the *Bismarck* had been sighted at Bergen, it could account for her loss without resort to fears for the Enigma. Had the Admiralty known of these German tendencies it might have been somewhat relieved, but it would still have had to take every possible precaution to conceal a precious asset in the struggle against the U-boats – the fact that the Enigma was at last being read currently.

---

* See Chapter 4, p 141.
† See Volume Two.

65. ADM 233/86, Excerpt from BNA Stockholm War Diary, p 24; McLachlan, op cit, pp 398–399.

CHAPTER 11

The Balkans and the Middle East from November 1940 to the German invasion of Greece

IN NOVEMBER 1940, when the Germans began preparations for the invasion of Greece with the immediate object of attacking British targets in the eastern Mediterranean and of preventing British attacks on the Romanian oilfields, the British assumed that they were bent on something more ambitious – a thrust through Turkey into the Middle East.* By the middle of December, when he ordered the preparations to continue, Hitler did indeed give more emphasis to his underlying purpose, the securing of the southern flank of the projected invasion of Russia, but Whitehall's earlier strategic assessment remained largely unchanged. Despite the feeling that Germany would not undertake a land offensive into the Middle East while her first priority remained an invasion across the Channel, and despite the fact that this feeling had been strengthened since Italy's reverses in Greece and north Africa, the British authorities continued to believe that Germany was planning to advance to Iraq and Suez via Turkey and Syria partly to seize the British oil and partly to divert British resources from the defence of the United Kingdom.† They lacked any reliable information about Germany's wider strategic intentions. And, as we have already seen, they would go on lacking reliable evidence on this subject throughout the early months of 1941.

About the timing and the scale of German preparations in the Balkans intelligence remained almost equally defective until the beginning of 1941. The inherent difficulty of getting good information at the early, planning, stage of any military operation was one reason for this, and there was the further difficulty that the German preparations for the attack on Greece (Operation *Marita*) via Bulgaria did not run smoothly. On 4 November the German Army High Command (OKH) was thinking of an offensive involving 3 or 4 divisions and estimated that the build-up would take 10 weeks. On 12 November Hitler set the scale of the attack at 10 divisions; in the same directive he ordered that the GAF should complete as soon as possible the aircraft warning system that it was installing on Bulgaria's southern frontier as a precaution against RAF flights to the Romanian oilfields from Greek bases. But Bulgaria's obstructiveness and her

---

* See Chapter 8, p 253 et seq.   † See Chapter 8, pp 259–260.

insistence on concealment delayed the installation of this system till the end of the year. By then Hitler had introduced further complications. Although it was not until March 1941, after the arrival of British troops in Greece, that he finally decided to occupy all the Greek mainland, as opposed to the northern Aegean littoral, he foresaw on 11 December that this might become necessary and decided that the force must be increased to 17 divisions. As for the timetable, OKH on 5 December had hoped that its troops would enter Bulgaria from 25 January and attack Greece on 1 March, but Hitler now settled that the first troops were to enter Hungary on 26 December; the build-up in Romania was to follow during January 1941, Bulgaria was to be entered on 7 February and Greece was to be invaded on 22 March. But the advance reconnaissance parties which had entered Bulgaria in civilian clothes before the end of 1940 encountered great physical problems and further Bulgarian recalcitrance while preparing for the crossing of the country, and it was not until 2 March that German troops entered Bulgaria.

In these circumstances it would in any case have been difficult for the British intelligence agencies to make an accurate assessment of the timing and scale of the German preparations. But they were also hampered by another consideration. Before the first German move into the Balkans – the despatch of the missions to Romania on 7 October 1940* – Whitehall had received various indications that it was imminent. Apart from the warning from A-54,† the diplomatic missions and the SIS in the Balkans had reported the arrival of German motorised AA units at Ploesti, the presence of German personnel and material at other places in Romania and a German offer to send four fighter squadrons to Romania, as well as some evidence that German divisions were expected in the south-east.[1] But it had, as always, been difficult to distinguish between these reports and many others that were less accurate, and the receipt of them had not prevented the Chiefs of Staff from complaining that they had been given inadequate warning.‡ After this move there was a great increase in the number of diplomatic and SIS warnings that Germany planned to enter Bulgaria, as well as in the information from these sources about the identification and deployment of the German forces in Romania;[2] and, needless to say, these warnings, of which there had been a steady stream since the previous summer,§ now received far more attention.

In the warnings a few items were remarkably accurate anticipations of German plans, but they were accompanied by many exaggerated and conflicting rumours. How much this was so may be judged from

---

* See Chapter 8, pp 249–250.   ‡ See Chapter 9, p 296.
† See Chapter 8, p 252.   § See Chapter 8, p 252 et seq.

1. CAB 80/19, COS (40) 783 (COS Résumé, No 56); CAB 80/20, COS (40) 801 (COS Résumé, No 57).
2. CAB 80/21, COS (40) 890 (COS Résumé, No 61).

the reports – some from the British diplomatic missions, others from GC and CS's decrypts of Axis diplomatic traffic, or from the SIS – made to the War Cabinet. On 29 October there was an unconfirmed Bulgarian report that 7 German divisions were moving down the Danube. On 13 November it was a report that rail preparations were being made for a German move into Bulgaria; on 20 November a rumour that GAF personnel had arrived in Bulgaria. On 22 November the Foreign Secretary reported, correctly, that Bulgaria was under pressure to join the Tripartite Alliance but, because great uncertainty existed on the matter, he did not suggest that Bulgaria was proving recalcitrant.[3] On the same day there was a telegram from the British embassy in Moscow suggesting that a German attack on Greece, probably through Bulgaria, was imminent; this information the Prime Minister forwarded to the C-in-C Middle East.[4] By 25 November, on the other hand, the Foreign Secretary had 'some grounds' for thinking that Germany did not wish to spread the war to the Balkans; and on 26 November he told the Cabinet of diplomatic reports from Hungary and Bulgaria to the effect that she was not contemplating any new initiative at present.[5]

The Service intelligence departments had by then come to a somewhat different conclusion. On 17 October they reported in the Chiefs of Staff résumé that German officers were infiltrating Bulgaria under the pretext of making a press and propaganda tour and that, as part of the preparation for the reception of GAF aircraft to form a forward defence line, aircraft warning posts were being installed at unspecified Bulgarian locations.[6] On 6 November they had heard that the number of divisions in Romania would be increased to 18 – a force far in excess of what was needed for training the Romanians and defending the oilfields – and re-affirmed their earlier view that Germany was preparing to thrust into Bulgaria and Thrace.[7] On 25 November the DMI surveyed for the CIGS 17 reports from diplomatic sources, the attachés and the SIS to the effect that German military personnel were already widely spread in Bulgaria and that the arrival of major forces (with Bulgaria's consent) was imminent.[8] On the basis of these reports and of its estimate of the number of German divisions in Romania, which it set at 5, MI had already informed the Chiefs of Staff on 21 November that German preparations to enter Bulgaria were now complete.[9] At the time of DMI's survey, though stressing

---

3. CAB 65/9, WM (40) 279 of 29 October; CAB 65/10, WM (40) 288 of 13 November, WM (40) 292 of 20 November and 294 of 22 November.

4. CAB 105/1, Hist (B) 1, No 24 of 22 November 1940.

5. CAB 65/16, WM (40) 295 CA of 25 November; CAB 65/10, WM (40) 296 of 26 November.

6. CAB 80/20, COS (40) 840 (COS Résumé, No 59).

7. WO 190/892, No 23B of 6 November 1940.

8. ibid, No 33 of 25 November 1940.

9. CAB 80/23, COS (40) 966 (COS Résumé, No 64).

that the completion of the preparations did not necessarily mean that Germany would move in the immediate future, MI repeated the view that 'the German General Staff had made all arrangements to carry out such movements at maximum speed' and calculated that it could have four divisions on the Greek-Bulgarian frontier within seven days.[10]

This appreciation was quoted at the Cabinet on 25 November.[11] On 26 November the Prime Minister, faced with these differing assessments, made his choice between the competing policies of the Foreign Office and the Chiefs of Staff. In favour of the attempt to bring Turkey into the war on the British side, which was preferred by the Chiefs of Staff, and against the line advocated by the Foreign Office, which would have limited the British initiative to persuading Turkey and Yugoslavia to consult together at the first sign of a German move against Bulgaria, he concluded that it was best to assume that the German entry into Bulgaria was imminent.[12] In doing so he was no doubt swayed by the circumstantial character of two of the reports which had impressed MI. Both from the Military Attaché, Sofia, one had announced that the head of a German reconnaissance party in Bulgaria had arrived in Sofia on 11 November and the other that bridges were being strengthened south of Simitli on the road to Salonika. But, like MI, the Prime Minister was probably influenced still more by the fact that on 1 November the German intention to install an aircraft warning system in Romania and Bulgaria had been confirmed by the GAF Enigma.[13]

The inclusion in the Enigma traffic of intelligence about the Balkans, a consequence of the arrival of a GAF mission in Romania, had begun on 23 October. Until the end of the year, before the German forces had begun to move to their forward areas and become dependent on W/T for their communications, the Balkan traffic was slight in bulk and, apart from the occasional message like the confirmation received on 1 November, its contents dealt only with routine matters like weather-reporting. In calmer circumstances, instead of leading it to over-value the non-Sigint warnings, this fact might have persuaded MI to discount them and to avoid the vastly exaggerated assessment of the state of German preparations which it made on 25 November. And it almost did. In the note he prepared for the Prime Minister the DMI stressed that the Enigma reference was the only 'known' evidence of German interest in Bulgaria. In the event, Whitehall had neither enough confidence nor, yet, enough experience with German W/T practice to enable it to realise that at least in such a case as this, involving a large build-up over long

---

10. WO 190/892, No 33 of 25 November.
11. CAB 65/16, WM (40) 295 CA of 25 November.
12. Butler, op cit, Vol II, p 374.
13. CX/JQ 417.

distances in under-developed country, where W/T was indispensable, it could reasonably put its trust in the lack of Enigma evidence.

□

December 1940 was a month of anti-climax after the November alarm, and it is possible that this was due to the fact that on 27 November the GAF Mission in Romania revealed in the Enigma that it was making its preparations 'in good time and for some distance ahead'.[14] Reports were still coming in from the diplomatic missions, Axis diplomatic decrypts and the SIS. Some of them, giving the locations of German AA units in Romania and indicating the consolidation of the German military position there, were confirmed by Enigma messages. But few of them now found their way into the Chiefs of Staff résumés. By 9 December MI had come to share the Foreign Office's view that Germany did not wish to spread the war into the Balkans at present.[15] On 16 December the Prime Minister believed that Germany was more likely to strike in Spain.*[16] On 24 December MI, with *Sealion* still very much in mind, repeated the view that Germany would wish to avoid fighting on two fronts,[17] and on 28 December it quoted approvingly an AI appreciation which found GAF dispositions in Romania to be consistent with defence of the oilfields rather than with plans for a Balkan offensive during the winter.[18] By that time, however, a sudden growth in the amount and the interest of the Enigma traffic had provided unmistakable evidence that the German preparations were entering a new stage; and its first effect was to revive the fear that a German advance against Greece was imminent.

On 21 December Enigma, which had so far given little information about the German Army in Romania, gave the first pointer towards its area of concentration.[19] On 24 December the decrypts gave the first reliable indication of the scale of the Army's involvement by mentioning the locations to be taken up by eight of 12 Army's Army Co-operation Staffeln; these, predominantly in southern Romania, were a powerful indication that Germany's advance was to be southwards against or through Bulgaria. Moreover, as a result of the increasing depth of GC and CS's intelligence records, three of the Staffeln were known to be specially trained for work with Panzer formations and two of them had operated with Panzergruppe Kleist in the Ardennes breakthrough in the campaign in France. On 26

---

* See Chapter 8, p 257.

14. CX/JQ 487.
15. WO 190/892, No 35 of 9 December 1940.
16. CAB 65/16, WM (40) 306 CA of 16 December.
17. WO 190/892, MI14 letter to FOES, 24 December.
18. WO 190/892, No 46A, DMI Minute to CIGS, 28 December.
19. CX/JQ 549.

December the GAF mission was instructed to 'push on with all energy' with the task of accommodating these Staffeln despite the bad weather. On the following day an Enigma decrypt carried the first mention of an operation *Marita*. In the last few days of the month it provided the first incontrovertible evidence of the entry of advanced German elements into Bulgaria by revealing that the GAF listening posts' parties referred to as long ago as 1 November were now arriving.[20] On 28 December, as we have already noted, AI dismissed the probability of a winter attack. But by that date it had already calculated that the GAF in Romania was to be built up to about 500 aircraft, had judged that figure to be consistent with the number of Romanian airfields inspected by the GAF mission – of which it had by now received precise details mainly from the Enigma – and knew that the force was to come under Fliegerkorps VIII, hitherto active over the Channel and associated with *Sealion*. And on 29 December the Enigma revealed that Fliegerkorps VIII had been subordinated to Luftflotte 4 and allocated a Romanian base.[21] Nor was the Enigma alone in suggesting that a dramatic change was taking place in the Balkans. It was confirming – at any rate it was supporting – information to the same effect from the other sources. In the last few days of 1940 the diplomatic missions and decrypts made it clear that German rail movements through Hungary were being increased. The British Minister in Budapest mentioned 1,800 trains – sufficient for 20 divisions – and an SIS report 'from a source which has proved reliable in the past' stated that the 12 Army Commander had moved south from Cracow to assume command of the troops in Romania, and that an attack on Greece through Bulgaria and Yugoslavia was planned for the beginning of March.[22]

At the insistence of the new DMI, MI drew attention to these developments in appreciations circulated to the CIGS and to many Whitehall departments on 30 and 31 December. As on other occasions in the first half of January 1941, its own inclination was still to think that, although Germany was intervening to redress the Italian setbacks, the object of her new moves was only to intimidate Greece, Yugoslavia and Bulgaria before advancing through Turkey to the Middle East.[23] On 5 January 1941, however, it judged that, if she found it necessary to attack these countries, she would make thorough preparations and defer the offensive until March. But it weakened this sound assessment by adding that Germany might consider herself forced to act before March. In this case she would do so before her preparations were complete and before the snows melted in February.[24] And no sooner had MI made this concession than the

20. CX/JQ 553, 554, 564, 566.
21. AIR 40/2322, Minute of 6 March 1941; CX/JQ 562.
22. WO 190/892, No 46 of 30 December 1940.
23. ibid, and No 51 of 31 December 1940; WO 190/893, No 1B of 5 January 1941.
24. WO 190/893, 5 January 1941.

sources began to mention dates. A-54 now announced that 'zero hour' for some unspecified move would be 15 January. On 7 January an Enigma decrypt seemed to confirm that his information was as accurate as it had been on previous occasions: the rear detachments for 'the intermediate landing grounds in Hungary and Romania' were instructed by Luftflotte 4 to arrive at their locations by 15 January and were told that 'they must be ready for the tasks assigned to them by 20 January'.[25] Earlier still, on 31 December, the German embassy in Bucharest had used the GAF Enigma to inform Berlin urgently that south-east Europe was humming with rumours of German troop movements and that the British legation in Bucharest was 'spreading the rumour' that a German attack on Greece would begin on 10 January.[26]

At its meetings on 7, 8 and 9 January the Defence Committee was not only confronted with this evidence. In a memorandum drawn up for the Chiefs of Staff on 6 January the Prime Minister had stressed another consideration. 'Nothing' he wrote, 'would suit our interest better than that any German advance in the Balkans should be delayed till the spring. For this very reason one must apprehend that it will begin earlier'.[27] Even while the committee was sitting, moreover, further intelligence was arriving. On 9 January the Enigma gave the news that yet more GAF personnel were moving into Bulgaria to establish telegraph and teleprinter links with Hungary and Romania and to lay down lines to the Bulgarian-Greek border along the main axis of advance towards Salonika. On the same day, the Chiefs of Staff résumé noted that Flak units were reported to be entering Bulgaria and that three GAF aircraft were carrying out photographic reconnaissance of the Bulgarian-Greek frontier.[28] The source of these two items is uncertain, but it is clear that, as well as the Enigma, the SIS and the diplomatic sources, particularly the Military Attaché, Sofia, were also supplying a stream of information. It included reports of troop movements across Hungary and of a sudden increase of GAF activity in Romania, including ground-air exercises and the building of advanced landing grounds, and several of the reports gave precise locations for the divisions and the GAF units that were arriving.[29] In all the circumstances it is perhaps not surprising that the Defence committee concluded that Germany intended to attack Greece on 20 January.[30]

On 10 January, the committee having also decided that it was of first political importance to provide Greece with the fullest possible support, the Cabinet instructed the C-in-C and the AOC-in-C Middle

---

25. CX/JQ 580.   26. CX/JQ 565.

27. Churchill, op cit, Vol III, p 8.

28. CAB 80/25, COS (41) 25 (COS Résumé, No 71).

29. CAB 80/25, COS (41) 42 (COS Résumé, No 72).

30. CAB 69/1, DO (41) 1st and 2nd Meetings, 8 and 9 January; Butler, op cit, Vol II, pp 395–396.

East to fly to Athens and offer immediate reinforcements. The C-in-C, his forces then in hot pursuit of the Italians in north Africa, questioned the instruction: 'it fills me with dismay'. He also challenged the intelligence assessment on which it was based. 'Our appreciation here', he telegraphed to London, 'is that the German concentration is a move in the war of nerves designed with the object of helping Italy by upsetting Greek nerves, inducing us to stop our advance in Libya and disperse our forces in the Middle East... We trust the COS will reconsider whether the enemy's move is not bluff'.[31] To this the Prime Minister replied on 11 January: 'Our information contradicts the idea that the German concentration is merely a move in the war of nerves or bluff... We have a mass of detail showing continual passage of troops to Romania, selection and occupation of airfields in Romania, movements of signals and other advanced agents into Bulgaria, and that a large-scale movement may begin on or soon after 20th instant'.[32]

Between 11 and 20 January the difference of view between the Middle East and Whitehall was somewhat narrowed. GS Int GHQ, ME had believed for some time that Germany's chief interest in the Balkans was the protection of the Romanian oil and that she would be deterred from occupying Bulgaria by the knowledge that this move would expose Ploesti to bombing.[33] It was still expressing the same opinion on 28 January,[34] and had no doubt come to hold it still more strongly since there had recently been several reports from the British mission and other sources in Athens that neither the Greeks nor the Turks thought a German advance likely.[35] GS Int was receiving from London, it must be stressed, very little of the detailed intelligence which showed Whitehall that Cairo's appreciation was wrong, and it had not yet been briefed about the existence or the extent of the Enigma. In Whitehall, on the other hand, the authorities were beginning to recognise by 15 January that they had once again been too hasty in warning that a German advance was imminent. By then they had, for example, received from an Italian diplomatic decrypt a statement by the German Chargé d'Affaires in Sofia to his Axis colleague that only small numbers of Germans were in Bulgaria as a sort of 'observer corps' with AA to co-operate with German batteries in Romania in the protection of the oil zone. And in an appreciation of 15 January MI, while again emphasising that Germany would act earlier if forced to do so, and while suggesting that she might feel forced to do so if Salonika was threatened (presumably by British or Turkish action), concluded that, otherwise, the German preparations were unlikely to be completed before the end of February.

31. CAB 105/1, No 42 of 10 January 1941.
32. ibid, No 44, 11 January 1941.
33. WO 169/19, DDMI ME Appreciation, 16 November 1940.
34. WO 201/1574, DDMI ME Appreciation, 28 January 1941.
35. CAB 105/1, No 43 of 10 January 1941.

In the appreciation of 15 January, and in another on 17 January, MI confessed to uncertainty about the direction the German advance would take: evidence from all sources about army dispositions pointed to an attack through Bulgaria to the south-east, but AI's knowledge of the location of the advanced landing grounds that were being prepared in Romania still pointed to plans for breaching the southern Bulgarian frontier.[36] By 20 January a Chiefs of Staff paper had concluded that Germany would occupy Bulgaria gradually during the next 2 months and would avoid hostilities in the Balkans until she had consolidated the position in Bulgaria; and earlier action was ruled out by the weather as well as by the state of her preparations. As for the purpose of the attack when it came, the Chiefs of Staff felt that, apart from German help to Italy in the central and western Mediterranean, the main threat was a drive to the Middle East. On 20 January itself this paper was considered by the Defence Committee. The committee was uncertain whether the German intention was to divert British forces from the United Kingdom or to continue beyond Bulgaria to some other destination, and equally uncertain as to what that destination might be; it even mentioned the Ukraine.[37] Because of the latest intelligence appreciations, and because the Greek government had by now rejected the offer of British forces, it allowed the C-in-C ME to go ahead and take Benghazi, but it also decided to instruct him to build up a mobile reserve in Egypt for possible use in Greece or Turkey within the next 2 months.[38]

□

In adopting this more relaxed attitude while remaining convinced, despite a second anti-climax, that Germany was preparing large-scale Balkan operations, Whitehall was guided mainly by the GAF Enigma. In the middle of January other sources had reported that the German Air Attaché in Sofia was still investigating airfield facilities in Bulgaria,[39] but an Enigma decrypt of 20 January, showing that the GAF mission in Romania was still discussing long-term arrangements for the supply of GAF fuel to Bulgaria, was more conclusive.[40] On the other hand, the Enigma yielded on 10 January the first definite figures of the GAF personnel for operation *Marita*, and on 18 January it disclosed that GAF hutments for *Marita* were being sent to Bulgaria.[41] On 17 January GC and CS summed up the recent Enigma evidence:

---

36. WO 190/983, Nos 3A and 5A of 15 and 17 January 1941; CAB 80/25, COS (41) 42 (COS Résumé, No 72).
37. CAB 80/56, COS (41) 14 (o) of 18 January; CAB 69/2, DO (41) 6th Meeting, 20 January.
38. Butler, op cit, Vol II, pp 377–378.
39. AIR 40/2322, Minute of 6 March 1941; JIC (41) 46 of 29 January.
40. CX/JQ 605.
41. CX/JQ 587, 603.

the concentration of Fliegerkorps VIII in Romania would be completed by early February; thereafter the launching of *Marita* would depend on the build-up of supplies, the concentration of the Army and the state of the weather[42] A week later MI calculated that the Germans could begin major operations at the beginning of March at the earliest.[43] British estimates of the timing, as of the scale, of German intentions were at last on target. In the middle of January OKH, anxious about its plans for the attack on Russia (Operation *Barbarossa*), still hoped to keep its schedule of 5 December for *Marita*: a Danube crossing from 25 January and the attack on Greece about 1 March.

During the second half of January the Germans were forced to accept postponements almost daily. On 28 January Hitler decreed that the Army should not cross into Bulgaria before 10 February and that 1 April should be the date for the attack on Greece. Because of Bulgaria's anxieties, he set the date for the entry into Bulgaria as late as possible, and not before the completion of camouflaged bases for Fliegerkorps VIII and of AA protection for Bulgarian strategic points. On 19 February he accepted another postponement: the bridging of the Danube was now to start on 28 February and the crossing into Bulgaria on 2 March, 6 weeks later than the date OKH had been hoping for.

After the middle of January the GAF Enigma traffic became steadily more voluminous with the advance of the German preparations. As before, however, it contained no explicit references to Germany's planning at the highest level. It was from the other sources, diplomatic or the SIS, that MI learned by 24 January that staff talks had begun between the German and the Bulgarian military authorities, as indeed they had on 22 January.[44] Not surprisingly, the Enigma traffic was also less reliable as a guide to the movement of German divisions than it was to the activities of the GAF, and up to the middle of February MI's calculations on the army build-up were exaggerated. It estimated that 9 divisions had reached Romania by 23 January, 10 by 30 January, 15 by 6 February and 22 to 23 by 13 February, whereas only 7 had arrived by 15 February to join the two already attached to the Military Mission.[45] But about the penetration of Bulgaria by the GAF, and about the scale of the force the GAF planned to move to Bulgaria, the Enigma provided a great wealth of detail. On 28 January the JIC surveyed all the evidence at the request

42. AI/JQ 4.

43. WO 190/893, No 11A of 26 January 1941.

44. ibid, No 9A of 24 January; M van Creveld, *Hitler's Strategy: The Balkan Clue 1940–41* (1974), p 115.

45. CAB 80/25, COS (41) 54 (COS Résumé, No 73), COS (41) 66 (COS Résumé, No 74), COS (41) 78 (COS Résumé, No 75) and COS (41) 98 (COS Résumé, No 76); Creveld, op cit, p 119.

of the Foreign Office. It estimated that the Germans had already moved into Bulgaria 4,000 GAF personnel, which included 500 to 600 in uniform, 1,500 Flak personnel, units for Y duties, airfield servicing and construction, signals and the Air Attaché's staff. 400 of the 550 aircraft scheduled for transfer to Romania would be deployed in Bulgaria. In the same paper the JIC estimated that no army formations had yet entered the country and, by way of conclusion, it repeated MI's assessment of the middle of January: the state of communications would prevent an offensive beyond Bulgaria before the beginning of March.[46]

At that point there was still no unequivocal evidence that Germany intended to advance beyond Bulgaria and, though the Whitehall authorities expected her to do so, they still remained uncertain as to the directions in which she would move. The Cabinet feared for both Greece and Turkey but, if only because it was itself striving to construct a Balkan bloc, it allowed that Germany's object might be merely to induce all the Balkan countries to succumb to pressure without fighting. MI in its almost daily appreciations in the first half of February struck the same note. On 9 February it stressed that the pointers 'do not take us beyond the occupation of Bulgaria'. From that time on, however, new intelligence piled up about the German order of priorities. From 7 February GC and CS decrypted a new variant of the Enigma traffic, introduced by the Germans on 23 January. Before that date GC and CS had obtained some railway instructions for the Balkan movements from the GAF Enigma. GC and CS and MI had encountered immense difficulties both in unravelling the code names, serial numbers and many other esoteric references used in the messages, the first of which was received at the end of December, and in working out a method by which orders for a given rail movement could be linked with others detailing such things as the contents of train-loads, routes and entraining and detraining points.[47] About the end of January 1941, however, the Railway Research Service – a unit belonging to the railway companies which had been incorporated into MEW at the outbreak of war – was brought in to deal with these problems, and progress in solving them was rapid when this step was followed by the breaking of the Railway Enigma.[48] As early as 6 and 7 February a massive movement by rail of GAF ammunition, fuel and other stores to destinations in south-west Bulgaria, on the axis of advance through the Rupel pass to Salonika, was identified from the Enigma traffic.[49] At about this time, while it was the Railway Enigma which provided the depth of information that made it possible to

---

46. JIC (41) 46 of 28 January; see also AIR 40/2322, Minute of 6 March 1941.
47. CX/JQ 562, 577, 583, 584, 586, 605, 622, 627.
48. WO 190/893, Memo from Head of the Railway Research Service, 12 February 1941.
49. CX/JQ 652, 655, 691.

elucidate the pro-formas and the serial numbers, the SIS began to supply additional intelligence about the railway movements, notably those through Hungary. Its agents independently discovered the code names – those of operas, motor cars and so forth – which the Germans gave to the movements and which were also being revealed by the Enigma. It was they, indeed, who established that there was a series named after mountains, for only one reference to these occurred in the Enigma traffic.[50] And by the middle of February their information, much of which was reaching London via the SIS's contacts in occupied France, together with the growing bulk of the Railway Enigma and some reports from the diplomatic missions,* was leaving little doubt that Greece was to be Germany's next victim.[52]

Supporting evidence came also from another source. In December 1940, after previously reading a number of minor cyphers used by German secret agents, GC and CS had broken the hand cypher of the main Abwehr group.† It was almost certainly this traffic which furnished evidence dated 10 December 1940 and 31 January 1941 revealing a switch in German intelligence priorities from the west to the east and south-east and certain consequential administrative changes, among them the intention to set up in Greece a secret intelligence centre of a type used in occupied countries. This led MI to appreciate on 14 February (though the information was certainly available to it earlier) that a German occupation of at least part of Greece was an immediate prospect, that an invasion of Britain was not imminent and that the Germans 'were thinking ahead' to Turkey, Iraq, Syria, Egypt and Iran.[53]

Not unnaturally, perhaps, all this evidence of increasing German preparations also produced the feeling in some quarters in Whitehall that 'intervention [was]...more certain and imminent every day'.[54] On 11 February the Defence Committee hastily summoned the DMI to give them a verbal appreciation of the strength, direction and timing of the German attack on Greece.[55] He gave them a summary of the findings made by his staff during the previous week. 23 divisions had now been identified in Romania, out of a possible future build-up of

---

* On 8 February the Chiefs of Staff agreed to the withdrawal of the British legation in Bucharest. This move was at the suggestion of the British Minister who no longer felt able to obtain information without danger of compromising his sources.[51]

† See above, Chapter 3, p 120.

50. WO 190/893, 9 April 1941.
51. CAB 79/9, COS (41) 46th Meeting, 8 February; CAB 80/25, COS (41) 75 of 6 February.
52. WO 190/893, Analysis of the sources of railway movements intelligence, 9 April 1941.
53. ibid, No 17B of 14 February 1941.
54. Churchill, op cit, Vol III, p 58, Memo of 12 February.
55. Davidson Papers; CAB 69/2, DO (41) 8th Meeting, 11 February.

35. In line with these over-estimates – only 9 divisions had actually reached Romania by 15 February, and the Germans contemplated sending only 17 until the Yugoslav coup forced them to increase this figure by 12 – the DMI no longer suggested that Germany might be hoping to secure Greece's capitulation without an attack. On the other hand, he also avoided any suggestion that her offensive was imminent. The Military Attaché Sofia and the British Minister in Bucharest had recently reported that her troops would cross into Bulgaria on 17 February.[56] If they entered on this date, MI calculated, they could reach the Greek frontier with 5 divisions on 12 March, reach Salonika a week after entering Greece and reach Athens with 10 divisions between mid-April and mid-May. The period of three to four weeks allowed between the crossing of the Danube and the attack on Greece was based on information then coming in from MA Sofia about the state of Bulgarian communications and Germany's 'feverish attempts' to improve them by repairs to roads and bridges.[57] The time allowed for the Germans to reach Athens after first entering Greece took into account the degree of resistance expected from the Greeks.

At a meeting of the Defence Committee later on 11 February, also attended by the DMI, the Prime Minister argued that the German advance through Greece would be more delayed, by British forces as well as by Greek redeployments. In the end, however, the committee accepted the DMI's timings.[58] It judged, further, that they gave time for British troops to be moved to northern Greece before the Germans attacked. In this belief, it ordered the C-in-C ME to give preparations for resistance in Greece priority over continuing his advance as far as Tripoli and to make the preliminary arrangements for the despatch to Greece of an expeditionary force. This decision was taken three days after the first German troops sailed from Naples to Tripoli but 11 days before it was learned that they had arrived in north Africa.* At the same time, and not least because it remained ignorant of Greek military planning, the Defence Committee decided to send Mr Eden, the Foreign Secretary, and Field Marshall Dill, the CIGS, to Cairo and Athens.[59] Throughout this period British intelligence of Greek, Turkish and Yugoslav plans was conspicuously less good than that about Germany's preparations, and it is also clear that Whitehall's hopes of co-operation from these countries were based on wishful thinking. As has been said by the official historian, 'it is indeed surprising that in view of Germany's military record, her vastly superior armaments and her proximity we should have expected the

---

* See Chapter 12, p 388.

56. WO 190/893, No 17A of 11 February 1941.
57. CAB 80/25, COS (41) 98 (COS Résumé, No 76).
58. 'High Level Intelligence', in Davidson Papers.
59. CAB 69/2, DO (41) 8th Meeting, 11 February.

Balkan countries to join the war against her or, if they did, to withstand her. It would appear that in such matters the Norwegian campaign had taught us little'.[60]

Different judgments have been passed on these strategic decisions. About the contribution made to them by intelligence there is no room for dispute. Although some German deployments had been detected on the Turkish-Bulgarian frontier, and it was far from certain that Turkey would not be invaded next, by 11 February, if not earlier, the Enigma had established Greece as the first objective of the German preparations for a large-scale Balkan campaign. By its lack of any reference to the transit of stores or personnel or to other preparations for an attack on or through Yugoslavia,* the Enigma traffic had left no doubt that the attack on Greece would come only through Bulgaria, but the timing of the attack remained unknown. The British diplomatic missions and diplomatic decrypts had suggested 17 February for the entry of German troops into Bulgaria at a time when the Germans were working to a date about 10 February; and the period of three to four weeks for the crossing of Bulgaria, calculated by MI mainly on the basis of information supplied by MA Sofia, was little less than OKH had in mind. MI's estimate of the scale of the offensive in its first phase – 5 divisions rising to 10 – was also reasonably accurate; in the event 10 divisions did operate from Bulgaria against Greece, though only 5 reached southern Greece by mid-April. But this approximation was reached fortuitously. MI greatly exaggerated the number of divisions being collected in Romania and, on the other hand, the Yugoslav coup was still to upset Germany's plans.

□

After the preliminary decisions of 11 February intelligence produced no change in British plans. On two occasions, however, it came near to doing so.

On 14 February MI reported that there was still no evidence that German ground forces had entered Bulgaria, but that the latest indications were that they were to move both to the Turkish and the Greek frontiers, the bulk to the latter.[61] During the next 10 days the GAF and the Railway Enigma traffic provided periodic returns of the strengths and locations of GAF units in Romania, and evidence of Fliegerkorps VIII's progress with the establishment of radar stations in Romania and Bulgaria, of the presence of armoured units in Romania and of the fact that individuals and small groups from the German Army were carrying out reconnaissance of Bulgarian

---

* See below, p 368.

60. Butler, op cit, Vol II, p 459.
61. WO 190/893, No 18A of 14 February 1941.

communications.[62] Enigma had already disclosed that radar sets in short supply in Germany were to be sent to Romania and Bulgaria.[63] The Enigma traffic, as before, yielded no information about dates, but soon after 17 February, the date previously given by the other sources for the entry into Bulgaria, the same sources announced a further delay: General List's postponed arrival at his HQ 12 Army, now located near Sofia, was timed for 25 February.[64] By 24 February, however, presumably by the SIS and the diplomatic sources, von Rundstedt and von Kleist had also been associated with Romania; and on that day MI, unaware of *Barbarossa* and thus of the fact that Rundstedt was in Romania as Commander-designate of Army Group South, which assembled there for the attack on Russia, interpreted this last item of intelligence as proof that the expected German offensive would be on a formidable scale.[65] On the same day, in a rare attempt by the intelligence authorities to intrude in the policy and planning sphere, the DMI developed MI's comments into a warning to the VCIGS that 'we must be prepared to face the loss of all forces sent to Greece', and he accompanied the warning with suggestions as to how the government might help Greece without committing the bulk of British forces in the Middle East.[66] The Chiefs of Staff were disposed to take the same view: in a paper dated 24 February they came to the conclusion that without co-operation from Yugoslavia or Turkey British support to Greece was 'unlikely to have a favourable effect on the war as a whole'.[67] But the Cabinet adhered to its earlier intention, deciding, also on 24 February, to send a major force to Greece, and confirming the decision on 27 February.[68]

In Cairo the Cabinet's decision was unwelcome for a different – indeed, for the opposite – reason. GS Int GHQ, ME remained sceptical of the constant warnings from London that the German occupation of Bulgaria was imminent. At least until the CIGS arrived in Cairo at the beginning of the last week in February, it believed that there was no real threat from Germany to Greece: Germany lacked fuel for large-scale active warfare and the British example in the desert would now suggest to her that an advance on Suez through north Africa was preferable to a northabout campaign. All the talk of her having a plan to drive through Bulgaria and Turkey to the Middle East was probably based on rumours, which she was spreading.[69] GS

---

62. CX/JQ 674, 677, 678.

63. AIR 20/1629, ASI Report No 13 of 10 January 1941.

64. CAB 80/26, COS (41) 124 (COS Résumé, No 78).

65. WO 190/893, No 20A of 24 February 1941; CAB 80/26, COS (41) 124 (COS Résumé, No 78).

66. Davidson Papers.

67. CAB 80/57, COS (41) 43 (o) of 24 February.

68. CAB 65/21, WM (41) 20 CA and 21 CA, 24 and 27 February.

69. WO 169/924, GS Int GHQ ME, Daily Intelligence Summary of 15 January 1941; WO 201/1574, DDMI ME Appreciations, 17 and 22 February 1941.

Int's scepticism was widely shared in Cairo.* It was thus ironical, to say the least, that further operational assessments made in Cairo at the beginning of March played no small part in persuading the Cabinet on 7 March to persist in sending a force to Greece after a second warning from the intelligence authorities in Whitehall had all but led it to reverse, on 5 and 6 March, its earlier intention.[71]

The Cabinet's doubts had set in with the news, on 1 March, that Bulgaria had joined the Tripartite Pact and, on 2 March, that German troops had crossed the Danube. It was not so much that the news came as a surprise. MI, who had noted the accumulation of pontoon bridging on the north bank of the Danube opposite Bulgaria as early as 15 January,[72] reported on 1 March that all was ready for the crossing and on 2 March the JIC expected the Germans to enter Bulgaria that day. This development coincided, however, with Eden's and Dill's discovery that the Greek Commander-in-Chief had not withdrawn his troops from the Bulgarian frontier to the Aliakhmon Line, as London had expected him to do, and this discovery came on the heels of an earlier shock. On 22 February Eden and Dill had learned that Greece's reinforcement of Albania had left her with only 3 weak divisions on her border with Bulgaria. On 24 February this information had led MI to fear that Germany might launch an attack, with only 2 divisions and airborne troops, at an earlier date than it had allowed. In its paper on 2 March the JIC, prompted by MI, repeated this alarming suggestion: with 1 armoured and 3 motorised divisions Germany could reach the Greek frontier by 6 March, and a further infantry division could be there by 11 March.[73] On 5 March the JIC thought the attack on Greece was 'imminent'; it had just been reported that German troops were already in the Struma valley, near the Greek frontier and on the route they were expected to follow.[74] On the same day the Chiefs of Staff, in an aide-memoire to the Cabinet, were still more alarmist: 1 German armoured division and 3 motorised divisions would be on the Greek frontier that very day, and by 22 March 5 German divisions might be approaching the defence line held by the Greeks.[75]

By this time, while the Greeks had reversed their earlier attitude and had accepted British support, the Turks had refused a limited offer of aid, and it was clear that neither they nor the Yugoslavs would combine with Greece and Great Britain against Germany. In addition, the arrival of the GAF in the Dodecanese had forced the British to

---

* See, for example, the marginalia written by General Marshall-Cornwall, GOC Egypt, on the PRO copy of DDMI, ME's appreciation of 22 February 1941.[70]

70. WO 201/1574.
71. CAB 65/22, WM (41) 24 CA and 25 CA, 5 and 6 March.
72. WO 190/893 of 15 January 1941.
73. JIC (41) 87 of 2 March.
74. JIC (41) 90 of 5 March; CAB 80/26, COS (41) 145 (COS Résumé, No 79).
75. CAB 65/18, WM (41) 24 of 5 March, Appendix.

abandon plans for an amphibious operation to seize Rhodes and presented a threat to the movement of the expeditionary force from Alexandria to the Piraeus. On the other hand, the British force had not yet begun to arrive in Greece – its movement had started only on 4 March. The Cabinet had much to make it hesitate besides the calculation that the Germans might attack on 5 March, a week earlier than the date estimated by MI on 11 February and repeated by the Prime Minister in the course of the Cabinet discussion on 24 February.[76] Nevertheless this last-minute calculation cannot have lightened its burden, and it may be safely assumed that in making its final decision to go ahead with its plans it was correspondingly swayed by the knowledge that the CIGS in Athens and authorities in Cairo did not accept this calculation. On 6 March, GHQ ME did not think that the Germans could reach the Greek frontier until 11 or 12 March and it felt that London 'had underestimated the time which the Germans would need to reach the Aliakhmon Line in force'.[77] The Cabinet's verdict was also influenced by GHQ, ME's over-optimistic assessment of the time that must elapse before Rommel could launch a serious offensive in the Western Desert.*

□

Whitehall's last-minute fear that Germany would make an immediate limited attack on Greece, like Cairo's dismissal of it, was an operational assessment based on strategic and logistic calculations, unsupported by firm intelligence about the enemy's intentions. At the time they crossed into Bulgaria the Germans were allowing for a delay of 36 days before the opening of the attack on Greece. The troops reported in the Struma valley on 5 March were in fact advanced units only.[78] Apart from this item, there had been no positive intelligence from any source to justify a modification in either direction of the earlier British estimate that the attack would not begin before 12 March. By 12 March, however, intelligence was making it clear that even that estimate had been over-generous. On 8 March the GAF Enigma reported that the remaining units of Fliegerkorps VIII were moving to Bulgaria but had not yet reached their battle stations.[79] On 11 March MI, after seeing a decrypted report from the Italian Military Attaché, Sofia, that the German dispositions would not be complete before 20 March, estimated that 13 divisions which had reached Bulgaria were not at full strength.[80] By 13 March it believed, correctly, that 5 German

---

* See Chapter 12, p 389.

76. CAB 65/21, WM (41) 20 CA of 24 February.
77. CAB 105/2, Hist (B) 2 No 76; Cab 65/22, WM (41) 25 CA of 6 March.
78. Creveld, op cit, pp 130, 156.
79. AIR 40/2322, Minute of 6 March 1941.
80. WO 190/893, No 27A of 11 March 1941.

divisions had reached the Greek-Bulgarian border but, having got wind from diplomatic sources in Ankara of secret negotiations between Greece and Germany, it took the view that Germany would decide between further negotiation and the use of force by the end of the month.[81]

In the event Hitler, if he had ever seriously pursued the path of negotiating with the Greeks, abandoned it when it became clear that British forces were arriving in strength. On 17 March he decided to occupy the whole of Greece in order to eject them. Since preparations had hitherto been made only for the seizure of the northern littoral – an operation which had been expected to take only one week – this decision necessitated the commitment of a larger force and involved the risk of further delay. In order to reduce delay, with all its implications for operation *Barbarossa*, OKH brought forward to 1 April the date for the Greek assault, which as late as 22 March had been 7 April. Although it knew that the enemy was keeping a close watch on the arrival of the British force,* London received no information of these German changes of plan. But the changes brought the German D-day into line with the date chosen in the British estimate in the middle of March and that estimate was reinforced on 23 March by an Enigma message in which Fliegerkorps VIII announced the move of its HQ to a position 100 miles north of Salonika and declared itself 'ready for action there on the 25th'.[85] On 27 March the Chiefs of Staff résumé declared in its turn that Germany's preparations for the attack on Greece were completed.[86]

Whitehall remained far from certain that Greece would be the sole objective of the attack. At one level its uncertainty arose from MI's continued exaggeration of the size of the force which Germany had collected. Thanks to the Enigma, AI's estimate of the GAF strength in the Balkans remained very accurate. On 13 March it gave the number of aircraft in Bulgaria and Romania as 482; the actual number was 490.[87] On 27 March, when the actual figure was 355, it calculated that the GAF had 320 aircraft in Bulgaria with 40 more expected soon.[88]

---

* On 14 March GC and CS disclosed that the German Military Attaché, Athens had informed Berlin of its approximate size.[82] The MA had counted the troops as they disembarked.[83] The Enigma carried estimates of the arrivals based on GAF reconnaissance of the Greek ports – they put the number of troops at 50,000 to 60,000 when it was in fact 58,000 – and estimates of the RAF strength in Greece, based on German interception of RAF signals, which were equally accurate: they assumed a force of 70 aircraft and the actual figure was 80.[84]

81. CAB 80/26, COS (41) 162 (COS Résumé, No 80).
82. CAB 105/2, No 110 of 14 March.
83. Playfair, op cit, Vol II (1956), p 81.
84. CX/JQ 781, 788.
85. CX/JQ 788.
86. CAB 80/26, COS (41) 196 (COS Résumé, No 82).
87. ibid, COS (41) 162 (COS Résumé, No 80); AIR 41/10, p 123.
88. CAB 80/26, COS (41) 196 (COS Résumé, No 82); AIR 41/10, p 123.

MI's estimates of the German Army order of battle, on the other hand, though correct in believing that 5 German divisions had reached the Greek border by 13 March, had not improved. On 13 March MI calculated that there were 30 to 32 divisions in the Balkan area.[89] On 27 March it gave 35 as the number.[90] In fact the Germans deployed 17 divisions in the theatre until extra forces were brought in for the attack on Yugoslavia,[91] when the figure rose to 29. On the same date MI similarly over-estimated the number of divisions moving from Romania into Bulgaria. 12 Army then had 13 divisions there, with 3 more en route, but MI put the figure at 16 with 5 more moving in.[92]

Another handicap, still more serious than imperfect knowledge about the size of the German Army concentration, was the lack of positive intelligence about Germany's wider strategic intentions – a lack that was reflected in Whitehall's continuing ambivalence about *Sealion* and its continuing failure to discern that Germany was preparing to turn against Russia. As it saw more and more GAF units withdrawn from the Channel to the Balkans, Whitehall weakened in its assumption that Germany had adequate air forces both for *Sealion* and for a second major campaign. The Enigma had provided another major piece of evidence against this assumption at the beginning of February by revealing that an entire GAF administrative formation which had supported the *Sealion* preparations in the Antwerp area was moving to Romania.[93] But anxiety about the renewal of the invasion threat still persisted.* So did the reluctance to conclude that Germany would attack Russia. MI first reviewed reports of this possibility on 17 January. It did so again on 18 March, but it again concluded that it was unlikely. Nor did it qualify that view until after the campaign in Greece.† In these circumstances the decline in anxiety about *Sealion*, such as it was, was necessarily balanced by increasing anxiety about the Middle East.

By 7 February MI had reached the conclusion that Germany would not follow up the invasion of Greece with an advance through Anatolia until she had defeated the United Kingdom.[94] On 5 March, however, the JIC was still in two minds about the likelihood of this further offensive, though granting that Germany would not be ready to undertake it before the middle of May,[95] and during the rest of March the staffs in Whitehall and Cairo spent many hours calculating

---

* See Chapter 8, p 262 et seq.   † See Chapter 14, p 457 et seq.

89. CAB 80/26, COS (41) 162 (COS Résumé, No 80).
90. ibid, COS (41) 196 (COS Résumé, No 82).
91. Creveld, op cit, pp 151, 166.
92. CAB 80/26, COS (41) 196 (COS Résumé, No 82); Creveld, op cit, p 138.
93. CAB 80/25, COS (41) 98 (COS Résumé, No 76); AIR 40/2322, Minute of 6 March 1941.
94. WO 190/893, No 14B of 7 February 1941.
95. JIC (41) 90 of 5 March 1941.

the rates of advance through the Levant that Germany might achieve.[96] A report (of which the source was probably the Abwehr cypher)* that Germany was preparing to establish an intelligence centre in Turkey persuaded MI on 25 March that she might be preparing to turn against Turkey.[97] And on 27 March it included in the Chiefs of Staff résumé the rumour that German military circles were openly talking of a campaign through Turkey against Iraq and Egypt.[98]

□

A week later the anxiety about German intentions in the Middle East, long-standing and already again on the increase, was sharpened by events in Iraq. Since the summer of 1940 Whitehall had known that the political situation in Iraq was deteriorating in the wake of Germany's successes in Europe and as a result of increasing Axis pro-nationalist propaganda.[99] Since September they had had repeated evidence from GC and CS's reading of Axis diplomatic telegrams that the Italian and Japanese governments and the Grand Mufti of Jerusalem were involved in anti-British machinations in Iraq and the supply of arms to Arab nationalists in that country, where most of the Army officers were sympathetic to the Axis and where the Italian legation was an important centre of intrigue.[100] In November, when the Whitehall authorities had concluded that the Germans intended to advance through the Balkans and Syria to the Middle East, the JIC had considered the possibility of a German airborne attack against Syria ahead of a general drive into the Middle East.[101] The JIC had then thought that the Germans were more likely to preface a serious thrust into the Middle East by infiltrating Syria and using it as a base for anti-British subversion, and in December the Joint Planners had judged an airborne attack on Iraq to be impracticable.[102] Neither then nor later, however, did Whitehall and Cairo discuss what steps they would take in the event of an internal crisis in Iraq, and Rashid Ali's *coup d'état* of 3 April 1941 found them unprepared.

This was not because of any decline in the flow of intelligence about conditions in Iraq. By the beginning of December good reporting from Iraq by the SIS was providing yet another source of information. As

---

* See above, p 358.

96. See, for example, WO 190/893, No 32A of 25 March; WO 201/1574, JPS (ME) paper No 23 of 19 March 1941.

97. WO 190/893, No 33A of 25 March 1941.

98. CAB 80/26, COS (41) 196 (COS Résumé, No 82).

99. Woodward, op cit, Vol I, pp 571–572; CAB 80/13, COS (40) 461 of 14 June and COS (40) 494 of 26 June; CAB 65/18, WM (40) 189, 1 July.

100. JIC (40) 426 of 21 December, Appendices I and II. See also Playfair op cit, Vol II, pp 177–178.

101. JIC (40) 351 and 354 of 2 and 16 November.

102. CAB 80/24, COS (40) 1004 (JP) of 3 December.

early as the beginning of January the SIS noted that the position of the Regent was deteriorating – and the Foreign Office brought this report to the attention of the Chiefs of Staff on 6 January.[103] In the two months between the resignation of Rashid Ali's government at the end of January and his coup on 3 April the Baghdad office of the SIS poured out a stream of warnings that all was not well. On 16 February it urged that the capacity for mischief of Rashid and his army and political supporters 'should not be belittled', and on 16 March it reported that Rashid was preparing to put pressure on the government or even force it to resign. It was no doubt this SIS information that led GS Int GHQ, ME to speak on 21 February of the possibility of a coup,[104] though the Italian diplomatic traffic was also indicating that a crisis was brewing. On 31 March the SIS warned that a military *coup d'état* was imminent. By then, it is true, the Iraqi government was taking steps to have Rashid's army supporters arrested and on 31 March itself the Regent fled the capital to take refuge with the British.[105] But it is not difficult to sympathise with the SIS's subsequent complaint to the Prime Minister that its warnings had been ignored by the Whitehall departments.

The SIS claimed that the fault lay with the failure of the Eastern Department of the Foreign Office to forward its reports to the Whitehall Service departments. And it is indeed the case that after 31 January, when the Chiefs of Staff took note of the suspect character of the new Iraqi government, Cabinet and COS papers expressed no special concern about Iraq or Syria until 2 April, when the COS agreed on the desirability of a forward policy to obtain a change of government in Iraq.[106] As against this, the Foreign Office was certainly pressing the Chiefs of Staff at the end of 1940 and in January 1941 to keep Rashid Ali in check by sending additional forces to Iraq.[107] However, immediate responsibility for strategic decisions in the Middle East theatre lay with the C-in-C Middle East, and he did not take action until on 2 April, the day before the coup, obviously anticipating a request from Whitehall that he should send reinforcements to Iraq, he took the unusual step of asking the JIC direct for an appreciation of the Soviet and Iranian reactions to such a move.[108] On 8 March 1941, on the other hand, military responsibility for Iraq had been transferred to the C-in-C India and, as it was not restored to Cairo until after the revolt in Iraq at the beginning of May,* it may safely be presumed that uncertainty about the chain of command

---

* See Chapter 13, p 412.

103. CAB 79/8, COS (41) 9th Meeting, 6 January.
104. WO 169/924, Daily Intsum, 21 February 1941.
105. Woodward, op cit, Vol I, p 573.
106. CAB 79/10, COS (41) 119th Meeting, 2 April.
107. Woodward, op cit, Vol I, p 572.
108. JIC (41) 134 of 2 April.

contributed something to the indecision of the British authorities. For the main explanations of their failures to make contingency plans, however, it is perhaps unnecessary to look beyond the acute shortage of resources in the Middle East and the fact that, throughout the first three months of 1941, the greater dangers in the Balkans and the western desert were monopolising their attention.

It was for the same reasons, no doubt, that, as yet, virtually no consideration was given to the possible need for intervention in Syria. By the end of 1940 reports from British diplomatic missions, from the Free French,[109] from the SIS and from the Italian diplomatic Sigint about the activities in Syria of the Italian Armistice Commission and of the arrival there of German civilians had already shown that the country was being developed, with Vichy's connivance, as a base for subversive activities in the Middle East. Similar reports continued to come in during the early months of 1941. On 18 March MI drew attention to German Press claims that the British government was planning to invade Syria and implied that they might be cover for Germany's own intentions.[110] But it was not until the third week of April, when the Greek campaign was drawing to a close, that anxiety about Syria came to a head.

□

Even before the *coup d'état* in Iraq had complicated the situation by increasing uncertainty about the Middle East, developments in Yugoslavia had produced another source of anxiety. The British Minister in Belgrade had kept Whitehall well informed about Germany's mounting pressure on Yugoslavia to sign the Tripartite Pact and grant transit facilities, but until the middle of March Whitehall had assumed, correctly, that Germany had made no preparations to attack Yugoslavia despite Germany's failure to secure her co-operation and despite the fact that the route through Belgrade was Germany's easiest approach to Greece. Guided by the absence of evidence for such preparations, MI had regularly reported to this effect since the middle of January.[111] Early in February A-54 had indeed reported that in connection with her intention to attack Greece 'before the end of March', Germany had no plan to invade Yugoslavia unless she refused transit facilities; but he had also warned that Germany was preparing an offensive against Turkey for 1 April, as well as sending reinforcements to France for an attack on Gibraltar, and the SIS in Belgrade believed he was becoming 'too alarmist'.[112]

---

109. CAB 80/24, COS (40) 1065 of 27 December.
110. WO 190/893, No 29A of 18 March 1941.
111. ibid, Nos 3A, 9A, 15A and 33A of 15, 24 January, 9 February and 25 March 1941.
112. Moravec, op cit, p 204; Amort and Jedlica, op cit, pp 102–103.

On 2 March the JIC excluded a move into Yugoslavia except possibly in the extreme south (the Petrich/Vardar valley).[113] As late as 23 March AI similarly discounted a simultaneous attack on Yugoslavia and Greece: it would require a still greater diversion of the GAF from the west than Germany had yet carried out.[114] As early as 20 January, however, the Prime Minister thought it seemed clear that the Yugoslav Prince Regent had warned the Greeks that if they let British forces into Greece Yugoslavia would allow the passage of German troops;[115] and on 22 January FOES had mentioned the possibility that Germany would risk war with Yugoslavia if Great Britain reinforced Greece on a large scale.[116] In March, with the arrival of the British forces, Whitehall and the commands in the Middle East became acutely aware that the British front in northern Greece could be turned if Germany attacked Yugoslavia and advanced through Monastir. MI drew attention to this danger on 11 March;[117] from 14 March it was calculating the likely scale of Yugoslav resistance to an attack.[118] On 19 March the British Military Mission in Athens feared that in their assault on Greece the Germans would cross Yugoslav territory and outflank the British and Greek defence line.[119]

The British agencies in Belgrade included not only the diplomatic mission and the attachés, but also SOE, which had originally been deployed in Yugoslavia to undertake sabotage projects for blocking the Danube and to organise resistance movements in Balkan countries that were threatened with German occupation, and the SIS, which lent its communications to SOE and provided it with essential contacts.[120] Up to mid-March they had hoped that, notwithstanding SOE's failure to obtain effective collaboration from the Yugoslav authorities in its sabotage operations, they would at least be able to prevent the government of the Prince Regent from yielding to German demands for transit facilities.[121] But by 18 March, judging that the Prince Regent had finally gone over to the German side, they decided that the time had come for an alternative policy – one that had hitherto been ruled out as premature by the Foreign Office[122] – and began to use their influence to have his government replaced by one which would, they hoped, join the war against Germany. On 19 March, at a meeting at the British legation, they discussed the plan in accordance with which

---

113. JIC (41) 87 of 2 March.
114. AIR 40/2322, Minute of 23 March 1941.
115. CAB 65/21, WM (41) 8 CA of 20 January.
116. CAB 81/64, FOES (41) 1 of 22 January.
117. WO 190/893, No 27A of 11 March 1941.
118. ibid, 14 March 1941.
119. CAB 105/2, No 126 of 19 March 1941.
120. CAB 80/56, COS (40) 27 (0) of 25 November and COS (41) 3 (0) of 8 January; CAB 69/2, DO (41) 4th Meeting, 13 January; Butler, op cit, Vol I, pp 403–415.
121. Woodward, op cit, Vol I, pp 515–516.
122. FO 371/25033, FO to Belgrade, 3 August and 24 October 1940; Woodward, op cit, Vol I, pp 521–528; J Amery, *Approach March* (1973), pp 171–178.

3 Ministers resigned from the Yugoslav Cabinet on 20 March, the day on which the Cabinet agreed to succumb to German pressure and sign the Tripartite Pact.[123] On 21 March the British Minister asked the Foreign Office whether the British government would approve of a *coup d'état* and support a new government. From Cairo on 23 March, after some hesitation, the Foreign Secretary gave him provisional authority to do what he thought fit to further a change of government, even at the risk of precipitating a German attack; and on 24 March the Minister received full authority to support any necessary subversive measures.[124] The coup was brought off on 27 March, two days after the Yugoslav government had signed the Pact, by Air Force and Army officers. That they had joined forces with the dissident political parties owed something to encouragement from the British attachés[125] and the SOE, and Whitehall was alerted to the fact that a coup was imminent before it occurred.[126]

While British participation in the plans no doubt contributed to their success, it is clear that even without direct British encouragement there would still have been a coup; its origins were deeply rooted in the Yugoslav political situation. On the other hand, it is clear that British expectations were belied by the new Yugoslav government. It refrained from denouncing the Tripartite Pact for fear of provoking immediate German retaliation and, in the hope of being left in peace, it refrained from making defence preparations until it became obvious that Germany in any case intended to invade. And despite warnings to this effect from Belgrade, Whitehall over-estimated the Yugoslav capacity to resist an invasion – and thus the number of additional divisions that Germany would have to bring up if she attacked Yugoslavia and Greece simultaneously. We have seen already that Germany brought up an extra twelve. MI calculated that she would have to bring up 32 or 33 additional divisions, including 4 motorised and 3 or 4 armoured.[127] Nor was it until 4 April, after the CIGS had talked with the new Yugoslav government, that London learned the full extent of Yugoslavia's unreadiness for war.

Of Germany's surprised reaction to the Yugoslav coup Whitehall was far better informed. Even before the Yugoslavs signed the Tripartite Pact the GAF Enigma showed that some German Army formations

---

123. B Sweet-Escott, *Baker Street Irregular* (1965); Amery, op cit; J B Hoptner, *Yugoslavia in Crisis, 1934–1941* (New York, 1962).

124. FO 371/30253, Belgrade to Cairo, 21 March and Cairo to Belgrade, 22, 23 and 24 March; Woodward, op cit, Vol I, pp 541–542; Churchill, op cit, Vol III, p 135.

125. FO 371/30253, Air Attaché, Belgrade, to D of I Air Ministry, 26 March; FO 371/30209 (R 3711/G), Air Attaché to Air Ministry, 31 March 1941; A Glen, *Footholds against a Whirlwind; an Autobiography* (1975), pp 63–64; J Tomasevich, *War and Revolution in Yugoslavia: the Chetniks* (Stanford, 1975), p 45; Dalton Diary, entry for 27 March 1941.

126. CAB 79/10, COS (41) 111th Meeting, 27 March.

127. WO 190/893, No 27C of 14 March 1941.

had been ordered to leave the Balkans for Poland. (This order was in fact a consequence of Hitler's decision of 17 March to transfer the armour from Army Group South to Cracow preparatory to *Barbarossa*.) On 26 March, the day after the signing, the Enigma revealed that these formations included three armoured divisions, SS Division Adolf Hitler, the HQs of Panzergruppe Kleist and of XIV Corps, and some troops of 12 Army. This was a powerful pointer to the German intention to attack Russia.* Of more immediate significance, however, was Whitehall's knowledge, also from the Enigma, that within 12 hours of the Belgrade coup the first of the rail movements out of the Balkans had been halted and orders given for it to be held in sidings, that Göring had ordered the German Chief of Air Staff back to Berlin for immediate consultations, and that AOC Luftflotte 4, the senior air command in the Balkans, was also expected in Berlin from Vienna on 28 March. Between 27 and 30 March the Enigma decrypts also revealed the start of a new series of rail movements (named after motor cars) bringing reinforcements to the Balkans, and preparations for a rapid army and air concentration in the Arad-Temesvar area, later seen to be the starting point for von Kleist's thrust into Yugoslavia.[128] The hasty assembly of forces for 2 Army's main attack on Yugoslavia from Austria and Hungary was less well reflected in the decrypts, but of this the SIS sent warning in good time from Carinthia.[129] In addition, A-54 provided from the end of March details of the plan and timetable for the attack on Yugoslavia, together with some information about the German preparations for *Barbarossa*.[130]

By 3 April the further transfer of German air forces from the west, the absence of which had led AI on 20 March to discount a simultaneous attack on Greece and Yugoslavia, was seen to be in full swing, the main concentration of the reinforcements being against Yugoslavia.[131] On 4 April the Prime Minister warned the Yugoslav government that GAF concentrations were arriving 'from all quarters'.[132] By 10 April AI estimated that 900 German aircraft were in the Balkans – that an additional 500 had arrived.[133] In fact the number was something short of 1,000 by that date,[134] and the Enigma and the low-grade GAF cyphers had shown that the reinforcements had been brought in from north-west Europe, Sicily and north Africa.

□

* See Chapter 14, p 451 et seq.

128. CX/JQ 803, 808, 821, 825, 849.
129. WO 190/893, No 35D of 1 April 1941.
130. Moravec, op cit, p 205; Amort and Jedlica, op cit, p 104.
131. CAB 80/27, COS (41) 221 (COS Résumé, No 83).
132. CAB 105/3, Hist (B) 3, No 43.
133. CAB 80/27, COS (41) 231 (COS Résumé, No 84).
134. AIR 41/10, pp 121, 123.

The Yugoslav coup and Germany's preparations for the attack on Yugoslavia entailed a final change in her plans for the attack on Greece. On 27 March she had been intending to launch the Greek operation on 1 April. The initial plan for the attack on Yugoslavia provided for the bombing of Belgrade on that day, postponed the attack on Greece until 2 or 3 April and set the date for the ground invasion of Yugoslavia at 12 April. On 29 March, however, it was decided to stage both the bombing of Belgrade and the opening of *Marita* on 5 April, with von Kleist's attack on Yugoslavia following on 8 April and that by 2 Army on 12 April. On 3 April Hitler intervened, fixing *Marita* and the bombing of Belgrade for 6 April. Except that 2 Army began its attack on 10 April, these dates were adhered to.

Of these last-minute changes of plan Whitehall received good tactical notice. On 28 March MI appreciated that, with complex troop train movements in progress between Germany and the Balkans, it might be a week or more before Germany could mount large-scale operations against Yugoslavia.[135] On 1 April it guessed, again correctly, that the attack on Greece had been imminent at the time of the Belgrade coup but would now be postponed to coincide with that on Yugoslavia.[136] It was probably relying partly on reports from the Greek-Bulgarian frontier that on 30 March the German 18 Corps with two mountain divisions had moved west of the River Struma – it was this Corps which performed the right hook through Yugoslavia which outflanked the Greek line and took Salonika in a few days[137] – and partly on an Enigma message of 29 March instructing all GAF units in the Balkans to establish signal communications with a single forward Battle HQ. On 2 April the Enigma provided further support for this appreciation by mentioning that a special operation (Strafgericht) was planned for 6 April.[138] Although there is no sign that the intelligence authorities ventured to predict that this operation was the bombing of Belgrade, the reference to it gave the intelligence authorities a date to work to. Also on 2 April the Enigma showed that the GAF had carried out reconnaissance of the railway from Nis to Belgrade, and MI quoted the decrypt of a message from the Italian Minister, Sofia stating that a simultaneous attack on Greece and Yugoslavia would come on the morning of 5 April.[139] This intelligence no doubt provided the basis for the warning issued to British troops in Greece on 4 April that the attack would probably start on the following day[140] and for General Wilson's open assumption of command on 5 April.

---

135. WO 190/893, No 35A of 28 March 1941.
136. Repeated in CAB 80/27, COS (41) 221 (COS Résumé, No 83).
137. Playfair, op cit, Vol II, p 82.
138. CX/JQ 823, 829.
139. WO 190/893, MI14 Appreciation of 2 April 1941.
140. Playfair, op cit, Vol II, p 82.

The German postponement of zero hour to 6 April was reflected in the Enigma, for the transmission of which a new direct service by GC and CS to the commands in Greece and the Middle East had recently been introduced.* At 0434† on 5 April, 24 hours in advance of the event, GC and CS informed the commands that GAF units had been instructed to begin hostilities at 0530 on 6 April. At 0015* on 6 April it notified them in a further Enigma message that the time had been postponed to 0600.[141]

---

* See Appendix 13.
† These are the times of origin of the messages from GC and CS; it is not known when the messages were received.

141. OL 34 of 0434/5 April 1941; OL 37 of 0015/6 April.

CHAPTER 12

North Africa and the Mediterranean, November 1940 to June 1941

IN THE Mediterranean after the Italian attack on Greece the next move was made by British forces. At the end of October 1940 the C-in-C Middle East decided that, instead of waiting for another move forward by the Italian Army in north Africa, he would himself attack, and the War Cabinet was informed of his intention on 5 November. From then on planning proceeded in conditions of deep secrecy – with the minimum of reference on paper and no reference whatever in signals – imposed by the correct assumption that the Italians had good intelligence about the British forces in Egypt. And British intelligence enjoyed the novel experience of contributing to the success of a large-scale British initiative. Nor is there any reason to doubt that its contribution was of decisive importance. Despite the fact that the Italians were expecting a British attack, Wavell's assault (*Compass*), which opened on 9 December, achieved complete surprise in terms of its timing and tactical execution. This owed something to Italian mistakes – the Italian Army Commander mis-interpreted the first British moves as preparations to meet the renewed advance that he himself was preparing – but it owed more to precise British planning and effective British deception measures, and these depended on the wealth and the accuracy of intelligence about the Italian forces and on the fact that, in view of its sources, the British commanders could now be confident of its reliability.

The strategic contribution of intelligence to the success of the British counter-offensive owed much to its work on the Italian Air Force. Nor was this limited to the provision of accurate information of the strength and the order of battle of the IAF before the campaign began. Until 31 December 1940, when it was changed again, and then from the beginning of the fourth week in January 1941, when it was again broken, the IAF high-grade cypher was 80 per cent readable and was yielding copious details almost currently. These included assessments both of the effects of RAF bombing raids and of the results of Italian reconnaissance missions over British forces at sea, in ports and on land. They also made it possible to keep a close watch on the Italian air effort – to see that this had reached its peak after the first week of *Compass*; that a serious repair situation had developed in Cyrenaica towards the end of December; that by the beginning of February 1941 the IAF in Cyrenaica had only 43 serviceable aircraft and, a week later, that it had withdrawn all its forces to Sirte or positions further west.

The high-grade Sigint contribution was not limited to intelligence derived from the Italian cypher. The GAF Enigma played its part by enabling RAF intelligence to discount at this stage a sudden appearance of the GAF in the north African theatre. As we shall see, the British Army authorities laboured under the perpetual fear that German armour might be despatched there. For the Air Ministry, on the other hand, the feeling that no considerable transfer of the GAF could take place without being reflected in the GAF Enigma decrypts was buttressed not only by the absence of any local GAF W/T traffic in the area but also by the knowledge obtained from Italian Sigint that a German delegation had arrived in Libya with three aircraft of different types at the beginning of September. From this and from information in the GAF Enigma about the activities of the delegation it correctly concluded that while the GAF was becoming interested in desert operations, and was probably subjecting its aircraft to climatic trials, German intervention was not imminent.[1]

On some items of strategic importance – the morale and the equipment of the IAF, for example – further information was obtained from the interrogation of Italian POW, who were also forthcoming about the tactical methods and procedure of the IAF. For two reasons, however, the supply of air intelligence of operational value was less satisfactory. In the first place, the IAF high-grade cypher decrypts rarely carried operational instructions. When they did, as was exceptionally the case during the Italian attack on Greece between November 1940 and the spring of 1941, special steps were taken to exploit them. From the end of November this source provided full coverage of the strength and dispositions of the IAF units engaged in the Italian attack on Greece, as well as information of the withdrawal of the Italian bombers from the campaign in April 1941, after the German invasion of Greece, but it also carried nightly reports from the Italian 4 Air Corps in southern Italy to Air HQ Albania giving details of the bomber targets for the following day. These were read within a few hours at GC and CS and the decrypts transmitted direct from GC and CS to the RAF HQ in Greece, where the material played a large part in the interception – often with heavy losses to them – of the IAF bombers and fighters over their targets. In relation to the north African fighting, however, it was sufficient for GC and CS to transmit a summary of its high-grade decrypts to the intelligence HQs at Cairo, as it did from September 1940, since the Italian Air Force, like the German, transmitted most of its operational

1. AIR 23/6767, HQ RAF, ME, Weekly Intelligence Summary, 2 September 1940 and following weeks.

W/T traffic in low-grade codes and cyphers, not to speak of plain language.

It was these other sources, not the high-grade cypher, which carried the data about airfield serviceability, aircraft movements and combat sorties. To take one example, the high-grade revealed the presence in Libya of a unit of torpedo-carrying aircraft – the first such enemy unit, Italian or German, to be identified – in September 1940, but did not carry any warnings of the attacks by these aircraft which seriously damaged HMS *Kent* in September and HMS *Liverpool* in October. And this illustrates the second problem that arose. Despite frequent changes, the low-grade codes continued to be readable at Cairo and GC and CS a good deal of the time, the changes being offset by frequent captures of code material. But the RAF had made no provision for the interception and exploitation of the IAF's operational traffic at its advanced HQs. RAF field Sigint was later to develop into an organisation employing over 1,000 men at a chain of stations along the north African coast and throughout the Levant. But no field unit was set up in the desert until August 1941; and until 1942 the advanced units there still passed their information back to HQ RAF, ME at Cairo, instead of being fully integrated with the intelligence section of the forward Group HQ, so that 'the excellent picture they accumulated of enemy organisation...was not fully used'. The same situation applied at Malta, Aden and Khartoum, the only places which had RAF Sigint units before August 1941. The results of their interception were passed to HQ RAF, ME for forwarding to the appropriate operational commands.

In these circumstances, given the difficulty of communications, the operational commands derived little immediate benefit from the available tactical air intelligence. At HQ RAF, ME the material was of great value; in March 1941, at the end of the desert offensive, the senior intelligence officer there reported that '"Y" information forms our most important source and is of direct operational use to us'. At the advanced HQs it was a different tale. In the western desert, as in connection with the defence of Malta and the Mediterranean Fleet against IAF attack, it proved impossible as yet to apply the system of early warning, based on low-grade Sigint and R/T, which was developed in the United Kingdom during the Battle of Britain and which would have been doubly useful in a theatre where the British forces, almost entirely lacking radar, were also almost entirely dependent on observer posts for information about raids. The local defences derived no benefit from Sigint during the IAF's offensive against Malta in the summer of 1940, the general situation being made still more difficult by the fact that the communications of the IAF in Sicily were by land-line, and could not be intercepted. As for the western desert, a report on the lessons learned during the British offensive singled out R/T for special mention, but it may be safely assumed that its criticism applied to all low-grade Sigint. It said that information from Y was of great strategic value, and that it would also have been of great tactical value if the service could have been extended to Group HQ and had been able to cope with R/T, but that as it was, tactical intelligence was not available from R/T and that for immediate action Y source intelligence usually arrived too late at Group HQ.[2]

As was the case with the Italian Air Force in Libya, Sigint was the chief source of the information about the Army order of battle. By the time the British advance was ready to begin, British knowledge of where the Italian Army was strong and where it was weak, and of its administrative layout, was very comprehensive, and this determined the final shape of the British plan. The fact that the location of some units proved to be faulty and that a last-minute increase of strength in the Italian forward areas went unnoticed proved not to be critical.[3] Work at Cairo on the lower-grade codes and cyphers of the Italian Army had been especially useful. In October the Army's crypt-analytic section in Cairo broke a new group of such cyphers, introduced for use by all Italian formations down to brigade level for all tactical communications and by intelligence staffs, and by the end of the campaign in Cyrenaica this source alone had yielded 8,000 decrypts. But work at GC and CS on the high-grade Army cypher was also beginning to yield some results before the advance, and before the Italians introduced further changes as a result of the capture of the cypher's books and keys at Bardia on 4 January GC and CS had read some 2,600 messages in it, of which about a third were teleprinted to the War Office for transmission to Cairo. Where Sigint, captured documents, POW and the censorship could not help – as in fixing the latest location of the enemy's units and revealing the current state of his defensive positions – good use was made of patrols by armoured car units[4] and of air reconnaissance.[5] In particular, two items of information obtained in this way were vital to the success of the initial breakthrough. On the night of 7–8 December 1940 a special patrol of 2 Rifle Brigade verified details of the gap in the minefield protecting the Italian position at Nibeiwa. This information finally decided the point of the assault.[6] Air reconnaissance determined the point at which the assault was made on the other crucial objective, Tummar East Camp.[7] It should be added that Whitehall had sent out

2. AIR 20/5466, Elmhirst, 'Lessons learned during Air Operations in the Western Desert, August 1940–February 1941', p 29.

3. Playfair, op cit, Vol I, pp 265, 273; Long, *Australia in the War of 1939–45*, Series I, Vol. I, 'To Benghazi' (1952), p 138; WO 169/53, HQ Western Desert Force, Intelligence Summary No 1.

4. Playfair, op cit, Vol I, p 212.

5. Richards, op cit, Vol I, p 269; AIR 41/44, p 74.

6. Playfair, op cit, Vol I, pp 266–267.

7. ibid, p 268; Richards, op cit, Vol I, p 271.

to Egypt a copy of one of MI's periodical notes on the German Army which summed up what had been learned of German planning and conduct of operations in France. This provided lessons in tactics which were used by the *Compass* planners.[8]

It is more difficult, not to say impossible, to document the part played by Army intelligence in the course of the campaign. Most reports of immediate tactical value went by word of mouth or were scribbled on message pads which have not been preserved. But it is known that No 3 Mobile Section of the Army's field Sigint organisation, attached to the Western Desert Force HQ, provided a steady supply of information from its decryption of the Italian tactical codes and cyphers. During December alone it produced 300 valuable decrypts. Later in the campaign its decrypts included the situation reports of the Italian Corps Commander in Bardia to the Italian Supreme Command during the Australia attack on that strongpoint early in 1941; a full strength return of the Italian garrison before the attack on Tobruk: and, despite Italian cypher changes after the fall of Bardia, details of the Italian withdrawal from Benghazi. These last played their part in General O'Connor's decision to thrust south-westward across the desert to Msus. This movement, unlike operations hitherto, took place across terrain of which the only knowledge was that provided by low-flying aircraft which pronounced the going 'difficult but possible'.[9] It was known that the Italian High Command had considered whether the British might make this move, but, after calculation, had dismissed it as impossible.[10]* The thrust brought on the battle of Beda Fomm on 5–7 February and the ejection of the Italians from Cyrenaica. Air reconnaissance also provided early evidence of the Italian retreat from Benghazi. At an earlier stage visual and photographic reconnaissance had provided the information on which the assaults on Bardia and Tobruk were planned.[12] Before the attack on Bardia, however, it is clear that the intelligence authorities in Cairo greatly over-estimated Italian losses during the battle of Sidi Barrani, and greatly under-estimated the number of men and guns withdrawn

---

* Sigint disclosed that the Italians were also perturbed about the operations of the Long-Range Desert Group, whose success in their operations to the south of the main theatre of operations stemmed largely from the first-hand experience of officers who had made a hobby of desert travel and exploration in peace-time.[11] The news of the whereabouts of the LRDG that reached Cairo came from decrypts of an Italian low-grade cypher since the Group was not allowed to take W/T transmitters with it on its operations.

8. WO 208/2914, War Office Periodical Notes on the German Army, No 30; WO 169/53, HQ Western Desert Force War Diary, December 1940.
9. Playfair, op cit, Vol I, p 357.
10. WO 169/19, GS Int GHQ ME, Weekly Review of the Military Situation (WRMS), of 10 February 1941.
11. Playfair, op cit, Vol I, p 294.
12. ibid, pp 282–283; AIR 41/44, pp 82–3, 88.

by the Italians to Bardia, and that this error cost the Australians many casualties.[13] This was an early example of the difficulty experienced by intelligence staffs throughout the war, no matter how well provided with information from Sigint, POW and captured documents, in making accurate estimates of the numerical strength of the forces facing them.

□

With the battle of Beda Fomm, which brought the British Army to El Agheila and to its first contacts with German forces, the war in north Africa entered a new phase. Meanwhile it had become imperative to bring about as quickly as possible the defeat of the Italian forces in east Africa. In January 1941, when the attack in this area was timed to begin early in February, intelligence left no doubt that the German penetration of the Balkans was gathering momentum, and the possibility that British forces would have to be despatched to Greece was already taking its place alongside another urgent reason for wishing to bring about a rapid destruction of the Italian forces – the need to clear the Red Sea for the passage of Allied and American shipping to Suez.

During Italy's early limited offensives in east Africa – against Kassala early in July 1940, against Moyale in Kenya in the middle of July, into British Somaliland early in August – intelligence had been of limited value to the British authorities. GHQ, ME had a fairly accurate picture of the Italian order of battle and some grasp of the strategic alternatives available to the enemy, but the Italians were generally successful in keeping secret their tactical moves.[14] Thereafter the Italian Army's high-grade cypher for the area was changed, and there was considerable uncertainty about its order of battle, and even more about its equipment and state of readiness, until the end of November, when larger-scale Italian advances against Kenya and the Sudan were beginning to be feared. But a very different situation prevailed by January 1941, when these advances had failed to materialise and British forces were ready to take the offensive. Partly because they benefited from valuable captured documents but mainly for two other reasons – the fact that British intercept stations were so sited as to be able to receive every Italian communication; and the fact that the Italians, isolated from metropolitan Italy and handicapped by the huge distances, could not make frequent cypher changes – the intelligence authorities in Cairo were able to turn the east African campaign into 'the perfect (if rather miniature) example of the cryptographers' war'.

In November 1940 the new high-grade cypher of the Italian Army in east Africa was mastered at GC and CS. In the same month the

---

13. Playfair, op cit, Vol I, pp 282–283; Long, op cit, pp 140, 143.
14. WO 169/18, GS Int GHQ ME, WRMS of 15 July 1940.

IAF's east African cypher was at last changed,* but the replacement was soon broken at CBME. By the end of the year CBME had in addition broken so many new lower-grade codes and cyphers, including those in use by the colonial authorities and the Carabiniere as well as by the Italian armed forces, that it had to suspend work on some of them in order to concentrate its limited staff on those that were of most operational value. From these sources, the value of which was all the greater in view of the shortage of air reconnaissance in the area and the lack of any SIS organisation, the British commanders were fully aware of the enemy's supply position and its many weaknesses when they began their advance, and throughout the early months of 1941 they were provided currently with complete details of virtually every Italian move.

Early in January the revelation that the Italians were withdrawing from Kassala enabled the British advance to begin nearly three weeks earlier than planned, on 19 January instead of 8 February. From then until the end of the campaign the Cs-in-C in Cairo were able to read the enemy's plans and appreciations in his own words as soon as he issued them; indeed, they sometimes received the decrypts while the Italian W/T operators were still asking for the signals to be checked and repeated. The flood of intelligence was not confined to any one sector or level of command, but was general throughout the whole area of operations and throughout the whole of the enemy's chain of command from the Viceroy himself down to the smallest garrison detachment. It extended from the reading of the Viceroy's daily situation report for the Italian government down to the reading of detailed instructions for the evacuation of Italian wives and families, and included by the way such material as the Air Force Command's regular previews of the operations it had planned for the coming week, its reports on the progressive disintegration of its resources and the orders and appreciations issued by the Italian Army Commander in connection with his successive withdrawals during the one important engagement, the battle of Keren. The material was read with so little delay, and so much of it contained advance information, that it was unnecessary to attach any Sigint units to the British commanders in the field. The work was shared between CBME at Cairo and a station at Nairobi, whose staff had been trained at CBME. The supply of information provided by these centres was so continuous that there was no time, and perhaps no need, to assess it before it was sent forward, and it was so complete that the DDMI in Cairo 'could not believe that any commander in the field had been better served by his intelligence than the Commander of the forces operating in East Africa'.

□

---

* See Chapter 6, p 206.

Italy's reverses in Greece, at Taranto and in the western desert had by this time precipitated the movement of German forces to the Mediterranean. By mid-November, after earlier changes of plan,* Hitler had decided to send GAF units to Italy: the RAF had to be prevented from attacking the Romanian oilfields from Greek bases, and the British Mediterranean Fleet had to be reduced before the German move into Greece in the following spring. These units – the formation selected was Fliegerkorps X – began their move at the end of December. At the end of December the Italians themselves had asked for ground support in Italy and Albania, and by the middle of January 1941, to prevent an Italian collapse, Hitler had agreed to supply a small force of armour to Libya from about 20 February and to send two and a half divisions to Albania. On 3 February, as a result of the British advance in north Africa, he had cancelled the Albanian move and had reluctantly decided to increase the troops earmarked for Libya by a complete Panzer division, the whole force to be called at this stage 'the German Africa Corps'. The movement of the first troops to Libya – 5 Light Division – followed in mid-February. Rommel arrived in north Africa on 12 February. The supplementary armoured division, 15 Panzer Division, was to begin crossing in mid-April.

Ever since the entry of Italy into the war the British authorities had allowed that German forces might intervene in the Mediterranean and had feared that, because of the shortage of long-range reconnaissance aircraft in the theatre and the lack of SIS agents in Italy and Libya, they would do so without advance warning being received.[15] In August 1940 the War Office and the Joint Planners had agreed that Germany was 'prepared to bolster up an Italian attack on Egypt or elsewhere with armoured and motorised divisions'.[16] It was on this assumption that the decision was then taken to send an armoured brigade from the United Kingdom to Egypt while the outcome of the battle of Britain was still undecided.[17]† The assumption had been based on reports from the SIS, British Service attachés and United States sources to the effect that Germany was planning to move to the Mediterranean. These reports were vague; they hinted at a great variety of projects,[18] they conflicted with what was known about

---

    * See Chapter 8, p 250.
    † On 25 August it was decided that the convoy might go round the Cape, and not through the Mediterranean, because of reconnaissance reports from Cairo that the expected Italian offensive was unlikely to begin for several weeks. See Chapter 6, p 216.

    15. WO 169/3, JPS (ME) paper of 20 June 1940; CAB 79/5, COS (40) 255th meeting of 8 August; CAB 95/2, ME (M) (40) 5th Meeting of 8 August, 6th Meeting of 12 August.
    16. WO 190/891, No 147 of 23 August; CAB 80/16, COS (40) 647 (JP) of 21 August, paragraph 64.
    17. Playfair, op cit, Vol I, pp 190–191; Butler, op cit, Vol II, p 308.
    18. WO 190/891, Nos 116 and 148 of 26 June and 30 August 1940; WO 190/892, No 30A of 20 March 1941; WO 169/18, WRMS of 15 and 22 July 1940; CAB 80/13, COS (40) 483 (COS Résumé, No 42); CAB 80/15, COS (40) 595 (COS Résumé, No 48).

Germany's concentration on *Sealion*, and even with evidence of the reverse movement of IAF squadrons into north-west Europe.[19] But the intelligence authorities had not been able to discount them – or, indeed, the danger that, given the poor state of their intelligence, German armour might reach north Africa without their knowledge.

Similar reports had continued to come in during the remainder of 1940. At the beginning of October, as already noted, the Cabinet had been advised by the Foreign Office of 'certain indications' that Germany's next move would be an attack from Libya rather than through Spain or into the Balkans.* But from the end of October Sigint had begun to provide some checks on the other sources. Italian cyphers had supplied the news that three GAF aircraft of different types had been sent to north Africa† and the information that a German Army mission was visiting Graziani's headquarters.[20]

At the same time the GAF Enigma, as well as revealing that GAF transport aircraft had arrived in southern Italy,[21] was uncovering the beginning of the German build-up in the Balkans.‡ In these circumstances the intelligence authorities in London and Cairo had regarded the Italian evidence as pointing only to tentative preliminary investigations by the Germans, and had remained unimpressed by the continuing stream of reports about the movement of German troops into Italy. None of these had found their way into the intelligence summaries and appreciations until 17 November, when their frequency had compelled MI to report on them to other intelligence departments and to the General Staff. The report had accepted that German Army units, including armour, had arrived in Italy, but emphasised that no units had been positively identified and that there was no reliable evidence as to their ultimate destination. It might be Albania, Yugoslavia, Malta, French north Africa or Libya, though it seemed improbable that Germany would send troops to north Africa in any number until she had seen how the situation developed throughout the Mediterranean.[22]

This assessment had reflected the state of thinking at the higher levels in Whitehall. Although the Foreign Office held that Germany was not yet determined on action in the Balkans, and might give priority to a drive on Egypt from Libya, the general feeling was that Germany would choose other alternatives – notably the Balkans and Gibraltar – in preference to Libya.§ In the Middle East those who were engaged in the planning of *Compass* were more worried than

---

* See Chapter 8, p 253.
† See above, p 370.
‡ See Chapter 8, p 259 and Chapter 11, p 350.
§ See Chapter 8, pp 259–260 and Chapter 11, p 349 et seq.

19. CAB 80/14, COS (40) 534 (COS Résumé, No 44).
20. WO 169/19, GS Int GHQ ME, Intelligence Summary of 23 October.
21. CAB 80/20, COS (40) 820 (COS Résumé, No 58).
22. WO 190/892, No 26 of 17 November 1940.

Whitehall by the possibility of the sudden and unannounced appearance of German tanks in north Africa; in addition, no doubt, they were tempted to dwell on this threat on account of their wish for reinforcements from the United Kingdom and their reluctance to divert to Greece any of the forces earmarked for *Compass*. But they had received no encouragement from their intelligence authorities. These were now recognising the value of negative Sigint evidence in connection with possible large-scale movements for which the enemy could hardly dispense with W/T. A JPS(ME) paper of 18 November had assumed that German land forces were bound to arrive some day, and had accepted that there would be no warning of their arrival from SIS reports or air reconnaissance. But it had insisted that their arrival would be betrayed not only by the appearance of GAF units – and of these there had been no trace – but also by German W/T transmissions. And it had pointed out that there was as yet no sign of German W/T traffic in the area and no Sigint reference to the presence of German forces.[23]

The growing reliance on evidence, negative and positive, from Sigint sources was justified during the next month. As late as 20 December AI in Whitehall had believed that the GAF was still being reserved for another attempt at invasion of the United Kingdom, that if aircraft were diverted it would be for an attack in the Iberian peninsula, and that Germany had no plans for operations from Italy.[24] But on 27 December AI reported that on 15 December German aircraft from two units which were known to have specialised in the attack on shipping in British waters – one of which, KG 26, belonged to Fliegerkorps X – had been in W/T contact with controls in Italy. In the interval between the two dates it had also obtained from GC and CS scraps of GAF Enigma pointing to a move by Fliegerkorps X to bases from which it could attack the Mediterranean Fleet; and these now enabled it to warn the Air Staff that such operations must be expected 'in the near future'.[25] On 4 January it was known in Whitehall that the GAF had established 'ground stations' in Sicily, a clear indication of where the new arrivals would be based.[26]

The speed with which the first of Germany's operational moves into the Mediterranean was detected – as late as 5 January 1941 only seven of her bombers had arrived in Sicily[27] – and the alacrity with which AI changed its views when the evidence changed were not matched in Whitehall's arrangements for disseminating the intelligence. The arrival of the GAF, marked by the attacks which severely damaged the

23. WO 169/3, JP (ME) paper of 18 November 1940.
24. AIR 40/2321, p 94.
25. ibid, pp 53–54; AIR 40/2323, Humphreys, 'The Use of Ultra in the Mediterranean and North African Theatre of War', p 4.
26. WO 190/893, No 8B, DMI minute to CIGS of 23 January.
27. CAB 80/25, COS (41) 25 (COS Résumé, No 71).

Illustrious on 10 January and sank the *Southampton* two days later, decisively changed the strategic situation in the Mediterranean. But, except that the Y officer on the flagship was able to give one hour's warning of the attack on HMS *Illustrious*,[28]* the first attack came as a surprise to the Mediterranean Fleet. Whether the Air Ministry was at fault, in taking no steps to alert the Admiralty beyond reporting in the Chiefs of Staff résumé on 9 January that GAF units had arrived in Sicily,[29] or whether the Admiralty, for judging that the information would be of no value to the Fleet, which would in any case be expecting heavy IAF raids, the information was not forwarded to C-in-C, Mediterranean, or to Force H, which was at sea at the time. That the Italians had, on 2 January, broadcast a welcome to GAF units arriving in Italy 'to partake in the severe air and naval struggle in the Mediterranean basin. . .' was promptly noted in Whitehall and Cairo: but while AI linked this item with the establishment of ground facilities in Sicily, there is no sign that it collated it with the Sigint clues which had a few days earlier led it to believe GAF attacks to be imminent. Indeed, AI's chief reaction to the broadcast was to discuss it in the context of Italian fears of a German takeover.[30]

With the help of the general GAF Enigma and the study of GAF low-grade traffic, AI was able from January 1941 to keep an accurate tally of the build-up of Germany's air power in the Mediterranean. At the end of January, when the true figures were 120 long-range bombers, 150 dive-bombers and 40 fighters, it put the numbers at 160, 150 and 40 respectively, and by 4 February it realised that it had over-estimated by 40 the number of long-range bombers.[31] Although it was unable to be certain of their dispositions at any one time, it was also able to give advance warning from Sigint of the deployment of Fliegerkorps X's aircraft from the main concentration in Sicily to other bases in southern Italy, Sardinia, Benina (near Benghazi) and Rhodes. On 21 January C-in-C Mediterranean was advised that 50 He IIIs were arriving at Benina and Rhodes; on 27 January, three days before their first mine-laying raid on the Suez Canal, he was warned that these included mine-laying aircraft.[32] By 26 January it was known that there were 80 long-range and dive-bombers at Benina.[33] The

---

* The source of this warning is not known. As the Y officers in the Mediterranean Fleet were not at this time familiar with GAF W/T procedures, it may have come from Italian intercepts.

28. ADM 223/89, Appendix XI, 10–11 January 1941; Playfair, op cit, Vol I, p 317.
29. CAB 80/25, COS (41) 25 (COS Résumé, No 71).
30. AIR 22/73, Air Ministry Weekly Intelligence Summary, No 71 of 1–8 January; WO 169/19, GS Int GHQ ME, Intelligence Summary of 3 January.
31. CAB 80/25, COS (41) 66 (COS Résumé, No 74), COS (41) 78 (COS Résumé, No 75); AIR 40/2322, Minute of 4 February.
32. ADM 186/801, BR 1736 (49) 2, p 68; AIR 40/2322, Minutes of 19, 21, 26 January, 12 February.
33. AIR 40/2322, p 54.

Sigint evidence was supplemented by other intelligence. The arrival of a PR Spitfire at Malta from No 1 PRU contributed to the effectiveness of the RAF raid on Sicilian bases on 13 January which reduced the scale of the GAF effort against Malta during the period when HMS *Illustrious* was undergoing emergency repairs there.[34] By the middle of March the SIS was providing regular information about GAF activities in the Dodecanese.[35] Of the available sources, however, only one, the low-grade GAF W/T traffic, could have provided good tactical intelligence of GAF raids, and then only if it was exploited locally. As early as 13 January this traffic had enabled Cairo to detect the presence of the GAF in the desert,[36] but during the early months of 1941 it was not possible to provide the necessary organisation and expertise elsewhere in the Middle East. Thus, the attack on the *Illustrious* led to the proposal that she should embark a Y officer in future, but neither officers nor interception sets were available. It was not until much later that RAF personnel qualified to interpret GAF low-grade traffic could be supplied for the Mediterranean Fleet.

□

Despite their knowledge of the arrival of the GAF in Libya, the intelligence authorities were slow to conclude that the German Army would follow. They continued to receive rumours of German troop movements through Italy, of practice embarkations in Sicily, even of the imminent arrival of German troops in Libya, from diplomatic sources, Italian POW and the SIS. One SIS source reported that huge quantities of colonial equipment and stores for warfare in African conditions were being transported southwards and that OKH, though regarding 'the Egyptian campaign' as an adventure, was preparing for it conscientiously. In addition the Poles were sending SIS information from a centre they had organised to report movements on the Italian railways.[37] Air reconnaissance disclosed that by 3 February close on half a million tons of shipping, consisting mostly of ships of 6,000 tons or over, had been concentrated in Naples. In Cairo the intelligence authorities noted this evidence but were far from certain that it pointed to a move by the German Army into Libya: on 26 January DDMI's summary of the situation made no reference to this possibility,[38] and on 8 February GS Int GHQ, ME assessed the position at El Agheila without any reference to German forces.[39] A

---

34. AIR 41/44, p 87.
35. AIR 40/2322, Minute of 31 March.
36. WO 169/19, WRMS of 13 January.
37. WO 169/19, Intelligence Summaries of 10, 20 and 31 January 1941, WRMS of 27 January 1941.
38. WO 169/924, DDMI Appreciation of 26 January 1941.
39. ibid, of 8 February 1941.

similar situation prevailed in Whitehall. On 22 January FOES, which on 9 January had judged that German intervention in Libya was not imminent;* gave a warning that Germany might be preparing to send armour to Libya in addition to providing air support to the Italians;[40] but, partly because they were distracted by the rumour that Germany planned to move into Tunisia,† the intelligence bodies did not repeat this warning before contact was made with the German forces. By 6 February, 2 days before the first convoy of German troops sailed from Naples, MI thought it probable that 2 or 3 German divisions, with armour, were in southern Italy or Sicily and sensed that an expedition of some kind was preparing. But it felt unable to decide whether the move would be against Malta, against Tunisia or into Libya. This was the order in which it listed the possibilities for the Chiefs of Staff in the résumé of 6 February.[41] So great, indeed, was Whitehall's indecision that it absorbed the first reliable indication of the destination of the German expedition with considerable reluctance.

On 9 February an IAF high-grade cypher message contained special instructions for IAF/GAF escort of convoys between Naples and Tripoli. The decrypt of the message was not completely certain, but GC and CS was reasonably sure that the convoys that were being referred to were German. The Whitehall intelligence staffs at first rejected this suggestion. On 12 February the Admiralty passed the information to C-in-C Mediterranean and stressed the unusual and elaborate involvement of the GAF, but it was not until 18 February that it told him that the convoys 'appeared' to be German. Even then it did not connect the decrypt with the abnormal shipping concentration at Naples.[42] There was, it appears, a similar delay before the Air Ministry indicated to HQ RAF, ME that the convoys were transporting German forces.[43] And until at least as late as 15 February AI clearly remained unimpressed by the evidence. On that date a minute reflecting the views of both the German and the Italian sections dwelt on 'the current atmosphere of evacuation' in Tripoli and Germany's 'lack of interest in the Italian African Empire'. An increase in German transport aircraft flights between Italy and Libya had been noted in the past fortnight, but it was thought to be more likely to be associated with the evacuation of treasure and notabilities than with the arrival of reinforcements 'other...than a rear-guard'.[44]

In Whitehall no further appreciations were attempted before news was received from GS Int GHQ, ME that British forces had made

---

* See Chapter 8, p 260.
† See Chapter 8, pp 258–259.

40. CAB 79/8, COS (41) 28th Meeting of 22 January, Annex.
41. CAB 80/25, COS (41) 78 (COS Résumé, No 75).
42. ADM 223/75, Admry signals 1623/12 February and 2203/18 February.
43. AIR 40/2322, Minute of 19 February.
44. ibid, p 61.

contact with German armoured cars at El Agheila,* and that similar vehicles had been sighted by aircraft to the west of that position, on 22 February. German broadcasts to the effect that Germany was reinforcing Tripoli were dismissed as propaganda, and it was not until 27 February that the departments, for the first time since 6 February, drew the attention of the Chiefs of Staff to the fact that reports of the presence of German divisions in southern Italy were still coming in from POW and the SIS. Even then, the COS résumé stressed that there was no confirmation for such of these reports as suggested that the divisions were bound for Libya.[46] The failure to foresee the German move was not, however, complete. By 17 February GS Int GHQ in Cairo had decided that these reports could no longer be discounted, and had concluded that Germany had probably abandoned her plans for a march on Turkey and Syria in favour of an attempt to advance on the Delta from north Africa.[47]

□

That Cairo had been slow to reach this conclusion, and Whitehall even slower, was not of great importance. Even if they had been given longer warning, it seems unlikely that British forces could have done much to prevent the passage of the German convoys: of the total of 220,000 tons of Axis shipping sent to Libya from Italian ports in February and March 1941 as much sailed after as before it was known that it was taking German reinforcements, and yet only 20,000 tons was intercepted.[48] Nor can it be assumed that earlier firm intelligence of the German intention to send forces to Libya would have affected the decision to transfer British troops from north Africa to Greece. The Cabinet had agreed in principle to this transfer on 24 February, before it had learned that German forces in small numbers had been encountered at El Agheila on 22 February. During a further discussion on 27 February – when the Cabinet had learned of this encounter – no one disputed the Prime Minister's refusal to draw pessimistic inferences from it in the absence of any signs of German preparations to advance across the desert.[49] And when the Cabinet eventually confirmed its decision on 7 March, after re-considering it during the first week of March and all but reversing it on 5 and 6 March, it knew something about the size of Rommel's force.†

---

* The first British armoured car to exchange fire with the Germans was that of Lt. E T Williams KDG who later became the senior intelligence staff officer in 8 Army and 21 Army Group.[45]   † See below, p 389.

45. Long, op cit, p 285.
46. CAB 80/26, COS (41) 124 (COS Résumé, No 78).
47. WO 169/19, WRMS of 17 February; WO 169/924, DDMI Minute of 17 February.   48. Playfair, op cit, Vol I, p 369.
49. CAB 65/21, WM (41) 21 CA of 27 February.

Of more significance was the miscalculation of the threat from Rommel's force. The Cabinet confirmed its decision to transfer troops to Greece on the assumption that the British flank in Cyrenaica was reasonably secure. It based this assumption on an appreciation sent by the C-in-C Middle East on 2 March, just before leaving Cairo for Athens to take part in last-minute discussions about the transfer of troops to Greece, in which he discounted the possibility that Rommel would constitute a serious threat before the summer.[50] Largely on account of this appreciation a Cabinet enquiry in April 1941 into the decisions of the previous month came to the conclusion that 'there would probably be some criticism that our Intelligence service had been defective'.[51] Even so, it is far from certain that the Cabinet's decision would have gone the other way if the threat to Cyrenaica had been more correctly assessed. The Cabinet was influenced not only by the C-in-C's appreciation but also by other considerations – the knowledge that against Greece the Germans were preparing an operation larger than any they could attempt in north Africa; and the calculation that there was still time to build up a defence position in Greece before the Germans struck there.*

In his appreciation of 2 March the C-in-C estimated that the Germans might test El Agheila without delay, and possibly push on to Agedabia, but would not try to reach Benghazi until they had landed more motor transport and built up to one infantry division and one, possibly two, armoured brigades. As their present strength was only a brigade group, it was unlikely that they would achieve this before the summer.[52] This estimate of the strength and the rate of build-up of the German contingent was accurate enough, and its accuracy was soon to be confirmed.† The mistake lay in underestimating what Rommel would attempt with a small force, without waiting for the build-up. It was a mistake that had been foreshadowed as early as 17 February in the appreciation in which GS Int GHQ, ME had at last accepted the probability that German troops were being sent to Libya. GS Int had then added that, because the sea-crossing would be a problem for the Germans and because they had no experience of desert warfare, 'a considerable time must elapse before any serious counter-offensive can be launched from Tripoli'.[53]

After the first week of March, when it had played its part in the decision to move British forces from north Africa to Greece, this mistake did not go entirely uncorrected. But Cairo was still surprised by Rommel's offensive. By 10 March GS Int was allowing that the

---

* See Chapter 11, p 363.
† See below, pp 391–392.

50. CAB 105/2, No 67 of 2 March 1941.
51. CAB 65/22, WM (41) 41 CA of 17 April.
52. CAB 105/2, No 67; Playfair, op cit, Vol II, p 10.
53. WO 169/19, WRMS of 17 February 1941.

enemy might risk a thrust beyond Agheila and Agedabia without making meticulous preparations,[54] and by 24 March – the day on which the Germans captured Agheila – it estimated that he could be ready to operate against Cyrenaica in a limited way with one German light and one Italian armoured division by 16 April. But on this second date, in what was its last appreciation before Rommel developed his advance on 31 March, it still thought it unlikely that he would try to retake Benghazi before bringing up armoured and motorised reinforcements, and that this would not be earlier than about mid-May.[55] By 20 March the C-in-C was admitting to some anxiety about the Cyrenaican front where 'growing enemy strength may indicate early forward movement'.[56] He may have been influenced by evidence for the strengthening of the GAF units under Fliegerführer Afrika (the north African sub-command of Fliegerkorps X set up at the beginning of February), which was coming in from the decrypts of the Fliegerführer's strength and serviceability returns during March, and by other GAF Enigma references to reconnaissance of the Agedabia area on 10 March; to the stoppage of leave on 19 March; to an expected increase in the scale of operations, also on 19 March.[57] After the event these were recognised to have been pointers to Rommel's coming attack. But the intelligence authorities did not have the experience to enable them to recognise such signs at the time; in any case no clues to the scale or the objectives of the attack were received. Accordingly the C-in-C felt on 20 March that the enemy's administrative problems 'should preclude anything but a limited advance'.[58] And on 30 March an operational instruction from GOC Cyrenaica Command reported that 'since occupying Agheila the enemy had shown no sign of a further advance' and that 'there is no conclusive evidence that he intends to take the offensive on a large scale'.[59]

Despite some earlier anxiety in MI, Whitehall did not dissent from this conclusion. On 28 February MI thought it unlikely that Germany would adopt a solely defensive role, especially if British forces did not advance to Tripoli; and did not rule out the possibility that Rommel would advance the 300 miles from Tripoli to Cyrenaica and then attempt a pincer movement.[60] On 4 March MI had 'indications' that Germany's strength in the desert might be raised to 2 armoured divisions and thought she would aim at surprise, doing everything she could to overcome the disadvantages of climate and terrain, and launch an attack at the earliest possible moment.[61] But within the JIC

---

54. ibid, WRMS of 10 March 1941.
55. WO 169/924, DDMI Appreciation of 24 March 1941.
56. CAB 105/2, No 131 of 20 March.
57. CX/JQ 744, 771, 773, 777.
58. CAB 105/2, No 131 of 20 March.
59. Playfair, op cit, Vol II, p 12.
60. WO 190/893, No 23A of 28 February.
61. ibid, 'Results of WO Intelligence' of 25 April 1941, para 2f (iii).

organisation this appreciation of the situation was not accepted:[62] and on 5 March the JIC itself felt that the German troops needed time to acclimatise themselves.[63] On 20 March MI pointed out that the Germans could now operate against Tunisia and mentioned indications that they were possibly preparing some sea-borne expedition from Tripolitania, but now had nothing to say about their preparations for an eastward advance.[64] The Chiefs of Staff résumés throughout March reported German troop movements east of Tripoli but refrained from guessing at what lay behind them. As for the Chiefs of Staff themselves, the CIGS agreed with Wavell that maintenance and other administrative difficulties would be a disadvantage to the enemy in any attack he might make.[65]

In the event Rommel's attack was made at about the strength that had been allowed for, and it was indeed brought to a halt by administrative difficulties. But his capability to go on to the offensive in Cyrenaica was thus under-estimated by a fortnight and the estimate of his ability to carry the offensive forward was still more seriously at fault for judging that he would not attempt to reach Benghazi with the limited forces at his disposal. The under-estimates owed something to the fact that as yet Rommel remained an unknown quantity; and they are understandable in the light of the state of intelligence at the time. As GC and CS was still unable to read the German Army Enigma – until September 1941 this was not broken extensively and it was not read regularly before April 1942 – the intelligence authorities depended on the GAF general Enigma for their most reliable information on German Army movements. Nor were they greatly inconvenienced by the fact that from the beginning of January 1941 the GAF had introduced a new variant or off-shoot of the general GAF Enigma for Fliegerkorps X and for Fliegerführer Afrika when this was established in February. On 28 February GC and CS overcame this set-back by breaking the new variant (called the Light Blue); and from then until 31 December 1941, when it went out of use, its daily change of cypher was solved within twenty-four hours. As was invariably the case when the GAF was engaged in operations with the Army, the new traffic carried Army intelligence. By 3 March it had revealed the extent of the German Army and Air Force contingents in Libya, established the location of their advanced elements, identified Rommel as GOC of the Africa Corps and, by referring to a sixth, seventh and eighth convoy, thrown some light on the Army build-up that was contemplated. Although some confusion still persisted as to whether Rommel had only parts or the whole of 5 Light Division, and as to whether or not he also had other units from 3 Panzer Division

---

62. ibid, paragraph 3b.
63. JIC (41) 90 of 5 March.
64. WO 190/893, No 30A of 20 March 1941.
65. Playfair, op cit, Vol II, p 6.

from which it had been lifted, the British authorities had a good idea of the strength of the Africa Corps well before he began his attack.[66] Nor was this information confined to Whitehall. Until 13 March, together with summaries of high-grade Italian Sigint, the gist of it went out to Cairo by Telex via the Air Ministry, and from 13 March a new type of signals service was at last inaugurated to carry Sigint decrypts direct from GC and CS to the CBME.* But while it was an invaluable supplement to the information Cairo was getting from air recon- naissance, the Enigma traffic, as we have seen, carried no indications of the scale of attack that Rommel might deliver.

This would not have been surprising in the best of circumstances; and for the British the circumstances were not favourable. In the first place, either from wishful thinking or from unfamiliarity with the material, operational authorities in Cairo under-rated the value of the Enigma evidence. As late as 27 March the C-in-C supported his earlier assessment that there was no real danger of a counter-offensive before May, when he expected to receive reinforcements, with the argument that the enemy's advanced forces were mainly Italian and that the Germans were a 'small stiffening' whose numbers were 'probably much exaggerated'[67] – and this despite the fact that his GS Int had warned on 17 March that the Germans amounted to the best part of a light division or 'a rather lesser proportion of a normal armoured division'.[68] This first difficulty was compounded by another. The Enigma revealed on 13 March that Rommel was going to Berlin but was silent on the purpose and the outcome of his visit.[69] As it happened, its purpose was to get approval for an offensive in May, and reinforcements for it over and above the 15 Panzer Division already promised him, and its outcome was that he was refused additional forces and instructed to act cautiously on account of administrative difficulties: on 21 March he was ordered to confine himself to defending Tripolitania until mid-May and then, 15 Panzer Division having arrived, to do no more than take Agedabia as a jumping-off point for an advance into Cyrenaica. In Berlin the estimate of the possibilities was thus much the same as that made by C-in-C Middle East. But on his return Rommel saw things differently. After taking El Agheila on 24 March, he decided on another limited thrust on 30 March and then, contrary to his instructions and against Italian protests, took advantage of the weakness of the British front to develop a full-scale offensive.

□

* See Appendix 13.

66. CX/JQ 712, 725, 733, 748, 753, 776, 791, 792, 813; WO 169/19, Intelligence Summary of 9 March, WRMS of 3, 10, 17, 24 and 31 March 1941.
67. Playfair, op cit, Vol II, p 12.
68. WO 169/19, WRMS of 17 March 1941.
69. ibid of 24 March.

Rommel's advance reached Agedabia on 2 April, Benghazi on 4 April, Derna on 7 April, and after by-passing Tobruk on 10 April it had taken him by the middle of the month to defensive positions in the Bardia-Sollum-Sidi Omar area: on 26 April he captured the Halfaya Pass. During this advance British intelligence was scarcely more successful in influencing the fighting than it had been in foreseeing it. Nor had it provided before the advance any warning of the superiority of Germany's equipment, the extent of which was now discovered for the first time.

At the tactical level intelligence was, indeed, virtually non-existent. The British forces were too weak to mount extensive patrols; moreover, their armoured cars were outgunned by Rommel's.[70] Though there was later to be much controversy on the point, the Army was dissatisfied with the reliability of the RAF's reconnaissance.[71] The Sigint unit at Western Desert HQ, which had performed so well during the earlier fighting, was now handicapped by the fact that the Italians had tightened up their communications security and in any case rarely referred to German movements. More serious still, the unit was untrained in the interception and exploitation of German W/T traffic. It took in some plain language traffic and some traffic in the GAF's daily-changing operational code – for there was still no forward RAF unit at this stage – but could do little with it. It intercepted for the first time the German Army's signals in a medium-grade code that was later to be a valuable source; but no systematic study of this was undertaken until June 1941. There was a similar delay before it undertook regular traffic analysis on the increasing amount of German W/T. In all these respects the British performance contrasted badly with that of Rommel's forces. From the time of their arrival in north Africa the Germans made excellent use of reconnaissance patrols, both on the ground and in the air, and their Sigint unit produced valuable intelligence. Before beginning his advance Rommel learned from Sigint of British withdrawals and weaknesses south-west of Agedabia; during the advance Sigint supplemented his air reconnaissance with a steady flow of information, especially from the interception of the British R/T traffic.[72]

British deficiencies in field intelligence could not be off-set by the fact that the GAF Enigma was being read in the United Kingdom. Until the middle of April this traffic contained little of value about the enemy's intentions, and the number of items sent out on the new direct service from GC and CS to Cairo averaged less than one a day.* Thereafter the traffic began to carry an increasing amount of tactical intelligence, including the daily intentions of Fliegerführer Afrika,

---

* See above, p 392, and Appendix 13.

70. Playfair, op cit, Vol II, p 11.
71. AIR 41/44, p 113 et seq.
72. Playfair, op cit, Vol II, pp 16, 25, 27, 169.

reports on the effectiveness of RAF raids, statements of the German supply situation and, particularly when they ran out of fuel and rations, reports of the locations and movements of the German and Italian ground forces.[73] But the British forces were rarely in a position to make operational use of this information. To make matters worse, the GC and CS messages went only to Cairo until August; in Cairo they were seen only by a restricted number of individuals at the Service HQs; and delay in forwarding the information from Cairo to the commands was increased by a further problem – the need to adopt tight precautions in view of the extent to which, as the Enigma revealed, the Germans were reading the British field codes and cyphers. Nor were these the only difficulties. At GC and CS the staff who selected the Enigma material for transmission to Cairo were still learning their trade and their inexperience in recognising what would be of immediate significance to an army engaged in operations sometimes led them to withhold information of great importance. On 8 April, for example, they failed to advise Cairo that the Germans were anxious to learn whether Tobruk was being reinforced or evacuated.*

It was not only the forwarding of tactical intelligence that suffered from GC and CS's inexperience and from the haste with which it had to work. On 2 April GC and CS informed Cairo that elements of 15 Panzer Division were moving from Trapani to Palermo, probably bound for Tripoli. But it failed to add that it knew that an advanced detachment of this division was already in Tripoli or that the date for the onward movement from Palermo had not yet been fixed; and it omitted to send a further signal when it learned that embarkation at Palermo could not be before 9 April.† It also failed to report when it learned, on the other hand, that other reinforcements promised to Rommel were cancelled after the beginning of the German campaign against Greece. Defects in the service to Cairo also arose from the fact that the German signals or the British intercepts of them were sometimes corrupt – so that false reports of the presence of 5 Panzer Division in north Africa were not corrected until June – and from the need to take the security precaution of paraphrasing the original German signals. When all this has been said, however, the Enigma traffic was still invaluable for its strategic information, if not on the tactical level, and it was so from an early stage in the German advance.

---

* There was an alarm over the security of the Enigma in connection with the German interest in Tobruk in the spring of 1941, as a result of which special procedures for the handling of decrypts were introduced. A similar alarm, this time connected with Rommel's illness on the eve of Alam Halfa, led to the reintroduction of these procedures in August 1941 – see Volume Two.

† But the Admiralty rectified this omission in a signal to C-in-C Mediterranean, and may have done so by arrangement with GC and CS to avoid delay in Cairo. See further below, p 395.

73. ibid, pp 26–27, 30, 35; eg CX/JQ 814, 829, 834, 881.

As early as 2 April it revealed that, because operations elsewhere had higher priority, Fliegerführer Afrika was being denied reinforcements. On 5 April it produced proof that in pushing on beyond Agedabia Rommel was flouting his instructions.[74] This evidence enabled the JIC to report that Rommel was exploiting his early successes by launching an improvised offensive, and that he was not under orders to conquer Egypt. More to the point it enabled the Prime Minister to press this conclusion on the C-in-C Middle East at a time when Wavell thought Rommel's objective was Egypt.[75] By 7 April the C-in-C had ceased to expect a large-scale attack on Egypt and on 10 April he accordingly made arrangements for holding Tobruk and for positioning his forces in the Bardia-Sollum area.[76] On 14 April the Enigma reported that the bulk of the German forces were taking up defensive positions in the Sollum-Sidi Omar sector and that Fliegerfuehrer Afrika was still pressing for fighter reinforcements. In signals intercepted on 26 April he was told that his forces were adequate for their allotted task, and this task was re-defined: the GAF in Libya was switched from close support of Rommel to attacks on British shipping off Tobruk and the defence of Axis shipping at Benghazi.[77] From the middle of the month the Enigma had carried frequent reports from Fliegerführer Afrika about his fuel shortage and on 28 April it revealed that the GAF in the forward area of Tobruk-Bardia was 'seriously impeded by casualties and non-replacements'.[78]

By that date the Enigma information reaching Cairo had been supplemented by captured documents and intelligence from POW which made it clear that the German advance had been hastily improvised.[79] Even so, far less was known about Rommel's supply difficulties than about the GAF's, and little had been learned about his plans and his losses – largely, no doubt, because GC and CS was not reading the Army Enigma. In addition, although it was beginning to look as if he had temporarily been fought to a standstill, particularly after the failure of his assault on Tobruk at the beginning of May, great uncertainty still prevailed about the timetable for his armoured reinforcements. At GC and CS, and in its forwarding of intelligence to Cairo, there had initially been some confusion on this score. There must have been further confusion at Cairo: on 18 April despite the fact that several references to the movement of 15 Panzer Division had by then been sent to Cairo, the C-in-C Middle East was

---

74. CX/JQ 829.
75. CAB 105/3, No 28 of 2 April and No 36 of 3 April 1941; JIC (41) 137 of 5 April.
76. CAB 105/3, No 70 of 7 April and No 84 of 10 April.
77. CX/JQ 814, 895, 899.
78. OLs 90, 92, 96, 108.
79. CAB 105/3, No 201 of 25 April 1941.

appalled to learn that the division then disembarking at Tripoli was a Panzer division, which must be expected to have 400 tanks.[80] Thereafter the situation was not fully cleared up. On 27 April the C-in-C had estimated from a variety of intelligence sources – air reconnaissance, captured documents, POW and the Enigma – that 15 Panzer Division had completed its disembarkation at Tripoli by 21 April, and could all be at Tobruk by 8 May, but he had calculated that an enemy force of 4 divisions (5 Light, 15 Panzer and 2 Italian) would be unable to move further forward before mid-June on account of supply difficulties – though he had added that he could not be confident that the Germans would not once again attempt more than he expected.[81] By the end of the month the Enigma had disclosed that elements of 15 Panzer Division were still arriving – in fact, though this was not known at the time, the attack by British destroyers on the convoys on 16 April* had delayed its timetable and its transfer was not due to be completed until mid-May[82] – but on 3 May the JIC judged that the C-in-C was overstating the enemy's transport and supply problems and overlooking 'certain indications' that Rommel would try to break the British defences with a smaller mobile force in May.[83] It was this view, at a time when there was unmistakable evidence that 15 Panzer Division was arriving but when uncertainty about its time-table had not yet been cleared up, which persuaded the Chiefs of Staff to take the risk of sending the *Tiger* convoy with armour reinforcements for Wavell through the Mediterranean to Alexandria.[84]

At this juncture the GAF Enigma illuminated the military situation. As the British were to learn only after the event, Rommel, whose objective on 10 April had indeed been Egypt, was asking in the last week of April for ground reinforcements to be sent by air, for GAF reinforcements and for the deployment of U-boats on the coast between Sollum and Tobruk, these measures being essential if he was to avoid the loss of Sollum and Bardia and the abandonment of the chance to take Tobruk, and OKH was becoming alarmed. On 27 April it sent General Paulus to Libya to discover Rommel's intentions and to make him understand what very limited resources there were with which to help him. Paulus's first step was to refuse to sanction the assault on Tobruk, which Rommel had planned for 30 April, until he had studied the situation.[85] This too the British were to learn only after the event. But on 2 May, when the attack on Tobruk had failed, Paulus

---

* See below, p 400.

80. ibid, No 140 of 18 April.
81. ibid, No 219 of 27 April and No 224 of 28 April.
82. CX/JQ 903; Enemy Documents Section Appreciation/9, p 39 fn 1.
83. JIC (41) 191 of 3 May.
84. Churchill, op cit, Vol III, pp 218–220.
85. EDS Appreciation/9, pp 32, 34, 41.

gave Rommel new instructions, and these were transmitted in full to Berlin in the GAF Enigma. The main task of the Africa Corps was to retain Cyrenaica with or without Tobruk, Sollum and Bardia. This task was not to be endangered by fighting round Tobruk. Given the 'thoroughly exhausted' condition of the troops the emphasis must be placed on re-organisation, the creation of mobile reserves and the establishment of a secure basis of supply. Further attacks on Tobruk, even on a small scale, were forbidden unless quick success without substantial losses could be expected. Except for reconnaissance, there was to be no advance beyond Sollum without OKH permission until the whole of 15 Panzer Division had arrived; at that point a decision must depend on the circumstances.[86]

Whitehall and Cairo had this intelligence at their disposal by 4 May.[87] In Whitehall it constituted only one element in the assessment of the strategic situation. In the second half of May a Chiefs of Staff strategic review ruled out a German attempt to advance on Egypt, but it had other reasons for doing so: so ambitious an offensive would involve an air commitment on a scale that would handicap the plan for an invasion of Britain, which the Chiefs of Staff still believed to be Germany's over-riding aim for 1941.*[88] On 30 May, when the JIC forecast that the German effort in Libya would be limited to what could be done with the forces already there, it was also influenced by the scale of the German build-up against Russia.†[89] On the operational level in Cairo the information was not unnaturally of greater significance. It directly influenced the character and the planning of operation *Brevity*, the first main counter-attack against the German positions at Halfaya, Sollum and Capuzzo which Wavell delivered between 15 and 17 May.[90] Plans for some operation, to take advantage of Rommel's difficulties after his failure at Tobruk and before 15 Panzer Division could reach the front, were in any case being made, but it was because he had received the full text of Paulus's instructions and the information that 15 Panzer Division had not yet arrived in full strength that the C-in-C committed all his available tanks to the attack despite the fact that the *Tiger* reinforcements had not yet arrived in Alexandria.[91]

As early as 6 May the intelligence that the German troops were exhausted and required time for rest and re-organisation had been passed to the commander of the *Brevity* forces.[92] On 16 May Cairo

---

* See Chapter 14, p 467.   † See Chapter 14, p 470 et seq.

86. CX/JQ 914.
87. CAB 105/4, Hist (B) 4, No 29 of 4 May and No 33 of 5 May 1941.
88. CAB 80/57, COS (41) 82 (0) of 27 May.
89. JIC (41) 229 of 30 May.
90. WO 169/1240, Western Desert HQ War Diary, 6 May 1941.
91. Churchill, op cit, Vol III, pp 288–300. See also CAB 105/4, No 50 of 7 May and No 62 of 9 May 1941.
92. WO 169/1240, Western Desert HQ War Diary, 6 May 1941.

learned from GC and CS that after the *Brevity* attack on the previous day the German situation at Sollum and Capuzzo was critical, ruling out the concentration of reserves and any counter-attacks, and that the Germans could not expect air support before 17 May. On 17 May it knew that Rommel had applied for help to Luftflotte 4, over the head of Fliegerführer Afrika, in an attempt to prevent a similar situation developing at Bardia.[93] But despite this excellent intelligence, and however narrow the margin, the attempt to defeat Rommel before he had been reinforced had come to nothing – except for the temporary reoccupation of the Halfaya Pass – by 18 May when the Enigma disclosed that Rommel hoped that the British forces might withdraw from Sollum to Mersa Matruh.[94]

One reason for the failure, the most important indeed, was the technical superiority of the German equipment, particularly armour and anti-tank guns. British intelligence had given no warning of this, and its extent was revealed for the first time during the British counter-attack.* At the same time, intelligence performed poorly during the fighting. Although the GAF Enigma contained much tactical information, it was often out of date by the time it was read at GC and CS. When it was sent out to the Middle East there was the same difficulty as before in getting the intelligence from Cairo to the British forces, a difficulty which can easily be appreciated if it is remembered that the British commanders were sometimes as much out of touch with the whereabouts and movements of their own forces as with those of the enemy.[95] More serious still – for even when, later on, these delays had been reduced, the Enigma would still be more valuable for what it said about order of battle and supply than for tactical battle intelligence – the British inferiority in field intelligence was as marked before and during the battle as it had been during the retreat.

Rommel's field intelligence intercepted the British signals and alerted him to the coming attack.[96] For their part, on the other hand, the British commanders failed to detect Rommel's success in bringing forward in good time a large part of his reserve armour. From air reconnaissance, including PR, they knew before the attack that Rommel had between 30 and 50 tanks in the Sollum-Capuzzo-Halfaya area and that the bulk of his armour lay at Tobruk, 70 miles to the rear, and they expected to have a tank superiority of two to one in the battle area. In the event, despite Rommel's grave fuel problems, they encountered rather more armour than they had themselves, and neither air reconnaissance nor any other source had betrayed the

---

* See Volume Two.

93. CX/JQ 958; OL 338 of 16 May and OL 352 of 17 May 1941.
94. OL 376 of 19 May.
95. Playfair, op cit, Vol II, pp 28, 155.
96. ibid, p 161; AIR 41/44, p 159.

movement forward of the enemy tanks.[97] Intelligence also failed during the operations which led to Rommel's recapture of the Halfaya Pass on 27 May – operations which began as bluff but which developed into a serious attack in greatly superior strength.[98]

A month later the second British counter-attack (operation *Battle-axe*), launched as soon as possible after the arrival of the *Tiger* reinforcements, had failed for the same reasons. As the C-in-C had feared in advance,[99] it was once again handicapped by its inferior equipment; the German tanks and armoured cars turned out to be too much, in performance as in numbers, for the British. Once again Rommel was well served by his field intelligence. As a result of intercepting British signals, he was expecting the attack on the day it was delivered, and he was supplied with good information from W/T and captured documents throughout the battle.[100] And once again British field intelligence was weak, both before and during the battle. Before the counter-attack began, it was known that Rommel was strengthening his defences; air reconnaissance had found no signs that he had received any important reinforcements during the past month; and the GAF Enigma, with its full information on the GAF order of battle, had established not only that there had been no increase in the GAF's strength in Libya, but also that its strength in Sicily had been drastically reduced by withdrawals to other theatres.[101] It was thus not difficult to rule out a German advance. But the evidence about the number and disposition of Rommel's tanks was unsatisfactory and the Army was again complaining that air reconnaissance and PR were inadequate.[102] How inadequate – and how defective – were all other sources of intelligence, including tactical reconnaissance by the British armoured car patrols, which were handicapped by air attacks and out-gunned and out-paced by the heavier German cars,[103] was revealed when the fighting began.[104] The British forces had counted on meeting 100 German tanks. They were met by more than twice that number, Rommel having once again brought up practically all his reserves from the Tobruk area at the right time without revealing their movement. In these circumstances it mattered little that the general lines of Rommel's counter-attack had been judged correctly: the British forces did not have strength enough to meet it.[105]

□

---

97. Playfair, op cit, Vol II, pp 159–161; AIR 41/44, p 159; Churchill, op cit, Vol III, p 305.

98. Playfair, op cit, Vol II, p 163; CAB 105/4, No 230 of 27 May 1941. See also EDS Appreciation/9, pp 56–60.   99. Playfair, op cit, Vol II, p 167.

100. ibid, pp 168–169; EDS Appreciation/9, pp 63–64, 68, 70–71, 73.

101. Playfair, op cit, Vol II, pp 163, 166; CAB 80/28, COS (41) 337 (COS Résumé, No 91), COS (41) 357 (COS Résumé, No 92), COS (41) 370 (COS Résumé, No 93).

102. AIR 41/44, p 165.   103. Playfair, op cit, Vol II, p 167.

104. AIR 41/44, p 173 et seq.

105. CAB 105/5, Hist (B) 5, No 234 and No 235 of 18 June 1941.

Up to the beginning of Rommel's advance into Cyrenaica the British had had little success in disrupting Axis supplies and reinforcements to north Africa. After the beginning of the advance, operations against the supply routes were stepped-up, and on 14 April the Prime Minister ordered that the highest priority should be given to them.[106] And whereas 10 Axis merchant ships had been sunk en route to Libya during the first three months of 1941, 8 of them by submarine, 21 were sunk during April and May – 8 by submarine and 9 by surface ships operating from Malta.[107] But this improvement was insufficient to bring about any serious damage to the enemy's supply position.

That more could not be done was due in the main to operational limitations. The RAF did something to interrupt work in the ports of Tripoli and Benghazi and the coastal shipping in the enemy's forward area, but it was unable to mount an effective attack against his trans-Mediterranean shipping because it could keep only a small striking force at Malta, where reconnaissance aircraft were also in short supply. The Navy's increased attack on that shipping followed from the decision of C-in-C Mediterranean to base 4 destroyers at Malta from 11 April. During May, however, while it became possible to increase the PR aircraft and the air striking force at Malta, the destroyers had to be withdrawn. At the same time, there was still a dearth of advance intelligence of operational value about enemy shipping – a dearth which is emphasised by the fact that it was exceptionally, as a result of a single item of Sigint, that the destroyers were moved to Malta by 11 April and were successful on 16 April in wiping out an entire convoy (5 merchant ships and 3 escorting Italian destroyers) that was carrying units of 15 Panzer Division to Africa.

The decision to base the destroyers at Malta was taken on 8 April in direct response to an Ultra signal from the Admiralty informing the C-in-C on the morning of 7 April that 'advanced elements of German 15th armoured division were embarking at Palermo on or after 9 April probably for Tripoli'.[108] To the same item of intelligence, if only indirectly, the destroyers owed their success against the convoy on 16 April, the only spectacular success at this time apart from the sinking on 24 May by submarine of the Italian liner *Conte Rosso* with 1,500 Italian troops on board. On the arrival of the destroyers, Malta intensified its air reconnaissance; one enemy convoy was sighted on 11 April, another on 12 April, and on both of these occasions the destroyers sailed to intercept but without success; but on 16 April they were guided to the convoy by a third sighting by reconnaissance aircraft.[109]

---

106. Roskill, op cit, Vol I, p 431.

107. Playfair, op cit, Vol II, pp 53–54, 58.

108. ADM 233/76, Admiralty to C-in-C Mediterranean, 0941/7 April 1941, C-in-C Med to Admiralty, 1506/8 April.

109. ADM 186/801, p 90; Playfair, op cit, Vol II, p 54.

As yet, however, it was rarely the case that air and naval reconnaissance and PR benefited in this way from Sigint. The Italian naval
cyphers were not being read, nor was there any German naval Sigint
for the Mediterranean area. From the middle of April the GAF
Enigma left no doubt that Rommel's advance had produced an acute
shortage of fuel and transport in north Africa. It showed, too, that
the enemy was making desperate attempts to overcome the shortage
by developing shipping on the coastal route from Tripoli to the front
and by flying especially urgent replenishments across the Mediterranean. But when the bulk of his supplies were going by sea – convoys
were leaving Naples for Tripoli every three or four days between
March and the middle of May, and there were individual sailings from
Palermo and Trapani – the GAF Enigma contained only occasional
convoy escort instructions from Fliegerkorps X. And although these
were passed to Cairo from GC and CS, or to the C-in-C Mediterranean
from the Admiralty,[110] they could rarely be forwarded to the naval and
RAF commands in time for them to act on them until the Sigint service
from GC and CS to the Mediterranean was overhauled and extended
in the autumn.* In these directions, as in British Army field
intelligence, things were to improve before the fighting in north Africa
was resumed; but none of the advances had been made by the end
of June.

---

* See Appendix 13.

110. ADM 233/76, Admry signals 1229/17 April, 2315/18 April.

CHAPTER 13

The Operations in Greece, Iraq, Crete and Syria

WHAT TURNED out to be the opening blows in the battles for Greece and Crete were exchanged at sea, on the day after the coup in Belgrade, in the battle of Matapan. Matapan eliminated the danger of attacks by the Italian surface fleet on the convoys that were taking British troops from Egypt to Greece, and it was later to have further important consequences.

By the middle of March the Germans were pressing the Italian Admiralty to strike against the British convoys. Quite apart from the fact that Axis air attacks on them were having little effect, the build-up for the German attack on Greece was in its final stage and a resounding naval victory would send the offensive off to a good start. Moreover, Rommel was demanding that the Italian Navy should help him by reducing the threat to his supply routes. By 20 March the Italians had agreed in principle to meet the German request. They were influenced by the fact that for the first time since the raid on Taranto as many as three of their battleships were operational, by the German promise that Fliegerkorps X would provide reconnaissance and escort, and by German claims to have scored torpedo hits on two British battleships and reduced to one the operational battleships of the Mediterranean Fleet. On 25 March, the day after the Mediterranean Fleet had returned to Alexandria after covering the year's second Malta convoy, they fixed 28 March as the date for the attack. On 26 March the Italian Fleet sailed for its first large-scale offensive of the war. It was to be the last of any importance.

Hitherto, while Italy continued to be well-informed about British movements, British intelligence about Italian naval movements had undergone little or no improvement and, as in the first few months after Italy's entry into the war, the British forces had had to make do with inadequate air reconnaissance and chance sightings.* In July 1940, when the cruiser *Colleoni* was sunk during an early and smaller attempt to raid shipping in the Aegean, a chance sighting by a British destroyer had provided the first evidence that she was at sea.[1] In November 1940 the Fleet Air Arm attack on the Italian Fleet at Taranto forestalled a movement to bombard Suda, but of this intention the British had no advance information.[2] During Force H's

---

* See Chapter 6, p 206 et seq.

1. ADM 186/800, p 53.   2. ADM 186/801, p 10.

bombardment of Genoa in February 1941 intelligence failed to disclose that the Italian Fleet had left Spezia and passed close to the British ships.[3] No warning was received, again, of the raid carried out by Italian explosive motor boats in Suda Bay on 26 March 1941, when they sank HMS *York*.[4] But before this last attack was made the British already suspected that some larger undertaking was being planned.

Their suspicions had been aroused not by the recognition that Axis air reconnaissance in the eastern Mediterranean was taking place on an unusual scale,[5] but by indications from the GAF Enigma that the Axis powers might be planning a landing on the Libyan coast for the end of March.[6] It soon turned out that these indications referred only to coastal supply operations, but C-in-C Mediterranean, who had been prompted by this intelligence to hold his ships at short notice for steam since their return to port on 24 March, was kept on the alert by the receipt on 25 March of further information. First, the GAF Enigma disclosed that all German twin-engined fighters from Libya had been ordered on the previous day to move to Palermo 'for special operations'. There was no clue as to the nature of these operations, but the German evidence was quickly followed by the decryption of an Italian message announcing that 25 March was D minus 3 for an operation involving the Rhodes Command. This message was transmitted in the Italian naval Enigma, which the Italians used only infrequently.* On 26 March further messages in the same cypher provided additional details. They showed that air reconnaissance and attacks on airfields in the Aegean had been ordered for two days before and on the day of a certain operation; that there had been requests for information about the British convoys between Alexandria and Greece; and that provision was being made to neutralise British air cover. The C-in-C Mediterranean received these decrypts, together with the Admiralty's appreciation that they pointed to the likelihood of a thrust into the Aegean or the eastern Mediterranean, in the forenoon of 26 March.[7] Early that afternoon the Admiralty was able to confirm what had so far remained uncertain – that the Italian Enigma messages of 25 and 26 March referred to the same set of operations.[8]

On the strength of this evidence the C-in-C took action during the evening of 26 March. He cancelled a southbound convoy that was due to leave the Piraeus, arranged that a convoy bound for the Piraeus should reverse course only at nightfall, in order to avoid arousing

---

* See Chapter 6, p 210.

3. ADM 186/797, p 30.
4. ADM 186/800, p 77.
5. Cunningham, op cit, p 325; Playfair, op cit, Vol II, p 61.
6. CX/JQ 791 of 25 March 1941; ADM 223/88, p 310.
7. ADM 223/88, pp 310, 314.
8. ibid, p 311.

Italian suspicions, and ordered a cruiser force that was already at sea (Force B) to be south of Crete at dawn on 28 March. He himself planned to sail with the 1st Battle Squadron and the *Formidable* after dark on 27 March. As yet he was uncertain whether the enemy intended a surface raid or a large-scale air attack on the convoys.[9] Soon after midnight on 26–27 March the Admiralty threw some doubt on its earlier appreciation by informing him that, as some of the Italian Enigma messages had been signed by a War Office official, the impending operation might be a landing operation.[10] But uncertainty was brought to an end at 1230 on 27 March when a flying-boat from Malta sighted 3 Italian cruisers and a destroyer about 75 miles east of Sicily steering towards Crete.[11]

The C-in-C sailed after dark that day, as previously planned.* Because the Fleet's chances of intercepting Italian movements depended on not arousing Italian suspicions as well as on having tolerably good evidence that their ships were at sea, the C-in-C was still sceptical that he would meet the enemy – he bet his Staff Operations Officer that there would be no encounter – but he personally took an additional precaution before sailing. Knowing that the Japanese Consul General at Alexandria regularly reported on the movements of the Fleet, and as regularly played an afternoon round of golf, he visited the club house with his clubs and an overnight bag, and let himself be sighted.[13] Whether the ruse was effective is not known, but later GC and CS decyphered the Italian estimate that 3 battleships and one aircraft carrier were still in Alexandria at 1900 on 27 March.[14]

The battle of Matapan followed on 28 March. It was the first important operation in the Mediterranean to be based on Sigint. It is true that no further Sigint came to hand after the Italian ships had been encountered on 27 March and that the battle manoeuvres were decided on the strength of sightings, those provided by HMS *Warspite's* Walrus reconnaissance aircraft being especially valuable.[15] But without the advance information provided by Sigint the presence at sea of the Italian forces would not have been suspected in time and the Mediterranean Fleet would not have been in a position to avert the probable destruction of at least one of the two important convoys at sea in the threatened area.[16] As it was, this information enabled the

---

* The conclusion that he decided to sail only after receiving the aircraft sighting of 1230 on 27 March is incorrect.[12]

9. ibid, pp 311, 315, 318; Cunningham, op cit, pp 325–326.
10. ADM 223/88, p 317.
11. Playfair op cit, Vol II, p 62.
12. Roskill, op cit, Vol I, p 428; ADM 186/795, BR 1736 (35), p 4.
13. Cunningham, op cit, pp 325–326.
14. ADM 233/88, p 312.
15. Playfair, op cit, Vol II, p 65.
16. ADM 223/88, pp 307, 309; Cunningham, op cit, p 327.

Fleet not only to prevent a heavy loss of shipping and a serious disturbance to British plans, but also to destroy 3 Italian cruisers and 2 destroyers and, with its naval aircraft, to torpedo the flagship, *Vittorio Veneto* – a fact which was confirmed by POW intelligence soon after the battle.*[17] These, moreover, were only the immediate results. In the longer term the severe handling received by the Italian Navy consolidated British control of the eastern Mediterranean and ensured that during their evacuation from Greece and Crete, although they suffered severely from air attack, the British forces were safe from the surface attack to which they would otherwise have been highly vulnerable.

□

It is difficult to reconstruct precisely what intelligence contributed to the British forces during the campaign in Greece which followed the German attack on 6 April. In general, however, the imperfect records bear out the following conclusions. Despite some improvements, sufficient to avoid serious errors, field intelligence was of little assistance. Despite continuing difficulties, the high-grade Sigint sent out from the United Kingdom was, in contrast, of enormous value for its effect in reducing the scale of the calamity.

Such tactical intelligence as was available was well used. This is suggested by the fact that the Australian official history, so critical of British field intelligence during the north African campaign against the Italians, makes no criticism of its performance during the fighting in Greece – and indeed gives some examples of information reaching the field commanders in time to help their decisions.[19] Equally clearly, the amount of information was severely restricted. Although there was a little air reconnaissance, and although arrangements were made for the interrogation of prisoners in Athens and further forward, the chief source was direct observation by the British and Greek forces – and it was not long before the Greek air observer system broke down and the GAF was able to make many attacks without warning.[20] There was still no photographic reconnaissance and field Y was still unable to make a valuable contribution.

---

* Errors in the use of intelligence by the Italian C-in-C played an important part. He received a good deal of accurate Sigint, both shore-based and from his ships. But having been initially misled by the faulty German reports of damage to two British battleships, and by the assumption that most of the British Fleet was still at Alexandria, he ignored an accurate aircraft sighting report and DF evidence which should have warned him of the proximity of the main British force. He thus judged it safe to send the cruisers *Zara* and *Fiume* with several destroyers to help the cruiser *Pola*, disabled by torpedo attack, when this was far from being the case.[18]

17. AIR 22/74, Air Ministry Weekly Intelligence Summary No 84 to 9 April 1941.
18. ADM 186/795, p 60; Playfair, op cit, Vol II, p 69.
19. Long, op cit, Vol II, 'Greece, Crete and Syria', (1953), pp 57, 80, 115.
20. Richards, op cit, Vol I, p 297.

The British field Y unit in Greece was the first fully mobile B-type (Corps HQ) unit to reach the Middle East. Arriving in Egypt in January 1941, its staff had been intended to deal mainly with Italian low-grade cyphers. But the unit had operated in France and Belgium in 1940 and most of its staff knew German as well as Italian. As they were equipped with copies of GAF codes and of the GAF bomber grid, they were able to exploit GAF tactical traffic and German plain language transmissions encountered in Greece. But GC and CS had as yet made no progress with the German Army field cyphers for lack of traffic, and partly for this reason – and partly because the unit had to be constantly on the move during the retreat – the service it provided was of little operational value.

Field intelligence might have played a more important role if the main British and German forces had come to grips with each other. That they did not do so was due at least in part to the value to the British forces during their retreat of the higher-level intelligence sent from London to General Wilson's HQ and to the forward HQs. It was during the Greek campaign that comprehensive appreciations based on the GAF Enigma decrypts were transmitted to the commanders in the field for the first time in the war, and that the commanders were told of the source and the reliability of the information. The service which had been opened to Cairo on 13 March* was extended to GHQ Greece and HQ BAF Greece by 27 March. Once the fighting had begun, those at GC and CS who were responsible for selecting the intelligence transmitted on the service became less inhibited in what they sent out. They still withheld some items that should have gone, but it was probably a fault on the right side that they lowered their security precautions only gradually.[21] The GAF Enigma was being read currently, each day's being broken within 24 hours except on one day, and they were understandably anxious lest the commanders should make operational use of it without adequate cover in messages that might be read by the Germans. Even so, the Enigma traffic, as well as providing London with its main information about the course of the fighting during the first week of the campaign, went out to Athens in the form of regular comprehensive appreciations based on the more important items – chiefly reports from GAF liaison officers giving information about division and corps identifications and locations and sufficient notice of intentions to keep the GAF informed of the German Army's tactical plans.[22]

Between 7 and 15 April similar appreciations were sent on the GC

---

* See Appendix 13.

21. AIR 40/2323, paras 6, 39.
22. AIR 40/2323, paras 1 and 4; CX/JQ 828–830, 832, 833, 836, 839, 842, 843, 845–847, 850, 852, 854, 857, 859, 861–866, 872, 873, 875, 877–880, 882, 883, 886, 890, 894–897, 899, 900, 904.

and CS service to the Military Attaché at Belgrade, who was given discretion to pass the intelligence to the Yugoslav authorities with suitable security precautions. No record remains of what use he made of the intelligence, but it must have been less valuable than it was in Greece for in the Yugoslav fighting GC and CS was unable to solve until after the end of the campaign the pro-forma used in the GAF liaison officers' reports.

About the way these appreciations were used in Athens and at the forward HQs – with what delays they were received, how they were combined with other intelligence, how they influenced operational decisions – little explicit evidence has survived. It is clear that the HQs were hampered by severe organisational difficulties. The intelligence staff for the British expeditionary force was provided by 27 Military Mission, already in Greece, because experienced officers could not be spared from Cairo. The staff provided was too small, so that when it was divided into two echelons – one at forward HQ and one at Athens – neither was sufficiently self-contained to be an efficient body. In Athens, moreover, there were several sources of information – the British legation with its Service attachés, 27 Military Mission and the Greek General Staff, as well as the intelligence section of the expeditionary force – and no time to organise effective co-ordination between them. Throughout the campaign the intelligence section of the force and 27 Military Mission reported separately to GHQ Middle East and to the forward HQs and on some matters, notably the state of the Greek forces, their views conflicted. To make matters worse, communications from Athens to the forward HQs were bad, as were those from Athens to Cairo where the C-in-C had considerable difficulty in getting a clear picture of the fighting.[23] But the surviving records at least establish that these difficulties were off-set by the fact that the C-in-C ME and GOC Greece had accurate and current intelligence from 'most secret sources', some of them German,[24] and it may safely be assumed that the Enigma was the most valuable among them. It is noteworthy that accurate and current information of the movements and intentions of German formations, said to be from such 'most secret sources', which was signalled to London by British Forces Greece and the C-in-C ME on 7 and 17 April respectively,[25] appears to have been derived from Enigma.[26] This may have been passed back because the two commands were either uncertain of the source or unaware that the information was already available to Whitehall. The Prime Minister's statement to the War Cabinet on 21 April that Thermopylae was threatened by 3 divisions was almost certainly based

23. Mockler-Ferryman, op cit, p 163; CAB 105/3, No 149 of 19 April 1941.
24. CAB 105/3, No 69 of 7 April, No 121 of 17 April 1941.
25. ibid, Nos 69 and 121 of 7 and 17 April 1941.
26. CX/JQ 829, 830, 862, 863.

on Enigma decrypts of that date[27] and furnishes a specific example of the type of information yielded by this source.

The GOC's main decisions concerned the timing of the repeated withdrawals that were forced on him. They appear to have been extremely well-timed as a result of the Enigma appreciations that were being sent to him. Thus, he made an early adjustment to his initial defensive line when it became apparent to him by 8 April that the German 40 Corps was going to be a threat from the direction of Monastir, and the Enigma decrypts were providing nearly current intelligence about the movements of the spearhead troops of 40 Corps as they advanced through Monastir,[28] outflanked the Aliakhmon line by a route which MI had thought them unlikely to use, as being extremely difficult for tanks, and compelled General Wilson to withdraw to Olympus.[29] Enigma information that German armour intended to operate to the south of Olympus reached the GOC on 15 April[30] and undoubtedly influenced his decision of that date to withdraw to Thermopylae – a decision of which it has been said by the Australian official historian that 'if the. . . withdrawal had begun a day later it would have been disastrous for the British force'.[31] It was the Enigma, again, which, early in the campaign, removed all uncertainty about a possible German threat to Turkey by revealing the movement of 5 and 11 Panzer Divisions westward from the Bulgarian–Turkish border to join Panzergruppe Kleist.[32] The same source provided British commanders with immediate confirmation of the capitulation of Yugoslavia and, on 21 April, of the Greek Army in the Epirus.[33]

□

On 7 April, the day after the German attack on Greece, the Chiefs of Staff considered what steps to take about Rashid Ali's coup of 3 April in Iraq. At this time, immediately after the opening of the campaign in Greece, Whitehall judged that the danger of an early move by Germany through Turkey to Syria and Egypt or Iraq had receded; it knew that the German armoured divisions on the Turkish–Bulgarian border had been moved westward after the Yugoslav coup, and it in any case felt that Germany would not embark on so large an undertaking so long as she still hoped to attempt an invasion of the United Kingdom in 1941. But it expected German political pressure

---

27. CAB 65/22, WM (41) 42 CA of 21 April; CX/JQ 872.
28. Playfair, op cit, Vol II, p 86; CX/JQ 845, 847.
29. Playfair, op cit, Vol II, p 86; CAB 80/27, COS (41) 248 (COS Résumé, No 85).
30. CX/JQ 856, 857.
31. Long, op cit, Vol II, p 81.
32. WO 190/893, No 40B of 8 April 1941; CAB 80/27, COS (41) 231 (COS Résumé, No 84).
33. CX/JQ 856, 872.

on Turkey and in Syria to continue. In the same way, while it thought that a German advance on Egypt from Libya would be difficult during the summer, it was afraid that a secondary offensive in Cyrenaica might be combined with pressure aimed at diverting British forces to Iraq and east Africa.[34] As for Rashid Ali, there was as yet no firm evidence that he had any military understanding with the Axis powers and in one diplomatic decrypt the Italian Minister in Baghdad had reported that he could give Rome no firm assurance that the coup had an anti-British character. The Foreign Office and the SIS were, however, warning that he was financed by the Axis and was under Axis pressure, and that he was growing stronger in the absence of British backing for his opponents.[35] In another decrypt, moreover, obtained by GC and CS on 5 April, the Italian Minister in Tehran reported that he had agreed with his German colleague that Syria would be the best route for the despatch of arms to the Iraqi nationalists; and the Whitehall authorities assumed that there was some collusion between Rashid and the enemy. In this climate of opinion the Chiefs of Staff favoured armed intervention in Iraq over the recognition of Rashid's government. From Cairo the C-in-C, though not responsible for military action in Iraq,* suspected that he would be asked to take such action and urged London to confine itself to diplomatic pressure. On 8 April he had received the JIC's answer to his request for an appreciation† – Russia and Iran were not likely to respond unfavourably to a British move into Iraq[36] – but he could not spare troops.[37] The Cabinet in these circumstances turned to India. The first British troops from India arrived at Basra on 18 April.

Within a week the soundness of this decision was confirmed by Axis diplomatic Sigint. This source disclosed that on 17 April Rashid Ali had made an appeal for assistance from the Axis, in particular for air support.[38] On 26 April another decrypt showed that on 23 April he had had no reply to this appeal and was asking that help should arrive immediately after the first clash with British forces, which he thought might occur within 3–4 days.[39] In addition there had been indications from the SIS that trouble was brewing. Before the first troops arrived from India the SIS warned that British inaction would encourage Rashid. In the last week of April it reported that he had been given

---

* See Chapter 11, p 367.

† See Chapter 11, p 367.

34. CAB 80/29, JP (41) 276 of 8 April 1941; JIC (41) 144 of 10 April 1941; CAB 80/27, COS (41) 231 (COS Résumé, No 84).

35. CAB 69/2, DO paper 14/33/8 (MICE telegram 05146), 7 April; CAB 65/18, WM (41) 36 of 7 April.

36. JIC (41) of 5 April.   37. Playfair op cit, Vol II, p 179.

38. cf G Warner, *Iraq and Syria, 1941* (1974), p 98, using *Documents on German Foreign Policy*, Series D (HMSO) Vol XII, No 372.

39. cf Warner, op cit, pp 99–100, using *DGFP*, op cit, No 401.

an ultimatum by the Iraqi Army: it would take over from him unless he turned out the British forces and established relations with Germany within a week. On 28 April the British Ambassador told him that a second contingent of troops would arrive on 30 April. On 29 April Rashid told the British Ambassador that he would not tolerate the arrival of further troops[40] and on 30 April he invested the RAF station at Habbaniya, where fighting broke out on 2 May. The RAF Commander there had broken the siege by 6 May, but he had received no warning of the Iraqi move. The first news of it to reach him came from visual reports of large numbers of troops leaving Baghdad for Habbaniya in the early hours of 30 April. There had been for a number of years an RAF intelligence staff, largely dealing with political intelligence, with HQ at Habbaniya, but this had failed to give any warning. Perhaps influenced by this, the C-in-C and the AOC-in-C ME soon set up the Combined Intelligence Centre Iraq (CICI) to co-ordinate and control all non-operational intelligence activities.[41]

What the Axis diplomatic decrypts did not yield was precise knowledge of the facts on the German side. A few days after the coup Germany informed the Mufti that she was willing to supply arms to Iraq if a way of delivering them could be found; but it was not until 6 May, Vichy having agreed to send arms by train from Syria and to allow the GAF to use Syrian bases, that Germany turned her general assurance of support into a detailed proposal.[42] Since the end of March, on the other hand, the Enigma, without throwing any light on the nature of her next move, had left no doubt that Germany was concentrating airborne forces in the Balkans. On 22 April the Chiefs of Staff had entertained the suspicion that, although there seemed to be indications that Crete was the object of the preparations Germany was making for a large-scale airborne operation, Crete might be cover for a descent on Cyprus and Syria.*[43] And on 27 and 28 April they had asked the Foreign Office to warn the Vichy High Commissioner in Syria of the danger of a German airborne attack and had invited the C-in-C Middle East to consider what forces he could spare to help the High Commissioner to resist an attack.[44]

The intelligence bodies did not disagree. On 1 May, as well as warning that Rashid would resist if he received air support, the Chiefs of Staff résumé reported 'reliable indications' of an imminent German

---

* See below, p 416.

40. Woodward, op cit, Vol II, p 578.

41. Mockler-Ferryman, op cit, p 164; CAB 105/4, No 74 of 10 May; JIC (41) 18th meeting, 19 June and JIC (41) 257 of 18 June; JIC (41) 481 of 19 December; CAB 80/60, COS (42) 245 (0) of 25 December, Annex IX, App III, para 8.

42. Playfair, op cit, Vol II, pp 193–195.

43. CAB 79/11, COS (41) 143rd meeting, 22 April.

44. ibid, COS (41) 150th meeting, 28 April; Butler, op cit, Vol II, p 517; CAB 105/3, No 218 of 27 April 1941.

airborne attack on Syria.[45] It seems that these 'indications' were a report from Jerusalem that the Italian Armistice Commission in Syria was preparing for a German landing and a diplomatic report to the effect that the United States Consul-General in Beirut surmised that German airborne troops might 'some day arrive in Syria'.[46] On 2 May MI recognised that an attack on Iraq was improbable without the establishment of some intermediate stage in Syria or possibly Cyprus, and it admitted that other intelligence indicated that an airborne attack on Crete was to be Germany's next step and that a simultaneous attack on Crete and Syria was unlikely on account of the German shortage of transport aircraft. 'On the other hand', it still thought that it would be possible for the Germans to launch an expedition from the Dodecanese direct to Iraq if the British position in Iraq deteriorated, the assault being accompanied by an attack on Syria, either direct or via Cyprus, and it listed 'the indications that an attempt to occupy one or both of these countries will be made. . .'.[47]

In terms of their intelligence content, the indications were not impressive.* On 5 May, moreover, the Enigma confirmed that Crete was the enemy's immediate goal† and the JIC ruled out the possibility of an early assault on Cyprus.[48] But by then Axis diplomatic Sigint was giving colour to the anxieties about Iraq by revealing that Rashid Ali was still appealing for German and Italian support and that the Axis powers were responding to his appeals.

The Chiefs of Staff had already decided – on 2 May – that Iraq should revert to Wavell's command and, since the Basra force could not be sent to Habbaniya because of floods, had asked him to consider the immediate despatch of a force to Habbaniya; and they had already overruled – on 4 and 5 May – the C-in-C's argument that, because any forces he could send would be too little and too late, it was better to rely on diplomatic pressure on the Iraqis.[49] Perhaps as a result of receiving the Enigma evidence about Crete by the morning of 6 May, the C-in-C was still reluctant to take action. But later on 6 May Whitehall could assure him that there was 'an excellent chance of restoring the situation by bold action, if it is not delayed', since 'Rashid Ali has all along been hand in glove with the Axis powers' and 'our arrival in Basra forced him to go off at half-cock before the Axis was ready'.[50] It had derived the information from the Italian diplomatic cypher. This had just revealed, in advance of British

---

* MI's paper is given as Appendix 14.
† See below, p 417.

45. CAB 80/27; COS (41), 279, (COS Résumé, No 87).
46. WO 190/893, No 56A of 2 May.
47. ibid.   48. JIC (41) 188 of 5 May.
49. Playfair, op cit, Vol II, p 185; Churchill, op cit, Vol III, pp 227–229; Butler op cit, Vol II, p 463.
50. CAB 105/4, No 40 of 6 May 1941.

reports, that Rashid Ali had failed at Habbaniya, that his stocks of bombs and ammunition were exhausted and that he was desperately entreating the Germans and the Italians to send him bomber and fighter aircraft.[51] And three days later the GAF Enigma began to uncover the action that Germany was taking in response to his appeals.

On 9 May the Enigma revealed that the GAF was preparing a small-scale operation near Athens, at an airfield that was not being used for the attack on Crete; and GC and CS suggested that its purpose might be to help the Iraqis. During the following two days further messages showed that He 111s and Me 110s with Iraqi markings, or no markings at all, were to be sent from Athens to Rhodes. On 12 and 13 May the Enigma confirmed the accuracy of diplomatic reports from Damascus that German aircraft had arrived in Syria and Iraq,[52] and also showed that the German effort was to be a limited one. On 14 May it revealed that several more GAF aircraft were in Syria awaiting instructions and that an arms train had left on 11 March for Iraq from Damascus, where the French High Commissioner had asked the Germans to keep their presence as unobtrusive as possible.[53]

As late as 8 May Wavell had still preferred a political solution; he had agreed that he could relieve Habbaniya but doubted whether the force he could spare was adequate to operate against Baghdad. But by 9 May, when he pressed the C-in-C to move on Baghdad, the Prime Minister was able to stress that 'every day counts, for the Germans may not be long'. He was also able to emphasise the poor state of Rashid's position. On the previous day the Italian diplomatic decrypts had shown both that Rashid was still appealing to Berlin and Rome for help against the decisive British air superiority and that, as the Defence Committee was at once informed, he was 'in desperate straits'.[54] In the next few days similar evidence was obtained from decrypted Japanese diplomatic messages. In a message decrypted on 12 May the newly arrived Japanese Minister to Baghdad reported that the Iraqi resistance could continue till 15 or 20 May but if British forces advanced from Palestine the Army would collapse sooner and abandon Baghdad. On 13 May the Prime Minister followed up his message of 9 May by transmitting to the C-in-C personally the text of the Japanese Minister's signal, adding no comment except 'burn after reading'. The British force from Palestine was then entering Iraq and the C-in-C now signalled that he would 'try to liquidate this tiresome Iraq business quickly'.[55]

---

51. OL 231 of 6 May and OL 238 of 7 May.
52. CAB 105/4, Nos 83 and 84 of 12 May.
53. OLs 261, 267, 272, 287, 300, 315, 316 and 318 dated 9 to 14 May 1941.
54. CAB 69/2, DO (41) 26th meeting, 8 May; OL 254 of 8 May.
55. Churchill, op cit, Vol III, pp 230–232; OL 295 of 13 May.

The GAF bombing of the British forces in Iraq began on 14 May. Though it temporarily put heart into the Iraqis, it was limited by inadequate supplies and therefore indecisive. An Iraqi counter-attack against the British troops advancing from Habbaniya to Baghdad, launched on 21 May, came to nothing; Baghdad surrendered on 31 May. During the campaign Sigint had kept London[56] and Cairo well-informed of developments. By 22 May the Enigma reported that the aircraft committed by the GAF, which AI had put at about 30 and which in fact numbered 24, were running into fuel difficulties.[57] On 24 May decrypts of Vichy's diplomatic traffic showed that the Iraqis were bewildered by the change in the situation in Iraq and upset at German and Italian delay in sending help.[58] On 25 May the Italian diplomatic traffic showed that IAF fighters were due to arrive in Iraq on the next day[59] and on 28 May it added that, because of shortage of fuel, no further supplies of war material would follow by air.[60] The same source painted the situation in Baghdad as 'very serious but not desperate' on 30 May,[61] but on 1 June Vichy diplomatic traffic reported that the government, the Mufti and the Italian and German Ministers had left the country.[62] The fact that the Germans had established diplomatic relations with the Iraq government and sent a Minister to Baghdad had emerged in the Japanese and Italian diplomatic traffic by the middle of May. On the day after the fall of Baghdad, Hitler intervened to order a last-minute stand, and the GAF Enigma carried his decision. Help to Iraq was to be continued despite the adverse situation. Further reinforcements were being planned and supply bases were to be organised in Syria and Iraq, for which purpose he had sent General Felmy to Aleppo. Since Turkey would not allow the passage of arms, an effort would be made to send bombs by sea. Troops would not be sent at present, but a reinforced battalion was being got ready in Germany.[63] Later on 1 June, however, the Enigma revealed that the GAF was to be withdrawn from Iraq to Syria and that operations in Iraq were to be suspended, and on 3 June the Enigma made it clear that the support base near Athens was being disbanded and the aircraft returned to their units.[64] On the same day the Italian diplomatic traffic revealed that the Axis advisers in Iraq considered it impossible to continue military support for the pro-Axis forces there.[65]

□

---

56. CAB 80/28, COS (41) 337 (COS Résumé, No 91), COS (41) 357 (COS Résumé, No 92), COS (41) 385 (COS Résumé, No 94).
57. OLs 287, 342, 413 and 414 dated 13 to 22 May; cf Warner, op cit, p 106.
58. OL 441 of 24 May; cf Warner, op cit, p 115, using DGFP, op cit, No 543.
59. OL(D) 456 of 25 May.   60. OL 493 of 28 May.
61. OL 517 of 30 May.   62. OL 254 of 1 June.
63. OL 523 of 1 June.   64. OL 525 of 1 June; OL 535 of 3 June.
65. OL 534 of 3 June.

The intervention in Iraq was undertaken in the interval between the British retreat from Greece and the beginning of the battle for Crete, and with full knowledge that that battle was imminent. The Enigma had given two weeks' notice of the date of the German assault and provided in advance crucial details about the German assault plans. And it was mainly on this account that the British were able to inflict on the enemy more damage than he had sustained during the whole of the earlier fighting in Greece, and to turn his achievement in taking the island into a Pyrrhic victory.

An airborne attack on Crete was not part of the original *Marita* operation. Not until March 1941 did General Student, AOC of the parachute and airborne troops of the newly-formed Fliegerkorps XI, draw up a plan for such an attack. And not until 21 April was it put to Hitler. He then set the starting date for 17 May. But he did not finally order the operation (*Merkur*) till 25 April. The force – Fliegerkorps XI with 500 Ju 52s – was not assembled in the Athens area until 14 May, on account of supply difficulties encountered during the move from Germany to the Balkans, and other delays postponed the start till 20 May.

In Whitehall, where it had long been expected that the Germans would use paratroops in the Balkans as they had done in Norway and the Low Countries,[66] the first signs of German preparations for airborne operations were received in the last week of March. On 25 March, the Enigma having revealed that Fliegerkorps XI was collecting Ju 52s for multiple glider-towing and that it had been ordered to prepare the temporary move of 5 or 6 Gruppen of Ju 52s to Plovdiv, MI reported that 250 transport aircraft had arrived in the Balkans.[67] By 30 March the Enigma had confirmed the arrival at Plovdiv of the advance party of a 'detachment Süssmann', a General known to be associated with Fliegerdivision 7 – the crack airborne formation of Fliegerkorps XI which was known to have carried out the paratroop landings in Holland – and of other units, including one which was known to have been training in night glider-towing in Brunswick, and MI warned that large-scale airborne operations in south-eastern Europe were being prepared. As yet, however, there was no information about the targets. Earlier, on the basis of 'most secret sources' other than the Enigma, MI had opted for Lemnos and Fliegerdivision 7 had indeed been allocated this first task.[68] On 30 March MI considered an attack on Salonika or the Greek rear to be more likely than one on the Greek islands.[69]

---

66. WO 190/892, Nos 27 and 28 of 22 and 24 November 1940; WO 190/893, No 9A of 24 January 1941.

67. WO 190/893, No 33A of 25 March; CAB 80/26, COS (41) 196 (COS Résumé, No 82).

68. Creveld, op cit, p 154; WO 190/893, No 33A of 25 March.

69. WO 190/893, No 35C of 30 March 1941.

Uncertainty on this last point continued throughout April. It was known from the Enigma by 18 April that 250 Ju 52s had by now been withdrawn from routine duties and placed under Fliegerkorps XI in the Plovdiv area and, by 24 April, that Göring had decided to use some of them on a special operation. What that was, however, was revealed only when a regiment of Fliegerdivision 7 dropped on the Corinth Canal on 26 April in an attempt to cut off the British retreat, which had begun two days earlier. By then the Enigma had established that a further operation was imminent: Fliegerkorps XI was given priority for fuel supplies, and there had been a reference to the importance of getting the supplies to Fliegerkorps XI's area by 5 May.[70] But there was still no evidence that Crete was the next German objective. It was presumably on this account that the Prime Minister, later so urgent an advocate of giving priority to defence measures in Crete, ruled on 18 April that, although the Cabinet had decided to defend Crete, the evacuation of Greece and the maintenance of the position in Libya must come first.[71]

If one reason for the uncertainty was the lack of positive evidence, another was the tense situation in Iraq. On 22 April the COS thought Crete a likely German objective, but also suggested that the enemy might be aiming at Cyprus as a stepping-stone to Syria and beyond, and on 23 April, before doing the same for Crete on 27 April, the JIC made an estimate of the possible scale of an attack on Cyprus.[72] So great, indeed, was the anxiety on this score that uncertainty persisted even after the Enigma revealed that Crete was the next German objective. On 26 April the Railway Enigma confirmed that a further operation was intended by announcing that a large-scale movement from Germany to the Balkans significantly codenamed *Flying Dutchman*, which on other Enigma evidence was clearly Süssmann's transfer of Fliegerdivision 7, would begin on 27 April.[73] Also on 26 April, the day after Hitler issued his *Merkur* directive, the GAF Enigma referred explicitly to Crete: Luftflotte 4 referred to the selection of air bases for 'operation Crete' and Fliegerkorps VIII requested photographs and maps of the island.[74] From this and other references Fliegerkorps VIII's role in supplying air support for the operation became clear. On 29 April, however, and again on 1 May, when the flight of the Regent from Baghdad had brought the crisis in Iraq to a head, the C-in-C Middle East was still uncertain as to where Germany would strike.[75] Nor was he alone in suspecting that the

---

70. CX/JQ 884, 886; AI/JQ 19.

71. Playfair, op cit, Vol II, p 124.

72. CAB 79/11, COS (41) 143rd meeting, 22 April: JIC (41) 163 of 23 April; JIC (41) 181 of 27 April.   73. CX/JQ 900.

74. CX/JQ 889.

75. Churchill, op cit, Vol III, p 241; CAB 105/3, No 233 of 29 April 1941; CAB 105/4, No 9 of 1 May 1941.

Enigma references to Crete might be part of a German cover plan for a descent on Cyprus and Syria; on 30 April the Chiefs of Staff still harboured this suspicion.[76] The Prime Minister had concluded by 28 April that 'it seems clear from all our information that a heavy airborne attack...will soon be made on Crete'[77] and he was later to be mildly critical of Wavell's hesitation;[78] but he himself admitted on 3 May that the enemy might be 'only feinting at Crete'.[79]

No great operational significance need be attributed to the delay that was caused by this hesitation. The authorities in Crete were fully alive to the danger to them. On 18 April the C-in-C Middle East had warned them that Crete might be one of the German objectives. By that date, moreover, the link which carried the Enigma direct from GC and CS to Cairo had been extended to Crete. On 16 and 21 April they were notified on this link that the GAF was preparing airborne operations from Bulgaria; on 22 April, just before the evacuation from Greece, they were warned to burn all the material they had received on the service. Thereafter, the Prime Minister having decided that the Enigma material must continue to go to Crete, General Freyberg, who took command on 30 April, received it from GC and CS disguised as information supplied by an SIS agent in Athens.[80] On assuming command General Freyberg warned his forces to expect an attack on 1 or 2 May.[81] It seems hardly possible that anything extra could have been done to strengthen the defences in the short interval which elapsed between 27 April, when the British authorities obtained Enigma's first mention of Crete, and the first few days of May, when their uncertainty was brought to an end.

On 1 May the Enigma revealed that in connection with *Merkur* Fliegerkorps VIII had been ordered to refrain from destroying airfields on Crete and from mining Suda, to make a photographic mosaic of Crete and to report on bomb stocks. On 4 and 5 May it provided further confirmation that Crete was the target by showing that extensive air reconnaissance of Cretan ports and airfields had been laid on.[82] By 5 May the JIC had ruled out an attack on Cyprus in the immediate future.[83] Even more important, the Enigma now established for the first time that the Crete assault was not imminent. On 2 May it reported the departure of the first and second wave of Fliegerkorps XI from Hanover and carried a request that Student should announce by 6 May when the Korps could arrive in Greece.

---

76. CAB 79/11, COS (41) 153rd meeting, 30 April.
77. Churchill, op cit, Vol III, p 241; CAB 69/2, DO (41) 19th meeting, 28 April.
78. Churchill, op cit, Vol III, p 244.
79. ibid, p 245.
80. OL messages, KOT series, 16, 21 and 22 April 1941.
81. DM Davin, Official History of New Zealand in the Second World War, 'Crete', (1953), p 77.
82. CX/JQ 917, 920, 921.
83. JIC (41) 188 of 5 May.

On 4 and 5 May it showed that Fliegerkorps VIII did not expect to move its HQ from Plovdiv to Athens until 8 May. And most important of all, on 6 May it vouchsafed nothing less than the German estimate of the probable date of the completion of their preparations – 17 May – and complete final operational orders for the execution of the assault. As is now known, these were a compromise resulting from last-minute debates among the German authorities, and it was perhaps for that reason that they were transmitted by W/T in great detail. They listed the exact stages of the plan from D-day, beginning with the landing of paratroops by Fliegerdivision 7 and other units of Fliegerkorps XI in the Maleme-Khania area (the main sector) and at Heraklion and Rethymnon, and proceeding, through the transfer of dive-bombers and fighters to Cretan bases, to the sea transport of flak units, supplies, equipment and three mountain regiments of ground troops.[84]

The flow of Enigma information during the next 2 weeks covered the concentration of Fliegerkorps XI in the Athens area, monitored the progress made by the Germans in establishing themselves in neighbouring islands and in assembling 27,000 tons of shipping, and reported the results of the GAF's softening-up attacks on Crete, which began on 14 May. On 15 May it revealed that the German Chief of Air Staff had requested a 48-hour postponement of the original date of 17 May and had received Göring's approval for his request.[85] On 19 May the Middle East was informed that Enigma had shown 20 May to be the probable date of the attack[86] and that on 19 May the German commanders were to meet with maps and photographs of Maleme, Khania, Rethymnon and Heraklion.[87]

These, the areas selected by the Germans for their airborne descents, tallied closely with those to which the British in Crete were already giving prominence in their defence preparations before 7 May, when they learned from the Enigma of the German operational plan.[88] But it was the fore-knowledge provided by the Enigma which gave the defenders the confidence and the time to concentrate all their forces at these points, and the value of the intelligence was all the greater because of the acute shortage of shipping, equipment and troops throughout the Middle East theatre. This had prevented the British from giving much attention to Crete's defences since their arrival there, though the RAF attempted to curtail the scale of the coming attack by bombing raids on the German assembly points disclosed by the Enigma. Nor was it until 14 and 15 May[89] that the Defence Committee was able to decide that the defence of Crete should have

84. CX/JQ 911.
85. CX/JQ 936, 941, 955, 958.
86. OL 370 of 19 May.
87. CX/JQ 967.   88. Playfair, op cit, Vol II, p 126.
89. CAB 69/2, DO (41) 29th and 30th meetings, 14 and 15 May.

priority over British projects in Iraq and Syria and the interruption of enemy supplies to north Africa, where the Enigma was only now establishing the subsidiary character of Rommel's offensive.

Despite Whitehall's other preoccupations, it was fully alive to the value of the intelligence about Crete. As the Prime Minister confided to Wavell on 9 May, this had presented a 'heaven sent' opportunity to deal the enemy a heavy blow.*[90] Plans aimed at inflicting the maximum losses on him, drawn up by the Director of Plans, Air Ministry, after discussions with the Naval Staff and the General Staff, were sent out to Cairo on 9 May.[91] On 12 and 13 May Cairo received in further despatches the results of Whitehall's close scrutiny of the Enigma material[92] and ideas from the Prime Minister, who later wrote that 'in no operation did I take more personal pains to study and weigh the evidence or to make sure that the magnitude of the impending onslaught was impressed upon the C-in-C and imparted to the General on the actual scene'.[93] On 12 May Wavell sent an officer to discuss the Prime Minister's messages with Freyberg.[94] On 14 May London repeated to the Middle East the warning that the attack could come any day after 17 May, and General Freyberg so informed his troops;[95] and from 17 May they expected the attack hourly.[96]

On 16 May the troops were given the final estimate of the likely scale of the attack: 25,000 to 30,000 airborne troops, 10,000 seaborne troops, 600 transport aircraft. This was an over-estimate, the numbers actually committed by Germany being 15,750 airborne troops, 7,000 seaborne and 520 transport aircraft.[97] There was uncertainty, also, about the scale on which the GAF would support the landing. On 27 April Whitehall had calculated this at 285 long-range bombers, 270 single-engined fighters, 60 twin-engined fighters and 240 dive-bombers.[98] At the beginning of May GS Int GHQ, ME had challenged these figures and suggested alternatives (150, 150, 40 and 100)[99] and the Cs-in-C Middle East had all agreed that London was exaggerating the threat.[100] In fact both estimates were wrong: the GAF used 280 long-range bombers, 90 single-engined fighters, 90 twin-engined fighters, 150 dive-bombers and 40 reconnaissance aircraft.[101] Nor did

---

* The Prime Minister estimated the value of the intelligence on Crete as £10 million.

90. CAB 79/11, COS (41) 170th meeting, 9 May, Annex I.
91. CAB 79/11, COS (41) 172nd meeting, 9 May.
92. CAB 69/2, DO (41) 28th meeting, 12 May; CAB 79/11, COS (41) 175th meeting, 13 May.
93. Churchill, op cit, Vol III, p 240; Davin, op cit, pp 37–38.
94. Davin, op cit, p 38.
95. CAB 105/4, No 102 of 14 May 1941; Davin, op cit, p 77.
96. Davin, op cit, p 77.
97. Davin, op cit, pp 77, 85; Churchill, op cit, Vol III, p 246.
98. JIC (41) 181 of 27 April.
99. Davin, op cit, p 33; CAB 105/4, No 9 of 1 May 1941.
100. CAB 105/4, No 19 of 2 May 1941.
101. Davin, op cit, p 85.

the Enigma assist by producing more reliable figures, despite the fact that last-minute decrypts, as well as identifying the army units that were to be used and thus reducing earlier uncertainty about the intended size of the seaborne assault, added significantly to what was already known about the units of Fliegerkorps VIII.[102]

It is unlikely that the conduct or the outcome of the battle were affected by the fact that the Enigma, while providing full details of the German plan and a date before which the attack would not take place, did not indicate the exact size of the assault. The British miscalculations on this point were small compared with those made by the Germans, who found the British garrison to be between three and five times stronger than they had assumed.[103] They also found, to quote the battle report of Fliegerkorps XI, that 'the area of operations...had been prepared for defence with the greatest care and by every possible means'[104] – and so much so that they had the impression that the defenders had known the time fixed for the invasion 'through their efficient espionage system in Greece'.[105] And the outcome was that, as well as sustaining more casualties on Crete than during all the fighting on the Greek mainland, they were left, after the decimation of Fliegerdivision 7, with a crippled airborne arm. Although the British were not to know this for many months, Fliegerdivision 7 was the only force of its kind in the GAF and the Germans made no attempt to rebuild it.

Aside from the advance Enigma information, which was clearly of overriding importance, it is difficult to establish how far other intelligence contributed to this result. During the battle the Enigma contained German situation reports, reinforcement rates, and identifications of units landed in the island,[106] and General Freyberg also got intelligence from POW and captured documents.[107] But we do not know how quickly he received this information or what he was able to do with it. One document, the German parachutist manual, captured as long ago as May 1940 and since then widely studied in the British Army, was undoubtedly of great assistance. In Crete the Germans used the landing pattern that they had adopted in Holland, and Student later said that he would have used different tactics had he known that the manual had been captured.[108] In Crete, too, to a greater extent than in Greece, field Sigint was of value. German R/T

---

102. CX/JQ 913.

103. Churchill, op cit, Vol III, p 269; A Clark, *The Fall of Crete* (1962), p 101; D Hunt, *A Don at War* (1966) p 39.

104. Quoted in Churchill, op cit, Vol III, p 269.

105. Air Historical Branch, AHB 6 Translation No VII/24, Report by Luftflotte 4 of 28 November 1941, p 24, para 2 (Ger DOC 8A-2026).

106. CX/JQ 923, 1001; MI/JQ 13.

107. Hunt, op cit, p 40; Clark, op cit, pp 77, 101.

108. WO 190/891, Nos 143 and 144 of 3 and 9 August 1940; Creveld, op cit, p 169; Clark, op cit, p 6.

bombing instructions were intercepted and information 'of great value' was produced by the exploitation of Fliegerkorps XI's tactical code. On account of shortage of aircraft and of German command of the air, there was little British reconnaissance north of Crete, while the British naval forces had to stand well south-west and south-east of Crete during daylight in order to avoid the GAF. However, on 21 May, as the result of Sigint information, an aircraft based on Egypt sighted a convoy of caiques, the only sea transport the Germans could muster, escorted by an Italian torpedo boat.[109] Shortly before midnight the Royal Navy sank a dozen of these ships and dispersed the rest: none of them reached Crete. News of this action induced the German admiral to order the second of the two convoys taking reinforcements and heavy equipment to return to the Piraeus, but the Royal Navy was able to make an attack on the caiques of the second convoy at dawn on 22 May. Though at heavy cost to itself, it prevented any German seaborne landings on Crete by stopping both convoys. Seaborne Y was also useful during these operations. The admiral commanding 7th Cruiser Squadron (CS 7), one of the two cruiser admirals involved, later reported that for a period of 24 hours the only information he obtained about the whereabouts of CS 12, his fellow flag-officer, was that which he received from his Y officer's interception of enemy sighting reports of the 12th Cruiser Squadron.[110]

The Navy's success failed to tip the balance in Crete. On 1 June Göring received – and GC and CS decrypted – a message from Luftflotte 4: Crete was 'clear of enemy forces' and its task had been completed.[111] As to whether, given the state of intelligence, the outcome should have been otherwise – not merely the severe mauling of the Germans which we have described, but their repulse – the Prime Minister commented at the time on Cairo's 'slowness in acting upon the precise intelligence with which [it was] furnished and the general evidence of lack of drive and precision' which filled him with disquiet about the Middle East staff.[112] It is perhaps fairer to conclude that, whereas the Germans had the strength to off-set bad intelligence, the British, whether from weakness or for other reasons, were not in a position to make better use of an intelligence service that was at last getting into its stride.

□

The discovery in the first week of May that Crete was the immediate objective of Germany's airborne preparations did not disperse the fear that Germany would move into Syria. On 8 May the Joint Planners

109. Playfair, op cit, Vol II, pp 135–137; Churchill, op cit, Vol III, pp 256, 261; Davin, op cit, pp 208–209; ADM 186/801, p 106.

110. ADM 223/89, p 12.

111. CX/JQ 1015.

112. PREM 3/109; PM Minute D186/1 of 14 June 1941.

in a memorandum for the Chiefs of Staff had still thought that Germany might make an airborne landing in Syria first, and possibly even a seaborne invasion.[113] On 9 May, in the same telegram in which he overrode the C-in-C's hesitations about Iraq, the Prime Minister had stressed the 'danger of Syria being captured by a few thousand Germans transported by air', and had suggested that General Catroux's Free French battalions in the Middle East should be assisted to enter the country.[114] From 14 May, when the Enigma had confirmed the arrival of GAF aircraft in Syria, en route for Iraq, and shown that the Vichy High Commissioner in Syria was providing them with landing facilities and conniving in the despatch of arms trains to Rashid Ali, the Whitehall authorities became convinced that Germany would move into Syria unless she was forestalled by early British action. On 19 May, when the assault on Crete was expected hourly and the position in Iraq had not yet been secured, they instructed the C-in-C Middle East to improvise the largest possible force for a movement into Syria at the earliest possible moment.[115]

When pressing the C-in-C to act quickly in Iraq, a week earlier, Whitehall had been guided by a good supply of Sigint. For its intervention over Syria it had no such intelligence support. From the British diplomatic missions and the SIS it had continued to receive reports of the arrival in Syria of German 'tourists'.[116] The Free French feared, as General Catroux told the C-in-C Middle East on 19 May, that the 'tourists' would soon be followed by a German airborne landing, and possibly by seaborne troops, and on 20 May they reported that in addition to 3 GAF squadrons the Germans already had one scattered division in the country.[117] These French reports, like those obtained from the other sources, were in fact occasioned by the activities of the staff of an Abwehr mission which had been in Syria since January and was now making the arrangements for the transport of arms and the transit of GAF aircraft to Iraq, and it is not difficult to see how they suggested preparations for German infiltration on a larger scale of the kind that had already overtaken other countries. On the other hand, the absence of any reference in the GAF Enigma to German preparations for military action in Syria stood in sharp contrast to the flow of intelligence the Enigma was providing about the preparations for the attack on Crete and the supply of air support to Iraq. Since 14 May, moreover, the RAF had been carrying out frequent reconnaissance flights over Syrian airfields without finding any other evidence of enemy activity.[118] But during the third

---

113. CAB 84/30, JP (41) 360 of 8 May.
114. CAB 105/4, No 61 of 8 May 1941.
115. ibid, No 142 of 19 May 1941.
116. AIR 22/74, Weekly Intelligence Summary, No 94, to 18 June – a retrospective survey.   117. CAB 105/4, No 155 of 20 May 1941.
118. Playfair, op cit, Vol II, p 201.

week of May, when the decision was taken to advance into Syria, the fear that Germany might continue her advance into the Middle East and the anxiety to forestall her had engendered in Whitehall an atmosphere in which no attention was given to such negative evidence.

How much this was so is shown by the nature of the intelligence appreciations. On 15 May the Chiefs of Staff résumé quoted reports that 'Germany intends to isolate Turkey by occupying Syria' and rumours that she had promised more help to Iraq in two weeks' time regardless of whether Turkey allowed the passage of troops. It went on to say that 'there are other indications that the centre of gravity of German activity has moved to south-east Europe, and it seems that the Germans have been led by developments in Iraq to concentrate on the eastern Mediterranean and beyond. By advancing through Turkey into Syria, and at the same time renewing their offensive in north Africa, they could develop once again the pincer movement which they have used so consistently in all their recent campaigns'.[119] On 21 May, the day after the first German landings on Crete, ACAS(I) took the unusual step of sending on GC and CS's Sigint link a personal message to the RAF's senior intelligence officer in Cairo to the effect that 'indications, though slight, point to another airborne expedition after Crete. Possibly Cyprus or Syria'.[120] These assessments did not merely ignore the significant fact that there were no such Sigint indications. They conflicted with the conclusion reached by the JIC on 11 May that damage to the communications in south-east Europe would prevent more than limited preparations for a major offensive through Turkey to the Middle East in the next six weeks.[121] They ignored the mounting evidence that Germany was concentrating major forces against Russia.*

At a time of crisis, with operations taking place simultaneously in Greece, Crete, Iraq and north Africa, the policy makers in Whitehall were in no mood to question these assessments or to demand more substantial evidence. On 19 May, the day on which he was instructed to improvise an advance into Syria, the C-in-C informed Whitehall that General Catroux was pressing him to invade at once with the arguments that French opinion in Syria was pro-British and that a German occupation was imminent, but that he, Wavell, distrusted some of the French information. On 20 May the Chiefs of Staff advised him to fall in with Catroux's wishes and he offered to resign. On 21 May the Prime Minister offered to accept his resignation. On the same day, however, the C-in-C reported that Catroux had

---

* See Chapter 14.

119. CAB 80/28, COS (41) 311 (COS Résumé, No 89).
120. OL 398 of 21 May 1941.
121. JIC (41) 205 of 11 May.

confessed that he had been misinformed about opinion in Syria: the French forces there would resist an Allied attack. Moreover, while distrusting the French rumours of a German seaborne landing and resisting the idea of a completely improvised Allied operation, the C-in-C had been fully convinced since 19 May of the danger of a German airborne descent on Syria. His dispute with Whitehall had been only about timing. Its outcome was that he secured a little more time in which to plan the invasion.[122]

During the next fortnight the absence of any intelligence pointing firmly to a German move into Syria gave way to positive indications that, while the French in Syria were preparing to resist an Allied occupation, no Axis threat existed. On 23 May the German Enigma disclosed that the French were reinforcing Syria with aircraft from north Africa.[123] Two days later it carried an order from Hitler that all German personnel in Syria and Iraq were to be volunteers and all GAF aircraft were to have Iraqi markings.[124] These precautions had been laid down from the outset and had been mentioned in Enigma messages on 9 and 11 May; this unusual way of placing further stress on them was good evidence both that the German force in the area was to remain small and that the German authorities were anxious to avoid provocation. During the first week of June, after revealing that Hitler had ordered on 1 June a last-minute stand in Iraq under General Felmy, the Enigma traffic showed the GAF withdrawing from Syria as well as from Iraq. At first, it is true, it disclosed that Felmy had been ordered later on 1 June to Aleppo to take over the GAF detachment withdrawn from Iraq and try to influence the French to resist a British advance; and on 2 June the German fighters were instructed to cease attacks in Iraq and to defend Syrian bases.[125] But on 3 June it gave the news that the GAF aircraft were being returned to their units and their Athens base disbanded,* though it was not until 10 June that the Enigma confirmed that Felmy's Aleppo detachment had been withdrawn.[126]

These clues were disregarded by the planners in Cairo and Whitehall. One reason was that, as the fighting in Crete drew to a close, there was no decline in their anxiety about Syria. On 25 May the C-in-C Middle East calculated that only small numbers of Germans were then in Syria, but that a larger body might arrive at any time by sea or air, and he asked the Chiefs of Staff whether the date of his advance should be made dependent on the arrival of this

---

* See above, p 414.

122. CAB 80/4, Nos 139, 140, 141, 163 dated 19 to 21 May 1941; Churchill, op cit, Vol III, p 290.
123. OL 429 of 23 May 1941.
124. OL 457 of 25 May.
125. OL 525 of 1 June; OL 530 of 2 June.
126. OL 548 of 8 June; OL 563 of 10 June. See also, Warner, op cit, p 141.

larger force. If he had changed his mind about the possibility of seaborne invasion, Whitehall had not altered its view on the need for speed. On 30 May the CIGS was still thinking that the Germans might attempt a large-scale leap-frogging descent on Cyprus.[127] Thereafter, a date having been set for the British offensive, the preparations for it no doubt acquired so much momentum that they could not have been re-phased even if the intelligence authorities had assessed the implications of the latest evidence correctly and brought them to the attention of the planners. They did not do so. On 28 May AI, in a second intervention into the stream of signals that were carrying the Sigint to Cairo, warned that 'if Crete is finished soon, Ju 52s could be used for further operations'.[128] And thereafter the Sigint went out without comment or appreciation by Whitehall until the British advance was launched on 8 June.

The advance was undertaken with forces that were known to be inadequate even for the French opposition that was expected, and the commanders, representing themselves as having come to fight Germans, not the French, must have been relieved to learn from the first prisoners that there were no German troops in Syria beyond a few airmen.[129] GHQ, ME, well briefed by the Free French and the SIS, put the French strength in Syria correctly at 25,000 regulars, 20,000 local troops and 90 tanks, and it had good information about the French dispositions.[130] Against opposition on this scale the C-in-C would have liked to have had 2 infantry divisions, 1 armoured division and some armoured brigades, but the force that could be made available for an early offensive was much less than this.[131] The outcome was a long campaign, and one in which the Allied troops had to be reinforced on more than one occasion before it was brought to an end on 12 July.

During the campaign, it is recorded, field intelligence was consistently good.[132] Topographical intelligence, of great value in a campaign in which terrain conditions played a big part, appears to have been excellent – mainly, no doubt, because of Free French information, but in part because, despite the fact that a ban had been imposed on the work in August 1940, the intelligence staff at Palestine HQ had continued to collect intelligence about the roads and tracks in Syria and the Lebanon.[133] The excellent order of battle intelligence available must have enabled the I staffs to make good use of the tactical information that came to them from sightings, POW and the

127. CAB 105/4, No 216 of 25 May; CAB 105/5, Nos 25 and 30 of 30 May.
128. OL 496 of 28 May.
129. 'Butler, op cit, Vol II, p 520.
130. Mockler-Ferryman, op cit, p 162; Playfair, op cit, Vol II, p 200.
131. Playfair, op cit, Vol II, p 203; Churchill, op cit, Vol III, p 293.
132. Mockler-Ferryman, op cit, p 162.
133. ibid, p 162.

field Sigint unit which had previously distinguished itself during the battle for Crete.

To these sources, those in the United Kingdom had nothing to add by way of intelligence bearing on the land fighting, but they provided valuable operational information about the GAF's share in the campaign and Vichy's naval and air intentions. Cairo and the C-in-C Mediterranean regularly received advance notice from the GAF Enigma of Fliegerkorps X's attacks on the units of the Mediterranean Fleet that were engaged in bombarding the French shore positions.[134] It was from the GAF Enigma, again, that the British authorities learned of the Vichy government's naval movements and intentions. The movements of French destroyers and submarines were regularly reported to Fliegerkorps X. On 27 June, having previously revealed that no further French naval units would be sent to Syria, the Enigma messages announced that the French government intended to carry out an operation in the eastern Mediterranean with one battleship, 4 cruisers and 4 to 6 destroyers, the force having GAF protection. This force was to have landed considerable French infantry reinforcements in Syria, and C-in-C Mediterranean, informed of this by the Admiralty, ordered submarines to concentrate against it.[135] But on 2 July London was able to inform the C-in-C Mediterranean that this operation, which would have been a momentous step in the development of German–Vichy-British relations, had been cancelled.[136]

No less valuable was the intelligence made available by GC and CS on the French view of the progress of the campaign and on French disagreement about the desirability of asking for additional German support. Because the Abwehr agent in Syria was using the GAF's communications, this also came from the GAF Enigma. On 14 June, when the British advance was being held up, the Enigma traffic disclosed that the Vichy High Commissioner in Syria had proposed that the GAF should be allowed to use Syrian bases, a step which Vichy had forbidden on 13 June, and on 15 June it emerged that the Germans were arranging for General Felmy to return from Athens to Syria. On the following day, however, it was learned that Vichy had insisted on maintaining the ban, though it continued to make requests for German assistance in transporting reinforcements by air.[137] On 21 June, in view of his shortage of material, the High Commissioner was again hoping for German support; and the messages carrying this information also confirmed that Turkey had refused to allow French arms and troops to cross her territory. By 25 June the Abwehr agent was reporting that the High Commissioner,

---

134. eg OL 591 of 14 June 1941.
135. ADM 223/77, Ultra signals 1159/27 June and 1006/28 June.
136. OLs 649, 677, 710 dated 21 June to 1 July 1941; JIC (41) 269 of 3 July.
137. OLs 581, 594, 602, 609, 666 dated 14 to 24 June 1941; OLs 718 and 719 of 2 July 1941. See also, Warner, op cit, pp 143–146.

his troops exhausted and suffering heavy casualties and himself depressed by his government's vacillation, was asking for German help direct. But on that day the agent announced that he was himself withdrawing to Aleppo, and on 4 July he expected the British to advance on Aleppo and doubted whether the situation was any longer tenable.[138]

---

138. OLs 649, 667, 670, 729 dated 21 June to 4 July 1941.

CHAPTER 14

'Barbarossa'

JUST WHEN they were completing their arrangements for the occupation of Syria the Commanders-in-Chief in the Middle East were instructed by the Chiefs of Staff to prepare for 'most energetic action' in yet another locality. On 31 May 1941 they were informed for the first time that Germany was concentrating large army and air forces against Russia, was demanding from the Russian government concessions that would be 'most injurious to us', and would march if her demands were refused. In the same telegram, on the ground that Russia might be persuaded to resist the German demands by the fear that Great Britain would otherwise attack the Baku oilfields, they were ordered to draw up plans for the seizure of Mosul as a base for possible attacks on Baku.[1]

As may be judged from the date and the contents of this telegram, the Whitehall authorities had been slow to reach agreement on the conclusion that Germany would make an attack on Russia, an undertaking which she had been preparing throughout the previous winter. Even when they had settled their differences, a bare three weeks before the attack, they were still failing to understand that what Germany had been preparing was not war in the event of the breakdown of negotiations, and after the despatch of an ultimatum, but an unconditional invasion, a surprise assault. In retrospect their slowness to realise this may seem to justify severe criticism of the intelligence bodies. We shall, indeed, see that weakness in organisation and the state of intelligence were partly responsible. But if we wish to be accurate about the nature and the extent of these deficiencies we must also recognise that during the year that ended with the German invasion in June 1941 many other considerations obstructed and distorted British outlooks on the relations between Germany and Russia.

Not the least important of these other considerations – and the first to exert its influence – was one that need cause no surprise. Political speculation about the possibility of a German attack on Russia ran ahead of Germany's preparations – ahead, indeed, of Hitler's first instructions that the attack should be prepared. In doing so, and in thus giving rise to rumours before there could possibly be any foundation for them in intelligence, it strengthened the disbelief with which the intelligence bodies later greeted such genuine pointers as they received to Germany's intention.

---

1. CAB 79/11, COS (41) 196th Meeting, 30 May, 197th Meeting, 31 May; CAB 105/5, No 42, 31 May 1941; Churchill, op cit, Vol III, p 318.

This speculation, which began at the time of the fall of France, was prompted at least in part by the wish of the British government to get on to closer terms with Russia after that set-back. British relations with Russia, poor enough before the last pre-war crisis, had deteriorated still further after the failure of the Anglo-French negotiations with Russia and the conclusion of the Russo-German pact in August 1939. British intelligence about Russia's aims and policies had been no better* – so that Whitehall had failed to foresee the Russo-German pact despite a flood of rumours on the subject[2] – and this had thereafter undergone no improvement. In these circumstances the Whitehall departments in the first nine months of the war had held that Russia's policy would be 'very unfavourable to German interests in the long run'[3] and that Germany would have to take account 'of a possibly hostile Russia',[4] but had at the same time shown no disposition to allow that Russia's objective in the war with Finland, as in her earlier move into Poland, might have a defensive character. Russia, like Germany, was assumed to be an expansionist state which regarded the British Empire as its main target. But on 14 June 1940 – the day on which Paris fell and Russia issued her ultimatum to Lithuania – the Foreign Office was taking the view that Russia was moving into the Baltic states against the time when she would have to defend herself against German aggression, and was advising Sir Stafford Cripps, the newly-appointed Ambassador to Moscow, that the Russians were alarmed by Germany's victories in France.[5] And from the same date Cripps in Moscow and the Prime Minister in London based a new approach to the Russian government on a series of warnings to it of the danger it stood in from Germany.

On 14 June Cripps told Molotov that Germany would be forced to turn east if France collapsed and that, 'according to our information', she would do so.[6] Earlier in June, on his way to take up his new post, he appears to have assured the Sofia correspondent of *The Times* that war between Russia and Germany was inevitable.[7] At the beginning of July – so the Germans learned from Italy's decryption of diplomatic signals[8] – he said the same thing to the Greek Minister in Moscow and added that, although Hitler would prefer to act that autumn, he would have to defer the attack until the spring. On 26 June the Prime Minister sent via Cripps a hint to Stalin to much the same effect.[9]

---

* See Chapter 2, p 46.

2. Aster, op cit, pp 155, 170–171, 181, 183, 263, 273, 275–276, 314–318; Dilks (ed), op cit, p 201; Bohlen, op cit, pp 77–84.
3. Woodward, op cit, Vol I, pp 37–38.
4. ibid, p 473; WO 190/865, MI 3 Appreciation, 23 November 1939. See also Appreciations in WO 190/874 and 883.
5. Woodward, op cit, Vol I, pp 464–465.   6. ibid, p 463.
7. B Whaley, *Codeword Barbarossa*, (1973), p 229.
8. Enemy Documents Section Appreciation/5, pp 90–91.
9. Churchill, op cit, Vol II, p 120.

There is no ground for doubting whether these warnings were sincere. On 27 June the Prime Minister expressed his opinion to Smuts: 'If Hitler fails to beat us here he will probably recoil eastwards. Indeed, he may do this without attempting invasion...'[10] On 8 July he repeated this to Lord Beaverbrook, Minister of Aircraft Production.[11] But the views expressed by Cripps and the Prime Minister had not been advanced in intelligence papers reaching the Cabinet or the Chiefs of Staff. Nor were they echoed there. On the contrary, in the Service intelligence branches, preoccupied as they were with the problem of divining the direction and the character of the enemy's immediate next moves and predisposed – as they had long been – to believe that Germany's chief objective was the defeat of Great Britain, the instinctive reaction to the fall of France was to lean in the opposite direction. On 18 April 1940 the JIC had concluded, as it had often done since the outbreak of war, that Germany could win the war only 'by knocking out Great Britain and France'.[12] When France was defeated the Service departments became still more convinced that she could win the war only by knocking out Great Britain. How much this was so, and how their conviction produced a divergence between their views and those of the Foreign Office, emerged during the preparation of the JIC paper on Germany's intentions that was issued on 2 July. As we have seen already, the Foreign Office and MI produced separate studies on this occasion, and while the Foreign Office cast some doubt on Germany's determination to invade the United Kingdom and, though not expecting it at once, allowed for a German move into the Ukraine, MI insisted that Germany would give absolute priority to *Sealion*.*[13]

Immediately, in the period after the beginning of July in which it became manifest that Germany was preparing for *Sealion*, the conviction of the Service staffs that the defeat of Great Britain must remain Germany's overriding objective was correct, and it was universally accepted as being so. On 5 August 1940 the JIC concluded unanimously, with no trace of dissension, that Germany and Russia both had the best of reasons for avoiding an open clash.[14] During August and September attention throughout the world was wholly taken up with the Battle of Britain. By the middle of October, however, when the threat of immediate invasion was receding, Cripps and the Prime Minister had returned to their earlier speculations and on the intelligence level the earlier dissension between the Foreign Office and MI had reappeared.

Cripps now told the Foreign Office that the Russians were so

---

* See Chapter 8, pp 251–252.

10. ibid, pp 227–228.   11. ibid, p 643.
12. JIC (40) 23 (S) of 18 April.
13. CAB 80/14, COS (40) 518 (JIC) of 2 July.
14. JIC (40) 225 of 4 August.

consumed with fear of Germany and Japan that it was unnecessary for him to warn them of the dangers of an Axis attack; and at the end of the month his response to the news that Molotov was going to Berlin was to repeat that in the long run, probably during 1941, the fundamental hostility between Germany and Russia would reassert itself.[15] On 31 October the Prime Minister – this time in a verbal briefing of senior military commanders – took the view that Germany would inevitably turn on Russia during 1941 for the sake of her oil.[16] By then this view had gained ground in the Foreign Office. On 29 September MI had asserted that 'the time will never come...when it will be safe to say that invasion of the UK is off,' and on 7 October, in a letter to the DMI, the Foreign Office chairman of the JIC had protested that this assertion was 'irrational': it was indisputable that Germany had enough ground forces to enable her to undertake more than one large campaign concurrently, but the GAF could not be switched to other theatres without seriously diminishing the sea and air threat to the United Kingdom. Moreover, MI's attitude was already 'crippling our strategy'.[17]

In so far as this protest applied to intelligence, it was prophetic. Until October 1940 the reluctance of the Service intelligence staffs to accept that Germany could cease to regard Great Britain as her main enemy was justified by the knowledge that Germany was giving priority to the *Sealion* front. From October 1940, when Hitler was in effect cancelling *Sealion*, it became another impediment to their correct assessment of the state of Russo-German relations, reinforcing their professional dislike of political speculation.

□

Until the end of October 1940 this reluctance was justified not only by the knowledge that Germany was giving priority to the *Sealion* front, but also by the state of intelligence about Germany's intentions towards Russia. In June Cripps had supported his warning to Molotov by referring to 'our information'. At the time he spoke, no such information had been received in Whitehall. At the beginning of August the JIC's opinion that both Russia and Germany wished to avoid a clash had been unsupported by the quotation of any items of intelligence, but the JIC had not overlooked or misinterpreted any important piece of intelligence. Nor was any intelligence obtained during the next three months that makes it reasonable to suggest that this conclusion might have been revised.

Up to the beginning of August 1940 the state of intelligence

---

15. Woodward, op cit, Vol I, pp 489, 491, 495, 498.
16. CAB 69/8, DO (40) 39th Meeting SSF of 31 October.
17. WO 190/892, No 11 of 29 September 1940 and attached correspondence to DMI 7 October 1940.

faithfully reflected the state of Germany's preparations. Since the autumn of 1939 – not to speak of *Mein Kampf* and other pre-war statements on the subject – Hitler had hinted from time to time to his senior staff that his 'next major task' was 'the conflict with Bolshevism'.[18] On 21 July, soon after he had issued his *Sealion* directive and learned that the British government had rejected his peace offer, he had ordered preliminary studies for an attack on Russia.[19] On 29 and 31 July, in further discussions with his military advisers, he had decided that preparations should begin for a five-month Blitzkrieg against Russia from May 1941, major operations against the United Kingdom being deferred to the autumn of 1941 or to 1942.[20] By the end of July OKH, which in anticipation of these discussions had already begun to reorganise itself 'for a military blow against Russia',[21] had increased the number of divisions in the east from 5 to 15,[22] and on 5 August it had received a first study for the invasion.[23] As yet, however, the German planning was confined to Hitler and a handful of his senior officers.

In these circumstances the German Service material that was being read at GC and CS was naturally silent about the planning, and the other sources of intelligence – the SIS, GC and CS's decryption of the diplomatic traffic of the Axis states, British diplomatic reports and other overt sources* – had nothing to contribute. After the fall of France these other sources became loquacious about Russo-German relations, but what they said merely duplicated the speculation in which people in Whitehall were themselves engaging.

During July 1940 the SIS reported that the Soviet Military Attaché in Berlin had warned his government that Germany was preparing to attack Russia. Other SIS reports in July announced that, in order to avoid provoking Germany, Russia would fulfil her undertakings under the trade agreement up to the last moment. In the same month, however, another SIS agent, one who was in touch with Ribbentrop, concluded that war with Russia 'was out of the question at present'. The reports from diplomatic sources were no less contradictory, some claiming that Russia and Germany were both preparing for a clash and others claiming that Hitler had renounced his earlier eastern aspirations. Among the later, one dwelt in some detail on the German anxiety to refute Cripps: the German embassy in Moscow was saying

---

* There was no RAF reconnaissance of eastern Europe.

18. B Leach, *German Strategy against Russia 1939–1941* (1973), pp 40, 48. See also EDS/Appreciation/5, p 30.
19. Leach, op cit, p 69; EDS/Appreciation/5, p 64; J M A Gwyer and J R M Butler, *Grand Strategy*, Vol III Part I, (1964) pp 50–51.
20. Leach, op cit, p 15; Gwyer and Butler, op cit, Vol III, p 52.
21. Leach, op cit, p 20.
22. EDS/Appreciation/5, Appendix B.
23. ibid, pp 79, 81.

that the warning he had put about was based on the movement of German divisions to Poland and was explaining that these divisions were not first-line troops and had been sent east because they could not be maintained in France. This might have been the basis for suspecting that Germany was protesting too much, but it would have been a flimsy basis and any tendency to make much of it must have been checked by the other overt evidence, such as it was. The most prominent public development was the Russian government's response to the warnings from Cripps and Churchill: on 1 August it denounced the attempts of Great Britain to drive a wedge between Russia and Germany.

If this was the burden of the intelligence sources up to the time of the JIC report of 5 August, it cannot be said that they had reported any decisive change by the end of October. By then the number of German divisions facing Russia had again been increased, from 15 to 33 (including 5 armoured, 2 motorised and 1 cavalry), and the logistic preparations in the east – the establishment of training centres and airfields, the transfer of supply depots and the development of communications – had begun in earnest. During September, following a concentration of Russian troops against Finland, Germany had negotiated the passage of German troops through Finland and increased her forces in north Norway.[24] Germany was concerned with the protection of the Romanian oil and the Finnish nickel in the event of Russian moves against them, but her attempt to explain her eastward deployments as being defensive and her insistence that the logistical preparations were being made for economic, not military, reasons did not wholly satisfy the Russians.[25] By mid-September another problem was creating friction between the two countries. In consequence of Hitler's verbal orders at the end of July that the German Army be raised to 180 divisions,* Germany's deliveries to Russia were falling so far behind what she had promised in the trade agreement of February 1940 that a crisis had arisen in trade discussions between the German and Russian governments as a result of which the Russians had temporarily cancelled all long-term projects for exports to Germany.[26] By 1 November they were complaining that Germany could apparently deliver war material to Finland but not to Russia.[27] Alongside these developments, which were increasingly difficult to conceal from the Russians, Germany had taken highly confidential steps to further the preparations for a Russian campaign. On 28 September Hitler had confirmed his verbal orders

---

* See Chapter 9, p 303.

24. EDS/Appreciation/5, p 59 and Appendix B.
25. ibid, pp 59, 82.
26. Medlicott, op cit, Vol I, p 642.
27. EDS/Appreciation/5, p 76.

for the expansion of the Army and the creation of new divisions for the east and had laid it down that these were to be ready by 1 May.[28] Also in September, the Abwehr had been instructed to improve its neglected coverage of Russia – though Hitler had vetoed OKH's wish to begin photographic reconnaissance of Russia for fear that this would disclose his intentions.[29] By mid-October Army Group East had been set up in Poland and OKH had moved its HQ from France to Zossen.[30]

On these developments Whitehall received three kinds of information. In October MEW obtained evidence from a variety of sources which, taken collectively, gave substance to current rumours of a breakdown in Russo-German trade relations. In particular, an SIS source reported that Mikoyan was opposing the export of materials which the USSR needed for its own defence plans. Having noted this intelligence, however, MEW did not attempt to draw conclusions from it;[31] nor was it commented on elsewhere in Whitehall. In the second place there were diplomatic and SIS reports about German and Russian intentions. During September there were several of these, most of them warnings that Russia was putting pressure on Finland (for such things as demilitarisation of the Aaland Islands) and that Germany was sending troops to Finland, garrisoning the nickel mines there and signing the agreement with Finland for the transit of German troops to north Norway. But the reports put different interpretations on these developments. Some spoke of an increase in Russia's military precautions against a German attack and indicated that some circles, particularly the Swedish government, were convinced that a German attack on Russia would not be long delayed. Others said that Germany was only reacting to a Russian threat or, as was the case with the SIS reports, stressed that Germany was taking every possible care not to antagonise Russia. Up to the last day of October, when the War Office weekly intelligence summary reported that the Russians were undertaking large-scale manoeuvres in order to improve standards in their Army,[32] the intelligence branches had commented on none of these reports. But given the nature of the reports they can scarcely be blamed for their reticence.

Up to the same date Whitehall had received two items of intelligence of a third kind to which it is arguable that it paid too little attention. One item came from A-54. On 22 August he reported that he had learned from an OKH officer that the German intelligence branch responsible for the Russian area – OKH's Foreign Armies East – had been expanding since June, that the Abwehr's counter-intelligence

---

28. Leach, op cit, p 72.
29. Whaley, op cit, pp 30–31, 33, 136.
30. EDS/Appreciation/5, Appendix B; Leach, op cit, p 82.
31. FO 837/439, MEW Summary of Enemy Economic Developments No 59 of 30 October 1940.
32. WO 208/2258, WO Weekly Intsum No 63 of 31 October 1940.

activities against Russia were also to be increased as a matter of urgency, and that the Abwehr in Romania had been reinforced by specialists on the southern Ukraine, the Crimea and the Caucasus. None of the intelligence branches in Whitehall drew the attention of the JIC, the Chiefs of Staff or the Cabinet to this item. Again they can scarcely be blamed: by the end of September A-54 was predicting that Germany's occupation of Romania was imminent, and would be followed by German advances through Turkey and Spain,* and much other evidence was accumulating to support the assessment of the British military authorities that, in so far and for so long as the Germans permitted any diversion of effort away from the United Kingdom, they would do so only for the purpose of overthrowing the British position in the Middle East.

The second item of intelligence that might have been thought significant concerned the eastward deployment of German divisions. On 27 August MI accepted that a further – and a very considerable – addition to the troops in Poland was taking place, and quoted a total of 60 divisions. There was no direct evidence for this increase, it appears, but the diplomatic sources were discussing it and the figure of 60 divisions may have come from the British Military Attaché in Ankara: a diplomatic rumour at the end of July had quoted him as saying that 60 divisions were massing against Russia. The figure was a considerable over-estimate; the number of German divisions in Poland reached 25 in September and did not increase till 1941. But as well as accepting the figure MI concluded that not even 60 divisions constituted an undue concentration of German forces in the east: the Germans had to keep their spare divisions somewhere, and from Poland they could use them to intervene anywhere in Europe.[34] In arguing thus, and in avoiding any association between the order of battle evidence and the rumours about a German attack on Russia, MI was basing itself mainly on the belief that Germany was giving priority to *Sealion,* but it was probably also influenced by a further consideration. On 10 July after its first brush with the Foreign Office, it had gone so far as to concede that Germany would not allow Russia to tie down large German forces. 'Germany's policy will be either (a) to fight her, or (b) to preserve the best possible relations.' But it had severely qualified the concession by adding that 'we must allow for (b), the worst possible case'[35] By the end of August, it is not unreasonable

---

* See Chapter 8, p 252. It has been claimed that on 27 October 1940 he transmitted a further report giving details – about the printing of maps and the preparation of espionage organisations – which established that Russia was to be attacked.[33] There is no evidence that this further report was circulated in Whitehall. The claim for it may be confusing it with the above report of 22 August and exaggerating its precision, but it is possible that he did send this more detailed warning and that it constitutes a third item of intelligence that was overlooked.

33. Amort and Jedlica, op cit, pp 96–97.
34. WO 190/891, No 147 of 27 August 1940.
35. ibid, No 123 of 10 July 1940.

to suppose, the feeling that it was necessary to discount any suggestion that Germany would go so far to lighten Great Britain's load as to turn on Russia – that is, the best possible case – strengthened the understandable conviction of the military intelligence authorities that Germany would continue to give priority to the defeat of Great Britain.

□

After the German entry into Romania in October 1940 the German threat to the Middle East replaced *Sealion* as the chief ground for the conviction that the defeat of Britain was Germany's chief priority. In the course of doing so it also appeared to supply continuing justification for the view that rumours about German preparations for an attack on Russia should be ignored.

At first, it is true, MI was reluctant to accept that Germany would allow herself to be diverted from *Sealion* even to the Middle East, and it also had some difficulty in deciding what to make of its knowledge that the German Army was expanding and embarking on a large mechanisation programme.* On 31 October it commented on both points in uneasy and ambiguous terms: 'It is clear that Germany is preparing for a campaign in areas suitable for operations by mechanised forces on a large scale...These areas might equally well be Russia or the Middle East. Furthermore,...in the Ukraine Germany can find her raw materials. In addition to which there have been signs recently of increasing nervousness on the part of the Russians as to Hitler's future intentions...'. To MI, however, it seemed probable that Hitler, yielding reluctantly to the advice of his military advisers, had decided to postpone *Sealion* and prepare for an advance through the Balkans to Turkey in an attempt to defeat Great Britain in the Mediterranean. 'The German admirals and generals, doubtful of the success of the invasion plans, are persuading Hitler that Germany's ability to stand a long war depends on a Drang nach Osten policy' – by which MI clearly meant not, as the phrase might lead one to expect, an invasion of Russia, but a drive through Turkey to the Middle East which might lead to complications between Russia and Germany. Its conclusion on 31 October was that Hitler 'sees dangers in this policy which may bring him into conflict with Russia and dislikes it because it will not yield quick results, but he is wise enough to see that he may have to adopt it. He is therefore making all necessary preparations to carry it through in case, either of his own accord or in consequence of events, he does accept it'.[36]

Once it had accepted that Hitler had temporarily turned away from *Sealion* and was contemplating operations against Great Britain in the Balkans and the Mediterranean, MI supplemented its earlier view,

---

* See Chapter 9, pp 303–304.

36. WO 190/892, No 18 of 31 October 1940.

to the effect that Germany would not wish to tackle Russia until she had disposed of the United Kingdom, with the argument that she nevertheless had to prepare against the possibility of a Russian attack on herself while she was engaged in the south and the south-east. On 27 October it was using both arguments to explain the move of German troops to Finland, of which it then had 'confirmed evidence', and the German-Finnish transit agreement of September, of which it had now obtained the details. There was nothing in these developments to indicate 'an early falling out of thieves'.[37] On 3 November AI adopted the same line: the move to Finland had completed Germany's European bulwark against Russia.[38] In further appreciations on 6 and 12 November MI extended the explanation to cover the German deployment in eastern Europe. The purpose of this, as of the move to Finland, was to hold Russia off while Germany advanced through Bulgaria and Thrace to the Middle East and helped Italy to subdue Greece.[39] On 16 December, in notes it prepared for a lecture by the Vice-Chief of the Imperial General Staff, it declared that 'Germany thinks that 58 divisions in Poland and 10 in East Prussia, as well as fortifications in Poland and a potential base in Finland, will keep Russia quiet'.[40] On 24 December, in a brief drawn up for FOES, it repeated the same view: Germany did not want a two-front war and would not fight Russia until she had disposed of Great Britain.[41] And in the War Office weekly intelligence summary that was issued on 1 January 1941 it used the same argument to cover a new intelligence development. By this time, at London's request, the Poles had established a network of agents to report on the German transport, depot and warehouse complex in eastern Europe.[42] By the end of the year MI had learned, presumably from this source, that a considerable amount of west to east road and rail construction was taking place in Slovakia. The intelligence summary of 1 January accounted for this by the German need to move troops from Poland and the Protectorate to Romania in readiness for the attack on Greece. It also said that the German position in Finland was intended to deter Russia from putting pressure on that country.[43]

On 9 January 1941, in the first inter-departmental study of German intentions that had been attempted since early November, FOES followed the line laid down by MI. German forces in eastern Europe had been moved there to guard against a Russian attack while

---

37. ibid, No 17 of 27 October 1940.
38. AIR 40/2321, Minute of 3 November 1940.
39. WO 190/892, Nos 23B and 25 of 6 and 12 November 1940.
40. ibid, No 40 of 16 December 1940.
41. ibid, No 44, MI 14 letter to FOES, 24 December 1940.
42. Whaley, op cit, p 48.
43. WO 208/2258, WO Weekly Intsum No 72 to 1 January 1941.

Germany advanced into the Balkans. Until she had defeated Great Britain Germany would not wish to fight Russia 'except in dire necessity'.[44]

On the same day – 9 January – Hitler reaffirmed his intention to invade Russia at the middle or the end of May 1941, the dates originally selected for the beginning of the operation. He was led to do so by expressions of anxiety about the undertaking from OKH and Admiral Raeder.[45] Their doubts had increased as they had watched Hitler's plans take shape in a series of decisions and directives during the previous two months. On 12 November, at the outset of Molotov's visit to Berlin of 12–13 November, he had confirmed in a directive the verbal orders for the preparation of the invasion which he had issued on 31 July.[46] After the Molotov visit he had decided that there should be no attempt to reach a negotiated settlement with Russia: diplomatic exchanges should be continued only for the purpose of deception and as a means of preserving for Germany the advantage of a surprise attack.[47] There had followed on 18 December the release of the *Barbarossa* directive. Based on plans submitted to Hitler by OKH on 5 December, this laid it down that Soviet Russia was to be defeated in one rapid campaign 'even before the conclusion of the war with England'. The Army was to assign all available units to this task subject only to the protection of the occupied countries against surprise attack. The GAF was to release units for the support of the Army in an eastern campaign in such strength as would ensure that land operations were brought to a rapid conclusion and that eastern Germany suffered as little as possible from enemy air attack. This concentration in the east was to be limited only by the need to protect supply bases and operational areas as a whole against air attack and to ensure that the offensive against Britain, and in particular against her supply routes, was not brought to a standstill. The Navy's main effort was to continue to be directed against Britain even during a campaign in the east. Orders for a deployment against Russia would be issued eight weeks before the operation was due to start. Preparations requiring a longer period, if they had not started already, would be put in hand at once and be completed before 15 May 1941. It was 'of decisive importance that the intention to attack should not become known'.[48]

Knowledge of these further decisions was confined to the highest levels in Germany and no whisper of them reached Whitehall. It is

---

44. CAB 80/25, COS (41) 23 of 9 January.
45. EDS/Appreciation/5, pp 92, 94–95, 102, 112; Butler, op cit, Vol II, p 540; Van Creveld, op cit, p 151.
46. Leach, op cit, p 77.
47. Whaley, op cit, p 17.
48. The directive is quoted in Gwyer and Butler, op cit, Vol III Part I, pp 67–68.

to be noted, for example, that A-54, who in December had followed up his earlier warnings about the Balkans with the information that an attack on Greece through Bulgaria and Yugoslavia was planned for March 1941,* obtained no inkling of the war games and the other planning for the Russian campaign that OKH and OKW were conducting during November and December. Nor was the lack of information confined to the subject of Germany's strategic discussions. Between October and the beginning of January there had been no reports of Germany's logistic preparations in eastern Europe and Scandinavia – and the absence of intelligence from those areas contrasted strongly with the increasing evidence that she was planning operations in the Balkan direction. Essentially, however, the failure of the Whitehall intelligence bodies at this stage was not such as can be accounted for by lack of intelligence. Upon the evidence available to them it would be unreasonable to expect that they should have decided that Germany planned to turn on Russia; their mistake lay in ruling out the possibility that she would do so.

When we ask why they did this, the question arises whether Germany's deception themes, even though primarily intended for Russian and not for British ears, had any effect in Whitehall. By the first of these themes, laid down by Hitler at the end of July, the logistic preparations in eastern Europe were to be presented as preparations for *Sealion* – they were being undertaken to enable training for invasion to go on in areas beyond the range of British bombing and reconnaissance.[49] In October this theme was continued in the directive postponing *Sealion*, which insisted that physical preparations for the operation were to be continued on the Channel. The second theme, first adopted when additional divisions were moved east in September, was intensified after Germany entered Romania in October. It was that the Army was being redeployed in order to hold Russia off while Germany tried to finish the war with Great Britain by striking south-east through the Balkans.[50] The *Barbarossa* directive of 18 December again insisted on this: the preparations for the operation were to be presented as precautionary measures in case Russia became hostile.[51] It will be obvious how closely the British assessment of the situation at the beginning of 1941 conformed to these themes. But it is equally obvious that the British conviction that Germany's chief aim was the defeat of Great Britain owed nothing to the German deception measures, and there is no evidence that those measures in any way influenced Whitehall's failure to question this conviction. If Whitehall had made some

---

* See Chapter 11, p 368.

49. Whaley, op cit, pp 172–173.
50. Leach, op cit, p 74.
51. Whaley, op cit, p 174.

attempt to consider Germany's war aims without prejudice it would have kept open the possibility that she would turn on Russia. It made no such attempt because of the strength of its conviction and, to a lesser extent, because it was not until the final establishment of the Joint Intelligence Staff on the eve of the German attack on Russia that it at last developed machinery that was formally responsible for bringing together at one point all the evidence that bore on enemy strategy and that was able to do so effectively.*

□

Two obstacles nevertheless stood in the way of a total acceptance of FOES's January conclusion.

The first was the fact that rumours about German preparations for an attack on Russia had been increasing. During November and December 1940 the SIS was reporting that its contacts among the Balt aristocrats were openly saying that they would soon regain their estates 'in the wake of the German army'. From November the world's Press – notably the *Neue Zürcher Zeitung* and the *Chicago Daily News* – began to carry stories of a coming Russo-German war.[52] By the end of November the eastward deployment of the German Army was the subject of constant and nervous speculation among the diplomatic corps in Moscow.[53] In November the SIS man in Helsinki reported that he had heard from Abwehr officers that Germany would attack Russia in the spring.

In an appreciation issued on 17 January 1941 MI noted that there had been 'a number of suggestions lately that Germany may be intending' an attack on Russia – and clearly felt that it ought to take account of them. It then proceeded to examine the rumours in the light of 'the military evidence'. In the previous October, in reply to the protest from the Foreign Office's chairman of the JIC,† it had already resorted to the argument that in strategic questions the Chiefs of Staff knew best.[54] By early February 1941 it would be insisting rather more emphatically that the military evidence, as opposed to political information and still more to political rumours, was the only reliable guide to Germany's intentions.[55] In the January appreciation this was already its central premise. The paper reviewed what was known about the German Army's deployments in each theatre and placed the information in a military context.

The 3 German divisions in north Norway were probably there to

---

* See Chapter 9, p 298.
† See above, p 432.

52. Whaley, op cit, pp 180, 182.
53. ibid, p 27.
54. WO 190/892, No 11 and attachments.
55. WO 190/893, No 15A of 9 February 1941.

guard against the danger of British raids. There were 1,500 troops in Finland – this was a lines of communication contingent. The 6 divisions in Slovakia evoked no comment. Of the presence of German divisions on the Romanian frontier with Russia there was no evidence. Improvements were being made to the communications between Germany and Russian Poland – these were 'probably intended for implementing more rapidly recent economic agreements rather than for any military purpose in the immediate future'. Similar work in Romania indicated preparation for operations in the south-east rather than against Russia. As for Poland, the number of German divisions there had now climbed to 70 in MI's estimates but MI stressed that most of them had been there since the previous summer and that many of them were internal security divisions, not part of the field army. Partly on this account, and partly because the Germans were undertaking a good deal of work on fortifications on the Russo-German frontier, it seemed unlikely that Germany contemplated any offensive action in the area. From these assessments, and above all from the last, the overall conclusion reached by MI was that German dispositions and preparations in the neighbourhood of Russia's frontiers 'cannot at the moment be described as anything but normal'.[56]

As may be judged from the tone of MI's paper of 17 January, the second obstacle was the lingering suspicion elsewhere in Whitehall that military intelligence was not everything – that there was some substance to the persistent rumours. This suspicion had flared up again in November 1940, at the time of Molotov's negotiations in Berlin in which Molotov had insisted on Russia's interest in Finland and the Balkans and resisted Hitler's suggestion that Russia should expand in the direction of Iran and India. Though the negotiations had been commented on in countless reports from British embassies and in the decrypts of Axis diplomatic traffic supplied by GC and CS, the British government had learned little about their true purpose or their outcome,[57] and the speculation of MI and the Foreign Office on these subjects had diverged. For MI, Molotov's visit to Berlin had been made necessary by the need for closer contact between the Russian and the German governments at a time when German troop concentrations on the Russian frontiers, made by Germany in order to secure her rear, were alarming the Russians and when the Germans were anxious to know Russia's attitude to their extension of the war into the Balkans and against Turkey.[58] In the opinion of the Foreign Office the important points had been that Russian policy in the Balkans was running counter to German designs and that Russia had not responded to Germany's attempt to get her to support a German move into the Middle and Near East.[59]

56. ibid, No 5A of 17 January 1941.
57. Churchill, op cit, Vol III, p 316.
58. WO 190/892, No 32B of 24 November 1940.
59. Woodward, op cit, Vol I, p 497.

In the first week of January 1941 the Foreign Office raised no objections to the FOES report. Later in that month, when it had learned that Russia and Germany had renewed their economic agreement and signed a Pact of Friendship, it was admitting that Russo-German relations 'appeared to be as close as at any time' since the summer of 1939.[60] On 22 January it was commenting with approval that in the appreciation of 17 January MI had on military grounds reached the same conclusion as it had itself reached on political grounds – that there was no reason to expect an early German attack.[61] This view was shared by some of the foreign diplomats in Moscow and the Foreign Office knew that this was so. On 17 and 23 January it learned that the Turkish Ambassador thought that the rumours of a German attack on Russia were part of a deception plan to cover Germany's intention to drive through Turkey, and that his Greek colleague agreed with him. But even if the Foreign Office was impressed by these reports – and it seems unlikely that it was wholly convinced – this was not the case with the Prime Minister. The FOES report made no impression on him, if indeed he saw it. On 6 January, when the final draft of the report was being prepared, he again referred to the possibility that Hitler would turn east. 'A great campaign in the east of Europe', he wrote, 'the defeat of Russia, the conquest of the Ukraine and an advance...to the Caspian would none of them, separately or together, bring him victorious peace.'[62] On 20 January, no doubt on his initiative, the Defence Committee of the Cabinet debated, inconclusively, whether, beyond Bulgaria, Germany's object was to operate against the British or to drive into the Ukraine and the Caucasus.[63] On 24 February he commented that Russia was now in an unenviable position and that her attitude was one of making concessions to Germany in order to gain time.[64]

This last comment was made at the meeting at which, as well as deciding that it must prepare to send an expeditionary force to Greece, the War Cabinet discussed a suggestion from Cripps that the Foreign Secretary should visit Moscow after his trip to the Middle East. The Cabinet decided that the Foreign Secretary and the CIGS should go no further than Ankara. Cripps, meeting them there at the end of the month, found that the CIGS believed that Germany was still giving priority to *Sealion*. He himself, in contrast, was still convinced that Germany would attack Russia first, and that she would do so 'not later than the end of June'. On his return to Moscow on 28 February he announced this to an informal press conference';[65] as in June 1940, he seems to have done so on his own initiative. Early in March the

60. ibid, Vol I, p 595.
61. FO 371/29470, N286/78/38.
62. Churchill, op cit, Vol III, p 10.
63. CAB 69/2, DO (41) 6th Meeting, 20 January.
64. CAB 65/21, WM (41) 20 CA, 24 February 1941, p 4.
65. Whaley, op cit, pp 35–36.

rumour was circulating around the embassies in Moscow that on his return from Ankara he had told Vyshinski, the Deputy Foreign Minister, most emphatically that in his personal opinion, based on reliable sources, Germany would turn on Russia after defeating Greece, Yugoslavia and Turkey.

Cripps's representations raise the question of what moved him to act. What, since it did not exist in Whitehall, was the source of his 'reliable' information? A possible answer is provided by what is known of American intelligence about the *Barbarossa* preparations. According to some American published accounts, the United States Commercial Attaché in Berlin had been kept informed of the initial planning between August and December 1940 by a senior member of the Nazi Party, and sometime between early January and mid-February 1941 he was given full details of Hitler's *Barbarossa* directive of 18 December and of the Führer conference on the subject of 9 January 1941. According to the same accounts, Washington received this information on 21 February and there was then a further delay before the United States government gave the information to the Russian Ambassador in Washington on 1 March – the further delay being in part due to consultations with the United States Ambassador in Moscow and to his advice that the Russians would distrust a warning and regard it as provocation.[66] Cripps was perhaps informed of this development by his American colleague.

□

While it is not unreasonable to suppose that Cripps learned of Washington's information from the American embassy in Moscow, there is no evidence that Whitehall received it at this time from the United States government. What was subsequently received, moreover, was not as precise as is suggested by the above accounts. The Foreign Office files show that on 21 March and 17 June 1941 – the latter only received on 25 June after the German attack had begun – the British embassy in Washington sent to London secret documents, dating from the previous January and April, which it had obtained from the State Department. Only the April documents survive in the files. They consist of very generalised accounts of German intentions and strategic objectives in the Mediterranean as well as against Russia, and the actual plans for the attack on Russia are only in broad outline. Major Morton's reaction to them seems fully justified: 'The Book of Revelations read backwards would be more helpful'; he added that they were clearly not official documents but only someone's comment on events and not nearly as good as the sort of material provided by

---

66. Whaley, op cit, pp 37–40, 227–228; US Department of State, *Foreign Relations of the United States, 1941* Vol I (1958), pp 712, 714; Cordell Hull, *Memoirs* (1948), pp 968–969; W Shirer, *The Rise and Fall of the Third Reich* (1959), Chapter 23.

the SIS.[67] The documents dated January and received from Washington in March were presumably no more revealing; at least in the Service intelligence branches they received no more attention than did the many other rumours that were coming in about *Barbarossa* from Axis diplomatic decrypts, from the British diplomatic missions and from the SIS. In the second half of March MI was reaffirming the assessment it had formed in January. It was doing so after some weeks of uncertainty that was produced, we can now see, by the fact that a further advance in Germany's preparations did not go entirely unnoticed by the intelligence sources.

For obvious reasons the German Army staggered the eastward movement of its formations and HQs, those headed by well-known generals remaining in the west for as long as possible, and the GAF, whose forward airfields and other installations had been under construction since October, deferred till April and May the deployment of the signals and administrative troops needed for the reception of its operational formations. The operational formations themselves were used against the United Kingdom or kept in Germany for refitting until a still later date; like the Army's main mechanised formations, they were not transferred to the east until the last three weeks before the opening of the offensive. At some levels, however, the German eastern build-up had to be intensified after the *Barbarossa* directive of 18 December 1940 and particularly after 3 February 1941, when OKH incorporated that directive into an operational order. On 3 February the Army Group commanders were appointed and indoctrinated. The number of divisions facing Russia grew from 34 in mid-January to 46 by 5 April after allowing not only for the despatch of 28 divisions from Poland to the south-east for the Balkan campaign, but also for the transfer of some divisions from the east to western Europe. In March the GAF intensified its vast programme for the construction of airfields and accommodation in the east.[68]

From the beginning of February reports on some of these activities began to reach Whitehall. One SIS report dated 31 January said that preparations for the invasion of Russia were almost open; troops were arriving in Poland from France; Russian speakers were being recruited into the Army and Russian emigrés into German intelligence units, regardless of suitability; preparations for operations by the GAF were particularly striking and included the construction of a continuous chain of aerodromes along the railway line from Poznan to Lodz. On 5 February MI commented on another report – probably from the Polish organisation in the area* – that large numbers of

---

* See above, p 438.

67. FO 371/26521, C6928/C7205/78/38.
68. US Department of Army, *The German Campaign in Russia*, p 26; EDS/Appreciation/5, p 103; Leach, op cit, p 169.

German troops, mainly armoured, were reaching East Prussia and that there was rail congestion between Berlin and Warsaw. Its comments were issued only in the low-level War Office weekly intelligence summary and were in the old vein: there was no other evidence to suggest that Germany was preparing for action against Russia and these moves were probably being made in order to keep Russia quiet while Germany occupied Bulgaria.[69] On 6 February – for the first time since 7 November, when it had given its view of the German activity in Finland[70] – it included an item bearing on Russo-German relations in the Chiefs of Staff résumé. Its comments on this item, which dealt with the German garrison in north Norway, also conformed to MI's earlier views: the garrison was not large enough to suggest that Germany was contemplating a descent on Iceland, a possibility which MI had mentioned on 23 January,[71] but it was not excessive as a safeguard against the danger of a Russian or a British attack.[72] On the same day, however, the DMI attached another appreciation to a letter he wrote to the chairman of the JIC and the other Directors of Intelligence. This said that the German Army, calculated by MI to be about the size of 250 divisions, was 'stronger than is necessary for actual operations, excluding a war against Russia which is unlikely for the present'.[73] At first sight the wording suggests that no change of ground has taken place; but the phrase 'for the present' has at last replaced the phrase 'until Germany has disposed of Great Britain'.

On 7 February MI issued another ambiguous appreciation. This stated that 250 divisions would be enough to hold off Russia if Germany attacked Turkey, but it also saw fit to add that 'Hitler is an opportunist'.[74] The implication behind this phrase might have been that Hitler was unlikely to undertake a venture which, like an attack on Russia, required long preparation. But it is no less possible that MI felt that it should concede that with his vast Army, and given its dispositions, he might easily switch to a surprise attack on Russia if it suited him.

A further sign of uncertainty – perhaps also of division of opinion – in MI occurred on 14 February. On that date MI notified the General Staff that a 'most reliable source' had recently reported an increase in German intelligence activity in the Near East, particularly against Turkey, Syria, Egypt, Iraq, Iran and Russia, at the expense of the intelligence staffs in west Germany. In the previous August it

---

69. WO 208/2258, Weekly Intsum No 77, to 5 February 1941.
70. CAB 80/22, COS (40) 915 (COS Résumé, No 62).
71. WO 208/2258, WO Weekly Intsum No 75, to 23 January 1941.
72. CAB 80/25, COS (41) 78 (COS Résumé, No 75).
73. WO 190/893, No 13B, letter from DMI to JIC Chairman and the other Ds of I, 6 February 1941.
74. ibid, No 14B of 7 February 1941.

had received similar information from A-54 and had not drawn it to the attention of the higher authorities.* It now took this step in part because the latest information had come from an even better source, the hand cypher of the Abwehr which GC and CS had broken during December 1940. No doubt for the same reason, its comments on the information, though primarily about Germany's intentions in the Balkans and the Middle East, included remarks about Russia which departed from its earlier views. One of them was that, although it would be 'dangerous' to let the information cast doubt on 'the serious intention of Germany to invade Great Britain in the coming months', 'it does certainly suggest that invasion is not imminent'. Another read as follows: 'The present changes do not seem to have the effect of weakening the intelligence centres charged with action against Russia' and 'they may be significant of German intentions in the later months of 1941'.[75] Given that the information was such as to foster Whitehall's grave anxiety about Germany's intentions in the Balkans, Syria and Iraq – that the DMI, indeed, in handwritten comments on it, dwelt only on its relevance to the danger in the Middle East – these remarks constituted no mean concession from MI's previous standpoint.

Between the middle of February and the middle of March, the intelligence branches, at full stretch in sifting the evidence and writing appreciations about German moves and intentions elsewhere, had little to offer about German-Russian relations. Their next report on that subject did not come until 5 March, when the Air Ministry drew attention to reports that German army and air officers were organising bases on the Finnish-Russian frontier.[76] On 7 March MI commented that German activity in Finland would not constitute a *casus belli* for Russia and also repeated its earlier interpretation of German activity in north Norway: this might be preparation for an expedition against Iceland or Ireland, or for defence against a possible British landing, or for support of Finland against Russian pressure.[77] It did not suggest that this activity in the north might be associated with such evidence as was coming in about eastern Europe. It was now keeping a sharper watch on that evidence, however. On 5 March it included in the War Office weekly intelligence summary the fact that several reports had been received suggesting conflict between Germany and Russia, including one to the effect that the Hungarian General Staff was convinced that Germany planned to attack Russia in June and July and another which claimed that the Germans had asked the Romanian government to supply plans of all bridges crossing the Pruth and the Dniester, the frontier rivers with the USSR. MI thought that

---

* See above, pp 435–436.

75. ibid, No 17B of 14 February 1941.
76. AIR 22/74, Air Ministry Weekly Intelligence Summary, to 5 March 1941.
77. WO 190/893, No 26A of 7 March 1941.

the first of these reports 'must be taken with reserve' but that the second was 'significant'. It also noted that the mobilisation of the Romanian Army was possibly relevant, and added the comment that Romanian and Hungarian forces could serve as a deterrent to Russian action in the Balkans 'for the time being, irrespective of a more active role in the near future'.[78] These reports and MI's comments on them should be considered against the fact that it was only on 17 January that Hitler confirmed an earlier decision to send two or three additional divisions to north Norway, partly to defend the area against possible British attacks and partly to prepare for two separate advances into Russia from Finland, and that it was not until the end of March that German troops first took up station on the Romanian-Russian frontier.[79]

But if MI was now on the alert, it was now, also, that Germany's deception measures had some impact there. On 10 January, in a directive announcing that *Sealion* and *Felix* were to remain temporarily postponed, and again on 6 February after approving OKH's operational order for *Barbarossa*, Hitler had ordered an intensified effort to disguise the *Barbarossa* preparations as preparations for invasion of the United Kingdom in 1941. The intensified effort involved actual movements and operations, beginning in March with the westward deployment of 21 divisions, mostly of second-class quality, from eastern Europe to Belgium and northern France, and incorporating especially heavy GAF raids on the United Kingdom in May.[80] On 5 March MI noted SIS reports of the beginning of this east-to-west movement[81] and, according to post-war testimony, was deeply divided as to what to make of it. Some of the specialists on the German order of battle were sure that the troops involved belonged to training formations which had been moved east before the attack on France; they suspected, moreover, that their return to the west might be a pointer to Germany's intention to turn on Russia. The DMI, by their account, dismissed this view as wishful thinking. By 11 March a compromise view had been adopted. On that date MI noted that the westward movement of troops was continuing and concluded, from the concurrence of westward and eastward movements, that the German Army was being redistributed, rather than concentrated in any one area.[82]

This conclusion paved the way for MI's return to its earlier position. On 18 March, in a new series of notes which appears to have been started primarily for the benefit of the Chief of the Imperial General Staff, MI did at last consider intelligence about Finland in the

---

78. WO 208/2258, WO Weekly Intsum, to 5 March 1941.
79. Creveld, op cit, p 135.
80. ibid, pp 150–151; EDS/Appreciation/5, pp 102, 105–106.
81. WO 190/893 of 5 March 1941.
82. ibid, No 27A of 12 March 1941.

same report with evidence about Russo-German relations on other fronts. Germany, it noted, was said to be strengthening her ties with Finland as a preliminary to closer military co-operation. A reliable report indicated that German Fifth Column activities in the Ukraine and Georgia were increasing. As for the continuing rumours of Germany's intention to attack Russia, MI conceded that 'the whispering campaign appears to have intensified', and that 'there are indications that Germany is less friendly, even on the surface'. But MI felt that some of the rumours arose from the fact that the Germans had been moving troops to Poland during the past three months, and that these troops 'may be to replace those which have moved to Romania and to dispose of some of Hitler's new divisions'. It did not speculate on the purpose that the new divisions might be put to, and its final conclusion was that 'so long as Germany has her hands full elsewhere, however, an attack on Russia is most unlikely'.[83]

On 19 March this conclusion was reaffirmed in a further report by FOES. The key to Germany's intentions after the end of the Balkan campaign was, this paper said, her determination to try to defeat Great Britain during 1941, and she would not attack Russia before she had defeated Great Britain. If Great Britain had not sued for peace by June Germany would give priority to a march through Syria to Suez and would do all she could to increase the strain on British resources by encouraging Japanese intervention, by stirring up insurrections in Latin America and by mounting such diversionary operations as an attack on Freetown. After making this far-ranging survey, the report admitted that she might also be contemplating other campaigns, in areas 'suitable for operations by mechanised forces where petrol was available'. But it attached less importance to them, and it did not stop to ask why, at the cost of enormous strain to her allegedly overstretched economy, Germany had built up a vast mechanised army.[84] In the week following the FOES report the Service intelligence branches continued to discount the rumours which conflicted with it. On 23 March AI was unconvinced by an SIS report that Germany intended to turn on Russia after occupying Greece, Yugoslavia and European Turkey in April: in its view the GAF was consolidating for a renewed onslaught on the United Kingdom[85] and, apart from the probability that Germany wanted to keep the war out of the Balkans, she would need three months to prepare for an attack on Russia.[86] Two days later, in an appreciation devoted mainly to the situation in Libya and the invasion threat to the United Kingdom, MI agreed with AI that *Sealion* was now unlikely unless renewed air attack and intensified blockade failed to reduce Great Britain, but it felt that Germany was

---

83. ibid, No 29A of 18 March 1941.
84. CAB 81/64, FOES (41) of 19 March 1941.
85. AIR 40/2232, Minute of 13 March 1941.
86. ibid, Minute of 23 March 1941.

in earnest about a Balkan campaign. It mentioned the fact that
reports continued to show that Germany was busy in Finland and to
suggest that she intended to attack Russia in the summer. But the
activity in Finland was 'possibly with a view to containing Soviet
troops; possibly to distract Soviet attention from the Balkans'. As for
the rumours about an attack on Russia, they 'were not convincing'.[87]
On 27 March MI repeated this assessment in the Chiefs of Staff
résumé.[88]

□

Whatever may be thought of the FOES strategic assessment, it must
be remembered that, for information about the enemy, FOES was
wholly dependent on the separate intelligence branches. In defence
of the intelligence branches, it must be conceded that, rumours apart,
they had as yet received only a few items of information that could
have been set with any great confidence against their own strategic
assumptions. Sir Winston Churchill has described the situation in his
own terms:

'Up till the end of March I was not convinced that Hitler was resolved on mortal
war with Russia, nor how near it was. Our intelligence reports revealed in much
detail the extensive German troops movements towards and into the Balkan
states... But none of these necessarily involved the invasion of Russia and all
were readily explainable by German interests and policy in [that area]... Our
information about the immense movement taking place... towards the main
Russian front... was far more difficult to acquire. That Germany should at
that stage and before leaving the Balkan scene, open another major war with
Russia seemed to me too good to be true... There was no sign of lessening
German strength opposite us across the Channel. The German air raids on
Britain continued with intensity. The manner in which the German troop
concentrations in Roumania and Bulgaria had been glossed over and
apparently accepted by the Soviet government, the evidence we had of large
and invaluable supplies being sent to Germany from Russia, the obvious
community of interest between the two countries in overwhelming and
dividing the British Empire in the East, all made it seem more likely that Hitler
and Stalin would make a bargain at our expense rather than war upon each
other.'[89]

From this description, moreover, as from what has emerged in the
foregoing pages about her response, or lack of response, to the
British and American approaches, it will be clear that the British
authorities were almost as much handicapped by ignorance of
Russia's assessments and intentions as they were by lack of incontrovertible evidence about Germany's. Nor could the intelligence
authorities make up for the absence of all but nominal diplomatic

---

87. WO 190/893, No 33A of 25 March 1941.
88. CAB 80/26, COS (41) 196 (COS Résumé, No 82).
89. Churchill, op cit, Vol III, p 317.

contacts with Russia. As well as being thwarted by her rigorous security measures, British intelligence about Russia suffered from the fact that since the mid-1930s it had concentrated almost all its efforts against the Axis powers. It was obtaining a trickle of information about Soviet military movements and personalities; but the intelligence available about Russia's industrial war potential was inadequate for an understanding of her capabilities, and virtually no intelligence was available about her political situation or her intentions.*

In relation to information from Russia, or intelligence about her, there was to be no improvement down to the time of the German attack. But where Germany was concerned the intelligence picture underwent a substantial change at the end of March. The COS résumé of 27 March noted without comment that Germany was again increasing her troops in Poland. This item reflected the intelligence, received from the GAF Enigma on the previous day, that 3 armoured divisions and other important elements in the German Army had been ordered to move from the Balkans to the Cracow area. On 27 March itself, the day of the Belgrade coup, the Enigma revealed that part of this transfer was being cancelled.†

For the Prime Minister, for some of the intelligence bodies – AI and GC and CS and, after some hesitation, the Foreign Office – the receipt of this intelligence provided the first confirmation that Germany's main preparations were directed against Russia. On 28 March the head of AI's German section issued the following minute:

'It is significant that the day after Yugoslavia signed the Tripartite Pact orders were issued for the transfer of a large proportion of the German "Balkan" forces to the Russian front. This, together with other reports and events such as the Lend-Lease Bill and the development of airfields in the east, leads me to believe that Germany's intention is to move into the Ukraine in the near future. A Balkan conflagration would necessarily postpone this. We have always believed that for economic reasons Germany must if possible avoid a war in the Balkans. On the other hand for the same reasons she may be forced to occupy part of Russia. A considerable time must, however, elapse before she could gain any appreciable economic advantages. There is therefore a possibility that Germany will accept diplomatic defeat in the Balkans and...concentrate on preparations for an aggressive policy against Russia.'

The minute suggested that the JIC should produce a paper on 'The Possible Invasion of Russia by Germany'.[90] On 30 March GC and CS also concluded that the Enigma evidence pointed to the possibility of some large-scale operation against Russia, 'either for intimidation or

---

* Germany was equally in the dark. For a discussion of Germany's virtually complete lack of intelligence about the military and economic capabilities of the USSR, see Albert Seaton, *The Russo-German War 1941–45* (1971), Chapter 3.

† See Chapter 11, p 371.

90. AIR 40/2232, Minute of 28 March 1941.

for actual attack'.[91] By then, and probably on 28 March, the Prime Minister had reached the same conclusion as AI.

At the news of the Yugoslav coup he had thought that 'if a united front were formed in the Balkan peninsula Germany might think it better business to take it out of Russia observing that we have had many reports of heavy concentrations in Finland and intrigues in Sweden and Finland'[92] That was on 28 March. Thereafter, according to his subsequent account, the receipt of the Enigma intelligence:

'illuminated the whole Eastern scene in a lightning flash. The sudden movement to Cracow of so much armour needed in the Balkan sphere could only mean Hitler's intention to invade Russia in May. This seemed to me henceforward certainly his major purpose. The fact that the Belgrade revolution had required their return to Roumania involved perhaps a delay from May to June.'[93]

His subsequent account is confirmed by the fact that on 30 March he put this conclusion in a telegram to the Foreign Secretary in Athens:

'My reading of the intelligence is that the bad man concentrated very large armoured forces etc to overawe Yugoslavia and Greece, and hoped to get former or both without fighting. The moment he was sure Yugoslavia was in the Axis he moved 3 of the 5 Panzers towards the Bear, believing that what was left would be enough to finish the Greek affair.* However, the Belgrade revolution upset this picture and caused the northward movement to be arrested in transit. This can only mean, in my opinion, the intention to attack Yugoslavia at earliest, or alternatively [to] act against the Turk. It looks as if heavy forces will be used in Balkan peninsula and that Bear will be kept waiting a bit. Furthermore, these orders and counter-orders in their relation to the Belgrade coup seem to reveal magnitude of design both towards south-east and east. This is the clearest indication we have received so far. Let me know in guarded terms whether you and Dill agree with my impressions'.[95]

On 3 April he sent a message to Stalin:

'I have sure information from a trusted agent that when the Germans thought they had got Yugoslavia in the net, that is to say after March 20, they began to move three out of the five Panzer divisions from Roumania to southern Poland. The moment they heard of the Serbian revolution this movement was countermanded. Your Excellency will readily appreciate the significance of these facts'.[96]

---

* Although this conclusion was correct, Hitler had in fact ordered this movement of armour on 17 March to implement his decision to transfer the armoured spearhead for *Barbarossa* from the Moldavian front to an area north of the Carpathians.[94]

91. CX/JQ/S/7 of 30 March 1941.
92. Churchill, op cit, Vol III, p 151.
93. ibid, p 319.
94. Creveld, op cit, pp 134–135.
95. Churchill, op cit, Vol III, pp 319–320.
96. Woodward, op cit, Vol I, p 604.

To the Prime Minister's indignation, this message did not reach the Russian government till 19 April.[97] One reason for the delay was Cripps' belief that the Russian government would regard it as provocative.[98]* Cripps did not doubt that a German attack was imminent, and already at the end of March he had again urged Whitehall to open discussions with the Russian government. During the delay he stressed to Vyshinski the seriousness of the German threat to Russia and the advisability of Russian support for the Balkan states.[99] On 19 April he gave Vyshinski both the Prime Minister's message and one from himself. His own note stated that 'the more recent developments of the war, and the apparent decision of Hitler to postpone the attempt to invade England, have in the view of His Majesty's Government increased the likelihood of German pressure to the east; and, according to their information, this view is confirmed by a great many independent sources in other countries, notably in Germany itself'. The evidence suggested that Hitler had decided that he had to secure food and raw materials for a long war. These could be secured only from Russia. Hitler could secure them either by agreement or force. 'Judging by the many indications we have received from usually reliable sources...a seizure by force of the sources of supply in the east is not a hypothesis at all but part of the planned German development of the war for the spring of this year'.[100]

The British warnings were by no means the only warnings conveyed to the Russian government at this time. Indeed, Moscow was by now alive with rumours of the coming assault, and Cripps probably based his warning not only on the Prime Minister's message, but also on information received from the other embassies, particularly the American. The Swedes had pieced together a fairly accurate estimate of Germany's intentions; they gave their information to the United States Ambassador in Moscow on 24 March.[101] By 1 April, it appears, the Yugoslav Military Attaché in Berlin had got wind of the German plan, and his government had passed his information to Moscow via London.[102] It has been claimed that since the beginning of 1941 the Vichy authorities had been giving the Soviet embassy their intelligence about the eastward movement of German divisions.[103] And it is beyond doubt that from 20 March the United States government had renewed its warnings to the Soviet Ambassador in Washington,

---

* For a discussion of what Soviet intelligence knew of German intentions see John Erickson, *The Road to Stalingrad* (1975), Chapter 2.

97. Churchill, op cit, Vol III, p 323.
98. Woodward, op cit, Vol I, p 605.
99. ibid, pp 606–607.
100. ibid, pp 608–609.
101. US Department of State, op cit, p 133.
102. M R D Foot, *Resistance: an Analysis of European Resistance to Nazism 1940–45* (1976), p 188, quoting P Auty, *Tito* (1970).
103. Paillole, op cit, pp 336–337.

advising him on the basis of decrypted Japanese diplomatic messages that Germany would attack Russia within 2 months.[104] Unlike Cripps, however, and unlike the Prime Minister and AI in Whitehall, the British Foreign Office remained reluctant to believe that Russia was to be attacked.

The Foreign Office was now receiving from the State Department via the British embassy in Washington information from the machine cypher used by the Japanese embassies for their most confidential telegrams, the source of the American warnings to the Soviet Ambassador.[105] But it does not seem to have been aware that the United States was giving warnings to the Soviet Ambassador; and up to the middle of April GC and CS's own exploitation of the Japanese diplomatic cyphers yielded only one item of intelligence bearing on the problem. This was a message of 23 March in which the Japanese Ambassador in Berlin reported that Admiral Raeder had expressed doubt about the wisdom of a German offensive against Britain, either directly or indirectly by advancing against British positions in the Middle East, and, hinting at German operations in other directions, had advised Japan to attack Singapore. What is perhaps more important, the Foreign Office did not receive the Enigma decrypts, and was in no position to judge the significance of the evidence from that source which had so impressed the Prime Minister and AI. And there were other reasons for its hesitation. On 1 April, having received from the embassy in Belgrade the rumour that Hitler had told Prince Paul that he intended to attack Russia on 30 June, it decided that it would be unwise to forward it to the Russians: the Soviet government, feeling that Russia was safe until Great Britain was defeated, might not wish to risk changing the policy of subservience to Germany, and warnings of the danger from Germany would only encourage it to maintain this attitude unless they were warnings which left no doubt that Germany would attack regardless of concessions Russia made to her.[106] It was no doubt on similar grounds that the Foreign Secretary at first counselled the Prime Minister against sending his warning to Russia on 3 April.[107] Early in April a Foreign Office minute was noting a 'significant' lack of evidence since the Yugoslav coup that Germany was going to attack Russia, and was approving the 'very sane point of view' expressed by MI at a Foreign Office meeting on 31 March that Hitler did not intend such an attack if he could avoid it.[108]

On the night of 2–3 April the Foreign Office obtained from

104. US Department of State, op cit, p 723. See also Whaley, op cit, pp 40, 45, 277–278.
105. FO 371/26518, C2045/C3309/19/18; FO 371/29482, N2617/78/38.
106. Woodward, op cit, Vol I, p 604.
107. ibid, p 606.
108. FO 371/29479, N1367/78/38.

Washington some justification for its caution. The embassy reported the receipt of the Prince Paul rumour from the State Department; in the same report, however, it also announced that the State Department had learned from the Japanese diplomatic cypher that Göring had told the Japanese Foreign Minister that Germany would attack Russia only after making another attempt to defeat Great Britain.[109] In the end, however – influenced, as we must suppose, by the impact of the Enigma evidence on the Prime Minister – the Foreign Office overcame its hesitation. On 11 April the Foreign Secretary followed up the Prime Minister's warning of 3 April by instructing Cripps to urge the Russians to do their utmost to encourage the Balkan states to resist Germany, and his message said that 'the German attack of which there are so many signs' would not be prevented by 'the fact that he [Hitler] is in conflict with us'.[110] On 16 April he told the Soviet Ambassador in London of the Prince Paul rumour and discussed with him the possibility of an Anglo-Russian rapprochement.[111]

MI had meanwhile refused to accept that the Enigma evidence of 26 and 27 March was decisive. On 1 April an MI appreciation conceded that the Enigma decrypts were 'of interest', but it also insisted that 'there is as yet no reason to believe the numerous reports that Germany intends to attack Russia in the near future'. On the contrary, 'the German object is undoubtedly to exert military pressure on Russia to prevent Russian interference in German Balkan plans'.[112] This conclusion MI repeated to the Chiefs of Staff on 3 April, when it added that the rumours of an impending attack might be being put about by Germany in order to influence Russia's diplomatic decisions.[113] On 2 April in its lower level and more widely circulated weekly intelligence summary it had indeed pointed out that the German Army now had 250 divisions, that this was the maximum that Germany could sustain without damage to her war production and supply, that she could not sustain so large a number in a long campaign, and that 'the policy seems to indicate that the German General Staff either contemplate in 1941 a short rapid campaign for which 250 divisions are considered sufficient, or hope to achieve their ends by an overwhelming display of force and...thereafter expect a period of quiescence'. In this paper, too, however, it had indicated its preference for the second of these interpretations by again referring to Germany's interest in holding off possible threats[114] On 9 April, again in the War Office weekly intelligence summary, it considered that reports of a German attack on Russia might well be

109. Woodward, op cit, Vol I, p 604; Whaley, op cit, pp 58–60.
110. Woodward, op cit, Vol I, p 605; Churchill, op cit, Vol III, pp 320–321.
111. Woodward, op cit, Vol I, pp 609–610.
112. WO 190/893, No 35D of 1 April 1941.
113. CAB 80/27, COS (41) 221 (COS Résumé, No 83) paragraphs 18, 20, 23.
114. WO 208/2259, WO Weekly Intsum to 2 April 1941.

German propaganda 'as part of a war of nerves against Russia during the Balkan campaign'.[115]

□

In the next inter-departmental assessment by the intelligence bodies – a paper on 'Germany Strategy 1941' drawn up on 5 April and issued by the JIC on 10 April – MI's views prevailed. On this occasion, as so often before, the intelligence bodies concluded that Germany's main objective remained the defeat of Great Britain during 1941, by blockade and air attack if possible, by invasion if necessary. It was beyond question that she also planned a drive through the Balkans as far as the Straits, but so long as she saw any chance of defeating the United Kingdom during 1941 she would not continue her advance as far as Syria, Egypt or Iraq – the more so as this would antagonise Turkey and Russia. As for Russia, a 'direct' German attack was unlikely at present. Germany would continue her military preparations in the east with the double purpose of keeping Russia amenable and of enabling herself to take immediate action when necessary. In the long run, of course, a Russo-German clash was inevitable unless Germany was defeated in the war with Great Britain. Germany undoubtedly had her eyes on the Ukraine and the Caucasus; Russia was fully aware of this. But Russia would do all she could to avoid the clash and – what was more to the point – so would Germany.

Germany, the JIC appreciation continued, would not have forgotten that her occupation of western Russia in 1918 had become a liability, and she must know that another occupation of Russia would severely reduce the forces available for offensive use elsewhere. Particularly because the strength of the GAF was insufficient for full-scale simultaneous operations on both fronts, a war with Russia would rule out an invasion of the United Kingdom, and would open up new possibilities for British offensive operations against Germany. It was doubtful whether Germany had enough strength even for simultaneous offensives against Russia and into south-eastern Europe. There was no evidence that she was under severe economic pressure and an attack on Russia would in any case bring about no improvement in her supply position in the short term. Weighed against these powerful strategic considerations, the evidence pointing to an early attack on Russia was judged to be unimpressive. The many rumours to this effect were probably designed to frighten Russia. Concentration and movements of German troops in the east, of which there was considerable intelligence, could have been undertaken for the same purpose. In any case, Poland was a useful training ground and a suitable location for reserves, and the preparations would enable

---

115. ibid, to 9 April 1941.

Germany to move against Russia if she later decided that her chances of eliminating Great Britain during 1941 were receding.[116]

After the completion of this report MI again showed signs of wavering. On 15 April it stressed that there was still no indication that Germany was increasing her total forces on the Russian frontier. But it also noted reports that the Russians were moving troops to the frontier, added that these 'suggest that they, at least, are taking the German threat seriously' and – all this in a summary of the evidence of the past six months prepared for the DMI – concluded that the rumours of a German attack 'were consistent both with a war of nerves and with an intention actually to invade'.[117] On the same day, in notes for the CIGS, it admitted that 'some colour' was lent to the rumours 'by troop concentrations in Poland and north Norway, the German interest in Finland, and fortifications in Poland'.[118] In the War Office weekly intelligence summary of 16 April MI repeated this admission: it was impossible to tell whether the 'persistent rumours coming from so many quarters...are merely being spread by Germany as part of a war of nerves or have some more solid basis in fact'[119] It repeated it again in the Chiefs of Staff résumé on 17 April.[120] Thereafter it inserted information and comment about Russo-German relations in every weekly résumé.

There were several reasons for MI's dwindling confidence in the opinion it had maintained up to 10 April. As the German Balkan offensive reached its climax, and began to move to its close, the argument that the rumours of Germany's designs on Russia and the evidence of her concentrations against Russia were explained by her need to keep Russia quiet was an argument that was losing its logical force. The same was true, as the spring advanced, of the belief that Germany was still giving priority to *Sealion*. On 17 April MI prepared an appreciation in which it showed that, if Germany adopted various ingenious arrangements, she could still bring back to France within three or four weeks sufficient armoured divisions for an invasion of the United Kingdom, but the tortuousness of the appreciation leaves little doubt that MI was unconvinced by its own argument.[121] These considerations no doubt played their part when the Service intelligence departments and MEW joined the Foreign Office in preparing an appreciation of the latest intelligence for despatch to Cripps on 20 April.

At the end of March the Polish underground organisation in eastern Europe had reported that Germany would attack on 15

---

116. JIC (41) 144 of 10 April 1941, covering APS (41) 3 of 5 April 1941.
117. WO 190/893, No 44B of 15 April 1941.
118. ibid, No 44C, Notes for CIGS, 15 April 1941.
119. WO 208/2259, WO Weekly Intsum No 87, to 16 April 1941.
120. CAB 80/27, COS (41) 248 (COS Résumé, No 85) paragraph 23.
121. WO 190/893, No 46A of 17 April 1941.

April,[122] and SIS's representative in Geneva had heard from a well-placed source with contacts in German official circles that Hitler would attack Russia in May. In the middle of April some diplomatic sources were predicting that the attack would be early in June and suggesting that Russia had some knowledge of the German plans. By then these sources – the Poles, the SIS and the diplomatic reports – had also sent in considerable detailed intelligence to support the general warnings. Germany had ordered a further call-up of men for military service and was developing airfields in Poland, mapping the Russo-German frontiers by air photography, training Russian refugees in Romania for administrative work, organising Ukrainian and White Russian emigrés, printing Russian currency notes, continuing preparations for Fifth Column activity in the Ukraine and the Caucasus. In the past month she had also increased her divisions in East Prussia and Poland. In commenting on this evidence to Cripps on 20 April the Foreign Office admitted that Whitehall did not know what to make of it. The reports might be part of a German war of nerves. A German invasion would result in much chaos throughout Russia and the Germans would have to reorganise everything in the territories which they might occupy. Meanwhile they would lose their supplies from Russia. The loss of material transferred across the Trans-Siberian railway would be even more important. Although the resources of Germany were immense, they would not allow her to continue her campaign in the Balkans, maintain the existing scale of air attacks against the United Kingdom, take the offensive against Egypt and at the same time invade and reorganise a large part of the USSR. All these arguments pointed against a German attack. On the other hand, a rapid success in the Balkans would enable Germany to throw most of her 15 armoured divisions against Russia. There was as yet no information about the movement of German aircraft towards the Russian frontiers; if the necessary preparations had been made in Poland, aircraft could be moved there at the shortest notice. The appreciation concluded by saying that the German General Staff appeared to be opposed to a war on two fronts and in favour of disposing of Great Britain before attacking Russia, but the decision rested with Hitler.[123]

Behind the inconclusiveness of this appreciation lay two increasingly prominent divergences of opinion. In MI itself there had been further evidence of restlessness in the ranks when a minute of 3 April had pointed out that among the German armoured divisions ready for action, estimated at 15, 9 were in the Balkans, 3 in central Germany and Poland, and 2 in Italy and north Africa. The minute had concluded that the Germans had more armour in the Balkans than MI had previously allowed, and that she clearly intended no immediate

122. Whaley, op cit, p 48.
123. Woodward, op cit, Vol I, p 612.

operations in the west. In the archive copy of the minute, which is marked for inclusion in a DMI note, the conclusion has been scored through.[124] Thereafter, of the intelligence items summarised for Cripps on 20 April, some of which had pointed to a German intention to occupy Russian territory, by no means all had been incorporated in the appreciations issued by MI. At the same time, while senior officers in MI could not bring themselves to accept this conclusion, the Foreign Office was becoming more convinced that Russia was soon to be attacked. This became clear when the Chiefs of Staff brought the divergence between MI and the Foreign Office into the open by calling for a verbal discussion with the JIC on 22 April about Germany's next move.

In a brief for the CIGS in advance of the discussion MI dwelt mainly on *Sealion* and discounted the rumours of a German attack on Russia because there were 'no immediate signs of the essential troop moves in the direction of the USSR'.[125] Another MI appreciation of 22 April stated that 'it appears certain that preparations for an eventual war with Russia are continuing, but there is absolutely no confirmation that Germany will attack this summer'.[126] These assertions were strictly correct: partly because Germany was deferring the eastward movement of her armour, and partly because for communications connected with the eastern deployment, as opposed to those connected with the Balkan campaign, she could use land-lines and forbid references to operational matters in messages going out by W/T, there were 'no immediate signs', 'no confirmation', and at the discussion itself the Foreign Office chairman of the JIC argued only that a threat to Russia might well develop as soon as the Greek campaign was over. But MI's position was that this development could be excluded, and this was because the absence of intelligence about the movements of the German Army ministered to its other and more fundamental doubts.

To the archive copy of DMI's brief for the CIGS there is attached a typewritten note in which an unidentifiable writer commented: 'If Germany can beat us, Russia is in the bag. Russia does not represent an obstacle to Germany in her battle with Great Britain. A pincer movement (on Suez) is the most likely course'. At the discussion the DMI disagreed with the chairman of the JIC, using the same general argument but giving it a somewhat different emphasis. There was no advantage to Germany in attacking Russia before the invasion of the United Kingdom; if she did so it would be after the harvest.[127]

□

---

124. WO 190/893, No 38A, Minute of 3 April 1941.
125. ibid, No 49B, DMI to CIGS, 22 April 1941.
126. ibid, No 49A of 22 April 1941.
127. CAB 79/11, COS (41) 143rd Meeting, 22 April.

At the meeting of 22 April, of which only a brief record survives, the two schools agreed to differ. At least they agreed that, if and when a German intention to attack Russia was confirmed, the movements of Germany's armoured divisions would provide the important evidence. In the event, however, with the Enigma remaining silent about the eastern deployment of the German armour, it was Germany's other activities that provided the next pointers to her intentions.

These pointers arose out of activity by the GAF from 24 April, two days after the meeting of the JIC with the Chiefs of Staff. On that day the GAF Enigma disclosed the first move of a GAF unit – a ground unit – from the Channel front to Poland. A signals regiment was ordered to Cracow, there to come under Fliegerkorps V which had hitherto been in France.[128] On 30 April AI summarised evidence pointing to a considerable programme for the construction in Poland of airfields and fixed GAF installations, including a signals and aircraft reporting system, and noted that, while this was 'probably for training purposes', the GAF could now transfer a substantial operational force to Poland at short notice.[129] On 3 May the Enigma revealed that aircraft of Fliegerkorps VIII, previously active in Greece, were to be hurriedly refitted in Gatow and that one of its units was to join a rail movement to Cracow a week later.[130] On 5 May it added that the air component of 12 Army was to join a movement for Oderberg, a major concentration point near Cracow, on 22 May. On 7 May AI reported that the GAF was over-flying Finland.[131] On 13 May Fliegerkorps II, which had been under Luftflotte 3 for attacks on the United Kingdom, was subordinated to Luftflotte 2, already associated with the eastern build-up.[132] On 17 May Luftflotte 4 signals troops in the Athens area were ordered to withdraw from operations and entrain for Moldavia between 20 and 25 May,[133] and elements of Fliegerkorps IV (hitherto in France) were ordered to the Bessarabian frontier and given an operational area from the south Carpathians to the Black Sea.[134] On 18 May elements of Fliegerkorps VIII were ordered to join a rail movement to Oderberg on 28 May.[135] This move was delayed by the operation against Crete, a fact which nearly delayed the already postponed *Barbarossa* campaign, but the final urgent withdrawal of this formation to the eastern front was reported in the Enigma on 1 June.[136] By 19 May Flakkorps I and II, previously associated with the *Sealion* preparations, had been ordered to be brought up to more than war strength, and the élite Flakregiment

---

128. CX/JQ/882.
129. AIR 22/74, Air Ministry Weekly Intelligence Summary, to 30 April 1941.
130. CX/JQ/913, 943.
131. AIR 22/74, Air Ministry Weekly Intelligence Summary, to 7 May 1941.
132. CX/JQ 1014.   133. CX/JQ 935/T8.
134. CX/JQ/963; AI/JQ 24.   135. CX/JQ 968.
136. CX/JQ/S/11 and 13; CX/JQ/954/T18, 958, 963, 968, 982, 1023.

'Hermann Göring' had been told to proceed to a point east of Cracow and place itself under Flakkorps II.[137] By the same date it was known from the GAF Enigma that GAF and Army units carrying bridging equipment were to join a movement starting for Moldavia on 6 June. This information was one of the first indications to be received of the earliest date at which operations might begin. The first mention of code-name *Barbarossa* had meanwhile occurred in the GAF Enigma on 8 May in connection with Luftflotte 4.[138]

The first reference to a Plan or Contingency B (*Fall-B*) was received on 14 May, when the GAF Enigma associated it with 12 Army.[139] By that date, from this source and from the Railway Enigma, Whitehall had obtained a considerable amount of information even about German Army movements. On 26 April it learned that the movement of ground forces from the Balkans to the Cracow area, halted at the end of March,* had been resumed.[140] By 5 May it knew that up to five motorised divisions were involved. As always, the GAF Enigma information on Army movements was fragmentary and its interpretation was anything but a straightforward matter. In connection with the movements in eastern Europe, moreover, the usual difficulties were increased not only by Germany's security precautions but also by British inability to intercept all the W/T traffic. For these reasons reliable deductions could be reached only after the analysis of much detail. By 19 May only about a dozen of the divisions known to be on the move had been identified, and their destinations remained unknown. Even so, it was clear by then that many of the divisions that had taken part in the Greek campaign, accompanied by some of the GAF ground and operational forces that had supported them there, had either left the Balkans or would soon be doing so; that a great many unidentified formations were also on the move; and that the moves were taking place with some urgency. Nor was there much doubt that most of the moves were towards the Russian frontier. The accompanying GAF signals and other units were known to be going to widely dispersed points in eastern Poland and Moldavia, and Poznan had been established as the HQ of Army Group B.[141] 12 Army – later to be taken out of the operation – had been connected with the Cracow area and it was known that three of its corps were taking part in the movements. As early as 5 May, moreover, it had been learned from the Enigma that a POW cage from 2 Army at Zagreb was to join a movement on 22 May on its way to join a division at Tarnow east of Cracow.[142]

It was not only the evidence of the Enigma traffic that indicated that

---

* See above, p 451.

137. CX/JQ/953, 961/T5, 964/T10 and T23.   138. CX/JQ 933.
139. CX/JQ 953.   140. CX/JQ 893.
141. CX/JQ 926.   142. CX/JQ/S/12.

exceptional activity was afoot. Invaluable for itself and as a check on the other information, it was also supplemented by the other sources. From the beginning of May the SIS's Polish connections reported on eight series of railway movements, all named significantly after Polish rivers, of which only one was mentioned by name in the Enigma.[143] In addition the SIS supplied, after the middle of April, from its Polish, Czech, Yugoslav and other connections a steady stream of individual reports about German troop movements to the east* and about the formation by the Germans of civilian administrations for the territories to be captured.

By the middle of May it could thus no longer be questioned either that exceptional German military preparations were in train or that they were aimed at Russia. But at that juncture the intelligence picture that was being built up by the military evidence was blurred by the diplomatic evidence – or rather by the assumptions of the diplomatic world.

□

Czech writers have subsequently claimed that the Czech authorities were obtaining much of their military intelligence from anti-Nazi circles in Berlin, and that it included the knowledge that the German attack would come in mid-May, when Yugoslavia had been defeated. In particular, they have claimed that as early as the end of March the Czech intelligence service's A-54 provided the news that the attack was definitely being prepared, together with information about the directions it was to follow and the number of divisions that were to take part in it, and identifications of the divisions and of their commanding officers. They have added that they passed this intelligence to the SIS; that, in addition, Benes relayed it to Mr Churchill at Ditchley Park on 9 or 19 April; and that the Prime Minister was excited by the news because it confirmed information he had just received from other sources.[144] In the British archives there is no record that such a report from A-54 was circulated in Whitehall at this time, and no circulation was given to whatever information the Prime Minister may have received from Benes. From the British diplomatic posts, however, many general warnings were being received, and from these it is clear that during April and May, with few dissentient voices, diplomats and attachés throughout the world were regularly reporting that Germany was about to turn on Russia. But what is equally clear from the reports is that from the middle of April the diplomatic world also began to canvass the possibility of a new German-Russian

---

* MI summarised the most important of these on 14 June 1941 and its summary is given in Appendix 15.

143. CX/JQ 978.
144. Whaley, op cit, pp 55, 235; Moravec, op cit, pp 205–206.

agreement. And by the middle of May it had become an article of faith in Whitehall that, while it could no longer be doubted that Germany was making preparations for an attack, the German decision as to whether to attack was being deferred pending the outcome of the Russo-German political negotiations.

Although this belief was without foundation – in accordance with Hitler's decision after the Molotov visit to Berlin in November 1940,* the German government made no attempt to reach a diplomatic settlement with Russia – it did not originate in Germany, as one of the German deception measures. Nor is this surprising. The overriding purpose of those measures was to mislead the Russians; the Russians could not have been deceived by the story that Germany was negotiating with them, which they knew to be untrue, and if Germany had encouraged the story the probable result would have been to make the Russians still more suspicious. During the spring, therefore, the German deception policy continued to be that of presenting the *Barbarossa* preparations partly as preparations for *Sealion* and partly as defensive measures against Russia, either in response to Russia's reinforcement of her frontier or as a precaution during the period of Germany's advance into the Balkans. In addition, against the time when this advance would have been completed, and the *Barbarossa* preparations could no longer be camouflaged, provision was made for an immense double bluff on the *Barbarossa* and the *Sealion* themes. From the middle of April the Russians were to be told that the *Barbarossa* preparations were intended to divert the attention of the British from the last stages of the preparation for *Sealion* by convincing them that Germany planned to attack Russia. In the event this final phase of the deception policy was not inaugurated until 22 May.[145] By then, when in the continuing trade negotiations between the two countries Russia had in fact forced the Germans to meet their obligations,†[146] the rumour that Germany and Russia were negotiating politically had swelled into the belief that Germany would soon link stringent demands, such as control of the Ukraine, to an ultimatum. The rumour appears to have originated and grown within the diplomatic community without encouragement from Germany.[147] Its persistence should be contrasted with the German efforts to suggest that *Sealion* might be renewed. These failed to impress London. At the end of May the Foreign Office was referring to the invasion bogey being given 'another little run' and the Directors of Intelligence both

---

* See above, p 439.

† In April 1941 Krutikov, First Deputy People's Commissar for Foreign Trade, arrived in Berlin for discussions which were confined to the Soviet-German economic agreement of 10 January 1941.

145. EDS/Appreciation/5, pp 106, 120, 122; Whaley, op cit, pp 173, 174.
146. Medlicott, op cit, Vol I, p 657.
147. Whaley, op cit, pp 175, 180–181.

then and again early in June were dismissing an invasion attempt that summer as 'nonsense'.[148]

An early version of the rumour about negotiations occurred in the middle of April. Cripps had reported to the Foreign Office that he expected the German Ambassador in Moscow to return from Berlin with a new request for whole-hearted Russian co-operation and a veiled threat of what would happen if the offer were refused.[149] At that time Cripps had not believed that Germany would be put off by Russian readiness to fall in with her demands and was predicting, as the Germans learned on 24 April, that she would in any case invade on 22 June.[150] But from 23 April, at just the time when the Enigma intelligence, the existence of which was unknown to him, was about to provide support for his long-standing views, he began to waver. On 23 April he reported that Russia's basic hostility to Germany had not been reduced by the danger of a German attack and that Germany could not secure real control of Russian supplies and transport except by an attack, but that, since Russia was anxious to postpone war at least until nearer the winter, the Soviet government would give way to any extent that did not vitally affect its preparations for war. 'The whole question therefore depends on the extent of Hitler's demands. The present actions of both governments are just as consistent with "pressure politics" as with preparations for war' – which is just what MI had said on 15 April.*[151] On 26 April he added that a Russo-German show-down would come within the next fortnight, that Germany's demands would be steep because her needs were increasing and could be met only by Russia, and that in the event of a Russian refusal she would have to take other steps to secure the key positions in the Russian economy.[152]

Cripps did not waver for long. On 2 May he reported that the German embassy had assured a reliable neutral that a German attack was out of the question. This source had been told that the Russians had carried out all their undertakings and the German government could rely on them to carry out a new agreement and that the Germans would not move in a new direction until they had completed the campaign against Egypt and the Middle East. Cripps added, however, that this was probably a new line in German deception. The Germans might be feeling that they had overdone the pressure and might now be trying to smooth away the annoyance it had provoked in Russia. On 6 May he reported that Yugoslav sources were saying that German operations against Russia were possible in the very near

---

* See above, p 457.

148. FO 371/26520, C5325/C5558/C6041/19/18.
149. Woodward, op cit, Vol I, p 607.
150. EDS/Appreciation/5, p 121.
151. Woodward, op cit, Vol I, p 613.
152. ibid, p 613.

future and that German officers had spoken of 6 June as the date.[153] Other diplomats shared Cripps's scepticism about the assurance given by the German embassy; most embassy rumours were to the effect that Stalin would not yield the widespread control of the Russian economy that Germany must be demanding, and that Germany would resort to force. None doubted, however, that Germany was making new demands on Russia and, while none could be sure of the outcome, even the suggestion that Russia had given way became more prominent from the middle of May. A report to this effect was broadcast at that time by Rome Radio – though it was publicly denied in Berlin and, privately, to the British government by the Russian Ambassador in London.[154]

The position of the Foreign Office was, in these circumstances, a difficult one. On the one hand it was unable to decide on the diplomatic evidence whether or not Germany would go beyond the pressure and the threats which that evidence assumed she was applying. Nor was it assisted in its efforts to do so by Hess's dramatic arrival on 15 May; he merely confessed that Germany had certain demands which Russia would have to satisfy and denied that Germany was planning an attack.[155] On the other hand, as we have seen, it did not regularly receive Enigma decrypts from GC and CS and was in no position to judge the significance of the mounting evidence from this source that Germany was preparing in earnest for a large-scale offensive.

For those who processed the GAF Enigma at GC and CS the position was quite different. Convinced that a new pattern was emerging from the Enigma decrypts, and rating it higher than the diplomatic intelligence, they had decided by 14 May that a German invasion of Russia, which they had thought possible since the end of March, had become a probability. GC and CS had been especially impressed by two developments, the revelation of 5 May that a POW cage was being moved to Tarnow, which it felt to be inconsistent with a German plan for intimidating Russia, and the urgency with which Fliegerkorps VIII, the unit which had spearheaded the attacks in France, Greece and Crete, was being prepared for despatch to Poland. Its judgment was then strengthened by the news that Flakkorps I and II were to be brought up to more than war strength and transferred to Poland, for these units belonged to the German AA field organisation which had played a decisive forward role during the invasion of France.[156] In the few days up to 23 May it pressed this judgment firmly on AI and there is little doubt that its arguments now exercised a decisive influence there.

---

153. ibid, p 614.
154. Whaley, op cit, p 180.
155. Churchill, op cit, Vol III, p 46.
156. CX/JQ 961/T5, 964/T10 and T23.

So far as can be judged – for the records of its appreciations at this time are incomplete – AI's position was one of great indecision until 23 May. On 7 May it noted that Russia was carrying out air reconnaissance in the eastern Baltic.[157] Also on 7 May it deduced correctly that the GAF was not yet ready to operate against Russia and would not be so for another month.[158] On 14 May it drew attention to the fact that in a speech on 5 May Stalin had said that Germany had embarked on an attempt to seize the whole of Europe and that Russia must be ready for any emergency.[159] On the following day it stressed, correctly, that apart from transport aircraft the bulk of the GAF was still in western Europe, but made no comment.[160] On 21 May by which time it had detected a drastic reduction in the GAF's effort against the United Kingdom, its only comment was that this reduction could be explained by the need for recuperation.[161] But on 23 May on the basis of the Enigma evidence – and notably of what this had revealed about the withdrawal of Fliegerkorps VIII for refitting by Luftflotte 2 and the move of Fliegerkorps II and other components of Luftflotten 2 and 3 from France to the east – it ceased to hesitate. Although it admitted that these preparations might be intended only to intimidate Russia, it now concluded that they pointed to a decision to 'satisfy German military requirements by occupying western USSR', Hitler having concluded that an early victory over Great Britain had become impossible, and estimated that the GAF would probably commit 1,070 aircraft (excluding army co-operation).[162]

In MI, the intelligence branch which claimed the chief responsibility for assessing the enemy's strategic intentions, the Enigma evidence again failed to carry the day. On 25 April, before the Enigma clues had begun to accumulate, MI, shaken perhaps by its encounter with the Foreign Office on 22 April, had produced for the first time a full-length appreciation devoted solely to Russo-German relations. In this paper it had conceded that there was 'an actual threat' to Russia. Many things pointed to this – the German troop movements in Finland; the movement of German troops, including armoured and motorised divisions, to Poland, as reported by GC and CS and the SIS; the evacuation of the families of German officials from Poland, which had been mentioned in a Japanese diplomatic decrypt; evidence from the SIS and Japanese and Italian diplomatic decrypts that Germany had been constructing airfields, building and improving roads, enlarging railway stations beyond what was needed for trade, and carrying out air reconnaissance over Russian territory. On the other

---

157. AIR 22/74, Air Ministry Weekly Intelligence Summary, to 7 May 1941.
158. ibid.
159. ibid, to 14 May 1941.
160. CAB 80/27, COS (41) 296 (COS Résumé, No 88), Appendix VIII.
161. AIR 22/74, Air Ministry Weekly Intelligence Summary, to 21 May 1941.
162. WO 190/893, No 66C, DDI3 Minute to D of I (O), 23 May 1941.

hand, MI had still disbelieved the rumours of a German intention to attack. Apart from feeling that they sprang from Germany's wish to contain Russia while Germany was fighting in the Balkans – an argument which it now used for the last time – it remained convinced that Germany's chief aim was the defeat of the United Kingdom. She was putting herself in a position to attack Russia, but her reasons were that she needed to ensure Russia's continuing economic collaboration, that she wished to keep Great Britain and Turkey guessing and, possibly, that she was feeling that she would have to invade Russia ultimately, if she failed in the Battle of the Atlantic.[163]

For another fortnight MI clung to its view that a German attack was most unlikely in the near future.[164] The state of mind in MI at this time was probably reflected faithfully in a paper put forward to the Prime Minister on 6 May by the CIGS 'on the highest professional authority'. It painted in great detail the danger of a German invasion of the United Kingdom, argued that Germany could only succeed if she defeated Great Britain, and made no reference to Russia.[165] A few days later, however, the tone of its appreciations underwent another change. On 12 May, after mentioning that it had received two reports to the effect that Germany was preparing to fight Russia at any moment, it judged that Germany's preparations for the attack would be completed by the end of May.[166] On 15 May, in the next weekly résumé for the Chiefs of Staff, it noted that, while 'such a policy does not necessarily indicate that an attack is being planned for the immediate future', Romanian military circles were expecting that they would shortly be expected to co-operate in an attack on Russia, that German-Romanian staff talks were in progress, and that Russian military maps were being issued to Romanian officers.[167] This information had been obtained from diplomatic sources. Furthermore – and this was a reference to the accumulating Enigma evidence – the gradual strengthening of German forces all along the Russian frontier from north Norway to the Black Sea had been confirmed, and this 'suggested that preparations for operations against Russia will soon be complete'. The summary drew attention to the SIS's evidence that SS contingents were being formed among emigrants from the Ukraine and the Baltic states and that pro-German governments for these territories were being organised. As for the continuing reports from many quarters of the German intention to attack, MI still felt that some of them were inspired by Germany, but it also noted that June and July, the earliest dates they gave for the attack, seemed

---

163. ibid, No 54B of 25 April 1941.
164. CAB 80/27, COS (41) 279 (COS Résumé, No 87), paragraph 23, COS (41) 296 (COS Résumé, No 88), paragraphs 40–41.
165. Churchill, op cit, Vol III, pp 373–377.
166. WO 190/893, No 60E of 12 May 1941.
167. CAB 80/28, COS (41) 311 (COS Résumé, No 89).

somewhat optimistic. Its final conclusion – and here it was perhaps influenced by a decrypt in which the Japanese Ambassador in Berlin reported that Hitler alone would settle this question – was that the Germans had probably not yet decided whether to use their preparations to threaten Russia into complying with their wishes or for an outright attack on her.[168] It will be remembered that is what the Foreign Office had said to Cripps on 20 April.*

In another paper of 15 May – a brief for the Axis Planning Section – MI said much the same thing. It now listed not only the strategic considerations that should deter Germany from turning against Russia before defeating Great Britain, but also, for the first time, the strategic arguments that might persuade her to do so – the need to cover her eastern flank and free most of her ground and air forces before invading the United Kingdom; the wish to forestall Russian intervention in Finland, Scandinavia and the Balkans. On the intelligence front it noted, once again, that the Germans might not yet have reached a decision to attack since there were reports that, although the General Staff was now in favour, the 'politicians' were against, but it went on to say that the presence of two Flakkorps in Poland and the evidence that armoured divisions were about to move there, coming on top of the earlier work on railway stations, airfields and roads, pointed to an offensive. The paper added that Germany had adequate forces to deal with Russia and that she would need two to three weeks to bring up the further armoured and motorised divisions that would be needed.[169]

The change in MI's position is underlined by two considerations. In the first place, since it had hitherto greatly exaggerated the number of German divisions in Poland and East Prussia,† it now underestimated the scale of the recent eastward deployment. Its mid-May estimate that 100 to 120 divisions faced the USSR, including 73 in Poland and East Prussia and perhaps 47 in the Balkans,[170] was accurate enough – the actual number on the day of the attack was 121 including 70 in Poland and East Prussia and 43 in the Balkans, as well as 28 in reserve and 4 in Finland – but this estimate obscured the fact that Germany had very largely built up to this figure since the end of March. In the second place, MI resisted the temptation to be entirely diverted by the German involvement in Crete and Iraq. Hitler hoped that the Crete offensive would draw attention away from the *Barbarossa* preparations. The planning of the Crete offensive, combined with the rigorous W/T silence which the Germans imposed on

---

* See above, pp 457–458.
† See above, pp 438 and 442 for MI's estimates of 60 divisions in the area in August 1940, 58 in December and 70 in January 1941.

168. ibid, paragraphs 30, 34, 35.
169. WO 190/893, No 64A, MI 14 Brief for APS, 15 May 1941.
170. ibid, and No 66C of 23 May 1941.

the *Barbarossa* preparations, did indeed lead to a southerly shift of Germany's W/T communications which persuaded some in MI to believe that the priority area of her land and air forces continued to be the Mediterranean despite the fact that her greatest strength was deployed on the Russian front. They made this point on 13 May[171] and on 15 May MI suggested in the Chiefs of Staff résumé that the centre of gravity was shifting to Iraq.*[172] As we have seen, however, anxiety for the Mediterranean no longer excluded considered appreciations of the situation on the Russian front.

But if MI had been forced by the evidence to accept, during the second week of May, that Germany was preparing for an early show of force against Russia, it still remained undecided as to whether her object was to attack Russia or to frighten her into submission to her demands. Fundamentally this was because it could not bring itself to accept that an attack would make sense. On 21 May the War Office weekly intelligence summary still maintained that many of the rumours of an impending attack were being put about by the Germans, and thought that it was difficult to find a logical reason why Hitler should attack unless he had 'made up his mind...to dispose of the Red Bogey once and for all'.[173] MI, however, did not believe that he had done such a thing, and it was for this reason that, notwithstanding its earlier insistence that military dispositions and military measures were alone significant as a guide to the enemy's intentions, it allowed its attention to be deflected from the military evidence by the diplomatic reports that were suggesting that Germany's object was only to intimidate the Russians, and that she was succeeding.

On 22 May, in the Chiefs of Staff résumé, MI acknowledged that the strengthening of German forces on the Russian frontiers was still being reported by several sources. It conceded, moreover, that even the diplomatic reports suggested that the situation remained tense: 'Two reports state that Hitler has not finally decided whether to obtain his wishes by persuasion or force of arms, and another indicates that the latter alternative will be chosen if the former does not give results by the end of May.' 'Nevertheless,' the résumé added, 'some reports of rapprochement suggest that German threats have been successful and that arrangements for German control of the despatch of supplies from Russia have been accepted by the latter country. German propaganda which was recently spreading rumours of war is now stressing co-operation.'[174]

□

---

* See Chapter 13, p 413.

171. ibid, No 61A of 13 May 1941.
172. CAB 80/28, COS (41) 311 (COS Résumé, No 89).
173. WO 208/2259, WO Weekly Intsum to 21 May.
174. CAB 80/28, COS (41) 325 (COS Résumé, No 90), paragraphs 27–28.

It was in this situation that, on 23 May, the JIC itself brought together all the intelligence in the first study it had specifically devoted to 'Germany's intentions against the USSR'.[175]

The study recognised that the situation had been transformed since the issue of the previous inter-departmental intelligence appreciation of German strategy on 5 April.* The Germans could not fight Russia at the same time as invading England – but 'present indications' were that *Sealion* was unlikely in the immediate future. More than that, the paper showed that the JIC was at last clearly acknowledging that 'the domination of Russia was a fundamental German objective'. It added that it was in Germany's interest 'for matters to be brought to a head as soon as possible'. These were the arguments which underlay the JIC's first conclusion: 'Germany cannot fight a long war without obtaining greater economic help from Russia than she is now receiving. She can only obtain this by an effective agreement or war.'

Which of these courses would Germany take? The study approached the problem in general terms. It recapitulated all that had been said in recent weeks of the disadvantages that Germany would incur by attacking Russia, adding only the new consideration that a war forced on Russia would strengthen the Soviet government's hold on the Russian people. Against these disadvantages it set down the arguments that might induce Germany to attack and these now included, alongside Germany's growing economic requirements for strategic purposes, the consideration that an invasion would enhance Germany's military prestige, which might be useful in off-setting the danger that the USA might enter the war, and enable Germany to resume 'the role of anti-Bolshevist champion – thus facilitating the consolidation of the "New Order" in Europe'. After weighing up these pros and cons the JIC reached its second conclusion: 'the advantages...to Germany of concluding an agreement with the USSR are overwhelming'. After all, Germany might do as much for her military prestige by imposing an agreement on Russia as by making an attack on her. 'From the general political standpoint Germany may hope to present to the world a picture of complete domination in Europe. With the addition of some agreement with the USSR she might hope to discourage the USA and to bring about a negotiated peace with ourselves.'

In its third conclusion the report considered one of the reasons why it was impossible to be certain that Germany would take her 'natural course', which 'would be to exert extreme pressure, backed by the threat of force, to obtain by negotiation from the USSR the concessions she requires'. This had to do with the position of the Soviet government. Its 'natural course' was to try to avoid a clash by yielding

---

* See above, pp 456–457.

175. JIC (41) 218 of 23 May.

to German demands; but it would refuse to sign any agreement that endangered its effective control of Russia, and it was making extensive preparations to meet the German threat should the worst happen. All depended on how much Germany demanded. 'It is on this issue, therefore, that the success or failure of the negotiations must depend and the possibility of friction is apparent.' And in its final conclusion the JIC pushed this argument to its logical end: 'It is essential for Germany to know quickly where she stands. If in the course of negotiations she sees no prospect of reaching agreement she will implement her threat of force'.

There was another obstacle to overcome before concluding that Germany would adopt her 'natural course' – the Enigma intelligence about the nature of Germany's military preparations which had by now persuaded GC and CS and AI, though not MI, that it was her intention to invade unconditionally. To this the JIC paid little atention. In the body of its report it summarised the evidence about Germany's preparations and the summary left no doubt that they were taking place on a gigantic scale. But it omitted just those items – the POW cage and the hurried withdrawal of key GAF formations from the Balkans – which had persuaded GC and CS that she was not negotiating about her demands. In the JIC's conclusions the assumption that Germany was negotiating with Russia appeared as a statement of fact: 'With her usual thoroughness Germany is making all preparations for an attack so as to make the threat convincing'. Moreover, the body of the report had a section added to it under the heading 'Latest Intelligence' and this announced that there were indications that Hitler and Stalin had reached an agreement on military as well as economic and political collaboration.

These indications had been received from, among other sources, the British Ambassador in Washington. On the day the JIC report was issued Lord Halifax reported that, according to information obtained from Berlin on 21 May, German troops were assembled in force on the Russian frontier, but that the Russian government had recently assented to German demands for a large increase in supplies and that the economic agreement might have military implications, with Russia allowing the passage of German troops and material to areas east of Suez and committing herself to take action against India.[176] It is reasonable to suppose that it was this rumour which prompted the JIC to add a last sentence to its final conclusion, and to do so at the last minute. After saying that Germany would implement her threat if she saw no prospect of reaching agreement the JIC ended its report with the observation that 'from present intelligence agreement is the more likely event'.

□

176. Woodward, op cit, Vol I, p 615.

However we explain the JIC's endorsement of the view that Germany was negotiating with Russia – and it is easy to see that its acceptance of diplomatic rumour owed much to Whitehall's reluctance to believe that Germany could be so irrational as to attack if she could possibly avoid it, and something, as we shall see, to Whitehall's fear that Russia might give way before the formidable threat that Germany had mounted – this belief continued for the next fortnight to close Whitehall's eyes to the possibility that Germany was preparing an unconditional attack.

It is fair to add that the entire diplomatic world continued to share the belief. On 22 May a decrypt from the Japanese Ambassador in Moscow did indeed report that it was 'not mere rumour that Germany may attack Russia shortly' and added that the rumours that Germany would fight unless Russia yielded to her economic demands were 'German propaganda'. But the Ambassador clouded his remarks by concluding that Germany was unlikely to attack as long as Russia continued to be acquiescent. Other Axis diplomatic decrypts pointed unequivocally in this last direction; in one decrypted on 25 May the Japanese Ambassador in Berlin mentioned the German interest in threatening India by advancing through Turkey and the Middle East. So did the talk of the embassies: Russia would yield and the Germans would then march to Suez via Syria; Germany was still determined to attempt an invasion of the United Kingdom. At the same time the rumour that the Germans were proposing direct participation in the Soviet economy – a rumour which had been circulating in the diplomatic community in Moscow for some time* – continued to reach London up to the middle of June.[177] There were diplomatic reports that Germany had proposed to Russia the joint development of the Ukraine and direct German control of the sources of supply from some areas of Russia; and there were even suggestions that Russia and Germany had reached agreement. On 2 June the Foreign Office's explanation for the apparent lack of negotiations in Moscow was that they might be taking place in Berlin so that Stalin could keep from his colleagues what was going on.[178]

To set against this stream of reports, Whitehall received on 23 May from A-54 the warning that Russo-German negotiations were 'just a delaying mechanism'; he also gave further details about the alternative regimes that the Germans were organising for Russian areas. It has been claimed that the same informant sent the Czech authorities a second report on 27 May in which he gave the correct date for the launching of *Barbarossa*; there is no trace of this in the British records and we may suspect that the claim rests on a garbled or exaggerated

---

* See above, p 465.

177. FO 371/29481.
178. FO 371/29481, N 2498/78/38.

version of the report of 23 May.[179] From 27 May, however, GC and
CS was supplying a steady stream of Sigint evidence. On 27 May the
GAF Enigma revealed that Fliegerkorps II was asking for maps of
Latvia, Lithuania, most of Poland and north-east Romania.[180] On
29 May it showed that the commanders of Luftflotten 1 to 5, AOC
Centre, Fliegerkorps I, II, IV, V and VIII, Flakkorps I and II and
Fliegerführer Baltic were, together with the GAF liaison officer with
OKM, all invited to attend a conference with their intelligence officers
on 4 June.[181] All these Fliegerkorps were known by then to be moving
east, and it was a reasonable assumption that the other authorities
were involved in the same operation with them. On 31 May the GAF
Enigma confirmed that Fliegerkorps V had been subordinated to
Luftflotte 4.[182] By then there was from the GAF and the Railway
Enigma ample evidence of an assembly for attack behind the
Bessarabian frontier,[183] and the assumption that Moldavia was to be
a jumping-off point had been confirmed in two ways. A newly
identified Army authority, the C-in-C of the High Command of
German Army Troops in Romania, planned to fly along the line of
the frontier river. Siebel ferries and an assault boat company which
had previously been in the English Channel were being included in
a rail movement destined for Moldavia.[184] Of the many rail movements
known to be running to Poland, the contents and destinations were
identified in only a few cases, but these few left no doubt that GAF
and Army units were being deployed along practically the whole length
of the frontier.[185] In north Norway – the area which was later to yield
the Enigma evidence that operations were imminent – the Enigma had
by now revealed the arrival of further reinforcements and had
provided some indications that the Germans were preparing to
attack.[186] During the first week of June the GAF Enigma established
that the transfer of Luftflotte 2 from northern France to the east was
substantially completed, that the delayed departure of Fliegerkorps
VIII from Greece was at last taking place and that the units of
Fliegerkorps VIII were not to transfer to their advanced landing
grounds for *Fall-B* before 16 June.[187] In a signal decrypted on 8 June
Luftflotte 2 told Fliegerkorps VIII not to mention operational matters
on W/T or land-line till further notice.[188] On 10 June in a further

---

179. Moravec, op cit, p 206.
180. CX/JQ 1002.
181. CX/JQ 1008.
182. CX/JQ 1014/T18.
183. CX/JQ/S/10, 11 and 13. See also, eg CX/JQ 882, 921, 963, 968, 978, 981, 984,
992, 1011, 1013, 1014, 1016, 1019, 1021, 1023, 1028, 1032; AI/JQ 24.
184. CX/JQ 989, 1019.
185. eg, CX/JQ 1060, 1074.
186. CX/JQ 504/T7, 907, 995, 1018, 1044/T7, 1080.
187. CX/JQ 1015, 1016, 1029.
188. CX/JQ 1040.

decrypt Göring summoned the commanders of all the GAF formations that had been mentioned in the Enigma signals to a conference at Karinhall, his personal HQ, for 15 June.[189]

For GC and CS this further evidence converted the probability that Germany might be planning a surprise invasion, a probability which it had urged since 14 May, into a virtual certainty by the end of that month. On 31 May it issued a special paper surveying the Enigma intelligence to that date:

'It becomes harder than ever to doubt that the object of these large movements of the German army and air force is Russia. From rail movements towards Moldavia in the south to ship movements towards the Varanger Fjord in the far north there is everywhere the same steady eastward trend. Either the purpose is blackmail or it is war. No doubt Hitler would prefer a bloodless surrender. But the quiet move, for instance, of a prisoner-of-war cage to Tarnow looks more like business than bluff. It would no doubt be rash for Germany to become involved in a long struggle on two fronts. But the answer may well be that the Germans do not expect the struggle with Russia to be long. An overwhelming eastward concentration, a lightning victory, an unassailable supremacy in Europe and Asia – such may be the plan behind this procession of troop trains from the Balkans to the eastern frontier'.[190]

On 7 June, by which time it had worked out the GAF order of battle on the Russian front, identifying the rough operational areas of most of its units, and had calculated that well over 2,000 aircraft were involved, GC and CS issued another special report. It concluded that there was little doubt that Germany was planning 'a very large-scale operation against Russia with the main front of attack in Poland and East Prussia'. On the evidence that Fliegerkorps VIII was not to transfer to advanced landing grounds for *Fall-B* before 16 June it calculated that Germany would be ready by 15 June. This further reference to *Fall-B*, first mentioned on 14 May,* suggested that some long-prepared plan was being implemented, but it remained uncertain whether there was any connection between *Fall-B* and *Barbarossa*. *Barbarossa*, first mentioned on 8 May,† had been twice mentioned again on 21 May in connection with naval preparations in the Black Sea and it seemed possible that *Barbarossa* was some separate operation in that area.[191]

These were not the only Sigint developments to occur during the first week of June. A noticeable increase in GAF W/T activity in north Norway led GC and CS to point out that 'any action against Russia would involve some move against northern Scandinavia'. In the same week GC and CS reported that five new naval W/T frequencies had

---

* See above, p 461.   † See above, p 467.

189. CX/JQ 1048.
190. CX/JQ/S/11 of 31 May 1941.
191. CX/JQ 979.

been introduced in the eastern Baltic and also noted that 'the introduction of army and GAF type call-signs into naval traffic pointed to imminent co-operation'. From about the same time GC and CS noticed that the GAF in the west was employing a form of radio deception (dubbed 'Sham') in an attempt to conceal the eastward movement of its formations.[192] From the quality and regularity of the transmissions, and with the aid of DF, it was able to detect that ground stations were broadcasting signals which simulated those normally passed between aircraft and their ground controllers.

GC and CS's conclusions were by no means ignored by the Service intelligence branches and the JIC. But in Whitehall the intelligence organisations judged the Sigint evidence on the assumption that Germany was negotiating with Russia, and in the light of the fact that this assumption was still receiving support from diplomatic sources they put a different interpretation on the Enigma clues. For them every further proof of the scale and urgency of Germany's military preparations was also further proof that Germany was determined to get her way in the negotiations and, while they could no longer exclude the probability that her determination would lead to war, they equally feared that Russia might give way. How much they still believed that Germany was applying pressure to Russia was shown on 30 May in a further appreciation by the JIC. This was less inclined than the report of 23 May to believe that an agreement would come, but was as convinced as before that agreement was being sought. It concluded that Germany would for the present consolidate in the Mediterranean with a view to turning south-east or south-west 'as soon as she is satisfied regarding the Soviet'. 'Although many reasons exist why Germany should decide, after her success in Crete, to exploit her success by action towards Egypt, all the evidence points to Germany's next move being an attempt to enforce her demands on the Soviet by means of a threat of force which can immediately be turned into action.' In an annex the report indicated that the JIC was paying no attention to the advantages to Germany of an unconditional surprise attack by noting that the GAF preparations were so thorough, and so like those which had preceded other offensives, that they could 'only portend such drastic demands on the Soviet government that Hitler is doubtful of their acceptance and is, therefore, prepared to implement his threat of force by actual operations'. The annex also attempted to estimate the date by which Germany would be ready to attack. It gave two assessments of the GAF measures. The first was that they were 'planned to be completed...by the second half of June', the second that 'the present indications are that the air force dispositions necessary to implement any threat to Russia cannot now be completed before the end of June'. As for the Army, until a large

---

192. Collier, op cit, p 277.

concentration of armoured and motorised divisions, and of air forces, is definitely established on the Soviet frontier we can hardly fix when the climax of pressure on the Soviet will come, or the imminence of actual attack'.[193]

It was at this point that the Chiefs of Staff warned the Commanders-in-Chief in the Middle East that Germany was demanding drastic concessions from Russia, that she would march if they were refused – and that it was to be feared that Russia might yield.* At least for the period up to its despatch, their telegram of 31 May disposes of the Prime Minister's subsequent claim that the Chiefs of Staff were 'ahead of their advisers'.[194] For the period between the end of May and the middle of June, when the growing feeling that war was probable between Germany and Russia had hardened into the certainty that Germany intended to attack, the claim may have more validity, for the process of conversion cannot be documented with the same detail at the different levels in Whitehall.

In the Foreign Office the conversion occurred sometime between 2 and 9 June. On 31 May and again on 2 June the Permanent Under-Secretary noted in his diary that, while he agreed with the Chiefs of Staff that Germany was fully prepared for an attack on Russia, he still believed that Russia would give way.[195] On 9 June itself the Foreign Secretary doubted if Russia would fight – 'a big if, I will admit'.[196] But by 9 June opinion in the Foreign Office had hardened into conviction that, as the Foreign Secretary then told the Cabinet, 'all the evidence points to attack'.[197] On 10 June, in a memorandum prepared for the Foreign Secretary on the motives that might lead Hitler to decide for war, it noted that in MEW's view Hitler could on the economic side obtain by negotiation practically everything Russia could supply; it was certain, moreover, that war would lead to a reduction of supplies for a considerable time. On the other hand, the memorandum went on, he might want complete control of the economic resources of European and Asiatic Russia because he had decided to prepare for a long war. He might also wish to eliminate Communism, a step which he might think welcome in the Nazi Party and to large sections of opinion throughout Europe and useful in turning American and even British opinion in his favour. The replacement of the existing Russian government by one linked to Germany would, moreover, facilitate German co-operation with Japan, and Hitler might think that this would also discourage the United States from entering the war. These political advantages would follow

---

* See above, p 429.

193. JIC (41) 229 of 30 May 1941.
194. Churchill, op cit, Vol III, p 318.
195. Dilks (ed), op cit, pp 382, 385, diary entries for 31 May and 2 June 1941.
196. FO 371/26521, C 6668/19/18.
197. CAB 65/22, WM (41) 58 CA, 9 June.

only if Russia surrendered quickly to diplomatic or military pressure. As against that, on the military side Hitler might be calculating that, if Russia put up effective resistance, he would still be able to arrange a compromise without upsetting his strategic position in the Atlantic and the eastern Mediterranean. A further military consideration was that, though constituted purely for defence, the Russian Army immobilised 50 German divisions. Hitler might think that a showdown with Russia would free these divisions, enable him to reduce his Army and put him in a position to set about organising the whole of Europe on a peace footing.[198] It is worth noting the comment on this memorandum of the Permanent Under-Secretary: he thought there was 'much force' in this last, military, argument and that it might be the explanation of the 'otherwise somewhat incomprehensible phenomenon' of German military action against Russia.[199] On the previous day another Foreign Office minute had described Hitler's apparent decision to attack Russia as 'the most astonishing development on the grand scale since the war began'.[200]

MI, AI and the JIC were also moving to the same conclusion by 9 June. MI's contribution to the Chiefs of Staff résumé of 5 June repeated that the preparations being made against Russia 'may be used merely to ensure compliance with Germany's demands in the negotiations that are believed to be taking place', but added that Germany was likely to use force if her demands were refused.[201] AI's paragraph – the two branches were even now making separate appreciations – said much the same thing: 'there are other indications that Germany is preparing to enforce her demands on the Soviet, if necessary by force'.[202] On 10 June the JIC appreciated that either war or agreement would come in the second half of the month* and on that date, to the extent that it was beginning to prepare a paper on 'The Effects of Russo-German Collaboration', it was still allowing that Russia might give way.[204] But by 9 June it had produced the first version of another paper, on the effects for Great Britain of a Russo-German war.[205]

As yet there had been only one new development on the intelligence front. A conflict of evidence had begun to emerge in the diplomatic

---

* According to the Prime Minister.[203] There is no record of a JIC appreciation on this date but the JIC may have issued this view in a daily summary and the file of the JIC's daily summaries has not come to light.

198. Woodward, op cit, Vol I, pp 618–619; FO 371/29483, N2891/78/38. See also for MEW views FO 371/29481, N2466/N2500/78/38; FO 371/29482, N2802/78/38.
199. FOR 371/29483, loc cit.
200. FO 371/26521, C6668/19/18.
201. CAB 80/28, COS (41) 357 (COS Résumé, No 92), paragraph 35.
202. ibid, paragraph 62.
203. Churchill, op cit, Vol III, p 318.
204. JIC (41) 251 of 13 June.
205. JIC (41) 234 of 9 June.

reports that Whitehall was receiving on the subject of Russo-German negotiations. Some of these reports continued to assume that political negotiations were taking place, and even to suggest that Russia was about to yield. On 3 June, however, GC and CS had decrypted a message in which the Italian Ambassador in Moscow reported that his German colleague had assured him that Germany was not negotiating with Russia, and on 7 June the Swedish government had warned the Foreign Office that Germany would bring force to bear about 15 June – a date that was now being frequently mentioned in diplomatic circles.[206] It was perhaps in the light of these indications that on 10 June, following the Cabinet meeting of the previous day, the Foreign Secretary gave the Russian Ambassador full details of the intelligence available about Germany's military dispositions and elicited from him the assurance that no political negotiations were proceeding between Russia and Germany and that there would be no Russo-German alliance.[207] But at its next meeting, on 12 June, the Cabinet remained hesitant. After being informed by the Foreign Secretary that Cripps, now on a visit to London, did not know whether Russo-German political negotiations were taking place, but expected Germany to issue an ultimatum when her military build-up was completed, it felt unable to decide whether Germany would prefer to destroy Russia's military forces or to demand complete control of the Ukraine and the Caucasus in the hope that Russia would yield; if Russia gave way to this demand, it noted, Germany would have outflanked Turkey to the north.[208]

No sooner had the Cabinet broken up on this uncertain note than Whitehall received from GC and CS the decrypt of a message sent out by the Japanese Ambassador in Berlin in his Chef de Mission cypher on 4 June. It was part of a long account of the interview he had just had with Hitler. Hitler, the Ambassador reported, felt that the Soviet attitude, though outwardly friendly, was habitually obstructive, and he had decided that Communist Russia must be eliminated. If sacrifices were not made now they would be twenty times greater in five or ten years' time. Romania and Finland would join Germany against Russia and the campaign would soon be over. 'If Japan lagged behind when Germany declared a state of war against Russia, it was quite open to her to do so.' The Ambassador added that, though neither Hitler nor Ribbentrop mentioned a date, the atmosphere of urgency suggested that it was close at hand.

This information convinced the JIC that Germany intended to turn on Russia. In a short paper issued on 12 June it announced that 'fresh evidence is now to hand that Hitler has made up his mind to have done

206. FO 371/29482, N2673/N2680/79/38; Woodward, op cit, Vol I, p 620; Whaley, op cit, p 106.
207. Woodward, op cit, Vol I, p 620.
208. CAB 65/22, WM (41) 59 CA, 12 June.

with Soviet obstruction and intends to attack her. Hostilities therefore appear highly probable, though it is premature to fix a date for their outbreak. It remains our opinion that matters are likely to come to a head during the second half of June'.[209] On 13 June, presumably on the strength of the same information, the Foreign Secretary, after consultation with the Prime Minister, told the Russian Ambassador that the evidence for a German offensive was increasing and offered to send a military mission to Moscow,[210] and the Chiefs of Staff instructed the Joint Planners and the JIC to make arrangements for the despatch of a mission when Germany attacked.[211]

□

By 10 June the Enigma had made it clear that the attack would not come till after 15 June.* Between 14 June and 22 June, the day on which Germany launched the offensive, the GAF Enigma, without disclosing the actual date, left no room for doubt about the imminence of the attack.

The weak link in Germany's security chain was her need to resort to W/T for last-minute communication with north Norway. On 14 June GC and CS decrypted messages which issued code-names to Luftflotte 5, apparently for operations against Russia from Norway and Finland, and carried most secret orders in connection with the arrival of a 'Chief War Correspondent' at Kirkenes.[212] On 15 June an aircraft reporting unit at Kirkenes was instructed in the GAF Enigma to prepare to cross into Finland but in no circumstances to occupy its posts there until authority was given.[213] By 18 June the same source had revealed that there were GAF battle and special operation staffs at Kirkenes and that the latter was receiving information about Russian orders for the camouflage and dispersal of aircraft. Three further GAF Enigma messages decrypted on 20 June dealt with the crossing of the frontier. One lifted the ban on flying over the prohibited frontier zone but limited flying there to the movement of aircraft to airfields near the frontier. Another warned the special operations staff at Kirkenes that, since minelaying was to be carried out before the crossing, surprise would not be possible. In a third, Kirkenes was instructed that any aircraft flying over the frontier before the general crossing must do so at a great height.[214] Apart from these messages to north Norway there had been other indications in the Enigma. On

---

* See above, p 474.

209. JIC (41) 252 (O) of 12 June.
210. Woodward, op cit, Vol I, p 621.
211. CAB 79/12, COS (41) 210th Meeting, 13 June.
212. CX/JQ 1057, 1060.
213. CX/JQ 1062.
214. CX/JQ 1079/T8 and T10.

14 June the staff of Luftflotte 4 received instructions to be at their new battle HQ, ready to operate, from 17 June.[215] On 19 June Luftflotte 1 was told that it could carry out minelaying before 'general crossing of the frontier'.[216] On 21 June GC and CS decrypted a message in which Luftflotte 4 gave Fliegerkorps IV a target for the first attacks.[217]

On 16 June GC and CS, in another special appreciation summarising this evidence up to that date, concluded that the attack could come at any time from 19 June.[218] On the same day MI singled out the Enigma information about the 'Chief War Correspondent' and judged from the other evidence that the invasion would not come before 18 June.[219]

To the end, however, the Whitehall intelligence branches found it difficult to discard the belief that Germany would present Russia with demands and an ultimatum. On 16 June MI, noting that there had been rumours that Russo-German relations were to reach a crisis about 20 June, did confess that much obscurity surrounded the nature of the German demands, but it still suggested that 'Germany anticipates the necessity of using force, possibly because she feels certain that Russia cannot bow to the very drastic demands she wishes to make'.[220] The Foreign Office, similarly, was never wholly convinced that 'Germany intended to attack Russia and not merely to use diplomatic and military pressure to intimidate the Soviet government' – that Hitler had decided to invade Russia 'without giving her the chance to surrender to the most stringent demands'.[221] Nor, it must be added, were other governments able to believe this. The Japanese Foreign Secretary appears to have thought that Germany would need a pretext before declaring war.[222] On 19 June the Swedish government informed the Foreign Office that it expected Germany to issue an ultimatum within a week.[223] As for Cripps, who had predicted so early and for so long that Germany would attack, his suspicion that Germany and Russia were negotiating increased as the crisis mounted.

If Cripps was already wavering on 12 June, when the Foreign Secretary reported his view to the Cabinet, he was even more undecided when he himself attended the Cabinet on 16 June. On this occasion, still expecting a German ultimatum, he spoke at some length and with much uncertainty about whether Russia would or would not meet German demands and threw out a further suggestion:

---

215. CX/JQ 914, 936, 953/T8, 964, 1060.
216. CX/JQ 1079/T10.
217. CX/JQ 1085.
218. AI/JQ 25.
219. WO 190/893, No 85A of 16 June 1941.
220. ibid.
221. Woodward, op cit, Vol I, p 620; Butler, op cit, Vol II, p 544.
222. Whaley, op cit, p 237.
223. Woodward, op cit, Vol I, p 623.

Stalin's assumption of supreme power as Chairman of Commissars in Russia on 6 May was probably due not only to his need to ensure that the High Command was on a war basis, but also to his conviction that he alone in Russia was strong enough to make to Germany the concessions she was demanding.[224]

Like the long-standing assumption that Russia and Germany were negotiating, the feeling that Russia might even now give way to Germany's last-minute demands owed something to the policy which Russia had adopted towards the threat from Germany since the beginning of 1941. She had been increasing her defensive preparations and issuing political warnings, backed by military movements, against Germany's expansion to the south-east; but she had also been doing her utmost to propitiate Germany – renewing the trade agreement in January, resuming her supplies to Germany and increasing them month by month, acquiescing in extensive German violations of her air-space, withdrawing recognition of the Belgian, Norwegian and Yugoslav governments in May, and maintaining towards other western governments not merely an uncommunicative attitude, but even a pose of unconcern which culminated on 14 June in her public denial of the rumours that Germany was about to attack her. In relation to the German threat this policy was no doubt well considered. It is sufficiently explained by the need of the Russian government to gain time and by its wish to make it plain in Russia and to the world, in the event of a German invasion, that Russia had not provoked it.[225] In Whitehall, however, as for other governments that watched from outside, it necessarily created uncertainty as to whether Russia would resist if Germany increased the pressure or if Germany attacked. For example, it is reported that Benes was impressed when Maisky told him on 26 May that no conflict between Russia and Germany was imminent and that if differences were to arise between Berlin and Moscow the Soviet government would do everything to resolve them peaceably.[226]

That this was its effect in Whitehall was all the more inescapable because of another consideration. Cripp's hesitation owed much to his uncertainty about the purpose of Russia's policy. But that uncertainty in its turn owed much to his conviction that, as he told the Cabinet on 16 June, Russia would be unable to hold out for more than three to four weeks if Germany did attack. In this belief he was at one with all the Whitehall departments, where the lack of intelligence about Russia, and information from Russia, was still well-nigh complete. In the paper on the effects of a Russo-German war which it compiled on 9 June the JIC had allowed Germany four to six weeks to occupy the

224. CAB 65/22, WM (41) 60 CA, 16 June.
225. EDS/Appreciation/5, p 129; Woodward, op cit, Vol I, p 595; Whaley, op cit, pp 32–33; Gwyer and Butler, op cit, Vol III, p 85.
226. Moravec, op cit, p 206.

Ukraine and reach Moscow; in a revised version of this paper issued on 14 June it had changed its estimate to between three and four weeks at the shortest but possibly as long as six weeks.[227] Even these estimates rested on the assumption that Germany would not use all her bombers for the attack: on 19 June AI thought the reduction in the scale of bombing effort against the United Kingdom in recent weeks might be due to a policy of conserving the GAF for simultaneous heavy air attacks on Russia and Great Britain.[228] In MEW's opinion 'the Germans would not incur heavy casualties or any high degree of military exhaustion in defeating the Red Army'.[229] The Foreign Office held much the same view; and only the Prime Minister 'did not share the prevailing pessimism about Russian powers of resistance'.[230]

It was against this background that from the middle of June, as the Enigma pointed more clearly every day to the imminence of *Barbarossa* and as doubt about Russia's readiness to withstand German pressure was replaced by certainty that she could not long survive a German attack, Whitehall's latent anxiety about *Sealion* returned to the surface. On 14 June the JIC calculated that, on the assumption that Germany reached Moscow in three to four weeks, there would be an interval of four to six weeks before she could attempt an invasion of the United Kingdom; if she took as long as six weeks to defeat Russia this interval would be between six and eight weeks.[231] On 17 June MI noted that the SIS's sources, including the valued Polish network, were reporting that further German troop movements into France were about to take place on a large scale.[232] It was in these circumstances that, urged on by the Prime Minister, the Chiefs of Staff on 25 June, three days after the opening of *Barbarossa*, ordered that the anti-invasion forces in the United Kingdom should be kept on the alert and be brought to their highest state of efficiency by 1 September.[233] Nor was this decision reconsidered until 23 July when the JIC, in its first attempt since the attack to assess the effect of the war in Russia on the prospects of invasion, concluded that an invasion attempt was unlikely before 1942. It based this view on the obvious grounds that, with the improvement of British defences, invasion was becoming an increasingly hazardous operation and that, given the need for redeployment from Russia, it had become a complex undertaking. It supported it with negative evidence from intelligence: the best sources, presumably Sigint and photographic reconnaissance, contained no sign of German redeployment, no indication that Germany

---

227. JIC (41) 234 of 14 June.
228. CAB 80/28. COS (41) 385 (COS Résumé, No 94), Paragraph 46.
229. Woodward, op cit, Vol I, p 615 (n).
230. ibid, p 615 (n).
231. JIC (41) 234 of 14 June.
232. WO 190/893, No 86A of 17 June 1941.
233. CAB 79/12, COS (41) 224th Meeting, 25 June.

had developed any new weapon or method of warfare, and, on balance, they told against invasion during 1941.[234] The JIC repeated this view on 1 August,[235] and on the following day the Prime Minister and the Chiefs of Staff decided to withdraw the directive in which they had required the highest state of readiness from the beginning of September.[236]

---

234. JIC (41) 295 (O) of 23 July.
235. JIC (41) 307 (O) of 1 August.
236. CAB 79/13, COS (41) 274th Meeting, 2 August.

APPENDICES

The Polish, French and British Contributions to the Breaking of the Enigma

The Enigma, an electro-mechanical wired encyphering machine with a series of drums or wheels, was put on the European commercial market in the 1920s. Adopted by the German Navy in 1926, by the German Army in 1929 and by the German Air Force in 1934, it was thereafter subjected by them to a series of modifications – mainly the addition of variable inter-connecting plugs between the keyboard and the wheels, the introduction of new wheels and the resort to a variety of different ways of setting the machine and to more frequent changes of settings – with the object of increasing its security.[1] By the outbreak of war, as a result of these modifications, the Germans judged that they had rendered it safe even in the event of capture; and they had indeed made it into a cypher system that presented formidable obstacles to the cryptanalyst. Instructions for arranging and setting the wheels could be changed as frequently as every 24 hours; anyone not knowing the setting* was faced with the problem of choosing from one hundred and fifty million, million, million solutions.

General Gustave Bertrand, one-time head of the cryptanalytical section of the French Intelligence Service and author of the most detailed book about how this problem was solved, says he was prompted to publish after seeing the garbled story given in Michel Garder, *La Guerre Secrète des Services Spéciaux Français, 1935–45* (Paris, 1967).[2] Garder's book does not mention the Enigma by name, though it states that the French obtained information about a German cyphering machine from an agent, beginning in 1937. Bertrand's account has in its turn provoked counter-claims and additional details. It is here summarised with additions and corrections from other sources.

Bertrand claims to have been in contact from 1932 (not 1937) to 1939 with a German, whom he calls Asché, who was employed in the cypher branch of the German Army till 1934 and in the Forschungsamt (Communications Intelligence Section) of the GAF thereafter. The claim has been supported by Colonel Paul Paillole, former chief of the

---

* See note on p 495.

1. *The Times*, Letters to the Editor, 10 October 1977, 29 October 1977; Rohwer, op cit, Appendix 10 ('Notes on the Security of the German Cipher Systems').

2. Bertrand, *Enigma ou la plus grande énigme de la guerre 1939–1945* (1973), pp 13, 265.

French counter-espionage, who adds that Asché's name was Hans-Thilo Schmidt and that he was a 'play-boy who spied for money'.[3] Paillole explains that he was prompted to issue his information by annoyance at Group Captain Winterbotham's false claim that the secrets of the Enigma machine were first uncovered when a Pole who had worked in an Enigma factory in Germany was smuggled from Poland to Paris just before the war by the SIS.[4]

From Asché, according to Bertrand, the French obtained no less than 303 documents graded Geheim or Geheime Kommandosache about the Enigma. They included instructions for one of the Enigma machines, Army Enigma keys* for 1932, 1933 and the first half of 1934, and a long text encyphered on the machine together with its clear text and all key data – everything in fact except information about the internal wiring of the wheels – and were indispensable for the break into the Enigma.[5]

Bertrand further claims that, armed with this information, he approached the British, the Poles and the Czechs for help in exploiting it; that little happened with the Czechs and that the British showed little interest; but that to the Poles, who had been working on the Enigma since 1928 with a strong team of mathematicians, but with no data beyond intercepted messages, it came 'as manna in a desert'.[6] GC and CS records are far from perfect for the pre-war years. But they confirm that the French provided GC and CS (they say as early as 1931) with two photographed documents giving directions for setting and using the Enigma machine Mark I which the Germans introduced in 1930. They also indicate that GC and CS showed no great interest in collaborating, for they add that in 1936, when a version of the Enigma began to be used in Spain, GC and CS asked the French if they had acquired any information since 1931; and GC and CS's attitude is perhaps explained by the fact that as late as April 1939 the ministerial committee which authorised the fullest exchange of intelligence with France still excluded cryptanalysis.q As well as saying that 'the British intelligence service...did not seem to show much interest', Paillole gives additional details about Franco-Polish collaboration – that following French contact with Warsaw in 1933 several experimental models of the Enigma machine were put together between 1934 and 1938; that Polish-French collaboration extended to the interception and decryption of German signals

---

* See note on p 495.   † See Chapter 1, p 39.

3. Paillole, op cit, pp 33, 63–64; *Sunday Times*, 'Now the French claim their Spy found the Code', 27 June 1976.
4. F W Winterbotham, *The Ultra Secret*, (London 1974) and *Sunday Telegraph*, 21 July 1974.   5. Bertrand, op cit, pp 23–26.
6. ibid, p 37.

between 1936 and 1938, when Bertrand made several trips to Warsaw.[7] A memorandum by the head of Polish Intelligence before the war, S A Mayer, which was written in response to Bertrand's book and is now filed with the GC and CS papers, makes no mention, on the other hand, of the Asché material. It claims that the Poles simply bought the commercial model of the Enigma and set to work with a group of mathematicians to discover how it had been modified and improved for use by the German armed forces.[8] In all probability the truth lies in between. This is suggested by three other accounts, based on interviews with some of the Polish mathematicians. One says that the Poles, using Bertrand's documentation, cracked the mathematical problem after buying a commercial version of the machine in 1932.[9] Another says that the Poles had discovered in 1928 that the German armed forces were using a modified version of the commercial Enigma and that 'in 1932...the Polish cypher bureau...had achieved a partial solution when...Bertrand provided some key Enigma documents obtained by Hans-Thilo Schmidt'.[10] The third accepts Bertrand's claim while thanking him for his praiseworthy objectivity in nevertheless conceding that the Polish mathematicians played the leading role in breaking the Enigma.*[11]

On the work of the Polish mathematicians the Polish accounts provide the following further information. Recruited in September 1932, they took barely four and a half months to 'crack the system of the early version of the Enigma'. From 1934, greatly helped by a Pole who was working in an Enigma factory in Germany, they began to make their own Enigma machines. However, these were crude and time-consuming, and it was only later that they developed mechanical versions of the Enigma machine. The first break-through, a mathematical one which 'resulted in the theoretical breaking of the Enigma machine at the beginning of 1933', and the construction of Polish copies of the Enigma machine from 1934 were followed from 1937 by the development of the 'cryptographic Bombe', a machine devised for 'finding' Enigma keys by the rapid automatic testing of several tens

---

* This account refers to another publication, W Kozaczuk, *Bitwa o tajemnice. Służby wywiadowcze Polski i Rzeszy Niemieckiej 1922–1939* (*The Battle of Secrets. The Intelligence Services of Poland and the German Reich, 1922–1939*) (Warsaw 1967), which appears to have been the earliest to reveal the fact that the Enigma had been broken. For a German translation of this Polish book see a series of articles under the title 'Enigma' in the journal *Horizont*, issues No 41–No 49 (1975).

7. Paillole, op cit, p 83; *Sunday Times*, 27 June 1976.
8. GC and CS Archive, Memorandum by S A Mayer.
9. *Sunday Times*, 3 November 1974 (interview with Thadeus Lisicki).
10. D Kahn, *New York Times Book Review*, 29 December 1974.
11. Colonel W Kozacsuk, 'The Key to the Secrets of the Third Reich (I)', *Poland* (Warsaw), No 6, 1975.

of thousands of possible combinations. Improved versions of the Bombe were constructed up to 1939.*[12]

This information by no means establishes from what date the Poles actually read the Enigma traffic, or how extensively they read it. The answer to these questions is complicated by the fact that during the 1930s the German armed forces were continuously improving the Enigma machine. A German report on the Polish work states that on this account it suffered from long interruptions from January 1935 and again from October 1938.[14] In addition, the Germans at first changed the Enigma keys only once every three months, but later began to change them monthly and eventually changed them daily. Another difficulty arises because the Poles do not give details of the extent of their success against this mounting problem; nor do they ever mention the contents of their decrypts. One of their accounts claims in very general terms that 'Nazi messages' were read regularly from the first break-through until 1938.[15] Another says only that after the introduction of the Bombe in 1937 an Enigma key could be broken in 'no more than 110 minutes'.[16] A third account – the Mayer memorandum – appears to be more precise. It claims that 'by the end of 1937 our cryptologists had completely mastered the reading of intercepted German radiograms' and adds that in January 1938, in a two weeks' test, 'circa 75% of this material was then decyphered'.[17] But it does not specify which Enigma keys were mastered or how extensive the material was. Nor does it say whether the material was read currently, and the reference to a two weeks' test may mean that current messages were not being decyphered.

On this subject the Poles informed GC and CS at a meeting in July 1939† that they made their initial break into a pre-1931 model of the Enigma that was used by the German Navy, and that up to the spring of 1937, having worked out the wiring of the wheels with help from a stolen copy of the keys for a three-month period, they read naval signals more or less currently. They admitted, however, that after the end of April 1937, when the Germans changed the naval indicators,

---

* The Bombe is described in some of the Polish accounts as an electronic device, as 'a forecast of the computer technique' and as being similar to the 'undoubtedly still more sophisticated' devices that were later produced in Britain. However, the brief description gives the impression that it was basically an electro-mechanical scanning machine.[13]

† See below, pp 491–492.

12. *Sunday Times*, 27 June 1976 (interviews with Thadeus Lisicki and Colonel W Kozacsuk); Kozacsuk, 'The Key to the Secrets of the Third Reich (II)', *Poland* (Warsaw) No 7, 1975.

13. B Randell, *The Colossus*, University of Newcastle upon Tyne, Technical Report Series, No 90, June 1976.

14. Rohwer, op cit, p 236.

15. *Sunday Times*, 3 November 1974 (interview with Thadeus Lisicki).

16. Kozacsuk in *Poland* No 7, 1975.

17. Mayer memorandum, p 2.

they had been able to read the naval traffic only for the period from 30 April to 8 May 1937, and that only retrospectively. Moreover, this small success left them in no doubt that the new indicator system had given the Enigma machine a much higher degree of security. With regard to military Enigma (by which they may have meant only army or both army and air) they stated that they had read it until 15 September 1938, when the Germans introduced two additional wheels, thus increasing the number for selection from three to five; that they had subsequently worked out the wiring of the new wheels; but that by mid-December 1938 they had ceased to be able to read the traffic.

The Poles were accordingly receptive when in December 1938 Bertrand took the initiative in calling a Franco-British-Polish conference of cryptanalysts to discuss Enigma. GC and CS was also interested by then. In April 1937 it had broken the Enigma used in Spain by the Germans, the Italians and Franco's forces after the outbreak of the Spanish Civil War;[18] this was a machine similar to the commercial model. By the end of 1937, on the other hand, it had given up hope of breaking the different model that the German Navy was using. And during 1938 another approach to or by the French – the British approach made in 1936 had led only to the exchange of Enigma intercepts and DF bearings – had aroused GC and CS's interest by producing the plain and cyphered texts of four Enigma messages and information about the wireless networks of the German Army. Bertrand, however, admits that the French could make no progress on their own.[19] He asked for the conference because the Poles had not reported any success to him, and he was becoming desperate.[20]

The conference met in Paris on 7–9 January 1939. There was, according to Bertrand, a useful exchange of technical ideas, and Bertrand's organisation and GC and CS agreed to exchange liaison officers and establish a teleprinter link.[21] But there was no exchange of Enigma results. Mayer explains why: the Polish cryptanalysts, under instructions not to disclose their achievements unless the other participants revealed that they had made some progress, formed the impression that the French and British had nothing to offer.[22] It was, however, at the invitation of the Poles that a second meeting of cryptanalysts from the three countries took place in Warsaw on 24–25 July, and at that meeting they revealed that they had broken the Enigma and proposed full collaboration in exploiting it.

Bertrand records that when suggesting the July meeting the Poles announced that something new had happened, and implies that they became more forthcoming not only because Poland had received her

---

18. *The Observer*, 8 July 1973.
19. Bertrand, op cit, pp 71–72.
20. ibid, p 57.
21. ibid, pp 58, 72.
22. Mayer memorandum, p 3.

guarantee from Great Britain and France in March, and was worried by the growing danger of war, but also because the Germans had again introduced new Enigma wheels on 1 July 1939.[23] As it happens, the Germans did not add extra wheels to the army and air Enigmas in the summer of 1939, though they made other changes, and Mayer's memorandum confirms that what was then worrying the Poles was the fact that, whether because they had too few staff or for other reasons, they had not yet overcome the difficulties caused by the much greater change of September 1938. It states that after the January 1939 meeting the Poles had continued their 'solitary battle against the Enigma' but that despite the development of the Bombe they were 'for the time being unsuccessful', and that, as the international situation was fast deteriorating, they decided to ask for close collaboration with France and Britain in 'solving the difficulties [that had] arisen out of the introduction of new wheels'.[24]

As well as confirming what GC and CS learned at the July meeting – that although they had recovered the wiring of the September 1938 wheels, the Poles had not been able to read the military Enigma since the end of 1938 – this evidence is supported by what is known about subsequent developments. At the July meeting the Poles, as well as explaining the methods they had developed for breaking the Enigma, agreed to present the British and the French with a copy, one each, of a Polish-built Enigma machine and technical drawings of the Bombe; and it was settled that the British would concentrate on finding a method of breaking the daily keys while the Poles retained responsibility for more theoretical work.[25] According to Bertrand, he took the British copy to London on 16 August and handed it over on Victoria Station to 'C' in person, 'C' being 'en smoking, avec rosette de la Légion d'Honneur à la boutonnière. Accueil triomphal!'[26] When the various papers from the Poles – and in particular the wheel wirings – reached GC and CS it was soon possible to decrypt the old messages for which the Poles had broken the keys, but more recent messages remained unreadable. It is clear, moreover, that the Polish cryptanalysts, who were transferred to Bertrand's Paris organisation at the beginning of October,[27] were not themselves reading the Enigma at the time: they believed that the Germans had again made wholesale changes to the Enigma on the outbreak of war, whereas the Enigma then underwent no change.

In the event the first war-time break into the Enigma was made with help from GC and CS by the Poles at Bertrand's organisation in Paris

---

23. Bertrand, op cit, pp 59–60.
24. Mayer memorandum, pp 3–4.
25. ibid, p 4; Bertrand, op cit, pp 59–60; *Sunday Times*, 3 November 1974.
26. Bertrand, op cit, p 60.
27. Mayer memorandum, p 4; Bertrand, op cit, p 69; Kozacsuk in *Poland*, No 7, 1975.

at the end of 1939. Bertrand implies that this break was made *on 28 October*.[28] The truth is that an Army Enigma key (the key named the Green at GC and CS) *for 28 October* was broken in the second half of December. In the autumn of 1939, as well as working on the improvement of the Bombe, GC and CS used the information it had obtained from the Poles at the July meeting to improve its own hand methods, which involved the preparation in large quantities of sheets with punched holes. By the middle of December, two copies of these sheets were completed, and one was sent across to Paris. 'At the end of the year', GC and CS records, 'our emissary returned with the great news that a key had been broken (October 28, Green) on the...sheets he had taken with him. Immediately we got to work on a key (October 25, Green)...; this, the first wartime Enigma key to come out in this country, was broken at the beginning of January 1940'. The GC and CS account continues: 'Had the Germans made a change in the machine at the New Year? While we waited...several other 1939 keys were broken. At last a favourable day arrived...The sheets were laid...and [the GAF] Red of 6 January 1940 was out. Other keys soon followed...'. The Mayer memorandum disagrees only in giving a later date for the solution of the key for 28 October. It says that 'the cryptologists [in Paris]...noted only that on 17 January they finally solved the key for 28 October and that by the end of January 1940 they were sure that no further changes had been made to the Enigma'.[29] Other Polish accounts agree with Mayer's date.[30]

In the interval between January and 23 June 1940, the date on which, on the defeat of France, Bertrand's organisation dispersed, the Paris organisation and GC and CS continued work in close collaboration. Bertrand claims that up to 14 June, in the period from 28 October 1939, 121 Enigma keys were solved; he also implies that the results were all produced by his organisation.[31] But Mayer states that as well as investing in the development of the Bombe, which the French left to the British, GC and CS broke 83 per cent of the keys that were read at this time; he adds that in all 126 keys were broken in this period, for 100 days from 6 July 1939 to 16 June 1940. He explains that GC and CS's preponderance was due to the agreed division of labour, by which Paris concentrated on research while GC and CS gave priority to technical development aimed at the quicker breaking of daily keys, and to the fact that GC and CS was better organised and equipped than Paris to intercept and decypher the German traffic.[32] It should

---

28. Bertrand, op cit, pp 76–77.

29. Mayer memorandum, p 6.

30: *Sunday Times*, 3 November 1974 (interview with Thadeus Lisicki); Korbonski, 'The True Story of Enigma – the German Code Machine in World War II', *East European Quarterly*, Vol XI, No 2, Summer 1977, University of Colorado, p 232.

31. Bertrand, op cit, pp 72–76, 79.

32. Mayer memorandum, pp 5–7.

be added that GC and CS's punched-hole sheets turned out to be much less laborious than the non-Bombe methods developed by the Poles and that by the end of May 1940 GC and CS had taken delivery of the first British-made Bombe.

The Bombe greatly increased the speed and regularity with which GC and CS broke the daily-changing Enigma keys. From the summer of 1940, as more and better models were built, it was the essential basis of GC and CS's continuing and increasing success. On this account, and because GC and CS had not thought of the possibility of using high-speed machine testing against the Enigma before the July 1939 meeting, it has been argued that the Poles made their most valuable contribution by then providing the diagrams of their Bombe. But the British Bombe was of quite different design from the Polish and much more powerful; and it is virtually certain that the GC and CS Enigma team would in any case have realised the need to develop analogue machinery for recovering the daily keys as soon as it had discovered the wirings of the Enigma wheels – the more so since the team included Turing, who already had an interest in machine computation. In the light of these considerations it seems likely that the most important outcome of the July meeting was that the Poles handed over the results of their brilliant technical work in recovering the wheel wirings, though an additional benefit – imponderable but potentially of great psychological value -- was the very discovery that the Poles had had such significant success.

If this is accepted, and if it is assumed that the delay in building the first British Bombe and in evolving the much improved logic for the later Bombes would have been the same as was in fact incurred, it is possible to arrive at an actual measure of the Polish contribution to the successes against the war-time Enigma. The first British capture of Enigma wheels was made from U-33 in February 1940. As this was seven months after GC and CS's receipt of details of the wheels from the Poles, the first Bombe would in the absence of Polish assistance have been delivered to GC and CS in January 1941 instead of in May 1940. In the interval between May 1940 and the following January GC and CS would have continued to read Enigma keys by hand methods with something like the frequency and something like the delay that it actually did between January and June 1940, and the regular and nearly current reading of a key, which in fact began on 22 May 1940, would have been correspondingly delayed. It must be added, however, that just as the operational keys that were actually read up to June 1940 were virtually confined to those of the GAF, the only important exception being an inter-Service key (the Yellow) which the Germans introduced for the Norwegian campaign,* so the only key that was actually read regularly from as early as the end of May 1940 was the

---

* See Chapter 3, p 109.

GAF general key (the Red).* The regular solution of German naval and army Enigma keys began so much later than the beginning of 1941, and was the outcome of so many other developments, that it is unlikely that the Polish contribution made any difference to the dates from which they were mastered.

---

* See Chapter 3, p 109; Chapter 4, p 144.

Note: In the early days of the war no distinction in terminology was made between an Enigma *key* and the daily *settings* of the machine for each key. There were different keys, both as between Army, Navy and Air Force keys, and different keys within each Service (eg GAF Red, Army Green). Over and above this, the setting for each key was changed daily. We have not always preserved the distinction between key and setting in this appendix but have sought to do so in the main text.

APPENDIX 2

The SIS Air Photographic Unit – the Activities of F S Cotton[1]

In the middle of 1938 Squadron Leader F W Winterbotham, who had himself been a pioneer of air photography at the end of the First World War, was concerned with the liaison between the SIS and the French Deuxième Bureau de l'Armée de l'Air. The French had provided the most recent photographs of German targets. They had been taken on reconnaissance flights in 1936, the year such flights had been resumed after a break dating from 1929, and were limited to targets of military interest and in particular to areas of Army interest; these included the Siegfried Line, the approaches to the Maginot Line and the area between the Moselle and the Rhine, but apart from sporadic missions as far east as Munich, no great penetration into Germany had been attempted.

As the normal means of obtaining such target information were likely to be reduced, and might cease altogether if the international crisis deepened, these photographs aroused interest in the possibility of extending aerial photographic reconnaissance, and as Winterbotham found that the French were also anxious to extend their aerial espionage, a co-operative venture was proposed. The reconnaissance, if it was to be clandestine, would have to be carried out at high altitude, using a high speed aircraft, to minimise detection and avoid interception. It would have to be done by a civil organisation and with some cover story. Various negotiations took place involving the Deuxième Bureau, Mr Paul Koster, the European representative of the American Armament Corporation, Mr A J Miranda of the New York branch of the Corporation and Mr F S Cotton, a business friend of Miranda. Eventually Cotton was introduced to Winterbotham, and the scheme was discussed. Thus began an association destined to play a vital part in the development of aerial photographic reconnaissance.

Sidney Cotton, an Australian, had served in the RNAS in the First World War and had done a great deal of flying in all sorts of circumstances in the intervening years. He had been accustomed to

---

1. This account has been compiled from:
   AIR 41/6, *Photographic Reconnaissance*, Vol 1
   ADM 233/54, PR Monograph
   R Barker, *Aviator Extraordinary; the Sidney Cotton Story* (1969)
   F W Winterbotham, *Secret and Personal* (1969), Chapter 14
   C Babington Smith, *Evidence in Camera* (1958), Chapter 1
   Morgan, *NID History 1939–1942*

flying his own aeroplane around Europe and was thus ideally suited for the proposed operation, under the 'cover' of a private company created for the purpose – the Aeronautical Research and Sales Corporation. After detailed discussions between Cotton and Winterbotham it was decided that a Lockheed 12A was a suitable aircraft, and one was obtained from America; it arrived at Southampton in January 1939. A co-pilot engineer was recruited in the person of Flying Officer R H Niven, a Canadian who was about to complete his Short Service Commission in the RAF.

Although it may have originally been intended that Cotton should fly the aircraft only when not on an operation, and that a French crew would carry out the reconnaissance missions, it was in fact Cotton who flew the first attempts to obtain photographs. He noticed that at 15,000 feet and above the windscreen became frosted over, and that it was only by allowing warm air from the cockpit to be sucked out past the windscreen that he was able to prevent frosting. This was to be of importance later. Cotton and Niven carried out the first reconnaissance missions over western Germany from Toussus le Noble which had been selected by the French as a suitable base of operations. The first, on 25 March 1939, covered Krefeld, Hamm, Munster and the Dutch frontier. Then on 1 and 7 April the Black Forest and Wurtemburg were photographed, and on the last German flight, on 9 April, the outskirts of Karlsruhe, Bruchsal, Heidelberg, Mannheim, Ludwigshafen and Ebersbach. The sorties were flown at approximately 5,000 m; a French camera of focal length 30 cms was used, giving photographs of a scale of about 1/16,700. The next mission, the last in co-operation with the French, was to photograph Italian targets in the Mediterranean area. On 25 April a sortie covered the coast from east of Tripoli to the Tunisian border, the aerodrome of Castel Benito and five other airfields, and a number of gun positions and communications targets. The flight was at 5,800 m, the French camera was used, and in all 282 overlapping photographs were obtained of a scale of 1/20,000.

Cotton relates that he encountered various difficulties in working with the French, and in any case, as already stated, the original intention appears to have been that they would fly the operational missions. At all events, after this mission the Lockheed was handed over to the Deuxième Bureau; using it, the French photographed Spezia, Sardinia and Sicily. But it was agreed that Cotton should continue with photographic reconnaissance, and two further Lockheeds 12A were obtained. They arrived in Southampton early in May 1939. One was flown on 20 May to Buc, and handed over to the French, the other, to be used by Cotton, was flown to Heston on 11 May.

Cotton now started the development of the system which he had had in mind. The normal range of the Lockheed 12A was 700 miles.

Believing this to be inadequate, he fitted extra tanks with the object of achieving a range of 1,600 miles. He decided to use the standard RAF F 24 camera with 5″ lenses, but fitted these in a group of three so that one pointed vertically down and the others inclined at 40°; with overlap they should photograph a strip 11½ miles wide from a height of 21,000 feet. To minimise detection, he also had the aircraft painted a pale duck-egg green, which he registered as 'Camotint'.

On 14 June, preparations complete, Cotton and Niven flew to Malta. There they made contact with Flying Officer M V Longbottom, who had been involved in the earlier RAF flying boat reconnaissance activities and who had developed a keen interest in photographic matters. Cotton had been looking for someone to help on the photographic side, and Longbottom joined the team. A series of highly successful missions were flown, between 15 and 25 June 1939. Eastern Sicily, the Dodecanese, Leros and Rhodes, Italian east Africa, Somaliland, and Cyrenaica were all covered. As the RAF Narrative puts it:

'Within ten days, a single aircraft, piloted by a supposedly wealthy Englishman with a taste for desert ruins, was able to secure photographs of key points in most of the areas of the Italian Empire, which during the past few years had been exercising the British and French naval and air staffs... It is a striking fact that in nearly every case the SIS was re-photographing vertically localities previously covered obliquely by RAF machines flying discreetly beyond the six-mile limit?'[2]

The next series of sorties was to be over German targets. During July Cotton had been, perhaps fortuitously, in contact with some Germans who were interested in colour film and in particular with a firm with which Cotton had business interests. The outcome was a flight to Berlin on 26 July. Cotton had modified the Lockheed to take concealed cameras in the wings, but after discussions with Winterbotham these were not fitted on this occasion. On 28 July, however, when on a visit to the international air meeting for sports pilots to which he had been invited when in Berlin, Cotton installed two Leicas in the wings, operated from the cockpit. Even though carrying a German passenger he succeeded in taking photographs in the Mannheim area, and of other targets on the return journey. On a second business trip to Berlin, on 17 August, he took photographs of targets north of Berlin. For this third trip to Berlin, on 22 August, no cameras were fitted, but Cotton and Niven had taken Leicas with them and they took the opportunity on the return journey to take some photographs of German fleet units at Wilhelmshaven.

The photographs of Wilhelmshaven, and other coastal German targets, were of great interest to the Admiralty, where it had become imperative to obtain all possible information about the whereabouts

---

2. AIR 41/6, p 41.

of the major German fleet units. These targets were again photographed in the last pre-war days. On 28 August Niven flew a
Beechcraft to Wilhelmshaven and the Schillig Roads and secured
evidence that the ships were still there. (A Beechcraft had been added
to the Heston flight some time previously, and had been used by Cotton
and Niven since March, but this was its first German operation.)
Another mission to the same area took place the following day. These
flights demonstrated that quite apart from the value of photographic
reconnaissance to obtain intelligence of installations, it could be used
with advantage to observe activities such as ship movements provided
frequent missions could be flown.

This completed the SIS photographic reconnaissance flights in
the pre-war period. However Cotton, Niven, and Longbottom were
also looking to the future. They realised that in addition to the
improvements which they might make in cameras and film, there
was an urgent need to improve aircraft performance. This had been
demonstrated by the Lockheed modifications, but even greater speeds
and range were required. The outcome of their deliberations was the
proposal to use a Spitfire, and to this end Longbottom prepared and
submitted a detailed proposal in August 1939.[3] In this he examined
the combined problems of aircraft, cameras, camouflage and tactics.
He also suggested the later use of the Whirlwind, which was then at
the prototype stage.

Once war had broken out Winterbotham discussed the future of the
Flight with DG Ops (AVM R H Peck) and agreement was reached in
principle to retain it as a special Flight within the control of the RAF.
The problem was how to do this without creating a conflict between
the unorthodox ideas which Cotton and his colleages proposed for
the future development of photographic reconnaissance and the
RAF's traditional concept of operational reconnaissance. Cotton
thought that 'the best answer, both for getting immediate results and
for the future development of RAF photography, was for the nucleus
already in being at Heston to be expanded on a war footing, proving
the system by taking whatever pictures were wanted. When the unit
and its methods had become properly established, the RAF could take
it over'.[4] The Admiralty was also in favour of this policy, although this
was not known to Cotton at that time. But after further negotiation
it was decided that the RAF should take over the Flight to form an
experimental unit for the purpose of testing and, if successful,
developing certain novel methods for making photographic reconnaissance over enemy territory. The Unit was formally handed over to
the Air Ministry by the SIS on 23 September 1939. It was to be based
at Heston, commanded by Cotton as a Wing Commander, and was
placed under Fighter Command for administration.

---

3. ibid, Appendix xii.
4. Barker, op cit, p 149.

APPENDIX 3

A Note on the Organisation of the German Economy at the Outbreak of War*

The Nazi system of government was based on the 'leadership principle', each minister being responsible personally to Hitler. There was no collective Cabinet responsibility and consultation between ministries for the co-ordination of policy was frowned upon by Hitler and the Nazi Party. Cutting across the structure of the ministries were the offices of 'commissioners' and 'plenipotentiaries', created to deal with particular problems and constantly growing in number. The central and regional authorities of the Party itself interfered in economic matters, creating a dualism with the bureaucracy. Decisions upon broad questions of economic strategy rested ultimately with Hitler himself.

The economic recovery of Germany after 1933 depended primarily upon the programme of rearmament initiated by the Nazis, and the armed services themselves played an important and independent role in shaping the economy in that they were given wide powers to require from industry the production of war material. Between the Services and the Reichswirtschaftsministerium (the Ministry of Economics) which carried the main responsibility for administering the civil economy, there were serious conflicts of jurisdiction, exacerbated by competition between the three Services for the products of industry.

Until 1936, when the Four Year Plan organisation was established, the primary responsibility for control of the supply of raw materials to industry lay with the Ministry of Economics, within whose jurisdiction came also the control of foreign trade and the management of foreign exchange holdings. To control and administer the supply of raw materials the Ministry early established Reichsstellen (Reich Offices) for each raw material and basic industrial product and, in theory at least, the 'planning' of industrial output rested upon the rationing of raw materials by the Ministry of Economics through these offices. In practice, however, this system was ineffective because although the Reichsstellen had the responsibility for issuing permits for the use of materials they had no control over the formulation of

---

* For fuller accounts see, eg, B H Klein, *Germany's Economic Preparations for War* (1959); A S Milward, *The German Economy at War* (1965); B A Carroll, *Design for Total War* (1968).

demands by competing users. Nor had the Ministry of Economics any control over the placing of industrial orders by the armed services.

By 1934 the unco-ordinated flow of demands for raw materials had already led to a shrinkage of stocks, sharp increases in imports and serious balance of payments difficulties. Two measures of reorganisation were then introduced in an attempt to remedy the situation.

One of these measures was the transfer in 1934 of the economic staff of the Army Ordnance Office to the War Ministry, where it was given inter-Service status under the title of Wehrwirtschafts-und Waffen-wesen (Defence Economy and Armament Affairs), and the conferment upon its head, Colonel (later General) Georg Thomas, of responsibility for co-ordinating economic support for the arms programmes of the three armed Services.

The other measure appeared to be more far-reaching, since it seemed to recognise the need for some form of central planning for the economy as a whole. In August 1934 Dr Schacht, Germany's leading financial expert, succeeded Kurt Schmitt, the Minister of Economics, first as Acting Minister and then, in January 1935, as full Minister. This appointment was an acknowledgement of the serious-ness of Germany's international financial problems. In May 1935, however, Schacht was given a further appointment which acknow-ledged the seriousness of the conflicts of economic jurisdiction within Germany. He was made Plenipotentiary General for the War Economy (Generalbevollmächtigter für die Kriegswirtschaft – GBK) with over-riding authority in economic matters.

Neither experiment succeeded in its object. The responsibilities of the Wehrwirtschafts-und Waffenwesen office were ill-defined and the three Services retained full control of current supply and weapon development for their own needs. The office was therefore incapable of reconciling the competing demands of the Services upon industry. What Schacht might have made of his position as GBK had his real powers been equal to those required by his task it is impossible to say. He was handicapped from the outset by being denied any authority over the armed Services' programme of mobilisation. He was regarded with suspicion by the Party. Nor was Hitler willing to confer upon anyone other than himself the real powers which the office of GBK implied. Finally Schacht was confronted in October 1936 with the creation of the Four Year Plan organisation and the appointment of Göring as Commissioner for the Plan, Commissioner for Fuel and 'responsible' for raw materials.

Hitler saw the primary purpose of the Four Year Plan as being to secure self-sufficiency in a number of raw materials of major strategic importance until a new Lebensraum could be obtained by conquest. He instructed Göring that he was to seek *total* independence of foreign sources only for fuels and rubber and it was in these two sectors that the Plan was most effective. Under its auspices great progress was made in the construction of synthetic oil plants and the development of artificial rubber production, and it also secured a considerable expansion of the output of artificial fibres.

Once again, however, the powers of the new organisation were ill-defined. Göring held that it was to exercise leadership and drive but not to take over the functions of existing offices. Most of its agencies were in fact set up within other ministries. To support his new role as 'responsible' for raw materials Göring established within the Four Year Plan organisation a Bureau for Raw Materials and Synthetics under the direction of Colonel Löb of the Air Force Staff, who in the spring of 1937 produced a long-range plan.

Nominally Göring as Commissioner was endowed with the powers of a supreme planning authority, although Schacht still remained GBK. Conflict between Schacht and Göring over jurisdiction was therefore inevitable. To this was added a direct conflict over policy, since the capital expenditure and raw material imports, coupled with a weakening of export trade, ran counter to Schacht's efforts to restore the financial situation. The final clash between the two men arose over Göring's plan for the exploitation of low grade German iron ore which was opposed by both Schacht and the steel industry. Schacht resigned as GBK and Minister of Economics in November 1937. His successor, Funk, was confirmed in office in February 1938.

With the fall of Schacht from ministerial office (he remained President of the Reichsbank for another year) Göring gave up his ineffectual attempt to plan the raw material balance: Löb's long-term plan was scrapped and the Bureau for Raw Materials transferred to the Ministry of Economics, where it continued its function of building up stocks. Göring dissipated his general planning authority amongst newly created plenipotentiaries and special commissioners and allowed the General Council of the Four Year Plan, which was to have served as a supreme planning authority, to lapse.

None of these experiments in organisation affected inter-Service rivalries in relation to the economy. Thomas' Wehrwirtschafts-und Waffenwesen office had already proved ineffective as a means of co-ordinating Service requirements when an event occurred which was to weaken its position still further. In February 1938 Hitler dismissed his Commander-in-Chief, von Fritsch, and the Minister for War, General von Blomberg, and took over the command himself. The armed Services directorate of the Ministry became the OKW under Keitel, of which Thomas' staff, re-named Wehrwirtschafts-und Rüstungsamt (Wi Ru), was a branch. Whereas Blomberg had at least endeavoured to make a reality of Thomas' co-ordinating function, Keitel made little effort to give it his support. Thomas, however, still tried to exert a general influence upon economic policy and, in doing so, became more and more clearly identified with policies unacceptable to Hitler and Göring, arguing for armament in depth and for total mobilisation of resources at the expense of the consumer. Not fully understanding Hitler's strategic ideas he was pessimistic about the raw material situation and even by 1939 did not consider Germany ready for war. Göring generally disregarded what he had to say.

During much of 1938 quarrels about jurisdiction between the GBK, the Four Year Plan and OKW (in the shape of Wi Ru) persisted. In September an attempt was made to put an end to them by a new Reich Defence Law under which Göring replaced Keitel as Hitler's deputy in national defence matters. It was decreed that in time of war German domestic administration would be in the hands of a group (chaired by Hitler or Göring) consisting of the Chief of OKW, the GBK (now re-named Generalbevollmächtigter für die Wirtschaft (GBW)) and a new Plenipotentiary for the Administration of the Reich (General-bevollmächtigter für die Reichsverwaltung (GBV)). Wilhelm Frick was appointed to the new office.

The new law made little difference to the positions of the contending authorities in the last months of peace. When, in May 1939, OKW and GBW staffs sat down together to draw up a joint 'Mob. Plan Wirtschaft' (Economic Mobilisation Plan) for the economy as a whole, responsibility for war planning was still divided between them, the OKW staff (Wi Ru) being theoretically responsible for the Wehrmacht programme and GBW for the civilian side, with the Four Year Plan organisation playing an ambiguous role in the background. They had not completed their work when war broke out in September.

In another important respect also the German economic system on the eve of the war fell far short of comprehensive planning. The supply of labour to the various sectors of the economy was administered centrally by the Ministry of Labour but there was no inter-departmental mechanism by which its decisions could be related to the supply of other resources. In practice such co-ordination as there was took place at the regional level, inspectors subordinate to Wi Ru being responsible for securing the labour required by the main armaments firms (A-betriebe) through the Regional Labour Offices. The authority of the Regional Labour Offices was, however, restricted by the existence of a 'Standing Change of Employment Order' requiring the consent of both employer and employee to any change of job.

It fell to Göring to attempt some solution to the administrative problems arising from competing demands for manpower. Characteristically he avoided the issue and in a decree of 14 June 1939 placed the responsibility collectively upon the GBW, the GBV, the Chief of OKW and the Führer's Party deputy. When, in December 1939, Göring succeeded in abolishing the office of GBW such influence as the Ministry of Economics could exert in manpower matters was further weakened. In practice the administration of labour supplies was to remain poorly co-ordinated with the administration of the economy as a whole throughout the war. Not even Speer could bridge the gap.

Thus at the outbreak of war the German economy was still without a central planning authority. Nothing comparable with the Soviet

'command' economy, with its Gosplan for the construction of a
self-consistent plan and its hierarchy of economic ministries responsible for plan-fulfilment, had been established. Nevertheless a method
of administering the actual production of goods and services had been
developed which adequately served Hitler's purposes and which by the
exercise of ingenuity on the part of industrialists overcame the defects
of the central administration to the extent that it provided Germany
with the economic basis for Blitzkrieg.

There was little state ownership in Nazi Germany. Agriculture,
industry and commerce remained in private hands, but they were
grouped in 'self administering' associations set up by the Nazis on
coming to power. There were four such 'co-operative' structures:
(1) the Reichsnährstand (the Food 'Estate' or administration), (2)
the Organization der gewerblichen Wirtschaft (the Organisation of
Industry and Trade), (3) the Deutsche Arbeitsfront (the German
Labour Organisation), and (4) the Aufbau des Verkehrs (the Cor-
porate Organisation of Transport).

The largest branch of the Organisation of Industry and Trade was
the 'Reichsgruppe Industrie' (Reich Industrial Group) comprising all
classes of industrial production, which for policy-making purposes was
formally subordinate to the Ministry of Economics. In practice,
however, apart from its authority over the supply of raw materials the
Ministry had little say in the conduct of industrial affairs.

In the face of confusion and bickering at the highest levels of
government and despite the absence of a national plan for economic
mobilisation for war the 'self-administering' organisations, under
strong and experienced leadership, provided without great difficulty
the material required by the armed Services in the campaigns in
Poland, Norway, western Europe and Russia up to the winter of
1941–42. This success was achieved in spite of a system of allocating
raw materials so defective that although by 1939 stocks were in fact
adequate for Hitler's purposes, industrialists clamouring for supplies
found themselves confronted with recurring shortages, especially of
steel. The wastefulness of the method of allocating resources was not
to become apparent until the real nature of the war in Russia was borne
in upon Hitler's government in the winter of 1941 and reform became
imperative. When introduced in 1942 the reforms demonstrated that
one of the most important areas of 'slack' in the German economy
had been in planning and administration. Many of the strains which
were being reported to Whitehall between 1936 and 1939 were due to
the fact that what was undeniably a war economy had not been fully
mobilised either by the subordination of all economic activity to the
production of armaments or by the establishment of an administrative
system by which the optimum use of resources could be made in a long
war.

APPENDIX 4

Displacement of German Capital Ships

Having repudiated the Treaty of Versailles on 16 March 1935, Germany signed the Anglo-German Naval Agreement on 18 June 1935. By this treaty the Germans agreed to limit their naval construction to 35 per cent of British strength except in submarines. They were accorded the right to build up to parity in submarine tonnage, but agreed not to exceed 45 per cent unless a situation arose which in their opinion made it necessary. In addition they agreed to limit the tonnage of battleships to 35,000 tons standard displacement.[1]

Before this, in March 1933, Germany had been considering her requirements for a new type of warship of about 26,000 tons. These were the battle-cruisers D (*Scharnhorst*) and E (*Gneisenau*). The keel plate of D was laid on 14 February 1934, but later that year reconsideration of the design – to mount 9 instead of 6 11″ guns, stronger armour, a 2 knot increase in speed – led to an increase in displacement of about 20 per cent. The naval requirements also included two battleships, F (*Bismarck*) and G (*Tirpitz*). In 1935 Hitler ordered a reconsideration of the main armament of all four ships. That of D and E remained unchanged, but it was decided that F and G should have 8 15″ guns. This caused an increase in their displacement to about 41,000 tons. A memorandum from the German Naval Plans Division to the Chief of Staff on 18 February 1938 contained the true (T) and the announced (A) displacements and draughts of these ships:

Type	Displacement (tons)		Draught (metres)	
	T	A	T	A
D, E	31,300	26,000	8.55	7.50
F, G	41,700	35,000	8.69	7.90

The memorandum added: 'The view of the Plans Division is that it is wrong to indicate a greater tonnage than has already been announced to Britain, Russia and Japan, so that we shall not be accused of starting an arms race'.[2]

The characteristics of the *Bismarck* were formally notified to the Foreign Office on 8 July 1936 as being a standard displacement of

---

1. Roskill, op cit, Vol 1, p 52.
2. Godfrey Memoirs, Vol V, Part II, Chapter XXXII.

35,000 tons, a draught of 26 feet and a main armament of 15" guns. The comparable RN battleship was the *King George V*; her main armament was of 14" guns, and she had been designed with constraints to ensure that any departure from the agreed limit, of 35,000 tons, should not exceed 5 per cent. The German declaration was accepted by the Admiralty, and it was assumed that although the *King George V* had inferior main armament, she would be superior to the *Bismarck* in such qualities as speed, endurance and protection.

The Naval Attaché in Berlin in his 1936 report accepted the German statement; he thought that although the Anglo-German naval agreement would go the way of other agreements in time, that time was not yet.*[3] The Director of Plans, Admiralty was more sceptical. In July 1937 he evolved a rough method of comparison by taking the products of length, beam and draught of capital vessels to establish a sort of coefficient of displacement. Using such information as was available, and taking 35,000 for Great Britain, he found that the figures were 37,200 for France, 39,300 for Germany, and 37,800 for Italy. This crude method was sufficient to cause anxiety, and anxiety was increased when the Italian 10,000 ton cruiser *Gorizia* was damaged on 25 August 1937 and had to dock in Gibraltar for repairs. The observations and measurements which were then made suggested that she had a displacement of between 11,280 and 11,440 tons, which showed that she was about 10 per cent over her declared tonnage. This matter was discussed by the CID at various times during 1937, but no representations were made to the Italian government.[5]

The Director of Naval Construction considered that the D of P's estimates were not in themselves sufficient to warrant the conclusion that a displacement of 35,000 was being purposely exceeded for the German battleships. He felt that in other countries designers were not pressed to be meticulously accurate, and suggested that a figure of 36,000 tons should be accepted. Opinion in NID was divided. Those in the German section tended to be suspicious of the figures announced by Germany; the technical section sided with the views of the other technical departments. NID had some SIS reports, but these were not sufficiently firm to settle the question, and no technical intelligence was available to resolve an admittedly difficult problem.[6]

---

* When the Naval Attaché's report went to the Foreign Office as an enclosure to the embassy's annual report in January 1937 his comment was deleted, but he had sent a copy of the original to the DNI.[4] However, after the war he was to admit that he might have expressed his doubts more forcibly if he had not been misled by Admiral Raeder's earnestness and apparent sincerity into thinking that Germany would abide by the Treaty.

3. ibid.
4. ibid, p 247.
5. ibid, Chapter XXXII; CAB 2/6, CID 294th Meeting, 17 June 1937, 299th Meeting, 14 October 1937, 300th Meeting, 28 October 1937.
6. Godfrey Memoirs, Chapter XXXII.

Discussion continued until the outbreak of the war, but with no satisfactory result.

The facts were finally established only when the *Bismarck* was sunk in 1941. In October of that year, using intelligence from the survivors, her true displacement was assessed as 41,150 tons, 17½ per cent above the declared tonnage, and her draught as 33 feet.[7]

---

7. ibid.

APPENDIX 5

The OSLO Report

(Translation)

1. *Ju 88 Programme.* Ju 88 is a two-engined long-range bomber and it has the advantage of being able to be employed also as a dive-bomber. Several thousand of these, probably 5,000, are being produced monthly. By April 1940, 25–30,000 bombers of this type alone are expected to have been completed.

2. *The Franken.* The first German aircraft carrier is in Kiel harbour. It is expected to be completed by April 1940 and is named 'Franken'.

3. *Remote-controlled Gliders.* The German Navy is developing remote-controlled gliders, i.e. small aircraft of some three metres wing-span and three metres length which carry a large explosive charge. They have no engines and are cast off from an aircraft flying at a great height. They contain:

(a) an electric altimeter, similar to the wireless altimeter (Bell Syst. Tech.J. Jan 39.p.222). This causes the glider to pull out at a height of some three metres above the water. It then continues its flight under rocket propulsion.

(b) a remote-control apparatus using ultra short waves in the form of telegraphic signals by which the glider can be steered to the right or left or straight ahead, eg from a ship or from an aircraft. In this way the glider may be directed against the side of an enemy ship, when the explosive charge should fall and explode under water.

The secret code number is FZ 21 (Ferngesteuerte Zielflugzeug = remote-controlled target-aircraft). The testing range is at Peenemünde, at the mouth of the Peene, near Wolgast, near Greifswald.

4. *Autopilot.* A pilotless aircraft, code number FZ 10, is being developed at Diepensee near Berlin, which is to be controlled from a manned aircraft and used, for example, for the purpose of destroying balloon barrages.

5. *Remote-controlled Shells.* The Army Ordnance Department (HWA) is the testing place for the Army. This centre is concerned with the development of shells of 80 cm calibre. Rocket propulsion is being used, and stabilisation is secured by built-in gyros. The difficulty in using rocket propulsion is that the projectile does not fly straight but describes uncontrollable curves. It has therefore a remote control by means of which the rocket's jet is steered. This development is still in its early stages and the 80 cm shells are intended to be used later against the Maginot Line.

6. *Rechlin.* This is a small place on Lake Meuritz, north of Berlin. The laboratories and test range of the Luftwaffe are there, a rewarding target for bombers.

7. *Methods of Attack on Bunkers.* Experiences in the campaign against Poland have proved that against concrete gun-emplacements an ordinary direct attack is useless. The Polish gun-emplacements were therefore completely screened by smoke shells, so that the smoke screen hung lower and lower over the gun positions. The Polish gun crews were in this way compelled to withdraw into their bunkers. Close behind the smoke screen German flame-throwers came forward and took up positions in front of the bunkers. Against these flame-throwers the gun-emplacements were powerless, and their occupants either died or had to surrender.

8. *Air Raid Warning Equipment.* At the time of the attack by English airmen on Wilhelmshaven at the beginning of September the English aircraft were already sighted 120 km from the German coast. Along the whole length of the German coast are short-wave transmitters of 20 kw power which send out quite short pulses of 10^{-5} secs duration. These pulses are reflected by aircraft. Near to each transmitter there is a receiver, tuned to the same wave-length. After an interval the reflected pulse from the aircraft reaches the receiver and is recorded on the cathode-ray tube. From the interval between the transmission of the pulse and the reception of the reflected pulse the distance of the plane can be computed. Since the transmitted pulse is much stronger than the reflected pulse, the receiver is cut off while the transmission takes place. The transmitted pulse is marked on the cathode-ray tube by a local sign.

In connection with the Ju 88 – The programme [is] for such transmitters to be installed all over Germany by April 1940.

Countermeasures. By means of special receivers, which can register pulses lasting 10^{-5} to 10^{-6} seconds, the wave-lengths of the pulses transmitted in Germany must be determined and then interfering signals must be transmitted on the same wave-length. These receivers can be on the ground as well as the transmitters, since the method is very sensitive.

While this method as a whole is being introduced, there is another method in preparation, which works on 50 cm wave-length. See Fig. 1.* The transmitter T sends out short pulses which are narrowly directed by means of an electric dish. The receiver R stands immediately next to the transmitter and likewise has a direction antenna. It receives the reflected [pulses. The transmitter and receiver are connected by a]† wiring system whose transmission time is continually adjustable. This artificial circuit has the following object:

---

* The diagrams were not attached to the copy available.
† Line omitted in the copy available.

the receiver is normally turned off and can receive no signals. The pulse from T also runs along the artificial circuit and renders the receiver active for quite a short time. If the period of the pulse in the circuit is equivalent to the duration of the reflected pulse, the latter can be registered by the receiver on a cathode-ray tube. With this procedure the distance of, eg, an aircraft, can be estimated very precisely, and it is very resistant to interference, since the receiver is open only for a very short time.

9. *Aircraft Range-Finder.* When airmen fly to carry out an attack on a foreign country, it is important for them to know how far they are from their base. For this purpose the following procedure has been developed at Rechlin.

At the base there is a radio transmitter (6 m band) which is modulated at a low frequency 'f'. The aircraft, at a distance 'a' receives the 6 m wave and the low frequency f, after demodulation. With this low frequency it modulates its own transmitter which has a somewhat different wave-length. The adjusted frequency of the wave-length from the aircraft is received at the base and demodulated. The low frequency f thus received is compared with the local low frequency f. They differ by the phase angle 4π f.a/c (c = speed of light). By measuring the phase, one can measure the aircraft range, and one can inform the aircraft of its position. In order that the measurement should be unambiguous, the phase angle must equal 2π*, but with so low a frequency, one cannot obtain any great precision. Therefore at the same time one transmits a second, higher, frequency, eg 1500 pps and then compares its phase angle. So 150 pps as a rough measure and 1500 pps as a fine measure.

10. *Torpedoes.* The German Navy has two new kinds of torpedoes.

a) For instance when it is desired to attack convoys from 10 km. Such torpedoes have a wireless receiving apparatus which can receive three signals. With these signals the torpedoes may be steered either from the ship which fired it, or from an aircraft, to the right or left or straight ahead. Long wave-lengths, of the order of 3 km which penetrate well under water, are employed. These are modulated by short audio frequency signals which steer the torpedo. In this manner the torpedo may be guided to within close range of the convoy. In order actually to hit a vessel there are on the head of the torpedo two acoustic receivers which constitute a direction receiver. The torpedo's course is guided by this receiver so that it moves automatically towards the source of sound. If, therefore, the torpedo has been brought to within a few hundred metres of any ship, it automatically makes straight for that ship, since any ship makes acoustic noises because of its engines. By means of acoustic or radio jamming signals, it is comparatively easy to protect a ship.

---

* Footnote in the original: – to remain below 2π, one chooses, therefore a low frequency f, eg 150 pps and then the phase angle = 2π for 1,000 km exactly.

b) The second type of torpedo is probably the type which sank the *Royal Oak*. These do not strike the ship's side, but explode under the ship's bottom. The fuze is initiated magnetically, an effect based on the following principle: Fig 2. The vertical component of the magnetic field is everywhere approximately the same, but it is altered by the ship S so that the field is weaker at A and C and stronger at B. A torpedo coming from the left moves first in a normal field, then in a weaker field etc.

In the torpedo's head a coil rotates about a horizontal axis in the manner of an earth induction coil. At the terminals of the coil an e.m.f. is set up proportional to the vertical component of the magnetic field. An equivalent back e.m.f. develops in series so that no current flows so long as the torpedo is in a normal magnetic field. But when the torpedo comes to A, the magnetic field there is smaller and the e.m.f. on the coil decreases. The two opposing forces are no longer equal, and a current flows and activates a relay mechanism which initiates the fuze. The retardation is so adjusted that the explosion takes place immediately under the ship's bottom.

It is perhaps possible to protect oneself against such torpedoes by stretching a cable along the whole length of the ship, at about the level of the ship's hold and as far out from the ship's side as possible. Then if a suitably adjusted direct current is passed through this cable, it will create a magnetic field and will remove the danger point A to a position far outside the ship. The torpedo will then explode too soon. It is perhaps possible also by means of appropriately selected compensating coils to counter-balance the alteration of the magnetic field by the large mass of the ship.

□

ELECTRIC FUZES FOR BOMBS AND SHELLS

In Germany they are discontinuing the use of mechanical fuzes and going over to electric fuzes. All bomb fuzes are already electrical. Fig. 1. shows the principle. When the bomb leaves the aircraft the condenser C_1 receives a charge of 150 volts from a battery by means of a sliding contact. This condenser charges the condenser C_2 through a resistance R. C_2 becomes charged only when the bomb is at a safe distance from the aircraft. When the bomb touches the ground, a mechanical contact K closes, and the condenser discharges itself through the coil Z. The advantage is that the bomb can never be live while it is still on the plane, and thus a plane can be safely landed with a bomb load on board.

Fig. 2 shows an electrical time fuze. It is on the same principle, only instead of a mechanical contact it has a lamp G*, which lights after

---

* Text has 'Glimmlampe', ie glowlamp.

a fixed time interval. This time can be regulated through the condensers and resistances.

The newest development makes use of the lamps with grids, Fig. 3. If the battery voltage is so selected to be below the voltage of the fuze, and the grid is insulated, then, by altering the part capacities C_{12} and C_{23}, the lamp can be made to activate the fuze. Extraordinary small changes in the part capacities are all that are necessary. Fig. 4 shows how it is built into a shell. The head of the shell is insulated and is connected to the grid of the lamp. If the shell passes near to an aircraft the part capacities are somewhat altered and the lamp lights, whereby the shell explodes. The fuzes can be so set that all the shells will explode at a precisely determined height, eg three metres, above the ground.

I include herewith such a lamp and grid. There is an improved version with an annular grid.

The bomb fuze bears the number 25; production is expected to increase from 25,000 in October 1939 to 100,000 from April 1940.

These fuzes are being manufactured at Sömmerda in Thuringen on the railway from Sangershausen to Erfurt. The firm's name is Rheinmetall.

APPENDIX 6

COS (40) 360
(Also JIC (40) 71)

17th May 1940

WAR CABINET
CHIEFS OF STAFF COMMITTEE

URGENT INTELLIGENCE REPORTS
*Directive to the Joint Intelligence
Sub-Committee*

The Joint Intelligence Sub-Committee are responsible for taking the initiative in preparing, at any hour of the day or night, as a matter of urgency, papers on any particular development in the international situation whenever this appears desirable to any member, in the light of information that may be received from time to time in the Foreign Office or in the Service Departments. The members of the Joint Intelligence Sub-Committee, who are in the closest touch with the intelligence situation, are in a better position than anyone else to decide when such papers should be prepared, and it is for this reason that the responsibility is placed on them.

2. The object of these papers, *which should be as brief as possible*, will be:

(i) To draw attention to any information received in the Foreign Office or the Service Departments which appears to be of special importance, to assess its value, and to supplement it with any other information available so as to present the broad deductions which are to be drawn concerning the particular situation in question.

(ii) To summarise broadly the available evidence regarding the intentions of the enemy or developments in any of the 'danger spots' in the international situation, and to set out the conclusions which may be drawn therefrom.

3. Papers prepared as a matter of urgency in accordance with paragraphs 1 and 2 above will be on a distinctive coloured paper different from that used for the S.R. summary.

4. The utility of such papers will very largely depend upon the rapidity with which they can be prepared and issued. If the process is slow there is a danger that action may be taken on information which

has not been properly considered and assessed by the Intelligence Staffs.

5. The distribution of these papers will be as follows:

(I) The Prime Minister. Major-General Ismay, in his capacity as senior Staff Officer to the Minister for Defence, will be responsible for bringing the paper to the notice of the Prime Minister at any hour of the day or night and of taking his instructions as to action.

(ii) The other members of the War Cabinet.

(iii) The Chiefs of Staff.

6. Nothing in this directive is intended to change in any way the other duties of the Joint Intelligence Sub-Committee in regard to the preparation of reports and memoranda on specific subjects, either on their own initiative or as directed by the Chiefs of Staff.

(Signed) *T. S. V. PHILLIPS*
V.C.N.S.

R. E. C. PEIRSE
V.C.A.S.

A. E. PERCIVAL
A.C.I.G.S.

(for C.I.G.S.)

Richmond Terrace, SW1

APPENDIX 7

(i)   AI3 Appreciation of 17 October 1940

Invasion of England (Operation SMITH) Air Ministry Summary

After the collapse of France the Germans spread much propaganda threatening invasion of the United Kingdom, and SIS sources produced many reports of the conversion of barges, fishing craft and motor-boats for this purpose. At the end of August towing craft did in fact assemble at Cuxhaven and Emden, and at the beginning of September these craft and large numbers of barges began to assemble in the enemy-occupied ports nearest England, that is, at Rotterdam, Antwerp, Flushing, Ostend, Dunkirk, Calais, Boulogne and Havre. Shipping, as opposed to barges, assembled at the two ends of this line of ports, at Rotterdam and Antwerp to the east, and at Havre to the west (some of these ships are known to be loaded with ammunition and fuel). At the same time the liners Bremen and Europa, now camouflaged, moved from their berths at Hamburg to Bremerhaven, and light German naval forces appeared in Cherbourg, Brest and Lorient.

2. On the 8th September, Sir Samuel Hoare reported from Madrid that a reliable source, returning from Berlin, stated that the invasion of England was known in offical circles there by the code-name SMITH. This was the first mention of the word, which first appeared in the special messages on the 21st of the same month. Later messages appear to identify SMITH beyond doubt with the attempted invasion of Great Britain.

3. Messages have been received in sufficient numbers to enable some picture of the invasion plan to be formed, and some small nucleus of an order of battle to be seen. Although most special messages identify the air side of the operation purely with Air Fleet 2 (now occupying the area between the Seine and the Zuider Zee), there are indications that air attack will be launched from the whole coast crescent from Brest to Norway, since aircraft recovery vessels will be stationed at

515

Brest, Schellingwoude, Borkum, List, Stavanger and Trondheim (in the gap from Brest to Schellingwoude there is already an efficient sea rescue service). It seems probable that Air Fleet 2 may direct air operations, and be swollen for this purpose at the expense of Air Fleet 3. The only Army specifically mentioned is the 16th Army (General-oberst Busch), now stationed in the Pas de Calais and Belgium, although there are slight indications that the 9th Army (Seine area) is also likely to take part. The German Navy is, of course, greatly interested.

4. Administratively, the following preparations appear to have been made – under Air Fleet 2 (Generalfeldmarschall Kesselring), Air Administrative Staff Belgium-North France (General der Flieger Wimmer) exercises supervision over Special Administrative Staff 300 (Generalmajor Andrae, at Roubaix), which seems to be responsible for detailed embarkation, supply and administration arrangements, and is known to have been employed on similar duties during the invasion of Norway. Unloading Detachments have been formed at Antwerp and three other places, presumably to unload stores and munitions arriving at these places. Loading (Embarkation) Staffs have been formed at Rotterdam, Antwerp, Ostend, Dunkirk and Calais, pre-sumably to embark the expedition and its supplies. Loading areas, one at Rotterdam, one at Antwerp, one believed to be North or East of Rotterdam, and no doubt others elsewhere, have been detailed and assigned to units requiring to load stores. In addition, Special Air Administrative Staff 16 (possibly the SAAS 16 which took part in the invasion of the Low Countries or perhaps a staff renamed to identify it with the 16th Army) has been detailed for the 'second crossing', no doubt to arrange the administration and supply of air bases captured or improvised in this country. An Air Force Landing Staff also takes part in the 'second crossing', presumably to supervise disembarkation of supplies and ancillary services. All the above arrangements seem to have to do solely with sea transport, but that air transport will also be employed is shown by the improvement of surfaces and landing facilities at certain aerodromes (one believed to be near St Omer, the others unlocated) intended for the use of air transport units, and by a mention of the assignment of the Air Transport Division (Flieger-division 7, which carried the Airlanding Division into Holland) to the Rotterdam area for loading purposes.

5. Operationally, the attempt to cross to British soil seems to be planned in three stages. These are –

(a) The First Crossing. Nothing positive is known about this, save that AA regiment 202 (now in the La Panne area) is detailed to take part in it, embarking at Rotterdam. It is thought that fighting troops mainly will take part in this crossing, and it is noteworthy that the Germans place great reliance in their AA guns (which can fire below the horizontal) for tank and pill-box destruction. There is much evidence that the AA artillery will play a large role in the adventure, as Flakkorps 2 (St Omer) is to embark supplies at Ostend, Dunkirk and Calais (though not necessarily for this first crossing).

(b) The Second Crossing. It is known that the following staffs and detachments will take part: the Air Force Landing Staff, Special Air Administrative Staff 16, Light AA Brigade (half a regiment) 74, and an Air Force Constructional Equipment Section (believed to be for the repair of aerodromes). In addition it is known that a tanker containing 200,000 gallons of aviation fuel will take part. It is known that this crossing will sail from Rotterdam and Antwerp and probably from other ports, and land in Landing Areas B and C (not yet located) and possibly in others.

(c) The Third Crossing. The following elements are known to be detailed for this crossing: the ground party of a Dive-Bomber Geschwader consisting of 3 groups (120 aircraft in all), the ground party of a Ground Attack Group (40 aircraft in all), a motorised Aerodrome Servicing Unit (Flughafenbetriebskompanie). Fuel and ammunition for the four groups will also be taken.

Other units or formations believed to be intended for landing in this country are 2 Telephone Construction Sections, the 1st Brigade of AA Regiment 12, and the Air Component of the 16th Army (which Air Component will take with it 20,000 gallons of fuel and 27,000 rounds of MG ammunition).

6. It is obvious from the above that it is the intention (from the German Air Force point of view, as part only of the larger plan) to capture by forces borne on the first crossing an area containing aerodromes or landing areas, to repair these aerodromes or improvise landing grounds with the services carried on the second crossing, and to bring on the third crossing ground parties and a servicing unit, with the aim of operating some Air Forces from bases in this country after the third crossing has taken place. These Air Forces will no doubt include, in addition to the dive-bomber, ground attack and army co-operation squadrons mentioned above, some fighter units. There is no real evidence as to the time-spacing of the three crossings, although a tiny clue suggests that 3 days may elapse between the first and second. No evidence is available as to what role will be played by Fliegerdivision 7, but this will presumably be, as in Holland, the landing of parachute troops, airlanding troops, and supplies by air.

7. The following timetable is available for that part of the expedition which will set sail from Antwerp:

S-9 (the ninth day before zero day)	Supplies are embarked.
S-8	Vehicles are embarked.
S-7	,,
S-6·	,,
S-5	,,
S-4	Troops and horses are embarked
S-3	Expedition sets out.

S−2	Expedition sets out
S−1	Expedition assembles.
S	Landing is attempted.
S+1	
S+2	
S+3	The Second Crossing begins(?)

It seems likely that the parts of the expedition setting sail from other ports of embarkation could load and assemble in less time than this, which is made so lengthy by the long journey down the Scheldt.

8. Other information which may bear on this crossing is that Fliegerkorps VIII has been given orders to move into the area of Luftflotte 2 'for attack on the long range batteries on the English South Coast. Target data to be obtained in consultation with the 16th Army'. Many exercises have taken place, at Carteret, Fecamp, and Harlingen, in which heavy and light AA guns have been carried on powered pontoons capable of a speed of 11 knots and good manoeuvrability. Exercises have taken place at Gravelines which included the 'locking-out' into the sea of barges from the canal and a landing. In some ports, the 16th Army is believed to hold loading and unloading exercises nightly. Directional wireless beam stations have been put in position on the French Coast, and may possibly be intended as aids to sea navigation in restricted visibility. Pioneer exercises have been carried out on the Lower Seine by the 9th Army, attended by representatives of an AA Corps. It is known that much parachute and glider training is in progress in Germany. The dive-bomber units, which were withdrawn from the attack on this country on the 18th of August and concentrated at forward aerodromes in the Pas de Calais area, have still not been re-employed and are presumably in readiness for (a) protection of German convoys in the Straits of Dover against British sea attack, and (b) attack of British sea and shore targets when favourable opportunity is offered.

9. All the evidence shows that operation SMITH is a planned barge-borne, ship-borne and air-borne invasion of the United Kingdom, to take place in these stages:

(a) Seizure, by barge-borne and perhaps air-borne troops, of a foothold in Great Britain, probably on the South or South-East Coast. Diversionary attacks may take place in Scotland and the North.

(b) The rapid establishment of air and sea bases in the occupied area.

(c) The arrival of the main expedition, accompanied by some air forces.

(d) The main battle.

10. The special messages show that preparations for SMITH were still continuing on the 13th October, but are now almost complete. There is no evidence that a decision has yet been made to put the plan into operation, but the temptation to take this decision will be great

when preparations are complete and when conditions appear favourable. In view of our naval superiority and unweakened air defences, it is possible that these conditions may include calm sea and restricted visibility, which would enable the German Army to get to grips with Home Forces without suffering too heavily from sea and air attack.

(ii)   MI14 Appreciation of 18 October 1940

Invasion of UK and/or Eire (SEELÖWE–SEALION Question)

---

1. The first reference* to the Sea Lion operation was contained in a report dated 21st September, 1940, which stated that the German Admiralty made the seaplane base commands of BREST, BORKUM, TRONDHEIM, SCHELLINGWOUDE, STAVANGER and LIST responsible for making all the preparations for the supply of air rescue vessels (one for each base) in connection with the Sea Lion operation. The HQ of Airfleets 2, 3 and 5 had to ensure compliance with these instructions in the event of the date of S1 day (presumed to be zero day for the operation) being notified before the seaplane base commands could receive their instructions: in any case the Airfleets had to notify the date of S1 day to the seaplane base commands in their respective areas.

2. On 25th September an air formation HQ known to be in charge of GAF equipment in Belgium and Northern France (LG Stab ZBV 300) asked permission of the Regional Air Command for that area and of the 2nd Airfleet to change the arrangements for an aerodrome construction unit (which could be used for repairing an aerodrome so as to enable aircraft to land) and send it on the second crossing instead of the first. This request was said to be 'connected with the Sea Lion operation' and to be due to lack of accommodation on the first crossing.

---

* A report of the 29th August spoke of an 'S detachment' of the 7th Air Division; this doubtless refers to the same operation.

3. This reference to crossings made it clear that some sea-borne operation was being contemplated. It was therefore natural to link it up with the report that on 11th September certain German Air Force officers were appointed to the embarkation staffs at ANTWERP, OSTEND, DUNKIRK and CALAIS. Other GAF officers were appointed liaison officers to embarkation staffs at the same ports. At the same time the GAF system of communications was linked up with the embarkation HQ at the ports mentioned. Certain immediate appointments were made on the same date: an officer of the GAF transport service for liaison duties with 16th Army and two officers to the disembarkation staff at Antwerp.

4. An order of 27th September from the 2nd Airfleet made alterations in the plans for crossing, relegating to the third crossing the ground personnel of certain dive-bomber and ground attack units.

5. No mention was made of the Sea Lion operation in the orders issued by the Regional Air Command on 2nd October concerning aviation fuel and ammunition, but as these had to be sent to CHERBOURG and LE HAVRE it is reasonable to suppose that part of the expedition was to start from these ports. At each of these over 3 million gallons of aviation fuel in barrels, together with bombs for 60 operations by a dive-bomber group (ie 39 aircraft) and MG ammunition for 12 operations each by one dive-bomber and one fighter group were to be provided.

6. The fact that about the same date the 2nd Airfleet found it necessary to issue special orders for the protection against British bombing of dumps and of vessels loaded with ammunition, fuel, etc may also be taken as being connected with the preparations for the same operation.

7. On 2nd October also the 2nd Airfleet sent an urgent request to the air formation HQ in charge of equipment for the provision of a tanker carrying at least 220,000 gallons of aviation fuel; this was expressly stated to be connected with the Sea Lion operation, the tanker being allocated to the second crossing.

8. Air Force Embarkation HQ 2 was reported to be in Antwerp; it could be reached by telephone through the Army exchange there. On 6th October the Signals Officer of the air formation HQ in charge of equipment made enquiries as to the possibilities of telephonic communication with all five embarkation staffs, and the above was one reply.

9. A document of 7th October from OC Signals of the 2nd Airfleet to the same air equipment formation HQ mentioned second and third crossings.

10. On 5th October an order, referring to the first crossing from Rotterdam, required AA Regiment 202 (stationed to the East of Dunkirk) to send a return of the precise amount, in kilograms, of fuel, rations and ammunition per unit which could not be taken in the regiment's own transport.

11. A document of 8th October asked the 2nd Airfleet to supply two tank vessels, each with 220,000 gallons of aviation fuel, for two different sectors: the one was required at ROTTERDAM and the other at ANTWERP. The were required for S+3 day. If only one were available it should be held ready at ROTTERDAM.

12. On 3rd October two documents issued by the Quartermaster General of the 2nd Airfleet referred to Landing Staff E (Air Force) as being allocated to the second crossing, the application for sea transport to be made to the Regional Air Command for Belgium and Northern France.

13. On 10th October the air equipment formation HQ already mentioned endeavoured to find out from the naval authorities in Antwerp when the extinguishing (? screening or dimming) of the lights on the Scheldt would be complete, by how much this would decrease the times required for sailing out (presumably from starting point down the Scheldt to assembly point), and which S-days were to be assigned for (a) taking over of goods, (b) the shipping of laden vehicles, (c) the embarkation of troops. The reply suggested a misunderstanding in connection with the Scheldt lights. They were already extinguished and the date for relighting them was 17th October. The intention was to set out without lights, but if lights were to be used the time of setting out could be postponed by 24 hours. With regard to the dates for loading, the reply stated that troops and supplies would be loaded on S minus 9 day, vehicles from S minus 8 to S minus 5 and troops and horses on S minus 4 day. The expedition would set out on S minus 3 and S minus 2 days and would assemble on S minus 1 day. Source indicated that S minus 1 day was presumably the day before the operation.

14. On 11th October an unknown unit was instructed to report to the Air Force Field Equipment unit for the West of France as soon as loading operations in the GIRONDE area were complete. This is not expressly stated to be connected with the Sea Lion operation, but it may well be.

15. A document of 13th October from an unidentified Regional Air Command HQ (possibly XVII) appeared to indicate that some form of sea-borne transport was leaving or had perhaps left STETTIN.

16. The Quartermaster General of the 2nd Airfleet on 13th October informed the air formation HQ already mentioned that the motor tanker MARIANNE was standing by with 198,000 gallons of aviation fuel at BRUNSBÜTTEL (KIEL Canal). On receipt of warning order it would be instructed by HQ 2nd Airfleet to proceed to ROTTER-DAM and report both to the naval authorities and to the Air Force loading staff. HQ 2nd Airfleet is arranging for the passage of this vessel in the second crossing to landing area B. The MARIANNE is a vessel of 523 tons gross with a speed of 8 knots and a draught of about 8 ft 2 ins. If, as is suggested, a second tanker is available, it is to be fitted into the second crossing from Antwerp to landing area C.

17. HQ 2nd Airfleet on 12th October notified the Air Liaison Service attached to HQ 16th Army that the following supplies would be needed by the air formations of the 16th Army for the first 20 days, beginning from S-day, of the Sea Lion operation: 300 barrels of aviation fuel (each of about 66 gallons) and 27,000 rounds of machine gun ammunition (13,500 rounds pointed steel core, 9,000 pointed steel core and tracer and 4,500 armour-piercing).

The Regional Air Command for Belgium and North France must have these stores so arranged that they can be loaded into the ships of the Army along with the ground personnel of the air formations concerned. The Air Liaison Service of the 16th Army will settle the details with the Regional Air Command.

18. On 12th October also HQ 2nd Airfleet, in reply to a question from the air formation HQ mentioned above, confirmed that the loading of supplies for the 7th Air Division (normally used for troop transport) had been assigned to ROTTERDAM.

19. HQ 16th Army on 14th October issued instructions that Army Corps should in future carry out nightly loading and unloading exercises with dimmed lights and that they should arrange adequate telephonic, visual or wireless communications with the local air-raid warning stations. If an alarm is sounded lights will be extinguished. HQ 16th Army asked for support to enable these exercises to be carried out without a hitch. HQ 2nd Airfleet requested the Air Force administrative services and the 2nd Anti-Aircraft Corps to give every assistance in these exercises.

20. *Conclusions from Sea Lion reports*

(a) From the preparations referred to, it seems reasonable to conclude that 'Sea Lion' designates a sea-borne invasion of UK and/or Eire.

(b) *Date*. The details concerning the arrangements at ANTWERP provide some clue as to the date. Troops and supplies will go on board on S minus 9 day, vehicles on the next four days and troops and horses on the last day before setting out. The vessels would then move off on S minus 3 day (or one day later if the Scheldt navigational lights are to be used) and would reach their place of assembly on S minus 1 day. The date for restoring navigational lights on the Scheldt is 17th October. S minus 2 day therefore cannot fall before that date, so that the earliest possible zero day (S or S 1) for the operation would be 19th October;* it will probably be later.

(c) *Starting points and destinations.* Reference is made to 'all five' embarkation staffs, and when these are first mentioned the ports of ANTWERP, OSTEND, DUNKIRK and CALAIS are named. Later there are frequent references to ROTTERDAM.

---

* In view of the date of the document, the earliest possible zero day seems to be 20th October.

But ROTTERDAM corresponds to landing area B and ANTWERP to landing area C. It might therefore be presumed that there is another starting point farther North corresponding to landing area A.

The reference to stocks of aviation fuel at CHERBOURG and LE HAVRE might suggest that they also are to be used as starting points in connection with the same operation. That would make a total of eight ports which there are some grounds for believing might be used.

The references to loading operations in the GIRONDE area and to some seaborne transport leaving STETTIN suggest the possibility of other starting points which may very probably be connected with the same operation.

There is no evidence to show where the landing areas lie, but one may presume that the starting points are selected with a view to the shortest possible lines of communication. It has been suggested that the distance from ROTTERDAM to area B is longer than that from ANTWERP to area C, because a tanker with aviation oil is absolutely necessary in the former case, but could be dispensed with in the latter.

(d) *Units concerned.* That part of the expedition with which the above information deals would seem to be largely in the hands of the 2nd Airfleet. The first reference to Sea Lion mentioned the 3rd and 5th Airfleets, but only in connection with the provision of air rescue vessels, two of which are to be based on Norwegian ports. It may therefore be concluded that the 5th Airfleet, which is in Scandinavia, is to participate. The 2nd, which is in N.W. France, is probably taking part, as BREST is another of the bases supplying a rescue vessel.

The 16th Army, Anti-Aircraft Regiment 202, Fl Corps 8 and the 7th Air Division are also mentioned, but these are doubtless only some of the formations and units concerned. The 7th Air Division, which is for airborne troops, will presumably operate in landing area B, as its supplies are being loaded in ROTTERDAM.

(e) *Number of crossings.* Three crossings at least would appear to be contemplated. Details concerning the first are unknown.

The second will include:

(i) One tanker (or possibly two) with aviation fuel. It will not proceed to ROTTERDAM until the preliminary warning for the operation is given.

(ii) Air Force landing staff and an aerodrome construction unit: the latter was originally to have been in the first crossing, but there was no available space. It is evidently required quite early, presumably to make aerodromes fit for use by aircraft.

The third crossing will include the ground personnel of certain dive-bomber and ground attack units (relegated from the second crossing).

There is also a reference to two tankers which had to be ready by S plus 3 day. These are presumably the same that are detailed to form part of the second crossing, but it hardly seems safe to conclude that the second crossing will not take place until the third day of the operation.

(f) *Miscellaneous.* In the schedule for ANTWERP four days are to be devoted to the loading of vehicles, but the nature of these is unspecified. It would seem that large numbers of vehicles are being taken. The horses may possibly be required for bringing vehicles or weapons ashore or for the pack transport of a mountain division.

Note

It should be clearly borne in mind that we have insight only into the preparations made by the 2nd Airfleet, which means that we see about one quarter of the picture in some detail and nothing or very little of the rest. We must suppose, however, that preparations are in fact in progress from the Baltic ports (or possibly Norway) down to BORDEAUX.

———

This message must be treated as OFFICER ONLY and must not be transmitted by telephone. The Admiralty and the Air Ministry are in possession of the information.

Signed   Lt Colonel, G.S.

MI14
1730 hours
18.10.40

APPENDIX 8

JIC (41) 112
22 March 1941

WAR CABINET
JOINT INTELLIGENCE SUB-COMMITTEE

AXIS PLANNING SECTION
Memorandum by the Joint Intelligence Sub-Committee
on the Object Status and Responsibilities of the
Axis Planning Section

1. *Foreword*

Until now there has been no adequate machinery *under* the JIC to study, appreciate and work out the plans and intentions of the Axis powers, and produce them in the form of 'All-Service' papers, complete with the political and economic picture. In fact, on the occasions when such papers have been produced by the JIC, this has to be done by a cumbersome and often untrained drafting Committee, provided ad hoc by all departments from their already fully occupied Intelligence sections.

2. *Object*

The object of the APS is to place under the Directors of Intelligence a body of selected and trained officers with full experience of the tactical and strategical methods and of the political and economic implications of modern warfare, combined with expert knowledge of drafting papers.

Although their detailed information must come from the various Ministries concerned the Axis Planning Section, in order to carry out their role, must 'get under the enemy's skin'. They must, therefore, resist any temptation to permit their judgment to be coloured by taking into account information that reaches them regarding British plans, operations, etc, unless they are likely to be known to the enemy, at any rate in substance.

3. *The Status and responsibilities of the APS*

As laid down by the Chiefs of Staff, the Axis Planning Section will be responsible to the Joint Intelligence Sub-Committee, and work within the Joint Intelligence organisation, as an 'All-Service' machinery, to keep under constant review all Axis intentions, plans, and strategy and reproduce this in the form of papers as required.

At the same time, the Joint Planning Staff will have the right to call upon the Axis Planning Section for any particular appreciation.

4. *Relations with the Directors of Intelligence*

When drafting papers as a collective body for the Joint Intelligence Sub-Committee, each representative will consult his own Director of Intelligence to ensure that the views put forward by him represent the views of his Ministry.

5. *The Duties of the Axis Planning Section*

It therefore follows that the Axis Planning Section must –

(a) Study and assimilate all existing papers on Axis strategy and intentions, produced either by the Joint Intelligence Sub-Committee or by the Future Operations (Enemy) Section, or by individual Ministries.

(b) Keep such papers under constant review, and be prepared, either under the orders of the Joint Intelligence Sub-Committee or on their own initiative, to produce amended papers as and when changes in the situation demand this.

This study should often assist them in the production of new papers on any new fields of Axis strategy not already covered. In fact, the initiative for producing new papers will as often come from the Axis Planning Section as from the Joint Intelligence Sub-Committee; in general, however, the Axis Planning Section should obtain Joint Intelligence Sub-Committee sanction before drafting, but not before studying the need for, any such new papers.

The Axis Planning section is not an Agency for collecting and collating information, which must remain the responsibility of the various Ministries concerned. Ministries, moreover, must ensure that all essential reports, information, etc, are conveyed to their Axis Planning Section representative, who will always have full access to the Country Sections of his Ministry, to obtain all information required for the drafting of papers and other purposes.

The above thus represents the collective responsibility of the Axis Planning Section.

Individually they also have responsibilities in regard to their own Ministries; as laid down in paragraph 3.

6. *Methods of Work*

Members of the Axis Planning Section will require to work –

(a) individually in their own Ministries, since it is there that they must obtain and assimilate detailed reports etc; and

(b) collectively in the Axis Planning Section joint office.

In addition Axis Planning Section representatives will attend any suitable Conference in their own Departments, and, if possible, the bi-weekly Joint Intelligence Sub-Committee conferences; and if necessary, any special conferences of the Combined Intelligence Centre.

7. *Future Planning*

Although the Axis Planning Section will be mainly concerned with drafting papers dealing with the immediate future, they will always bear in mind enemy intentions in the more distant future. They should, therefore, be in a position to produce both long-term and short-term appreciations on Axis strategy.

8. *Composition of Axis Planning Section – Personnel*

  (a) *Officers*
    (i) An officer of the equivalent rank of GSO1 from each of the Service Departments and a representative from the Foreign Office and the Ministry of Economic Warfare.

(ii)   An officer of the equivalent rank of GSO2 from each of the Service Departments.

  (b) *Clerical*
    The clerical staff will be provided by the Cabinet Office.

9. *Accommodation*

  (a) *In the Offices of the War Cabinet*
    The Axis Planning Section will occupy rooms in the War Cabinet Offices.
  (b) The Axis Planning Section will also be accommodated in their own Ministries.

ANNEX

Programme for Axis Planning Section

1. The Axis Planning Section will start with a full examination of the problem of Axis Strategy –

  (a) *Through Turkey*: thereafter to –
    (i) Egypt, via Syria etc, and/or
    (ii) Iraq.
  (b) Followed by a similar study of Axis Strategy from Tripolitania against, or towards –
    (i) Egypt.
    (ii) Tunisia and Algeria.

2. The Axis Planning Section should next turn their attention to the Far East.

3. The Axis Planning Section will keep under constant review JIC (41) 70, particularly as regards Spain.

APPENDIX 9

Intelligence in Advance of the GAF Raid on Coventry, 14 November 1940

After predicting on 18 October that the GAF would before long concentrate on night raids using as many as 600 bombers, the Intelligence Branch of the Air Ministry received by 12 November, from two different sources, the warning that a new type of raid might be imminent.

It received on 11 November from GC and CS the decrypt of an Enigma message of 9 November giving the signals procedure to be used by KG 100 for 'Moonlight Sonata'. The message gave the meanings of a number of code groups to be used by the aircraft in certain contingencies. Some of these meanings were self-evident but the first was the single word 'Korn'. There was nothing to indicate that 'Korn' was the code name for a target; indeed, the last four code groups in the list were for 'Target Areas 1, 2, 3 and 4'. The message specified the W/T frequencies to be used by KG 100, and stated that *Knickebein* beams would be used. It laid down that, should the operation not take place on account of the weather report from KG 100, the code group 'Mond' would be sent by W/T and the beams shifted to alternative targets. It ordered, further, that tuning signals should start at '1300 on the day of operation'. At Luftflotten 2 and 3 and the C-in-C of the GAF were concerned in these arrangements, and as the message indicated that the CO of KG 100 would lead the operation, 'Moonlight Sonata', whatever it was, was clearly unusually important. The message contained no date for the operation and no clue as to the whereabouts of target areas 1 to 4.*

When sending the decrypt to the Air Ministry GC and CS commented only that 'Moonlight Sonata' was assumed to be the code name for a particular operation. In a subsequent commentary on the decrypt GC and CS stated that 'there is no evidence that this [the code name "Korn"] was correctly interpreted as Coventry'. In fact, as there was nothing in the decrypt to suggest that 'Korn' concealed the identity of a target, it is perfectly understandable that AI, in its attempt to work out the objective of the operation, concentrated on those parts of the message which referred specifically to the four target areas.

AI's interpretation of the decrypt was given in a memorandum to

---

* See Annex 1.

the Air Staff dated 12 November from AI 1(w) – the round-the-clock section responsible for advising about enemy operations.* This suggested that the word 'Sonata' might indicate 'that the operation will be carried out in three waves, ie KG 100 (who may start the fires) followed by the two air fleets in pre-arranged order', that the word 'Moonlight' might indicate that the operation would be carried out at or near full moon and that 'the use of wireless beams including Knickebein and a VHF beam' indicated that the operation would be a night attack. It thought this interpretation was consistent with the GAF's evident intention to use 'all available aircraft'.† It drew attention to the fact that AI had received evidence from another source that the GAF planned a very heavy night raid on the most suitable night 'between 15/11 [full moon] and 20/11'. As regards the GAF's targets the memorandum said: 'The following target areas are mentioned in the signals instructions:

    (i) Target Area I. It is uncertain where this area lies. It is possibly central London. There is, however, a possibility that it is in the Harwich–Ipswich district.

    (ii) Target Area II. Greater London and within the circle Windsor–St Albans–Epping–Gravesend–Westerham–a little south of Leatherhead–Windsor.

    (iii) Target Area III. The Triangle bounded by lines connecting Farnborough Aerodrome–Reading–Maidenhead.

    (iv) Target Area IV. The district Faversham–Rochester–Sheerness.'

Finally, and no doubt as a result of the arrangements made in the decrypt for a shift to alternative targets, it added that 'it is not known whether the target areas referred to above are all primary target areas or whether they include both primary and secondary targets'.

As already stated, these identifications of the target areas were not derived from the 'Moonlight Sonata' decrypt, which merely listed target areas Nos 1, 2, 3 and 4. The three areas that were firmly defined were obtained from a recently captured map. However, in judging that these targets were the targets for the raid AI 1(w) was making an assumption which is perhaps explained by a commentary from GC and CS to AI, drawn up on 14 November, but no doubt recapitulating earlier discussions between the two. This stated that the captured map's identification of target areas 2, 3 and 4 'confirms intelligence already obtained or inferred by source CX/JQ (ie the GAF Enigma)...'[2]

When deciding to adopt these areas as the targets for the 'Moonlight Sonata' operation, AI 1(w) relied on the above evidence

---

   * See Annex 2.

   † Contemporary estimates of the strength of the German long-range bomber force, which was concentrated in Luftflotten 2 and 3, set it at 1,800 front line aircraft.[1]

1. AIR 40/2321, Minute of 2 December 1940.
2. CX/JQ/450 of 15 November 1940.

to the exclusion of that which it had obtained from its other source, a POW pilot who had been shot down on 9 November. He had not only told a stool-pigeon the date which AI 1(w) quoted – 'between 15/11 [full moon] and 20/11 ' – and said that every long-range bomber would be engaged and every *Knickebein* route used, but had also claimed that the targets would be Birmingham and Coventry. This information was passed to the D of I in a note by AI 1(k), the section responsible for POW interrogation, on 12 November. The note makes it plain why AI 1(w)'s memorandum to the Air Staff did not mention the POW's reference to Coventry and Birmingham. After summarising the POW's evidence, AI 1(k)'s note went on:

'As this [the POW intelligence] came after S/L Humphreys's visit this afternoon when he mentioned that a gigantic raid under the code-name 'Moonlight Sonata' was in preparation, I thought it well to bring this information to your notice although on account of the source it should be treated with reserve as he is untried. I believe S/L Humphreys has pretty definite information that the attack is to be against London and the Home Counties...The objective should also be regarded as doubtful as probably his [Humphreys's] information is later.'*

Squadron Leader Humphreys, the senior AI liaison officer at Bletchley, was responsible for advising on the interpretation of the decrypts of GAF Enigma traffic.

Although a copy of AI 1(k)'s note to the Director of Intelligence was passed to the Directorate of Home Operations, the Directorate naturally made its plans on the basis of the memorandum which AI 1(w) had addressed to the Air Staff. On 12 November the Director of Home Operations minuted the DCAS that the memorandum was 'good enough upon which to prepare a plan', particularly as it stated that 'the same source' would probably provide short notice of the night upon which the German attack would be made.[3] But while Home Operations was drawing up its counter-plan further intelligence was received from the same two sources.

In the early hours of 12 November, before AI 1(w)'s memorandum had been issued to the Air Staff, GC and CS sent to AI the decrypt of an Enigma signal of the previous day from Vannes, KG 100's HQ. This stated 'prepare for new targets as follows', gave the words 'New Targets 51, 52 and 53', and listed against each of the three targets five beam bearings from transmitters with river code names.† These transmitters, those of the new *X-Gerät* navigational beams, had by this time been located by ADI (Sc), and their location was known in the appropriate divisions of AI, including AI 1(w).[4] There should thus

---

* See Annex 3. † See Annex 4.

3. N E Evans, *RUSI Journal*, September 1976, p 68.
4. AIR 20/1669, 1670 and 1671, ASI interim reports on *X-Gerät*, 11 and 24 September and 5 October 1940; AIR 20/1627, ASI Report No 10, *X-Gerät*, of 12 January 1941.

have been no difficulty in at once laying off the bearings and discovering that for targets 51, 52 and 53 their intersections indicated Wolverhampton, Birmingham and Coventry respectively. But the surviving records indicate that AI did not associate the second decrypt with the 'Moonlight Sonata' preparations and that, for that reason, it either did not lay off the bearings or, more probably, having laid them off, still failed to recognise their relevance to the coming raid despite the fact that the intersections coincided with what the POW had said about the targets.

This conclusion will seem less surprising if it is noted that Enigma messages from KG 100 quoting new targets, followed by numbers, had been quite common since September in connection with KG 100's use of the *X-Gerät* navigational system, and that of the targets located by laying off the beam transmissions in these messages some had been large industrial cities, including Coventry,[5] so that though by no means a routine signal, the second decrypt, unlike the 'Moonlight Sonata' decrypt, was not particularly unusual. Moreover, earlier signals of this type had given the time at which the beams would transmit, whereas the decrypt of 11 November gave no date or time.

Before giving the evidence for this conclusion it should be noted that there is one item in the records which at first sight tells against it. This is the text of a summary of the intelligence received up to 14 November which was written on 17 November, after the event, by the Directorate of Home Operations. The summary gave in the first paragraph the intelligence obtained from the POW on 11 November. In the second paragraph it gave the intelligence received 'from another source that the Germans were planning a gigantic raid under the code name "Moonlight Sonata"'. Its third paragraph read:

'3. On the 12th November Air Intelligence was able to amplify this information sufficiently to confirm that a heavy-scale attack was probable at the full moon; that the Knickebein and VHF beams (River Group) would be employed; that Air Fleets 2 and 3 together with KG 100 (amounting to some 1,800 first-line aircraft) would be participating; and that the operation would be undertaken in 3 phases; and that there were 3 target areas which were alternatives. Finally the C-in-C of the GAF would be controlling the operation in person.'*

Most of the information in this third paragraph is extracted from the 'Moonlight Sonata' decrypt. But this does not apply to the reference to 'VHF beams (River Group)' or to the reference to '3 target areas

---

* See Annex 5.

5. See, for example, CX/JQ/345 of 29 September 1940; CX/JQ/351 of 3 October; CX/JQ/401 of 26 October; CX/JQ/408 of 30 October; CX/JQ/409 of 30 October; CX/JQ/412 of 31 October; CX/JQ/417 of 2 November; CX/JQ/423 of 3 November; CS/JQ/429 of 5 November; CX/JQ/435 of 7 November; CX/JQ/439 of 8 November 1940.

which were alternatives'. For these there are three possible explanations:

  (a) they were taken from the second Enigma decrypt, and taken from it on 12 November, as the summary says;

or (b) they were taken from the second Enigma decrypt but, despite what the summary says, were taken from it after the event, when it had been recognised that the decrypt was connected with the 'Moonlight Sonata' operation;

or (c) they had nothing to do with the second decrypt, the reference to VHF beams being a repetition of AI 1(w)'s mention of these in its appreciation of the 'Moonlight Sonata' decrypt and the reference to 3 targets being a slip for the four targets listed in that appreciation – a slip that could be due to the fact that, as we shall see, the POW later spoke of 3 targets or 3 separate raids.

At this distance of time it is impossible to choose between these explanations. But there is some difficulty in accepting that the first is the right one, and that the summary is evidence that the second decrypt was seen to be associated with 'Moonlight Sonata' on 12 November. Professor R V Jones appears to give some support for it by claiming that the second decrypt was unusual in giving three targets, whereas earlier *X-Gerät* decrypts of the same type had given only one, and in specifying beam directions which did not meet the standards of bombing accuracy to which KG 100 had previously been operating and that he 'duly alerted the proper authorities'.[6] In fact, however, he is inaccurate on the second of these points* and he does not claim that he associated the second decrypt with the expected 'Moonlight Sonata' raid; on the contrary, he is at pains to stress that until 14 November neither he nor the proper authorities knew where that raid would come.[7] We may add that the third paragraph of the Home Operations summary does not say that the second decrypt confirmed the POW's reference to Coventry and Birmingham, as it would surely have done if it had been associated with 'Moonlight Sonata' and its bearings had been laid off, but uses it only as further evidence that a large raid was being planned.

We may now turn to the evidence which positively indicates that AI missed the relevance of the second decrypt. Its chief items are the operational instructions for the counter-measures (code name 'Cold Water'), which the Air Ministry issued in the early hours of 14 November, and a memorandum in which, later on the morning of 14 November, the Air Staff informed the Prime Minister of what was afoot. The Operational Instructions stated that the GAF's targets would be those in London and the south-east that had been listed in

---

* See Annex 4, which gives directions down to seconds.

6. Jones, op cit, p 147.
7. ibid, Chapter 18.

AI 1(w)'s memorandum of 12 November, thus discounting the POW's evidence. On the other hand, they relied on the POW for the probable date: the raid was to be expected on 'the night of the full moon (15/11) or the most suitable moonlight night subsequent to that date'. The memorandum to the Prime Minister gave the same expected time and the same targets, and stated that the targets 'are probably alternative to each other'.*

It is true that in the memorandum to the Prime Minister the Air Staff expressed some reservation about the targets. They concluded by saying: 'We believe that the target areas will be those noted in paragraph 1 above, probably in the vicinity of London, but if further information indicates Coventry, Birmingham or elsewhere, we hope to get instructions out in time'. This does not sound like the language of men who had been warned that the POW's reference to Coventry and Birmingham had been corroborated by the bearings given in the second Enigma decrypt. It seems clear, moreover, that the reservation, together with a qualification which had appeared in the 'Cold Water' operational instructions themselves, had been prompted by the receipt of further information from the POW.

The D of I had passed the results of an interrogation of the POW to DCAS at 1900 on 13 November. The POW had now added that the operation was to consist of three separate attacks on consecutive nights, each using 500–800 aircraft, and that there was a code-word for each attack, the first being 'Regenschirm' (Umbrella) and the second 'Mondschein Serenade' (Moonshine Serenade); he did not know the third. He had also repeated that the targets were to be in 'the industrial district of England'. With regard to the code-words the D of I had commented. 'You will see that the code-word for second day is somewhat like code name for the general operation – "Moonlight Sonata" '.[8] On receiving the D of I's report the DCAS had minuted: 'I really can't believe that this is a three night show. "Umbrella" is KG 100. "Moonshine Serenade" is the main attack. No 3 phase is something else. How can even the optimistic Boche hope to get 3 consecutive nights of fine weather?'.[9] Nevertheless, the original assumption that the GAF intended to use 'all available aircraft' on one night in a single operation was qualified in the light of the POW's remarks when the operational instructions were issued. They said that 'the operation will be carried out in 3 phases in a single night or on 3 consecutive nights. It is, however, considered that the former is more likely, and that the attack will be concentrated into a single night'.

---

* See Annex 6.

8. AIR 2/5238, D of I's Minute to DCAS of 13 November 1940. See also Evans, op cit, p 70.

9. Evans, op cit, p 70.

Although the operational instructions made no such concession to the POW's repetition of the claim that the targets were to be in 'the industrial district of England', there was enough discussion of it to show that this was the reason why the Air Staff took the precaution of warning the Prime Minister that the targets might be Coventry or Birmingham. On seeing the instructions the D of I minuted on 14 November his agreement with their interpretation of the three phases of 'Moonlight Sonata' – 'it will probably be an attack on *one* night *in 3 waves*' (his italics). He also commented that 'P/W states 500–800 aircraft, but mentions "The Industrial District of England" '.[10] On the same day the Director of Home Operations noted that 'the 4 target areas only were indicated in the Order, and not Birmingham and Coventry. CAS agreed'.[11]

The decision to omit any reference to Coventry and Birmingham from the operational instructions for the counter-measures, though clearly reached after some debate, was made easier by two considerations. In the first place, many of the counter-measures were aimed at crippling the German assault at its known bases, and would have been the same whatever the target. Secondly – and this argument appeared in the Air Staff's memorandum to the Prime Minister in the phrase 'if further information indicates Coventry, Birmingham or elsewhere, we hope to get instructions out in time' – the operational instructions stated, as had been announced in the first of the Enigma decrypts, that final proof of enemy intentions was expected by 1 pm and not later than 3 pm on the day chosen for the attack. Moreover, as well as expecting further information, AI knew where it would come from. Accordingly the Duty Group Captain at the Air Ministry, who would advise the commands to give the executive order bringing the counter-measures into effect, was informed that GAF beam tunings and weather reports would provide reliable proof that 'Moonlight Sonata' was due and that these would be followed by intelligence on beam paths and beam intersection points which would give final confirmation of targets and approach routes.[12] And the 'Cold Water' counter-measures included instructions that a specially close watch should be kept on the W/T signals of the GAF and on the beam transmissions.

Even without these instructions, these signals and transmissions would have been continually monitored. In the remaining record of what was intercepted, on the other hand, there is no sign that the authorities were alerted on 14 November by the *text* of any signal either to the fact that the raid was imminent or to the fact that Coventry was to be the target.

---

10. AIR 2/5238, Enclosure 4A. See also Evans, op cit, p 70.
11. AIR 2/5238, DHO Minute of 14 November 1940.
12. Evans, op cit, p 70.

The files of the Directorate of Home Operations contain two minutes dated 14 November. The first instructed the Duty Officer to issue the telegram 'Executive "Cold Water"' as soon as he was informed that the enemy calibration signal had indicated the night chosen for 'Moonlight Sonata', and to issue a further telegram as soon as the direction and point of intersection of the beams had indicated the target selected. The second states that, the calibration signal having been made at 1300, and acknowledged by Luftflotte 3, the CAS decided to go ahead with 'Cold Water' and the Directorate 'spoke to commands' and issued the 'Executive' telegram at 1615. The files contain the text of this telegram marked with TOO 1615 and time of despatch 1641. They contain only a draft of the further telegram; in this the space left for the announcement of the target remains blank and there is nothing to show that the telegram was despatched.[13] But as the Directorate was using the telephone to the commands, and as it can have had no motive for subsequently claiming that it was better informed than it was in fact, there seems no reason to question the account of the final developments that is given in the summary drawn up by the Directorate of Home Operations on 17 November. This reads:

'At about 1300 hours on the 14th November German radio beam activity coupled with enemy reconnaissance reports, and the interception of messages from the Central Control for the operation at Versailles, indicated that operation "Moonlight Sonata" was to commence on the night of 14–15 November. An executive order to implement counter-plan "Cold Water" was thereupon issued to all concerned.

By 1500 hours on the 14th November the Radio Counter-measures Organisation was able to report that the "River Group" beams were intersecting over Coventry. All RAF Commands were informed, and Home Security and Home Forces put into the picture'.*

□

In the light of the above analysis we may briefly comment on some of the statements that have been published on the subject. Mr R P Bateson[14] is right to say that the Air Ministry got two days' notice 'of this raid', but wrong in claiming that it was clear by 12 November that a series of raids against three targets was to be expected and that Coventry's defences were strengthened as a result. Coventry's defences were strengthened by 14 November, but were so in response to representations made to the Cabinet early in November.[15] There is no

---

* See Annex 5.

13. AIR 2/5238.
14. Letter to *Sunday Telegraph*, 28 July 1974.
15. Evans, op cit, p 71.

basis for Mr A Cave Brown's claim[16] that Whitehall had known for two days that Coventry was to be the target and that no counter-measures were taken in order to safeguard the security of Ultra: extensive counter-measures were not only prepared but also put into effect, as Mr Evans' study has shown. Mr Evans[17] is, however, in error in accepting that the Ultra message of 9 November, decrypted on 11 November, showed the targets to be in south-eastern England, and thus in his speculation that, possibly because it suspected a breach in signals security, the GAF may have changed the objective between 9 and 14 November. The message contained no target information, only a list of target numbers; these, we can now see, all referred to alternative targets but were preferred to the POW reference to Coventry as the primary target from the conviction that Enigma clues pointed to the GAF's intention to attack the areas marked on the map. Group Captain Winterbotham[18] is right to say that Coventry was not identified as the target until about 3 pm on 14 November, but wrong to suggest that counter-measures were limited by the need to safeguard the source; and wrong in claiming that the word Coventry was spelt out in an intercepted signal. Mr P G Lucas[19] indeed thinks that on the afternoon of the raid a low-grade GAF signal was intercepted announcing that the target was 'Korn'. But he may be misremembering the reference to 'Korn' made in the Enigma signal decrypted on 11 November: in any case he adds that 'we were not bright enough to guess that "Korn" might be Coventry'.

Sir David Hunt[20] and Sir John Martin[21] have contributed the further information that the Prime Minister abandoned a visit to Ditchley Park on the afternoon of 14 November on receiving a message about the beams, but that he returned to Downing Street under the impression that the raid was to be on London, and remained under that impression for the rest of the day. If their recollection is perfect this must mean either that the Prime Minister, who had been warned earlier that London was the probable target, got the first general warning, received about 1 pm, but never got the second warning, received about 3 pm, to the effect that Coventry had been identified by the beams; or that his knowledge that Coventry had been identified did not prevent him from assuming that London would also be attacked.

---

16. *Sunday Express*, 14 March 1976.

17. Evans, op cit, p 73.

18. *The Ultra Secret*, (1974), pp 60–61; *Sunday Telegraph*, 21 July 1974; letter to *Times Literary Supplement*, 25 June 1976.

19. Letter to *The Times*, 31 August 1976.

20. Letter to *The Times*, 28 August 1976; Times Literary Supplement, 28 May 1976; letter to TLS, 9 July 1976.

21. Letter to *The Times*, 28 August 1976.

ANNEX 1
to APPENDIX 9

Excerpt from CX/JQ/444 of 11 November 1940

GERMANY
AIR
OPERATIONS

4. '*Moonshine Sonata*'

Source saw following secret instructions issued by the Senior Signals officer, Fliegerkorps 1 and dated 1400/9/11/40:–

'W/T data of K.G. 100 for "Moonlight Sonata" ':

(1) Frequency 4492 kcs., alternative 4730 kcs. K.G. 100: Ground Station's call-sign F4G; Hptm. ASCHENBRENNER's aircraft, F4GA; other aircraft use F4G with letters B, C, D, etc, added. Aircraft three-letter code LM4, with following 'Verfuegungs-signale':–

No. 9 – KORN (sic).
No. 10 – Weather at English coast.
No. 11 – Weather at target.
No. 12 – Bombing conditions over the target.
No. 58 – KNICKEBEIN Beam 3.
No. 59 – KNICKEBEIN Beam 4.
No. 60 – Beam interference.
No. 61 – Beam very broad.
No. 62 – Intersection of beams is over the target.
No. 63 – Beam is to left of target.
No. 14 – Beam is to right of target.
No. 15 – Target Area 1.
No. 16 – Target Area 2.
No. 17 – Target Area 3.
No. 18 – Target Area 4.

K.G. 100 will give the tuning-signal at 1300 hours on day of operation, to be repeated at 1315 hours by Airfleet 3, call sign D3R.

(2) In case the attack is not to take place on account of the weather report from K.G. 100, instructions to this effect will be issued:–

(a) By telephone via the Fliegerkorps (plural: but number of them unspecified).

(b) By W/T: the main W/T station of the C-in-C, German Air Force, will send the code group 'MOND MOND' (ie MOON MOON) three times. Airfleets 2 and 3 will repeat the group three times.

Call-signs:–

C-in-C, GAF – MOR
    Airfleet 2 – ROS
    Airfleet 3 – BUR
    K.G. 100 – F4G.

(3) Five minutes after the signal 'MOND MOND' the KNICKEBEIN beacons will be shifted on to alternative targets: duration of shift over about twenty minutes. KNICKEBEIN will continue to operate during the shift over.

(Reliability (A) except for paragraph 3, which is (B). Source assumes that 'Moonlight Sonata' is a code name for a particular operation.)

ANNEX 2
*AI 1(w) Memorandum to Directorate of Home Operations of
12 November 1940*

From PRO S 7248 (AIR 2/5238), and quoted in N E Evans,
RUSI Journal, September 1976, p 67

MOONLIGHT SONATA

1. On 11.10.40 information was received from our SPECIAL SOURCE which indicated that the GAF is about to carry out an air operation of very considerable dimensions against this country.

2. The code name of this operation is 'MOONLIGHT SONATA'.

Possible date of this Operation

3. Signals instructions for this operation were issued at 1400 hours on 9.11.40. The date for which the operation is planned was not specified. The following factors assist in determining likely dates.

(i) The name 'Moonlight Sonata' suggests that the operation is to be carried out at night when the moon is near or at the full.

(ii) The use of wireless beams including 'KNICKEBEIN' and a VHF beam indicate a night operation.

(iii) A night operation involving a large number of aircraft is more conveniently carried out by moonlight.

(iv) From another source information has been received which indicates that a very heavy night raid is to be carried out against this country on the most suitable night between 15.11 (full moon) and 20.11.

It therefore seems likely that 'Moonlight Sonata' is to be played on the night of the full moon (15.11) or the most suitable moonlight night subsequent to that date.

Possible strength of the operation

4. The call signs to be used indicate that Airfleets 2 and 3 and KG 100 are participating. The operation is being controlled by the C in C of the GAF. It seems therefore safe to conclude that these formations will be putting out all available aircraft. The importance of the operation is further stressed by the fact that the CO of KG 100 will be flying. It is believed that KG 100 has a maximum operation strength of 30 aircraft. On this occasion not more than 26 can be participating, but it is not known how far the number detailed to take part falls short of this figure.

Execution of the operation

5. It would appear that the plan is for KG 100 using the very accurate VHF beam, in the use of which it is specialised is to commence the operation. The Aircraft of this unit are to carry out the following tasks.

(i) Send reports of the weather on the coast of England and in the target areas and on bombing conditions in the target areas.

(ii) Report on the satisfactory functioning of Knickebein beams and whether the intersection of beams is over the selected targets.

Presumably if KG 100 reports conditions to be satisfactory, the other aircraft will follow. The choice of the word 'SONATA' may indicate that the operation will be carried out in three waves, ie KG 100 (who may start fires) followed by the two air fleets in pre-arranged order.

6. In the event of KG 100 reporting the weather to be unfavourable over the primary target areas arrangements have been made to move the Knickebein beams to alternative target areas.

Target Areas

7. The following target areas are mentioned in the signals instructions.

(i) *Target area I*. It is uncertain where this area lies. It is possibly central London. There is, however, a possibility that it is in the Harwich–Ipswich district.

(ii) *Target Area II*. Greater London and within the circle Windsor–St Albans–Epping–Gravesend–Westerham–a little south of Leatherhead–Windsor.

(iii) *Target Area III*. The Triangle bounded by lines connecting Farnborough Aerodrome–Reading–Maidenhead.

(iv) *Target Area IV*. The district Faversham–Rochester–Sheerness.

8. It is not known whether the target areas referred to above are all primary target areas or whether they include both primary and secondary targets.

AI 1(k) Memorandum to Director of Air Intelligence
of 12 November 1940

From PRO S 7248 (AIR 2/5238), and quoted in Evans, op cit, p 67.

A pilot from 2/KG 1 from MONDIDIER shot down on the 9th inst. has told the following story to his roommate. (A SP installed two days ago [if this isn't clear Group Captain Davidson will explain].) He believes that riots have broken out in London and that Buckingham Palace has been stormed and that 'Hermann' thinks the psychological moment has come for a colossal raid to take place between the 15th and the 20th of this month at the full moon and that Coventry and Birmingham will be the towns attacked. P/W stated he had recently made 2 to 3 attacks on London nightly but that this attack will only entail one flight per night and that every bomber in the Luftwaffe will take part. He says that workmen's dwellings are being concentrated on methodically in order to undermine the working clases who are believed to be so near revolt. He thinks that every Knickebein route will be employed and that in future they will concentrate on 50 kg shrieking bombs.

As this came after S/L Humphrey's visit this afternoon when he mentioned that a gigantic raid under the code name of 'Moonlight Sonata' was in preparation, I thought it well to bring this information to your notice although on account of the source it should be treated with reserve, as he is as yet untried.

I believe that S/L Humphreys has pretty definite information that the attack is to be against London and the Home Counties and he believes that it is in retaliation for Munich. The objective should also be regarded as doubtful as probably his information is later.

ANNEX 4

Excerpt from CX/JQ/445 of 12 November 1940

GERMANY
AIR
NAVIGATIONAL BEAMS

4. Source saw following telegram dated 11/11, signed MATT-IESEN (VANNES): 'Prepare for new targets as follows;–

New target 51 WESER 356 degrees
49 minutes 54 seconds

SPREE 357 degrees
41 minutes 45 seconds

ELBE 304 degrees
10 minutes 14 seconds

RHEIN 304 degrees
09 minutes 17 seconds

ISAR 307 degrees
17 minutes 54 seconds

New target 52 WESER 359 degrees
57 minutes 58 seconds

SPREE 0 degrees
51 minutes 17 seconds

ELBE 304 degrees
00 minutes 29 seconds

RHEIN 303 degrees
59 minutes 28 seconds

ISAR 307 degrees
26 minutes 26 seconds

New target 53 WESER 04 degrees
37 minutes 41 seconds

SPREE 05 degrees
31 minutes 12 seconds

ELBE 305 degrees
02 minutes 08 seconds

RHEIN 305 degrees
01 minutes 00 seconds

ISAR 308 degrees
52 minutes 30 seconds'

ANNEX 5

DDHO Summary of 17 November 1940

From PRO AIR 20/2419

Note on German Operation 'MOONLIGHT SONATA', and
Counter-plan 'COLD WATER'

Intelligence

On the 11th November it was reported that a Prisoner of War, in
conversation with a room mate, said that a colossal raid had been
planned to take place between the 15th to 20th November, at the full
moon, and that Coventry and Birmingham would be the towns
attacked. Every bomber in the Luftwaffe would take part, and
workmen's dwellings would be methodically attacked in order to
undermine the working classes, who were believed to be near revolt.
The prisoner thought that every Knickebein route would be used.

2. On the same day information was received from another source
that the Germans were planning a gigantic raid under the code name
'Moonlight Sonata'.

3. On the 12th November Air Intelligence was able to amplify this
information sufficiently to confirm that a heavy scale attack was
probable at the full moon; that the Knickebein and VHF beams (River
Group) would be employed; that Air Fleets 2 and 3, together with
KG 100 (amounting to some 1,800 first line aircraft) would be
participating; and that the operation would be undertaken in 3 phases;
and that there were 3 target areas which were alternatives. Finally, the
Commander-in-Chief of the GAF would be controlling the operation
in person.

Air Staff Counter-Plan

4. On receiving the above information the Air Staff issued a
counter-plan (code-named 'Cold Water'), the principal features of
which were:–
   (a) Continuous watch on German radio activity, and maximum
       radio interference with enemy navigational beams and beacons:
   (b) Security patrols by Bomber aircraft over the German aero-
       dromes occupied by Air Fleets 2 and 3:
   (c) A heavy scale of attack on the aerodromes at Vannes and St
       Leger used by the specialist beam flyers of KG 100.
   (d) A special bombing attack on the Knickebein and VHF beam
       transmitters near Cherbourg by aircraft flying up the beams and
       dropping sticks of bombs in the silent zone, which has been
       discovered immediately above the transmitters:
   (e) A heavy bombing attack on a selected city in Germany.

(f) The maximum scale of night fighter and anti-aircraft artillery to be concentrated against the enemy raiders.

5. The operation orders to implement this plan were issued at 0300 hrs. on the 14th November.

History of the Action

6. At about 1300 hours on the 14th November German radio beam activity coupled with enemy reconnaissance reports, and the interception of messages from the Central Control for the operation at Versailles, indicated that operation 'Moonlight Sonata' was to commence on the night of the 14–15th November. An executive order to implement counter-plan 'Cold Water' was thereupon issued to all concerned.

7. By 1500 hours on the 14th November the Radio Counter-measures Organisation was able to report that the enemy 'River Group' beams were intersecting over Coventry. All RAF Commands were informed, and Home Security and Home Forces put into the picture.

Action by Coastal Command

8. One Squadron bombed Vannes aerodrome and started one large, and several small, fires. Bursts were also seen on the runways and in an aircraft dispersal area.

9. The aerodrome at St Leger was bombed by 8 Blenheim aircraft, but results were not observed.

10. Eight Hudson aircraft attacked aerodrome at Rosendail, Gravelenes, and the jetty at Calais. At Rosendail an Me.110, which took off to engage our bombers, was shot down.

11. All Coastal Command aircraft returned from these operations.

Action by Bomber Command

12. A heavy attack by 30 aircraft was delivered against military objectives in Berlin, during which 17 tons of high explosive bombs, 4,000 incendiaries, and 6 – 1,500 lb land mines were dropped. A number of large fires and explosions resulted.

13. 43 Bomber aircraft attacked aerodromes of Air Fleets 2 and 3. The results were good. For example. At Melun fires were started in the hangers and bursts were seen close to 14 aircraft on the ground. At Chartres an enemy aircraft was set alight on the flare path.

14. Our casualties during the night amounted to 10 bombers missing, 2 in the sea, and 1 crashed on return.

Action by special Radio Bombers

15. Two special aircraft and crews attacked the beam transmitting stations on the Cherbourg Peninsula, by dropping sticks of bombs in

the silent zone immediately above the stations. One stick of bombs was observed to straddle (no. IV Knickebein Beam), which became silent and did not open up again during the night. An intercepted instruction to the VHF Beam Station at Cherbourg, to switch to a new target, produced the reply that the apparatus was unserviceable. It is presumed therefore, that the special bombing attacks succeeded in putting 2 beam transmitters out of action during the night.

Radio Counter-measures

16. All radio counter-measures were put into effect. These included 'meconing' the enemy radio beacons and spoiling the beams. While these operations were technically successful they are unlikely to have contributed materially to the defence, since the night was so clear and bright that radio navigational aids were not essential.

Fighter Action

17. A total of 121 fighter sorties were despatched during the night, consisting of 10 AI Beaufighters, 39 AI Blenheims, 22 Defiants, 45 Hurricanes, 4 Gladiators and 1 Spitfire. The fighter operations resulted in 11 AI detections, culminating in one enemy sighting: one sighting assisted by searchlights and 9 unassisted sightings. Two engagements resulted from these sightings and one enemy aircraft was damaged.

18. The disappointing number of combats which followed on the 21 interceptions or enemy detections is attributed, inter alia, to the exhaust glow from Hurricanes and Defiants, which has the double disability of interfering with the pilots' vision and acting as a warning beacon to enemy bombers. The poor vision through the perspex screens of Blenheims and Hurricanes is also a contributory cause.

19. The fighter deployment provided for patrols over the target area, patrols across the beams and on enemy lines of approach, and also for vectoring on to specific enemy raiders.

Balloon Defence

20. The Coventry barrage of 56 balloons was reinforced on the 14th November by 16 further balloons, 8 of which were deployed on the night 14–15. The Barrage was flying throughout the enemy attack, and no enemy aircraft came below the level of the balloons. Balloon casualties resulting from the bombardment were slight.

AA Gun Defences

21. Forty high angle guns were deployed for the defence of Coventry, and these remained in action throughout the bombardment. Although the Gun Operation Room was bombed it soon returned to

action, and at the end of the operation was in control of all the heavy anti-aircraft except for 6 guns.

22. The light anti-aircraft deployed in Coventry had been increased on the 12th November by 12 Bofors provided by Home Forces.

Enemy Action and Tactics

23. It is estimated that some 330 enemy aircraft were engaged in the attack on Coventry, which was opened by some 10 aeroplanes of KG 100, which flew up the beams and started fires in the target area. The remaining aircraft then bombed the fires. While earlier raids followed the beams they were soon abandoned by subsequent sorties, which took full advantage of the bright moonlight and approached the objective over a wide front.

ANNEX 6

*Air Staff Memorandum to the Prime Minister
of 14 November 1940*

From PRO AIR 2/5238, and quoted in Evans, op cit, p 70

NOTE FOR THE PRIME MINISTER ON PROJECTED OPERATION BY GAF – 'MOONLIGHT SONATA' AND THE COUNTER OPERATION BY THE METROPOLITAN AIR FORCE – 'COLD WATER'

From a good source of information we learn that the enemy propose to carry out a heavy night bombing attack on targets in an area in this country. The areas, which are probably alternative to each other, are Central London (not absolutely definite), Greater London, the area bounded by Farnborough–Maidenhead–Reading and the area bounded by Rochester–Favisham–Isle of Sheppey. The areas are apparently alternative and the selection would be on the point of weather or visibility.

2. The whole of the German long range Bomber Force will be employed. The operation is being co-ordinated, we think, by the Commander-in-Chief, GAF. It is probably a reprisal for our attack on Munich. KG 100, led in person by the Geschwader Commander, will carry out the first phase of the operation and the first attacks.

3. The attack will probably take place on a night between 15th and 20th November, ie during the full moon period. At 1300 hours on the day preceding the night on which the attack is to be launched, KG 100 (the experts of Knickebein type radio navigation) will carry out a reconnaissance over the target areas to discover whether the intersection of the beams is in fact over the selected objective and at this time will transmit a weather report, which will be replied to by Air Fleet Headquarters. This will be our signal that the party is on.

4. The information which comes from a very good source indeed is confirmed to some extent by a Prisoner of War shot down on the 9th. In his report he states that Goering is convinced that the people in London are on the point of revolution and that Buckingham Palace has been stormed. He has therefore arranged a great raid to take place on Coventry and Birmingham with the object of destroying workers' dwellings in order to undermine the morale of the working classes.

5. We believe that the target areas will be those noted in paragraph 1 above, probably in the vicinity of London, but if further information indicates Coventry, Birmingham or elsewhere, we hope to get instructions out in time.

6. On our part, we propose to meet this situation by a maximum effort of the Metropolitan Air Force.

(a) On the part of 80 Wing reconnaissance of beams will be carried out each day and a close watch will be kept on wavelengths to enable all information, including the 1300 hour reconnaissance information, to be got. The aircraft of 80 Wing on the night of the operation will operate down the beams and bomb in an attempt to attack the beam stations.

(b) On the part of Fighter Command and the anti-aircraft defence the maximum number of AI and 'Cats Eye' fighters will be operated on the avenues of approach as disclosed by the beams and in the vicinity of the objectives with the object of destroying enemy bombers. The Anti-Aircraft command will be on their toes and C-in-C Fighter Command has been asked to concentrate, if practicable, a number of AA guns on the avenues of approach. We have also arranged for the night fighters to intercept enemy bombers on their homeward journey as they switch on their navigation lights in the vicinity of Fecamp Light. We did consider operating Blenheim night fighters over the German Aerodromes. This idea, however, was abandoned as it would have meant removing the AI equipment from at least one Squadron of Blenheims. This would have put the Squadron out of action for operations over this country – possibly for a number of days. This was not considered worthwhile, especially as the Medium Bomber Force had already been detailed to attack the enemy aerodrome in question.

(c) On the part of Bomber Command, we considered a knock-for-knock policy by the heavy Bomber Force would provide the best course of action. C-in-C has therefore been told that he should select a City in Germany, eg Berlin, Essen or Munich – depending on weather conditions – and concentrate the force on this. The Whitley Force is already committed to the attack of industrial targets in Northern Italy. We did not, therefore, include this in our plan. The Medium Bomber Force at maximum sorties will be employed on security patrols over the night bomber aerodromes in France, Belgium and Holland.

(d) On the part of Coastal Command, a heavy attack will be launched at dusk or early night on Vannes Aerodromes – the home of KG 100 with the object of imposing delay, confusion, and loss to this Geschwader – whose operation is the key of the German Plan. The remainder of the Coastal Command bombing sorties will be co-ordinated with the Bomber Command Medium Force in the attack of enemy night bomber aerodromes.

7. The attack is to be in three phases or to be carried out over a period of three nights. On the information available at this time it seems that the former is the more likely. If, however, later information indicates that it is a three night operation our counter measures – 'Cold Water' – can be repeated.

Operational Chain of Command in the German Air Force (GAF)

The largest operational sub-division of the GAF was the Luftflotte. These were numbered 1, 2, 3, 4 and 5 and were directly subordinated to the High Command of the GAF (OKL).

To each Luftflotte one or more Fliegerkorps (I, II, IV, V, VIII, IX etc) were assigned according to operational requirements. The Fliegerkorps, called Fliegerdivision early in the war, consisted of all types of flying unit – bomber, dive-bomber, fighter and reconnaissance. To each Fliegerkorps were assigned a varying number of Geschwader, the nearest equivalent of the RAF Groups. The types of Geschwader were as follows:–

Bomber   – Kampfgeschwader (KG)
Dive Bomber   – Sturzkampfgeschwader (St.KG)
Single Engined Fighter   – Jagdgeschwader (JG)
Twin Engined Fighter   – Zerstörergeschwader (ZG)
Night Fighter   – Nachtjagdgeschwader (NJG)
Ground Attack   – Schlachtgeschwader (SG)
Transport   – Zur Besonderen Verwendung (ZBV)
                               (later Transport Geschwader TG)

Each Geschwader comprised 3 or 4 Gruppen (a Gruppe was the rough equivalent of an RAF Wing) and each Gruppe 3 or 4 Staffeln (a Staffel was the rough equivalent of an RAF squadron).

The Geschwader and Gruppe were given Arabic and Roman numerals respectively. Thus, for example, the third Gruppe of Bomber Geschwader 27 was numbered III KG 27. Kampfgruppe 100 (KGr 100) was an independent unit and was often referred to as KG 100).

The administrative sub-division of the Luftflotte was the Luftgau.

APPENDIX 11

GAF Navigational Aids

(i) *GAF Medium Frequency Beacons*

It was well known before the war that, unlike the RAF, the Germans strongly favoured the use of radio aids to aircraft navigation, and that an extensive network of medium frequency radio beacons existed. At the outbreak of the war 24 beacons were known. By March 1940 these had been increased to 46, the new beacons being installed mainly along Germany's western frontier. As well as the beacons several German broadcasting stations were used in a similar manner. After the occupation of France and the Low Countries this network was redeployed to form an elaborate system extending from Norway to Bordeaux, and at 1 September 1940 it totalled 38 beacons and 11 broadcasting stations in addition to those in Germany.

The beacon transmissions, a call-sign followed by a 20-second continuous note which enabled the aircraft to determine a bearing to the known location of the beacon, were sent out on selected frequencies within the band 176–580 kc/s. The initial system of call-sign and frequency change, made daily at midnight, was a simple one, and the Y Service had no difficulty in passing beacon information rapidly to RAF commands for operational purposes and in particular to the counter-measures organisation.

When it became clear that the network was being used for a variety of purposes by the GAF – the fixing of turning points en route to the target, homing on the return flight, as well as for general navigation in the bomber offensive – counter-measures were pressed ahead in spite of the then usually accepted theory that the night-effect rendered MF beacons useless for accurate navigation at night. The counter-measure adopted was a masking beacon – the 'meacon' – which had been developed by the Post Office in case it might be required to counter illicit beacons should they be used by enemy aircraft over the United Kingdom. The 'meacon' reradiated the original beacon signal with the same characteristics but with a different point of radiation. The resulting effect could not be detected in an aircraft with normal equipment, so that false bearings would be obtained.

The meacons were ready in July 1940, and three stations were deployed on 14 August; by the end of the month these were increased to 15 at five sites. Their successful operation required that the call-sign and frequency of each beacon to be countered should be known, in advance if possible. Frequencies were measured on the ground by the Y Service at Cheadle and in the air by aircraft of No 80 Wing RAF, and beacon power information was compiled from measurements made at the Air Ministry's Research Station at Great Baddow.

The strength and tactics of meaconing soon worried the GAF; many references to the failure of airborne DF equipment were heard in intercepted messages and enemy air-crews were frequently lost and crashed or landed in the United Kingdom. However, the best indications of the success of the counter-measures were the steps taken by the Germans to overcome them. The original simple system, which allowed for forecasting frequencies, persisted until December 1940. Then the first system change occurred, with frequencies being altered once a day but at differing times. This made forecasting impossible, and delays before the Y Service intercepted and located the beacons were inevitable until the system was broken. Further changes in procedures occurred on 1 April 1941, 1 September 1941, 10 October 1941, this last change not being broken until early November. Yet another change was made on 20 December 1941 and another on 1 April 1942. By this time the complexity was such that 15 call-sign and frequency changes took place daily, mostly during the hours of darkness. Although the Y Service allocated every DF equipment it could spare to fixing the beacons, 15 to 25 minutes were now required to meacon all beacons after a change. Later, even more complex procedures were to follow.

Further evidence of the success of the counter-measures was provided by the knowledge that GAF bombers used the German Wireless Safety Service organisation to obtain bearings. This service had a network of high grade DF stations operating in the 150–600 kc/s and 3–6 Mc/s bands. It assisted any aircraft in difficulty by receiving at a number of its stations a series of long dashes sent out by the aircraft and then fixing the aircraft by bearings. As the meaconing became more effective, the Service started to give fixes to operational aircraft and was thus no longer merely an SOS organisation. Its method of operation in its new role was soon understood by Cheadle and in fact had been anticipated. Special meacons had been prepared for the new frequencies and had been installed on 7 December 1940, the day before this new navigational aid started as expected.[1]

---

1. AIR 41/46, No 80 Wing RAF Historical Report 1940–45.

(ii) *Knickebein*

The Intelligence Problem

In March 1940 a He 111 of Kampfgruppe 26 was shot down and a note recovered from it referred to a radio beacon as a navigational aid and also to 'Radio beacon *Knickebein* from 0600 on 315°'. Two months later a diary was discovered in the wreckage of another He 111 from the same unit (it was, as it happened, the replacement aircraft of the one first referred to). This contained an entry of 5 March which read: '...we studied *Knickebein*,'. In the meantime POW had provided some information on a bombing apparatus called the *X-Gerät*, and one prisoner suggested that *Knickebein* was something like the *X-Gerät*, and that it had a very narrow beam. For a short time the intelligence authorities were uncertain whether one system or two systems existed, but there was no doubt that the references were to a navigational aid.[2]

GC and CS, alerted to the term *Knickebein*, produced the next relevant intelligence. An Enigma signal, intercepted on 5 June and decrypted on 9 June, read:

'Knickebein at Kleve is confirmed (or established) at point 53° 21' N, 1° W.'

It had been sent by the Chief Signal Officer of Fliegerkorps IV, whose aircraft had been known to have been active in the Retford area, to which the geographical co-ordinates referred. A search for a possibly illicit beacon produced nothing, thus disposing of one possibility. A more probable explanation appeared to be that *Knickebein* was a beam system which could fix a target by intersecting beams.[3] This suggestion had been among those which had been made in March in the attempt to explain the incomplete information from POW.[4]

GC and CS was able to supply the information that Fliegerkorps IV consisted of KG 4 and 27, which were equipped with He 111. Fortunately much was known of the equipment of the He 111; the first aircraft to land in the UK, in October 1939, had been a He 111, and it had been thoroughly examined. No specialist equipment had been found, but the aircraft carried a Lorenz 'blind-landing' receiver. It was now realised that the receiver had a sensitivity unnecessarily high for its declared purpose. Its operational frequency band was between 28 and 35 Mc/s.[5]

Dr R V Jones suggested that the system consisted of a Lorenz-type beam transmitted from Kleve which a bomber could follow until it

---

2. AIR 20/1623, ASI Report No 6 of 28 June 1940.
3. ibid.
4. AIR 20/1622, ASI Report No 5 of 23 May 1940; Jones, op cit, p 85.
5. AIR 20/1623.

met a crossing-beam from another transmitter to give the target position. Professor Lindemann initially did not accept this theory as he doubted whether a beam on 30 Mc/s would follow the surface of the earth at the required ranges. However, when he was shown an unpublished paper by Mr E T Eckersley – an expert on radio propagation – he withdrew his objections and advised the Prime Minister that the matter should be fully investigated. As a result Air Marshal Joubert was appointed to take charge of an investigation. Lindemann and Joubert agreed that the case was strong enough to justify an attempt to find the beams and take counter-measures. This view was endorsed by the Night Interception Committee on 16 June, and it was decided that the recently disbanded RAF Blind Approach Training and Development Unit – the only unit with beam flying experience – should be re-formed as the Wireless Intelligence and Development Unit (WIDU).[6]

By that time more evidence had become available. On 14 June a POW from KG 26 gave detailed information which went a long way to confirming the theory. He stated that *Knickebein* was a bomb-dropping device involving two intersecting radio beams; that the beams were picked up by one Lorenz receiver, which released the bombs (automatic release was not a property of *Knickebein* – a confusion with the *X-Gerät*); and that the device had been developed at Rechlin.* Further intelligence soon followed. On 18 June documents which had been recovered from an aircraft crashed in France gave the co-ordinates of two stations:

1 Knickebein, (near Bredstedt, NE of Husum) 54° 39′ 8° 57′,
2 Knickebein, (near Kleve) 51° 47′ 5″ 6° 6′.

A note taken on 20 June from a POW gave the same stations and co-ordinates except for referring to the first as Stollberg, and it added that the frequencies were 30 and 31.5 mc/s respectively.[7]

On 21 June the Prime Minister called a meeting at which all the facts were presented to him, with the theory which had been evolved. He ordered that the existence of *Knickebein* should be accepted, and that work on counter-measures should have absolute priority. There was an unexpected development after the meeting when Eckersley withdrew his figures on range of interception as being inapplicable in the present circumstances. R V Jones, however, persisted and was proved right. That same night, 21–22 June, one of the Ansons of WIDU found the transmissions on a frequency of 31.5 Mc/s in a narrow beam 400–500 yards wide and discovered that a second beam synchronised with and intersected the first.[8]

---

* See the Oslo report, Appendix 5.

6. ibid; AIR 41/46, p 2; Jones RUSI Lecture, in *RUSI Journal*, August 1947.
7. AIR 20/1623.
8. ibid; AIR 41/46, Appendix B; Churchill, op cit, Vol II, p 339.

The initial investigation completed, the other stations, frequencies, and procedures of the *Knickebein* system were soon identified. One item, however, the identity of the transmitter, was not established until 7 September, when photographic reconnaissance of a site at Beaumont-Hague revealed a small aerial whose characteristics were suitable for the transmission of a narrow beam in the appropriate frequency band.[9]

The aircraft intercept of the beam signals was confirmed by ground intercept on 24 June, when it was established that three frequencies, 30, 31.5, 33.3 Mc/s were in use. In July recovered aircraft documents gave a general description of the system which confirmed what had been postulated, together with information about the beam pattern and some performance figures: the beam could be aimed to an accuracy of 0.1°, the beam width was 0.3°, which was later confirmed by aircraft intercept, and the ranges at which the system could be operated for various aircraft heights up to 6,000 m were given.[10] By the end of August 1940, two more *Knickebein* stations were known, and from then until May 1941 information on the system and its operational procedures gradually accumulated. That month another captured document revealed that the number of stations was to be increased to twelve. It also gave details of a new receiver which could be used with the latest transmissions in such a way that 34 spot frequencies between 30 and 33.3 Mc/s could be chosen.[11]

Counter-measures

Once the beams had been detected in June 1940, two methods of countering the system were investigated. In both cases improvised equipment had to be used to begin with. The first consisted of straightforward jamming; the second was to transmit signals synchronised with the enemy signal. By the latter method it was hoped to distort the equi-signal, at the centre of the beam, and so divert the bomber from its true course without its knowledge; that is to 'bend the beam'. Both methods were tried and flight tests were made during enemy raids to test efficiency.

It was found that the jammers were effective when they did not wander in frequency and blot out the signal in the neighbourhood of the jammer, which led to frequency control. The second method, which had been employed whenever possible, did not conclusively show the distortion of the beam but the equi-signal was masked. In view of these results, and the problems of large-scale deployment, it was decided to go ahead with unsynchronised methods. As time went on various improvements were introduced, eg self-monitoring by the

---

9. AIR 20/1626, ASI Report No 9 of 18 September 1940.
10. AIR 41/46, Appendix A, quoting AI 1(e) Memo, 30 July 1940.
11. ibid, p 30.

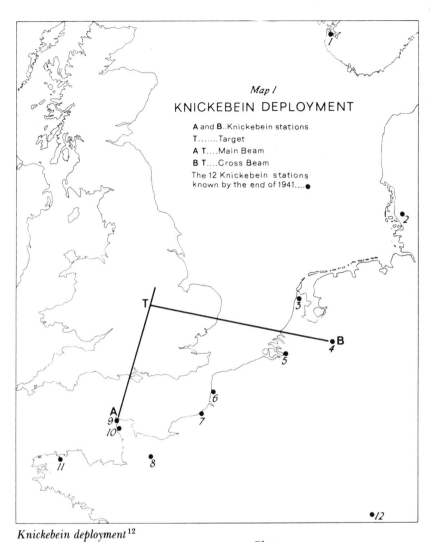

Map I

KNICKEBEIN DEPLOYMENT

A and **B**..Knickebein stations
T.......Target
A T....Main Beam
B T....Cross Beam
The 12 Knickebein stations
known by the end of 1941....●

Knickebein deployment [12]

Kn No.	Location	Position	Photograph date	Frequency and intercept date	
1	Stavanger	58° 46′ N 05° 37′ E	29. 9.40	30 or 31.5	—
2	Stollberg	54° 39′ N 08° 57′ E	1. 9.41	30	Jun 40
3	Julianadorp	52° 55′ N 04° 43′ E	10. 3.41	33.3	Nov 40
4	Kleve	51° 47′ N 06° 06′ E	15.10.40	31.5	Jun 40
5	Bergen-op-Zoom	51° 27′ N 04° 18′ E	24. 9.41	31.5 or 33.3	Oct 41
6	Mt. Violette	50° 37′ N 01° 41′ E	21. 6.41	30 or 31.5	May 41
7	Greny	49° 58′ N 01° 18′ E	1.10.40	,,	Aug 40
8	Mt. Pincon	48° 58′ N 00° 37′ W	17. 6.41	,,	May 41
9	Beaumont-Hague	49° 40′ N 01° 51′ W	7. 9.40	,,	Aug 40
10.	Sortosville-en-Beaumont	49° 25′ N 01° 43′ W	3. 7.41	,,	May 41
11	Morlaix	48° 40′ N 03° 44′ W	4. 1.41	,,	Oct 40
12	Lörrach	47° 38′ N 07° 46′ E	13. 5.40	,,	—

12. ibid, Appendix A.

jamming stations, extension of listening stations. In retrospect it seems clear that No 80 Wing RAF, was able to keep ahead of enemy developments due in part to close co-operation with the Y Service and the intelligence bodies.

The effect of the counter-measures was illustrated by enemy changes in tactics and by reports of enemy discontent with the system. As early as 24–25 September 1940 an interchange of frequencies between two stations was observed. Afterwards POW reports indicated a growing mistrust of *Knickebein* and by January 1941 it was apparent that the GAF was beginning to believe pilots' reports of unreliability. This continued until the new equipment was introduced in 1943.[13]

(iii) *X-Gerät*

The Intelligence Problem

Although the first indications that there were probably two German navigation systems had come in March 1940, and although after a brief period of confusion one had been resolved as *Knickebein*, nothing was learned about the other, *X-Gerät*, for some time. But during August 1940 a group of four beam transmissions on about 74 Mc/s, which appeared to originate on the French coast were intercepted by the Y Service; another on about 66.3 mc/s was also intercepted from the Cherbourg area. They differed in detail from *Knickebein*, but were similar in character. Their purpose was unknown until the start of September, but GC and CS then obtained GAF Enigma decrypts which contained a wealth of information. Some of the decrypts were operational messages giving beam settings, bearings and references to numbered targets. Others gave details about the fitting of the *X-Gerät* to aircraft and mentioned that coarse and fine beams were used. Most important was the fact that the intelligence connected these operations with a single unit KG 100. On 11 September an ASI report stated that it was possible tentatively to conclude that the new 74 Mc/s transmissions were associated with KG 100 and the *X-Gerät*.[14]

A second interim ASI report of 24 September showed that the system was understood and that much more detail of its organisation and procedures had been learned from the Enigma. Six transmitters were identified, all having the names of German rivers, and in two cases their positions were quoted. The advanced base of KG 100, known to be at Vannes, was passing target instructions for the night to the

---

13. ibid, pp 10–12.
14. AIR 20/1669, ASI Interim Report on X-Gerät of 11 September 1940.

various stations in France for the named transmitters. The experimental evidence of the transmissions could be linked with the *X-Gerät* operations, a conclusion which was confirmed by the fact that in the Enigma traffic reference had been made to the use of crystals with natural frequencies in the 8–9 Mc/s region.[15]

On thirteen nights between 23 August and 20 September the GAF Enigma had contained operational information giving times, targets denoted by numbers between 5 and 30, the beams either fine or coarse from named transmitters, and beam bearings. Although the data were incomplete on many nights, it was possible to make a number of deductions. The targets had been numbered on a 'new target' system showing an increase in number with dates and it seemed from this that *X-Gerät* activity had started shortly before 23 August. The distinction between fine and coarse beams led to a suggestion that the former were in the decimetre region and the latter in the known 65–75 Mc/s band. This conjecture came from an incorrect deduction that one of the transmitters had been referred to as FuD2, the other as B1. But this mistake was soon to be corrected.[16]

Dr Jones then analysed the likely accuracy of the system. In the light of the fact that the transmitter stations were given in geographical co-ordinates to the nearest 0.01″ (that is to about a foot), that the settings of the fine beams were given to 5″ (which implied an accuracy of 12½ feet at 100 miles) and that on 1 September a beam width was quoted as 8–10 seconds, the theoretical accuracy over London appeared to be 35–40 feet, 'however incredible it may seem'.[17]

With the available information it was also possible to postulate the manner in which the system operated. An aircraft from KG 100 would fly from Vannes, pick up the direction beam, coarse and fine, from a transmitter in the Cherbourg area, fly along it until it met, first the coarse and then the fine beams from a transmitter in the Calais area, and then a second cross beam also from near Calais. The time between the two intersections would, given that the position of the second crossing point relative to the target was known, provide sufficient data for the point of bomb release to be determined.[18]

Although by this time, 24 September, the principle of the *X-Gerät* had been correctly established, the positions of some of the transmitters were undetermined, and other details had still to be worked out. With the assistance of Dr L J Comrie of the Scientific Computing Service, these were solved, the positions of two more transmitters were determined and it was also established that the distance between the intersections of the cross beams was exactly 15 km. Dr Jones was able to say on 5 October that it would be possible to determine all

---

15. AIR 20/1670, ASI Interim Report No 2, 'The X-Gerät' 24 September 1940.
16. ibid.   17. ibid.
18. ibid.

the elements in the system and to solve the target numbers that had been given in the Enigma messages.[19]

Although the frequency band had been established for some of the beams, ie 65 to 75 Mc/s, it was not yet known what frequency would be used in an operation. The Enigma decrypts referred to the settings of the beams as 'Anna Grad' and it was clear that Anna referred to an instrument in the aircraft. It was finally established that the relationship between frequency and grad was

$$\text{Frequency in Mc/s} = 66.5 + \text{Anna Grad}/10.*$$

Later the examination of equipment found in a crashed aircraft, a He 111, established that the Anna was not, as had been expected, a wave-meter but a complete VHF receiver. The examination of equipment in another crashed aircraft made it possible to explain references in the Enigma decrypts to another piece of equipment, AVP. It was an audio filter which was found to peak at 2,000 c/s. This discovery corrected the modulation and enabled the counter-measure transmitters to be modified. From an earlier measurement it had been assumed that the modulation frequency was 1,500 c/s, and in consequence the transmitters had been ineffective.[20]

The evidence that the GAF was developing what appeared to be a very accurate aid to bombing, with an inherent accuracy of about 120 yards, led Lindemann to draw Churchill's attention not just to the gravity of the threat but to the suggestion that the GAF might adopt new tactics: 'There is some reason to believe that the method adopted is to send a few KG 100 aircraft fitted with special devices to assist in blind bombing on these expeditions in order to start fires on the target which any subsequent machines without special apparatus can use'.[21] This was written three weeks before the GAF bombed Coventry using the pathfinder technique for the first time.

The X-Gerät system

To simplify, the system was one by which an approach beam was directed to the target and crossed by two transverse beams at points P and Q (see map) a fixed distance, 15 km, apart, and at a fixed distance, 5 km, from the target. The time between P and Q enabled the ground speed to be determined and thus the point of bomb release, R. In operations all that was required was for the clock to be started and stopped as the first and second beams were met; thereafter the system was automatic.

---

* See (v) below.

19. AIR 20/1671, ASI Interim Report No 3 of 5 October 1940.
20. AIR 20/1627, ASI Report No 10 of 12 January 1941.
21. Jones, op cit, p 139.

Since the beams were very narrow, about 0.05°, and thus difficult to identify, the actual system involved a more elaborate system of seven beams on seven different frequencies. The approach beam was three beams, one wide (coarse) and two narrow (fine); the wide beam was about 4°; a coarse beam intersected the approach beam 30 km before the first intersection P, to act as a warning; the first cross beam was fine, the second cross beam was two fine beams. The frequency band was 66.5 to 75 Mc/s and frequency steps of 0.5 Mc/s were used.[22]

Counter-measures
Counter-measures were not instituted without difficulty, as suitable transmitters were not readily available. Eventually the Army provided a Gun Laying Pulse transmitter (GL/T Mk 1) and the Navy also provided one in the appropriate band. Modifications to cover the audio modulation frequency, then reported to be 1500 c/s, were made, but this was not the correct frequency and it was not until the recovery of the audio filter from the crashed He 111 that effective jamming of the 2000 c/s modulation could be made. The first jammers were brought into operation in November 1940, and once the modulation modifications had been made the deployment of seventeen transmitters widely spread over the country could proceed. In January 1941 the Germans realised that interference was being caused by radio counter-measures (RCM). The steps taken to overcome this were largely procedural, and were ineffective. From mid-January 1941 beams were no longer set up before raids, or, if they were, they were changed for the operation. In February more complexity was introduced, with rapid changes in frequency during attacks. When attacks were resumed in April 1942 the GAF attempted to defeat counter-measures by using double modulations, but this measure had essentially been anticipated and it was successfully dealt with. It was probably the close co-operation between the ground watching stations and the flights made to provide such warning as was possible, and particularly the flexibility of the RCM equipment and methods, which convinced the Germans that it was useless to continue after 1942.[23]

(iv) *Y-Gerät*

In July 1940 Air Scientific Intelligence Report No 7 concluded that the Germans had developed a system involving a *Knickebein* beam and some form of distance measuring. There had been an Enigma report

22. AIR 20/1627, Sections 1 to 6; AIR 41/46, Appendix H.
23. AIR 20/1627, Section 14; AIR 41/46, pp 13–14.

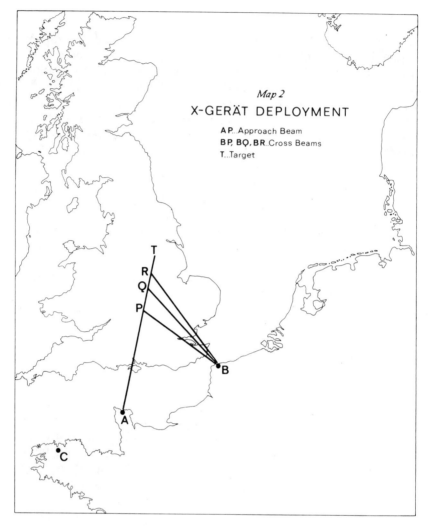

Map 2

X-GERÄT DEPLOYMENT

A P...Approach Beam
B P, B Q, B R..Cross Beams
T...Target

X-Gerät deployment[24]

Initially the transmitters at the operational sites were referred to in the Enigma by the names of German rivers, eg WESER, ELBE, RHEIN, ISAR, ODER and SPREE.

WESER was at 49° 42′ 19.28″ N 1° 51′ 24.87″ W
SPREE   49° 41′ 43.13″ N 1° 55′ 37.10″ W

RHEIN and ELBE were together near 50° 49.0′ N 1° 38.7′ E.

The stations at which the many transmitters were situated when the system was fully deployed were given by the British authorities, in order to protect the Enigma, the names of the German leaders.

A.   Cherbourg Area   49° 42′ N 01° 55′ W
         1940/41   GÖRING, HITLER
         1941/42   GÖRING, HITLER, QUISLING*
B.   Calais Area   50° 52′ N 01° 42′ E
         1940/41   HIMMLER, RIBBENTROP,* HESS*
         1942   LEY, GÖBBELS,* HESS*
C.   Morlaix Area   48° 25′ N 03° 53′ W SHIRACH
Stations* Fine beams only.

---

24. AIR 20/1670 and 1671; AIR 41/46, Appendix H.

of 27 June that the GAF was 'setting up *Knickebein* and *Wotan* Anlagen near Cherbourg and Brest'.[25] Later POW divulged that *Wotan* had one beam and that it depended on distance measurement along that beam. The Oslo report, it was recalled, had described a means by which a pilot could determine, or be informed of, his range by a radio method involving ground and aircraft transmitters.[26]

Little more intelligence was received during the next few months. However the Enigma traffic associated with the *X-Gerät* navigational system contained on 6 October a message from KG 100 at Vannes to a station known as *Wotan II* on the Hague peninsula near *Knickebein* 4 which gave information of a different character from that given in *X-Gerät* messages. It referred to 'Target 1 Co-ordinates 50° 41′ 49.2″ N, 2° 14′ 21.2″ W'. (Bovington Camp, Dorset, on which a few bombs were dropped a few nights later.) Two similar messages were sent on 13 October, as 'practice', and on 2 November another quoted 'Target 5229' (using the old system). In November, also, transmissions were intercepted on 46.2 and 47 Mc/s of a beam type from III KG 26, known to be at Poix. Shortly afterwards two signals were recorded which could only have meant that one station in an aircraft was relaying the modulation of another station on the ground.[27]

By January 1941 it had been established that the system was used only by III KG 26 and that there were transmitting stations in three areas. The general principles were known but operating details were not. The method of ranging and its accuracy had been determined, but the beam characteristics were unusual and differed from the previous blind-bombing raids. However these uncertainties were removed by the recovery of a *Y-Gerät* from a crashed aircraft of III KG 26 on 3–4 May 1941. Its examination not only fully explained the system, but also disclosed its vulnerability to counter-measures. The crews of this and other aircraft shot down described the lack of confidence of the GAF in the *Y-Gerät* but expansion of the system continued and by September 1941 six areas were known. Throughout 1942 the *Y-Gerät* transmitters continued to radiate from time to time but it was difficult to know whether the few attacks that took place used these beams,[28] for there was little evidence of beam flying.

Counter-measures

The first counter-measure adopted was a form of meacon, in which the ranging signal was received and re-radiated to confuse the enemy range indications. The first equipments were installed in February 1941. About that time messages passed by GAF ground stations

---

25. AIR 20/1624, ASI Report No 7, 17 July 1940.
26. AIR 20/1627, Section 12.
27. ibid.
28. AIR 41/46, pp 22, 46.

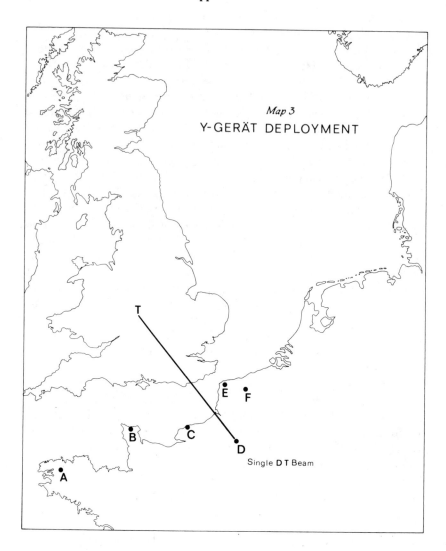

Map 3

Y-GERÄT DEPLOYMENT

Single **D T** Beam

Y-Gerät Deployment[29]
A. Commanna 48° 24′ N 03° 55′ W Oct 1941
B. Cherbourg 49° 41′ N 01° 33′ W Nov 1940
C. St. Valeri   49° 50′ N 00° 33′ E July 1941
D. Montdidier 49° 38′ N 02° 37′ E March 1941
E. De Boursin 50° 47′ N 01° 51′ E May 1942
F. Cassel   50° 49′ N 02° 28′ E Nov 1940
Two stations were deployed at Cherbourg from March 1941.
A station was set up at Stavanger in June 1943.
The numbers of available channels were increased at B, C, E in 1943.

---

29. ibid, Appendix K.

indicated that all was not working smoothly. For instance, out of a total of 89 aircraft under possible control only 18 were known to have been given the bomb-drop signal. There was no evidence that this was due to counter-measures. In March, however, although during heavy attacks 50% of aircraft were instructed to bomb, a number of events occurred to show that the RCM were beginning to have some effect. In April and May attacks on a relatively large scale and over a wide area made counter-measures difficult, but it was noted that only on two occasions did more than 25% of aircraft get the dropping signal. When the *Y-Gerät* apparatus was recovered in May interrogation of the crews disclosed that III KG 26 was losing confidence in the system and attributing the troubles experienced to jamming. Examination of the recovered equipment showed that it was very susceptible to jamming which prevented the synchronising device from operating, and steps were taken to alter the RCM accordingly.[30]

(v) *The Anna Investigation*

This was an early, probably the first, example of what is sometimes referred to as the numbers game, that is the use of factory marks or numbers in the intelligence process.

An instrument, known as Anna, was mentioned in equipment returns in the Enigma at various stations believed to be connected with the *X-Gerät*. Among the data were references to settings in 'grad' and a series of seven digit numbers. The equivalent returns also gave the natural frequencies of specified quartz crystals held at the stations.

In the course of time the Anna grad numbers collected were 10, 15, 25, 30, 35, 44, 47, 55, 60, 75 and 85. Two of them are clearly not correct. The quartz frequencies, multiplied by eight to give the transmitted frequencies, gave in all the series 66.5, 67.0 . . . 72.5 and 75.0. A chance remark by a German officer indicated that so many grad represented a frequency. The answer to the question of what was the relationship between grad and frequency was provided when on a particular day a station was given orders to operate the settings on Anna 30 and 35. The station was known to have crystals including 69.5 and 70.0. Thus the required relationship was

Frequency in Mc/s $= 66.5 + $ Anna Grad/10.

The works numbers, or factory markings, for Anna were numbers between 90699-37 and 90714-37. An examination of equipment from a crashed He 111 from the KG known to use the system found an

---

30. ibid, p 22.

apparatus which bore a label 90708-37. This was Anna. It had a
maximum dial reading of 85, which was also the highest one reported,
and this determined that the maximum frequency in operation was
75.0. Anna was not merely a wave-meter, as had been expected, but
a complete VHF receiver. The works number – 37 clearly showed the
date of manufacture.

Associated with Anna was a secondary equipment known as AVP.
Its works numbers were in the range 5005 to 5250. A later search in
another crashed He 111 for a box with a number in this range
revealed an audio filter unit marked 5017. The 5000 series was
known to be unique, and so this was identified. This established the
modulation frequency, and enabled the counter-measures to be
corrected and made effective.[31]

---

31. AIR 20/1627, Appendix 1.

APPENDIX 12

GC and CS Naval Section Reports on German Weather-Reporting Ships

(i) *Z/320 of 26 April 1941*

A. *The Ships.*

The following trawlers are known to be in use as weather-reporting ships:

Sachsenwald	650 tons
Muenchen	306 tons
Coburg	344 tons
Ostmark	438 tons
Sachsen	284 tons
August Wriedt	407 tons
Lauenburg	344 tons
Hohmann	?

All but *Sachsenwald* and *Wriedt* were included in a list of weather-reporting ships issued by Admiral Norwegen at Oslo in January 1941. All but *Lauenburg* and *Hohmann* are known to have been at sea as weather-reporting ships in February and April 1941. There may be others, of which no mention is yet available.

B. *Bases*

Ships operating North of Iceland are based at Drontheim: those working in mid-Atlantic are based on the French West Coast: eg

Ostmark was returning to Drontheim on 14/2.
Wriedt returned to the Gironde on 17/4.

It is probable that the ships in Admiral Norwegen's list are those based at Drontheim, and that *Sachsenwald, Wriedt* work from the French West coast.

C. *Areas occupied.*

The two main areas, North of Iceland and mid-Atlantic, are 46°–50° N., 32°–40° W. and 67°–71° N. 1°–7° W. Evidence for this, other than d/fs, is as follows:

1) *Z evidence*: a) On 14/2 *Muenchen's* position was announced as 71° N. 1°–4° W.

b) On the same day *Coburg's* position was announced as 67° N. 4°–6° 15′ W.

c) *Sachsenwald* was ordered to take up a new operational area on 3/2, in 48° 50 N., 33°–37° W.

d) On 22/2 *Sachsenwald* was ordered to move into the area 48° 18–49° 12 N., 29° 30–32° 30 W., to report on British forces thought to be in that position.

2) *German Met. broadcasts of weather received from the following positions.*

19/3: 71° N. 2° W.
20/3: 70° N. 5° W.
7/4: 67° N. 5° W.
9/4: 49° N. 36° W.
   71° N. 3° W.
10/4: 49° N. 36° W.
11/4: 48° N. 26° W.
   70° N. 4° W.
13/4: 70° N. 9.7° W.
   67° N. 5° W.
14/4: 70° N. 4° W.
15/4: 70° N. 4° W.
   70° N. 5° W.
16/4: 48° N. 33° W.
17/4: 67° N. 5° W. (0300)
   49° N. 40°(?)W.
   67 N. 5° W. (1400)
   71° N. 5° W.
20/4: 67° N. 5° W.
   70° N. 5° W.
23/4: 67° N. 4° W.

D. *Number of ships at sea.*

Signals in February and on 2 days in April, and the evidence of the above positions, indicate that 2 ships are stationed North of Iceland, one in 70°–71° N. 2°–5° W. and the other in 67° N. 5° W., and that one is stationed in 48°–49° N. 33°–36° N. approx.

E. *Activities.*

(1) These ships are responsible for the bulk of weather reports received from sea, although

a) a U-boat is ordered to report the weather each day, between 2300 and 0300 GMT, from the N.W. Approaches.

and b) tankers and supply ships may report the weather occasionally, but only when requested (Reference signal 2107/8/2).

Weather reports (WW signals) are usually made for 0200, 0300, 1200, 1400 and 0000 German time.

(2) Sightings of enemy shipping are also reported, and the order to *Sachsenwald* on 22/2 to move into an area where British forces were suspected suggests that as much use as possible is made of these ships for reconnaissance against our shipping.

(3) Ships apparently remain at sea for at least a month. eg *Sachsenwald* was at sea throughout February. *Coburg* went out on 9/2 and was still operating on 25/2.

F. *W/T.*

Permanent listening watch is kept, by ships in both areas, on Kootwik frequencies.

Signals from the ships are made on frequencies in the Kootwik, Series B or Norddeich Services, on which the weather reporting ships are responsible for almost all WW traffic. In general, although there are occasional exceptions, weather-ships in mid-Atlantic use Norddeich or Series B for transmissions, and weather-ships North of Iceland use Kootwik only. Series A might be used occasionally – eg:

WW signal on Series A at 0232/16/2 was made by *Sachsen.*

G.   *Cyphers carried.*

a) *Naval Enigma*: ships both receive and transmit Naval Enigma signals, cyphered on Home Area keys (Schluessel M, allgemein).

b) *Weather Cypher*: WW signals are cyphered on the *Wetterkurzschluessel* to which there are occasional page and table references in the material at present available.

c) *The Short Signal Book*: This was not carried in February, but evidence on 16 and 17/4 makes it probable that it is now carried by the weather reporting ships operating in the mid-Atlantic area. It may or may not be carried by those ships operating North of Iceland: there is no evidence that they have used it. (See appendix).

H.   *Future Movements.*

Wriedt was not at sea during February. A signal 3/2 suggests that she had just returned to base. Assuming a week's passage in each direction *Sachsenwald* must have been at sea for six weeks – the last week of January to the first week in March (inclusive). *Wriedt* was back in Gironde on 17/4 and could therefore have been at sea only 6 weeks including passage time.

Again allowing a week for passage, *Sachsenwald* has been on patrol since 10/4. Assuming the procedure is repeated *Sachsenwald* will be on patrol for 6 weeks and will therefore begin the return passage on 22/5, and *Wriedt* may leave her base in time to relieve *Sachsenwald* on that date i.e. about 15/5.

I. *Conclusions.*

The seizure of one of these ships, if practicable, would:

1) deprive the enemy of valuable weather reports for a considerable period,

2) remove a potential source of information concerning our fleet and shipping movements.

3) offer an opportunity for obtaining cyphers including the Short Signal book (extensively used by German raiders and supply ships) in the case of those ships in mid-Atlantic, as well as

4) do something to remove German confidence in their ability to sail infested seas.

Appendix.

Evidence that the Short Signal book is carried by some weather reporting ships:

In February the book was not carried. Because she did not carry it, *Sachsenwald* on 3/2 (T.O.O. 1656) was given a code table, by W/T signal, for use when reporting enemy shipping. When using this the sighting report was attached to the weather signal and took the following form:

0448/14/2 WW KYPL BNYY VVVV WEVS
1217/26/2 WW EXEW PIOG VVVV ZUYR

It is probable that this code has now been superseded by the Short Signal book in the case of those ships operating in mid-Atlantic, for the following reasons:

(1) the above type of signal is no longer intercepted and has not been for more than a month.

(2) Naval Enigma acknowledgements of short signals from *Sachsenwald* and *Wriedt* on 16 and 17/4 no longer, as in February, refer to 'Short weather report and short signal received' but only to 'Short signal received', independently of the weather traffic.

(3) although none of the short signals from these two ships were intercepted, their contents, available in the Naval Enigma acknowledgements, are more comprehensive than if they had been cyphered on the system used in February. eg a typical February signal reads 'Merchant ship, course East'. A signal from *Sachsenwald* on 17/4 (ref. T.O.O. 1635) reads 'Medium sized merchant ship 5–10000 tons, 175°, speed 14 knots' and could only be sent in short signal by use of the Short signal book.

Both *Sachsenwald* and *Wriedt* are ships which operate in the mid-Atlantic area. In the case of the weather-ships working from Drontheim to the North of Iceland, there is no evidence that they have used the Short Signal book or that they carry it.

(ii) *ZG/3 of 19 June 1941*

W B S Lauenburg

(1) *Lauenburg* is a weather reporting ship of 344 tons, based at Drontheim.

(2) She left Drontheim overnight 27–28/5, to take over from *Sachsen*, and had therefore been 3 weeks at sea (including days on passage) by 17/6 and will have been at sea almost 5 weeks at the end of June.

(3) Evidence of her predecessor's patrol suggests that *Lauenburg* intends to be out after the end of June, ie for more than 5 weeks:

Sachsen patrolled (exclusive of passage time) from about 13/4 to 28/5, when she was relieved by *Lauenburg*, after being out for more than 6 weeks.

Evidence for the patrol-periods of other ships is less complete, but evidence of a tendency to overstocking with cypher material in addition to the *Sachsen* evidence, suggest that *Lauenburg*, leaving in the last few days of May, will be carrying keys both for June and July.

(4) Positions given by her in weather reports during her patrol are as follows:

0413/2/6	72 N	9 E
0412/6/6	72 N	1 W
1213/7/6	72 N	2 W
0842/8/6	72 N	2 W
1443/8/6	72 N	2 W
0417/9/6	73 N	3 W
0646/13/6	73 N	4 W
1711/15/6	72 N	3 W
0613/16/6	72 N	3 W
0812/17/6	72 N	3 W
1411/17/6	72 N	3 W
0613/18/6	72 N	4 W
1411/18/6	72 N	4 W
0613/19/6	72 N	4 W

(5) Her reports are made daily at 0600–0640 GMT and 1410–20 GMT (approx.) on 12040 kcs.

APPENDIX 13

The Special Signals Service from GC and CS to the Middle East

The proposal that Sigint from the German Enigma should be transmitted direct from GC and CS to the Middle East was first made in November 1940 when the establishment of CBME, a possible channel for such a service to Cairo, coincided with the fact that the Enigma began to provide intelligence about Germany's penetration of the Balkans. But four months elapsed before the difficulties were overcome.

One difficulty, that of persuading the intelligence branches in Whitehall to allow GC and CS to select what material should be sent, was by then declining in importance. Intelligence from the GAF Enigma had been sent to the BEF and to the Howard Vyse mission to the French GQG in May 1940 direct from GC and CS (but disguised as agents' reports), and during the summer preparations had been made for introducing a similar service to the Home Commands in the event of an invasion of the United Kingdom. The need for speed dictated that responsibility should again be delegated to GC and CS in a service to the Middle East, particularly when GC and CS began to read the Enigma traffic of Fliegerkorps X and Fliegerführer Afrika at the end of February 1941. Moreover, the intelligence branches had by then posted experienced Service officers to Bletchley to advise GC and CS; and by retaining the power to amplify, to modify and to comment on GC and CS's signals in signals of its own, Whitehall further safeguarded the convention by which GC and CS supplied intelligence and it alone interpreted it.

A more serious difficulty was to find room for the service when the wireless channels to the Middle East were already greatly over-loaded. But this consideration, while it was one cause of delay, in the end helped to precipitate the decision to inaugurate the service. Much of the growing volume of signals to and from the Middle East arose from the need to pass Middle East intercepts of foreign wireless traffic to GC and CS and to return to the intelligence bodies in the Middle East the results of GC and CS's cryptanalytical work on the intercepts, especially the Italian traffic; and there was also much signalling between the two sides on technical and administrative matters. In addition the gist of the Italian and German Sigint was already being signalled to the Middle East via the Air Ministry and the War Office. So long as these communications were carried on a variety of different Service wireless channels their management constituted a considerable problem and there was constant anxiety about delays and insecurity. Thus, quite apart from the need for a special channel to carry the Enigma intelligence to the Middle East, there was growing pressure for the rationalisation and simplification of the signals between GC and CS and the Middle East on other Sigint business.

These requirements finally overcame the most weighty reason for hesitation. This was the problem of how to safeguard the security of the source of the Enigma if intelligence from it was transmitted to the Middle East and distributed there. In Whitehall itself it had become impossible by the spring of 1941 to conceal the true source of the increasing flow of Enigma decrypts from their recipients within the intelligence branches, and the mounting security problem was being met by the introduction of strict precautions to prevent the reproduction of Enigma items in such intelligence documents as the Chiefs of Staff résumés and MI appreciations to which the branches gave a wide circulation. But to the extension of the intelligence to the commands Whitehall remained anxious to apply its own earlier and stricter rule by which knowledge of the source was withheld even from its immediate recipients. The inauguration of the service to the Middle East was held up until arrangements which met this requirement had been negotiated and laid down.

When the service was introduced on 13 March 1941, the intelligence selected by GC and CS had to be paraphrased before it was transmitted by an RAF W/T link to Cairo, in signals distinguished by a special prefix – to begin with the prefix was the digraph OL, but the digraph was generally changed after every 9,999 signals – and by a sub-prefix for each individual addressee. In Cairo it was initially handled personally by the Director of CBME, who distributed it to a very limited number of recipients at the three major intelligence HQs. Though he suspected that it was the Enigma, he was not formally told this until the beginning of May. Thereafter he continued to withhold from the recipients any information as to its source: they were told only that the source was 'completely reliable'. They, in turn, were instructed not to distribute it outside Cairo and Alexandria; and though the HQs could take it into account in framing operational orders to lower commands, such use of the intelligence was permitted only when it could be made to seem that it had been disclosed by other sources like reconnaissance or low-grade Sigint. In the spring of 1941 the service was extended to the British commanders in Greece and Crete* and to the British Military Attaché in Yugoslavia.q

Together with the fact that the selection of the intelligence for Cairo was 'patchy and capricious' while GC and CS was gaining experience, these security precautions, however understandable, blunted the

---

* See Chapter 13, p 407.
† See Chapter 13, p 408.

impact of the intelligence in Cairo and limited its usefulness to the Middle East Commands. At the same time, they placed an onerous round-the-clock burden on the Director of CBME and added to the strains which already marked the relations between the CBME and the separate Service intelligence HQs in the Middle East.* During the first few weeks of the new service, when GC and CS was sending no more than one signal a day to Cairo, these problems did not greatly matter. But by the end of April, when the volume of Enigma decrypts bearing on the Middle East and north Africa was increasing, and was containing an increasing amount of tactical and operational intelligence, it became obvious that the initial arrangements would have to be changed. From the beginning of May two Army officers assisted the Director of CBME and they, at least, were indoctrinated as to the source, while preparations were made to place the GC and CS/Cairo service under the SCU/SLU organisation which was later to be extended to every HQ that received high-grade Sigint.

The SCU/SLU link with Cairo, a development of the arrangements which had been adopted briefly in May 1940 for sending selections from the GAF Enigma decrypts to the BEF, was established in August 1941. It involved Special Communications Units (SCUs), which were equipped with hand-speed morse facilities that could be brought into use when normal Service communications were inadequate or non-existent, and Special Liaison Units (SLUs), which were responsible for decyphering all signals on a link, for circulating them within the HQ and for supervising the security precautions laid down for the handling of their contents. The Army provided most of the personnel for the SCUs; the SLUs were predominantly staffed by the RAF. Both were organised and operationally controlled, however, by CSS's organisation, which set up a new section for the control and development of the SCUs and which supervised the SLUs through section I(c) of the Intelligence Branch in the Air Ministry.†

With the institution of the SCU/SLU system it became possible to modify the security precautions which had hitherto governed the handling of Sigint at the Cairo HQs. Its authorised recipients were now indoctrinated as to the source of GC and CS's product. The same relaxation was adopted at other commands as the system was extended to them. In the Middle East the extension began in September 1941, from which month GC and CS was sending signals direct to Alexandria, Malta, the western desert and Jerusalem, which was a centre for the preparations that were being made against a possible German attack on the Middle East from the north, as well as to Cairo.

---

* See Chapter 6, p 221.

† For a good account of the work of the SCU/SLU organisation see R. Lewin, *Ultra goes to War* (1978).

APPENDIX 14

MI 14 Appreciation of 2 May 1941
Possible German Action in
Syria and Iraq

Conclusions

1. If the Germans should launch an attack on Syria or Iraq by
airborne troops –
   (a) *SYRIA*
      They might succeed in establishing a hold on a part of Syria and
      perhaps raise the country against the French, unless we can send
      military aid to General Dentz.
   (b) *IRAQ*
      (i) they could support the Iraqi Army at MOSUL and BAGH-
         DAD and ultimately threaten our position at BASRA,
         unless we can provide additional Forces;
      (ii) they could capture RATBAH and cut the oil pipe line.
2. It is improbable that an attack on Iraq would take place without
some intermediate stage being established in Syria or possibly in
Cyprus.
   We have information pointing to an attack on CRETE as the first
step, and this is believed to be imminent. On the other hand, if the
British situation in Iraq seriously deteriorates, it would be possible to
launch an expedition from the DODECANESE direct to Iraq.
3. The maintenance of a force in Syria and Iraq would in existing
circumstances be completely dependent on airborne supply and on
existing stocks in Syria. If the latter are not extensive or suitable the
Germans might attempt to occupy CYPRUS even before attacking
Syria.
4. The indications that an attempt to occupy one or both of these
countries will be made, and the evidence in support of the above
conclusions, are summarised below.

SYRIA

5. According to a report from JERUSALEM the Italian Disarmament Commission in Syria is preparing the way for the landing of
German airborne troops. In particular landing grounds near HOMS
have been reconditioned; a large quantity of motor transport has been
sent to HOMS and dumps of petrol and munitions are available in
the vicinity. This is confirmed by another source. Petrol dumps are
also reported at PALMYRA.

6. The occupation of Syria and Iraq would have a profound effect on the Turkish will to resist, and the Germans are undoubtedly considering the attempt.

7. Airborne troops could reach the HOMS area easily from the DODECANESE Islands. If all the troop-carrying aircraft now in the Balkans were available a total of 3,000–4,000 troops could be landed on the first day, including ground staffs for aerodromes and some 2,000–3,000 fighting troops. Mobility would be ensured by the use of MT available on the spot. These forces would be largely dependent on air transport for supplies.

8. It is also believed that fighter aircraft and dive-bombers (fitted with extra tanks) could reach HOMS. The operation of bombers would probably be much handicapped unless French stocks of bombs could be used. This, however, would meet with considerable technical difficulties.

9. When HM Consul General BEIRUT approached General DENTZ, the latter replied categorically that he had orders to resist all aggression. On the other hand, according to some reports from Syria, the state of French morale is so low that resistance to the Germans could be counted on only if tangible British support in AFVs and aircraft were forthcoming. What would be the attitude of General DENTZ, in the event of Vichy ultimately acquiescing in the German occupation, is hard to foresee.

10. At the present moment other reports indicate the imminence of an airborne attack on CRETE. A simultaneous attack on Syria and CRETE is unlikely on account of the shortage of transport aircraft.

IRAQ

11. Once the HOMS area had been occupied the flight of further airborne troops to any part of IRAQ would be simple, but in the case of Southern Iraq, aircraft would have to refuel before returning to Syria.

12. Communication between Syria and Northern Iraq could then be established by road through RATBAH or MOSUL by the use of MT stocks in Syria.

13. In addition an airborne force could reach the neighbourhood of RATBAH from the Dodecanese direct in one flight. The aircraft would then have to refuel before returning, but some petrol stocks are probably available at RATBAH.

14. The Iraqi Government are calling for Axis support.

Author's Note: The last phrase in the draft paragraph 14 for this appreciation was deleted from the final version. It read: 'and an actual attack on British forces may begin at any moment'.

APPENDIX 15

MI Summary of German Troop Movements to the East April–June 1941

APRIL

Move of Divisions through BANAT to BUDAPEST

1. 18/4
Large concentration German troops in the vicinity of UZHOROD.

2. 23/4
Majority movement of German troops through Hungary was now via ORODEABISTRITZA. German troops in Moldavia have been reinforced.

3. 25/4
Mechanised troops to total of 20,000 have begun return journey BUDAPEST-VIENNA. German forces continue to go to BUKOVINA.

4. 27/4
Two motorised divisions have passed through VIENNA from Balkans.

POLAND.

5. 4/4
Civilian rail movements considerably curtailed.

6. 8/4
Constant movement of troops eastward through KATTOWITZ.

7. 18/4
Two motorised divisions passed by road through BRNO in direction of MORAVSKA OSTRAVA.

8. 23/4
Large concentration of troops are reported in SE Poland. Eighty trains of infantry passed through OLOMOUC.

9. 23/4
Billets prepared on west bank of VISTULA. Unconfirmed rumour of mass transports to East Prussia.

10. 25/4
Large armoured unit passed LODZ going east.

MOLDAVIA

11. 25/4
    About 12 divisions in MOLDAVIA.

FINLAND

12. April
    One new division sent to KIRKENES via Finland.

MAY

Movement of Divisions through BANAT to BUDAPEST

1. 8/5
   Large numbers of German troops trains and A/C passing to MOLDAVIA.
2. 9/5
   90 divisions now massed on USSR border. Movement will be completed by 20/5.
3. 27/5
   Heavy movement continues to Roumania. 25–30 trains a day.

POLAND

4. 31/5
   Large concentration trains at PRZEMYSL (SE Poland).
5. Considerable movement of trains and heavy artillery from CRACOW eastwards.

ROUMANIA

6. 6/5
   12 divisions in MOLDAVIA. More arriving.
7. 9/5
   6 divisions at PRUTH.
8. 29/5
   Serious curtailment of civilian rail requirements to be ready to transport German troops on 15 June to Moldavia.

FINLAND

9. 27/4–5/5
   1,500 troops passed through Finland into Norway.
10. 6/5
    5 divisions in Finland.

11. 8/5

   15,000 to 16,000 troops around KIRKENES. Throughout the month troops and material continue to be sent by sea, to Finland.

12. 26/5

   2 armoured divisions sent to Finland.

13. 29/30.5

   Troops quartered in ROVANIEMI area.

JUNE

POLAND

1. 12/6

   Considerable movements in Poland towards Russian frontier.

MOLDAVIA

2. 3/6

   Marshals LIST and REICHENAU in Moldavia.

3. 4/6

   2 German armoured divisions may be being transferred to BUKOVINA. Heavy German military movements in progress to Roumania.

4. 4/6

   Evacuation of civilian population from Moldavia reported completed. Persistent rumours German attack on Russia 15 June.

FINLAND

5. 8/6

   20,000 troops in PETSAMO area.

6. 11/6

   2 Mtn divisions moving into Finland.

7. 12/6

   2 divisions centred on ROVANIEMI. Another coming from OSLO by sea. About 20,000 troops in Finland.

8. 12/6

   About 12,000 German troops moved into Finland from Norway. 2 German divisions in Finland.

9. 12/6

   Large numbers of ships have arrived during the month at Finnish ports, with German troops and material.

Index

British Embassies and Legations—*continued*
  Berne
    MA sends Polish intelligence on German
    intentions in the West 1940 130

  Budapest
    Reports on German troop movements 352

  Copenhagen
    Reports on German intentions in
    Scandinavia 122; 123; 124

  Madrid
    Reports on German strategic intentions
    189; 253–255; 256; 257; Ambassador's
    attitude to SIS activities 275–276; NA
    advises Defence Committee on Spanish
    attitude to war 257

  Moscow
    Difficulties in obtaining information 46;
    Reports on German-Russian rapprochement
    46; Ambassador's views on German
    preparations for *Barbarossa* 430; 432;
    443–444; 453; 464; 478; 480–481

  Oslo
    Receives Oslo Report 100; Reports on
    Altmark 105–106; on German intentions in
    Scandinavia 117

  Stockholm
    Reports on German intentions in
    Scandinavia 116; 117; 118; 122; on
    invasion threat to Britain 183; on
    Barbarossa 453; 478; 480; NA reports on
    German movements in Baltic 333; on
    Bismarck 340–341; 346; 506; As source of
    information generally 285; 333

  Washington
    Reports on Axis intentions in Mediterranean
    258; on *Barbarossa* 444–445; 454; 455; 471
    NA on US problems in collection of
    intelligence 313
    see also Diplomatic sources of intelligence
British Joint Staff Mission in Washington
    Established 1941 313; A1 section 314;
    British Army delegation 313; JIC section
    314; NID delegation 313
British Military Mission Greece 369; 408
British Military Mission Poland 39
British Military Mission Romania 39
British Military Mission Turkey 39
Brooke, Lieut. General Sir Alan
    As Commander, British II Corps BEF 143
Brown (Enigma key)
    see Enigma machine; GAF Traffic (Brown)
Budapest
    For embassy and attaché reports from
    see British Embassies and Legations

Bulgaria
    German preparations for entry 347–348;
    Intelligence collection and evaluation on
    254; 255; 348–366

'C' (Head of Secret Service)
    Post created 17; Presses for amalgamation
    of intelligence services 1925–1927 19;
    Agreements with DNI about GC and CS
    Naval Section 22; Anxiety over SIS
    finances 49; 51; 91; Defence of SIS 56;
    Receives Enigma machine from Colonel
    Bertrand 1939 492; Reactions to DMI's
    letter on Sigint policy 1940 270–277;
    Instructions from Prime Minister to send
    him all Enigma messages 295–296
Cabinet War Room
    Daily reports 97; 294
Cadogan, Sir Alexander
    As Permanent Under-Secretary 56;
    476–477
Cairo (Heliopolis)
    see RAF. Sigint organisation
Captured documents
    Importance to GC and CS attack on
    Enigma 336–338; Admiralty instructions
    on searching for 163; 337–338; Exploitation
    in Middle East 205; Documents captured
    from Army Group B 1940 143; 161; 162
    and footnote; 304; GAF instructions for
    German offensive 1940 114–115; on GAF
    strength in Blitz 318; on GAF order of
    battle 1940 319; *Knickebein* from Heinkel
    aircraft 324; 552; 553; *X-Gerät* from
    Heinkel aircraft 326; Parachutist manual
    Crete 1941 420; from *Krebs*, *München* and
    Lauenburg 337; from U-49 140; 231; 333;
    U-110 337–338; from VP 2623 163; 336;
    from *Galileo Galilei* 209; from *Uebi Scebeli*
    206; from Italian Army at Bardia 378
CAS
    In Singleton enquiry 299–302; and
    Moonlight Sonata 534; 535
Catroux, General
    As C-in-C Free French battalions in Middle
    East 422; 423–424
CBME
    History 197; 219; Terms of reference 215;
    219; Organisation and administration 197;
    219–221; 570–572; Relations with GC and
    CS 219–221; 392; 570–572; with Service
    departments 219–221; with W Committee
    221; W/T link with GC and CS 570–572
Censorship
    Organisation and administration 94; 287;
    As source of intelligence 90; 224; In Middle
    East 205 and footnote; 206; Ministry of
    Information assumes responsibility for 287
Central Interpretation Unit
    see CIU

Chamberlain, Neville
Policy towards German resistance groups
56–57 footnote; As chairman of FPC 73;
Suspicions of intelligence from opposition
groups 81; Announces guarantees to
Poland and Romania 82–83; Authorises
investigation into Secret Service 1939 91
Cheadle (RAF main Y station) 14; 179;
180 footnote; 319; 320; 321; 329;
Development of radio counter-measures
322–323; 551; Intelligence collection to
1939 25; Battle of Britain 1940 180–182;
Blitz 1940–1941 315; 319; Interception of
long-range German bomber call-signs
301–302; Relations with GC and CS 268;
320; 321
Chief of Air Staff
see CAS
Chief of Imperial General Staff
see CIGS
Chief of Naval Staff
see CNS
China
JIC investigation of air warfare in 37 and
footnote
Christie, Group Captain M G
Assessments of European situation 47;
Relations with Foreign Office 47; with
Sir Robert Vansittart 47–48; with SIS
47 footnote
Churchill, Winston
Attempts to form Naval Staff 1912 9; As
Secretary of State for War 1920s 18–19; 50;
Pre-war assessments of threat from GAF 78;
As First Lord of the Admiralty 1939–40 120;
121; As Prime Minister, role in Singleton
enquiry 102; 299–300; 302; Orders COS
to review intelligence procedures 160;
Asks to receive all intelligence on occupied
France 275; Complains about JIC
reports 294–296; Agrees with USA to pool
intelligence 312; Alerted about Moonlight
Sonata 317; 532–534; 536; Orders priority
for counter-measures against Knickebein
324; 553; Receives Enigma material on
Greece 408–409; Sends Enigma material
to Crete 417; Views on invasion threat 1940
175–176; on threat to Egypt 215; to Spain
257; to Balkans 350; 351; 353; 354; 359;
363; to Yugoslavia 369; 370; 371; to north
Africa 388; 395; 400; 416; to Crete 416;
417; to Syria 423–424; to USSR 431; 432;
443; 450–451; 452; 462; 482; Sends
warning to Yugoslav government 371;
to Stalin 430–431; 452–453; 454; Sends
personal message to C-in-C ME on Iraq 413
CIC
Terms of reference 168–169; 171;
Membership 168; Intelligence collection
and evaluation on invasion threat 1940
172; 174; 183; 184; 187; 189; 261–264;

Relations with Coastal Command 170;
with PRU 279
CICI
Terms of reference 411
CID (Committee on Imperial Defence)
History 7–8; Investigation into state of
intelligence 1902 16 footnote; Attitude to
PR 27; Relations with IIC 33–34
CIGS
Concern about invasion threat 1940 190;
On visit to Mediterranean 1941 359; 361;
362; 363; 443; Assessment of threat to
Cyprus 425
CIU
cont of PIU
Organisation and administration 279; 281
see also PR Interpretation
Civil Defence
Sigint contribution 321
CNS
Direct access of DNI to 10; Receives
Wegener book on German naval strategy
117–118; Receives report of Darlan's
orders to French Fleet 1940 150; Memo on
invasion 1940 175; Informed of German
capital ship displacements 505
Coast watching
In Norway 105–106; 276
COIS China Station
Relations with FECB 40 and footnote
COIS Mediterranean
Warning of Italian attack on Greece 218
Cold Water (codeword) 532
see also Coventry raid 1940
Colonial Office
Relations with SIS 17
Combined Bureau Middle East
see CBME
Combined Intelligence Centre Iraq
see CICI
Combined Intelligence Committee
see CIC
Combined Services Detailed Interrogation
Centre
see CSDIC
Commercial codes and cyphers
Interception of 26
Communications networks
Analysis of see TA
Compass (codeword) 214; 375
see also Libya
Comrie, Dr L J 557
Conte Rosso (Liner)
Sinking of 400
Co-ordination of Defence, Minister for
Appointed 36; Member of FPC 74;
Chairman of MCC 97
Co-ordination of W/T Interception

Committee (GC and CS)
cont of Cryptography and Interception
Committee History 23; Membership
23 footnote
Copenhagen
For embassy and attaché reports from
see British Embassies and Legations
COS
Demands for intelligence at outbreak of war
89; Relations with JIC 93; 291–299;
Discussion of establishment of ISPB 93
footnote; Instigation of weekly résumés of
Allied and enemy military developments
97; 294; of weekly summaries 93; Review
of intelligence system 1940 160
COS. Joint Intelligence Sub-Committee
see JIC
COS. Joint Planning Sub-Committee
see Joint Planning Sub-Committee
Cotton, F Sidney 28–30; 136; 171; 281–282;
496–499
see also PR; PR operations
Coventry raid 1940
German use of *Knickebein* 316; 528–531;
537–538; 539; 542; of *X-Gerät* 530; 531;
532; Intelligence before raid 316–318;
523–548; Sigint contribution 316–317;
528–533
Crete. German Invasion of
German plans 415; 418; Intelligence on
411–412; 415–421; Sigint contribution
411–412; 415–421
Cripps, Sir Stafford
As British Ambassador to Moscow 430;
432; 443–444; 453; 464; 468; 478; 480–481
Cromwell (codeword) 185
see also Great Britain. Invasion threat 1940
Cryptanalysis
Definition 20
see also Enigma machine;
GC and CS
Cryptography and Interception Committee
(GC and CS)
History and membership 23 and footnote;
24 footnote;
cont as Co-ordination of W/T Interception
Committee
Cryptography and Interception Committee.
Y Sub-Committee
see Y Sub-Committee
Cs-in-C Middle East
Requirement for strategic intelligence 191;
Attitude to MEIC 194; to CBME 219–220;
Estimate of Italian threat to Egypt 1940
216; Instructions to offer help to Greece
353–354; Handling of east African
campaigns 381; COS instructions to in
connection with *Barbarossa* 429; 476
see also Cunningham; Wavell
CSDIC (ME)
Creation of 205

CSDIC (UK)
Terms of reference 90 and footnote; 283;
Relations with Service departments 282
see also POW Interrogation
CSS
see 'C'
Cunningham, Admiral Sir Andrew
As C-in-C Mediterranean, warning of
Italian attack on Albania 1939 84; In
action against Mers-el-Kebir 150; 154;
155; Scepticism about invasion of Britain
176 footnote; Freedom from Admiralty
operational control 194; Critical of
intelligence about Italy 199; Moves to
Alexandria 202; Receives RAF warning
of Italian intentions 202; Views on Italian
intentions 204; 205; In Battle off Calabria
209 and footnote; Warned of GAF arrival
in Mediterranean 385; and of convoys to
Tripoli 387; Bases destroyers at Malta 400;
Receives Enigma material on convoys 401;
and during Syrian campaign 426; In
Battle of Matapan 404 passim
CX material 138
see also Enigma decrypts
Cyprus
Assessments of German threat to 411; 412;
416–417; 423; 424
Czechoslovakia
Cabinet Committee on 73; Collapse of SIS
organisation in 57; Intelligence on German
entry into Prague 58; 83; Czech
Intelligence recruits A-54 58; Its liaison
with SIS 277; 462; Its collection of
intelligence on German invasion of
USSR 462

Dakar
Anglo-French Operation 1940 149–158
Darlan, Admiral
and French Mediterranean Fleet 149–152
DCAS and Coventry raid 533
DCM
Relations with DRC 49 footnote
DCNS
see James, Vice-Admiral
DCOS
Recommendations for co-ordination of
intelligence 1936 26–27; 31; and
establishment of ISIC 34–35
DD (Ph) (Air Ministry)
Post created 279; Relations with ADI (Ph)
281
DDI (Air Ministry)
Post created 1935 12; 14
DDI 3
see AI. DDI 3
DDIC (Admiralty) 12
DDMI (Middle East) 195 and footnote

Gibraltar
Attack by midget submarines 1940 211;
German plan for attack 249–250; 257–258;
Intelligence on 252–253; 256–259
HMS *Glorious*
Sinking by *Gneisenau* and *Scharnhorst*
141–143; 268
Gneisenau
see Germany. Navy: *Gneisenau* and
Scharnhorst
Gördeler, Dr Carl 68 footnote; 69 footnote
Göring, Marshal Hermann
Involvement in German economic
organisation 501–502; 503; Comments on
mismanagement of Directorate of Air
Armament 308; Declarations on air
warfare against Britain 315; Corinth canal
operation 416; Invasion of Greece 418;
Invasion of Crete 421; Tells Japanese
Foreign Minister of German intention to
invade Russia 455; During preparations
for *Barbarossa* 474
Gort, General Lord
As C-in-C BEF 143
Government Code and Cypher School
see GC and CS
GPO
Radio counter-measures against GAF
medium frequency beacons 323; 550–551;
Y Stations 26
Graf Spee
see Battle of River Plate
Great Britain. Invasion threat 1940
German plans 164–166; 184–189; 249–251;
261; Intelligence on 165; 168; 171–174;
182–190; 261–264; 431; 432; 437; 440;
443; 463–464; 482; 515–524; Sigint
contribution 166; 173–174; 183–184;
185–186; 188–189
Greece
Italian preparations for invasion 217–218;
250; 255; Intelligence on Italian invasion
217–219; 376–377; Institution of Inter-
Service operational intelligence summary on
Greek situation 294
German plans for invasion 251; 257; 258;
260; 347–348; 356; 363–364; 372;
Intelligence on 253; 259; 260; 349–350;
351–364; 369; 371; 372–373; Sigint
contribution 352; 355–363; 364; 371–373;
British assistance to 251; 353–355; 359;
361–363; 369; 372; 388–389; lack of
intelligence of Greek plans 359; 362;
Intelligence contribution in fighting in
Greece 406–409
Green (Enigma key)
see Enigma machine. German Army traffic
(Green)
Greenland
German attempt to set up weather reporting
system 286

GS Int, GHQ, ME
Formation 193–194; 195 and footnote;
Relations with CBME 215; Use of captured
documents 205; Limitations in assessment
of strategic intelligence 217; Assessment
of Axis plans 1940 255; Intelligence reports
on Italian threat to Libya 204; 215–217; to
Greece 217–219; Italian order of battle in
east Africa 380; on German offensive in
Balkans 353; 354; 361–362; in Greece 363;
in Iraq 367; in Crete 419; in Libya 386;
387–388; 389; 392

Halifax, Lord
As Foreign Secretary 57 footnote; 68; 69;
81–83; 99; 202; 349; 370
As British Ambassador Washington 471
Hall, Admiral 'Blinker'
As DNI 9
Hankey, Sir Maurice (later Lord)
As Secretary of CID 30; 34; 36 and footnote
Investigation into Secret Service 91–92;
267
Hankey Committee (on Axis oil) 103;
233–234; 235; 237; 243; 305–306
Harris, Sir Arthur 78
Hartley Committee (on Axis oil)
cont. of Lloyd Committee
History 102; 103 and footnote
Harwood, Commodore
In Battle of River Plate 105
Hatston
GAF attacks on Fleet Air Arm base 119;
120; PR flight by RN aircraft from Hatston
1941; 342
HDU
Organisation and administration 180 and
footnote; 327; Relations with Service
departments 180 and footnote; 327; During
Battle of Britain 1940 180–182
see also Kingsdown
Heliopolis
see RAF Sigint Organisation
Hess, Rudolf 465
Admiral Hipper
see Germany. Navy: *Admiral Hipper*
Holland
SIS activities in 57 footnote; Liaison with
SIS 277; FPC assesses implications of
German occupation 82–83
see also France and Low Countries. German
Invasion
Home Defence Executive
Terms of Reference 165; 169; Defence
plans against invasion threat 1940 173
Home Defence Units
see HDU
Home Fleet
see Royal Navy. Home Fleet
HMS *Hood*
Sinking by *Bismarck* 342

James, Vice Admiral Sir William
Head of Room 40 21 footnote; Orders formation of OIC 10; Attitude to PR 27
Jamming
see Radio counter-measures
Jan Mayen Islands
German attempt to set up weather reporting system 286; 341
Japan
Attack on codes and cyphers 24; 40 footnote; 52; 53 and footnote; 454
Joint Intelligence Committee (JIC)
Formation and terms of reference 4; 5; 32; 36–43; Membership 36; 41; 42–43; 160 and footnote; Organisation and administration 93–100; 159–160; 291–299; 513–514; Daily summary 294–295; Dominions Wire 292; and its extension to USA 312; Situation reports 97 and footnote; 513–514

Relations with Air Targets Sub-Committee 37 and footnote; with APS 297–298; with COS 93; 292–299; with DDMI 41; with Directorate of Combined Operations 293; with FOES 296–297; with FOPS 293; with Foreign Office 39–40; 42–43; 292; with IIC 32; 36; with ISSB 93 footnote; 94 footnote; with JPS 36; 38; 39 and footnote; 93; 95–96; with MEIC 193; with MEW 101; 102; 290; with NID 17; 287; with Service departments 37–38; 291–299; with Situation Report Centre 41–42; with SOE 293; with USA 314

Sub-committees on air warfare in Spain and China 37 and footnote; 79 and footnote; on topographical information 292
JIC appreciations and reports
Preparation of 38 and footnote; 39 and footnote; 95–96; 111; 293–294; 296; Customers' dissatisfaction with 294–295 Far East appreciation 1936–1937 38 footnote; Mediterranean, Middle East and North Africa appreciation 1937 38 footnote; on Situation in event of war with Germany 1938 38 footnote; on possible action by Germany spring 1940 95; 129; 310; 431; 434; against Sweden 1940 96; in Norway 129; on German plan to invade Holland 1940 129; on invasion threat 1940 166–167; 173–175; 184–185; 186–187; 188; 190; 1941 262–263; 482–483; Review of Italian intentions 1940 203–204; on Italian plans to invade Greece 1940 217–218; 294; on present situation in Germany 1940 235–237; 297; 432; on possible supply position of German Europe 1940 237 and footnote; 239; on German armaments industry 1940 235–247; on German intentions in Romania 1940 251–253; 294;

on military value of Vichy forces 1940 294; On Weygand's actions in north Africa 1940 294; on situation in French colonies 1940 294; on German economy 1941 310–311; on German plans to invade Greece 1941 356–357; on Soviet and Iranian reactions to possible British intervention in Iraq 1941 367; on German troops in north Africa 1941 391; on possible scale of an attack in Cyprus 1941 416; on German strategy 1941 456–457; on German intentions against USSR 1941 470–471; 475–476; 477; 478–479; 481–482; on effects of Russo-German collaboration 1941 477
Joint Intelligence Staff (JIS)
Development out of APS 298; 441; Relations with NID 17 287
Joint Planning Staff (JPS)
Organisation and administration 32; 35–36; 38–39; 93–98; 293; Demands for intelligence at outbreak of war 89; Proposes establishment of 'Enemy Syndicate' 296; Relations with FOES 296; with Foreign Office 41; 42; 74; with ISIC 36; with JIC 36; 38; 39 and footnote; 93; 95–96
Jones, Dr R V
see ADI (Science) (Air Ministry)
Jutland
Sigint contribution to battle 1916 21 footnote

Keitel, Field Marshal Wilhelm
68 footnote; 503
HMS *Kent*
In Mediterranean 1940 377
Kiel
Warship construction 1934 50; Use of canal during Norwegian campaign 116
Kielmansegg, Major
In French campaign 1940 135 footnote
HMS *King George V*
Comparison with the *Bismarck* 505–506
Kingsdown RAF station, main HDU
180 and footnote; 319; 320, 322, 325; 327
Kleist, General Ewald von
As Panzergruppe leader in France 148; 351; in Balkans 361; 371; 409
Knickebein
Airborne interception 271 footnote; 553; Enigma decrypts on 324; 552; First detected by AI 315; Intelligence on 316; 324–325; 552–554; R V Jones' work on 324–325; Modifications to 328; Radio counter-measures 182; 324–325; 554–556; Use in Coventry raid 1940 316; 528–531; 537–538; 539; 542
'Knock-out blow' by GAF
AI assessment of 78; 79; 82; 110
'Korn' (codeword) 316; 528; 536; see also Coventry raid

Poland—*continued*
445–446; 451; Polish Intelligence's reports
on German build-up for *Barbarossa* 438;
445; 457–458; 462; 482
see also Enigma machine. Polish contribution
to breaking
Political Warfare Executive
see PWE
Portal, Air Chief Marshal Sir Charles
see CAS
Portugal
SIS activities in 275
POW interrogation
Organisation and administration 90;
282–283; 288; techniques 282–283;
Interrogation of U-boat crews, U-31 231;
U-32 231; 333; U-39 93 footnote; about
Moonlight Sonata 316–317; 530–533; on
GAF strategy in Blitz 321; 328; on
effectiveness of radio counter-measures 325;
on *Knickebein* 324; 552; 553; *X-Gerät* 327;
556; *Y-Gerät* 327; 328; 561; 563; about
German intentions in Italy 388; in north
Africa 395; in Crete 420; 425; about IAF
strength and morale 376; about Matapan
405–406
PR
Organisation and administration 26–30;
48; 90; 94; 169; 279–282; 496–499; Use in
assessment of bomb damage 28; 102; 149
footnote; 279 280; 281
see also PDU : PRU
PR interpretation
see CIU : PIU
PR operations
By Cotton 28–30; 136; 171; 281–282;
469–499
By RAF to 1939 26; 28–30; of Caucasian
oilfields 198; 199 and footnote; In 1940
Atlantic Islands 257; Belgium 114; 133;
171–172; France 148–149; 171; 172; 183;
184–189; Germany 104; 105; 110; 113;
114; 116; 123; 133; 136; 171; 183; 186;
Holland 172; of *Knickebein* locations 325;
of *Wotan* sites 327; Italy 203; 211;
Mediterranean 202; North Africa 211;
Norway 171–172; 183; Spain 207; In 1941
Crete 421; France, of German capital
ships 332; 345; Germany 332; 340;
Holland 327; Mediterranean 400–401;
North Africa 386; 398; Norway, of
German capital ships 341; Syria 422
By France before French campaign 28;
132–133; 496; 497
By Germany, of Norway 123; of Scapa
Flow 340–341
PR techniques 28–30; 497–499
Mosaics 133; Night photography 279–280;
Oblique photography 28; Photographic
scale 280; Use of Wild machine 104;
Vertical photography 28

Prime Minister's Office
Daily receipt of selected Enigma decrypts
and GC and CS summaries 295–296;
Receipt of intelligence on occupied Europe
275; Sifting of original intelligence
documents 295–296
HMS *Prince of Wales*
In hunt for the *Bismarck* 1941 341
Prinz Eugen
see Germany. Navy : *Prinz Eugen*
Prisoners of war
see POW
Private intelligence sources 47–48; 56; 81
see also Vansittart, Sir Robert
Propaganda
Analysis of German press and radio
propaganda 90; by MI Branch 287
see also PWE
PRU
cont of PDU
Organisation and administration 90;
170–171; 279–281; 332; Relations with
Admiralty 279; with CIC 279; with
Bomber Command 279–280
PRU, ME 207–208; 279
PWE
Digest of foreign press and radio 90

Quisling, Vidkun
Warns Hitler of British plans to enter
Norway 115

Radar
Allied 15; 107; 179; 180; 181; 182; 319;
321; 324; 327–329; 335; 342; 377
Enemy 15; 271 footnote; 360; 361
Radio counter-measures
Against GAF medium frequency
navigational beacons 322–324; 550–551;
Against *Knickebein* 324–325; 554–556;
Against *X-Gerät* 326–327; 559; Against
Y-Gerät 327; 328; 561–563
Radio fingerprinting
see RFP
Radio Intelligence Service (USA)
see RI
Radio Security Service
see RSS
Radio telephony
see R/T
RAE
Development of cameras and equipment for
PR 281; Examination of intercepted
navigational beams 271 footnote
Raeder, Admiral Erich
115; 250; 439; 454; 506 footnote
Railway Research Service
Assistance to Sigint attack on German
Railway Enigma 357–358
Rashid Ali
see Iraq

HMS *Rawalpindi*
  Sinking by *Gneisenau* and *Scharnhorst* 1939
  105
RCM
  see Radio counter-measures
Red (Enigma key)
  see Enigma machine. GAF traffic (Red)
Resistance groups
  see Germany. Opposition
RFP
  Definition 271 footnote; 342
  Of signals from *Bismarck* 1941 342; 344
  see also TINA
Rhineland. German occupation 11; 58; 73
RI
  Definition 21 (footnote)
Ribbentrop, Joachim von
  As Foreign Minister 433; 478
River Plate, Battle of 105–106; 331
Rivet, Colonel
  As head of French espionage and
  cryptanalysis 131 footnote
HMS *Rodney*
  In chase for *Bismarck* 343; 344
Romania
  British guarantee to 83–84; German entry
  into 249–251; 252–255; 348–366; As base
  for German preparations for *Barbarossa* 442;
  447–448; 458; 467; 473–474
Rommel, Greneral Erwin
  Arrival in Libya as GOC Afrikakorps 382;
  Counter-attack from Agheila 389 et seq;
  Use of field Sigint 393; 398; 399
  see also Libya. Intelligence on German
  intentions
Roosevelt, President Franklin D
  Approves SIS contact with FBI 312; Sends
  special representative to London 312;
  Agrees to pool intelligence with Britain
  312–313; Receives Dominions Wire 312
Royal Aircraft Establishment
  see RAE
Royal Air Force. No 80 Wing
  Counter-measures against navigational
  beams 271 footnote; 324–325; 326–328;
  554–556; 559; Takes over WIDU 325;
  Relations with Service departments 328
  see also Coventry raid

Nos 138 and 419 (SD)
  SIS special flights 276

Bomber Command
  Intelligence Staff at 14; C-in-C as
  recipient of high-grade Sigint 319; Use of
  low-grade in Blitz 321–322; in attacks on
  KG 40 bases 329; Attitude to PR 28;
  Relations with PDU 136; 149 and footnote;
  Operations by No 3 PRU 279–280; In
  Norwegian campaign 319; in attack on
  synthetic oil plants 1941 305

British Air Forces in France (BAFF) 133;
  136; 143; 144
  Sortie over Ardennes 136; Inability to
  co-ordinate Enigma with low-grade Sigint
  145

Coastal Command
  Intelligence Staff at 14; C-in-C as recipient
  of high-grade Sigint 139; Value of low-
  grade 108; Patrols between Scotland and
  Norway 107; Reconnaissance
  responsibilities 169–170; Relations with
  CIC 170; Sighting of *Altmark* 106; of
  German ships en route to Norway 122;
  In Battle of Atlantic 335

Fighter Command
  Intelligence Staff at 14; Value of low-grade
  Sigint 108; Use of Enigma material and
  low-grade Sigint in intruder operations
  321–322
  see also Dowding, Air Chief Marshall; and
  Battle of Britain

Habbaniya station
  Iraqi attack on 411; 412–413

HQ Greece
  Contribution of Italian Sigint to successes
  against IAF 376; Receipient of high-grade
  Sigint from GC and CS 407

HQ Middle East
  Area of responsibility 195; Intelligence
  Staff 195–197; Value of Sigint 377; PR for
  British offensives 208; Delay in being
  warned of sailing of German convoys to
  Libya 387

Sigint Organisation
  Baghdad and Cairo (Heliopolis) stations 196

Royal Navy. Force B
  In Battle of Matapan 405

Force H
  In Mediterranean 210; 211; 403–414; In
  chase for *Bismarck* 343–345
  see also Mers-el-Kebir

Home Fleet
  Pre-war alert 84; First OIC war-time
  report to 106; C-in-C's criticism of
  intelligence 112; Recipient of high-grade
  Sigint 104; 138–139; 144; Opposes
  Admiralty policy on invasion of Britain 176
  and footnote; GAF operations against 108;
  RAF over-estimate of threat to Scapa Flow
  110; In Norwegian campaign 122–123;
  140–143; 144; Sails as result of TA on